Lecture Notes in Computer Science 16339

Founding Editors

Gerhard Goos
Juris Hartmanis

Editorial Board Members

The series Lecture Notes in Computer Science (LNCS), including its subseries Lecture Notes in Artificial Intelligence (LNAI) and Lecture Notes in Bioinformatics (LNBI), has established itself as a medium for the publication of new developments in computer science and information technology research, teaching, and education.

LNCS enjoys close cooperation with the computer science R & D community, the series counts many renowned academics among its volume editors and paper authors, and collaborates with prestigious societies. Its mission is to serve this international community by providing an invaluable service, mainly focused on the publication of conference and workshop proceedings and postproceedings. LNCS commenced publication in 1973.

Vincent G. Duffy
Editor

HCI International 2025 – Late Breaking Papers

27th International Conference on
Human-Computer Interaction, HCII 2025
Gothenburg, Sweden, June 22–27, 2025
Proceedings, Part IX

 Springer

Editor
Vincent G. Duffy
Purdue University
West Lafayette, IN, USA

ISSN 0302-9743   ISSN 1611-3349 (electronic)
Lecture Notes in Computer Science
ISBN 978-3-032-13011-2   ISBN 978-3-032-13012-9 (eBook)
https://doi.org/10.1007/978-3-032-13012-9

This Springer imprint is published by the registered company Springer Nature Switzerland AG
The registered company address is: Gewerbestrasse 11, 6330 Cham, Switzerland

If disposing of this product, please recycle the paper.

Foreword

The HCI International (HCII) conference was founded in 1984 by Gavriel Salvendy (Purdue University, USA, Tsinghua University, P.R. China, and University of Central Florida, USA) and the first event of the series, "1st USA-Japan Conference on Human-Computer Interaction", was held in Honolulu, Hawaii, USA, on 18–20 August. Since then, HCI International has been held jointly with several Thematic Areas and Affiliated Conferences, with each one under the auspices of a distinguished international Program Board and under one management and one registration. Twenty-seven HCI International Conferences have been organized so far (every two years until 2013, and annually thereafter).

Last year, we celebrated 40 years since the establishment of the HCII conference, which has been a hub for presenting groundbreaking research and novel ideas and collaboration for people from all over the world. Over the years, this conference has served as a platform for scholars, researchers, industry experts, and students to exchange ideas, connect, and address challenges in the ever-evolving HCI field. The conference has evolved itself, adapting to new technologies and emerging trends, while staying committed to its core mission of advancing knowledge and driving change.

The 27th International Conference on Human-Computer Interaction, HCI International 2025 (HCII 2025), was held as an 'on-site' conference at the Gothia Towers Hotel and Swedish Exhibition & Congress Centre, in Gothenburg, Sweden, on June 22–27, 2025, with the additional option for 'on-line' participation. It incorporated the 21 thematic areas and affiliated conferences listed below.

A total of 7972 individuals from academia, research institutes, industry, and government agencies from 92 countries submitted contributions. 1430 papers and 355 posters (as short research papers) were included in the volumes of the proceedings published just before the start of the conference. Additionally, 439 papers and 104 posters were included in the volumes of the proceedings published after the conference, as "Late Breaking Work". The contributions thoroughly cover the entire field of human-computer interaction, highlight the evolving role of computers in diverse contexts, and demonstrate how HCI research is shaping and improving user experiences across a wide range of domains, influencing technological progress and its effective integration into various sectors. The volumes constituting the full set of the HCII 2025 conference proceedings are listed on the following pages.

I would like to thank the Program Board Chairs and the members of the Program Boards of all thematic areas and affiliated conferences for their contribution towards the high scientific quality and overall success of the HCI International 2025 conference. Their manifold support including paper reviews (via a single-blind review process, with a minimum of two reviews per submission), session organization, and their willingness to act as goodwill ambassadors for the conference is most highly appreciated.

This conference would not have been possible without the continuous and unwavering support and advice of Gavriel Salvendy, founder, General Chair Emeritus, and Scientific Advisor. For his outstanding efforts, I would like to express my sincere appreciation to Abbas Moallem, Communications Chair and Editor of HCI International News.

September 2025   Constantine Stephanidis

HCI International 2025 Thematic Areas and Affiliated Conferences

- HCI: Human-Computer Interaction Thematic Area
- HIMI: Human Interface and the Management of Information Thematic Area
- EPCE: 22nd International Conference on Engineering Psychology and Cognitive Ergonomics
- AC: 19th International Conference on Augmented Cognition
- UAHCI: 19th International Conference on Universal Access in Human-Computer Interaction
- CCD: 17th International Conference on Cross-Cultural Design
- SCSM: 17th International Conference on Social Computing and Social Media
- VAMR: 17th International Conference on Virtual, Augmented and Mixed Reality
- DHM: 16th International Conference on Digital Human Modeling & Applications in Health, Safety, Ergonomics & Risk Management
- DUXU: 14th International Conference on Design, User Experience and Usability
- C&C: 13th International Conference on Culture and Computing
- DAPI: 13th International Conference on Distributed, Ambient and Pervasive Interactions
- HCIBGO: 12th International Conference on HCI in Business, Government and Organizations
- LCT: 12th International Conference on Learning and Collaboration Technologies
- ITAP: 11th International Conference on Human Aspects of IT for the Aged Population
- AIS: 7th International Conference on Adaptive Instructional Systems
- HCI-CPT: 7th International Conference on HCI for Cybersecurity, Privacy and Trust
- HCI-Games: 7th International Conference on HCI in Games
- MobiTAS: 7th International Conference on HCI in Mobility, Transport and Automotive Systems
- AI-HCI: 6th International Conference on Artificial Intelligence in HCI
- MOBILE: 6th International Conference on Human-Centered Design, Operation and Evaluation of Mobile Communications

Conference Proceedings – Full List of Volumes

1. LNCS 15766, Human-Computer Interaction — Part I, edited by Masaaki Kurosu and Ayako Hashizume
2. LNCS 15767, Human-Computer Interaction — Part II, edited by Masaaki Kurosu and Ayako Hashizume
3. LNCS 15768, Human-Computer Interaction — Part III, edited by Masaaki Kurosu and Ayako Hashizume
4. LNCS 15769, Human-Computer Interaction — Part IV, edited by Masaaki Kurosu and Ayako Hashizume
5. LNCS 15770, Human-Computer Interaction — Part V, edited by Masaaki Kurosu and Ayako Hashizume
6. LNCS 15771, Human-Computer Interaction — Part VI, edited by Masaaki Kurosu and Ayako Hashizume
7. LNCS 15772, Human-Computer Interaction — Part VII, edited by Masaaki Kurosu and Ayako Hashizume
8. LNCS 15773, Human Interface and the Management of Information: Part I, edited by Hirohiko Mori and Yumi Asahi
9. LNCS 15774, Human Interface and the Management of Information: Part II, edited by Hirohiko Mori and Yumi Asahi
10. LNCS 15773, Human Interface and the Management of Information: Part III, edited by Hirohiko Mori and Yumi Asahi
11. LNAI 15776, Engineering Psychology and Cognitive Ergonomics: Part I, edited by Don Harris and Wen-Chin Li
12. LNAI 15777, Engineering Psychology and Cognitive Ergonomics: Part II, edited by Don Harris and Wen-Chin Li
13. LNAI 15778, Augmented Cognition, Part I, edited by Dylan D. Schmorrow and Cali M. Fidopiastis
14. LNAI 15779, Augmented Cognition, Part II, edited by Dylan D. Schmorrow and Cali M. Fidopiastis
15. LNCS 15780, Universal Access in Human-Computer Interaction: Part I, edited by Margherita Antona and Constantine Stephanidis
16. LNCS 15781, Universal Access in Human-Computer Interaction: Part II, edited by Margherita Antona and Constantine Stephanidis
17. LNCS 15782, Cross-Cultural Design: Part I, edited by Pei-Luen Patrick Rau
18. LNCS 15783, Cross-Cultural Design: Part II, edited by Pei-Luen Patrick Rau
19. LNCS 15784, Cross-Cultural Design: Part III, edited by Pei-Luen Patrick Rau
20. LNCS 15785, Cross-Cultural Design: Part IV, edited by Pei-Luen Patrick Rau
21. LNCS 15786, Social Computing and Social Media: Part I, edited by Adela Coman and Simona Vasilache

85. CCIS 2772, HCI International 2025 — Late Breaking Posters: Part II, edited by Constantine Stephanidis, Margherita Antona, Stavroula Ntoa, George Margetis and Gavriel Salvendy
86. CCIS 2773, HCI International 2025 — Late Breaking Posters: Part III, edited by Constantine Stephanidis, Margherita Antona, Stavroula Ntoa, George Margetis and Gavriel Salvendy

https://2025.hci.international/proceedings

27th International Conference on Human-Computer Interaction (HCII 2025)

The full list with the Program Board Chairs and the members of the Program Boards of all thematic areas and affiliated conferences of HCII 2025 is available online at:

http://www.hci.international/board-members-2025.php

HCI International 2026 Conference

The 28th International Conference on Human-Computer Interaction, HCI International 2026, will be held jointly with the affiliated conferences at the Montréal Convention Centre (Palais des congrès de Montréal), in Montreal, Canada, 26–31 July 2026. It will cover a broad spectrum of themes related to Human-Computer Interaction, including theoretical issues, methods, tools, processes, and case studies in HCI design, as well as novel interaction techniques, interfaces, and applications. The proceedings will be published by Springer (part of Springer Nature) in a multi-volume set. More information will become available on the conference website: https://2026.hci.international/.

General Chair
Constantine Stephanidis
University of Crete and ICS-FORTH
Heraklion, Crete, Greece
Email: general_chair@2026.hci.international

https://2026.hci.international/

Contents

Artificial Intelligence and Smart Services in Digital Human Modeling

Health Monitoring, Decision-Making, and Care Optimization

Ergonomics and Digital Human Modeling

Ergonomics and Digital Human Modeling – a Literature Review and Case Study

Satyaswaroop Nanda[(⊠)], Aashish Kumar Maduri, Andre Luebke,
and Vincent G. Duffy

Purdue University, West Lafayette, IN 47906, USA
`{nanda11,amaduri}@purdue.edu`

Abstract. Ergonomics is the study of optimizing the interaction between workers, equipment, tasks, and their environment to improve efficiency and comfort. The term "ergonomics" is derived from two Greek words: "ergon," meaning work, and "nomos," meaning laws. This article presents a literature review on ergonomics and a case study focused on the ergonomic analysis of an excavator operator using the 3D analysis software RAMSIS. A 3D CAD model of the excavator is provided, with manikins created based on an anthropometric database. The analysis includes three manikins representing the 5th percentile male, 50th percentile male, and 95th percentile male. Each manikin is positioned as the driver within the excavator cabin, and an ergonomic assessment is carried out for both the current and neutral postures. The report focuses on the application of advanced RAMSIS analysis features to conduct a detailed ergonomic assessment. Specifically, it examines comfort analysis to evaluate posture data and identify potential discomfort areas within the cabin following adjustments to the steering wheel position. The report documents posture data results after incremental adjustments to the steering wheel position. For the literature review, databases such as Scopus and Scite.ai, along with the bibliometric software Biblioshiny and VOSviewer are utilized.

Keywords: Ergonomics · RAMSIS · Scopus · Scite.ai · Biblioshiny &
VOSviewer

1 Introduction and Background

Ergonomics is a broad field that explores the interaction between individuals, machines, and their work environments, with a diverse array of research and practical applications. According to the International Association of Ergonomics (IEA), ergonomics is the study of various factors in human anatomy, physiology, and psychology in a certain working environment (Wu, 2022). The study of how humans interact with machines and their surrounding environments focuses on factors such as work efficiency, human health, safety, and comfort, addressing these concerns in various settings like the workplace, home, and during leisure time. Interactions between machinery and the environment provides a more comprehensive basis for the design and use of the human-machine system by revealing the law of the relationship between the three elements of human,

© The Author(s), under exclusive license to Springer Nature Switzerland AG 2026
V. G. Duffy (Ed.): HCII 2025, LNCS 16339, pp. 3–20, 2026.
https://doi.org/10.1007/978-3-032-13012-9_1

machine, and environment, thereby ensuring the optimization of the overall performance of the human-machine system(Wu, 2022). Figure 1 shows the 3 elements of Ergonomics design and their interactions.

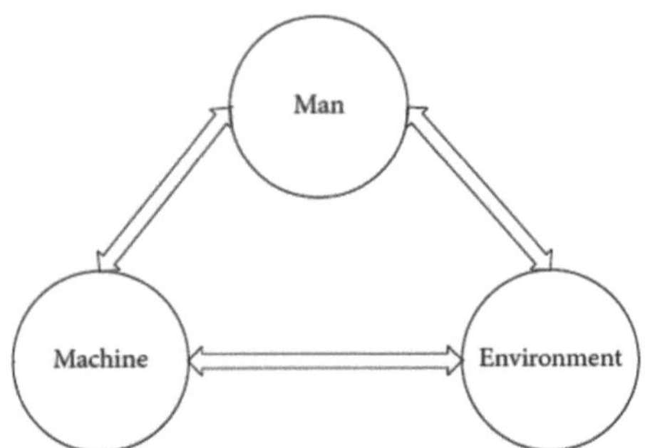

Fig. 1. Three Elements of Ergonomics Design (Wu, 2022)

DHM has emerged as state-of-art technology for ergonomic evaluation of product and/or workstations in virtual environment and is on the verge of becoming an integral part of computer-aided ergonomics and computer aided engineering (Sanjog et al. 2015). Simulations using digital mockups and digital human models are cost-effective in the long term compared to the traditional ergonomic evaluation methods in a typical product or process development scenario. DHM technology is gaining increasing interest among researchers because it allows for obtaining realistic results both in the design process and in the assessment of ergonomic indicators in the workplace (Lasota and Hankiewicz 2024).

The objective of this paper is to present a brief literature review on Ergonomics and Digital Human Modeling, along with an ergonomic analysis of three operators seated in an excavator under typical environmental conditions using advanced RAMSIS features. Anthropometric databases are employed in product design and human ergonomics evaluation, while digital human modeling facilitates ergonomics analysis from the early stages of product and workstation design (Dahibhate et al. 2023). In this study, three manikin models representing the 5th, 50th, and 95th percentile males were created using an anthropometric database. Each manikin was assigned the role of an operator, collectively representing a broad range of the population.The excavator geometry, imported from a 3D model, was utilized as the simulated vehicle environment. The manikins were positioned within the cabin based on predefined constraints applied in the RAMSIS software. Subsequently, the steering wheel location was adjusted to determine the optimal position that accommodates all three manikins while minimizing ergonomic stress.

1.1 Purpose Statement

In the RAMSIS 3D software, male manikins representing the 5th, 50th, and 95th percentiles were positioned within the excavator cabin. The initial ergonomic assessment identified significant discomfort levels, with elevated posture values recorded in the neck, shoulders, and back of all three manikins. This finding highlights the impact of suboptimal seat design, steering wheel placement, and control panel configuration on operator comfort. Such poor ergonomic conditions can lead to musculoskeletal issues, including joint and back pain, as well as fatigue. Over time, these factors may also increase the likelihood of accidents in the workplace.

2 Literature Review

2.1 Data Collection and Analysis

A brief analysis using Google Ngram underscores the importance of Safety Engineering in relation to Ergonomics and Digital Human Modeling. Figure 2 illustrates the frequency of references to these terms in Google Books from 2010 to 2022. The data shows that while mentions of Safety Engineering and Digital Human Modeling have remained fairly consistent throughout this period, the frequency of references to Ergonomics has significantly increased in research publications.

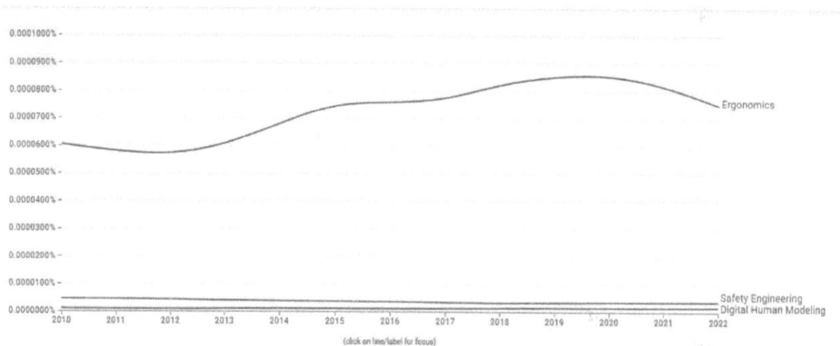

Fig. 2. A graph from GoogleNgram compares the keywords "Ergonomics", " Digital Human Modeling" & "Safety Engineering" (https://books.google.com/ngrams/, n.d.)

To explore the current research in the field of Ergonomics, particularly in relation to Engineering and Digital Human Modeling, research articles were downloaded from the Scopus and Scite.ai databases. The search terms used in these databases were "Ergonomics" and "Ergonomics and Digital Human Modeling." These databases include all peer-reviewed literature, such as scientific journals, books, and conference proceedings. The metadata analysis was performed using bibliometric software, including Biblioshiny and VOSviewer. Bibliometrix software-Biblioshiny is an application that allows the importing of data from Web of Science, and Scopus for performing bibliometric analysis and building data matrices for co-citation, coupling, scientific collaboration analysis, and co-word analysis. (Aria, 2017). Table 1 summarizes the Database used, Keywords searched, and Number of research articles yielded. For Scopus and Scite.ai, the articles were searched for the period 2020–2024.

For this paper, only articles related to Ergonomics within the subject area of Engineering were collected from the Scopus database for the period 2020–2024, totaling 1929

Table 1. Data Collection on Research Areas – Ergonomics and Digital Human Modeling

Database	Keyword Search	Number of Articles
Scopus	Ergonomics	1929
Scopus	Ergonomics, Digital Human Modeling	66
Scite.ai	Ergonomics	760

articles. A similar search was conducted for "Ergonomics" and "Digital Human Modeling," yielding 66 published articles. Figure 3 illustrates the annual number of articles published on Ergonomics within the Engineering field from 2020 to 2024. The number of articles remained relatively steady between 2020 and 2022, with the highest number of articles published in 2024, reaching to 504. However, there was a slight decline in 2023, with only 324 articles published. Figure 4 shows a similar trend in the number of articles published related to 'Ergonomics and Digital Human Modeling (DHM)'.

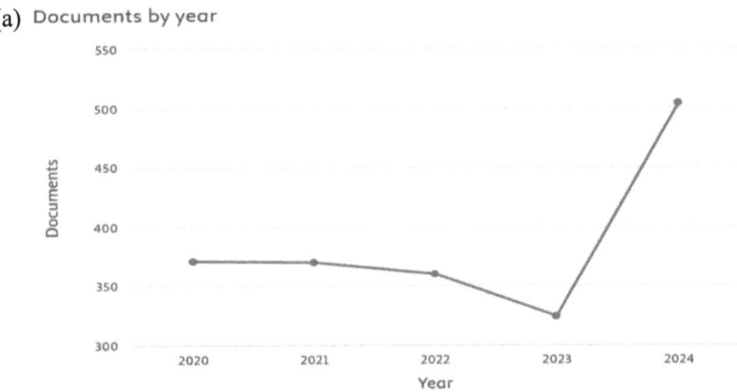

Fig. 3A. Articles published on Ergonomics 2020–2024(Scopus, n.d.)

Figure 5 and 6 shows the articles published based on the country between the period 2020–2024. From the trend, it is evident that USA is the leading publisher followed by the China, India and Italy.

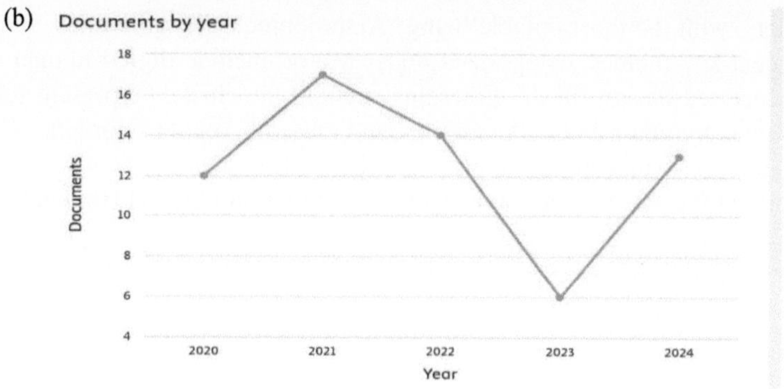

Fig. 3B. Articles published on Ergonomics and DHM 2020–2024(Scopus, n.d.)

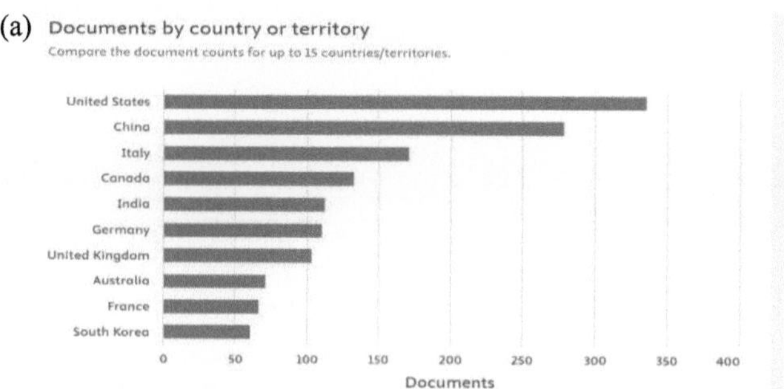

Fig. 4A. Top 10 Country Articles Published on Ergonomics 2020–2024(Scopus, n.d.)

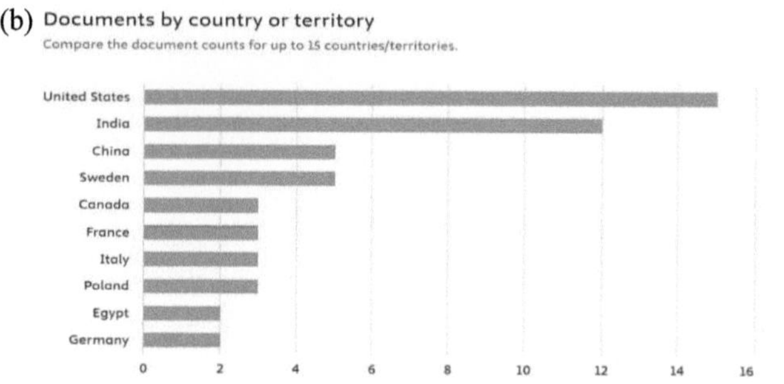

Fig. 4B. Top 10 Country Articles Published on Ergonomics & DHM 2020–2024 (Scopus, n.d.)

2.2   Thematic Map on Ergonomics and Digital Human Modeling

The thematic map organizes the cluster distribution into four quadrants, using a coordinate system where centrality is represented on the x-axis and density on the y-axis. Figure 5 presents the thematic map for articles related to "Ergonomics and Digital Human Modeling." Eleven distinct clusters are identified based on the following parameters: 225 words, a minimum of 3 clusters, and 2 labels. The primary themes consist of four clusters, with the most notable being "Anthropometry," ergonomics, and Industry 4.0. The next key themes, categorized under Motor, include digital human modeling and user-centered design. In the Emerging section, the clusters represent topics such as digital twin, human-robot collaboration, and musculoskeletal disorders. Niche areas explored include healthcare ergonomics and human-product interaction. The thematic maps highlight the various applications of Ergonomics and Digital Human Modeling.

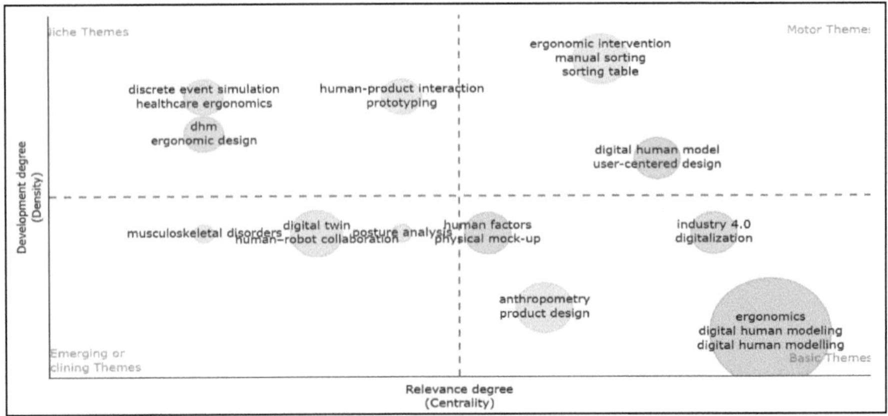

Fig. 5. Thematic related to Articles Published on 'Ergonomics & DHM' (Aria, 2017)

2.3 Word Cloud on Ergonomics and Digital Human Modeling

To generate the word cloud and word table, data from Scopus, comprising 66 published articles between 2020 and 2024 related to "Ergonomics and Digital Human Modeling," were imported into Biblioshiny software. The parameters were set to display the top 30 words (Fig. 6).

Fig. 6. Word Cloud from articles published on 'Ergonomics & DHM' (Aria, 2017)

The larger words, such as "digital human modeling," "ergonomics", "anthropometry," and "digital twin, optimization" and "productivity" clearly highlight the focus of research and the application of Ergonomics and DHM.

2.4 Co-Citation Analysis

VOSviewer software is used to conduct co-citation analysis on the topics of "Ergonomics and Digital Human Modeling," utilizing data sourced from Scopus. Co-citation analysis is a bibliometric method that examines how often two papers, authors, or journals are cited together by a third document. To identify the most highly cited papers related to Digital Twin (DT) in Manufacturing and DT in Ergonomics, data from both Scopus and Web of Science were imported into VOSviewer software.

Figure 7 displays the co-citation analysis network, where the minimum number of citations for a referenced paper was set to 3, and the top 5 most cited references were selected. The figure reveals five distinct clusters and the strength of their connections. Table 2 lists the top 5 research papers, published and highly cited between 2020 and 2024, that are relevant to "Ergonomics and Digital Human Modeling".

Fig. 7. Co citation analysis on 'Ergonomics and DHM' (VOSviewer, n.d.)

Table 2. Data Collection on Research Areas – Ergonomics and Digital Human Modeling (VOSviewer, n.d.)

Selected	Cited reference	Citations	Total link strength
✓	bubb h., engstler f., fritzsche f., mergl c., sabbah o., sch...	3	7
✓	feyen r., liu y., chaffin d., jimmerson g., joseph b., com...	4	6
✓	karhu o., kansi p., kuorinka i., correcting working postu...	4	6
✓	marshall r., case k., porter m., summerskill s., gyi d., da...	3	6
✓	zhu w., fan x., zhang y., applications and research trend...	3	3

Table 3. Steps followed for the RAMSIS setup and Ergonomics Analysis

	Tasks
Step 1	Launch RAMSIS Software–Click on *'launchNextGenAutomotive'*.Add the License code and change the background color of the screen from Black to Blue
Step 2	Add the following Plugin. From the 'Extra – Option' dropdown. *NextGen Ergonomics,NextGen Project Manager, NextGen Bodybuilder, NextGen Congnitive*
Step3	Right-click and select the following from the drop-down – *'Framework View' 'Framework Operation', 'Ergonomics Analysis', 'Ergonomics Operations', and 'Ergonomics Project'*

3 Ergonomics Analysis Using RAMSIS Software

For our ergonomic analysis, we utilized RAMSIS software to create three driver manikins representing the 5th, 50th, and 95th percentile males. The initial setup of the RAMSIS software, including the creation and positioning of the manikins are detailed in the procedure below which involved generating the manikins and positioning them in the driver's seat using the RAMSIS constraint application. This report will specifically demonstrate the application of advanced RAMSIS features (Figs. 7, 8, 9, 10, 11 and 12).

Fig. 8. Step 1–3 – Initial Setup

(*continued*)

(continued)

| Step 4 | a. Select from the Start menu *'NextGen bodybuilder'*
b. Select the *'Anthropometric Database'* from the Anthropometry dropdown. From the popup window select *'German2004'* & *'Male'*
c. From the same dropdown select *'Typology – Control measurements'* For this project we have selected created 3 male manikins
   1. *Male Manikins – 50th percentile*
   2. Alter the percentiles in the control measurements section and click OK
d. From the same dropdown select *'Add Body Measure list to structure tree'* and in the popup window name as *50_Male_Body Measure* |
| Step 5 | a. Select the Ergonomics plugin from the Start menu
b. Click on the 'Role Definition' and create a Name as 'Tom-Operator'
c. Click on the 'Test Sample' icon and give Manikin's Name as Tom-Operator. From the *Anthropometry* tab select Male and corresponding Body Measure list from the dropdown. Assign the Tom-Operator role in the *Role Assignment* tab. Under *Additional Option* select ' No Skinpoints' and 'No shoes'
d. Click Create, Tom-Operator, 50 percent of male manikins is created
e. Follow the same steps in creating 5th-Jim and 95th-Harry percentile Male manikins |

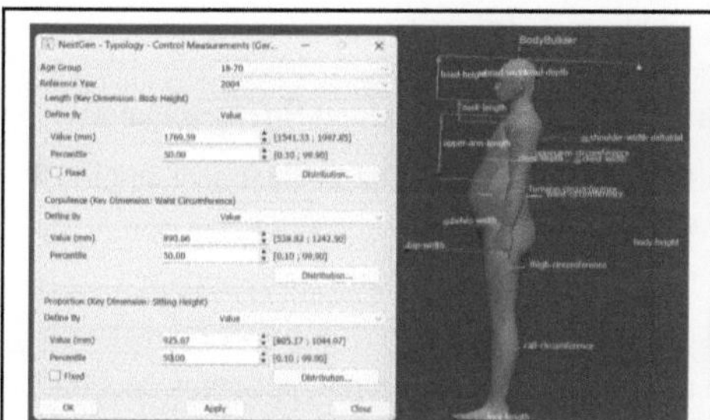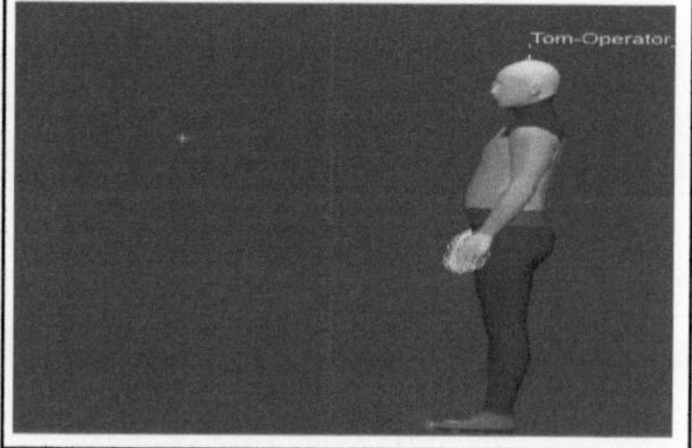

Fig. 9. Step 4 / 5 Manikin Creation _ 50P Tom Operator

Step 6	Add the 3D geometry file of the Excavator into the design environment
Step 7	The Manikin Tom Operator H-Point is now aligned with the floor level. Click on the icon 'Translate Object' to move the manikin near the Truck
Step 8	Click on *'Geometry'* in the structure and hide the exterior parts, Floor, and the doors of the Heavy Truck
Step 9	a. Add the skin points provided along with the Geomtry into the manikin Mike Driver b. Assign 'Workshoe' to the Manikin by selecting the object properties and Additional options in the popup window

12   S. Nanda et al.

Fig. 10. Steps 6–9 – Manikin Position near the Excavator

Step 10	Place the Manikin onto the seat of the Excavator. To do this a. Select *Define Restriction'* from the dropdown ' Operations ' b. In the popup window set 'Target' under *'Restriction Type'* c. In the section *'Manikin Comp'* box, type H-point d. To select the *'Env. Object'* click on the seat surface adjustment e. Press Create to execute the command f. **The H-Point of Manikin is now constrained to the Seat Surface Plane**
Step 11	Repeat the above steps to execute the constraint between the Shoe heel and Floor surface. **RightHeel / Floor and LeftHeel /Floor**
Step 12	Repeat the above steps to execute the constraint between the Shoe and the Footrest. **RightBall / Line_5 and LeftBall /Line_3**
Step 13	Repeat the above steps to execute the constraint between the Steering wheel and hand. **HAL2_1/STW_Left and HAR2_1/STW_Right**

Fig. 11. Step 10–13 – Manikin Target Constraints

| Step 14 | Move the manikin to the seat of the Excavator Cabin
a. Ensure all the 7 constrains have been applied to the Manikin – Tom Driver
b.In the **'Define Restriction'** popup window click on Posture calculation
c.From the popup window that appears, click the Start icon. Once the computation is completed the status will show whether the Posture calculation will indicate whether successfully completed based on the constraints applied
d.In the *Define Restriction* popup window select the Restriction type as *Manual Grasping* and Grasping mode as *Grasp Firmly* for left and right hands
d.For the manikin Tom Driver's initial Posture calculation was successfully completed |

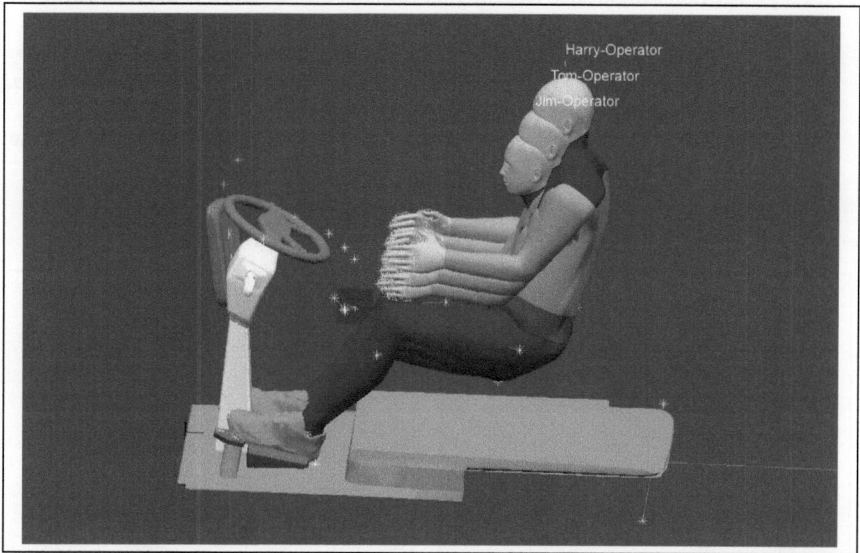

Fig. 12. Three male manikins positioned in the Excavator cabin

| Step 15 | Follow Steps 10–14 to move the Manikin Jim and Harry to Excavator Cabin and perform the Posture calculation |

(continued)

(*continued*)

Step 16	**Align the bottom heel of the shoes of all the 3 manikins**

a) From the Geometry drop down menu, select *'Point'* and create two points on the Floor level

b) Select Line from the Geometry drop down and draw the *'line'* joining the two above points

c) Select *Define Restriction'* from the dropdown' Operations '. In the popup window set 'Target' under *'Restriction Type'*

d) In the section*'Manikin Comp'* box, select the Left Heel / Right Heel

e) To select the *'Env. Object'* click on the Line15 as created above

f) Press *'Create'* to execute the command

g) The Left / Right shoe Heel of Tom Operator isconstrained to the Line 15

h) Click on *'Posture calculation'* to positon the manikin shoeheel to the Line15

   i) Select Tom Operator and from the edit drop down menu, select *'special copy'*

j) Select the manikins Harry and Jim.From the edit drop down menu select *'special paste'* and restriction section within in

Click on Posture calculation to positon the manikin Harry and Jim shoe heel to the Line15 as shown in Fig. 13

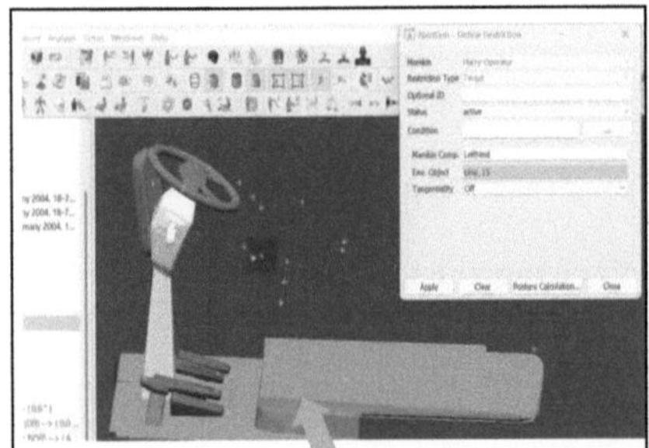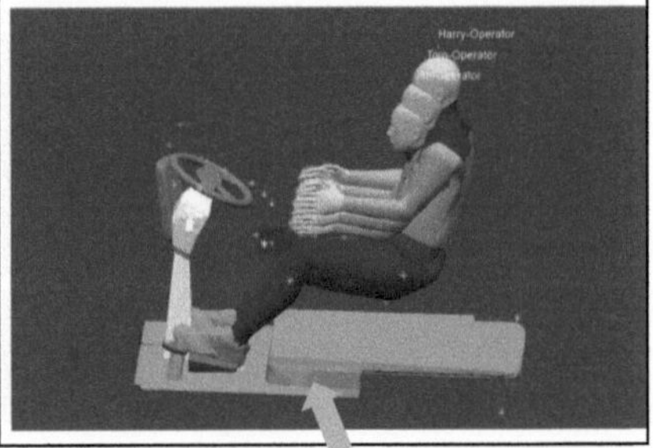

Fig. 13. Step 16 – Align bottom Shoe heel position

Step 17	**Kinematic Analysis Process set up –Steering Wheel – Translational**

a) From the 'Geometry' dropdown select 'Define Kinematics'

b) Select the origin by clicking on any point on the steering column

c) Click Add Degrees of Freedom select the type of DOF as 'Translation'

d) For Direction box, select X-axis and Z-axis to form a vector

e) Set the Maximum Value as 100mm as initial values

f) Click on Add object and select 'Steering Wheel' from structure tree

Click Create – Ref Fig. 2 (Fig. 14)

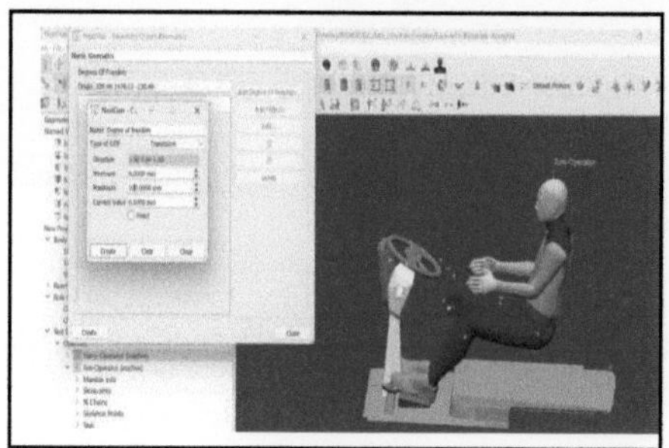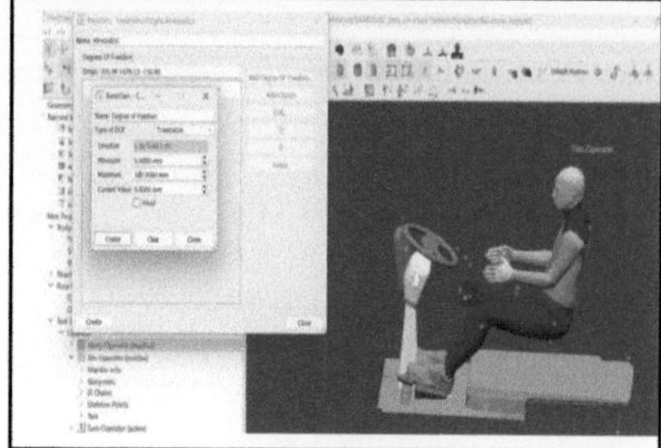

Fig. 14. Step 17 – Kinematics Analysis Set Up –– Translational

Step 18	**Kinematic Analysis Process set up –Steering Wheel – Rotational** a) Create a point on the Steering wheel column and select that as 'Origin Point' b) Click Add Degrees of Freedom select the type of DOF as 'Rotational' c) For Direction box, select Y-axis to form a vector d) Set the Maximum Value as 30 deg and Minimum Value as -30 deg e) Click on Add object and select 'Steering Wheel' from structure tree Click Create – Ref Fig. 15

Step 19	**Kinematic Analysis and Comfort Feeling Assessment of all three Manikins** a) Constraint application of Steering Wheel and Manikin b) Repeat Step 16 from c) to k) to execute the constraint between the Steering wheel and hand. **HAL2_1/STW_Left and HAR2_1/STW_Right** c) For the Kinematic Analysis – Set initial values for **Transnational** to **0mm** and **Rotational** to **0deg** d) Comfort Feeling Assessment of 50P manikin – Tom Operator. To do this select the *'Comfort Feeling'* tab from the *Analysis* drop-down. Repeat the same for other manikins Figure 16 shows the initial comfort assessment of three manikins

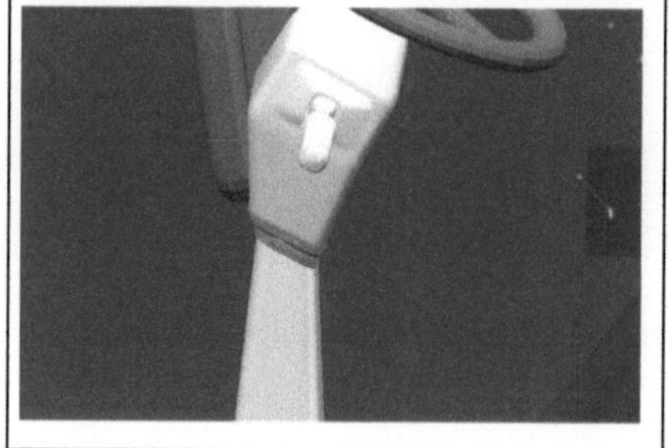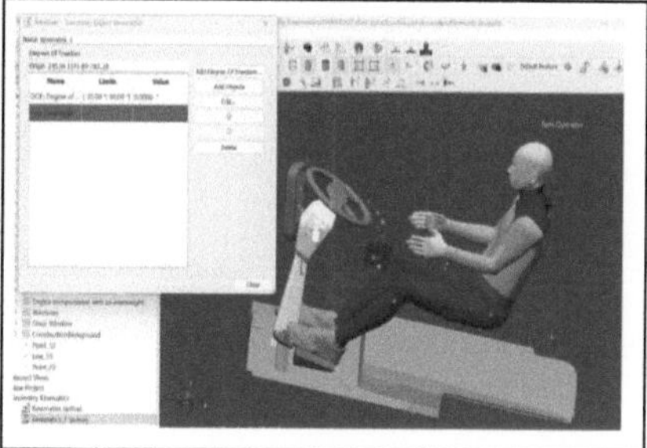

Fig. 15. Step 5 – Kinematics Analysis Set Up – Rotational

Step 19	**Kinematic Analysis and Comfort Feeling Assessment of all three Manikins**
	e) Constraint application of Steering Wheel and Manikin
	f) Repeat Step 16 from c) to k) to execute the constraint between the Steering wheel and hand. **HAL2_1/STW_Left and HAR2_1/STW_Right**
	g) For the Kinematic Analysis – Set initial values for **Transnational** to **0mm** and **Rotational** to **0deg**
	h) Comfort Feeling Assessment of 50P manikin – Tom Operator. To do this select the *'Comfort Feeling'* tab from the *Analysis* drop-down. Repeat the same for other manikins
	Figure 16 shows the comfort assessment of three manikins

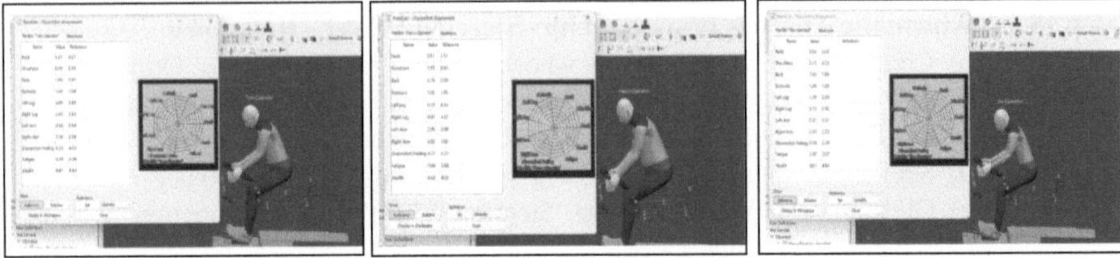

Fig. 16. Step 19 –Kinematic Analysis - Steering Wheel -Translational & Rotational

Step 20	**Kinematic Analysis and Comfort Assessment of all three manikins**
	a) For the Kinematic Analysis – Set initial values for **Transnational** to **10mm** and **Rotational** to **10deg**
	b) Comfort Feeling Assessment of 50P manikin – Tom Operator. To do this select the *'Comfort Feeling'* tab from the *Analysis* drop-down. Repeat the same for other manikins
	Figure 17 shows the comfort assessment of three manikins

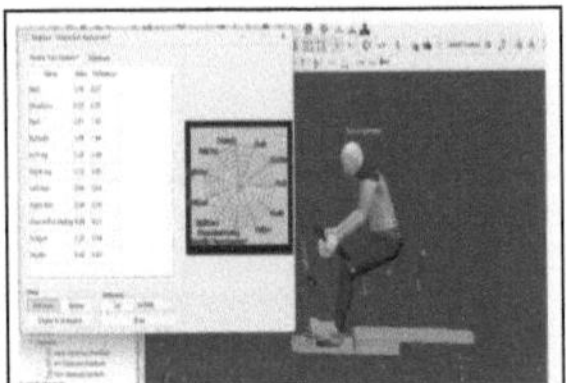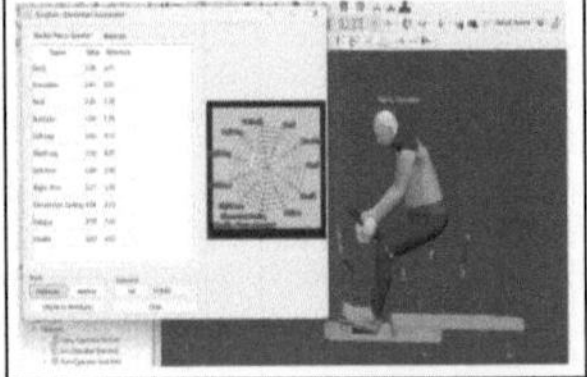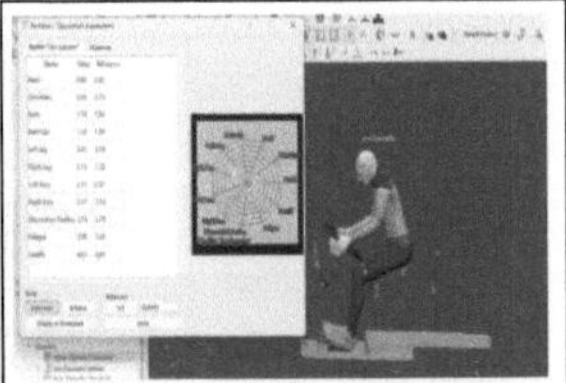

Fig. 17. Step 20 –Kinematic Analysis - Steering Wheel -Translational & Rotational

(continued)

(continued)

Step 21	**Kinematic Analysis and Comfort Assessment of all three manikins** c) For the Kinematic Analysis – Set initial values for **Transnational** to **50mm** and **Rotational** to **20deg** d) Comfort Feeling Assessment of 50P manikin – Tom Operator. To do this select the *'Comfort Feeling'* tab from the *Analysis* drop-down. Repeat the same for other manikins Figure 18 shows the comfort assessment of three manikins

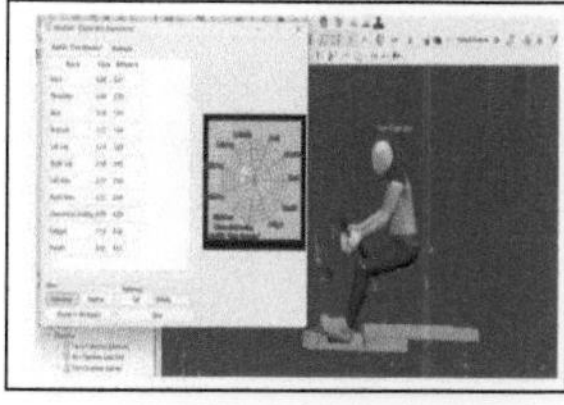 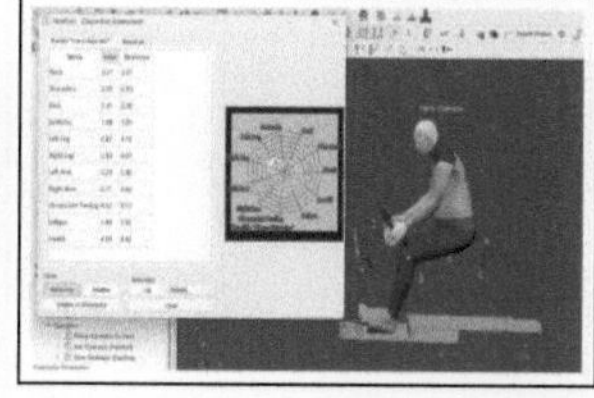 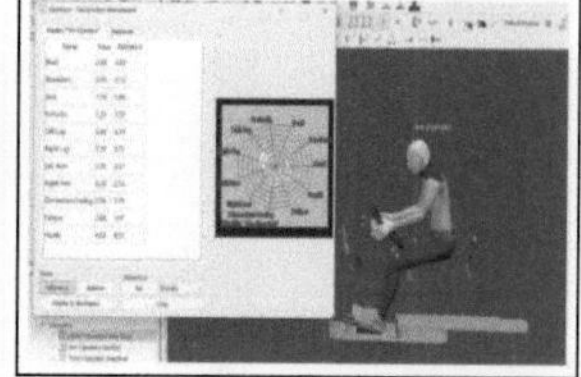

Fig. 18. Step 21 –Kinematic Analysis - Steering Wheel -Translational & Rotational

Step 22	**Kinematic Analysis and Comfort Assessment of all three manikins** e) For the Kinematic Analysis – Set initial values for **Transnational** to **100mm** and **Rotational** to **30deg** f) Comfort Feeling Assessment of 50P manikin – Tom Operator. To do this select the *'Comfort Feeling'* tab from the *Analysis* drop-down. Repeat the same for other manikins Figure 19 shows the initial comfort assessment of three manikins

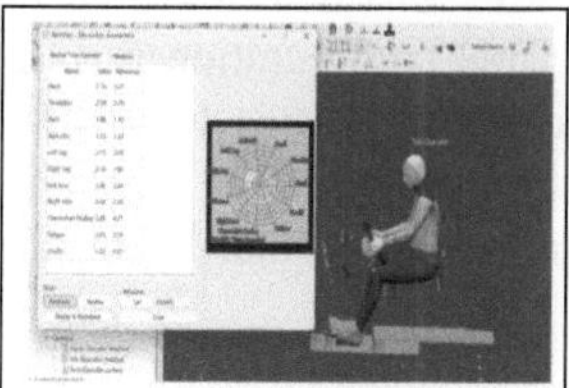 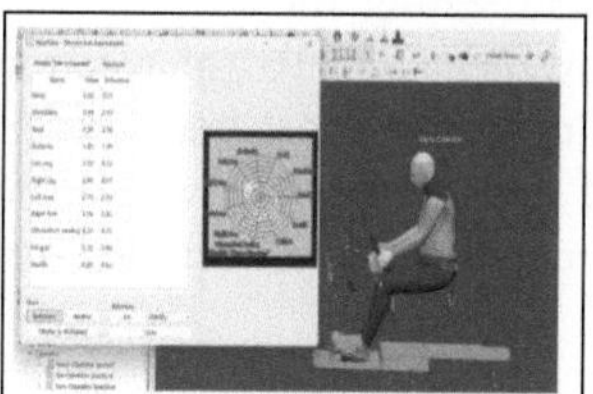 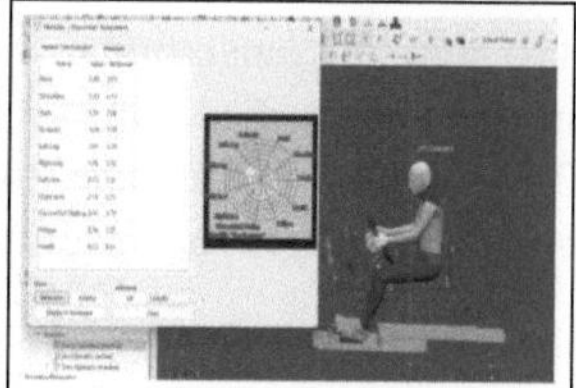

Fig. 19. Step 22 –Kinematic Analysis - Steering Wheel -Translational & Rotational

(continued)

(continued)

Step 23	**Kinematic Analysis and Comfort Assessment of all three manikins** g) For the Kinematic Analysis – Set initial values for **Transnational** to **110mm** and **Rotational** to **16deg** h) Comfort Feeling Assessment of 50P manikin – Tom Operator. To do this select the *'Comfort Feeling'* tab from the *Analysis* drop-down. Repeat the same for other manikins i) Fig. 20 shows the initial comfort assessment of three manikins

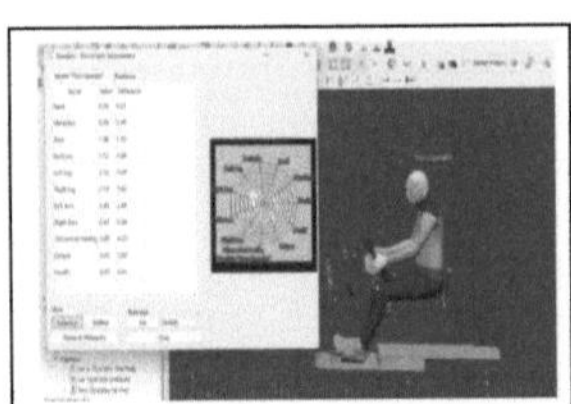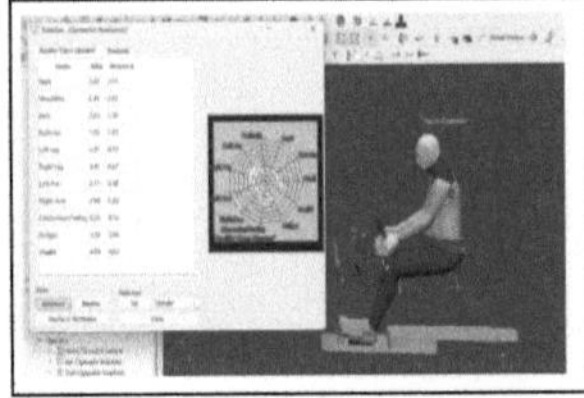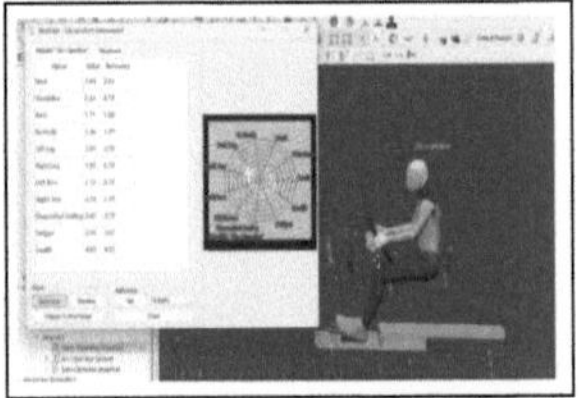

Fig. 20. Step 23 –Kinematic Analysis - Steering Wheel -Translational & Rotational

4   Results

Table 4 presents the consolidated discomfort values derived from the ergonomic comfort assessment conducted for three manikins representing the 5th, 50th, and 95th male percentiles. The table summarizes discomfort levels across five different steering wheel positions evaluated through kinematic analysis. These five iterations involved varying both the translational and rotational adjustments of the steering wheel to identify its optimal position using the advanced RAMSIS Kinematic Analysis feature.

The optimal steering wheel setting for all three manikins was determined to be 110 mm of translational movement and 16° of rotation. This configuration resulted in the lowest discomfort values, with most body parts recording scores well below 3.5. Figure 21 illustrates the optimal steering wheel position for the three manikins, representing a broad spectrum of the population based on the kinematic analysis results.

Table 4. Posture Values after Steering Wheel position adjustment

Body Parts \ Steering Wheel Position	Comfort Assessment - Kinematic Analysis														
	Translational - 0 mm Rotational - 0 deg			Translational - 10mm Rotational - 10deg			Translational - 50mm Rotational - 20deg			Translational - 100mm Rotational - 30deg			Translational - 110mm Rotational - 16deg		
	J5P	T 50P	H 95P	J 5P	T 50P	H 95P	J5P	T 50P	H 95P	J5P	T 50P	H 95P	J5P	T 50P	H 95P
Neck	3.03	3.27	3.51	2.88	3.18	3.38	2.66	2.98	3.21	2.49	2.76	3.02	2.26	2.39	2.77
Shoulders	2.73	2.70	2.93	2.60	2.59	2.81	2.45	2.48	2.61	2.33	2.39	2.44	2.18	2.16	2.36
Back	1.66	1.93	2.36	1.74	2.01	2.40	1.70	2.00	2.31	1.71	1.98	2.25	1.22	1.33	1.78
Buttocks	1.29	1.64	1.95	1.32	1.69	1.94	1.23	1.63	1.90	1.26	1.53	1.85	0.82	0.96	1.42
Left Leg	3.79	3.89	4.12	3.21	3.38	3.63	2.43	2.64	2.87	2.01	2.13	2.37	2.07	2.12	2.36
Right Leg	3.72	3.83	4.07	3.15	3.32	3.58	2.37	2.58	2.83	1.95	2.18	2.41	1.95	2.00	2.26
Left Arm	2.31	2.64	2.90	2.31	2.66	2.84	2.20	2.57	2.79	2.13	2.45	2.71	1.85	2.00	2.42
Right Arm	2.33	2.58	2.82	2.31	2.60	2.77	2.20	2.51	2.71	2.14	2.43	2.66	1.75	1.98	2.32
Discomfort Feel	3.79	4.23	4.72	3.75	4.24	4.66	3.56	4.09	4.51	3.47	3.89	4.33	2.88	3.11	3.77
Fatigue	3.07	3.34	3.66	3.00	3.32	3.59	2.84	3.19	3.46	2.74	3.03	3.32	2.38	2.54	2.97
Health	4.61	4.61	4.62	4.61	4.62	4.67	4.62	4.62	4.69	4.63	4.63	4.69	4.61	4.62	4.63

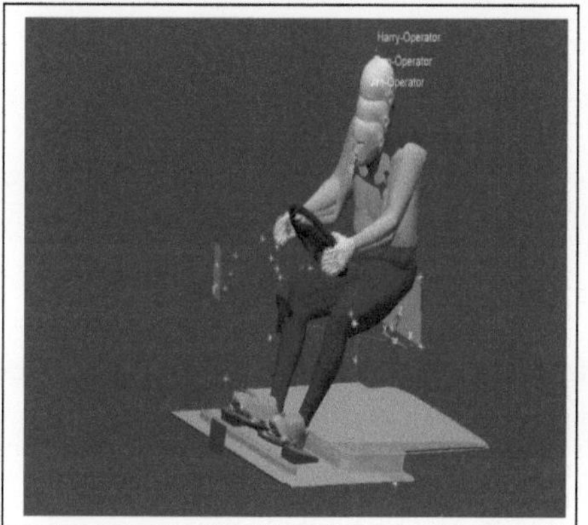

Fig. 21. Final Optimal Position of all the 3 three manikins after Kinematic analysis

5 Conclusion

This report presents a concise literature review on Digital Human Modeling and Ergonomics, with relevant research articles sourced from the Scopus and Scite.ai databases. A preliminary analysis was conducted using the Bibliometrix software, specifically through the Biblioshiny interface. The ergonomic assessment was performed using the RAMSIS Digital Human Modeling software.

A CAD model of an excavator was imported into the RAMSIS environment, where three manikins representing diverse population percentiles were created: Tom (50th percentile male), Harry (95th percentile male), and Jim (5th percentile male). All three manikins were designated as "Operators" to simulate their interaction with the excavator controls.

The Target Constraint application in RAMSIS was utilized to position each manikin in the driver's seat of the excavator cabin. The report leverages the advanced RAMSIS Kinematic Analysis feature to identify the optimal steering wheel position that minimizes ergonomic stress on key body parts, including the neck, shoulders, and back.

The initial discomfort assessment, detailed in Table 4, presents posture values for each manikin without any kinematic adjustments to the steering wheel. The findings indicate that all three manikins experienced significant stress in the neck region, followed by the shoulders and back. This underscores the need for adjustments to the steering wheel position to mitigate discomfort.

Subsequently, a kinematic analysis was conducted to determine the optimal steering wheel setting. When the steering wheel position was adjusted to align with the neutral posture of the manikins, posture values for the neck, shoulders, and back decreased significantly, falling well below the discomfort threshold of 3.5.

The results section presents the posture values obtained through multiple iterations of steering wheel adjustments in both translational and rotational directions. The optimal steering wheel position for each manikin is established, ensuring a significant reduction in ergonomic stress across the assessed body parts.

References

Aria, M., Cuccurullo, C.: An R-tool for comprehensive science mapping analysis. Journal of Informetrics (2017)

Dahibhate, G., Shinde, R., Sakle, N.: The use of digital human modeling in ergonomic design and product development. In: Journal of The Institution of Engineers (India): Series C **104**(5), pp. 1133–1138 (2023). Springer. https://doi.org/10.1007/s40032-023-00982-5

https://books.google.com/ngrams/. (n.d.). Google Ngram

Lasota, A.M., Hankiewicz, K.: Digital Human Modeling in Improving the Ergonomics of Industrial Workplace – a Methodological framework. Management and Production Engineering Review **15**(1), 182–192 (2024). https://doi.org/10.24425/mper.2024.149999

Sanjog, J., Karmakar, S., Patel, T., Chowdhury, A.: Towards virtual ergonomics: aviation and aerospace. In: Aircraft Engineering and Aerospace Technology **87**(3), 266–273 (2015). Emerald Group Holdings Ltd. https://doi.org/10.1108/AEAT-05-2013-0094

Scopus. (n.d.) Scopus : https://www.scopus.com/search/form.uri?display=basic#basic

Wu, C.: Application of ergonomics in product design based on computer-aided design. Mathematical Problems in Engineering, 2022 (2022). https://doi.org/10.1155/2022/7523367

VOSviewer. (n.d.). https://www.vosviewer.com/

Analysis of Ergonomic Risks Based on Physical and Postural Characteristics in the Food Industry

Luis Alberto Revilla-Vivar[1] and Jorge Buele[2]([✉])

[1] Facultad de Ingenierías, Universidad Tecnológica Indoamérica, Ambato 180103, Ecuador
[2] Centro de Investigación en Mecatrónica y Sistemas Interactivos (MIST), Universidad Tecnológica Indoamérica, Ambato 180103, Ecuador
jorgebuele@uti.edu.ec

Abstract. Musculoskeletal disorders are one of the leading causes of occupational disability worldwide, affecting workers across various industries, particularly in the food industry. These disorders are caused by factors such as improper postures, repetitive movements, and manual handling of loads. Despite efforts to mitigate these risks, ergonomic assessment in many work environments remains insufficient, as it is often limited to posture observation and does not include precise anthropometric measurements. This study aims to integrate anthropometric measurements with the Rapid Entire Body Assessment method for a more accurate and personalized evaluation of ergonomic risks in the food industry. Through a quantitative approach, anthropometric measurements of workers in a food production plant were analyzed and the Rapid Entire Body Assessment method was applied to assess working postures. The data obtained were statistically analyzed to identify correlations between the physical characteristics of employees and musculoskeletal discomfort. The results showed a significant correlation between anthropometric dimensions, such as elbow height and functional reach, with discomfort in areas such as the elbow, knees, and lower back. These findings emphasize the need to adapt workstations to the physical characteristics of employees to prevent injuries. The integration of anthropometric measurements and the Rapid Entire Body Assessment method provides a more accurate tool for assessing ergonomic risks and designing personalized interventions that improve occupational health and productivity in the food industry.

Keywords: Musculoskeletal disorders · Anthropometry · Ergonomics · Food industry

1 Introduction

Musculoskeletal disorders represent one of the leading causes of occupational disability worldwide, with a significant percentage of workers in industrial sectors [1, 2], such as manufacturing and the food industry, affected by these issues. According to recent studies, up to 79.89% of workers in the food industry experience musculoskeletal disorders, primarily in the back and upper limbs [3]. In sectors such as manufacturing, the

© The Author(s), under exclusive license to Springer Nature Switzerland AG 2026
V. G. Duffy (Ed.): HCII 2025, LNCS 16339, pp. 21–33, 2026.
https://doi.org/10.1007/978-3-032-13012-9_2

prevalence of musculoskeletal disorders in the limbs can reach up to 30% [4], seriously affecting employee health and company productivity [5]. According to the World Health Organization, approximately 60% of workers in industrial sectors face musculoskeletal disorder-related problems due to factors such as improper postures, repetitive physical exertion, and manual handling of loads [6]. In particular, the food industry, due to the nature of tasks such as product handling and the need to maintain prolonged postures, increases the risk of musculoskeletal injuries, impacting both worker health and company productivity [7, 8].

In food industry work environments, working conditions such as task repetition, prolonged static postures, and manual product handling contribute to a high prevalence of musculoskeletal disorders in areas such as the lower back, elbows, and knees [9]. Although various strategies have been implemented to mitigate these risks, reducing worker injuries remains a challenge due to the lack of a comprehensive ergonomic assessment that combines both postural evaluation and anthropometric measurements of workers. Employees in these industries are exposed to a higher likelihood of suffering from musculoskeletal disorders, which directly impacts their performance and the overall efficiency of companies [10].

Ergonomics and anthropometry have been extensively studied to address health issues in the workplace. In this context, Chung and Pérez [11] highlight the effectiveness of the Rapid Entire Body Assessment method for evaluating working postures and their relationship with the incidence of musculoskeletal disorders in the food industry. However, this approach is limited to posture evaluation without considering the specific physical characteristics of workers. Anthropometry, as a field dedicated to measuring human body dimensions, has proven to be important for customizing workstations and better adapting them to employees' physical characteristics [12].

The study by Benítez Pérez et al. [13] shows that, although some studies focus on posture measurement and others on anthropometry, the combination of both approaches remains insufficient. This highlights a significant gap in research, as the interaction between these areas allows for a more comprehensive analysis of ergonomic risks and the implementation of more effective solutions.

Despite advances in research on ergonomics and anthropometry, there is a significant gap in integrating these approaches into the analysis of occupational risks, particularly in the food industry [14]. Most studies have evaluated these two dimensions separately, without exploring how they interrelate and how this affects workers. This gap creates an opportunity to investigate the combination of postural and anthropometric evaluation, which could improve the accuracy of risk assessment and provide personalized ergonomic interventions [15].

This research seeks to integrate anthropometry with the Rapid Entire Body Assessment method to provide a more comprehensive evaluation of ergonomic risks among workers in the food industry. By combining anthropometric measurements, such as body height, shoulder width, and arm length, with the assessment of working postures through the Rapid Entire Body Assessment method, it will be possible to more accurately identify the ergonomic risk factors present in the work environment. This integration will enable the creation of a database that facilitates the development of personalized ergonomic solutions aimed not only at reducing musculoskeletal disorders but also at promoting a healthier and more efficient work environment.

The objective of this research is to develop a correlation between specific anthropometric measurements and the Rapid Entire Body Assessment evaluation in order to offer a personalized approach to the identification of ergonomic risks. Through the implementation of this methodology, a database will be created to support the design of ergonomic interventions adapted to the physical characteristics of the workers. This approach will not only contribute to the reduction of musculoskeletal injuries but also to the improvement of working conditions and overall well-being in the food industry.

2 Methodology

2.1 Study Approach

This study employs a quantitative approach to identify and analyze the ergonomic and anthropometric factors present in food industry workstations. The collected data are organized into tables and compared with international ergonomic standards, facilitating the analysis of awkward postures, repetitive movements, and other factors that impact workers' health [16].

2.2 Type of Research

The study is descriptive and applied, aimed at characterizing the working conditions of employees using standardized tools. The analysis of variables such as awkward postures and repetitive movements allows for the identification of the main risk factor [17]. The use of an inductive, non-experimental, and cross-sectional methodology provides a foundation for understanding the relationships between workers' physical characteristics and their musculoskeletal discomfort. By collecting specific data on anthropometric measurements and postures, the research seeks to identify associations that explain how ergonomic factors affect health. As a non-experimental study, the methodology focuses on observation without manipulating working conditions, allowing for a realistic and applicable view of the situation. In addition, the cross-sectional design, centered on the analysis of a single point in time, provides a snapshot of the existing risks without requiring longitudinal follow-up.

2.3 Population and Sample

The target population included all production plant workers. The sample was selected using non-probabilistic convenience sampling. The final sample consisted of 51 workers who met the established inclusion criteria: employees with at least six months of tenure, performing production tasks, and voluntarily agreeing to participate in the study.

2.4 Instruments and Procedure

To assess ergonomic risks, the Rapid Entire Body Assessment method was used to evaluate postures and physical workload at the workstations. The Nordic Musculoskeletal Questionnaire by Kuorinka was applied to identify musculoskeletal discomfort in various body regions, such as the back, shoulders, and wrists.

Anthropometric measurements were conducted using standard tools such as measuring tapes and calipers to collect data on height, limb length, and other key physical characteristics of the workers.

The data collection procedure consisted of the following steps:

- Obtaining informed consent from the participants.
- Direct observation of the workstations and application of the Rapid Entire Body Assessment method.
- Administration of the Nordic Musculoskeletal Questionnaire to assess musculoskeletal discomfort.
- Measurement of the workers' anthropometric characteristics.

2.5 Statistical Analysis

The data collected were analyzed using SPSS (version 26.0). Descriptive analyses (means, standard deviations, and frequencies) were performed. To evaluate the relationships between variables, the point-biserial correlation coefficient and Somers' D statistic were used.

2.6 Ethical Considerations

This study was conducted in accordance with the ethical principles established by the Helsinki Declaration [18], ensuring the confidentiality of personal data and the informed consent of participants at all times. The results obtained will be used exclusively for academic and scientific purposes, respecting the rights and privacy of those involved.

3 Results

3.1 Participant Profile and Anthropometric Characteristics

The following section presents the sociodemographic data of the participants in this study. Table 1 summarizes the main characteristics of the workers, including gender, age, marital status, family responsibilities, education level, type of transportation, and months of employment. These factors were collected to better understand the participants' profiles and how they may influence the results of the ergonomic assessment and Rapid Entire Body Assessment scores. The distribution of participants according to each variable provides key insight into the social and occupational context in which the study was conducted.

Table 2 shows the key anthropometric measurements of the participants, revealing that total body height has a mean of 160.2 cm with a standard deviation of 7.4 cm, indicating moderate variability among participants. Elbow height in the standing position

Table 1. Sociodemographic characteristics of the participants.

Variable	Category	n	%
Gender	Female	16	31%
	Male	35	69%
Age	18 - 24	13	25%
	25 - 30	21	41%
	31 or older	17	33%
Marital Status	Single	33	65%
	Married / Cohabiting	15	29%
	Divorced	3	6%
Family Responsibilities	None	23	45%
	1 person	11	22%
	2 or more people	17	33%
Education Level	Primary education	3	6%
	Secondary education	21	41%
	Higher education	27	53%
Type of Transportation	None	6	12%
	Private	22	43%
	Public	23	45%
Months of Employment	Less than 6 months	0	0%
	Between 6 and 12 months	17	33%

shows a mean of 99.5 cm and a standard deviation of 3.8 cm, suggesting that this measurement is relatively homogeneous among workers. Likewise, functional reach has a mean of 74.7 cm, standing out as one of the measurements with greater variability, with a range from 56 cm to 79 cm. These measures provide an overall view of the workers' physical dimensions.

Table 2. Summary of descriptive statistics (anthropometric measurements).

Anthropometric Measurement	Mean (cm)	Standard Deviation	Minimum (cm)	Maximum (cm)
Total body height	160.2	7.4	142	177
Elbow height (standing)	99.5	3.8	88	112
Elbow height (sitting)	73.0	4.5	63	78
Seat height	54.1	3.2	46	60

(continued)

Table 2. (continued)

Anthropometric Measurement	Mean (cm)	Standard Deviation	Minimum (cm)	Maximum (cm)
Leg length	95.2	4.2	88	104
Thigh depth	50.9	3.8	44	56
Shoulder width	43.4	2.3	40	49
Hip width	41.5	2.7	38	45
Arm length	63.7	3.5	56	69
Functional reach	74.7	4.2	66	79
Hand circumference	19.0	1.0	17.0	20.9
Finger length	8.0	0.5	7.0	9.0

3.2 Correlations Between Anthropometric Measures and Musculoskeletal Discomfort

Table 3 presents the results of the relationship between anthropometric measurements and musculoskeletal discomfort reported by the participants. The correlation coefficients indicate the strength and direction of the relationships between the different variables, while the p-values reflect the statistical significance of these associations. The correlations reveal important patterns that help to understand how certain anthropometric measurements may be associated with discomfort in different body areas, such as the neck, back, knees, ankles, and others.

Table 3. Associations between anthropometric measurements and musculoskeletal discomfort across different body regions.

Anthropometric Variable	Body Area with Discomfort	Coefficient r_{pb}	p-value
Total body height	Neck discomfort	−0.329	0.018
Total body height	Knee discomfort	−0.298	0.034
Total body height	Knee discomfort in the past 12 months	−0.305	0.030
Total body height	Neck discomfort	−0.283	0.044
Elbow height (standing)	Neck discomfort	−0.283	0.044
Elbow height (standing)	Knee discomfort	−0.305	0.030
Elbow height (standing)	Neck discomfort	−0.327	0.019
Elbow height (standing)	Ankle or foot discomfort	−0.297	0.035
Elbow height (sitting)	Elbow or forearm discomfort	−0.300	0.032
Elbow height (sitting)	Knee discomfort	−0.378	0.006

(continued)

Table 3. (*continued*)

Anthropometric Variable	Body Area with Discomfort	Coefficient r_pb	p-value
Hand circumference	Neck discomfort	−0.327	0.019
Hand circumference	Ankle or foot discomfort	−0.297	0.035
Leg length	Ankle or foot discomfort	−0.337	0.016
Shoulder width	Shoulder discomfort	−0.279	0.047
Shoulder width	Dorsal or lumbar discomfort	−0.291	0.038
Functional reach	Ankle or foot discomfort	−0.291	0.038
Functional reach	Ankle or foot discomfort	−0.297	0.035
Shoulder width	Shoulder discomfort	−0.291	0.036
Hand circumference	Neck discomfort	−0.344	0.013
Finger length	Neck discomfort	−0.289	0.039

r_pb = point-biserial correlation

The results show that several anthropometric measurements are significantly associated with musculoskeletal discomfort. For example, elbow height in the sitting position presents a significant correlation with knee discomfort ($r = -0.378$, $p = 0.006$), indicating that as this measurement increases, knee discomfort tends to decrease. In addition, functional reach also shows a significant relationship with ankle discomfort ($r = -0.297$, $p = 0.035$) and foot discomfort ($r = -0.291$, $p = 0.038$), suggesting that greater reach length may be associated with less discomfort in these areas. Overall, the data indicate that anthropometric measurements such as shoulder width, hand circumference, and finger length have significant relationships with discomfort in different parts of the body, highlighting the importance of adjusting working conditions to the physical characteristics of employees to reduce the risk of musculoskeletal injuries.

3.3   Associations Between Ergonomic Risk and Musculoskeletal Discomfort

Table 4 shows the Somers' D coefficients and their p-values for analyzing the relationship between ergonomic risk scores and musculoskeletal discomfort in different body areas. The Somers' D coefficient is a measure of association that helps determine the strength and direction of relationships between variables. This table highlights the body areas where significant relationships exist between ergonomic risk levels and reported discomfort, which is crucial for understanding how ergonomic conditions may affect workers' physical well-being.

Table 4. Associations between ergonomic risk levels and reported musculoskeletal discomfort in specific body regions.

Discomfort Area	Somers' D coefficient	p-value	Interpretation
Elbow/Forearm	0.251	0.030	Significant relationship
Knees	0.278	0.013	Strong association
Elbow/Forearm (Mild or more)	0.245	0.036	Significant relationship
Knees (Mild or more)	0.278	0.013	Strong association

The results indicate a significant relationship between ergonomic risk scores and musculoskeletal discomfort in several body areas. The strongest association is observed in the knees, with a Somers' D coefficient of 0.278 ($p = 0.013$), suggesting that higher ergonomic risk is strongly related to greater discomfort in the knees. A significant relationship is also found for the elbow/forearm, with a coefficient of 0.251 ($p = 0.030$), indicating a moderate correlation. These findings reinforce the importance of conducting ergonomic assessments focused on specific body areas to reduce the risks of musculoskeletal injuries, especially in more affected areas such as the knees and elbow/forearm.

Figure 1 shows the relationship between various anthropometric measurements (such as total body height, elbow height in standing position, leg length, etc.) and ergonomic risk scores. It can be observed that the anthropometric measurements (represented by lines of different colors) exhibit a relatively consistent dispersion pattern, while the ergonomic risk scores (in green) fluctuate with greater variability over time. There does not appear to be a clear or direct correlation between physical measurements and ergonomic scores, although some peaks in ergonomic scores coincide with certain height or length values, suggesting that some workers with specific anthropometric characteristics may be exposed to higher ergonomic risks.

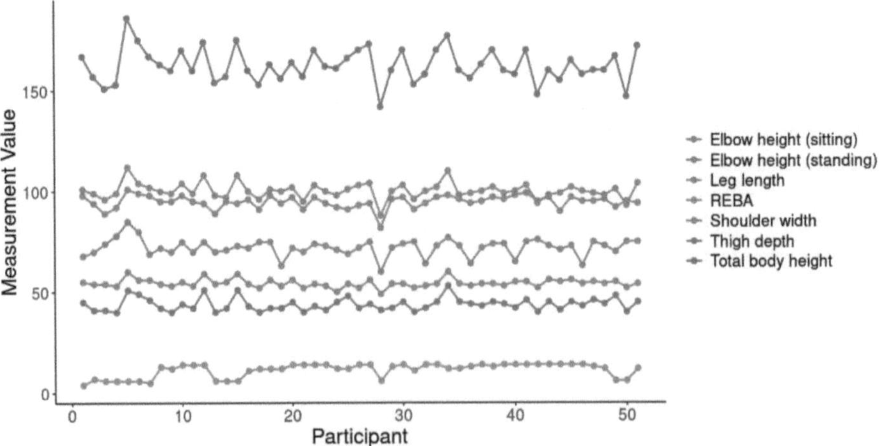

Fig. 1. Scatter plot of anthropometric measurements and ergonomic risk scores.

3.4 Distribution of Anthropometric Measurements and Ergonomic Scores by Gender

Figure 2 shows the distribution of total body height according to the gender of the participants. It is observed that males have a wider distribution, with a height range approximately from 155 cm to 185 cm, and a median close to 170 cm. In contrast, females present a narrower distribution, with a range between 145 cm and 165 cm, and a median near 160 cm. Additionally, an outlier is visible among males (closer to 190 cm). This suggests that, within this sample, males tend to be taller and exhibit greater variability in body height compared to females.

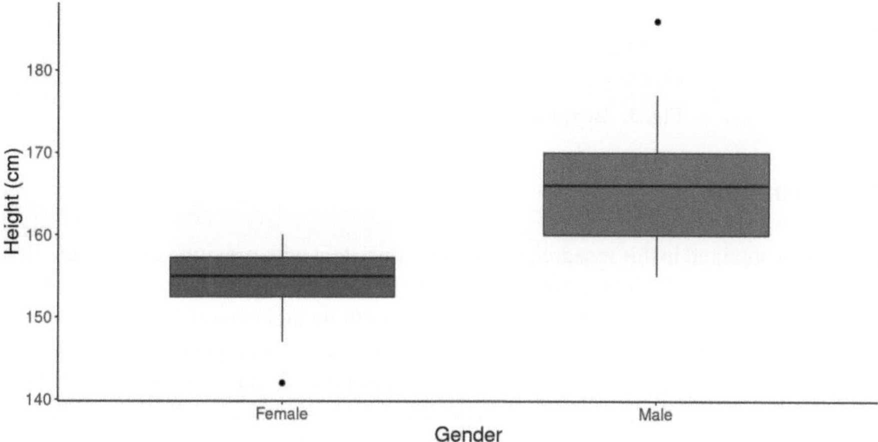

Fig. 2. Boxplot of total body height by gender.

Figure 3 shows the distribution of ergonomic risk scores according to the gender of the participants. Males exhibit a narrower distribution, with a median around 11, and a range from 7 to 13, with few lower outliers. In contrast, females show a wider distribution, with a median near 13, and a score range between 5 and 15, with some lower outliers. This graph suggests that, on average, females tend to have higher ergonomic risk scores, which may indicate greater exposure to ergonomic risk, while males show more consistency in their ergonomic risk scores.

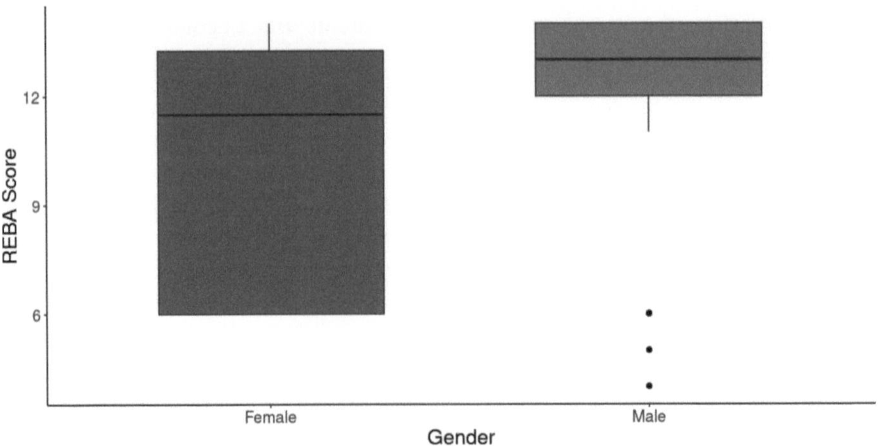

Fig. 3. Boxplot of ergonomic risk scores by gender.

4 Discussion

The results obtained in this research are largely consistent with previous studies but offer a different perspective by integrating anthropometric measurements with the Rapid Entire Body Assessment method, allowing for a more accurate and personalized evaluation of ergonomic risks. In line with the conclusions of Krishnan et al. [19], who also found a strong relationship between improper postures and musculoskeletal disorders (MSDs), our study reinforces the importance of adjusting workstations according to employees' physical characteristics. However, unlike their study, which focused on postures, this research incorporates anthropometric variables, providing a more comprehensive analysis of risk factors. By integrating both methodologies, a more complete and precise assessment of risks is achieved, which may be crucial for designing more effective ergonomic interventions.

The findings are consistent with those of Hita-Gutiérrez et al. [20], who emphasized the relevance of postural ergonomics in the prevention of MSDs in the food sector. However, our approach, by incorporating measurements such as elbow height and functional reach, allows for a more individualized and effective adjustment of workstations. This aspect is important for designing personalized ergonomic interventions that not only prevent injuries but also improve workers' comfort and productivity. This more personalized approach allows for better adaptation of workstations and more effective prevention of musculoskeletal disorders by addressing the needs of each worker.

Furthermore, as noted by Dapari et al. [21], the lack of workstation adjustments significantly contributes to MSDs, and our results support this premise. However, the integration of anthropometric measurements into ergonomic interventions, as proposed in this study, represents a key distinction by providing a more comprehensive evaluation that considers both physical characteristics and postures adopted during work. These findings highlight the importance of personalizing ergonomic interventions, not only by adjusting work equipment but also by considering employees' physical dimensions to maximize intervention effectiveness.

Compared to other studies, this research offers a more comprehensive approach by integrating two important tools: anthropometric measurements and the Rapid Entire Body Assessment method. This combination enables a more effective evaluation of ergonomic risks and offers practical solutions to reduce MSDs in the food industry, improving not only workers' health but also companies' productivity. By considering both perspectives, this research provides a more robust model for injury prevention that has the potential to transform traditional ergonomic approaches, promoting a safer and healthier work environment.

5 Conclusion

This research demonstrated that the combination of anthropometric measurements with the Rapid Entire Body Assessment method provides a more accurate and personalized evaluation of ergonomic risks in the food industry. The results indicate that workers' physical dimensions, such as elbow height and functional reach, are significantly associated with musculoskeletal discomfort in specific body regions, reinforcing the need to design ergonomic interventions tailored to employees' physical characteristics. Furthermore, the implementation of a database integrating these measurements will enable the development of customized ergonomic solutions that not only reduce musculoskeletal disorders but also promote a healthier and more efficient work environment.

However, this study has certain limitations. The sample size was limited to a single production plant, which may restrict the generalizability of the findings to other sectors or populations. Additionally, the cross-sectional design does not allow for the evaluation of long-term effects or causal relationships. Future research should include larger and more diverse samples, as well as longitudinal designs that assess the long-term impact of personalized ergonomic interventions. Expanding the range of measured anthropometric variables and incorporating additional ergonomic assessment tools may also contribute to a more comprehensive understanding of the interaction between physical characteristics and ergonomic risk.

Acknowledgments. A special thanks to Universidad Tecnológica Indoamérica for its support through project IIDI-022–25 titled "Innovación en la Educación Superior a través de las Tecnologías Emergentes" and to the EDUTEM research network for assisting in the dissemination of results.

References

1. Cruz-Salazar, R., Buele, J.: Analysis of musculoskeletal disorders in university administrative staff: a necessary ergonomic assessment. In: Montenegro, C., Rocha, Á., Cueva Lovelle, J.M. (eds.) Management, Tourism and Smart Technologies, pp. 233–242. Springer Nature Switzerland, Cham (2024). https://doi.org/10.1007/978-3-031-44131-8_24
2. Aimar, D.: Chapter 6: the invisible disability of dyslexia in French organizations: framing disability as a skill through global diversity management. In: Research Handbook on Global Diversity Management, pp. 79–90. Elgaronline (2025)

3. Torres-Ruiz, S.: Riesgo ergonómico y trastornos musculoesqueléticos en trabajadores de industria alimentaria en el Callao en el 2021. Horiz. Méd. Lima **23** (2023). https://doi.org/10.24265/horizmed.2022.v23n3.04

4. Balderas López, M., Zamora Macorra, M., Martínez Alcántara, S., Balderas López, M., Zamora Macorra, M., Martínez Alcántara, S.: Trastornos musculoesqueléticos en trabajadores de la manufactura de neumáticos, análisis del proceso de trabajo y riesgo de la actividad. Acta Univ. **29** (2019). https://doi.org/10.15174/au.2019.1913

5. Skamagki, G., Carpenter, C., King, A., Wåhlin, C.: Management of chronic musculoskeletal disorders in the workplace from the perspective of older employees: a mixed methods research study. Int. J. Environ. Res. Public Health **19**, 9348 (2022). https://doi.org/10.3390/ijerph19159348

6. World Helath Organization: Protecting workers' health. https://www.who.int/news-room/fact-sheets/detail/protecting-workers'-health. Accessed 15 June 2025

7. Ahmad, M.A., Shafie, F.A., Masngut, M.I., Mokhtar, M.A.M., Abdullah, A.M.: Work-related musculoskeletal disorders among workers in food manufacturing factories in Hulu Langat, Selangor, Malaysia. Malays. J. Med. Health Sci. **17**, 74–79 (2021)

8. Ayaga, F., Mburu, C., Karanja, B.: Assessment of ergonomics hazards and associated health effects in selected food and beverage industries Nairobi Kenya. J. Agric. Sci. Technol. **23**, 1–11 (2024). https://doi.org/10.4314/jagst.v25i1.1

9. Malý, S., Mesto, N., Kubás, J., Hollá, K., Osvaldová, L.M.: Occupational Health and Safety of Food Industry Employees with Emphasis on Specific Diseases (2023)

10. Ariyanto, J., Palutturi, S., Russeng, S.S., Birawida, A.B., Warsinggih, W., Rosyanti, L.: Control of the risk of musculoskeletal disorders in the food industry: systematic review. Ann. Romanian Soc. Cell Biol. **25**, 4254–4261 (2021)

11. Chung, J.F.C., Pérez, G.L.R.: La evaluación de factores de riesgo ergonómico en el taller automotriz el chino de la ciudad de Portoviejo. Rev. Científica Cienc. Tecnol. **23**, 101–117 (2023). https://doi.org/10.47189/rcct.v23i40.626

12. Moustafa, A.W., Gharib, I.: Anthropometry of the Hand and Product Design. Int. Des. J. **14**, 21–39 (2024). https://doi.org/10.21608/idj.2024.378407

13. Benítez Pérez, S.B., Charris Gómez, S.C., Colpas Ruiz, M.A., Herrera Villalobos, Y.P.: Percepción de los empleados sobre el clima ergonómico en la empresa, la calidad de vida y la presencia de síntomas osteomusculares en Clínica Reina Catalina S.A.S. y Unidrogas S.A.S. (2021)

14. Fazi, H.M., Mohamed, N.M.Z.N., Rashid, M.F.F.A., Rose, A.N.M.: Ergonomics study for workers at food production industry. MATEC Web Conf. **90**, 01003 (2017). https://doi.org/10.1051/matecconf/20179001003

15. Martelo Lora, L.F., Mercado Pérez, J.A., Flórez Álvarez, E.G.: Analysis of the impact of ergonomics on office workstations. Int. J. Manag. Sci. Oper. Res. **8**, 25–37 (2023)

16. Akyıldız, S.T., Ahmed, K.H.: An overview of qualitative research and focus group discussion. Int. J. Acad. Res. Educ. **7**, 1–15 (2021). https://doi.org/10.17985/ijare.866762

17. Taherdoost, H.: What are different research approaches? comprehensive review of qualitative, quantitative, and mixed method research, their applications, types, and limitations. J. Manag. Sci. Eng. Res. **5**, 53–63 (2022). https://doi.org/10.30564/jmser.v5i1.4538

18. World Medical Association: World Medical Association Declaration of Helsinki: Ethical Principles for Medical Research Involving Human Subjects. JAMA. **310**, 2191–2194 (2013). https://doi.org/10.1001/jama.2013.281053

19. Krishnan, K.S., Raju, G., Shawkataly, O.: Prevalence of work-related musculoskeletal disorders: psychological and physical risk factors. Int. J. Environ. Res. Public Health **18**, 9361 (2021). https://doi.org/10.3390/ijerph18179361

20. Hita-Gutiérrez, M., Gómez-Galán, M., Díaz-Pérez, M., Callejón-Ferre, Á.-J.: An overview of REBA method applications in the world. Int. J. Environ. Res. Public Health **17**, 2635 (2020). https://doi.org/10.3390/ijerph17082635
21. Dapari, R., et al.: Prevalence of recent occupational injury and its associated factors among food industry workers in Selangor. PLOS ONE. **18**, e0293987 (2023). https://doi.org/10.1371/journal.pone.0293987

Assessing the Suitability of an Upper Body OpenSim Model for Simulations of Horizontal and Overhead Drilling Use Cases

Carina Spengler[1], Susanne Sutschet[1(✉)], Alfredo Saucedo[1], Martin Fleischer[2], Rebecca Rack[2], Klaus Bengler[2], and Sven Matthiesen[1]

[1] Institute of Product Engineering, Karlsruhe Institute of Technology (KIT), Karlsruhe, Germany
{susanne.sutschet,sven.matthiesen}@kit.edu
[2] Chair of Ergonomics, Technical University Munich (TUM), Munich, Germany
bengler@tum.de

Abstract. This study evaluates the ability of OpenSim musculoskeletal simulations to estimate upper limb muscle activation during hammer drilling. A user study was conducted with six subjects performing different drilling tasks while varying drilling postures (horizontal - two-handed, upwards - two-handed, upwards - one-handed) and drill bit size. Body motion, external forces, and surface electromyography (sEMG) of muscle groups of the upper body were measured. Muscle activations were simulated in OpenSim using an upper limb musculoskeletal model and results were compared to the experimental data. Overall, simulated activations aligned qualitatively with EMG trends across different tasks, although quantitative agreement was limited depending on muscle and subject. The results indicate the potential of such models for early-stage ergonomic evaluations of power tools. Key challenges include scaling of muscle forces in the model, user-specific variability, and vibration effects.

Keywords: Digital Human Models · Biomechanical analysis · Muscle activation · Power tools

1 Introduction

Construction workers have one of the highest risks for work-induced musculoskeletal disorders (WMSDs), such as tendonitits and joint pain. These occur mainly due to repetitive high-force tasks. Using power tools, these issues are further exacerbated by ergonomically unfavorable quasi-static body postures and additional vibrational load. Unsuitable tool design can further increase the risk of WMSDs [1]. In the past, power tools, such as hammer drills, were often designed with a focus on technical performance, without paying particular attention to ergonomics [2]. Considering ergonomic aspects is often costly and time-consuming, as it typically requires interactive physical prototype testing in user

V. G. Duffy (Ed.): HCII 2025, LNCS 16339, pp. 34–49, 2026.
https://doi.org/10.1007/978-3-032-13012-9_3

studies. This could be reduced using digital human models (DHMs) by estimating the impact of product changes on the user's posture and musculoskeletal stress. Musculoskeletal simulations, enabled by platforms such as the open-source software OpenSim [3] or the commercial AnyBody Modeling System (AnyBody Technology, Aalborg, Denmark), allow for a comprehensive representation of the human musculoskeletal system and can provide valuable insights into joint loads and muscle activity.

While many musculoskeletal models primarily focus on the lower limbs, some also include the upper body musculature. Full-body models such as the model by Rajagopal et al. [4] provide a basis for full-body simulations. Miehling et al. [5] created a full-body OpenSim model by combining several particles models: the lower body model by Thelen et al. [6], the upper body by Holzbaur et al. [7], the flexible lumbar spine by Christophy et al. [8], and the neck model by Vasavada et al. [9]. It was applied, i.a., for estimating user stress during upwards screwing with a screwdriver [10]. Chang et al. [11] developed a full-body OpenSim model by combining Raabe's lumbar-spinal model [12] with Saul's upper limb model [13], and using it to simulate overhead drilling tasks. However, posture and external loads were synthetically defined, and no experimental data were used for validation. The model allows analysis of joint and muscle loading in the upper extremities, spine, and lower limbs, supporting the study of physically demanding tasks.

The problem is that it is unclear whether, and to what extent, OpenSim models can accurately simulate the user's muscle activation during high-force power tool tasks such as hammer drilling using experimental data from the application. From this gap, we formulated the following research question:

To what extent can muscle activation during different use cases of hammer drilling be accurately estimated using OpenSim simulations compared to experimentally measured EMG data?

This work aims to address this question by conducting a drilling user study, simulating the drilling tests using the freely available OpenSim upper body model of Saul [13], and verifying its accuracy by comparing simulated muscle activation with measured EMG data.

2   Materials and Methods

2.1   Experimental Subject Study

Test Subjects. To collect experimental data for musculoskeletal simulations, we conducted a drilling study with six healthy, right-handed subjects. Demographic and anthropometric data were obtained through questionnaires and direct measurements (s. Table 1). Body segment lengths were measured for the motion capture system and for scaling the digital human models. The physical activity level was assessed using a classification scale ranging from 0 ("You avoid all physical activity whenever possible") to 10 ("More than 15 h per week").

Participation was voluntary and all subjects gave their consent after receiving a detailed explanation of the study protocol. The study could be interrupted or terminated at any time. During the planning phase of the study, a consultation was conducted with the Data Protection Office and the Ethics Committee of the Karlsruhe Institute of Technology (KIT).

Table 1. Demographic and anthropometric data of the test subjects.

No.	Sex (m/f)	Age	Body height [cm]	Body weight [kg]	Physical activity level (0–10)
1	m	32	193	100	7.0
2	m	29	186	93	8.5
3	f	25	165	65	7.0
4	m	32	180	76	6.0
5	f	29	175	83	5.0
6	m	24	173	70	7.5

Sensor-Equipped Hammer Drill. We used a cordless hammer drill Hilti TE 2-22 (Hilti AG, Schaan, Liechtenstein). The hammer drill weighs 2.3 kg and is specified with an impact energy per stroke of 1.5 J at a rate of 4860 impacts per minute at the nominal rotational drill speed of 1090 rpm. The hammer drill was equipped with 12 piezo resistive force sensors (FlexiForce A201 Sensor 25lbs, Tekscan, Inc., Norwood, MA, USA) positioned at the main handle, as depicted in Fig. 1. To determine the optimal sensor placement, the handle was marked with color prior to the study to identify the areas with the most wear, indicating the primary zones of user interaction. To measure the hammer drill vibrations, an accelerometer (356A02, PCB Piezotronics, Depew, NY, USA) was attached at the top of the main handle (s. Figure 1), according to ISO5349-2:2015-12 [14].

Test Procedure. To record upper body muscle activation during the drilling tests, surface electromyography (sEMG) was employed using wearable sEMG shirts (MShirt Plus, Myontec Ltd., Kuopio, Finland) with the MCell3 sensors (Myontec Ltd., Kuopio, Finland). The system enables bilateral measurement of the following muscle groups: trapecius, pectoralis, latissimus, shoulder (deltoid), upper arm (biceps, triceps), and forearm extensors and flexors. To improve the signal transmission capability, the sEMG shirts were moistened on the inside before use. For each muscle, maximum voluntary contraction (MVC) tests were performed twice to facilitate normalization. In addition, full-body posture was

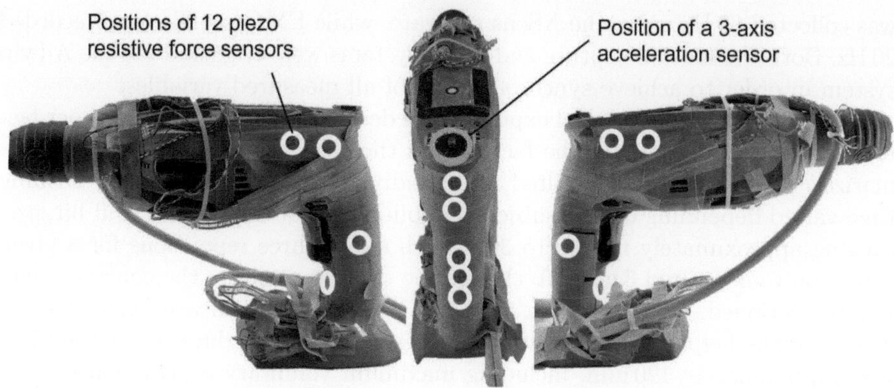

Fig. 1. Modified hammer drill Hilti TE 2-22 with positions of 12 piezo resistive force sensors (white circles) and position of three-axis accelerometer (blue circle), depicted without battery (Color figure online)

captured using an inertial motion capture system (XSens Technologies B.V., Enschede, The Netherlands). 17 inertial measurement units (IMUs) were placed on predefined body segments of the subjects and subsequently calibrated. After the XSens sensor configuration, a static T-pose of the subject was recorded for approximately 5 s, which was later used for calibrating the subject-specific OpenSim model.

The drilling tests were performed based on the setup in Fig. 2. The subjects were standing on a force-torque measuring plate (BP600900-1000, AMTI, Watertown, MA, USA), which enabled measuring the push force. The subjects used the sensor-equipped hammer drill for drilling into a concrete plate (concrete type C3037, Rau-Betonfertigteile GmbH & Co KG, Ebhausen, Germany). The concrete plate was adjusted in height and orientation depending on the drilling position and subject's body height. Three different drilling positions were investigated: a) horizontal, two-handed drilling, b) upwards, two-handed drilling, and c) upwards, one-handed drilling. For horizontal drilling, the drilling position was set to be at the subject's chest height, while the concrete plate was set vertically. For upward drilling, the subject's position was set so that the elbow angle was about 90°, with the concrete plate set horizontally and adjusted in height. The hammer drill was equipped with the following two different drill types: 6 mm - 4 cutting edges and 12 mm - 4 cutting edges (type TE-CX, Hilti AG, Schaan, Liechtenstein). The drilling depth in all configurations was set at five times the diameter, 30 mm for the 6 mm drill bit and 60 mm for the 12 mm drill bit. To minimize variability in the applied load across drilling trials, the drill bits were replaced after approximately 30 uses due to wear.

Throughout the drilling measurements, force and acceleration data at the hammer drill, as well as ground reaction forces were recorded at 5 kHz using an Adwin data acquisition system (Adwin Pro II, T11 processor, Jaeger Computergesteuerte Messtechnik GmbH, Lorsch, Germany). Motion capture data was collected 60 Hz using the XSens software, while EMG signals were recorded 20 Hz. Both the motion capture and EMG systems were triggered via the Adwin system in order to achieve synchronization of all measured variables.

A randomized full-factorial experimental design with three replicates per factor combination was used. The factors and their corresponding levels are summarized in Table 2. This resulted in 18 individual trials per subject. Drilling time varied depending on the subject's applied push force and the drill bit size, ranging approximately from 5 to 30 s. Each set of three repetitions for a given condition took around 3 min. To change the drilling position, the concrete plate was repositioned, which led to a 5–10 min break between measurement blocks. These breaks helped minimize subject fatigue. The total duration per subject was approximately 120 min, including maximum voluntary contraction (MVC) measurements and motion capture sensor calibration. The experiment could be paused at any time upon request. All six participants completed the study without any issues.

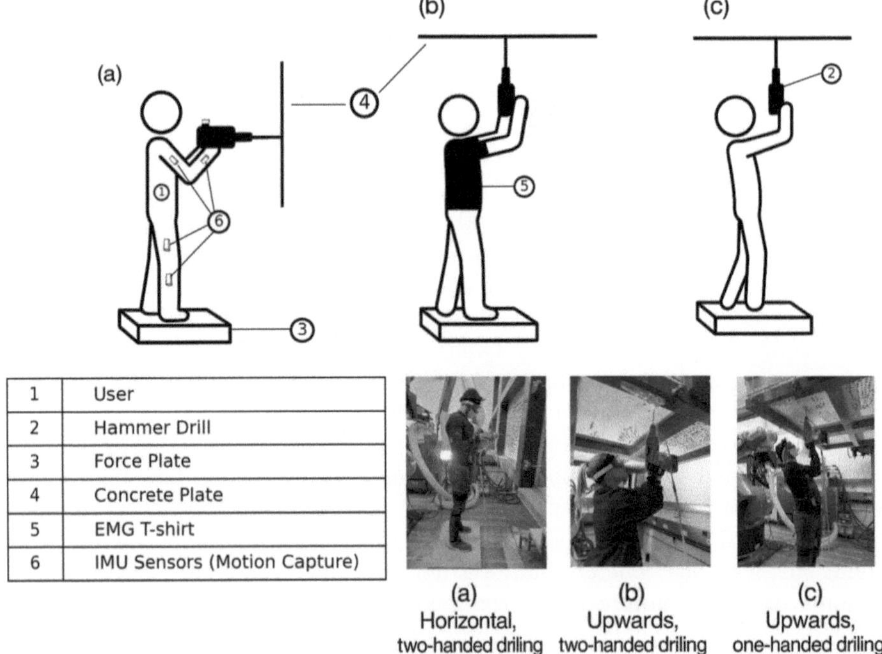

1	User
2	Hammer Drill
3	Force Plate
4	Concrete Plate
5	EMG T-shirt
6	IMU Sensors (Motion Capture)

Fig. 2. Experimental setup: subjects wearing IMU motion capture sensors and an EMG shirt and standing on a force-torque measurement plate drilled into a concrete plate using a sensor-equipped hammer drill. The task was performed in three different drilling postures: a) horizontal – two-handed, b) upwards – two-handed, and c) upwards – one-handed.

Experimental Data Postprocessing. All data were cut using the acceleration signal to ensure that the analysis was based on data during stable drilling. Depending on the use case, one-handed or two-handed, different piezo resistive force sensors were considered to calculate the interaction forces per hand between the hammer drill and the subject. To evaluate the overall push force, data from the force-torque measuring plate were analyzed according to the drilling orientation: x-direction for horizontal drilling, z-direction for vertical drilling. To obtain the push force in z-direction, the weight of the subject and the hammer drill were subtracted. The total vibration value of the effective values of the frequency-weighted acceleration (a_{hv}) was calculated from acceleration data for each drilling measurement according to ISO 5349-1:2001 [15]. To evaluate the elbow and shoulder flexion angles, root mean square (RMS) values were computed for each drilling trial. The mean and standard deviation of push forces, a_{hv} values, and joint angles were then calculated across all trials for each drilling use case.

Table 2. Factor levels included in the evaluation.

Factor	Levels	Details
Drilling position	3	horizontal - two-handed, upwards vertical - two-handed, upwards vertical - one-handed
Drill bit size	2	6 mm - 4 cutting edges, 12 mm - 4 cutting edges

2.2 Musculoskeletal Simulations

To simulate the drilling trials in OpenSim (Version 4.3, Stanford University, Stanford, California, USA), the bilateral Upper Extremity Dynamic Model [13] was used (s. Fig. 3). For each subject, a subject-specific scaled model was created using the OpenSim Scale Tool and the measured body segment lengths of the subjects. IMU motion capture data were transformed to .sto files using Matlab (R2022b, MathWorks, Matick, MA, USA). The recorded T-pose was used to place the IMU sensors on the subject-specific scaled models using the OpenSim IMU Placer Tool. The cutted IMU data from each drilling trial was used to compute the joint angles of the scaled and calibrated upper body model using the IMU Inverse Kinematics (IMU IK) Tool. Interaction force data calculated from the piezo resistive force sensors were transformed to .mot files using Matlab. To simulate muscle activation of the shoulder-arm system, the Static Optimization (SO) Tool was used by applying the interaction forces to each hand. Beforehand, the motion was filtered with the integrated Butterworth filter 6 Hz. Reserve actuators from Table 3 were additionally applied to the models.

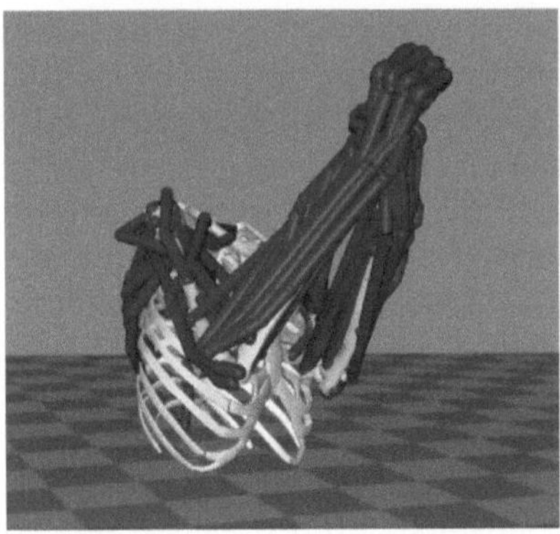

Fig. 3. Bilateral upper extremity model by Saul [13] in simulated two-handed upward drilling position.

Table 3. Upper body reserve actuators used for Static Optimization simulations.

Model coordinates	Optimal force
elv_angle_r/l	50
shoulder_elv_r/l	60
shoulder_rot_r/l	20
elbow_flexion_r/l	10
pro_sup_r/l	10
deviation_r/l	10
flexion_r/l	10

2.3 Data Postprocessing

For each drilling test, the RMS for the SO-simulated and experimental measured muscles was calculated over time. Muscle activation was expressed as a percentage of MVC by normalizing the EMG signals to the RMS of the corresponding muscle-specific MVC measurements (%MVC). SO-simulated muscle activations were summed up for each muscle group. For the comparison between simulations and EMG measurements, we averaged the data across all subjects for each drilling use case. We selected the right deltoid, biceps, triceps and forearm muscle group for the comparison. To assess whether there were statistically significant differences in muscle activation across different drilling positions and drill bit sizes, a one-way analysis of variance (ANOVA) was performed. The test was applied separately for simulated (SO) and measured (EMG) muscle activation. ANOVA was performed per muscle group across all subjects with a significance threshold of $p < 0.05$. For subject 6, measurements were excluded due to EMG recording errors.

3 Results

This study investigates the accuracy of musculoskeletal simulations using an OpenSim upper limb model to estimate muscle activation of various hammer drilling use cases by comparing the results to experimentally measured EMG data.

3.1 Comparison Between Simulated and Experimentally Measured Muscle Activation

Figure 4 and Fig. 5 presents a comparison between simulated muscle activation (blue) and EMG data (grey) in %MVC for the right biceps, triceps, deltoid, and forearm muscles across multiple drilling use cases. RMS values for each drilling test were calculated over time and averaged for each use case across all subjects. The background color zones provide a qualitative indication of activation intensity based on criteria, based on recommendations of the Institute for Occupational Safety and Health of the German Social Accident Insurance (IFA) [16]: green (low), yellow (moderate), orange (high), and red (very high).

General Key Observations. The agreement between simulated and measured muscle activations is generally consistent with the qualitative activation intensity classifications (low/moderate/high/very high activation). Notable exceptions include the one-handed upward drilling task for the right deltoid muscles and the horizontal drilling position for the right triceps muscles, where the models in average underestimate the muscle activation. For the biceps, triceps, and deltoid muscle groups, some high outliers can be seen, even above 100% muscle activation. Muscle-specific observations include:

- **Right biceps muscles:** The simulated muscle activation is slightly overestimated compared to the EMG data. However, there is a good alignment between simulation and EMG measurements with a max. absolute mean error (AME) of about 13%. Also, simulation and measurement consistently classify the right biceps activation as low. The simulation shows high outliers during certain upward drilling tasks, with values occasionally exceeding 100% activation.
- **Right triceps muscles:** For horizontal drilling, simulated activation remains in the low range, while EMG data indicate moderate to high activation (AME > 30%). Measured EMG activation is higher during horizontal than upward drilling. For upward drilling tasks, simulated and measured values are more closely aligned (AME <15%) and both decrease within the low to moderate activation range. EMG data show high outliers (> 100%) in some use cases.
- **Right deltoid muscles:** Muscle activation is consistently underestimated in the simulation. In the upwards one-handed drilling use cases, there is big scattering in EMG data, even values higher than 100% were measured. The upwards, two-handed drilling tasks show the closest alignment between simulations and EMG measurements (AME <10%).
- **Right forearm muscles:** Simulations and measured EMG data have a good agreement (AME < 10%) and indicate a mainly low activation level for all tasks. Overall, the simulation leads to a higher scattering in muscle activation, while the deviation of the median values is comparatively small with a maximum of 5%.

Subject-Specific Comparison. Table 4 presents the absolute mean errors (AME) and standard deviations between simulated and EMG-measured muscle activations, calculated per subject and muscle over all drilling tasks. The results show considerable inter-subject variability. For example, subject 3 showed the lowest AMEs across most muscles (e.g., 4.46% for the deltoid), while subject 5 had the highest deviations in several muscles (e.g., 51.05% for the biceps). The overall average AME across all subjects was highest for the right deltoid (24.78%), followed by the triceps (19.78%), biceps (17.46%), and forearm muscles (11.74%). These subject-wise results align with the boxplot-based observations.

3.2   Comparison Between Drilling Postures and Drill Bit Sizes

Table 5 summarizes the p-values obtained from the one-way ANOVA tests for each muscle. A significant difference in muscle activation across postures was observed for the right deltoid muscle in the EMG data ($p = .0223$). However, none of the simulated (SO) values showed significant posture-dependent effects, including the right deltoid ($p = .9563$). For the other muscles (right biceps, triceps, and forearm), no significant differences in muscle activation were found with respect to posture in either the EMG (all $p > .68$) or SO data (all $p > .12$).

No significant differences in muscle activation were found between the 6 mm and 12 mm drill bit sizes for any muscle, in either the EMG (all $p > .59$) or SO data (all $p > .54$). The smallest p-value was observed for the triceps in the SO data ($p = .5427$), confirming the absence of any statistically relevant effect of drill bit size.

3.3   Drilling Loads

Averaged loads and joint angles during the captured drilling use cases are listed in Table 6. Push forces with 12 mm drill diameter are in average 10–35 N higher than with a 6 mm drill. The mean flexion angle of the right shoulder is in average similar for the two-handed drilling postures and is around 10° higher for the one-handed vertical position. The mean flexion angle of the right elbow is comparable for upwards drilling and almost 30° higher for the horizontal drilling use case.

Table 4. Absolute mean errors (AME) between root mean square (RMS) values per drilling test over time of SO-simulated and measured muscle activations (normalized EMG) per subject and muscle. Values are shown as mean ± standard deviation.

Subject	Right deltoid	Right biceps	Right triceps	Right forearm
1	20.66 ± 14.50	7.53 ± 4.89	17.99 ± 15.16	5.63 ± 6.96
2	29.87 ± 25.84	5.12 ± 4.27	17.95 ± 15.38	7.11 ± 5.39
3	4.46 ± 2.88	20.53 ± 9.43	10.66 ± 8.50	9.52 ± 2.60
4	48.92 ± 36.77	5.07 ± 4.64	19.20 ± 22.66	15.88 ± 8.51
5	18.01 ± 11.22	51.05 ± 42.51	30.11 ± 31.91	20.55 ± 11.77
Mean	24.78 ± 15.94	17.46 ± 19.21	19.78 ± 7.57	11.74 ± 6.34

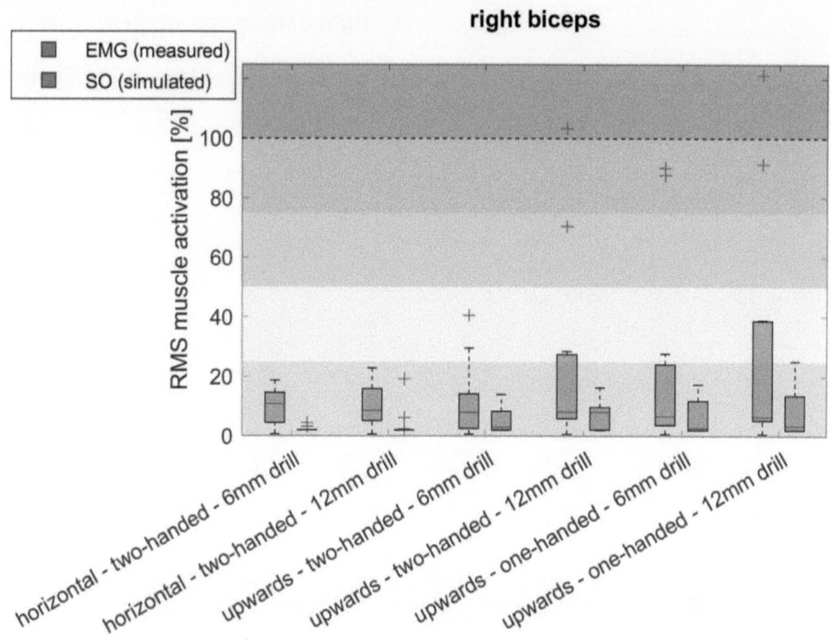

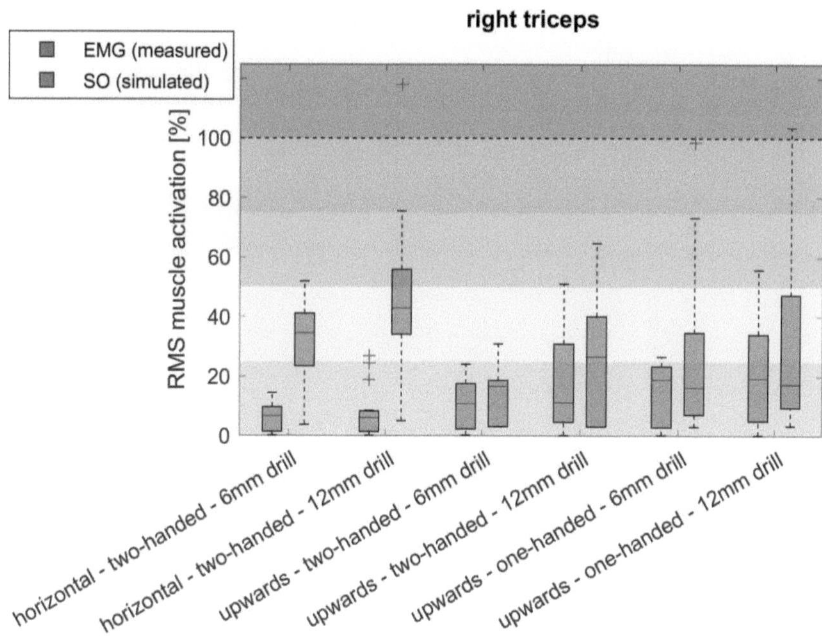

Fig. 4. Comparison of EMG data in %MVC and SO simulated muscle activation of right biceps and triceps muscles, $N = 15$, color-coded in the background with the criteria of muscle activation: green (low), yellow (moderate), orange (high), and red (very high) [16] (Color figure online).

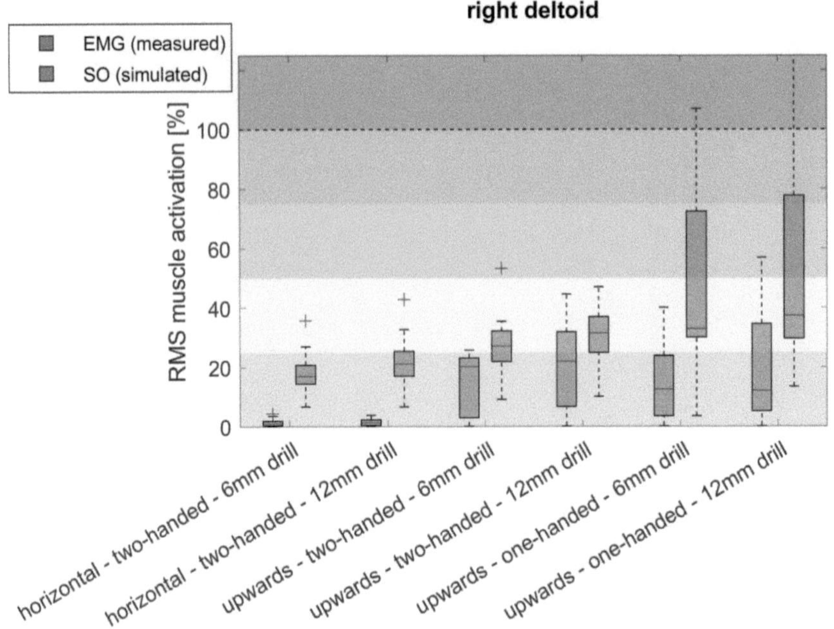

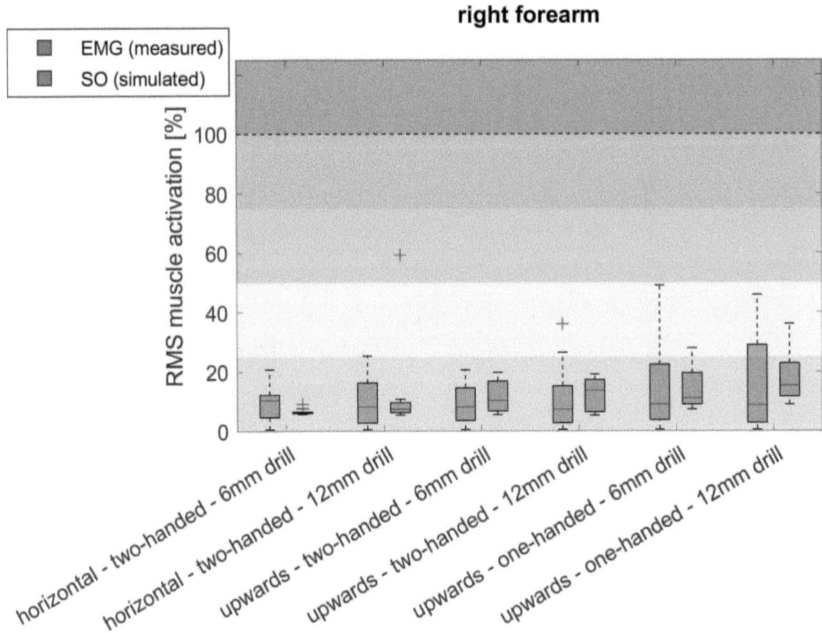

Fig. 5. Comparison of EMG data in %MVC and SO simulated muscle activation of right deltoid and forearm muscles, $N = 15$, color-coded in the background with the criteria of muscle activation: green (low), yellow (moderate), orange (high), and red (very high) [16] (Color figure online).

Table 5. ANOVA p-values for differences in muscle activation across drill positions and drill bit sizes (EMG and simulated SO data). A p-value < 0.05 indicates a statistically significant difference.

Muscle	Drilling position		Drill bit size	
	EMG	SO	EMG	SO
right deltoid	$p = .0223$	$p = .9563$	$p = .7512$	$p = .6068$
right biceps	$p = .9651$	$p = .1243$	$p = .6729$	$p = .6074$
right triceps	$p = .6856$	$p = .1624$	$p = .5995$	$p = .5427$
right forearm	$p = .9626$	$p = .7870$	$p = .7389$	$p = .9990$

Table 6. Overview of drilling loads (push force, acceleration along the drilling axis at the main handle, right elbow and shoulder flexion angle) for the different use cases. Values are mean and standard deviation of RMS over time for each drilling test, $N = 17$.

	Horizontal	Upwards, two-handed	Upwards, one-handed
	6/12 mm	6/12 mm	6/12 mm
Push force [N] mean	86.8/109.4	119.6/128.5	87.1/122.3
std	20.7/20.4	33.8/34.3	20.8/49.7
$\mathbf{a}_{hv}$ [m/s^2] mean	24.38/20.96	23.70/22.40	26.43/26.06
std	5.09/1.62	4.73/3.16	4.80/4.59
Elbow flexion [°] mean	36.2/39.0	9.7/10.2	8.3/10.8
std	8.1/8.5	9.6/8.2	7.9/8.5
Shoulder flexion [°] mean	10.0/10.6	9.6/10.9	23.2/25.4
std	2.9/2.0	7.1/8.3	10.8/12.3

4 Discussion

4.1 Comparison Between Simulated and Experimentally Measured Muscle Activation

In general, there was good qualitative agreement between the simulated and experimentally measured muscle activation across the different drilling use cases. The simulation was able to capture task-specific trends, such as an increased activation of upper arm and shoulder muscles during overhead drilling compared to horizontal drilling. However, achieving quantitative agreement proved to be challenging. The following factors contribute to the observed deviations:

- **Scaling of muscle forces:** High external loads during drilling exceeded the physiological capacity of certain simulated muscles ($>100\%$). To achieve more plausible simulation results under 100% activation, additional reserve actuators were added (s. Table 3). This indicates that the default maximum isometric muscle forces defined in the model are too low for certain muscles during high-force tasks such as hammer drilling. An approach for systematic scaling of the isometric muscle force such as the Strength Mapping Algorithm (SMA) of Miehling and Wartzack [20] may increase the accuracy of the simulations.

- **Number and diversity of subjects:** The study included only six participants, limiting generalizability. Muscle strength was scaled only indirectly via body size, without subject-specific strength parameters. Additionally, identical reserve actuators were used for all participants. This likely contributed to the inter-subject differences in simulation accuracy seen in Table 4. As shown in Table 1, the subjects varied in height, weight, and activity level, which may have influenced coordination strategies and led to higher EMG values in some cases without corresponding increases in simulated activation. Differences in expertise levels in hammer drilling may contribute to variations in push forces and muscle activation between subjects.

- **Influence of vibration:** Vibrational loads increase EMG amplitudes due to involuntary muscle responses, which static optimization-based simulations cannot capture. This may explain higher EMG values compared to simulated activations, particularly in the deltoid and triceps. Kihlberg [17] reported increased activity in forearm and upper arm muscles under impact vibration, while hand muscles remained unaffected. Similarly, Widia [18] observed rising muscle activity with increasing vibration level and exposure duration.

- **Limitations of the EMG system:** The use of the Myontec EMG shirt may have influenced the absolute accuracy of the signal. According to Steinebach et al. [19], the system is only conditionally suitable for evaluating absolute muscle activation levels in dynamic and static scenarios, although high correlation and precision were achieved compared to established systems. This could explain discrepancies such as unexpectedly high median triceps activation during horizontal drilling. Furthermore, EMG values obtained from MVC measurements are highly affected by the quality of execution and the subject's motivation, which can introduce additional potential inaccuracies in EMG normalization.

- **Further model simplifications:** Beyond actuator scaling and muscle force limitations, other simplifications, such as omission of fatigue, tissue compliance, and neuromuscular control variability, as well as discrepancies between simulated and actual body posture, may contribute to mismatches between simulation and EMG data.

Comparison to Related Studies. Chang et al. [11] simulated overhead drilling with a full-body model using only tool weight, without additional reserve actuators. For the posture most similar to our study's upward one-handed drilling (*high-middle reach*), the summed activation of the deltoid was approximately 45%, the triceps around 27%, and the biceps below 1%. This aligns well with our EMG observations: deltoid activation around 35–40%, triceps 15–20%, and biceps 5–10%.

4.2 Comparison Between Drilling Postures and Drill Bit Sizes

Statistical analysis revealed a significant effect of posture on muscle activation only in the right deltoid based on EMG data ($p = .0223$), while all other comparisons produced nonsignificant p-values ($p > .05$). This aligns with biomechanical expectations, as upward drilling requires increased shoulder elevation and stabilization. In contrast, simulated deltoid activation did not differ significantly between postures ($p = .9563$), suggesting that SO-based simulations may underestimate posture-dependent activation dynamics, particularly for shoulder muscles.

No significant differences in muscle activity were observed between the drill bit sizes 6 mm and 12 mm in EMG or simulated data ($p > .5$ for all conditions). The increase in diameter led to only small changes in muscle activation, although the mean push forces were 10- 35 N higher with the 12 mm bit. These effects were smaller than the variability between subjects.

5 Conclusion and Future Work

This study assessed the suitability of Saul's bilateral Upper Extremity model for simulating muscle activation during horizontal and overhead hammer drilling tasks. The simulations demonstrated in general good qualitative agreement with the EMG measurements. Quantitative agreement varied depending on the muscle and subject. With further refinement, the model could be used for simulations of several power tool use cases. This could help to inform design decisions in early product development, e.g., optimizing handle orientation or weight distribution and thereby reducing the need for extensive physical testing. Key future enhancements could include:

- adjusting maximum isometric muscle forces to reflect high-force industrial tasks,
- incorporating vibration effects into simulation interpretation,
- validating results with a high subject number and broader user population, including professional users.
- and using a full-body model to consider compensatory mechanisms.

Such improvements would enhance the accuracy of application modeling. As a result, more reliable user stress estimations could reduce the number of subjects required to obtain generalizable results. In the long term, virtual optimization of products and workplaces could support the early integration of ergonomic aspects in a more resource-efficient way during product development.

Acknowledgments. The study was conducted as part of the ExoTool project, which was commissioned by the KME - Kompetenzzentrum Mittelstand GmbH on behalf of the Bavarian metal and electrical industry associations bayme vbm. Phrases were reformulated with DeepL and ChatGPT 4.0.

Disclosure of Interests. The authors have no competing interests to declare that are relevant to the content of this paper.

References

1. Chaffin, D.B., Andersson, G.B.J.: Occupational Biomechanics, 2nd edn. Wiley, New York (1991)
2. Vedder, J., Carey, E.: A multi-level systems approach for the development of tools, equipment and work processes for the construction industry. Appl. Ergon. **36**(4), 471–480 (2005)
3. Delp, S.L., et al.: OpenSim: open-source software to create and analyze dynamic simulations of movement. IEEE Trans. Biomed. Eng. **54**(11), 1940–1950 (2007)
4. Rajagopal, A., Dembia, C.L., DeMers, M.S., Delp, S.L., Hicks, J.L., Uchida, T.K.: Full-body musculoskeletal model for muscle-driven simulation of human gait. IEEE Trans. Biomed. Eng. **63**(10), 2068–2079 (2016)
5. Miehling, J.: Musculoskeletal modeling of user groups for virtual product and process development. Comput. Methods Biomech. Biomed. Eng. **22**, 1209–1218 (2019)
6. Thelen, D.G.: Adjustment of muscle mechanics model parameters to simulate dynamic contractions in older adults. J. Biomech. Eng. **125**(1), 70–77 (2003)
7. Holzbaur, K.R.S., Murray, W.M., Delp, S.L.: A model of the upper extremity for simulating musculoskeletal surgery and analyzing neuromuscular control. Ann. Biomed. Eng. **33**(6), 829–840 (2005)
8. Christophy, M., Faruk Senan, N.A., Lotz, J.C., O'Reilly, O.M.: A musculoskeletal model for the lumbar spine. Biomech. Model. Mechanobiol. **11**(1–2), 19–34 (2012)
9. Vasavada, A.N., Li, S., Delp, S.L.: Influence of muscle morphometry and moment arms on the moment-generating capacity of human neck muscles. Spine **23**(4), 412–422 (1998)
10. Molz, C., et al.: A co-simulation model integrating a musculoskeletal human model with exoskeleton and power tool model. Appl. Sci. **14**(6), 2573 (2024). https://doi.org/10.3390/app14062573
11. Chang, J., Chablat, D., Bennis, F., Ma, L.: A full-chain OpenSim model and its application on posture analysis of an overhead drilling task. In: Duffy, V.G. (ed.) HCII 2019. LNCS, vol. 11581, pp. 33–44. Springer, Cham (2019). https://doi.org/10.1007/978-3-030-22216-1_3
12. Raabe, M.E., Chaudhari, A.M.: An investigation of jogging biomechanics using the full-body lumbar spine model: model development and validation. J. Biomech. **49**(7), 1238–1243 (2016)
13. Saul, K.R., et al.: Benchmarking of dynamic simulation predictions in two software platforms using an upper limb musculoskeletal model. Comput. Methods Biomech. Biomed. Eng. **18**(13), 1445–1458 (2015)
14. DIN EN ISO 5349-2: Mechanical vibration – Measurement and evaluation of human exposure to hand-transmitted vibration – Part 2: Practical guidance for measurement at the workplace (ISO 5349-2:2001 + Amd 1:2015); German version EN ISO 5349-2:2001 + A1:2015. Beuth Verlag, Berlin (2015)
15. DIN EN ISO 5349-1: Mechanical vibration – Measurement and evaluation of human exposure to hand-transmitted vibration – Part 1: General requirements (ISO 5349-1:2001); German version EN ISO 5349-1:2001. Beuth Verlag, Berlin (2001)
16. DGUV: Bewertung physischer Belastungen bei beruflichen Tätigkeiten. Institut für Arbeitsschutz der Deutschen Gesetzlichen Unfallversicherung (IFA), Sankt Augustin (2020). https://www.dguv.de/medien/ifa/de/fac/ergonomie/pdf/bewertung_physischer_belastungen.pdf. Accessed 12 June 2025
17. Kihlberg, S., Attebrant, M., Gemne, G., Kjellberg, A.: Acute effects of vibration from a chipping hammer and a grinder on the hand-arm system. Occup. Environ. Med. (1995)

18. Widia, S.Z.M.D.: The effect of vibration on muscle activity and grip strength using an electric drill. In: Proceedings of 2013 International Conference on Human Factors and Ergonomics

19. Steinebach, T., Wakula, J., Giese, C., Vedder, J.: Evaluierung eines in Textilien integrierten EMG-Messsystems für den Oberkörper in einer Laborstudie. In: GfA, Dortmund (Hrsg.): Frühjahrskongress 2021, Bochum, Beitrag B.4.4. Arbeit HUMAINE gestalten (2021)

20. Miehling, J., Wartzack, S.: Strength mapping algorithm (SMA) for biomechanical human modelling using empirical population data. In: Proceedings of 20th International Conference on Engineering Design (ICED15), vol. 10: Design Information and Knowledge Management, pp. 97–106. The Design Society, Milan (2015)

Self-quantification and Data Engagement: Insights from Smartwatch Users

Fang-Wu Tung[(⊠)]

National Tsing Hua University, Hsinchu 300, Taiwan
`fwtung@mx.nthu.edu.tw`

Abstract. Wearable devices have revolutionized personal health management by enabling continuous, real-time tracking of physiological and behavioral metrics. The rapid innovation and development of these technologies is reshaping industries, driving advancements in digital health, enhancing user engagement, and enabling data-driven healthcare solutions. This study examines how varying levels of health motivation and consciousness influence users' interactions with self-tracked data. It identifies six key dimensions of self-quantification and data interpretation: data awareness, data interpretation & trust, goal setting & health management, intuition vs. data reliance, collaborative & contextual data interpretation, and tolerance for inaccuracy. A survey then clusters participants into four user groups: active goal-setters, casual health observers, reactive health monitors, and proactive health managers. Findings indicate that highly motivated users seamlessly integrate wearable-generated data into their health routines and adapt to minor inaccuracies, whereas those with lower motivation exhibit intermittent usage and skepticism. As wearable technologies continue to play a critical role in modern healthcare, these insights underscore the need for tailored mHealth systems to address diverse user needs—ultimately fostering sustained engagement and healthier behaviors.

Keywords: Self-quantification · Wearable health technology · mHealth engagement · Data interpretation · User behavior segmentation

1 Introduction

Recent advances in digital health technologies have redefined the way individuals track and manage personal well-being. Wearable devices, mobile health (mHealth) applications, and IoT-integrated sensors now offer real-time information on a range of physiological and behavioral metrics [1, 2]. This shift from clinic-based assessments to continuous, user-driven monitoring creates opportunities for earlier detection of potential issues, more proactive health management, and deeper insights into population-level health data [3]. In turn, these developments contribute to broader public health strategies and more personalized medical interventions.

Among these emerging tools, smartwatches have become particularly influential thanks to their ease of integration into daily routines. In contrast to traditional health

V. G. Duffy (Ed.): HCII 2025, LNCS 16339, pp. 50–60, 2026.
https://doi.org/10.1007/978-3-032-13012-9_4

trackers that might only capture a single metric, smartwatches seamlessly gather multiple data points, such as step counts, heart rate variability, and sleep quality, while requiring minimal user effort [4]. The near-instantaneous feedback provided by these devices has been shown to encourage behavior change and improve adherence to fitness or wellness goals [5]. Wearer engagement is further enhanced by the ability to synchronize smartwatch data with mobile health applications and electronic health records, enabling a more holistic understanding of personal health trends over time [6].

Despite these advantages, existing studies often concentrate on technical accuracy—for instance, comparing wearable-derived metrics to clinical gold standards—or on discrete health outcomes, such as cardiovascular improvements. Far fewer investigations explore how individuals interpret or integrate the data they receive from their smartwatches. In practice, user experiences vary widely. Some people depend heavily on the device's numbers to guide daily decisions, while others treat the data as a secondary reference, often filtered through personal intuition or prior habits [7]. Trust in accuracy, personal motivation, and general health awareness all appear to mediate these differences, ultimately determining whether wearable data truly fosters long-term, meaningful change [8].

Addressing this gap, the present study examines self-quantification and data engagement patterns among smartwatch users, exploring the roles of health motivation and consciousness in shaping these patterns. We begin by defining the key dimensions of self-quantification and data engagement, building on established literature in digital health and behavioral science. We then segment smartwatch users based on their motivational profiles, illustrating how different groups interpret data and incorporate wearable insights into daily health routines. By examining these variations, our research provides a nuanced understanding of smartwatch-based health tracking and offers practical guidance for designing mHealth interventions that better align with user needs and preferences.

2 Literature Review

2.1 Self-Quantification and the Role of Wearable Devices in mHealth

Self-quantification, closely associated with the Quantified Self movement, involves systematically tracking personal health and lifestyle metrics to guide behavior and inform decision-making [9]. Recent advances in wearable devices have accelerated this practice by transitioning from sporadic, manual recordings to continuous, automated data collection [10]. Researchers have shown that these technologies can potentially foster long-term well-being through timely feedback, personalized goal setting, and early detection of health risks [11, 12].

One critical enabler of this shift has been the proliferation of smartwatches, which offer not only step-counting functions but also more advanced sensors that measure heart rate variability, sleep quality, and stress indicators. Through round-the-clock monitoring, smartwatches can bolster proactive health management, including real-time adjustments to exercise or sleep routines. Additionally, they act as pivotal interfaces within mobile health (mHealth) ecosystems, transmitting data to smartphone applications, cloud-based analytics, and even electronic health records (EHRs) for more comprehensive assessments.

However, existing research has often prioritized device-level metrics such as accuracy, battery performance, and sensor validation [13]. While these technical dimensions are important, they do not fully capture how wearers interpret or integrate the voluminous data that smartwatches generate. Motivations for self-tracking can vary widely—some users meticulously scrutinize every metric, whereas others remain largely passive, occasionally glancing at daily summaries. This variability implies that data alone may not suffice to induce behavioral change unless accompanied by meaningful interpretation and personalized feedback loops [14].

Moreover, several challenges and critiques have emerged, as continuous data streams may overwhelm users, causing information fatigue or even anxiety, particularly among those less comfortable with technology or self-tracking. In some cases, individuals may grow increasingly skeptical if they perceive inconsistencies or inaccuracies in the device's metrics [15]. This underscores an ongoing tension between the promise of automated health monitoring and the need for transparency, contextual relevance, and user trust. Indeed, the same metrics that can empower individuals to adjust behaviors may also cause confusion if the connection between numbers and health outcomes is not made explicit.

These observations highlight a central gap in the literature. Despite acknowledging the potential for data-driven insights, few studies have examined how users make sense of wearable outputs in their day-to-day routines. Equally underexplored is how social and psychological factors—such as individual motivation, subjective health beliefs, or cultural norms—may mediate the process of adopting and acting upon smartwatch data. Addressing these human-centered dimensions is crucial if the field is to move beyond validating devices toward ensuring that self-quantification effectively supports sustainable behavior change.

While self-quantification via wearables holds considerable promise, significant questions remain regarding user engagement, interpretation strategies, and the broader contexts in which individuals employ these devices. Researchers and developers alike stand to benefit from frameworks that capture the interplay between device capabilities, user motivation, and real-world health outcomes. By doing so, the next generation of mHealth solutions can better accommodate diverse user profiles, ultimately enhancing the technology's potential to drive lasting improvements in personal and population health.

2.2   User Segmentation Based on Health Motivation and Consciousness

Segmentation in digital health research aims to categorize users into subgroups whose attitudes, behaviors, and engagement with technology differ in systematic ways [16]. In the context of wearable devices and mobile health (mHealth) applications, scholars frequently focus on health motivation—the degree of personal drive to achieve wellness goals [17, 18]—and health consciousness—the ongoing awareness of bodily signals and willingness to reflect on lifestyle choices [19, 20].

Health motivation has been widely recognized in key behavior change theories [21]. Individuals with higher intrinsic motivation are generally more consistent in health-related behaviors, find greater value in feedback mechanisms, and consult wearable data more frequently. By contrast, those with lower motivation may track metrics sporadically or dismiss wearable outputs as irrelevant, potentially affecting their loyalty to devices and overall health outcomes [22].

Health consciousness, meanwhile, influences users' interpretation of physiological signals and their reactions to discrepancies between device metrics and subjective experiences [23]. More conscious individuals seek to confirm or refine their intuitive perceptions with objective data, whereas those with lower consciousness may overlook subtle shifts or fail to recognize health risks. By segmenting users based on these factors, researchers can better understand how psychological dispositions intersect with the practical aspects of self-tracking, ultimately informing mHealth solutions that accommodate diverse user profiles.

2.3 Data Engagement and Interpretation

Understanding how individuals engage with and interpret data from mobile health (mHealth) applications is crucial for designing effective digital health interventions. Although wearable devices generate abundant physiological and behavioral metrics, these potential benefits only materialize if users interact with the technology and derive practical insights from the information provided [24, 25]. Research into engagement and sense-making processes can thus guide critical enhancements in usability, personalization, and the long-term effectiveness of mHealth tools.

Engagement in mHealth encompasses behavioral, cognitive, and emotional dimensions, reflecting the degree to which people integrate self-tracking tools into their day-to-day activities [26]. Eaton et al. [27] summarized engagement in the context of mHealth interventions as the behavioral and experiential interaction users have with the technology, encompassing both the frequency and quality of use. Engagement includes objective measurements, such as app logins, SMS replies, or completion of intervention modules, and subjective experiences, like user satisfaction, perceived usefulness, or qualitative interviews. Improved engagement is theorized to correlate with meaningful behavior change, such as better adherence to self-management tasks. While many individuals start with strong motivation, app usage often diminishes over time [28]. For example, an app may achieve frequent logins yet fail to promote lasting health improvements if users only check metrics without interpreting or acting on them. Consequently, a holistic view of engagement is needed—one that accounts for how well the interface aligns with user goals and whether its features continue to offer relevance as user needs evolve [29].

Sense-making refers to the process by which users interpret and transform raw data into actionable information [30]. It plays a critical role in translating constant streams of mHealth metrics into concrete strategies for positive health outcomes. Nonetheless, numerous apps present information without adequate context—such as trend analyses, personalized benchmarks, or concise explanations—leaving users confused or overwhelmed. According to Dervin's Sense-Making Theory [30], individuals deliberately construct meaning when confronted with gaps in their understanding, implying that mHealth solutions must provide guidance (e.g., interactive data visualization, targeted coaching) to help users interpret biometric fluctuations.

Investigating engagement and data interpretation behaviors offers insights into designing more user-friendly and adaptive mHealth technologies. Incorporating real-time feedback, personalized recommendations, and intuitive data presentation can foster sustained interaction and empower users to manage their health autonomously [31]. Beyond individual benefits, these improvements can enhance public health efforts, enabling mHealth initiatives to support self-management and long-term well-being at the population level.

3 Methodology

To investigate self-quantification and data engagement among smartwatch users, this study developed and validated a structured questionnaire. Building on relevant literature and measurement scales, the questionnaire was refined through pilot testing and exploratory factor analysis to ensure construct validity and reliability. Subsequently, an online survey was administered to gather data on smartwatch usage behaviors and attitudes, allowing for the examination of engagement differences across user groups.

3.1 Questionnaire Development

A questionnaire was developed to systematically measure smartwatch engagement behaviors. Informed by relevant studies, academic literature, and online user discussions. These items were refined through a structured process involving pilot testing, exploratory factor analysis (EFA), and reliability testing to ensure construct validity and internal consistency. During the pilot study, participants assessed each item's clarity, relevance, and comprehensibility. Based on user feedback and statistical analyses, eight items were removed due to low factor loadings or redundancy, resulting in a final 20-item questionnaire. The instrument encompasses six key dimensions of smartwatch engagement: (1) Data Awareness & Device Preference, (2) Data Interpretation & Trust, (3) Goal Setting & Health Management, (4) Intuition vs. Data Reliance, (5) Collaborative Data Interpretation, and (6) Tolerance for Inaccuracy.

3.2 Online Survey and Data Collection

An online survey was administered to collect information on smartwatch usage, self-quantification behaviors, and health motivation and consciousness. The survey was divided into three main sections:

Demographics: Collected participant information on age, gender, and duration of smartwatch use.

Self-Quantification and Data Engagement: Measured smartwatch engagement using the validated 20-item questionnaire developed in the previous stage.

Health Motivation and Consciousness: Assessed the extent to which participants prioritize health management and remain aware of bodily signals.

This organization provided a comprehensive overview of participants' backgrounds, attitudes, and engagement with smartwatch-generated data.

3.3 Data Collection

A total of 926 survey responses were initially gathered. After removing incomplete responses, duplicate IP addresses, and participants who lacked smartwatch experience, 846 valid responses remained. The final sample included 47.3% male and 52.7% female participants and encompassed a broad age range. Most respondents (37.4%) were between 26 and 35 years old, followed by those aged 36 to 45 (35.5%).

4 Results and Discussion

4.1 Engagement and Health Data Interpretation in mHealth Systems

This study identified six key dimensions that reflect how smartwatch users engage with and interpret self-tracked health data, offering a structured framework for understanding engagement behaviors, trust in data, goal setting, reliance on technology, contextual interpretation, and adaptive expectations of data accuracy. Collectively, these dimensions illuminate self-quantification processes in mHealth systems and highlight new avenues for research and practical implementation.

Data Awareness and Device Preference captures the frequency with which individuals interact with smartwatch data and the extent to which device trust influences these interactions. Previous studies indicate that engagement increases when users perceive their devices as reliable and user-friendly [32]. The current findings extend these observations by emphasizing the role of usability, trust, and familiarity in shaping self-tracking behaviors.

Data Interpretation and Trust addresses how users evaluate wearable-generated data for accuracy and how they respond to inconsistencies. While earlier research identifies accuracy concerns as a primary determinant of engagement [33], this study illustrates how users rationalize discrepancies—some disengage when data appear unreliable, whereas others selectively trust certain metrics. These outcomes support calls for greater algorithmic transparency and contextual feedback to enhance user trust in wearable technologies.

Goal Setting and Health Management highlights the integration of mHealth data into goal-directed health behaviors. While goal-setting fosters sustained engagement, this study reaffirms that users with well-defined objectives engage in more consistent self-tracking. However, some participants reported difficulties in translating raw data into actionable insights, underscoring the need for AI-driven goal-setting tools and personalized recommendations to maintain motivation.

Intuition vs. Data Reliance captures the contrast between users who prioritize quantified metrics and those who rely more on bodily intuition. This divide influences engagement, as data-centric users adjust behaviors based on measured outcomes, whereas those who favor subjective interpretations treat self-tracking as a supplementary tool. These differences suggest that hybrid models—integrating both self-reported experiences and automated metrics—may better accommodate diverse engagement preferences.

Collaborative and Contextual Data Interpretation emphasizes the role of social validation and contextual understanding in making sense of self-tracked information. Without explanatory context, users may struggle to interpret data meaningfully, highlighting the importance of supportive social and informational environments.

Tolerance for Inaccuracy and Adaptive Expectations offers a nuanced perspective on how users manage perceived inaccuracies in mHealth outputs. While accuracy issues are often considered barriers to sustained use, these findings reveal that some users adopt an adaptive perspective, accepting minor errors while focusing on broader trends. Strategies such as incorporating confidence intervals, error margins, and clear explanations may help sustain engagement.

Collectively, these six dimensions provide a validated framework for examining self-quantification behaviors in mHealth settings, bridging gaps between wearable adoption models and digital health engagement theories. From a practical standpoint, these findings offer insights for developers, technology companies, and healthcare professionals. By integrating these dimensions into system design and intervention planning, mHealth platforms can foster more meaningful engagement, ensuring that wearable devices serve as catalysts for behavioral change rather than merely collecting data.

4.2 User Segmentation Based on Health Motivation and Consciousness

The study then employed K-means clustering to categorize participants along two self-reported dimensions: health motivation (drive to set and pursue health goals) and health consciousness (awareness of bodily signals and readiness to reflect on them). While five clusters emerged, one was extremely small and thus is not discussed further. The four major clusters each exhibited distinct patterns in smartwatch usage and data interpretation:

Proactive Health Managers (32.7%, N = 277). Representing the most engaged and data-driven segment, these individuals scored highly on both motivation and consciousness. They routinely monitored their health status, set preventive goals, and integrated multiple data sources (e.g., nutrition apps, other trackers). Their pursuit of comprehensive and accurate data reflected an emphasis on both structured goal-setting and everyday bodily awareness.

Active Goal-Setters (24.2%, N = 205). Participants in this cluster demonstrated high health motivation but did not consistently exhibit strong health consciousness. They relied heavily on quantitative metrics to inform their decisions and frequently tracked progress toward predefined goals. Although firmly committed to managing their well-being, they were sometimes less attuned to day-to-day physiological cues, focusing instead on numeric targets.

Reactive Health Monitors (17.8%, N = 151). This group exhibited high consciousness (sensitivity to bodily changes) yet relatively limited motivation. They primarily used smartwatch data in a reactive manner, checking metrics such as heart rate or sleep when experiencing symptoms or concerns. Though adept at noticing bodily fluctuations, they were less inclined to set or pursue health goals consistently.

Casual Health Observers (18.1%, N = 153). These individuals reported low health motivation and comparatively low consciousness. They tended to view smartwatches as convenience tools rather than resources for deliberate health management. Their sporadic use of self-tracking features suggests that wearable data serve more as supplementary information than a catalyst for behavioral change.

4.3 Differences in Engagement and Data Interpretation Among User Groups

This Building on the six previously identified dimensions of mHealth engagement and data interpretation, this section examines how varying levels of health motivation and consciousness shape individuals' use and perception of wearable device metrics. The resulting four user groups differ notably in the extent to which self-tracked data informs daily health management decisions.

Proactive Health Managers. Exhibiting the highest engagement across all dimensions, these users track and analyze multiple biometric indicators to set goals, monitor progress, and adjust behaviors. Their substantial trust in wearable technology makes device outputs an integral part of health management. Rather than demanding absolute precision, they focus on identifying trends over time and often integrate multiple applications and tools, cultivating a personalized self-monitoring ecosystem.

Active Goal-Setters. Also active in data use, this group centers on achieving specific objectives—improving fitness, sleep quality, or weight management. More sensitive to data discrepancies, they frequently seek higher accuracy and cross-verify results through medical consultations or alternative digital resources. Their engagement can wane when confronted with inconsistent or unreliable metrics, reflecting a strong results-oriented mindset.

Reactive Health Monitors. Taking a situational approach, these individuals use wearable devices primarily in response to immediate health issues (e.g., illness recovery or chronic conditions). Although they trust device data when it aligns with subjective sensations, unexplained fluctuations prompt them to rely on personal intuition. This cautious stance often results in intermittent, rather than sustained, tracking.

Casual Health Observers. Demonstrating minimal engagement, casual observers view wearable technology as a convenient source of general health information rather than a tool for active health management. Their limited reliance on self-tracked data leads to fewer behavioral changes and seldom includes setting long-term goals. Over time, these users may disengage further, perceiving wearable feedback as peripheral to their daily routines.

Collectively, these findings underscore distinct segments in wearable health data engagement. Proactive health managers leverage trends rather than absolute accuracy; Active goal-setters demand rigorous data validation; Reactive health monitors track selectively based on situational needs; and casual health observers engage infrequently, treating data as supplemental rather than essential. Correspondingly, trust in wearable outputs varies: proactive users accept minor inaccuracies, goal-oriented users require consistent reliability, reactive users revert to intuition under uncertainty, and casual observers rarely act on device-generated metrics.

Given these patterns, mHealth solutions should accommodate diverse motivations, trust thresholds, and data interpretation styles. Personalized engagement strategies, contextual explanations for data anomalies, and adaptive feedback loops can effectively address each user profile. Ultimately, tailoring design and communication to these four segments can promote deeper data sense-making, sustained adoption, and healthier long-term behaviors.

5 Conclusion

This study underscores the increasingly prominent role of wearable technology in everyday health management, revealing how user engagement is shaped by levels of health motivation and consciousness. By analyzing distinct user segments, it highlights a spectrum of behaviors—from active reliance on data insights to minimal trust in device accuracy—and affirms the ongoing relevance of personal intuition in interpreting self-tracked metrics.

Conceptually, the six key dimensions of self-quantification and data interpretation—data awareness, trust, goal setting, intuition, collaborative interpretation, and tolerance for inaccuracy—form a cohesive framework for understanding digital health engagement. Future research could employ longitudinal designs or incorporate broader public health perspectives, exploring how these dimensions evolve over time and influence outcomes at both individual and population levels.

Practically, the findings indicate that tailored mHealth interventions are essential. Proactive users who value comprehensive analytics require feature-rich platforms, while those with lower motivation benefit from streamlined interfaces and minimal manual input. By differentiating users based on motivation and consciousness, health technology companies can optimize product design, expand market reach, and enhance long-term engagement.

Although the study contributes a clear segmentation model and robust theoretical grounding, limitations such as sample composition or cross-sectional data collection warrant further investigation. Ultimately, balancing data-driven monitoring with intuitive, human-centered design promotes sustained behavior change, ensuring wearable devices transcend mere data collection to become catalysts for improved health and well-being.

Acknowledgments. This material is based upon work supported by the National Science and Technology Council of Taiwan under grant NSTC 113–2410-H-007–014 -MY2.

Disclosure of Interests. The authors have no competing interests to declare that are relevant to the content of this article.

References

1. Piwek, L., et al.: The rise of consumer health wearables: promises and barriers. PLoS Med. **13**(2), e1001953 (2016)
2. Tung, F.-W., Lai, C.-Y.: Development of a co-creation toolkit for designing smart product–service systems: a health device–related case study. In: International Conference on Human-Computer Interaction. Springer (2023)
3. Higgins, J.P.: Smartphone applications for patients' health and fitness. Am. J. Med. **129**(1), 11–19 (2016)
4. Baig, M.M., Gholamhosseini, H., Connolly, M.J.: A comprehensive survey of wearable and wireless ECG monitoring systems for older adults. Med. Biol. Eng. Compu. **51**, 485–495 (2013)
5. Gimpel, H., Nißen, M., Görlitz, R.: Quantifying the Quantified Self: A Study on the Motivations of Patients to Track Their Own Health (2013)

6. Patel, M.S., Asch, D.A., Volpp, K.G.: Wearable devices as facilitators, not drivers, of health behavior change. JAMA **313**(5), 459–460 (2015)

7. Shull, P.B., et al.: Quantified self and human movement: a review on the clinical impact of wearable sensing and feedback for gait analysis and intervention. Gait Posture **40**(1), 11–19 (2014)

8. Lupton, D.: The diverse domains of quantified selves: self-tracking modes and dataveillance. Econ. Soc. **45**(1), 101–122 (2016)

9. Swan, M.: The quantified self: fundamental disruption in big data science and biological discovery. Big data **1**(2), 85–99 (2013)

10. Schüll, N.D.: Data for life: Wearable technology and the design of self-care. BioSocieties **11**, 317–333 (2016)

11. Anikwe, C.V., et al.: Mobile and wearable sensors for data-driven health monitoring system: state-of-the-art and future prospect. Expert Syst. Appl. **202**, 117362 (2022)

12. Lin, C.-C., Tung, F.-W., Chen, C.-H.: Exploring user engagement with smartwatch health services: a comparative study between Taiwan and Singapore. in International Conference on Human-Computer Interaction. Springer (2024)

13. Fuller, D., et al.: Reliability and validity of commercially available wearable devices for measuring steps, energy expenditure, and heart rate: systematic review. JMIR Mhealth Uhealth **8**(9), e18694 (2020)

14. Coşkun, A., Karahanoğlu, A.: Data sensemaking in self-tracking: towards a new generation of self-tracking tools. International Journal of Human-Computer Interaction **39**(12), 2339–2360 (2023)

15. Boldi, A., et al.: Exploring the impact of commercial wearable activity trackers on body awareness and body representations: a mixed-methods study on self-tracking. Comput. Hum. Behav. **151**, 108036 (2024)

16. Wen, H.-C., Tung, F.-W.: Exploring user requirements for mobile health service systems. Journal of Design Service and Social Innovation **2**(3) (2024)

17. Moorman, C., Matulich, E.: A model of consumers' preventive health behaviors: the role of health motivation and health ability. J. Consumer Research, pp. 208–228 (1993)

18. Feng, S., et al.: How self-tracking and the quantified self promote health and well-being: systematic review. J. Med. Internet Res. **23**(9), e25171 (2021)

19. Parashar, S., Singh, S., Sood, G.: Examining the role of health consciousness, environmental awareness and intention on purchase of organic food: a moderated model of attitude. J. Clean. Prod. **386**, 135553 (2023)

20. Michaelidou, N., Hassan, L.M.: The role of health consciousness, food safety concern and ethical identity on attitudes and intentions towards organic food. Int. J. Consum. Stud. **32**(2), 163–170 (2008)

21. Ryan, R.M., Deci, E.L.: Self-determination theory and the facilitation of intrinsic motivation, social development, and well-being. Am. Psychol. **55**(1), 68 (2000)

22. Jin, D., et al.: Self-tracking behaviour in physical activity: a systematic review of drivers and outcomes of fitness tracking. Behaviour & Information Technology **41**(2), 242–261 (2022)

23. Gurrin, C., Smeaton, A.F., Doherty, A.R.: Lifelogging: personal big data. Foundations and Trends® in information retrieval **8**(1), 1–125 (2014)

24. Perski, O., Short, C.E.: Acceptability of digital health interventions: embracing the complexity. Translational Behavioral Medicine **11**(7), 1473–1480 (2021)

25. Szinay, D., et al.: Influences on the uptake of and engagement with health and well-being smartphone apps: systematic review. Journal of medical Internet

26. Riley, W.T., et al.: Health behavior models in the age of mobile interventions: are our theories up to the task? Translational behavioral medicine **1**(1), 53–71 (2011)

27. Eaton, C., et al.: User engagement with mHealth interventions to promote treatment adherence and self-management in people with chronic health conditions: systematic review. J. Med. Internet Res. **26**, e50508 (2024)
28. Gouveia, R., Karapanos, E., Hassenzahl, M.: How do we engage with activity trackers? A longitudinal study of Habito. In: Proceedings of the 2015 ACM International Joint Conference on Pervasive and Ubiquitous Computing (2015)
29. Tung, F.-W., Liang, P.-K.: Wearable wellness: exploring user experiences with fitness systems on smartwatches. In: International Conference on Human-Computer Interaction. Springer (2024)
30. Dervin, B.: Sense-making theory and practice: an overview of user interests in knowledge seeking and use. J. Knowl. Manag. **2**(2), 36–46 (1998)
31. Didžiokaitė, G., Saukko, P., Greiffenhagen, C.: The mundane experience of everyday calorie trackers: beyond the metaphor of quantified self. New Media Soc. **20**(4), 1470–1487 (2018)
32. Shin, D.-H., Biocca, F.: Health experience model of personal informatics: the case of a quantified self. Comput. Hum. Behav. **69**, 62–74 (2017)
33. Pingo, Z., Narayan, B.: "My smartwatch told me to see a sleep doctor": a study of activity tracker use. Online Inf. Rev. **44**(2), 503–519 (2020)

Digital Human Modeling in Fashion and Textiles

Utilizing Artificial Intelligence (AI)-Assisted Digital Modelling for Modern Chinese Qipao 3D Visualization

Kaiyun Chen[1], Lyu Xu[1(✉)], and Ziwen Qiu[2] (iD)

[1] College of Textile and Apparel, Shanghai University of Engineering and Technology, Shanghai, China
xulyu@sues.edu.cn
[2] Zeis Textiles Extension, North Carolina State University, Raleigh, NC 27606, USA

Abstract. In recent years, modern Chinese-style clothing (New Chinese Fashion) has gained popularity in the Chinese market. However, traditional qipaos face development challenges due to costly materials, labor-intensive craftsmanship, and fragmented design processes. Artificial intelligence (AI)-assisted technology and digital fashion modeling offer promising solutions by reducing material costs and accelerating design iterations, helping address production inefficiencies in modern qipaos. This study explores the potential of integrating AI-assisted technology with commercial 3D fashion CAD software. We propose a workflow using a well-trained AI model developed for modern Chinese qipao design based on the Stable Diffusion (SD) model. To evaluate software compatibility and adaptability, five designers specializing in New Chinese Fashion implemented this workflow using two leading 3D CAD programs—Style3D and CLO3D. They participated in follow-up interviews to assess AI model integration, simulation accuracy, and ease of use. Additionally, renderings from both platforms were shared on social media to gauge market acceptance through user feedback and engagement metrics. Results indicate that CLO3D aligns more effectively with AI-generated qipao design elements, offering vivid visual effects that better represent intricate features such as Chinese-style buttonwork and silk fabric textures. This study identifies suitable AI models and CAD platforms for modern Chinese-style qipao workflows, contributing to innovation in digital fashion design and enhancing the development of contemporary Chinese apparel.

Keywords: New Chinese Style Clothing · 3D Apparel Visualization · AI Generated Content (AIGC) · Generative AI · Pattern Generation · Design Efficiency · Smart Assistance in Design · Chinese Market

1 Introduction

Artificial Intelligence (AI) tools, especially generative AI, are revolutionizing the fashion industry by enhancing efficiency across design, production, and supply chain management (McKinsey Global Institute, 2023; Stanford Institute for Human-Centered Artificial Intelligence, 2024; Zhu and Zhang, 2022). Traditional fashion design processes

V. G. Duffy (Ed.): HCII 2025, LNCS 16339, pp. 63–74, 2026.
https://doi.org/10.1007/978-3-032-13012-9_5

require designers to manually create multiple sketches and undergo numerous rounds of revisions. In contrast, generative AI can rapidly produce a diverse range of design proposals, thereby reducing both the design cycle and labor costs (Wu, 2019; Ren et al. 2021). Tools such as DALL·E and other AI-driven design platforms can generate multiple style variations within minutes, enabling designers to explore and optimize options with unprecedented speed.

For instance, after adopting AI-assisted design, one fashion brand reduced its new collection development time from six weeks to just ten days, while increasing the diversity of design proposals by 50% (McKinsey Global Institute, 2023). In apparel manufacturing, AI systems further enhance operational efficiency by analyzing production data and recommending optimal workflow configurations. This is a substantial shift from traditional production planning, which relies heavily on the experience of engineers and is often time-intensive. According to industry reports, AI-enabled production line reconfiguration led to a 30% reduction in material transportation distances, a 22% increase in production capacity, and a 35% decrease in maintenance costs due to predictive maintenance strategies (Stanford Institute for Human-Centered Artificial Intelligence, 2024).The integration of AI has thus streamlined the entire fashion pipeline from design to manufacturing, accelerating innovation and reducing operational costs, while increasing flexibility and market competitiveness.

As AI adoption continues to rise, data-driven approaches are becoming mainstream in the fashion industry (Zhu and Zhang, 2022; Yu and Zhu, 2024). In the design domain, advanced AI models can deeply learn from databases of style images, consumer preferences, and trend information to generate new designs aligned with both trained knowledge and consumer expectations. Figure 1 illustrates how AI technology influences fashion design and development, showing its potential for improving production and retail efficiency.

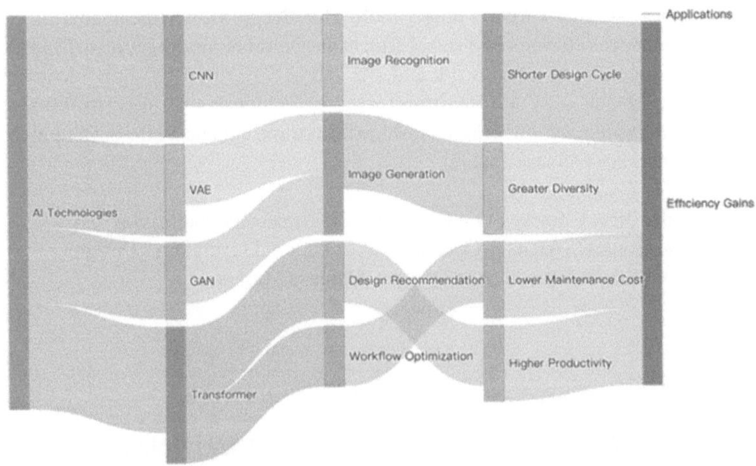

Fig. 1. Sankey Diagram: The Impact of AI on Fashion Design

As shown in Fig. 1, three key generative models support the AI-powered fashion design process (Behrens and Noteboom, 2022). Convolutional Neural Networks (CNNs), known for their ability to extract spatial hierarchies from image data, play a foundational role in parsing massive visual datasets to identify patterns and textures for design input, thereby reducing trend research time. Variational Autoencoders (VAEs), which combine variational inference and autoencoder architectures, facilitate style variation through their capacity to generate new data based on compressed representations of existing inputs. This model enables designers to mitigate the risk of design homogenization. Generative Adversarial Networks (GANs) use adversarial training between generators and discriminators to produce highly realistic visual samples (Li et al., 2022). The addition of Transformer structures further expands the possibilities for data augmentation and cross-modal design innovation.

Building upon the capabilities and impacts of AI technologies, this study aims to integrate AI-assisted design models with commercial 3D apparel Computer-Aided Design (CAD) tools. Specifically, it investigates and evaluates the adaptability of this integrated workflow in using the leading 3D CADs in Chinese market, Style3D and CLO3D, to design modern Chinese-style clothing (Xu and Dong, 2021; Pan, 2023).

2 Method and Results

2.1 Qipao-Specific AI Model Training

Given its cultural significance and popularity in today's Chinese market, the qipao was selected as the focal apparel category for this study (Liu, 2013). To support AI model training, a comprehensive dataset of qipao images was constructed using professional-grade photography equipment (Nikon Z7 II). All images were captured in a standardized lighting environment using a D65 light source at 2000 lx, ensuring consistent color temperature (5500 ± 100 K) and high resolution (45 MP).

The dataset includes a diverse range of qipao styles representative of the Beijing School and Shanghai School, featuring various decorative elements (e.g., lace trim, traditional buttonwork, embroidery), fabric types (e.g., silk, cotton), historical influences (ancient, modern, Chinese, Western), and lighting conditions. In total, 12,800 high-quality qipao images were collected and categorized according to geographical characteristics—Beijing School (32%), Shanghai School (41%), and Hong Kong School (27%)—and historical periods—Qing Dynasty (18%), Republic of China (35%), and modern era (47%). The dataset also reflects diversity in design features: lace trim (76%), buttonwork (89%), and embroidery (63%); and fabric materials including silk (52%), cotton (28%), and blended fabrics (20%).

Each image was annotated with descriptive keyword labels such as "high-collar qipao" and "high-slit design." As illustrated in Fig. 2, the training process began with image data acquisition and annotation. A realistic style base model, *Moyou Artificial Man XL*, was selected for this study. A LoRA (Low-Rank Adaptation) model was trained using the annotated images, binding descriptive keywords to visual features to enable sample generation from text prompts. The generated results were then evaluated and used to iteratively fine-tune model parameters, forming a continuous loop of improvement guided by researcher feedback.

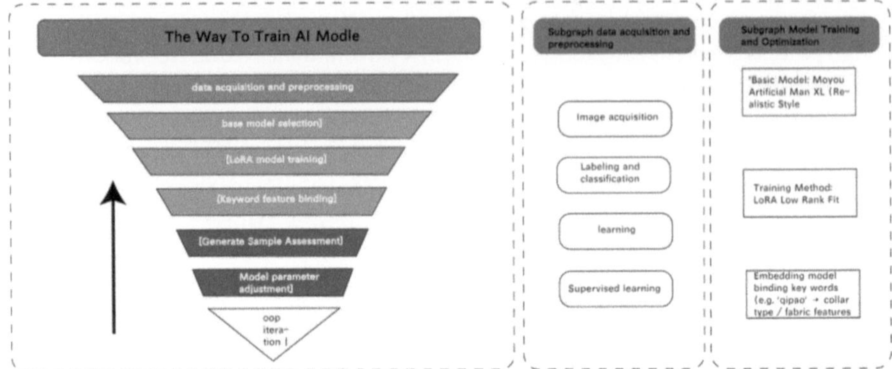

Fig. 2. AI Model Training.

To enable precise model training for qipao image generation, a three-level structured annotation system was established. The first level includes fundamental garment styles (e.g., mandarin collar, lapel, collarless), the second level captures design features (e.g., slit height, sleeve shape, hem silhouette), and the third level focuses on decorative details (e.g., button type, embroidery pattern, piping width). A hybrid annotation strategy was adopted: initial labeling was conducted using the CLIP-ViT-L/14 model, followed by manual verification by the research team, achieving a high annotation consistency (Cohen's $\kappa = 0.87$).

A dual-path adaptive fine-tuning scheme was implemented. In the LoRA path, low-rank adaptation layers were inserted into the cross-attention layers of the UNet, with a rank of 64, scaling factor $\alpha = 0.85$, and learning rate of 1e-4 using the AdamW optimizer. In the semantic binding path, a qipao-specific concept embedding space was constructed:

$$E(qipao) = \sum (\lambda_i \cdot E(termi)) + \Delta E$$

where terms like "qiapao", "silk", and "mandarin collar" were semantically embedded and optimized using contrastive learning, improving image-text alignment by 37.2% (CLIP Score from 0.82 to 0.94).

The training workflow involves structured data preparation (including directory setup for training, validation images, and textual annotations), LoRA training configuration using a Stable Diffusion base model, and parameter tuning—such as resolution settings, LoRA rank and alpha values, batch size, and learning rate—followed by execution through a defined training script. The training was summarized as depicted in Fig. 3.

Following the construction of the annotation system and fine-tuning paths, the data preparation phase began with organizing the dataset into a structured directory layout, including folders for training images, validation images, and text-based annotations. Image preprocessing was performed using a standardized pipeline that resizes images to the target resolution (recommended 1024 for SDXL), applies center cropping, converts them to tensors, and normalizes pixel values to the range of $[-1, 1]$.

For LoRA training, the base model used was "runwayml/stable-diffusion-v1–5", with an image resolution set to 768. The training configuration included LoRA-specific

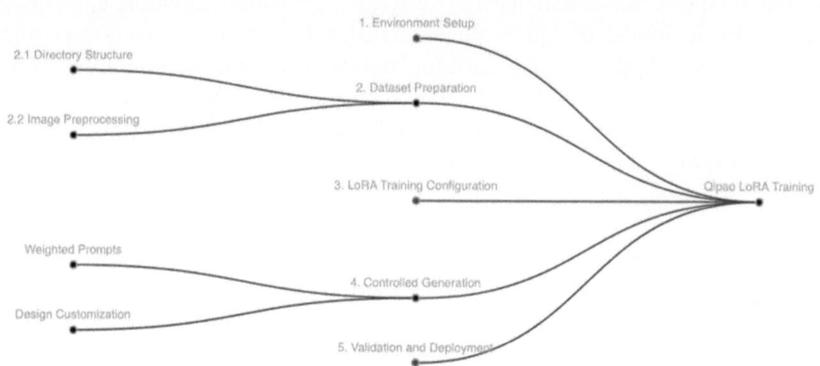

Fig. 3. Qipao LoRA Training.

parameters such as a rank of 128 to capture fine texture details, a scaling factor (alpha) of 64, and a learning rate of 1e-4. The batch size was set to 4 with gradient accumulation steps of 2, resulting in an effective batch size of 8, and the model was trained for up to 2000 steps.

The training script initialized the Stable Diffusion pipeline and injected LoRA adaptation layers into the cross-attention blocks of the UNet model (to_k, to_q, to_v, to_out.0), using Gaussian initialization. To focus learning on the image generation module, the VAE and text encoder components were frozen during training. The training loop involved sampling image latents, encoding corresponding text captions, and computing the mean squared error (MSE) loss between predicted and true noise values, followed by backpropagation for parameter updates in the LoRA-adapted UNet.

2.2 Software Application of the AI Model

Once the AI model was trained, it was deployed using the Stable Diffusion framework to generate qipao-style concept images. These AI-generated outputs are visual bases for designers to manually refine into finalized flat sketches. The refined sketches were then imported into 3D garment design software, Style3D and CLO3D, for further development.

In Style3D, the workflow began with DeepModelA, which rapidly optimized the base pattern and adapted it into 2D patterns suitable for multiple body types. These patterns were then edited and refined, including modifications to fabric properties. Printed patterns were created in Adobe Illustrator, and virtual samples were simulated within Style3D. In CLO3D, the base patterns were imported and adjusted using 2D/3D point editing tools to fine-tune the garment structure. Similarly, prints were created in Adobe Illustrator and applied using CLO3D's texture editor, followed by 3D simulation. While Style3D excels in fast pattern generation via DeepModelA, CLO3D offers greater compatibility, more realistic fabric simulation, and intuitive adjustment of both patterns and surface prints. However, CLO3D encountered limitations in layered fabric rendering, where Style3D performed more reliably.

68   K. Chen et al.

The AI-generated qipao visuals served not only as creative inspiration for designers but also to rapidly iterate and materialize stylistic directions. Building upon the visuals proposed by the model, designers quickly translated these ideas into corresponding pattern structures and print designs, ensuring that the output maintained cultural relevance to traditional Chinese aesthetics while also being commercially viable and production-ready. This AI-assisted workflow largely accelerated the design iteration cycle. Examples of the final results are shown in Fig. 4.

Fig. 4. AI-Generated Qipao Design.

2.3 3D Qipao Apparel Modeling

Building on the established AI-generated visuals and digital pattern workflows, the study proceeds to explore the application of 3D garment modeling software in the design and simulation of qipao garments. While prior studies have thoroughly demonstrated the advantages and feasibility of 3D garment modeling over traditional methods (Peng and Liu, 2024; Yuan, 2025), this research focuses on comparing Style3D and CLO3D specifically in the context of modern Chinese qipao design.

The operational workflows of Style3D and CLO3D have been detailed in previous literature (Qi, 2024; Peng and Liu, 2024). The digital garments were created using a standard Asian female avatar (bust: 84 cm, waist: 68 cm, hips: 90 cm), with adjustments made to the neck circumference (34 cm) and shoulder slope (14°) to suit the mandarin collar. A base qipao pattern (length: 120 cm) was imported, with side slits starting 10 cm below the hipline and extending 25 cm in length. The front seam was shifted 1.2 cm, and the mandarin collar height was set at 4.5 cm with a neckline curvature radius of 7.5 cm to ensure a smooth surface for later print application. Two silk fabric were selected with a particle distance of 10 mm for rendering (see Fig. 5). Transparent organza overlay was added (thickness: 0.12 mm, transparency: 70%), with physical properties fine-tuned (e.g., bending stiffness: 25 mN·m^2/m, stretch stiffness: 80 N/m^2, density: 1.1 g/cm^3) to simulate lightweight drape. Layer spacing was set to 0.05 mm to prevent fabric collision.

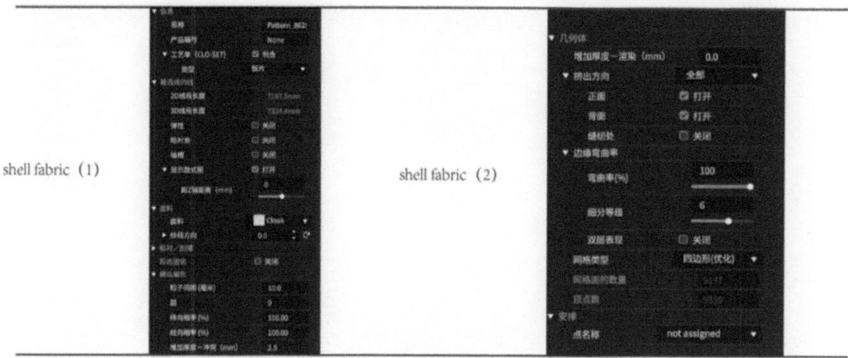

shell fabric（1）   shell fabric（2）

Fig. 5. Shell Fabric Selection (Using Style3D as Example).

Print patterns designed in Adobe Illustrator (800 dpi) were imported into the fabric editor. UV mapping was scaled to 90% and offset by 1.5 mm on both X and Y axes to eliminate misaligned seams. Normal maps were enabled at 60% strength to enhance dimensionality, along with ambient occlusion effects. Additional 3D details were incorporated, such as frog button designs (thickness: 0.5 mm, chamfer radius: 0.2 mm, surface roughness: 0.3) and embroidery motifs as shown in Fig. 6 in transparent PNG format mapped to collars and cuffs with a Z-axis elevation of 0.4 mm. Lace trim (0.1 mm thick) was applied to the slit and hemline with a friction coefficient of 0.6. Each trim had independent UV mapping and was scaled to 95% to match the main print.

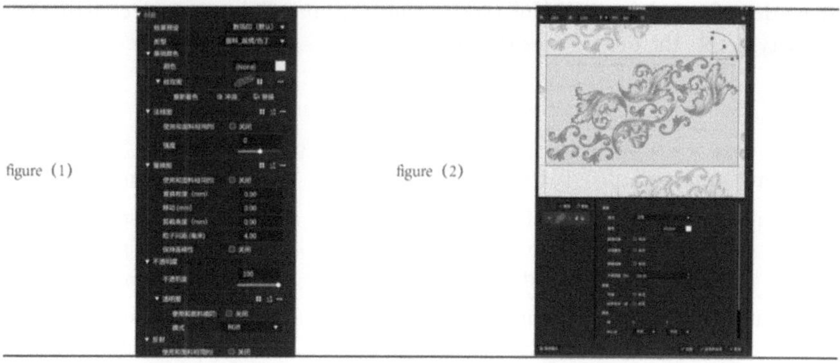

figure（1）   figure（2）

Fig. 6. Lace Trim Properties (Using Style3D as Example).

Fit refinement included testing garment tension in a sitting pose, adjusting waist ease from 2 cm to 3 cm, and reducing side seam tapering by 0.2 cm to prevent excessive fabric wrinkling. To enhance fabric realism, subsurface scattering (SSS) was enabled (density:

0.6, radius: 1.5 mm), with primary lighting set to 1200 lx and rim lighting at 30% to highlight embroidery and pattern depth. The final effect was shown in Fig. 7.

Fig. 7. Final Rendered Effect (Using Style3D as Example).

2.4 Design Effectiveness Evaluation

To evaluate the effectiveness of these tools, a dual-track validation approach was adopted, integrating both human designers and AI models for multidimensional scoring (out of 5 points per criterion).

Specifically, expert designers conducted visual assessments, and AI-based scoring models (downloaded from GitHub) were applied in parallel to ensure consistency and objectivity across the dimensions shown in Table 1.

Table 1. Evaluation System.

Evaluation Dimension	Criteria	Evaluation Tools
Visual Realism	Material texture, lighting, and resemblance to historical artifacts	Expert visual evaluation + AI material recognition algorithms
Local Simulation Accuracy	Fidelity of pattern reproduction	Super-resolution image comparison (error ≤ 0.5 pixels) + AI analysis
Aesthetic and Cultural Value	Color coordination and expression of cultural symbolism	AIGC-based style transfer analysis + designer survey
Software Compatibility	Hardware support and cross-platform integration	Designer interviews + research team feedback

(continued)

Table 1. (*continued*)

Evaluation Dimension	Criteria	Evaluation Tools
Ease of Use	Software integration, learning curve	Designer interviews + research team feedback

Regarding expert designers' evaluation results, Table 2 and 3 present the average scores and representative feedback from five experienced designers who evaluated the outputs created using CLO3D and Style3D. Their assessments cover the realism, technical quality, aesthetic appeal, software compatibility, and ease of use of each platform.

Table 2. Human Designer Evaluation for CLO3D.

Dimension	Avg. Score	Typical Comments
Visual Realism	4.7	"Silk texture closely resembles the real material; organza appears appropriately light and sheer."
Local Simulation Accuracy	4.7	"Pattern resolution is very high."
Aesthetic and Cultural Value	4.8	"Elegant yet gentle—nicely blends Eastern and Western aesthetics."
Software Compatibility	4.9	"Highly compatible, supports integration with MD, Illustrator, and Photoshop."
Ease of Use	4.3	"Offers high flexibility in parameter adjustments; well-integrated but slightly complex."

Table 3. Human Designer Evaluation for Style3D.

Dimension	Avg. Score	Typical Comments
Visual Realism	4.2	"Silk appears glossy, but lacks texture realism."
Local Simulation Accuracy	3.2	"Pattern resolution is insufficient; appears smudged when zoomed in."
Aesthetic and Cultural Value	4.8	"Elegant yet gentle—nicely blends Eastern and Western aesthetics."
Software Compatibility	3.0	"Project files aren't compatible with other software; panel edits are not supported on macOS."
Ease of Use	4.9	"Highly integrated, intuitive UI, and very fast 3D rendering."

In addition to human evaluation, AI models were used to assess the visual and stylistic fidelity of the garment outputs based on algorithmic criteria. Figure 8 summarizes the AI-generated scores across the same five dimensions, ensuring an objective and scalable comparison.

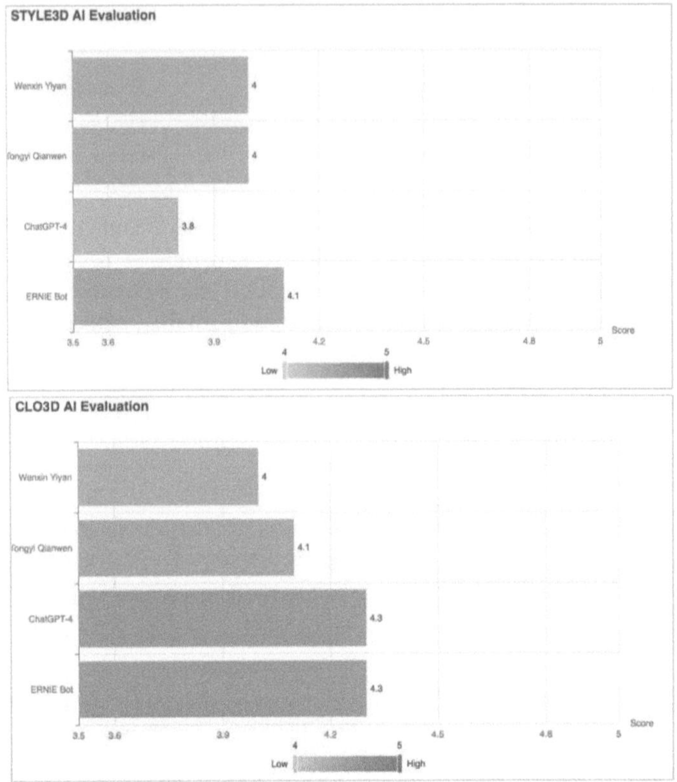

Fig. 8. AI Evaluation for Style3D and CLO3D.

3 Discussions

By synthesizing scores from various evaluators, particularly those from human designers who tend to align more closely with real-world standards, we can better gauge the practical validity of the results. For example, human evaluators rated CLO3D's virtual realism and local simulation accuracy at 4.7, indicating that the overall realism of digital garments is considered acceptable and trustworthy.

From this, we conclude that Style3D, with its highly integrated user interface and intelligent design modules, effectively lowers the technical barrier to 3D garment modeling. It is especially suitable for fast-paced applications such as fast fashion and e-commerce visualization. The software's built-in smart material simulation and auto-patterning system enhance modeling efficiency while still producing visually compelling results. Furthermore, Style3D's lighting simulation and virtual runway features strengthen its capabilities in rapid visual presentation. However, when it comes to modeling precision and physical fabric simulation, Style3D falls short compared to professional-grade tools. It has limited capacity in reproducing complex drape behavior and fine material textures, making it less ideal for highly detailed or realism-sensitive design tasks. Additionally, its support for file formats and cross-platform collaboration is restricted, which hinders its integration in multi-software workflows.

In contrast, CLO3D demonstrates a higher level of professional performance in digital garment modeling through its refined parameter control system and high-fidelity fabric simulation. It excels in representing structural details, fabric behavior, and realistic physical responses, particularly elasticity, drape, and deformation—making it well-suited for custom high-end garment design and the recreation of traditional craftsmanship. CLO3D also performs well in software interoperability, supporting seamless data exchange with tools such as Marvelous Designer, Adobe Illustrator, and Photoshop, which greatly enhances efficiency in cross-platform design collaboration. Although it presents a steeper learning curve and a more complex workflow, its high accuracy and fidelity make it particularly appropriate for garments like the modern qipao, where structural curvature and fabric expressiveness are essential for conveying traditional cultural aesthetics and contemporary craftsmanship.

This study is subject to limitations due to sample size and experimental duration, which prevented full coverage of existing design variations, creative directions, and standardized frameworks. It is important to note that the AI model used in this study did not integrate a comprehensive historical dataset encompassing the full evolution of qipao designs. Therefore, when applying the model in practice, one must remain aware of its historical constraints and the ongoing need for human creativity and design intuition. Moreover, the evaluation system is inherently limited by its reliance on subjective, perceptual criteria. While AI-generated scores serve as digitized representations of aesthetic attributes, they cannot replicate the depth of human aesthetic judgment nor replace the creative agency of designers. As such, the AI system developed in this research should be clearly defined as a supportive tool, not a replacement for human-led design.

From a technical perspective, although 3D digital modeling offers the ability to defy physical constraints and produce hyper-realistic renderings, it still faces significant challenges in accurately simulating the dynamic behaviors of real fabrics. Our experiments show that, for garments involving specialty materials, verification through traditional sample garment construction remains essential for accurately assessing the final fit and visual presentation of the design.

4 Conclusion

The results of this study indicate that CLO3D demonstrates stronger compatibility with AI models specifically trained for modern Chinese-style qipao elements. CLO3D offers more vivid and accurate visual outputs, effectively capturing intricate design details such as traditional frog buttons and the distinctive texture of silk fabrics commonly used in qipao construction. This research successfully identifies and establishes an integrated workflow that combines AI modeling with 3D CAD software, contributing significantly to fashion innovation and the contemporary development of Chinese-style qipao design and visualization.

Disclosure of Interests. The authors have no competing interests to declare that are relevant to the content of this article.

Acknowledgments. Research on the Future Trends of Digital Clothing from the Perspective of East Design Studies, Project Approval Number: 23YJC760130].

Shanghai University of Engineering Science's Innovation Fund.

References

McKinsey Global Institute. *Generative AI and the future of work in America* (Report). McKinsey & Company (2023). https://www.mckinsey.com/~/media/mckinsey/mckinsey%20global%20institute/our%20research/generative%20ai%20and%20the%20future%20of%20work-in-america/generative-ai-and-the-future-of-work-in-america-vf1.pdf

Stanford Institute for Human-Centered Artificial Intelligence. (2024). Artificial Intelligence Index report 2024 [Report]. Policy Commons. https://policycommons.net/artifacts/12089781/hai_ai-index-report-2024/12983534/

Zhu, W.M., Zhang, J.X.: Research on interaction of clothing design based on users' big data. Journal of Zhejiang Sci-Tech University (Social Sciences) **48**(2), 222–229 (2022)

Yu, J., Zhu, W.: The application of big data-driven generative AI in fashion design: taking Midjourney as an example. Silk **61**(09), 20–27 (2024)

Wu, Q.: Innovative design thinking in the era of artificial intelligence. Decoration **11**, 18–21 (2019)

Ren, R., Shen, L., Li, X.: The current situation and trend of the transformation and upgrading of intelligent marketing channels in the garment industry. Maotex Technology **49**(12), 98–103 (2021)

Behrens, A., Noteboom, C.: Generative adversarial networks in tumor-related research: a review and agenda for moving forward. SAIS 2022 Proceedings. **3** (2022). https://aisel.aisnet.org/sais2022/3

Li, M., Liu, B.Q., Peng, Q.L.: A camouflage suit pattern design based on the CycleGAN algorithm. Journal of Silk **59**(8), 100–106 (2022)

Xu, C., Dong, X.: Create the future of digitalization! Lingdi Style3D China Garment Forum 2021 successfully concluded. Textile and Apparel Weekly **13**, 10–11 (2021)

Pan, L.S.: Design change in the digital age. Art & Design Research **4**, 86–91 (2023)

Liu, F.: Research on "New Chinese Style" clothing design (Master's thesis, Qingdao University). Qingdao University (2013)

Peng, X., Liu, W.: Visualization analysis of CLO 3D technology in the field of virtual clothing application in China. Fashion Designer, (09), 81–86 (2024). https://doi.org/10.20100/j.cnki.cn11-4548/ts.2024.09.017

Yuan, X.: Research on variable dress customization scheme based on 3D technology—Taking small wedding dresses as an example. Textile Report **44**(02), 45–48 (2025)

Qi, W.: Virtual design and application of Style 3D knitted sportswear. Journal of Zhejiang Textile and Apparel Vocational College **23**(01), 9–13 (2024)

3D Scanning Technology for Assessing Soft Tissue Displacement in Running: An Exploratory Study on Compression Garments and Fatigue

Javier Gámez-Payá[1,2]($\boxtimes$) , Sandra Alemany[3], José Pérez-Maletzki[1,2], Alfredo Ballester[3], and Alfredo Remón[3]

[1] Department of Physiotherapy and Sport, Faculty of Health Sciences, Universidad Europea de Valencia, Valencia, Spain
`Javier.gamez@universidadeuropea.es`
[2] Biomechanics & Physiotherapy in Sports Research Groups (BIOCAPS), Valencia, Spain
[3] Instituto de Biomecánica de Valencia, Valencia, Spain
`sandra.alemany@ibv.org`

Abstract. The displacement of soft tissues during activities such as running can influence athletic performance, according to previous research. Fatigue, on the other hand, is a condition that causes changes in running biomechanics. One strategy to reduce soft tissue displacement is the use of compression garments. This exploratory study aims to apply a novel methodology to quantify soft tissue displacement and analyse body shape changes during movement using dense 3D information of the body surface. Specifically, the study recruited one recreational runner to examine the effects of compression garments and fatigue on the lower limb during running. The technology used is MOVE4D (IBV, Valencia, Spain), which enables the analysis of variables such as thigh and calf perimeters and the Shape Variability Index. To assess the system's reliability, the Intraclass Correlation Coefficient (ICC) was calculated under each experimental condition.

The results show that the scanning system can distinguish between compression and no-compression conditions in the leg and provides consistent measurement of the running cycle. Additionally, fatigue was found to increase soft tissue movement, while the use of compression garments reduces soft tissue displacement in the lower limbs. The MOVE4D system emerges as an innovative, non-invasive technology for analysing soft tissue motion and presents a promising tool for the design of compression garments in sports applications.

Keywords: soft tissue movement · compression garments · running · fatigue

1 Introduction

Running is a complex activity that involves repetitive impacts, that can reach 10 g, also ground reaction forces of 1.5 to 3 times the human body weight within 30 ms [1]. The above mentioned generates soft tissue (including muscles, tendons, adipose

V. G. Duffy (Ed.): HCII 2025, LNCS 16339, pp. 75–92, 2026.
https://doi.org/10.1007/978-3-032-13012-9_6

tissue, ligaments and skin) vibrations (STV) and movement in various physiological systems. These vibrations can influence muscle function, energy dissipation, and overall performance. Soft tissue vibrations during running can lead to neuromuscular fatigue, particularly in the lower extremities. Studies have shown that prolonged running induces changes in muscle activation patterns, with significant increases in electromyographic (EMG) activity in muscles such as the gastrocnemius medialis and vastus lateralis [2, 3].

Soft tissue vibrations and movement during running are closely linked to energy dissipation and running economy. A study investigating the relationship between soft tissue energy dissipation and leg stiffness found that higher step frequencies reduce energy dissipation, potentially improving running efficiency. This suggests that optimizing running mechanics to minimize unnecessary energy loss could enhance performance [4].

Runners adapt their biomechanics to minimize the effects of soft tissue vibrations and movement. For example, changes in foot strike patterns, stride frequency, and muscle pre-activation can reduce the amplitude and frequency of STV. These adaptations are critical for maintaining efficiency and reducing injury risk during prolonged running [5, 6].

Compression garments (CGs) are widely used in many sports to reduce and control STV and movement, and there is an increasing interest on the design and performance evaluation of these type of products. Studies have shown that CGs can lower blood lactate concentrations during exercise [7]. For instance, one systematic review found that compression garments were associated with reduced blood lactate levels during running and cycling [8].

Some research suggests that CGs can improve muscle oxygenation during and after exercise. For example, a study on lower-body compression garments found that they increased muscle oxygen saturation (SmO2) and facilitated faster reoxygenation after exercise-induced muscle fatigue [9]. Another study observed improved muscular oxygenation following endurance exercise when wearing CGs [8].

Compression garments are known to reduce muscle oscillation during running, which may contribute to improved running efficiency. A study using accelerometers found that full-leg compression pants significantly reduced muscle oscillation compared to loose-fitting control garments [10].

Wearing CGs may enhance proprioception, which is the perception of body position and movement. A study on half-marathon runners found that compression running pants improved knee proprioceptive acuity, particularly at longer running distances [11].

The use of CGs has been associated with reduced impact force during activities such as vertical jump landing. For example, custom fit compression shorts were found to decrease impact force by 27% compared to non-compressive garments [12].

The most commonly used methodologies for the analysis of STVs and movement are accelerometry, 3D motion analysis, and surface electromyography (sEMG), each with its own strengths and weaknesses. Accelerometry allows for high sampling frequencies (above 2,500 Hz) [13]; however, it is only capable of analysing vibration at the initial contact phase (first 50ms) and not throughout the entire stance phase of running. Additionally, it typically only measures vertical oscillation.

On the other hand, 3D motion analysis measures the displacement of markers placed on soft tissues in three dimensions, with sampling frequencies ranging between 100 Hz and 250 Hz [13]. EMG measures the electrical activity of muscles, which can be correlated with soft tissue vibrations. By analysing EMG signals alongside vibration data, researchers can understand how muscle activity influences vibration characteristics [14].

However, all of these methods share common weaknesses: they can only take localized measurements at specific points on the legs and are susceptible to artifacts caused by relative movement between the measurement technology and the athlete's equipment and/or skin [13].

Given this context, it is considered necessary to propose methodologies for analysing the movement of soft tissues throughout the entire running cycle in a global and direct manner, taking into account all anatomical points of interest in the leg, while avoiding artifacts caused by the use of material external to the athlete (markers, sensors…).

This paper presents a new methodology to quantify soft tissue movement and shape variations during running using dense 3D information of the body surface of the athlete in motion. Our methodology is used in an exploratory study on a single runner to assess the effect of a lower limb compression garment when running under two conditions: non-fatigued and fatigued.

The initial hypotheses are as follows: (1) the MOVE4D measurement system is capable of distinguish, throughout the entire leg, between compression and non-compression conditions in both fatigued and non-fatigued states, whether in a static position or during running. (2) Additionally, the MOVE4D system represents the phases of the running cycle using the perimeters of the calf and thigh. (3) Under compression conditions, the leg perimeter and movement of soft tissues decrease regardless of fatigue. Furthermore, (4) fatigue causes greater soft tissues displacements throughout the leg during the running cycle.

2   Methodology

2.1   Participant

This study aims to conduct an exploratory study. Accordingly, a single participant was recruited, a runner with a weekly mileage of 30 km and no reported injuries within the last three months.

Table 1 includes basic data of the runner, including his foot strike pattern. Foot strike pattern defines running biomechanics. Different muscular activations have been identified for different foot strike patterns. The non RFS (rear foot strike) runners activates their gastrocnemius muscles before ground contact, whereas non-RFS runners activate this musculature after the impact [15]. On the other hand, researchers have observed that knee load is larger in RFS runners [16]. Consequently, foot strike pattern impacts the runner's soft tissues dynamics.

Table 1. Participant description.

Variables	Runner
Age	53 years old
Height	180 cm
Weight	71 kg
Gender	Male
Personal best marathon	3h 15'
Personal best half marathon	1h 28'
Foot strike pattern	Rearfoot striker
Cadence	168 steps/minute
Dominant leg	Left
Perceived effort after the fatigue protocol (Borg scale)	17

2.2 Compression Garments

In the last years, compression garments have gain relevance in sports. As a consequence, most of the sportwear manufacturers include compression garments in their catalogue, including compression socks, tights and shorts. The garment employed in this study is a medical compression stocking from Jobst ® (Stockholm, Sweden). It presents an evolutive compression that ranges from 22 to 29 mmHg. Just before the experimentation, experts measured the runner's limbs to decide the convenient size of the compression stocking, based on the sizing guide provided by the manufacturer.

2.3 Experimental Design

This study was approved by the Research Commission of the European University (Code CI: 2024–866). The runner completed the experimental session within a single visit to the laboratory. At an initial stage, the technician informed the user about the experiment and the runner signed a consent allowing the capture of personal data and its subsequent study. Afterwards, the experiment included the following stages:

1. Following the manufacture instructions, the runner was measured to identify the convenient size of the compression garment. This involves the measuring of girths at thigh, calf and ankle. Subject's weight and height were also collected.
2. The runner warmed-up running in a treadmill for 10 min. The last 5 min of the warm-up mimic the test running speed. Also, the running cadence was measured to reproduce the same running conditions (168 spm for the participant in the study) in the rest of the experimentation.
3. The runner was scanned with the scanner in A-pose position (see Fig. 1 left) and running without compression garment. The capture lasted 3 s (at 178fps for a total of 534 frames). A metronome set the cadence and the running speed was determined

depending on the runner, and set to his personal best time of a half-marathon (1h 28' for the participant in the present study).

4. The runner was scanned again wearing the compression garment in A-pose position and running. Duration, constant running speed and cadence are controlled to equals the one in the previous scan.
5. The runner runed for 1h out of the laboratory at half-marathon pace.
6. The runner defined its level of fatigue using the Borg 6–20 scale.
7. The runner was scanned in A-pose position and ran without compression garment. Duration, running speed and cadence are controlled to equals the prefatigued conditions
8. The runner was scanned in A-pose position and ran wearing the compression garment. Duration, running speed and cadence are controlled to equals the once in the previous scans.

The experimental design results in four test conditions that were analysed separately:

- Test 1: no compression garment and non-fatigued runner.
- Test 2: compression garment and non-fatigued runner.
- Test 3: no compression garment and fatigued runner.
- Test 4: compression garment and fatigued runner.

2.4   Technology

MOVE4D (IBV, Valencia, Spain) [17] is a cutting-edge scan technology able to capture 3D objects in movement. It is especially suitable to scan persons, as it includes a sophisticated software that can reproduce human body shape with high accuracy. This software employs mathematical models of human body shape, human postures and soft tissues displacements, to enhance accuracy of the result. The software processes the accurate raw data reported by the scanning modules i.e., a 3D points cloud, and generates digital human models that reproduce the person with an error lower than a millimetre. MOVE4D is a technology developed by IBV and can work under different layouts. The one employed in this study includes 18 capture modules, with a scanning volume of 2x3x3 meters, which refers to width, large and height respectively. The system was set to capture at its maximum rate, 178fps.

The technology also presents some interesting tools to analyse data. In particular, it includes a digital measuring tape with more than 100 body metrics, including girths, distances, areas and volumes. It also allows to compute body metrics of humans in movement, called dynamic body metrics. Meaning that metrics are not related to a specific posture and therefore, they can be measured in any posture. Digital dynamic body metrics permit to evaluate the impact of movement in body human shape and play a key role in this study.

On the top of this, the technology includes a GUI that guides the user on the definition of customized body metrics. This tool allows the user to define its metrics of interests, as we already did during this research.

This study is based on the evaluation of a set of dynamic body metrics and the digital models which describe the body shape of the runner at every single frame. This is in fact a huge amount of data and requires an initial phase of the study to identify and define the relevant data to analyse.

2.5 Data Treatment and Variables

MOVE4D technology was used to capture the runner and also to process the capture and obtain digital models of the running cycle. It is important to note that in MOVE4D, all digital models are defined with a known mesh topology formed by 49530 vertices, meaning that the mesh and body surface have vertex-to-vertex anatomical correspondence. As this is a constant for all the digital models computed by the system, we can exploit this correspondence to compare digital models within a captured sequence and even to compare digital models of different sequences [18]. Anatomical correspondence facilitates the computation of geometric measurements such as lengths, widths, sections, surfaces, volumes or inertial moments, as well as to compute joint centres and motion variables. In this research, we focus on the evaluation of shape measurements in the calf and the thigh areas.

In order to compare metrics in the four tests' sequences, the sequences were aligned starting from their first heel strike of the left foot. Therefore, frames previous to that moment were neglected. In addition, the duration of all sequences was set to include, exactly, three steps. As a result, the four sequences present the same number of frames.

Exploiting the scanning technology functionalities, we defined 3 girths to study the movement of each thigh. They were set at different levels of the thigh. In particular, giving the segment defined by the related femur, the girths were set 35%, 50% and 65% (last being closest to the knee) of its length. To evaluate the behaviour of the calf, we measure its girth at 35% of lower leg (closest to the last). Figure 1 includes a graphic representation of the described girths over the subject on a static standing posture, called A-pose (left) and at a given moment of the experiment, i.e., running (right).

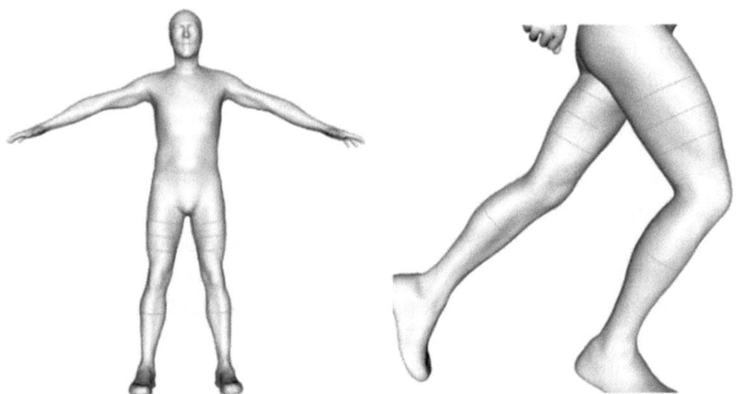

Fig. 1. Girths evaluated in A-pose (left) and during running (right).

The body metrics were evaluated during the whole running sequence, but also having into account several running key moments (see Fig. 2). Up to 6 phases were identified in the movement: heel strike right/left, midstance right/left and toe off right/left.

Heel strike is the moment when the foot touches the ground. Midstance refers to the instant when knees are in the same position in the sagittal plane. Toe-off phase refers to the moment when the foot leaves the ground.

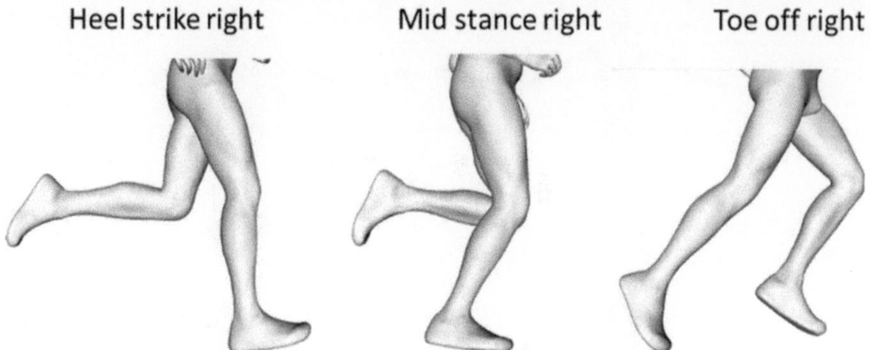

Fig. 2. Key moments in running identified.

Length of the girth is a 1D representation of a 3D girth and therefore, there is a leak of information. We exploit the outputs of the technology, which include the 3D objects during the whole sequence (see Fig. 3), to evaluate girths shapes and their variations.

To perform such a study, it was necessary to align all girths. This requires the alignment of 3D objects with similar but different shapes. To perform this alignment, we exploited the digital skeleton computed by MOVE4D (version 1.6) for every single digital model computed, and also the anatomical correspondence of all meshes. We make use of the anatomical correspondence to partition every mesh and obtain sub meshes of the anatomical segment of interest, i.e., the right/left calf. Using the digital skeleton joints, an initial alignment of body segments of different frames is performed. This initial alignment is improved with a 3D objects alignment algorithm (implemented by class vtkLandmarksTransform in library VTK [19]). Figure 4 shows the alignment process presented. Avatar in the left is the reference A-pose avatar, avatar in centre represents the same subject during running, and in the right shows the alignment of both avatars (left and centre) using its left calf body segment.

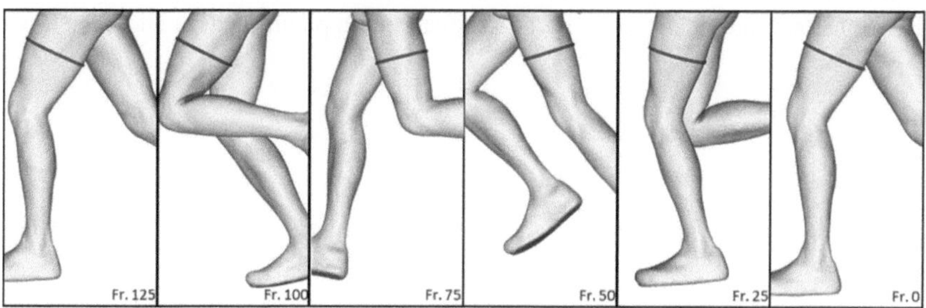

Fig. 3. Girth of left thigh at 50% in different captured frames. Frame number is labeled at the bottom-right corner of every picture.

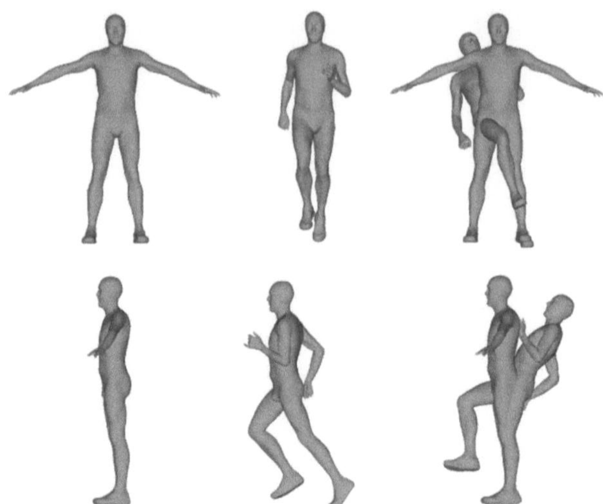

Fig. 4. Alignment of avatars based on the left calf. A-pose reference avatar (left), running avatar (centre) and aligned avatars (right).

Once the alignment is completed, we compute the girths and obtain a set of overlapped girths. Due to the runner homogeneous cadence, a sequence of a single step involves 127 frames, and subsequently, a sequence of 3 steps is formed by 381 frames. Having this into account, the evaluation of the left calf's girths creates a superimposition of 381 girths. This is showed in Fig. 5 (right). In order to quantify the variation of the girths, we compute the minimal area that covers all the lines of the girths (Fig. 5 centre). From here on, we will refer this area as the shape variability index (SVI). In addition, we can use the segment that joins knee and ankle to estimate the frontal and rear sections of the girths (Fig. 5 right). This way, we can evaluate the shape variability index for the anterior and posterior part of the limb. This is especially appealing as they present different functional zones during running: the anterior part (associated with dorsiflexion and knee extension) and the posterior part (associated with plantarflexion and knee flexion).

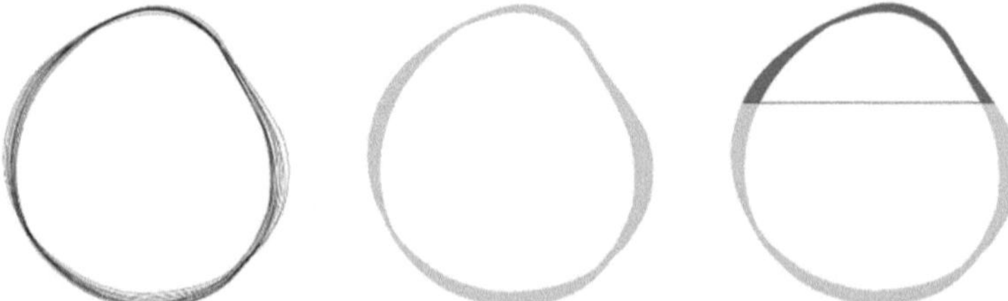

Fig. 5. Superimposition of aligned girths of the left calf at 35% (left), area defined by all girths in grey, or shape variability index (SVI) (centre), partition of SVI into anterior (dark grey) and posterior (light grey) parts (right).

Additionally, the SVI must be normalized in order to compare its values among all tests. Note that the A-pose scans showed differences in length and shape of the calf girths among the four tests performed. We normalize the SVI values using the area enclosed by the related girth in A-pose.

Same processing (alignment, computation of SVI and its normalization) was applied to the studied thigh girths.

In this sense, we focused our study on the evaluation of:

- The above-mentioned girths in A-pose.
- The circumference of the girths during running cycle.
- The shape variability index, as an estimation of the soft tissues' displacements, and its distribution in the anterior and posterior part of the leg.
- The shape variability index normalized by the area of the girth in A-pose, to enable the comparison of this variable among different tests.

2.6 Reliability Analysis

To analyse the repeatability and consistency of the measurements, the Intraclass Correlation Coefficient (ICC) was calculated using the Seolmatrix module of the Jamovi software (version 2.6.26.0). The results were reported as the mean ICC values along with 95% confidence intervals ($p < 0.05$). To interpret the results, we followed the guidelines proposed by Koo and Li (2016): ICC < 0.5 indicates poor reliability; 0.5–0.75, moderate reliability; 0.75–0.90, good reliability; and > 0.90, excellent reliability [20].

3 Results

Figure 6 and Tables 2 and 3 show the different captures taken during the four tests conducted in A-pose. By analysing the leg perimeter variables, it can be observed that the scanning technology is able to distinguish between compression and non-compression conditions in both fatigue and non-fatigue scenarios across all analysed perimeters. Additionally, a clear difference is observed between the fatigue condition (tests 3 and 4) and the non-fatigue condition (tests 1 and 2). When the runner is fatigued, regardless of compression, a smaller perimeter is observed throughout the leg.

Table 2. Calf perimeter in A pose (mm).

Test	Calf_L_35	Calf_R_35
Test 1	382	396
Test 2	380	395
Test 3	368	384
Test 4	366	381

Table 3. Thigh perimeter in A pose (mm).

Test	Thigh_L_35	Thigh_L_50	Thigh_L_65	Thigh_R_35	Thigh_R_50	Thigh_R_65
Test 1	524	498	451	551	518	469
Test 2	524	495	447	547	514	465
Test 3	514	485	440	541	507	457
Test 4	514	482	438	537	501	454

3D scanning also enables the description of the running cycle. The following figures display the perimeter of the calf (35% of the total length) and the thigh (35% of the total length), highlighting key moments of the running cycle. In the calf, a peak is observed corresponding to the midstance phase, and a trough associated with the impact phase (Fig. 7). In contrast, the thigh shows a peak during the aerial phase of the leg and a minimum related to the midstance phase (Fig. 8). Moreover, in both cases, larger perimeters are observed in the non-fatigued state, while smaller values are recorded under compression conditions.

A

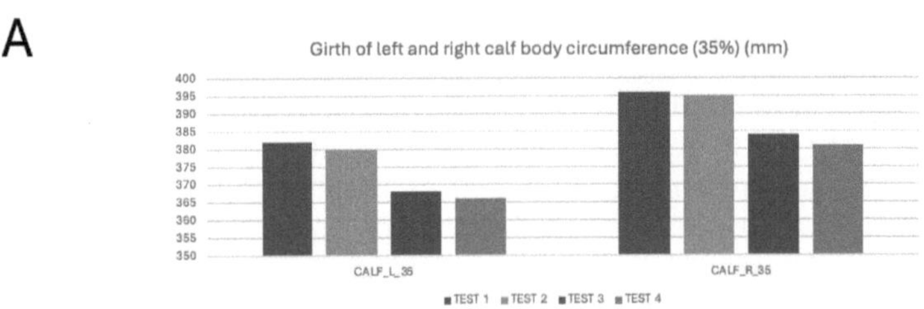

B

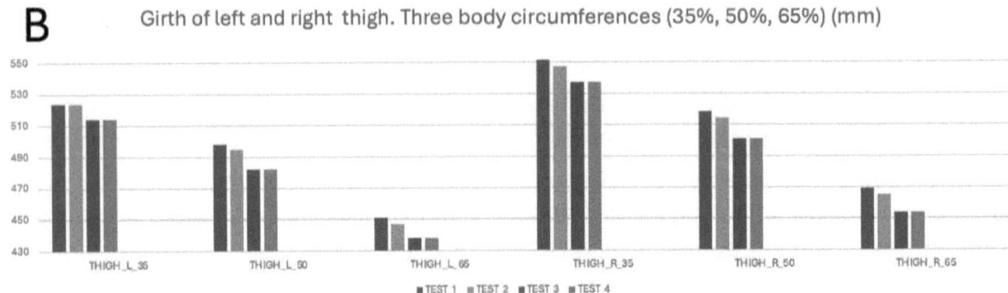

Fig. 6. Calf (35%) and Thigh (35%, 50% and 65%) perimeter in A-pose (mm).

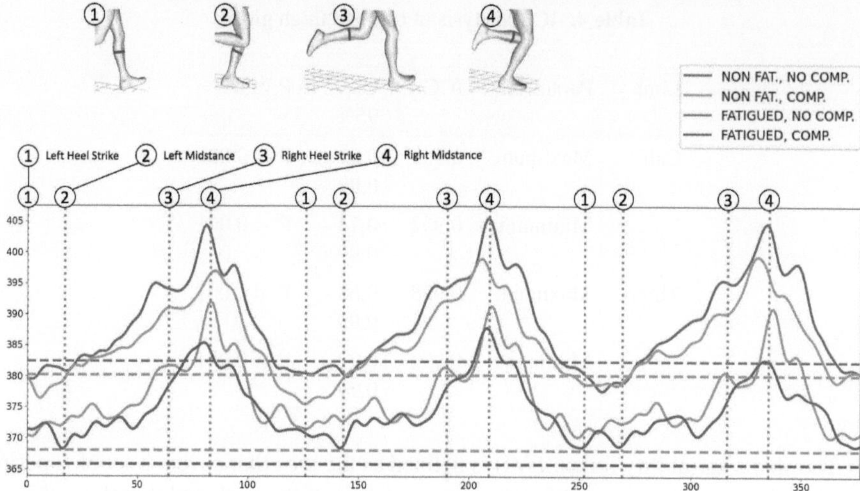

Fig. 7. Left calf girth 35% during running cycle.

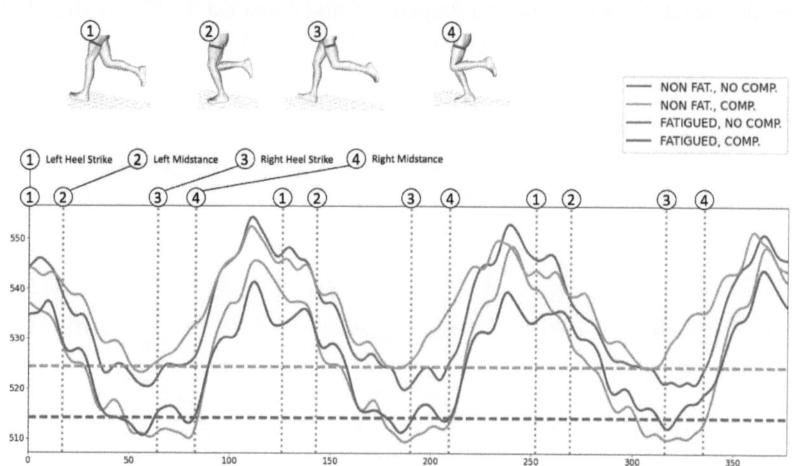

Fig. 8. Left thigh girth 35% during running cycle.

The table below shows the result of the ICC analysis of the calf and thigh girths; all mean values of ICC are above 92% (p < 0.05) showing an excellent reliability (Table 4).

Table 4. ICC analysis of calf and thigh girths.

Limb	Parameter	ICC	CI 95%	P value
Calf	Maximum	0.963	0,81 - 0,99	P < 0.001
	Minimum	0.952	0,74 - 0,99	P < 0.001
Thigh	Maximum	0.928	0,68 - 0,99	P < 0.001
	Minimum	0.994	0,97 - 0,99	P < 0.001

The shape variability index (SVI) is defined as the area that covers a set of superimposed girths and aims to quantify the shape variation of the girth and therefore, the soft tissue displacement in the girth. Figure 9 shows the superimposition of left calf girth 35% in the four tests. Girths are plotted in grey such that the black areas refer to several girths overlapping. Visually, we can see that the effect of compression garment clearly reduces the variability of girths (test 2 against 1 and 4 against 3). SVI is slightly larger under fatigued conditions (test 3 against 1 and 4 against 2).

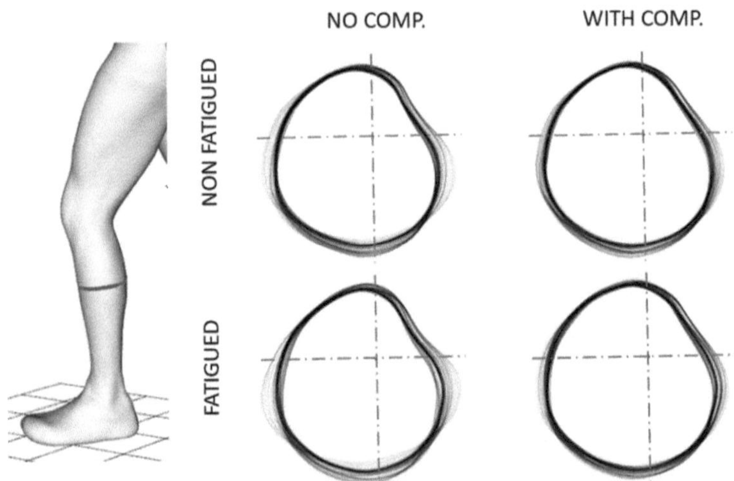

Fig. 9. Superimposition of the left calf girth 35% of the whole capture (3 steps) for the 4 tests performed.

To carry out the analysis, the leg was divided into two functional sections. It is clearly evident that during running, there is greater movement in the posterior part of the leg, as a larger area is observed across all the anatomical regions analysed, on both the right and left sides (see Table 5 and Figs. 10, 11 and 12).

Regarding the analysis on the impact of the compression garment during running, it can be observed that the compression conditions, i.e., Test 2 and Test 4, result in a smaller SVI compared to their non-compression counterparts, Test 1 and Test 3, respectively. This is consistent for both body segments under study, the calf and the thigh. Across all values, in both the anterior and posterior parts of the leg, it is consistently observed that T1 is greater than T2, and T3 is greater than T4 (see Table 4, Figs. 10, 11 and 12).

On the other hand, the effects of fatigue on body perimeters can be observed, particularly in the posterior part of the leg, when comparing conditions T1 against T3 and T2 against T4. In the three analysed regions (calf at 35%; thigh at 35%; and total thigh, sum of perimeters 35%, 50% and 65%), the movement of soft tissues (represented by the total area) shows that T1 is lower than T3, and similarly, T2 is lower than T4, with the exception of a few perimeters where the values are very similar (see Table 5).

When comparing the runner's dominant leg (left leg) with the non-dominant leg, differences can be observed. In the posterior region of the dominant leg, under non-compression conditions with and without fatigue, movement appears to be similar. However, in the non-dominant leg under the same conditions, greater movement is observed in the posterior region of the leg during fatigue, both in the calf and the thigh (Figs. 10, 11 and 12).

Table 5. Shape variability index (SVI) in calf and thigh compared to A pose area (%).

Calf	T1 anterior	T2 anterior	T3 anterior	T4 anterior
Left	18,41	15,27	18,19	14,99
Right	15,10	14,03	16,54	14,12
Calf	T1 posterior	T2 posterior	T3 posterior	T4 posterior
Left	22,94	16,94	22,48	18,34
Right	21,38	18,16	24,84	18,62
Thigh total	T1 anterior	T2 anterior	T3 anterior	T4 anterior
Left	59,80	56,44	59,81	56,94
Right	62,23	58,02	61,79	57,19
Thigh total	T1 posterior	T2 posterior	T3 posterior	T4 posterior
Left	70,22	63,37	71,26	65,95
Right	70,42	66,18	72,73	66,04
Thigh 35%	F1 anterior	F2 anterior	F3 anterior	F4 anterior
Left	20,33	20,21	20,35	19,61
Right	24,93	21,98	26,86	23,92
Thigh 35%	F1 posterior	F2 posterior	F3 posterior	F4 posterior
Left	21,72	19,49	21,29	20,17
Right	25,95	23,40	26,55	24,67

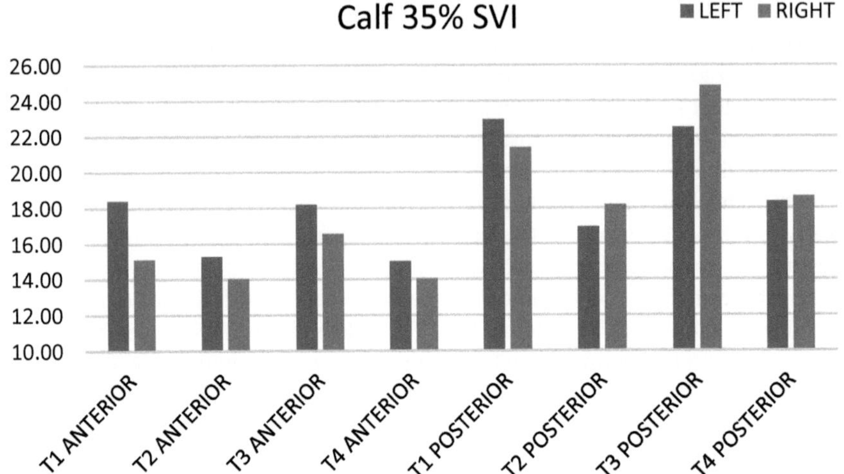

Fig. 10. Calf SVI in all tests (T1- T4) in the anterior and posterior part of the limb w.r.t A-pose girth area (%).

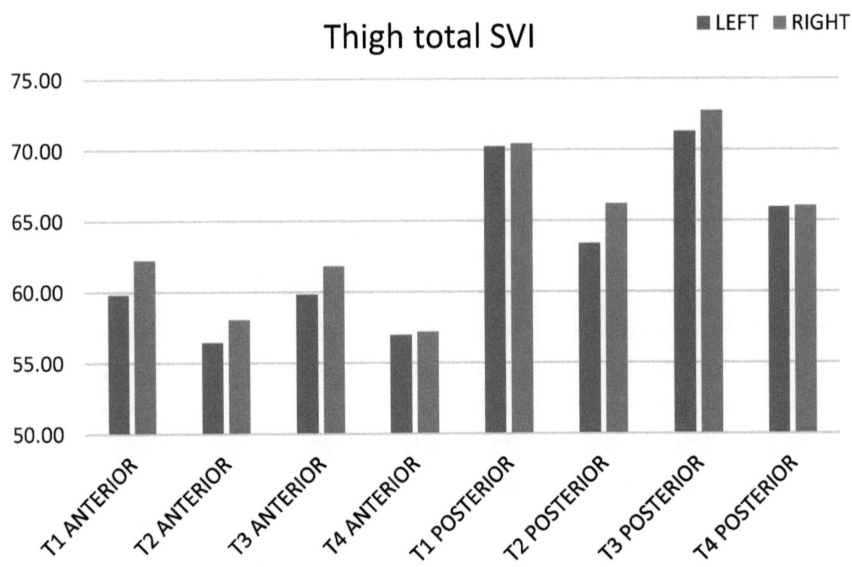

Fig. 11. Thigh (overall measurement) SVI in all tests (T1- T4) in the anterior and posterior part of the limb w.r.t A-pose girth area (%).

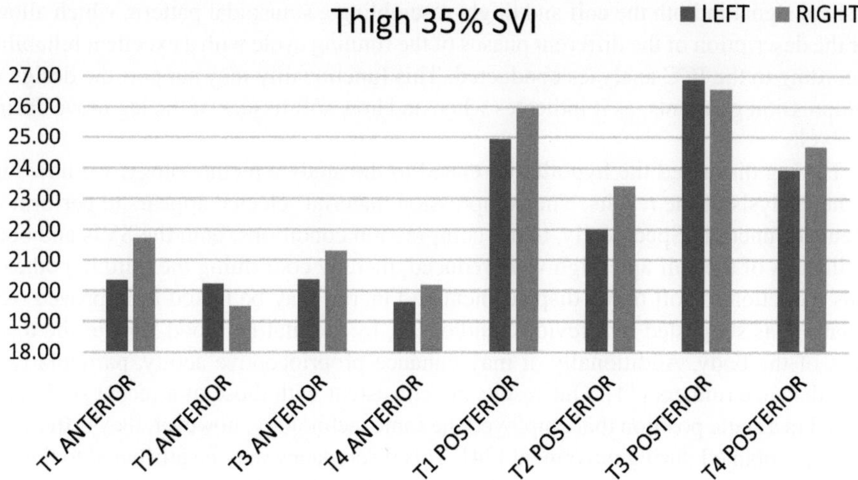

Fig. 12. Thigh (35%) SVI in all tests (T1- T4) in the anterior and posterior part of the limb w.r.t. A-pose girth area (%).

4 Discussion

Before discussing the study's hypotheses, it is important to highlight the differences observed when dividing the leg into two functional regions. The posterior part of the leg, which is associated with hip and knee extension as well as ankle plantarflexion, exhibits greater movement than the anterior chain, where more bony structures such as the tibia and the knee extensor musculature are located. This functional difference between regions of the leg may play a significant role in the design of compression garments, as it suggests differing biomechanical needs. This methodology and technology could be used to improve the design of compression garments, permitting the customization of garments, as proposed at a previous study [21].

An unexpected finding was the difference observed in the girths' length between fatigue and non-fatigue conditions. In both, the compression and non-compression tests, lower limb circumferences were smaller under fatigue, which may be attributed to reduced venous pressure and increased tissue pressure during muscle contraction [22], as well as factors such as dehydration, muscle fatigue, and/or decreased muscle tone.

In the present study, we proposed four working hypotheses: the first two related to the methodology and analysis technology, and the other two concerning the results obtained. Based on the data collected, we can confirm the first hypothesis. Differences were observed throughout the leg between compression and non-compression conditions, in both fatigued and non-fatigued states, and in both static position and running, using the MOVE4D technology. This aligns with recent research demonstrating the potential of 4D scanning systems like MOVE4D to detect volumetric and kinematic changes in human movement, offering a non-invasive and highly detailed method for biomechanical analysis [23].

The second hypothesis referred to the ability of the MOVE4D system to identify the phases of the running cycle. We have confirmed that the measurement system provides a cyclical signal in both the calf and thigh, resembling a sinusoidal pattern, which allows for the description of the different phases of the running cycle with a excellent reliability according to the ICC analyses conducted. This functionality may support the design of compression garments, as it indicates when and how soft tissues of the leg move during the cycle.

Having discussed the hypothesis related to the study's methodology, we now turn to the analysis of the results. The compression material selected appears to perform its intended function. Specifically, under compression conditions, both the SVIs and body perimeters of the calf and thigh were reduced, thereby confirming the third hypothesis. This reduction in soft tissue displacement and inertia may be linked to improved oxygenation, as suggested by previous studies [8], by facilitating blood flow to the distal parts of the body. Additionally, it may enhance proprioceptive acuity, particularly in long-distance runners [11]. Our results are consistent with those of a recent study conducted in a static position that employed the same technology; however, they differ from findings obtained during movement [24]. This discrepancy may be attributed to the fact that our study involved running, which is a more dynamic activity compared to walking.

Results also confirm the fourth hypothesis referred to the effect of fatigue during running. Fatigue was found to cause greater soft tissues displacement than the non-fatigued state, particularly in the non-dominant leg. It is possible that the dominant leg, which is stronger [25], is better prepared to limit the effects of fatigue. However, the non-dominant leg, being less strong and less skilled, may experience increased soft tissue movement under fatigue, resulting in greater inertia and reduced running economy [4]. These results highlight the importance of strength training in runners, as this strategy may help to improve athletes' response to fatigue. The increase in soft tissue movement may also be related to muscle fatigue during running, as analysed through EMG in various studies [2, 3].

The design of this study entails a methodological limitation: as it is an exploratory study, we are not in a position to generalize the results to a larger population. It is considered necessary to continue collecting data from more runners, taking into account their running technique. The runner analysed used a rearfoot strike (RFS) pattern. It would be interesting to understand how foot strike technique may influence the movement of soft tissues with and without fatigue, under compression and non-compression conditions, since RFS generates greater impacts during running and increased knee loads [16]. Therefore, the initial hypothesis would be that the RFS running technique generates more soft tissue movement than a non-rearfoot strike pattern.

5 Conclusions

In summary, the final conclusions of the study are: (1) the MOVE4D system is capable of differentiating in a non-invasive way between compression and non-compression states of the lower limb, (2) the MOVE4D system describes the cyclic pattern of running technique with an excellent reliability, (3) compression garments cause the soft tissues of the leg to move less, and (4) fatigue increases the soft tissues displacement in the leg. The MOVE4D system emerges as a valuable tool for the design of compression materials in both the sports and physical activity industry, and the healthcare sector.

Disclosure of Interests. The authors have no competing interests to declare that are relevant to the content of this article.

References

1. Chadefaux, D., Gueguen, N., Thouze, A., Rao, G.: 3D propagation of the shock-induced vibrations through the whole lower-limb during running. J Biomech. (2019) **96**, 109343. https://doi.org/10.1016/j.jbiom ech.2019109343
2. Play, M., et al.: Soft-tissue vibrations and fatigue during prolonged running: does an individualized midsole hardness play a role? Scandinavian Journal of Medicine & Science in Sports (2024). https://doi.org/10.1111/sms.14672
3. Ehrström, S., Gruet, M., Giandolini, M., Chapuis, S., Morin, J.-B., Vercruyssen, F.: Acute and delayed neuromuscular alterations induced by downhill running in trained trail runners: beneficial effects of high-pressure compression garments. Frontiers in Physiology (2018). https://doi.org/10.3389/FPHYS.2018.01627
4. Dewolf, A.H., Ivaniski-Mello, A., Peyré-Tartaruga, L.A., Mesquita, R.M.: Relation between soft tissue energy dissipation and leg stiffness in running at different step frequencies. Royal Society Open Science (2024). https://doi.org/10.1098/rsos.231736.
5. Chadefaux, D., Berton, E., Rao, G.: How runners deal with the shock induced vibrations propagating through their body. Journal of the Acoustical Society of America (2017). https://doi.org/10.1121/1.4989079
6. Boyer, K.A., Nigg, B.M.: Muscle Tuning During Running: Implications of an Un-tuned Landing The impact force in heel-toe running is an input signal into the body that (2006)
7. Leabeater, A.J., James, L.P., Driller, M.W.: Tight margins: compression garment use during exercise and recovery—a systematic review. Textiles (2022). https://doi
8. Engel, F.A., Stockinger, C., Woll, A., Sperlich, B.: Effects of Compression Garments on Performance and Recovery in Endurance Athletes (2016). https://doi.org/10.1007/978-3-319-39480-0_2
9. Hong, W.-H., Lo, S.-F., Wu, H.C., Chiu, M.-C.: Effects of compression garment on muscular efficacy, proprioception, and recovery after exercise-induced muscle fatigue onset for people who exercise regularly. PLOS ONE (2022). https://doi.org/10.1371/journal.pone.0264569s
10. Craig-Jones, A., Greene, D.R., Ruiz-Ramie, J.J., Navalta, J.W., Mercer, J.A.: The effect of compression garments on biomechanical and physiological factors. Biomechanics (2024). https://doi.org/10.3390/biomechanics4010007
11. Chang, L., Fu, S., Li, J., Wu, S.S.X., Adams, R., Han, J., Han, C.: Effects of compression running pants and treadmill running stages on knee proprioception and fatigue-related physiological responses in half-marathon runners. Frontiers in Physiology (2022). https://doi.org/10.3389/fphys.2022.1035424
12. Doan, B.K., et al.: Evaluation of a lower-body compression garment. Journal of Sports Sciences (2003). https://doi.org/10.1080/0264041031000101971
13. Play, M.C., Trama, R., Millet, G.Y., Hautier, C., Giandolini, M., Rossi, J.: Soft tissue vibrations in running: a narrative review. Sports Med Open. **8**(1), 131 (2022). https://doi.org/10.1186/s40798-022-00524-w. PMID: 36273049; PMCID: PMC9588116
14. Behling, A.-V., Giandolini, M., Tscharner, V. von, Nigg, B.M., Nigg, B.M.: Soft-tissue vibration and damping response to footwear changes across a wide range of anthropo-metrics in running. PLOS ONE (2021). https://doi.org/10.1371/JOURNAL.PONE.0256296
15. Ahn, A.N., Brayton, C., Bhatia, T., Martin, P.: Muscle activity and kinematics of forefoot and rearfoot strike runners. J Sport Health Sci. **3**(2), 102–12 (2014). https://doi.org/10.1016/j.jshs.2014.03.007

16. Kulmala, J.P., Avela, J., Pasanen, K., Parkkari, J.: Forefoot strikers exhibit lower running-induced knee loading than rearfoot strikers. Med Sci Sports Exerc. **45**(12), 2306–13 (2013). https://doi.org/10.1249/MSS.0b013e31829efcf7
17. Move4D. https://move4d.net. Accessed 15 June 2025
18. Parrilla, E., Ballester, A., Uriel, J., Ruescas-Nicolau, A. V., Alemany, S.: Capture and automatic production of digital humans in real motion with temporal 3D scanner. In: Eurographics Conference (2024). https://doi.org/10.2312/cl.20241048
19. Schroeder, W., Martin, K., Lorensen, B.: The Visualization Toolkit (4th ed.), Kitware, ISBN 978–1–930934–19–1 (2006)
20. Koo, T.K., Li, M.Y.: A guideline of selecting and reporting intraclass correlation coefficients for reliability research. J. Chiropr. Med. **15**, 155–163 (2016). https://doi.org/10.1016/j.jcm.2016.02.012
21. Kyzymchuk, O., et al.: Compression covers for limbs – towards automatic analysis of the profile geometry of limbs. In: Tokarska, M., Barburski, M. (eds.), Textile Futures: Engineering Advanced Materials for a Changing World (Proc. InnovaTex Conference, Łódź, Poland, January 2025), Monograph No. 2583, pp. 61–87 (2025). Łódź University of Technology Press
22. Stick, C., Heinemann, W., Witzleb, E.: Slow volume changes in calf and thigh during cycle ergometer exercise. Eur. J. Appl. Physiol. **61**, 428–432 (1990). https://doi.org/10.1007/BF00236063
23. Kuncová, M., Štěpánková, H.: The effect of compression stocking on legs' geometry changes within different movement. Applied Research in Textiles, 2, Article 007 (2024). https://doi.org/10.15240/tul/008/2024-2-007
24. Kyzymchuk, O., Riabchykov, M., Kyosev, Y., Melnyk, L., Boll, J.: The effect of compression stocking on legs' geometry changes within different movement. Fibres and Textiles **31**(2), 50–55 (2024). https://doi.org/10.15240/tul/008/2024-2-007
25. Kalata, M., et al.: Bilateral strength asymmetry in elite youth soccer players: differences between age categories. Symmetry **13**(11), 1982 (2021). https://doi.org/10.3390/sym13111982

Research of Sustainable Development and Fashion Application on Plants Dyeing Technique

Xinxian Han[1], Yueding Zhou[2], Xuenan Cai[2], and Wei Zhou[2](✉)

[1] Henan Institute of Science and Technology, Xinxiang, He'nan, People's Republic of China
[2] Zhejiang Sci-Tech University, Hangzhou, Zhejiang, People's Republic of China
{vinazhou6,zhousarah}@zstu.edu.cn, lghzzdy@163.com

Abstract. Plants Dyeing, employing plant-based materials, boasts a long and rich history within Chinese folk traditions, representing a shared intangible cultural heritage across numerous ethnic groups. Beyond its role as a traditional textile dyeing technique, it stands as a precious embodiment of Chinese folk art. This paper, adopting a sustainable fashion perspective, traces the history and evolution of traditional plant dyeing, analyzes its current application landscape encompassing its inherent advantages, technical status, and utilization in contemporary textiles. Furthermore, it identifies the challenges and issues confronting plant dyeing, such as limited economic viability, technical shortcomings, and constrained market demand. Looking ahead, this paper posits that plant dyeing will encounter new opportunities in future trends, technological innovations, and market expansion through the integration of genetic engineering, nanotechnology, and intelligent production methodologies. Through these means production efficiency and product quality can be enhanced. Simultaneously, by incorporating emotional design approaches, Plants Dyeing is poised to assume a significant role within the sustainable fashion, serving as a bridge connecting traditional culture with contemporary design. Ultimately, it is hoped to offer a unique green lifestyle to global consumers, promoting ecological civilization construction and sustainable development of the economy and society.

Keywords: Plants Dyeing · Traditional Dyeing Technique · Plant-based Dyes · Design Applications · Sustainable Development

1 Introduction

China stands as one of the pioneering nations globally to utilize organic plants as dyes for textile printing and dyeing. After thousands of years of practical exploration and technological refinement, it has gradually formed the unique and ingenious "plant dyeing" technique, which blends the unique charm of "timing, local conditions, superb materials, and skilled craftsmanship" [1], showcasing the profound cultural heritage and superb craftsmanship of China. However, with economic development, a large number of chemical dyes have been applied in the industrial and fashion industries, leading to a global ecological crisis while pursuing economic benefits [2]. In the 21st century, with the awakening of green revolution consciousness, sustainable fashion has received much attention. Against this background, Plants Dyeing, as an ancient dyeing technology, has become an important research direction for environmentally friendly dyeing of textiles again due to its unique environmental and health characteristics. This article starts from the perspective of sustainable fashion, analyzes the current application status and existing problems of the traditional Plants Dyeing technique, and looks forward to its future development trends, in order to provide useful reference for research and practice in the field of environmentally friendly dyeing of textiles.

2 History and Development of Plants Dyeing Technique

2.1 China

The Plants Dyeing technique has a long history in China, almost spanning the entire history of the Chinese civilization. In the era of Yellow Emperor, people began to use plant juices for dyeing and clothing making [3]. According to "Da Dai Li Ji·Xia Xiao Zheng(大戴礼记·夏小正)", the ancestors of Xia Dynasty had already used blue plants for dyeing and mastered the cultivation method of blue plants [4]. During the Shang and Zhou Dynasties, the dyeing technique in China had developed rapidly, people mastered various methods of dyeing with natural dyes, the Plants Dyeing technique has became mature, and dyeing industry also had became an important sector in social production. According to 'Zhou Li · Di Guan(周礼·地官),' there is a designated role titled 'Zhang Ran Cao(掌染草)', responsible for overseeing the vegetation utilized in the dyeing process. This specialized official, known as 'Ran Ren(染人)', is tasked with the management of textile dyeing. In the Spring and Autumn Period and the Warring States Period, people were proficient in the technique of making indigo, and also invented the method of dyeing with fermented yeast waste [5]. By the Qin and Han Dynasties, the plant dyeing industry had greatly developed, with madder plants being extensively cultivated and developed. In the "Shiji·Huozhi Liezhuan(史记·货殖列传), it is recorded that A thousand acres of madder(Qian Cao, 茜草) plants are equivalent to the status of a marquis with a thousand households." This indicates that madder had already begun to be cultivated on a large scale and had developed significantly. In the Eastern Han Dynasty's "Shuo Wen Jie Zi(说文解字)", there are records of 39 color names, reflecting the richness of the plant dyeing technique at that time. The renowned scholar Jiasi Xie(贾思勰) documented the method of making indigo from blue plants for the first time in his "Qi Min Yao Shu(齐民要术)". By the period of the Southern and Northern Dynasties, the preparation of plants dyes had become quite complete and could be stored and used throughout the year [6]. In the Tang Dynasty, the Plants Dyeing technique had reached a high level. The "Tang Liudian(唐六典)" explicitly mentioned the concept of Plants Dyeing [7]: "Generally, dyeing is mainly made from plants, using flowers and leaves, stems and fruits, or roots and bark, collected from various regions, and picked at specific times and months." This indicates that Plants Dyeing had become the main method and technique of dyeing in the Tang Dynasty, far more widely used than other natural dyes, with a diversified range of mordants and a richer spectrum of colors. According to the chromatic analysis of Tang textiles unearthed in Turpan, there were as many as 24 colors, showing the superb dyeing skills [8]. After the Song Dynasty, the Plants Dyeing technique continued to develop, and with the opening of the Maritime Silk Road, its sales range further expanded. By the Ming and Qing Dynasties, the Plants Dyeing technique in China reached its peak. With technological advancements, the types and proportions of dyes became more precise, and the dyeing process was meticulously divided into pre-dyeing, simultaneous dyeing, and post-dyeing processes [9]. The variety of plants that can be used for dyeing had greatly increased, with dyes not only being mass-produced to ensure self-sufficiency but also being exported overseas on a large scale. This not only promoted the further development of Plants Dyeing technique but also boosted the prosperity of the textile industry and commercial economy at that time. In India, Plants Dyeing was not only used for dyeing textiles but also widely applied in food, cosmetics, and medicines. Historically, India had over 450 species of dye plants, many of which also had medicinal value [10]. In Europe and America, Plants Dyeing technique held an important position in the Middle Ages and the Andean civilization, but gradually got replaced by synthetic dyes after the Industrial Revolution [11].

2.2   Japan, Indonesia, South Korea, North Korea and Europe

Since the Han Dynasty, Chinese textiles have gradually been introduced to Japan through the Maritime Silk Road. By the Tang Dynasty, the government actively promoted international exchanges, attracting a large number of Japanese envoys and scholar-monks to visit China. During the Wei, Jin, Northern and Southern dynasties, the techniques recorded by Jia Sixie for extracting indigo from woad, using safflower to dye fabrics, as well as techniques such as intaglio printing and resist dyeing, all were introduced to Japan. In the Ming and Qing dynasties, a large number of plant-based dyes were exported to Japan. Japanese textiles dyed with plants were deeply influenced by China but also had their own innovations. Batik(蜡染), originally introduced from China gradually disappeared, while tie-dyeing(绞缬) and resist-dyeing(夹缬) became increasingly popular. The plants dyeing techniques in Japan gradually developed into three main categories: pattern dyeing(型染), yuzen dyeing(友禅染), and tie-dyeing [13].

In addition, in places like Java, Indonesia, the local dyeing technique twists the fabric to create nodes, and then dyes it to produce various beautiful patterns [14]. The dyeing techniques of the South Korean and the North Korea can be traced back to the Western Zhou Dynasty to the Warring States period in China, were both introduced from China. Both have attached great importance to the advancement of dyeing techniques, such as the JinJiao Dyeing Method(锦绞染色法). In Europe, plants dyeing technique has been recorded since the early period of Christianity, with Rome mastering the technique of dyeing wool with plant dyes as early as the 7th century BC. However, it was not until the 9th century AD that the dyeing techniques of Germany began to spread, as for London, England, its dyeing techniques did not gradually become popular until the 11th century. Today, the study of plants dyeing has penetrated various fields of textile industry, demonstrating broad industrial development prospects.

3 Current Development Status of Plants Dyeing Technique

3.1 Analysis of Current Situation of Plants Dyeing Process

The ethnic minorities in the Dali area of Yunnan still maintain a relatively complete traditional Plants Dyeing technique [15], and have abundant plant dye resources, with 23 types of plant dyes used by the local Bai ethnic group [16]. Building on the inheritance of traditional dyeing techniques using plants, the current Plants Dyeing techniques continue to develop and innovate. Currently, researchers are tirelessly exploring new types of plant materials to broaden the range of dyes and meet the growing environmental and personalized needs. In addition to the long-used traditional dyes such as madder, indigo, and safflower, many emerging natural dyes such as tea, coffee, onion skins, mulberries, wormwood, black beans, pagoda tree husks, pomegranate peels, bayberries have also been discovered and successfully applied in the dyeing field, injecting new vitality into traditional dyeing techniques. These new types of dyes are not only bright in color and eco-friendly, but also possess special properties such as antibacterial and UV resistance. For example, plant dyes containing elements such as anthraquinones, flavonoids, α-phthalocyanines, dihydrofurans, and tannins such as rhubarb, lithospermum, pagoda tree husks, baicalin, pomegranate peels, tea polyphenols have good UV absorption capabilities, with molecular structures typically containing conjugated systems or aromatic rings, which can absorb UV light and form stable excited states, providing good protection for the human body.

In terms of technological innovation, the current Plants Dyeing techniques not only inherit ancient wisdom, but also cleverly integrate modern technologies such as nanotechnology and biotechnology, significantly improving the dyeing effect, making the colors more bright and long-lasting. For example, the Japanese company Kanebo has improved the dispersibility and penetration of dyes, making the colors more even and vibrant, while also enhancing the color fastness by using nanotechnology. The Max Planck Institute for Molecular Plant Physiology in Germany has successfully bred a plant species rich in specific pigments using genetic engineering technology. This plant has vibrant colors that are not easily affected by environmental factors, providing higher quality raw materials for Plants Dyeing [17]. In recent years, many research institutions in China have also actively engaged in the research field of plant dyes. The China Textile Academy, with the advantage of modern biotechnology, has significantly optimized the extraction process of plant dyes. By precisely controlling key extraction conditions such as temperature, pH, and extraction time, the efficiency and purity of pigment extraction in dyes have been effectively improved. At the same time, with the help of biotechnology, the color stability, light fastness and wash fastness of plant dyes have been further enhanced, making Plants Dyeing more competitive in modern textile industry and expected to promote their application in the high-end textile market. In addition, research institutions such as Dalian Institute of Chemical Physics of the Chinese Academy of Sciences, Beijing Institute of Fashion Technology, the Ecological Textile Laboratory of Jiangnan University, and Suzhou University all have professional researchers dedicated to this field [17]. They continue to explore and innovate, aiming to make significant breakthroughs and advancements in the research and application of plant dyes.

3.2 Technique and Advantages of Plants Dyeing

The process of traditional Plants Dyeing techniques can be roughly divided into five key steps. First, collect plants. It is necessary to select the appropriate parts of the plants and collect them at the best time to ensure the richness and stability of the pigments. Then, the pigments in the plants are effectively extracted into water through soaking and boiling. Heating and boiling help to break down the plant cell walls and release the pigments. Next, filter and extract the boiled plant solution, add an appropriate amount of water and alkali to optimize the extraction efficiency of the pigments. After that, immerse the fabric into the solution containing plant pigments and complete the dyeing process through steps such as soaking, dehydration, and drying. Finally, wash the dyed fabric to remove excess pigments and impurities, ensuring the purity and durability of the dyeing effect. In terms of dyeing techniques, Plants Dyeing covers various methods such as mordant dyeing, resist dyeing, and oxidation-reduction dyeing. Mordant dyeing combines pigments with the fabric tightly using a medium, resist dyeing produces new color effects by overlaying different colors, and oxidation-reduction dyeing changes the fabric color through chemical reactions. The use of these methods not only enriches the color expression of Plants Dyeing but also improves the efficiency and stability of dyeing.

Traditional Plants Dyeing is a gift from nature to humans, and the use of plant dyes is the core advantage of Plants Dyeing. The dyes used in dyeing come from plants, are non-toxic and harmless, and do not cause pollution to the environment. In addition, the dyes and mordants used in Plants Dyeing are both biodegradable and do not leave behind difficult-to-treat waste. Furthermore, the raw materials for Plants Dyeing are widely available, can be sourced locally, and reduce resource consumption and transportation costs. At the same time, Plants Dyeing produces less wastewater and waste gas, resulting in less environmental pollution. In comparison, the production and use of chemical synthetic dyes not only generate a large amount of toxic by-products, but also consume a lot of energy and water resources, exacerbating environmental pollution. Additionally, some herbal plants used for dyeing have medicinal effects. The medicinal properties of plants dyes are absorbed by the fabric along with the dyeing process, providing special health benefits to the body. For example, the leaves of the woad plant used for dyeing blue can be used as indigo leaves, which have a strong bactericidal effect against various dysentery bacilli and meningococci, with significant therapeutic effects and no bacterial drug resistance. Dyeing with mugwort has the effects of sterilization, detoxification, and hemostasis. And the purple gromwell has pharmacological effects such as antibacterial and anti-inflammatory, antiviral, and anti-tumor properties, treating dermatitis, eczema, psoriasis, and other conditions [12].

3.3 Application of Plants Dyeing Technique in Fashion Design

The color of Plants Dyeing contains a unique natural charm with its fresh and simple visual impression. It emotionally conveys an elegant and gentle atmosphere. It not only demonstrates the profound cultural heritage of Chinese civilization, but also cleverly achieves the harmonious unity of the ethereal and the solid, the empty and the rich. This transcendent aesthetic characteristic of the East has become an important source of inspiration for designers. Currently, the application range of Plants Dyeing is gradually expanding in the field of fashion design. Many well-known brands and designers are cleverly integrating Plants Dyeing technique with fashion design.

Li Wei(李薇) used the traditional Plants Dyeing technique to present more than 30 sets of garments with the theme of "Jade in Paris" at the 2024 Paris Fashion Week. Drawing inspiration from the magnificent mountains and rivers of the Sanjiangyuan(三江源) region and the unique ethnic culture. She perfectly integrates tradition with modernity, nature with humanities, and expresses the traditional cultural connotation of Chinese Plants Dyeing in a modern and innovative design language. The show received high praise from international audiences, not only exploring cultural heritage and beauty but also the blending and exchanging of the Chinese and Western cultures, allowing Chinese culture and design to confidently voice out to the world. Part of Li Wei's 2024 design works is shown in Fig. 1. Chu Yan(楚艳) has always insisted on combining traditional Chinese culture and aesthetic interests with fashion design. She founded the brand named Chu He Ting Xiang(楚和听香) using the Plants Dyeing technique. The brand is a pioneer in the fashion design field, creatively incorporating various traditional dyeing techniques such as natural Plants Dyeing, Song Jin(宋锦), Zhang Duan(漳缎), Xia Bu(夏布), and Tang Jin(唐锦) into contemporary fashion design. Give the traditional elements new life by integrating the eco-friendly concept of Plants Dyeing with design. Part of Chu Yan's design works is shown in Fig. 2. Domestic brand ICICLE Zhi He(ICICLE之禾) collaborated with pioneering Japanese fabric brand Food Textile in 2023, launched the S/S series named "Natural Way" capsule collection, transforming surplus plant-based ingredients from our daily lives such as coffee grounds after brewing coffee, unused food from farms and food factories, into natural dyes for cotton, silk, linen, and wool fabrics. These lightweight and soft fabrics fully absorb the essence of food, presenting clothing in subtle and delicate colors, exuding the beauty of nature. Part of Zhi He's 2023 Capsule Collection is shown in Fig. 3. The womenswear brand Tianyi(天意) extensively uses ramie fabric in its design. The fabric is made by impregnating the tubers of ramie plants multiple times with the juice, drying them, and then dyeing them with river mud after washing, resulting in a black front and a coffee-colored back. Liang Zi(梁子), the brand's design director, as a protector and excavator of traditional ramie fabric, continuously integrates Eastern culture and fashion elements, bringing out an unprecedented charm in ramie fashion. Part of Chinese womenswear brand Tianyi works is shown in Fig. 4.

The S/S 2023 collection "Silent Dance(沉默中舞蹈)" by Chinese original brand Mutedance is centered around plants dyeing, blending Eastern aesthetics with European retro styles, showcasing a unique romantic and gentle vibe. By using plants dyeing techniques, each garment presents a unique color tone, creating a hazy beauty akin to "watching flowers in mist". The collection continues the unique beauty of traditional Chinese clothing, interpreting a graceful "New Chinese Style". The iconic plants dyeing technique gives the fabrics a natural texture, presenting an abstract beauty reminiscent of flowers and plants, conveying a poetic sense of tranquility and brokenness, significantly enhancing the brand's wearability and recognition (Figs. 5 and 6).

UMA WANG was founded by Uma Wang in London(UK) in 2003. The brand uses special techniques to extract pigments from plants, which differ from the bright colors

Fig. 1. Li Wei's 2024 design works.

Fig. 2. Chu Yan's design works.

Fig. 3. Zhi He's 2023 Capsule Collection

Fig. 4. Chinese womenswear brand Tianyi.

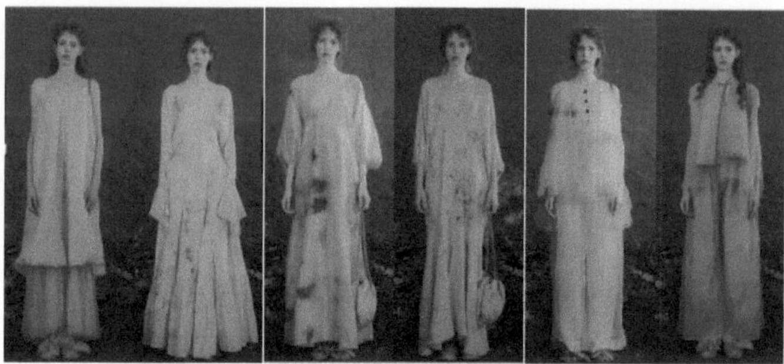

Fig. 5. Mutedance's S/S 2023 collection.

brought by chemical dyes, but give the garments a natural, gentle, and unique tone. This pursuit of natural colors, in harmony with the brand's minimalist style, adds depth and artistry to the clothing visually, while conveying respect for nature and Chinese culture. In general, UMA WANG successfully integrates Eastern aesthetics, traditional craftsmanship, and modern design through the use of plants dyeing techniques, creating a

Fig. 6. UMA WANG's S/S 2022 collection.

unique brand identity. Its designs not only showcase a profound cultural and natural heritage, but also reflect forward-thinking considerations for sustainable fashion, injecting new vitality and meaning into contemporary fashion (Figs. 7, 8, 9 and 10).

Fig. 7. Sou Sou's official website products.

Fig. 8. Kapok Knot's official website products.

The Japanese brand Sou Sou is a brand that combines traditional Japanese craftsmanship with modern lifestyle, known for its unique pattern designs and color combinations. The use of plants dyeing is a feature of the brand, with some products using natural plant dyes such as indigo and madder to create distinctive Japanese cultural characteristics. The brand's design retains the artistic nature of traditional dyeing while also paying great attention to the functionality of the clothing. Kapok Knot, as another Japanese

Fig. 9. Yohji Yamamoto's S/S 2018 Menswear.

Fig. 10. Make's Wuyong Land Series.

brand deeply rooted in the concept of sustainable development, is committed to using natural dyes and organic materials to create clothing. It cleverly integrates traditional Japanese plants dyeing techniques such as Aizome and Kakishibu with modern design concepts, nurturing unique textures and colors. Kapok Knot's design features mainly natural colors, highlighting not only the importance of environmental protection, but also showcasing the unique value of craftsmanship. In addition, in Yohji Yamamoto's S/S 2018 menswear, the use of plants dyeing techniques has also become one of the key highlights of the collection, showing the designer's profound understanding of nature and craftsmanship. This series, themed "Return to Nature", presents a unique aesthetic language through plant dyed fabrics. The loose silhouette and draping fabrics complement each other, while the natural texture of plants dyeing and Yohji Yamamoto's iconic deconstructive cutting form a clever contrast.

The brand Wuyong(无用) founded by Chinese designer Make(马可), known for its profound respect for traditional craftsmanship and innovative application, especially in the use of plants dyeing techniques, showcasing the brand's unique understanding of nature and culture. The brand uses a variety of natural plant dyes such as indigo, madder, su mu, walnut husk, etc., to imbue the fabric with soft natural tones and unique texture effects through handmade dyeing techniques. These colors not only present a serene and profound sense of beauty, but also convey a simple and poetic atmosphere through the gradient and mottled textures. In the "Wuyong Land Series(無用之土地系列)", the plants dyeing techniques are not only used in color, but also further enhance the brand's aesthetic language through the combination of fabric texture and cutting.

In the field of underwear and home clothing, Plants Dyeing textiles have become the first choice for children, individuals with sensitive skin, and green product enthusiasts due to their skin-friendly and safety characteristics. Brands such as "Hu Xi(乎兮)" and "Ai Mu Children(爱慕儿童)" under Beijing Aimer(北京爱慕) and "Le Town(乐町)" under Ningbo Peacebird Group(宁波太平鸟集团) have emerged in the market which are using natural dyes such as indigo, turmeric, and purple grass to design and develop a variety of close-fitting clothing and home clothing.

In addition, Plants Dyeing is also widely used in the peripheral products of fashion. There are a variety of products such as scarves, hats, backpacks, gloves, socks, etc., which meet consumers' demand for personalized and environmentally friendly products. For example, the Plants Dyeing series products launched by the famous American sock brand Stance not only have rich colors, but also focus on the design concept of antibacterial, deodorant, harmless and pollution-free. So the application of Plants Dyeing in fashion design has shown a trend of diversification and personalization, bringing new development opportunities to the fashion industry.

4   Challenges and Issues Faced by Plants Dyeing Technique

Technique with Plants Dyeing is facing multiple challenges and issues in the process of modernization transformation. Firstly, poor economic benefits become a key factor restricting its development. Due to the low efficiency of pigment extraction, long growth cycles, labor-intensive collection, complex processes, and the need for multiple repetitions of dyeing for the desired effect, the high production costs make it difficult to compete with chemical synthetic dyes. At the same time, many dye plants also have medicinal properties, if they are used for dyeing instead of medical production, which is actually a waste of their high added value potential. Especially in the context of the booming traditional Chinese medicine market, this mismatch of resources highlights the economic inefficiency of plant dyes. Secondly, imperfect technology is also a bottleneck in the development of Plants Dyeing techniques. Traditional dyeing techniques have significant deficiencies in dyeing reproducibility, color fastness, and the selection of mordants, making it difficult to meet the strict requirements of modern industry for production consistency and environmental standards. Additionally, limited market demand is also a major challenge that Plants Dyeing is facing now. Although consumers' demand for green and sustainable products is increasing, in the textile field, Plants Dyeing products are difficult to attract a large number of consumers due to high prices, limited color choices, and poor dyeing reproducibility. At the same time, the incomplete Plants Dyeing industry chain, lack of policy support, and other issues also limit the expansion of its market share.

5 Prospects for the Development of Plants Dyeing Technique

5.1 Future Trends

Nature provides habitat and resources for human beings, which are the foundation for human survival and development. Since the Industrial Revolution, the issues of excessive resource exploitation and environmental destruction have become increasingly prominent. The concept of sustainable development is gradually influencing the values and lifestyles of the public. In order to adapt to this change in social values, many fashion brands are incorporating sustainable concepts into fashion design, sparking a sustainable trend in the fashion industry. Against this background, Plants Dyeing, a green and environmentally friendly dyeing technique, will gradually become a hot issue in future research and application in the fashion industry.

At the same time, with the re-evaluation and respect for traditional culture on a global scale, Plants Dyeing, carrying the cultural value of thousand-year wisdom and natural philosophy, will gradually move from the periphery to the center, becoming a bridge connecting the past and the future. The current emerge of intangible cultural heritage has provided new opportunities for the protection and inheritance of traditional Plants Dyeing technique. The participation of multiple parties such as government, enterprises, designers, and consumers has promoted the revitalization and commercialization of Plants Dyeing techniques. By establishing intangible cultural heritage workshops, conducting skills training, and organizing cultural exhibitions, not only can effectively help to preserve the traditional knowledge and skills of Plants Dyeing, but it can also help to spark the interest and enthusiasm of the younger generation in this cultural heritage, forming a good inheritance ecosystem.

In conclusion, under the concept of sustainable design, the development prospects of the Plants Dyeing techniques are not only in the inheritance and innovation of the techniques themselves, but also in the promotion of cultural symbols and green lifestyle. It has immeasurable value in promoting ecological civilization, enhancing national cultural confidence, and promoting sustainable economic and social development.

5.2 Technological Innovation and R&D

The future development of Plants Dyeing relies heavily on continuous technological innovation and research. Modern biotechnology can be used to optimize the raw materials of plant dyes. For example, by using gene editing technology to cultivate new plant varieties with higher pigment content or easier extraction of pigments, not only can improve the production efficiency of dyes, but can also significantly reduce the dependency on natural plant resources, thereby mitigating environmental pressure caused by overharvesting. This initiative not only embodies the sustainable use of resources but also lays a solid foundation for the industrialization of Plants Dyeing. The optimization of mordanting techniques is equally important. Although traditional mordants have certain advantages in dyeing effects, some chemical components may have negative impacts on the environment and human health. By developing green chemistry technology and applying new materials, more environmentally friendly and efficient mordants can be developed. This innovation can significantly reduce pollution emissions during the dyeing process, enhance the adhesion and stability of dyes on fibers, and improve the consistency and durability of product quality. In terms of production techniques, the introduction of intelligent technology provides new possibilities for the standardization and large-scale production of Plants Dyeing. By precisely controlling key parameters such as dyeing temperature, time, and dye concentration with intelligent devices, not only can the repeatability of the process be enhanced, but also dye and energy waste can be reduced, achieving a more efficient and sustainable production process [18]. In addition, the application of modern equipment can not only significantly improve production efficiency but also preserve the unique natural textures and artistic expression of Plants Dyeing in large-scale production, meeting the market's demand for high-quality handicrafts. From raw material optimization, improvement of mordanting techniques to intelligent production process and functional development, each innovation provides important support for the future of Plants Dyeing, injecting new vitality into the continuation and development of traditional techniques in modern society.

5.3 Market Demand Expansion

The market demand challenge of Plants Dyeing lies in its high cost and niche positioning. Emotion-oriented design strategies can touch consumers' emotional resonance, and precise positioning and innovative expansion can be implemented in market strategies. Participatory design, actively advocates for consumers to deeply engage in design and production process of clothing, emphasizing the collaborative creation between designers and users. Inviting consumers to participate in collection, extraction, and dyeing process of Plants Dyeing not only allows consumers to intuitively experience the unique charm of Plants Dyeing, but also helps them deeply understand the environmental concept and cultural connotation behind it. Through the design concept of "created by me," expressing personal preferences and emotional needs, showcasing a unique self-image and taste. Under this model, Plants Dyeing products achieve a harmonious unity of intrinsic and extrinsic value, enhancing emotional identification and sense of belonging, and increasing added value. Recycled design, recycles textile waste before consumption. These waste materials, such as inventory fabrics, end-of-roll fabrics, sample fabrics, and defective fabrics, are of high quality and clean, making them ideal for reuse. By upgrading and remanufacturing Plants Dyeing, products are endowed with more emotional feedback, saving a considerable amount of labor and resource costs, and effectively extending the life cycle of raw materials. Customized design, this "one-on-one" customized service not only meets consumers' personalized pursuit of plans dyeing products but also embodies respect and love for nature and ecology. Positioning plans dyeing as high-end customized products, integrating their unique natural texture and cultural value into the high-end fashion, making it an ideal dyeing technique for high-end custom clothing and artistic home furnishings. This strategy not only meets the personalized needs of high-consumption groups but also enhances the market attractiveness of products through their scarcity and cultural connotation.

The sustainable development of Plants Dyeing will be based on technological innovation and will follow the path of market expansion. By developing fashion products that are more in line with modern aesthetics, deepening its environmental concept and cultural connotation can not only play an important role in the field of sustainable fashion, but can also become a model of combining traditional technique with modern design, providing global consumers with a unique green lifestyle.

6   Conclusion

The technique of Plants Dyeing, as a precious cultural heritage of China, not only reflects the concept of harmonious coexistence between humans and nature, but also demonstrates the innovative vitality of traditional technique in modern society. Faced with challenges, Plants Dyeing techniques need to improve production efficiency and product quality through technological innovation, enhance market competitiveness through market demand expansion, and achieve sustainable development through policy support and cultural inheritance. In the future, the Plants Dyeing techniques are expected to occupy an important position in the field of sustainable fashion, becoming a model of the combination of traditional technique and modern design. By deepening its environmental philosophy and cultural connotations, Plants Dyeing will provide global consumers with a unique green lifestyle, promote the construction of ecological civilization, enhance national cultural confidence, and promote sustainable economic and social development. In the context of globalization and informatization, the inheritance and innovation of Plants Dyeing will contribute significantly to the sustainable development of human society.

Disclosure of Interests. The authors have no competing interests to declare that are relevant to the content of this article.

References

1. Zhao, F.: 草木染的起源. Journal of Silk **03**, 54–57 (1984)
2. Zheng, J.X.: 浙江传统印染手工艺调研. Literature & Art Studies **1**, 112–119 (2002)
3. Wu, G.H.: Application and analysis of natural dyeing in costume design. Textile Auxiliaries **36**(06), 9–12 (2019)
4. Pan, C.Y., Jiang, W.: Inheriting and development of traditional chinese industry grass and wood printing and dyeing. Hundred Schools in Arts **08**, 55–57 (2011)
5. Liu, Y.C., Guan, Y.: Promoting the development of cultural undertakings and cultural and creative industries with aesthetic spirit of vegetation dyeing. China Dyeing & Finishing **49**(10), 96–98 (2023)
6. Wang, W.: 草木染的工艺技术与艺术审美特征探析. Journal of Silk **01**, 52–55 (2009)
7. Qiu, C.L.: 从《诗经》看周代的植物染工艺和服色审美. National Arts **05**, 152–156 (2023)
8. Wang, L.: 魏唐时期敦煌吐鲁番地区的绫织物. Journal of Dunhuang Studies **02**, 111–118 (2017)
9. Han J, Quye A.: A comprehensive study of textile dyeing techniques of the Ming and Qing Dynasties, China. In: Kirby, J. (ed.) Dyes in History and Archaeology 33/34. Archetype Publications, pp. 82–91 (2021). ISBN 9781909492806
10. Siva, R.: Status of natural dyes and dye-yielding plants in India. Curr. Sci. **92**, 916–925 (2007)
11. Mayolo, A.D.: Peruvian natural dye plants. Econ. Bot. **43**, 181–191 (1989)

12. Wang, H.: Health care & anti bacteria finish of traditional natural plant medicine and textile. Journal of Textile Research **25**(01), 109–111 (2004)
13. Wu Q. 浅谈草木染的起源、东传及在日本的发展. 明日风尚, (23), 328 (2016)
14. Fu, R.: Research on the Development of Grass Dyeing Art and its Application in Infant Clothing. Qingdao University (2021)
15. Huang, Z.W., Xue, Z.B., Wang, Y.X.: Current situation and prospects of sustainable fashion design. Journal of Silk **56**(10), 50–55 (2019)
16. Wang, W.J., Hui, R.M., Zu, Y.D., et al.: Development application and sustainable development of plant dyed garment products. Shanghai Textile Science & Technology **49**(06), 1–4 (2021)
17. Sivakumar, V., Vijaeeswarri, J., Anna, J.L.: Effective natural dye extraction from different plant materials using ultrasound. Ind. Crops Prod. **33**(1), 116–122 (2011)
18. Arsheen, M., Aleem Ahmed, M., Naheed, K., et al.: Study the effect of metal ion on wool fabric dyeing with tea as natural dye. J. Saudi Chem. Soc. **14**(1), 69–76 (2010)

Comparison of Different Embroidered Electrode Designs for Functional EMG Monitoring

Paolo Perego[1(✉)], Nicola Francesco Lopomo[1], Marco Loddo[1], Giulia Cappoli[1], Emanuele Gruppioni[2], and Giuseppe Andreoni[1,3]

[1] Design Department, Politecnico Di Milano, Milano, Italy
paolo.perego@polimi.it
[2] Centro Protesi INAIL, Vigorso Di Budrio (BO), Italy
[3] Bioengineering Laboratory, Scientific Institute IRCCS "E. Medea", Lecco, Bosisio Parini, Italy

Abstract. The integration of electrodes into textiles for monitoring physiological signals like surface electromyography (EMG) represents a critical area of development for wearable health technology. In this context, this paper reported a comprehensive evaluation of different embroidered textile electrode designs for surface EMG applications. Electrodes using silver-coated polyamide yarn on a neoprene substrate were specifically fabricated, exploring various embroidery pattern (i.e., Satin, Spiral, Moss stitch) and geometries. The electrodes underwent a multi-faceted evaluation, including impedance check and functional EMG signal acquisition during operating conditions, i.e., walking and step climbing. Preliminary key performance metrics, such as Root Mean Square (RMS) and Signal-to-Noise Ratio (SNR), were analyzed while maintaining the dry conditions. The results indicate that embroidered electrodes can reliably detect muscle activation, with performance levels dependent on the specific design. Notably, the SNR of several embroidered designs was found to be on par with conventional pre-gelled Ag/AgCl electrodes. This research underscores the viability of technical embroidery as a robust method for producing high-fidelity and durable textile electrodes for wearable monitoring physiological systems, paving the way for more comfortable and user-friendly healthcare and sports applications.

Keywords: Embroidered Electrodes · Textile Electrodes · Smart Garments · EMG · Smart Textile

1 Introduction

Electromyography (EMG) is a widely used technique for measuring muscle activity in clinical and research settings. In fact, signals acquired through EMG provide valuable information about the timing and intensity of muscular activation, thus supporting the diagnosis of neuromuscular disorders, underpinning the assessment of muscle function and providing biofeedback during personalized rehabilitation programs [1–3].

In the last decade, EMG systems have been significantly advancing compared to past years, achieving the ability to collect a larger number of channels and to use greater

© The Author(s), under exclusive license to Springer Nature Switzerland AG 2026
V. G. Duffy (Ed.): HCII 2025, LNCS 16339, pp. 107–118, 2026.
https://doi.org/10.1007/978-3-032-13012-9_8

bandwidth even in wireless mode, but in increasingly smaller sizes and without the need for bulky and uncomfortable cables during their use. On the contrary, the electrodes used to acquire EMG signals – above all when considering surface EMG - have undergone few advancements, particularly concerning geometry and interfaces [4].

Traditional surface EMG electrodes, typically made of silver/silver chloride (Ag/AgCl), generally require conductive gel to establish a stable electrical interface with the skin. However, these gel-based electrodes have several drawbacks, including skin irritation, discomfort, and signal degradation over time as the gel dries out [5]. In response to these limitations, there is a growing interest in developing dry electrodes that do not require conductive gel [6]. Among these, textile electrodes have emerged as a promising alternative due to their flexibility, conformability, and potential for seamless integration into clothing [7]. Furthermore, pros/cons of textile electrodes can be managed since various effective manufacturing techniques - such as weaving, knitting, and embroidery - can be used for their implementation [8].

In the last decade, several attempts have been made in the field of smart textiles to develop electrodes that can be seamlessly integrated into sensorized and intelligent garments [8]. In fact, the use of textile technologies in this context allows the continuous and seamless detection of physiological parameters without any constriction in time or space, proving useful information in several fields such as healthcare, fitness, and work [9]. Textile-based electrodes offer a unique advantage in wearable systems, conforming to the body's contours and maintaining consistent contact even during movement. Such systems need the sensor to be closely and firmly in contact with the body and without moving over the skin [10]. On the other hand, the attempts to obtain reliable textile-based electrodes need to face challenges in terms of signal quality, durability, and user comfort. Indeed, the integration of EMG electrodes into textiles requires careful consideration of factors such as electrode placement, skin contact pressure, and moisture management. Moreover, the design must balance the need for reliable signal acquisition with the comfort and aesthetic requirements of wearables [7]. Eventually, it is worth noting that integrating electrodes within clothing inherently required testing the overall washability of these solutions [11].

The main aim of the presented research was to introduce innovative textile electrode designs intended to enhance the comfort and functionality of EMG monitoring in smart garments. In particular, this study presents various designs for textile electrodes primarily based on the embroidery technique and considering the main aspects of signal quality within an effective testing framework [12].

2   Material and Methods

Within this section, we will first describe the embroidery process used for the fabrication of textile electrodes, including the choice of conductive materials and technical parameters specific for each defined design. Following manufacturing, a comprehensive characterization protocol established to assess electrode performance in term of signal quality is detailed; this includes also the analysis of electrical impedance to evaluate the reliability of the skin-electrode interface, alongside dynamic tasks to measure electrical stability under operating conditions. In this context, the testing protocol included plain walking and step climbing both focused on the vastus lateralis muscle; all the electrodes were benchmarked against standard Ag/AgCl disposables.

2.1 Electrode Fabrication

All the electrodes were produced using a silver-coated polyamide conductive thread (Madeira HC40, 117x2 dtex, resistance $< 300\ \Omega$/m). Without loss of generalizability, a neoprene fabric was chosen as substrate; in fact, this material reflected the main intended application focused on implementing functional liners for prostheses.

A technical embroidery machine (ZSK JGVA 0109) was specifically employed for fabrication. This system presented three different embroidery heads:

- *F-Head*: This 9-needle head is very similar to that of traditional embroidery machines; in general, it is used for conventional embroidery tasks with conductive threads, allowing the creation of flexible circuits, sensors, and other electronic components directly on the fabric.
- *W-Head*: This head is the most innovative one in the system; it allows for the precise laying and fixing of metal wires, optical fibers, and other technical materials onto a textile substrate, thus allowing the integration of heating systems, antennas, interconnections for electronic components, and preforms for composite materials.
- *K-Head*: This head can specifically create chain stitch and moss stitch embroidery; this technique is particularly useful for creating textile surfaces with large and voluminous areas, ideal to produce *soft-to-the-touch* areas.

In our study, the F-head was specifically used to fabricate the skin-contacting surface, while the W-head was chosen to embroider the conductive pathways, and the K-head specialized in moss stitching. This multi-head approach enabled the implementation of isolated circuits, thereby preventing direct contact of the primary conductive path with the skin.

To assess the impact of geometry and stitch type on performance and comfort, several electrode designs were developed. These designs, detailed in Table 1, were crafted using specialized software (EPC_win, Embroidery Studio, DE). The designs encompass variations in stitch type (Satin, Run, Moss), dimensions, and area.

Table 1. Characteristics of Fabricated Embroidered Electrodes.

Identifier	Stitch Type	Electrode Diameter(mm)	Total Area (mm^2)	Key Feature
S10	Satin	20	100	Filled design, 10 mm max stitch length
S20	Satin	20	100	Filled design, 20 mm max stitch length
Sp	Run	20	-	Single spiral line
FSp	Run	25	-	4-line spiral (flower shape)
M	Moss	20	100	Filled design with surface loops

2.2 Electrode Characterization

As previously emphasized, the primary objective of this experimental phase of the study was to comprehensively evaluate the performance of EMG signals acquired using embroidered textile electrodes during specific tasks that emulate operating conditions. It is noteworthy that the performances were directly compared against standard pre-gelled wet electrodes (H124SF, Kendall).

EMG Signal Acquisition Protocol. To minimize inter-subject variability and sharpen the focus on electrode performance, the study exclusively involved a single participant (a 37-year-old female, 174 cm tall, 64 kg weight). The subject was screened for pre-existing muscular pathologies, neurological disorders, or skin lesions in the electrode application areas; she provided explicit consent to participate in the experiment. Due to the defined operating tasks, the right rectus femoris was selected as the target muscle.

The placement on the skin was determined by identifying the midpoint of the target muscle using anatomical landmarks. Electrodes were positioned along the muscle longitudinal axis following the standard SENIAM guidelines and maintaining consistent inter-electrode distance.

The test sequence was repeated three times for each electrode type, utilizing between one and three distinct specimens per electrode geometry. All measurements were carried out under dry conditions. Environmental settings were controlled, with a constant temperature of 25 °C and relative humidity of 60%.

Walking. The participant was trained to walk on a straight line on a flat surface at self-pace. EMG signals were recorded during 3 different walking trials for each sample; within each trial, three consecutive gait cycles were obtained and only the central cycle was considered for the further analysis.

The measurement protocol included an initial reference acquisition using conventional pre-gelled Ag/AgCl electrodes, followed by the trials performed with the embroidered electrode samples under the very same conditions; the embroidered electrodes were maintained at the same place of the standard ones by marking the subject's skin with a dermographic pen. This approach enabled direct intra-subject comparisons between standard and textile-based electrodes.

For walking task, the acquisition was specifically conducted using a commercial system specifically designed for gait analysis (Smart DX, BTS Bioengineering, Italy), which integrated optoelectronic cameras, force platforms for synchronized motion capture and ground reaction force (GRF) measurement; furthermore, a wireless solution for EMG acquisition (FreeEMG, 1 kHz sampling rate) was present and inherently synchronized. In order to segment all the gait cycles, four reflective markers were placed on anatomical landmarks of the right lower limb, i.e., the lateral femoral condyle of the knee, the lateral malleolus, the head of the fifth metatarsus, and the calcaneus; marker tracks were captured using 10 infrared cameras, whereas GRF data were acquired via an embedded force platform positioned along the walkway to detect heel-strike and toe-off events. The EMG wireless probe was connected to the various electrodes using standard clip buttons. An elastic band was further used to secure all the electrodes and the corresponding probe; the tension of this band was maintained in all the trials (Fig. 1).

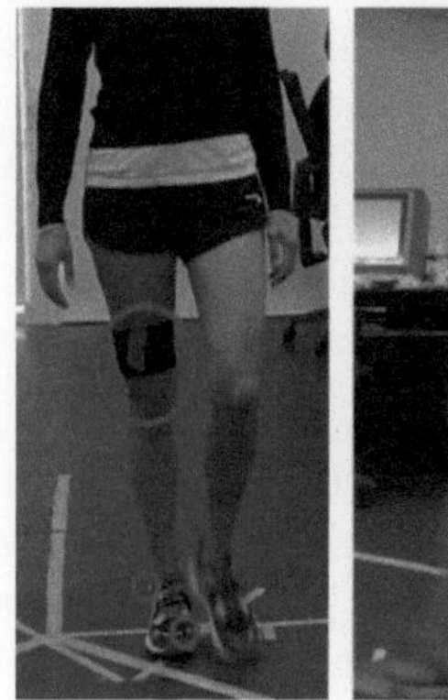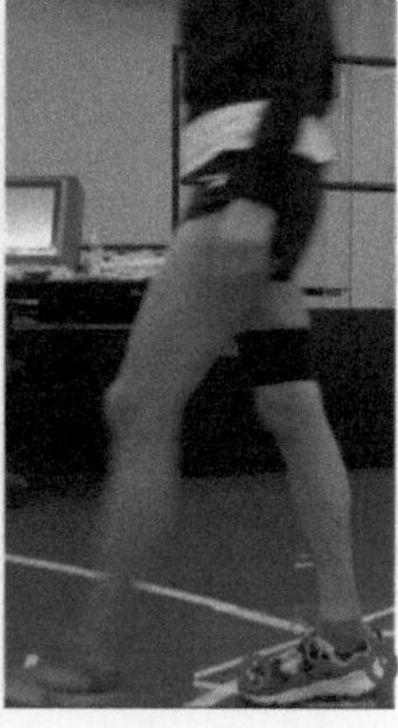

Fig. 1. Experimental setup showing the embroidered electrodes on the right rectus femoris secured by an elastic band, with reflective markers for motion capture. (a) Frontal view (b) Lateral view during walking.

Step Climbing. A second experimental test was conducted to evaluate the performance of the embroidered electrodes during step climbing, a task which specifically involves an important use of the thigh muscles.

The participant was instructed to perform a controlled step-up onto a 25 cm platform, starting from a neutral standing position and leading with the right leg. The movement was executed at self-pace and visually monitored by an expert to ensure repeatability. Each trial consisted of a single, complete ascent, and it was repeated three times per electrode type. As realized for the walking test, to optimize the skin–electrode interface, an elastic band was applied on electrodes with consistent manual tension to stabilize contact; furthermore, a two-minute waiting period was observed prior to each recording to allow for signal stabilization.

Surface EMG signals were acquired from the right rectus femoris muscle, adopting the same electrode positioning protocol used during walking tests (Fig. 2).

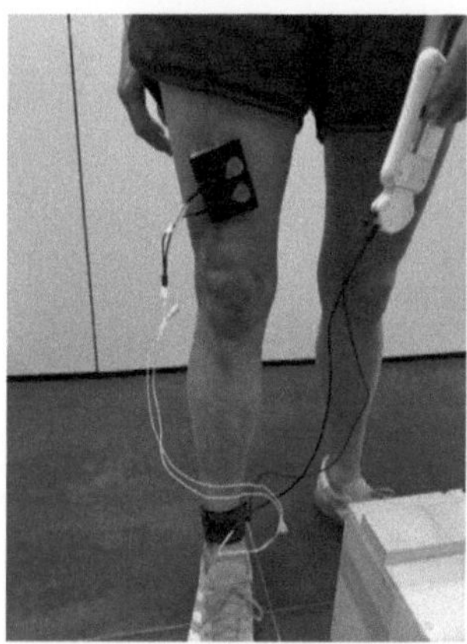

Fig. 2. Experimental setup showing the embroidered electrodes on the right rectus femoris and reference electrode on the right ankle.

The acquisition session began with a reference recording using standard pre-gelled Ag/AgCl electrodes, followed by trials employing the embroidered electrodes. EMG signals were sampled at 2000 Hz with 16-bit resolution (Sessantaquattro +, OTBioelettronica, Italy) and recorded via dedicated software (OT Biolab +, OTBioelettronica, Italy), which also handled synchronization and preliminary signal processing. The acquisition system was connected via cables to the various electrodes using standard clip buttons.

Signal Processing and Analysis. Data processing involved several key steps. First, the raw signal underwent high-pass filtering at 20 Hz to mitigate low-frequency noise and low-pass filtering at 500 Hz to prevent aliasing. Subsequently, the filtered signal was rectified, and its Root Mean Square (RMS) value was calculated. Signal quality was then quantified by determining the Signal-to-Noise Ratio (SNR), defined as the ratio between the active surface EMG signal and the baseline noise. For a comprehensive evaluation, both RMS and SNR values were averaged across the repetitions performed on each individual electrode specimen and then further averaged across the three electrode specimens overall.

Contact Impedance Estimation. Additionally, contact electrical impedance between the electrode and the skin was measured by using the Sessantaquattro + system (OTBioelettronica, Italy) and analyzed offline by a custom routine implemented in MATLAB (The Mathworks, USA).

More in detail, the system allowed us to measure the skin-electrode contact impedance, for each electrode connected, at a frequency equal to ¼ of the used sampling frequency (i.e., 2000/4 = 500 Hz) by pulling individually each electrode line to the positive and negative supply alternatively through a pull up and pull-down resistors, thus generating an AC signal, which amplitude was inversely proportional to the skin-electrode impedance. The value of the impedance was then obtained by considering that the power supply was 3.3 V and the pull up and pull-down resistors all had a value of 100 kΩ.

The system was interfaced with the various electrodes using a standard clip button connection, specifically designed with conductive thread and dedicated hardware.

3 Result and Discussion

3.1 Walking

Several representative examples of the EMG signals acquired during walking are presented in Fig. 3.

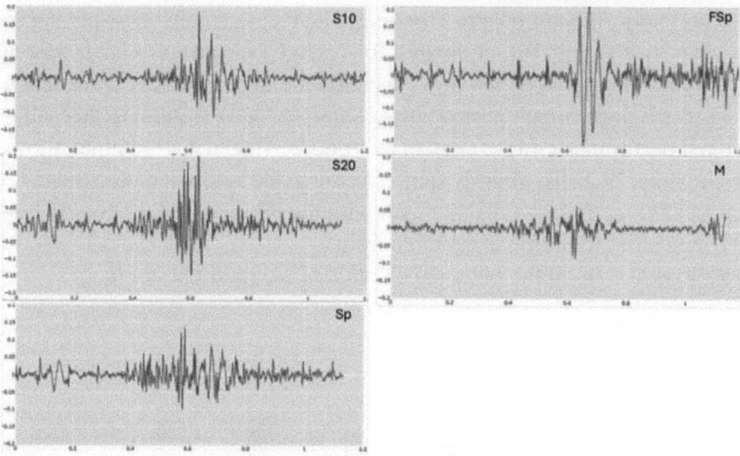

Fig. 3. Examples of acquired EMG signals (in mV) during walking; central gait cycle is reported for S10, S20, Sp, Fsp, and M designs of the embroidered electrodes.

The RMS values obtained from our analyses align with existing literature, which typically reports ranges of 0.05–0.3 mV for conventional EMG electrodes while walking for the rectus femoris muscle; t is reasonable to expect embroidered electrodes to yield values within a similar order of magnitude, though potentially with more variability and noise [13]. In fact, these values are influenced by electrode size, contact quality, and application context [14]. Specifically, results for S10 and S20 samples are encouraging since their RMS values ranged between 0.02 and 0.03 mV; indeed, S10 and FSp samples showed the highest values of RMS, which were above 0.03 mV, suggesting efficient signal pickup. On the other hand, M and Sp electrodes – the latter with a structure similar to the FSp electrodes - reported the lowest RMS, although still similar to the reference electrodes. It is worth noting that the presence of high variability observed between electrode specimens suggested potential instability or variability mainly due to motion artifacts. The RMS values of all the obtained electrodes, including reference ones, are reported in Fig. 4.

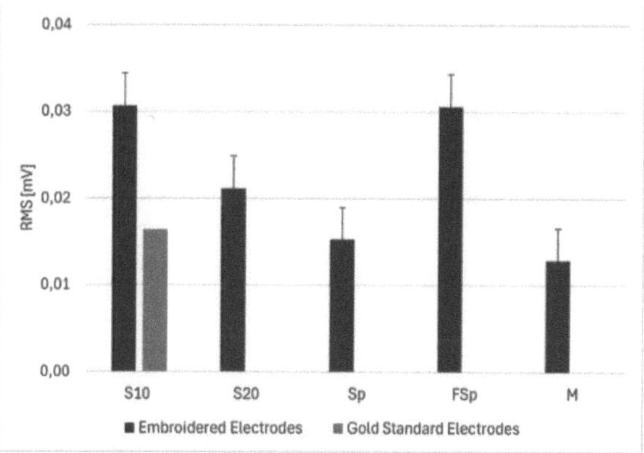

Fig. 4. Bar chart of the average RMS values for each electrode type during walking.

Regarding SNR, literature values for textile EMG electrodes show greater variability (typically 20–30 dB) [15, 16], compared to Ag/AgCl electrodes which generally offer 27–33 dB. Our FSp electrode notably exceeded the upper bound of this range with an SNR of 32.05 dB, indicating optimal noise immunity and positioning this solution close to the typical performance of Ag/AgCl electrodes. S10 and S20 samples showed SNRs of approximately 29.2 dB, slightly outperforming the reference electrodes (28.9 dB). While Sp and M electrodes – in agreement with the RMS values - recorded lower SNRs (~27 dB), they still fall within acceptable limits.

The SNR values of all the obtained electrodes are reported in Fig. 5.

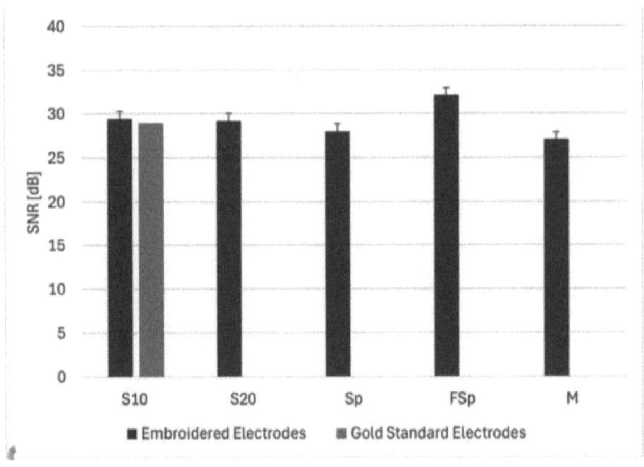

Fig. 5. Bar chart of the average SNR values for each electrode type during walking.

3.2 Step Climbing

All tested embroidery-based textile electrodes effectively recorded muscle activation signals. Examples of the recordings are reported in Fig. 6.

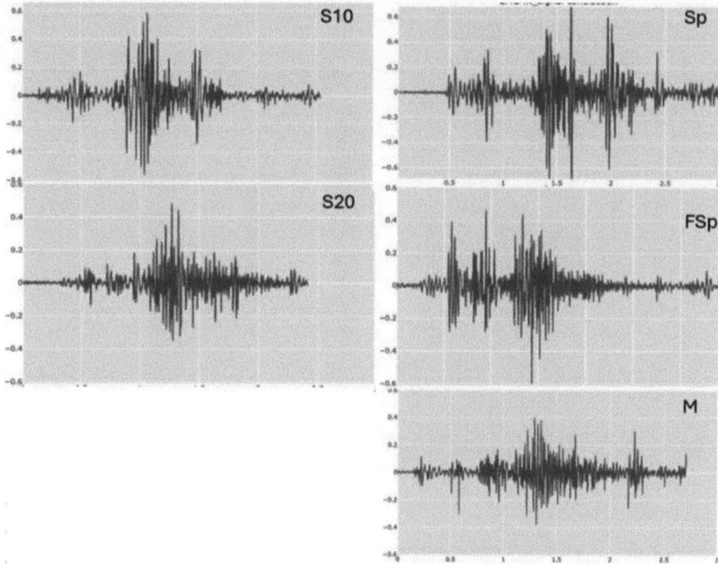

Fig. 6. Bar chart of the average RMS values for each electrode type during step climbing.

The reference electrode demonstrated a low mean RMS of about 0.07 mV and an excellent mean SNR of about 122 dB, coupled with very low contact impedance ($<$ 1 kohm), serving as an ideal benchmark. Among the embroidered electrodes, designs S10 (mean RMS: 0.06 mV; mean SNR: 121 dB) and S20 (mean RMS: 0.06 mV; mean SNR: 120 dB), along with M (mean RMS: 0.06 mV; mean SNR: 116 dB), showed performance values highly comparable to the reference electrode, indicating their capability for high-fidelity signal acquisition. Conversely, electrodes Sp (mean RMS: 0.11 mV; mean SNR: 95 dB) and FSp (mean RMS: 0.07 mV; mean SNR: 98 dB) showed significantly reduced SNR even if with quite high RMS values, indicative of poorer signal quality and increased noise contributions.

This degradation in performance for Sp and FSp is apparently correlated with their critically high values of contact impedance; in fact, FSp recorded the highest mean impedance of about 155 kohm, followed by Sp at 90 kohm. While the reference electrodes exhibited negligible impedance, electrode S20 achieved a good contact impedance (23 kohm), followed by S10 (34 kohm), and M (32 kohm). These contact impedance values for our embroidered electrodes are consistent with the broader literature on dry or textile electrodes, which commonly report impedances ranging from tens to hundreds of kilohms, substantially higher than traditional gel electrodes [14].

The RMS, SNR and impedance values of all the obtained electrodes are reported in Fig. 7, Fig. 8 and Fig. 9, respectively.

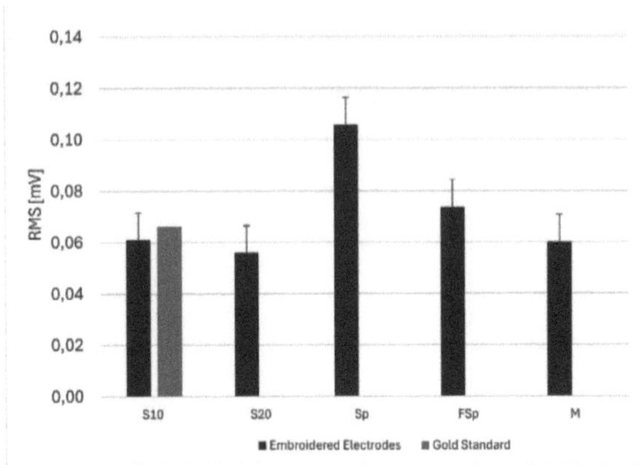

Fig. 7. Bar chart of the average SNR values for each electrode type during step climbing.

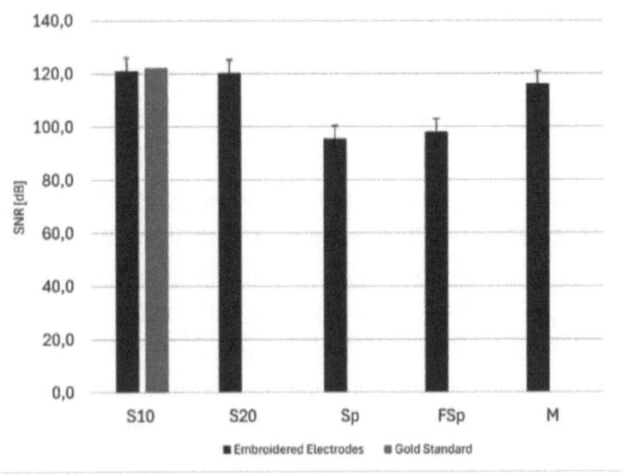

Fig. 8. Bar chart of the average SNR values for each electrode type.

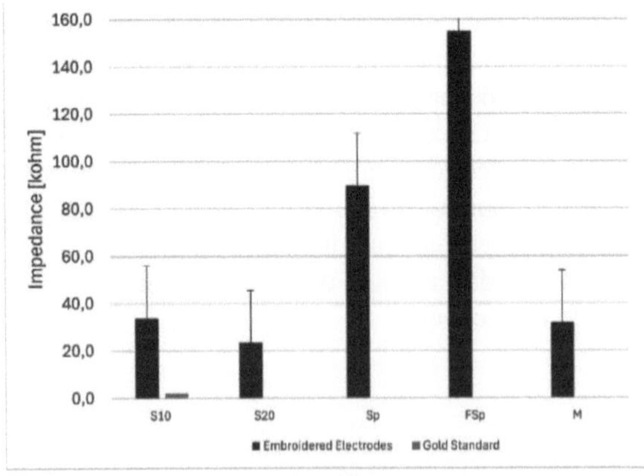

Fig. 9. Bar chart of the average values of the contact electrical impedance for each electrode type.

4 Conclusion

This study successfully demonstrated the viability of using technical embroidery to fabricate textile-based electrodes for functional surface EMG monitoring. Through a comparative analysis of various designs - differing in stitch type and geometry – the presented analysi shown that embroidered electrodes can achieve signal quality comparable to conventional pre-gelled Ag/AgCl electrodes under operating conditions.

Indeed, our findings indicate that the electrode design represent a critical determinant of performance. During dynamic tasks such as walking, the flower-shaped spiral (FSp) design yielded the highest Signal-to-Noise Ratio (SNR), suggesting its suitability for applications involving movement. In the more controlled step-climbing task, the filled satin stitch (S10, S20) and moss stitch (M) electrodes demonstrated performance metrics (RMS and SNR) almost identical to the reference pre-gelled Ag/AgCl electrode, which was strongly correlated with their lower skin-electrode contact impedance. Conversely, the spiral designs (Sp and FSp) exhibited higher impedance and a corresponding decrease in signal quality during the step-climbing test, highlighting those different designs must be optimized for different conditions.

In summary, this research validates technical embroidery as a robust and versatile manufacturing method for producing high-fidelity, textile-based surface EMG sensors. The ability to customize electrode patterns allows for the optimization of performance based on the specific application, balancing signal quality, comfort, and stability.

Future work should focus on long-term durability, including performance after repeated wash cycles, and testing on a more diverse subject population. The successful designs presented here pave the way for their integration into functional smart garments for continuous, unobtrusive monitoring in fields such as rehabilitation, sports science, and clinical diagnostics, ultimately enhancing the usability and comfort of wearable health technology.

Acknowledgments. This work is supported by INAIL (Istituto Nazionale per l'Assicurazione contro gli Infortuni sul Lavoro), with the PR23-PAI-P2– eLiner project.

Disclosure of Interests. The authors have no competing interests to declare that are relevant to the content of this article.

References

1. Merlo, A., Campanini, I.: Applications in movement and gait analysis. In: Surface Electromyography: Physiology, Engineering, and Applications, pp. 440–459 (2016)
2. Baudry, S., Minetto, M.A., Duchateau, J.: Surface EMG applications in neurophysiology. In: Surface Electromyography: Physiology, Engineering, and Applications, pp. 333–360 (2016)
3. Rainoldi, A., Moritani, T., Boccia, G.: EMG in exercise physiology and sports. In: Surface Electromyography: Physiology, Engineering, and Applications, pp. 501–539 (2016)
4. Etana, B.B., Malengier, B., Timothy, K., Wojciech, S., Krishnamoorthy, J., Van Langenhove, L.: A review on the recent developments in design and integration of electromyography textile electrodes for biosignal monitoring. Journal of Industrial Textiles, **53** (2023)
5. Trindade, I., et al.: Design and evaluation of novel textile wearable systems for the surveillance of vital signals. Sensors **16**(10), 1573 (2016)

6. Lam, E., et al.: Exploring textile-based electrode materials for electromyography smart garments. Journal of Rehabilitation and Assistive Technologies Engineering, **9** (2022)

7. Vidhya, C.M., Maithani, Y., Singh, J.P.: Recent advances and challenges in textile electrodes for wearable biopotential signal monitoring: a comprehensive review. Biosensors **13**(7), 679 (2023)

8. Guo, L., Sandsjö, L., Ortiz-Catalan, M., Skrifvars, M.: Systematic review of textile-based electrodes for long-term and continuous surface electromyography recording. Text. Res. J. **90**(2), 227–243 (2019)

9. Angelucci, A., et al.: Smart textiles and sensorized garments for physiological monitoring: a review of available solutions and techniques. Sensors **21**(3), 814 (2021)

10. Andreoni, G., Standoli, C.E., Perego, P.: Sensorized Garments for biomedical monitoring: design issues. In: Proceedings of the ECSA-2 (2015)

11. Standoli, C.E., Guarneri, R., Perego, P., Mazzola, M., Mazzola, A., Andreoni, G.: A smart wearable sensor system for counter-fighting overweight in teenagers. Sensors **16**(8), 1220 (2016)

12. Hermens, H.J., et al.: European recommendations for surface electromyography. Roessingh Research and Development **8**(2), 13–54 (1999)

13. Kim, H., Kim, S., Lim, D., Jeong, W.: Development and characterization of embroidery-based textile electrodes for surface EMG detection. Sensors **22**(13), 4746 (2022)

14. Etana, B.B., Malengier, B., Krishnamoorthy, J., Van Langenhove, L.: Improved skin-electrode impedance characteristics of embroidered textile electrodes for sustainable long-term EMG monitoring. Engineering Proceedings **52**(1), 29 (2023)

15. Kim, H., Rho, S., Lim, D., Lee, S.: Characterization of embroidered textile-based electrode for EMG smart wear according to stitch technique. Fashion and Textiles **10**, 32 (2023)

16. Song, J.E., Kim, H., Lim, D., Lee, S.: The improvement of body signal measurement using adhesive intermediate electrode between skin and textile. Journal of Engineered Fibers and Fabrics **19** (2024)

Research and Analysis of Risky Behavior in College Students' Sewing Craft Teaching

Zhen Qin[(⊠)], Hanze Ge, and Zejun Huang

South China University of Technology, Guangzhou, Guangdong, China
qinzhen1988@scut.edu.cn

Abstract. In the teaching of fashion and apparel majors at universities, sewing technology training is an indispensable component. However, college students often suffer injuries and strains during the learning process of sewing skills, which are related to multiple factors such as individual students, teaching methods, and laboratory environments. Through a survey of the main injuries and strains that occur during college students' sewing processes, the vulnerable body parts prone to injury and strain are summarized. Additionally, through in-depth interviews, observational research, professional judgment, and other methods, it is concluded that the primary causes of injuries and strains include inattention, unskilled techniques, incorrect sewing postures, and other factors. This paper proposes teaching improvement methods from three aspects, such as the teaching process, teaching hardware, and emergency support systems.

Keywords: college students · sewing technology · teaching · risky behaviors · strain

1 Introduction

The textile and garment industry is a traditional pillar industry in China, accounting for 40% of the global total textile trade. According to the 2024 college enrollment catalog, there are 204 universities in China offering the major of Fashion and Apparel Design. In the teaching of this major, the sewing technology course is an indispensable part. However, as college students generally have no prior sewing experience before entering this major, when using high-speed sewing equipment, they often suffer physical injuries due to dangerous behaviors or physical strain caused by long-term improper postures.

2 Theoretical Description

The health, safety, and well-being of workers during the sewing process have long been one of the focuses in fields such as ergonomics. The main research directions include the following:

First, studies on high-risk behaviors in sewing. Some scholars argue that the high-speed operation of sewing machines may cause needle stabbings, finger pinching, or

V. G. Duffy (Ed.): HCII 2025, LNCS 16339, pp. 119–128, 2026.
https://doi.org/10.1007/978-3-032-13012-9_9

injuries from flying fabric debris. The risks are higher when operators are distracted or fatigued (Smith, 2015). Some scholars have established an ergonomic evaluation decision tree for working postures and used machine learning to assess risks to different body parts during sewing. They found that the upper and lower arms are critical risk areas in the sewing process (Su, 2023), providing a reference for the body regions to be prioritized in this study's sewing risk assessment.

Second, in addition to the immediate injuries during the sewing process, scholars have studied the long-term physical damages caused by sewing work. For example, long-term repetitive movements such as stepping on pedals and maintaining fixed arm postures are prone to causing carpal tunnel syndrome, shoulder and neck pain, etc., with the mismatch of workbench height being the main inducement (Jones, 2018). Some scholars used surface electromyography to study the muscle load and activity patterns of the neck and shoulder muscles of female sewing machine operators, and prevented musculoskeletal diseases of sewing machine operators by intervening in the critical period of muscle fatigue (Zhang, 2011). This provides a foundation for the research on sewing postures and the identification of fatigue-induced incorrect postures in this study.

Third, the harm of the sewing environment to the human body is also one of the focuses of ergonomics. For example, some scholars have pointed out that the noise in industrial sewing workshops often exceeds 85 decibels, and long-term exposure can cause hearing damage (Brown, 2017). Formaldehyde and dye residues in fabric processing may trigger respiratory diseases or skin allergies (Garcia et al. 2019). In addition to physical injuries, some studies have also explored the harm of sewing work systems to workers. The high-intensity work under the piece-rate wage system is prone to causing anxiety and depression (Lee et al. 2020). These studies inspire this research to consider issues needing attention in college students' sewing technology teaching from multiple comprehensive factors.

The above studies provide a preliminary theoretical foundation and reference examples for this study. However, none of these studies have involved college students as a group. College students have particularities in their sewing experience, sewing learning environment, and sewing learning models. Conducting specific research on them can more pertinently promote the acquisition of sewing skills among college students and reduce the occurrence of hazards during the sewing process.

3   Research Framework

This study primarily employs a mixed-methods approach combining literature research, observational records, questionnaire surveys, and in-depth interviews. On the one hand, a questionnaire survey will first be conducted on the hazards and strains that occur during college students' sewing processes to summarize the main types of injuries and strains. On the other hand, in-depth interviews and analyses will be carried out on the affected body parts and causes of different injuries and strains to identify their root causes, which will serve as the basis for proposing improvement suggestions. The research is divided into three main parts:

A) Study on Primary Injuries During College Students' Sewing Learning

Through investigations into injury incidents and affected body parts, this section analyzes the causes of hazardous behaviors and seeks solutions. It aims to systematically document injury patterns and explore the underlying factors contributing to safety risks in sewing practice.

B) Regional Investigation and Analysis of Strains and Discomforts

Based on the interaction between the body and the sewing machine, the body is divided into four regions—head and neck, upper limbs, waist and back, and lower limbs—for targeted investigation and analysis. This part surveys the strains and discomforts experienced by college students during sewing learning, summarizing the common regions and causes of strains in the process of acquiring sewing skills.

C) Analysis of Optimization Pathways

Drawing on the causes of hazards and strains identified in the previous sections, this part explores optimization strategies to reduce hazardous behaviors in teaching. It focuses on developing practical methods and interventions to enhance safety and ergonomic design in college sewing education (Fig. 1).

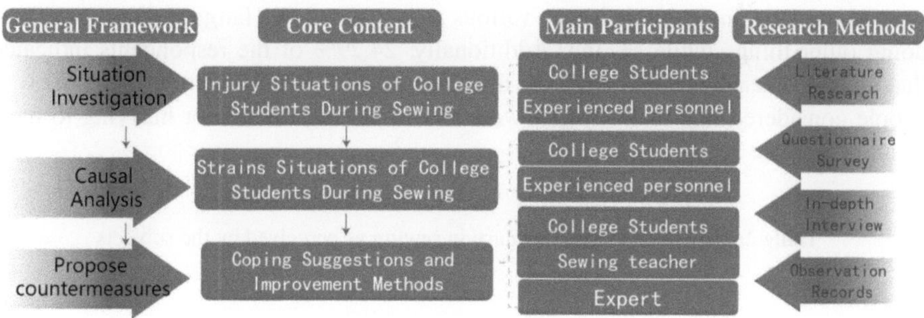

Fig. 1. Main Research Framework.

4 Specific Research

4.1 Investigation of Main Injuries

First, an investigation was conducted into the injury history of college students during sewing. By comparing historical injury data, the most vulnerable body parts were observed. Through a survey of 70 students' sewing learning processes, 61.4% of respondents identified needle stabbings, burns, and cuts as the most hazardous behaviors during sewing. Among them, needle stabbings were universally recognized as the most common injury in sewing, accounting for 20%, followed by burns (12.8%) and cuts (1.43%). Additionally, some respondents mentioned potential injuries such as electric shocks or machine tipping during sewing (Table 1).

Table 1. Proportions of main injury-causing behaviors in sewing as perceived by the subjects.

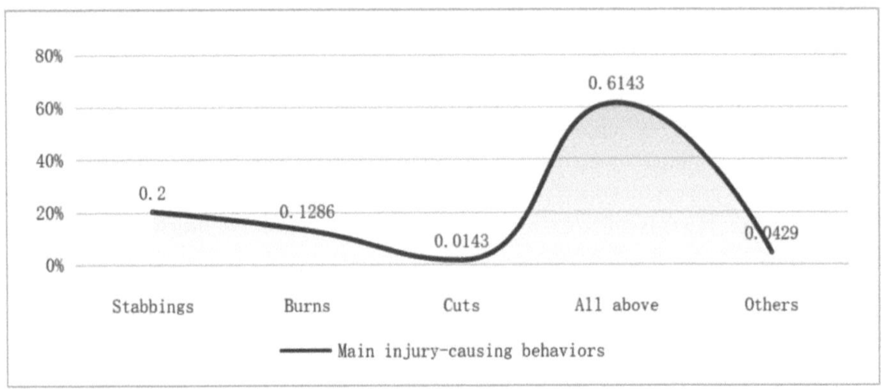

In terms of the causes of injuries, 68.75% of the subjects believed that the injuries were caused by inattention due to various reasons such as fatigue, distraction, and doing other things while sewing. Additionally, 24.29% of the respondents indicated that unskilled sewing techniques were the cause of their injuries. Furthermore, 5.7% of people considered that their injuries were due to sewing too fast or hurrying to meet deadlines (Table 2).

Table 2. The main causes of injury in sewing as perceived by the subjects

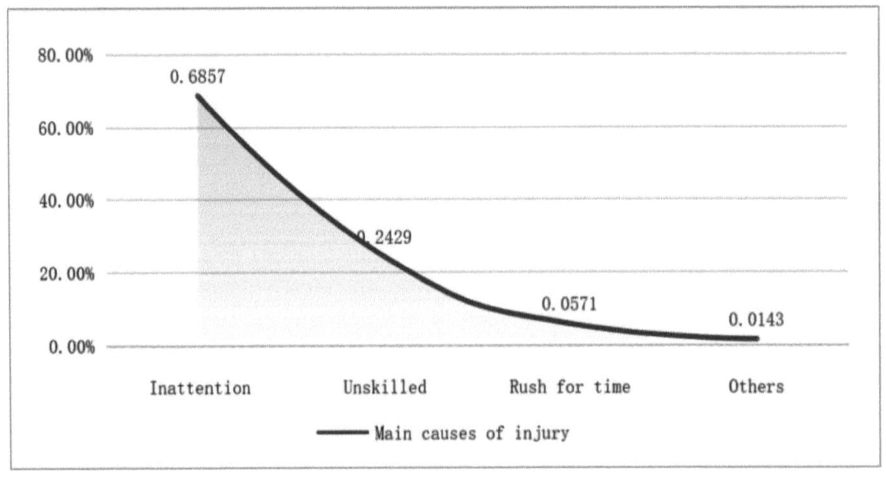

A) Needle Stabbings

Through in-depth interviews with respondents, the following scenarios of needle stabbings were identified:

First, high-speed inertial injuries. Industrial flat-sewing machines used in teaching generally have a rotation speed of $\geq$ 2,500 r/min, with some reaching 4,500 r/min. The kinetic energy generated by the needle bar movement can reach 15 J, sufficient to penetrate bone. Mechanical inertia persists for 3–5 s even after the power is turned off, making it easy for inertial injuries to occur after sewing has stopped during operation.

Second, operating without powering off is another major cause of injury. For example, changing needles, clearing thread ends, or performing maintenance without shutting down the machine may trigger accidental startup. This aligns with the Textile Industry Safety Guide published by OSHA (U.S. Occupational Safety and Health Administration) in 2021, which highlights that 70% of sewing machine injuries originate from maintenance operations conducted without powering off.

Third, coordination issues with feed dogs and presser feet. During sewing, one hand feeds fabric to the feed dogs while the other pulls it out from in front of the sewing needle. When fabric feeding is uneven, operators frequently adjust it manually, increasing the likelihood of fingers entering the danger zone. Improper pulling of fabric, such as excessive force or fabric slipping, may cause the hand to be accidentally stabbed by the needle. Notably, most needle stabbings occur on the non-dominant hand, and usually the left hand, with the index and middle fingers injured most frequently, directly related to their contact position during fabric feeding.

B) Burns

Interviews on burns revealed that they are primarily caused by improper equipment management, with the main reasons for such negligence including the following:

First, there is a discrepancy between sewing education in schools and factory sewing operations. In factories, tasks are divided into steps and specialized roles— cutting, ironing, stitching, and post-processing are each handled by separate workers, with each worker typically specializing in one step. In school sewing classes, however, students are required to learn and complete multiple steps, such as cutting, ironing, stitching, and post-processing. During the transition between steps, equipment management is prone to oversight. For example, most burns reported by surveyed students were caused by temporarily placing a plugged-in steam iron improperly.

Second, there is a cognitive bias regarding equipment performance. A continuously plugged-in steam iron can reach temperatures of 200°C, and its residual heat persists for a long time after being unplugged. Experiments show that it takes 12 min for the temperature to drop from 200°C to 100°C. Some students reported burns occurring during the movement or storage of the equipment after it was turned off. Additionally, interviews revealed that most students are unaware of the temperature requirements for ironing different fabrics. For example, synthetic fiber fabrics should be ironed at 120–160°C, while woolen fabrics require 160–200°C Although irons have fabric-type prompts, students often ignore these temperature thresholds in an attempt to iron fabrics quickly, leading to overuse of high temperatures.

C) Cuts

Among the respondents, the probability of cuts is approximately 1.4%, with fewer injured individuals. Cuts occur during and after the use of scissors.

First, the main causes of cuts during use are twofold: one is inattention due to fatigue, distraction, or doing other things while cutting. The other is misjudgment of fabric properties, such as excessive force during cutting, leading to scratches or cuts.

Second, cuts after use mainly occur due to improper placement of scissors or negligence during cleaning, resulting in falls that cause stabbings or scratches.

4.2 Investigation of Main Injuries

The second part of the study focuses on investigating the strain and discomfort experienced by college students during sewing learning. The *Occupational Safety and Health Report by the International Labour Organization* (ILO) states that the strain rate among sewing workers due to repetitive movements and static postures is as high as 62%. During the process of learning sewing techniques, some individuals do not suffer immediate mechanical physical injuries, but prolonged sewing still causes latent discomfort. According to the survey results, prolonged sewing mainly causes comprehensive discomfort in multiple aspects, including the eyes, muscles, and skeleton (Table 3).

Table 3. Main Discomfort Areas Reported by Subjects Caused by Long-Term Sewing.

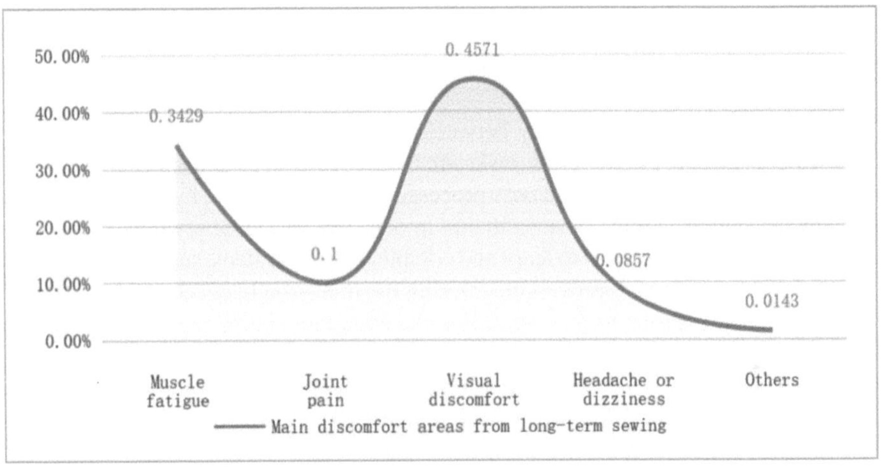

First, eye fatigue and visual discomfort have the highest proportion, accounting for 45.7%. The survey results are consistent with the content mentioned in the World Health Organization (WHO) White Paper on Occupational Eye Fatigue, such as "long-term close-range fine work is a high-risk factor for vision loss." Sewing requires long-term focus on close-range fine operations, usually with a visual distance of less than 30cm, causing the ciliary muscles to contract continuously and trigger regulatory spasm, manifesting as blurred vision, dry eyes, headaches, etc. (Hayashi et al. 2018). In addition, low-light environments or fabric reflection may exacerbate visual fatigue.

Second, muscle fatigue accounts for 34.29%. Sewing requires maintaining static postures of the shoulders, neck, and arms, as well as repetitive wrist movements, which easily lead to lactic acid accumulation in the muscles and cause soreness. Long-term labor can easily develop into tendon diseases or carpal tunnel diseases.

Third, joint pain accounts for 10%. Sewing operations require long-term sitting. According to the spinal biomechanics model, when the human body leans forward by 20°, the lumbar load increases to 1.5 times that in the upright position. Long-term bending or forward-leaning postures increase the pressure on the cervical and lumbar intervertebral discs, easily inducing degenerative lesions. In particular, improper height of the sewing machine can lead to scoliosis or thoracic compression (OSHA, 2020).

Fourth, dizziness and headache account for 8.57%. Dizziness or headache caused by long-term sewing is associated with multiple factors, including visual fatigue, musculoskeletal tension, cervical spine compression, and environmental factors. Prolonged sitting in an enclosed space with shallow breathing may lead to decreased blood oxygen saturation and brain hypoxia, triggering dizziness. Additionally, experiments on long-term sewers have found that 65% of headaches are significantly correlated with visual fatigue (Khan et al. 2019).

To understand the locations where muscle fatigue and joint pain occur, this study also conducted further investigations into discomfort in different body parts (Table 4).

Table 4. The Parts of Most Musculoskeletal Discomfort Caused by Long-Term Sewing by Subjects.

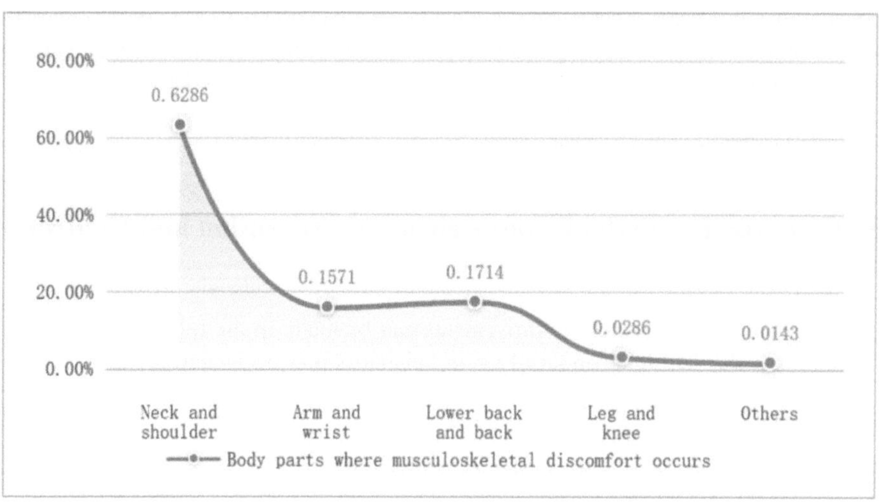

Musculoskeletal discomfort during sewing primarily concentrates in the neck and shoulders. First, this is related to prolonged maintenance of static postures. Sewing requires long-term head-down and neck-forward postures, causing continuous tension in the trapezius muscle, levator scapulae, and posterior cervical muscle group, which hinders local blood circulation and leads to lactic acid accumulation and soreness. Second, repetitive movements can cause muscle strain. When frequently operating a sewing machine, the shoulder joints and arms need to repeatedly perform actions such as pushing fabric and adjusting stitches, which may lead to overuse of shoulder rotator cuff muscles, such as the supraspinatus and deltoid muscles, and trigger chronic inflammation, such as scapulohumeral periarthritis or tendinitis.

Second, the lower back and back are affected. When sewing, maintaining a sitting posture without proper lumbar support can easily reduce the lumbar lordosis and increase the pressure on the intervertebral discs. At the same time, to see the stitching or manipulate the fabric clearly, sewers often involuntarily lean forward, leading to thoracic kyphosis and cervical extension, forming a "C-shaped" poor posture that exacerbates the load on the lower back and back. Prolonged exposure to this posture can weaken the deep abdominal and lumbar muscles, such as the multifidus and transversus abdominis, which fail to effectively stabilize the spine and accelerate strain.

Third, the arms and wrists are impacted. Hand discomfort caused by long-term sewing is mainly due to tendon and synovial membrane injuries from high-frequency repetitive movements. During sewing, the fingers repeatedly press the fabric and adjust the stitches, while the wrists frequently flex, extend, or deviate laterally, causing excessive friction in the flexor digitorum tendons and wrist extensor muscles, which can induce tendon sheath diseases. Static loading in unnatural postures, such as keeping the wrists suspended or in prolonged dorsiflexion when operating the sewing machine, can compress the median nerve, leading to finger numbness and other symptoms.

Fourth is the legs and knees. The main causes are blood circulation obstruction due to static sitting posture and joint load caused by repetitive pedaling movements. Prolonged sitting weakens the calf muscle pump function, reduces venous return, and easily causes leg swelling, numbness, or heaviness, which may increase the risk of varicose veins in the long term. Operating the sewing machine pedal requires repeated flexion and extension of the knee joint. Especially during high-speed sewing, if the pedal resistance is too high or the stroke is too long, the pressure on the patellofemoral joint surface increases. Sustained pedaling with one foot can easily induce plantar fasciitis or Achilles tendinitis.

5 Construction Path of Comprehensive Prevention and Control System

Based on the above research, improvements can be made in the following aspects for the various risky and labor-induced strain behaviors that occur during sewing among college students.

5.1 Innovative Management of the Teaching Process

In the pre-teaching phase, first establish the concept of safe sewing for students by setting up a special safety training stage, adopting a three-level progressive model of "cognition - simulation - practical operation." In the cognition stage, students directly understand the danger of tools by observing the puncture ability of sewing needles of different specifications. In the simulation stage, simulate and restore fault scenarios such as sewing machine thread jams to cultivate emergency response capabilities.Students must pass a safety operation assessment before using professional equipment such as high-speed sewing machines, after which they can enter the practical operation phase.

In teaching, attention should be paid to the setting of teaching duration. In previous investigations into needle stick injuries and cuts, many students mentioned that such incidents were caused by inattentiveness. Therefore, during the teaching process, attention training should be further strengthened. For example, the "20–20-20" attention training method can be implemented: after every 20 min of operation, students should gaze into the distance for 20 s and stretch for 20 s. Appropriate relaxation can improve students' concentration. Additionally, methods such as improving the teacher-student ratio, setting personalized teaching durations, and flexibly designing learning tasks can enhance students' learning focus and reduce the occurrence of injuries.

After teaching, sewing safety should be incorporated into the curriculum evaluation system. A dual-dimensional evaluation system integrating "safe operation" and "technical standards" should be established. During teaching evaluations, attention should be paid to students' technical operation specifications—such as whether the iron is powered off after use—and these should be given evaluation status equally important as technical proficiency. Alternatively, a safety points system can be developed to quantify standardized operations as components of credit requirements.

5.2 Technical Improvements to Teaching Hardware

First, standardization of the teaching environment. In terms of sewing equipment layout, according to OSHA standards, the spacing between sewing workstations should be $\geq$ 1.2 m. However, general teaching laboratories often fail to meet this standard, leading to some injuries caused by interference between adjacent workstations, such as bobbin ejection or fabric falling and tangling. Meanwhile, attention should also be paid to the stroboscopic effect of lighting. Since sewing is a long-term process, in laboratories using lighting with a stroboscopic frequency < 200 Hz, operators are prone to faster visual fatigue, which can lead to misjudgments in stitch distance accuracy.

Second, special teaching aids for sewing instruction can be upgraded. For example, traditional sewing machines can undergo safety modifications by installing infrared induction devices that automatically stop the machine when fingers enter the dangerous area near the needle. Pressure sensors can be added to iron handles to automatically cut off power when the iron is idle. Magnetic needle holders can be promoted to replace traditional needle packets, reducing the risk of needles scattering. For areas prone to fatigue, machinery can be introduced to relieve and treat fatigued body parts. For instance, shoulder-neck and eye relaxation devices can be designed to alleviate strain.

5.3 Construction of Emergency Support Systems

In terms of infrastructure, a mini first-aid station should be established in the laboratory, equipped with professional injury disposal supplies such as hemostatic gels and antibacterial dressings; a specialized outpatient clinic for process operation injuries should be set up in the campus hospital, stocked with biological agents including tetanus vaccines.

In terms of personnel management, a "safety partnership system" should be implemented, where every two students form a safety mutual-aid group to provide safety reminders for each other. Regular trauma first-aid drills should be carried out, requiring teachers and students to master the standardized disposal procedures of "hemostasis - disinfection - bandaging - reporting."

6 Conclusion

In summary, the sewing process is a multi-dimensional process requiring full-body coordination, especially among college students, who have concentrated learning time and no prior skill foundation in sewing. Through research and analysis, the causes of injuries and strains can be effectively identified, allowing for the development of optimal improvement strategies.

Acknowledgments. This study was funded by the Special Fund for Basic Scientific Research Business Expenses of Central Universities, and the project is the Surface Project for Cultivating Top-Notch Young Talents (QNMS202417), Youth Project of Guangdong Provincial Philosophy and Social Science Planning (GD24YYS03).

References

Smith, J., Lee, K.: Occupational hazards in garment manufacturing: a case study of needle injuries. Journal of Occupational Safety and Health **12**(3), 45–60 (2015)

Su, J.M., Chang, J.H., Indrayani, et al.: Machine learning approach to determine the decision rules in ergonomic assessment of working posture in sewing machine operators. Journal of Safety Research **87**, 15–26 (2023)

Jones, R., et al.: Ergonomics in sewing: impact of workstation design on musculoskeletal disorders. Ergonomics **61**(5), 678–695.Author, F.: Contribution title. In: 9th International Proceedings on Proceedings, pp. 1–2. Publisher, Location (2010) (2018)

Zhang, F.R., He, L.H., Wu, S.S., et al.: Quantify work load and muscle functional activation patterns in neck-shoulder muscles of female sewing machine operators using surface electromyogram. Chinese Medical Journal **124**(22), 3731–3737 (2011)

Brown, T., Zhang, L.: Noise-induced hearing loss in textile workers: a longitudinal study. Noise Health **19**(89), 231–239 (2017)

Garcia, M., et al.: Chemical exposure in textile workers: a hidden threat. Environ. Health Perspect. **127**(6), 065001 (2019)

Lee, S., et al.: Mental health challenges in fast fashion supply chains. Work Stress. **34**(4), 398–416 (2020)

Hayashi, R., et al.: Visual fatigue induced by near work. Invest. Ophthalmol. Vis. Sci. **59**(6), 2405–2412 (2018)

OSHA. Ergonomics for Sewing Machine Operators. Occupational Safety and Health Administration (2020)

Khan, M.A., et al.: Occupational headache in tailors. J. Occup. Health **61**(1), 45–53 (2019)

Effect of Fused Deposition Modeling Printing Parameters on the Accuracy of Virtual Drape Using 3D Printed Textiles

Sheng Zhan[1], Seonyoung Youn[2], and Kavita Mathur[1(✉)]

[1] Department of Textile and Apparel Technology and Management, North Carolina State University, Raleigh, NC 27606, USA
{szhan3,kmathur}@ncsu.edu
[2] Cornell University, Ithaca, NY 14853, USA
sy836@cornell.edu

Abstract. This study evaluates virtual drape simulation reliability for Fused Deposition Modeling (FDM) 3D printed textiles by systematically comparing physical measurements with digital simulations. We analyzed the effects of key production parameters (layer height, layer number, and infill density) on drape coefficient prediction accuracy across 60 measurements from 15 primary physically printed samples. Results showed virtual simulations consistently overestimated drape coefficients by an average of 13.53% points (18.20% relative error) compared to physical measurements (paired t-test: t(14) = 8.50, p < 0.001), with discrepancies increasing significantly for samples with 0.15 mm layer heights (16.15% error) versus 0.20 mm (11.29% error). Statistical analysis identified layer number as the most significant parameter affecting both physical and virtual drape behavior (F(2,12) = 125.47, p < 0.001), followed by subsequent layer height and infill density. The findings provide specific guidelines for the 3D printing community: designers should prioritize 0.20 mm layer heights with one or two layers to achieve simulation accuracy within 10–12%, while our calibration model reduces prediction errors by 35.3%. This research enables more reliable virtual prototyping of 3D printed textiles, reducing physical sampling requirements significantly and accelerating the integration of these innovative materials into sustainable digital design workflows.

Keywords: 3D printing · Virtual drape simulation · Textile drape · FDM · CLO3D · Digital prototyping · Apparel design

1 Introduction

The convergence of three-dimensional (3D) printing technology with digital apparel design represents a transformative development in textile manufacturing. 3D printing enables highly individualized parametric and modular garments tailored to specific body shapes [17,29]. Major fashion brands have implemented these technologies at scale—Adidas employs Digital Light Synthesis for 4DFWD

© The Author(s), under exclusive license to Springer Nature Switzerland AG 2026
V. G. Duffy (Ed.): HCII 2025, LNCS 16339, pp. 129–143, 2026.
https://doi.org/10.1007/978-3-032-13012-9_10

sneakers with 20,000 optimized lattice structures [2], while Dior reproduced archival garments using bio-based materials [11]. Within modern apparel design, reliably simulating mechanical parameters becomes critical for accurate 3D virtual garment simulation in CAD systems [10].

Virtual simulation tools like CLO3D, Browzwear, and Optitex have become industry standards, demonstrating considerable accuracy for conventional textiles while reducing cost and development time [24,30]. However, their reliability for 3D printed textile structures remains less validated. Unlike traditional textiles whose properties derive from fiber and yarn interactions [15,22], 3D printed textiles achieve mechanical properties through geometric structure and design parameters [3,18].

Recent research shows promise—Shea and Wirth [26] developed empirically tuned models for 3D-printed weaves, accurately estimating load-extension curves when properly calibrated. However, no comprehensive study has examined how FDM production parameters affect virtual drape simulation accuracy, creating a significant validation gap that limits integration into mainstream apparel applications.

Therefore, this study uniquely contributes by: (1) providing the first systematic validation of virtual drape simulations for FDM 3D printed textiles across multiple production parameters, (2) quantifying specific relationships between layer height, layer number, and infill density on simulation accuracy, and (3) developing a calibration model that reduces prediction errors by 35.3%, enabling reliable virtual prototyping. This work facilitates the integration of 3D printed textiles into digital design pipelines, directly address the 3D printing community's need for parameter-specific guidelines that optimize both physical properties and simulation reliability.

2   Literature Review

2.1   Evolution of Virtual Simulation in Textile Design

Commercial platforms such as CLO3D, Browzwear, and Optitex employ physics-based models, with CLO3D utilizing a mass-spring model that balances computational efficiency and visual realism [23]. Research demonstrates high correlation between virtual and physical drape tests for conventional textiles, with coefficients exceeding 0.94 for woven fabrics [30]. However, complex textile structures require specialized frameworks—James et al. [16] developed yarn-level modeling for intricate knits, while Stig and Hallström [28] presented methods for 3D textiles with curved yarns. Current simulation tools lack verification of 3D printed structures.

2.2   Structure, Properties, and Simulation Challenges Of 3D Printed Textiles

FDM technology enables soft, flexible 3D printed textiles whose properties depend critically on print settings [20,25]. Key parameters include structural factors (weave pattern, yarn spacing) and process parameters (layer height, infill density, print orientation). Research shows layer thickness and orientation effects vary with infill density [5], while optimized parameters can enhance properties by up to 60% [12]. For TPU materials, thinner layers (0.15 mm) increase hardness but may compromise inter-layer adhesion [21].

While prior work examined isolated aspects—Kabir et al. [19] studied auxetic structure drapeability, and Shea et al. [27] analyzed pattern geometry effects— no study has systematically validated how these parameters affect simulation accuracy. This gap limits practical virtual prototyping of 3D printed textiles, requiring comprehensive validation across parameter combinations.

2.3   Integration with Anthropometric Data and Sustainable Design

3D printing enables personalized, functionalized clothing [7] with enhanced properties like 70% increased abrasion resistance [13]. Virtual simulation technologies reduce material waste and energy consumption through digital prototyping [6,9]. Without validated simulation accuracy for 3D printed textiles, designers cannot fully leverage these sustainability benefits, as unreliable virtual prototypes lead to excessive physical sampling and material waste.

3   Methodology

3.1   Sample Preparation and Experimental Design

Materials. All samples were fabricated using an FDM 3D printer (TRILAB DeltiQ 2) with Thermoplastic Polyurethane (TPU 95A HF) filament. TPU was selected for its flexibility and elasticity, suitable for textile applications requiring drapeability. The material exhibits Shore hardness of 95A, providing balanced flexibility and structural integrity. Samples were printed on a heated bed at 50 °C to prevent warping.

Experimental Design. This study investigated three key production parameters:

1. **Layer Height**: 0.15 mm and 0.20 mm (subsequent layer height for multi-layer structures)
2. **Layer Number**: 1, 2, and 3 layers
3. **Infill Density**: 20%, 40%, and 60%

To ensure optimal adhesion between the printed material and the print bed, the first layer height was set to 0.20 mm for all samples, while subsequent layer heights were varied according to the experimental design (0.15 mm or 0.20 mm). This separation of first and subsequent layer heights is a standard practice in FDM printing to prevent warping and ensure print reliability.

The design consisted of 15 primary physical samples with key parameter combinations, as shown in Table 1 and Table 2. Additionally, one sample tested temperature effects (210 °C vs 230 °C, measurements 61–64) and one validation sample verified the calibration formula (measurements 65–68). Each physical sample was measured four times, yielding 60 primary measurements plus 8 supplementary measurements.

Samples were printed as 240 mm diameter circular discs for standardized drape testing. This diameter represents the maximum sample size achievable with the printing bed dimensions. Honeycomb infill pattern was selected for its balance of print speed and structural integrity.

3.2 Physical Drape Measurement

Physical drape measurements used a modified Cusick drape tester with a 96 mm diameter circular pedestal, as shown in Fig. 1. Samples draped naturally under their own weight while a digital camera captured the projected area.

Drape coefficient (DC) was calculated as:

$$\text{DC } (\%) = \frac{\text{Draped Area}}{\text{Undraped Area}} \times 100\% \tag{1}$$

where:

– Draped Area = projected area of draped sample (cm^2)
– Undraped Area = total flat sample area ($452.39\,cm^2$)

Higher DC values indicate stiffer materials with less draping capability. Image analysis was performed using Adobe Photoshop CC with calibrated scale references.

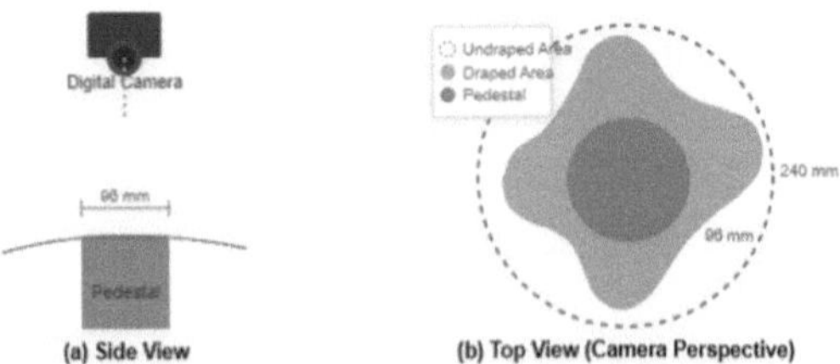

Fig. 1. Experimental setup for physical drape measurement showing the modified Cusick drape tester with 3D printed sample

3.3 3D Printed Textile Digitization and Simulation Methodology

3D Printed Textile digitization used CLO 3D simulator (version 7.3) implementing Baraff and Witkin's [4] physically based model. Physical properties were quantified using the CLO Fabric Kit 2.0 in Emulator mode, as illustrated in Fig. 2, which requires 23 input parameters to measure weight, thickness, stretch,

Table 1. Summary of Experimental Printing Parameters

Design Parameter	Conditions	Description / Illustration
First Layer Height	0.20 mm	Constant for all samples
Subsequent Layer Height	0.15 mm, 0.20 mm	Primary parameter
Layer Number	1, 2, 3	Primary parameter
Infill Density	20%, 40%, 60%	Primary parameter
Print Temperature	210°C, 230°C	Secondary parameter (supplementary samples)
Material	TPU 95A	Constant
Infill Pattern	Honeycomb	Constant
Sample Diameter	240 mm	Constant

*Note: For single-layer structures (n = 3), only the first layer height of 0.20 mm applies. The subsequent layer height parameter is relevant only for multi-layer configurations.

and bending behavior. These values are manually entered into CLO's Fabric Editor to generate realistic simulations.

For the virtual drape simulation, a digital model of each sample was created to match the exact dimensions and structural pattern of the physical samples. A cylindrical base with 96 mm diameter and 100 mm height represented the physical test pedestal. Simulations ran with gravity = 9.800 and 1 mm particle distance until stabilization. The virtual drape coefficient (DC) was then analyzed in ImageJ software using physical measurement protocols. Images were converted to binary format, and boundary-enclosed areas were calculated via pixel-counting

Table 2. Experimental design parameters for 3D printing samples

Sample ID	Layer Height (mm)	Number of Layers	Infill Density (%)	First Layer Height (mm)
S1	0.20	1	20	0.20
S2	0.20	1	40	0.20
S3	0.20	1	60	0.20
S4	0.15	2	20	0.20
S5	0.20	2	20	0.20
S6	0.15	2	40	0.20
S7	0.20	2	40	0.20
S8	0.15	2	60	0.20
S9	0.20	2	60	0.20
S10	0.15	3	20	0.20
S11	0.20	3	20	0.20
S12	0.15	3	40	0.20
S13	0.20	3	40	0.20
S14	0.15	3	60	0.20
S15	0.20	3	60	0.20

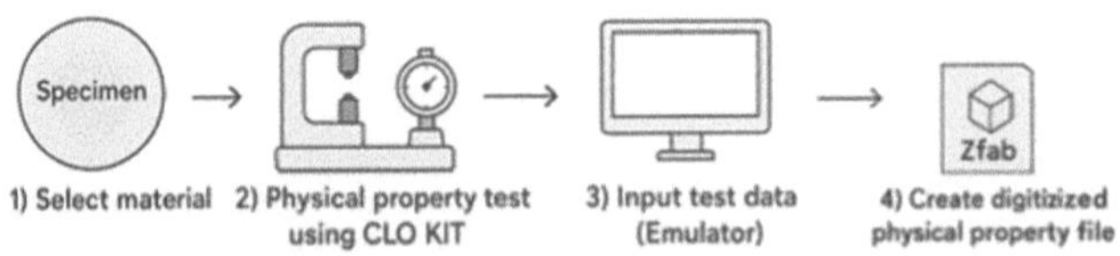

Fig. 2. Textile digitization process using CLO Fabric Kit 2.0 for measuring weight, thickness, stretch, and bending behavior

methods. Conversion to physical units was calibrated using a reference scale included in each image.

3.4   Statistical Analysis

Statistical analysis used Claude 3.5 Sonnet (Anthropic, 2024) for primary analysis with R software (Version 4.3.1) verification, This approach leverages recent advances in AI-assisted data analysis, which has demonstrated high consistency and efficiency in statistical computations while maintaining exceptional user-friendliness [14].

To avoid pseudoreplication, analyses used means of 15 physical samples rather than 60 individual measurements. Each sample's mean was calculated from four repeated measurements, ensuring n=15 accurately reflected independent experimental units.

The analysis included descriptive statistics, paired t-tests comparing physical and virtual drape coefficients, independent samples t-tests for subsequent layer height effects (using only multi-layer samples), one-way ANOVA to evaluate parameter effects, post-hoc Tukey HSD tests, multiple regression analysis for predictive modeling, and Pearson correlation analysis. All tests used $\alpha = 0.05$ with effect size calculations.

4   Results and Discussion

4.1   Overall Comparison of Physical and Virtual Drape Coefficients

Analysis of 15 3D printed textile samples revealed systematic overestimation by virtual simulations. Physical measurements yielded mean DC of 74.36% (SD = 11.25%), while virtual simulations produced 87.90% (SD = 12.10%), representing 13.53% points overestimation (18.20% relative error). This difference was statistically significant (paired t-test: t(14) = 8.50, p < 0.001, Cohen's d = 2.19), as summarized in Table 4 and Table 5.

Despite absolute differences, physical and virtual measurements showed strong correlation (r = 0.854, p < 0.001), indicating simulation algorithms preserve relative draping behavior across parameters. This supports calibration-based improvements for 3D printed textiles, as shown in Fig. 3.

The visual comparison of all samples is presented in Table 3, which shows the physical and virtual drape patterns for each of the 15 samples along with their corresponding DC values.

4.2   Effect of Subsequent Layer Height on Drape Coefficient

Analysis of multi-layer samples (n = 12) revealed critical insights into layer height effects. Physical measurements showed 0.20 mm subsequent layers (M = 80.97%, SD = 6.62%) produced higher DC than 0.15 mm (M = 76.81%, SD = 6.62%), though not statistically significant (t(10) = 1.09, p = 0.301).

Virtual simulations showed minimal sensitivity to layer height, with nearly identical values for 0.15 mm (M = 92.96%, SD = 5.77%) and 0.20 mm (M = 92.26%, SD = 6.63%) samples (t(10) = 0.19, p = 0.850).

Most critically, 0.15 mm samples showed significantly higher prediction errors (M = 16.15%, SD = 3.46%) than 0.20 mm samples (M = 11.29%, SD = 4.82%; t(10) = 2.01, p = 0.036, one-tailed), as detailed in Table 6.

This divergence highlights fundamental simulation limitations. Virtual simulations model idealized geometries without manufacturing defects. While thinner layers theoretically improve surface quality [8], our findings reveal 0.15 mm layers in flexible TPU can cause under-extrusion and inconsistent inter-layer bonding. These manufacturing defects create variable mechanical properties in physical samples that deviate significantly from the idealized models used in simulations. Virtual simulations assume perfect material deposition and bonding, failing to account for the real-world manufacturing challenges that affect draping behavior. This explains why physical samples with 0.15 mm layers show unexpected flexibility (lower drape coefficient) due to bonding defects, while virtual simulations predict uniform behavior regardless of layer height. For practical applications, designers must recognize that simulation accuracy depends not only

Table 3. Physical and virtual samples with their Dice Coefficient (DC) values

Sample ID	Sample Group				
	S1	**S2**	**S3**	**S4**	**S5**
Physical Sample					
Virtual Sample					
DC (Physical)	55.18%	59.11%	54.45%	68.48%	74.05%
DC (Virtual)	55.14%	74.71%	77.27%	86.96%	80.28%
Sample ID	Sample Group				
	S6	**S7**	**S8**	**S9**	**S10**
Physical Sample					
Virtual Sample					
DC (Physical)	70.88%	74.89%	72.68%	76.16%	81.73%
DC (Virtual)	83.82%	88.30%	94.91%	96.02%	96.94%
Sample ID	Sample Group				
	S11	**S12**	**S13**	**S14**	**S15**
Physical Sample					
Virtual Sample					
DC (Physical)	83.42%	82.96%	86.80%	84.14%	90.52%
DC (Virtual)	92.89%	97.19%	98.40%	97.95%	97.67%

Table 4. Overall Comparison of Physical and Virtual Drape Coefficients (n = 15 physical samples)

Measurement Type	Mean (%)	SD (%)	Min (%)	Max (%)
Physical DC	74.36	11.25	54.45	88.98
Virtual DC	87.90	12.10	58.41	99.78
Prediction Error	13.53	6.17	3.96	24.29

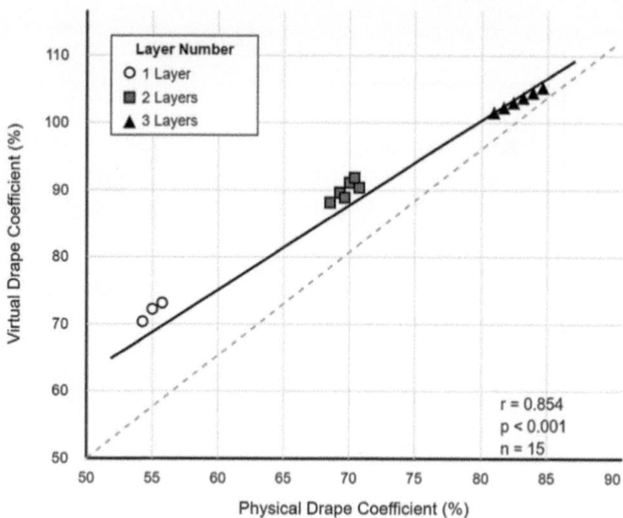

Fig. 3. Scatter Plot Physical vs. Virtual DC

Table 5. Statistical Comparisons

Statistical Test	Value	p-value	Effect Size
Paired t-test	$t(14) = 8.50$	< 0.001	Cohen's d = 2.19
Pearson correlation	$r = 0.854$	< 0.001	-

on geometric parameters but also on the manufacturing quality achievable with those parameters-making 0.20 mm subsequent layer heights preferable for both simulation reliability and consistent physical properties.

4.3   Effect of Layer Number on Drape Coefficient

Layer number showed the strongest influence on draping behavior, as illustrated in Fig. 4. Physical DC increased linearly: 56.25% (SD = 2.41%) for single-layer, 72.86% (SD = 2.80%) for two-layer, and 84.93% (SD = 3.14%) for three-layer structures. ANOVA confirmed highly significant effects ($F(2,12) = 125.47$, p < 0.001, $\eta^2 = 0.954$), with all pairwise comparisons significant (p < 0.001).

Virtual simulations amplified this effect: 69.04% (SD = 10.57%), 88.38% (SD = 5.92%), and 96.84% (SD = 1.92%) for one, two, and three layers respectively ($F(2,12) = 28.89$, p < 0.001, $\eta^2 = 0.828$). Three-layer samples approached saturation, suggesting algorithmic limitations.

Prediction errors (12.79%, 15.52%, 11.91% for 1–3 layers) were not significantly different ($F(2,12) = 0.48$, p $= 0.630$), indicating proportional overesti-

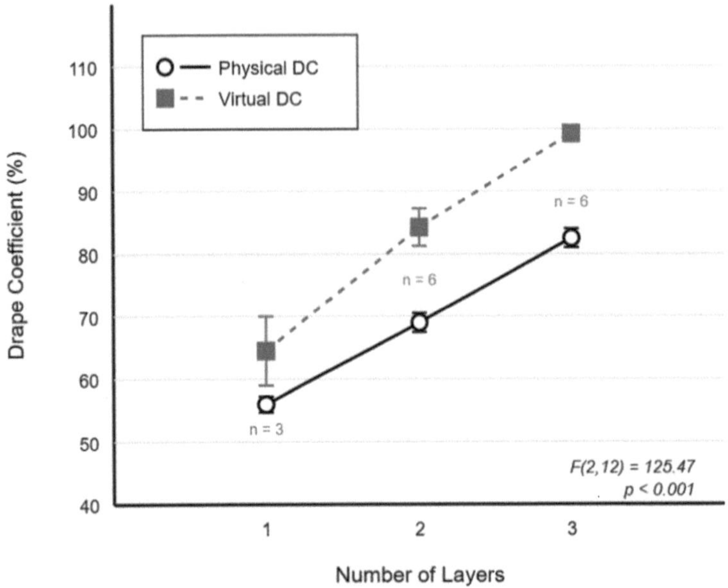

Fig. 4. Layer Number Effect on Drape Coefficient

mation across layers. This consistency enables reliable calibration for graduated stiffness applications. These results are summarized in Table 6.

4.4 Effect of Infill Density on Drape Coefficient

Physical DC showed modest increases with infill density: 72.57% (SD = 10.68%) at 20%, 74.93% (SD = 10.27%) at 40%, and 75.59% (SD = 12.94%) at 60% ($F(2,12) = 0.11$, p = 0.899, not significant).

Virtual simulations showed stronger effects: 82.44% (SD = 15.54%), 88.48% (SD = 9.24%), and 92.76% (SD = 8.23%) for 20%, 40%, 60% respectively ($F(2,12) = 1.28$, p = 0.313).

Single-layer 60% infill samples showed anomalous behavior (M = 54.45%, SD = 1.08%), with increasingly linear infill trajectories compromising inter-line adhesion. This effect may extend to multi-layer samples, as the modest 3% physical DC increase from 20% to 60% infill suggests manufacturing constraints limit expected stiffness gains.

Prediction error increased significantly with infill density: 9.87% (20%), 13.56% (40%), 17.17% (60%), approaching significance ($F(2,12) = 3.12$, p = 0.081). The simulation's inability to account for inter-line adhesion limitations causes growing discrepancies at high densities, as shown in Table 6.

Notably, the porous and mesh-like nature of 3D printed textiles increases modeling complexity and reduces simulation accuracy, as fine structural details are often oversimplified during the simulation process.

Table 6. Effects of Production Parameters on Drape Coefficients

Parameter	n	Physical DC (%)		Virtual DC (%)		Prediction Error (%)	
		Mean	SD	Mean	SD	Mean	SD
A. Layer Number Effects							
1 Layer	3	56.25	2.41	69.04	10.57	12.79	10.25
2 Layers	6	72.86	2.80	88.38	5.92	15.52	5.62
3 Layers	6	84.93	3.14	96.84	1.92	11.91	3.05
ANOVA	$F(2,12) = 125.47^{***}$			$F(2,12) = 28.89^{***}$		$F(2,12) = 0.48$	
B. Subsequent Layer Height Effects (Multi-layer samples only)							
0.15 mm	6	76.81	6.62	92.96	5.77	16.15	3.46
0.20 mm	6	80.97	6.62	92.26	6.63	11.29	4.82
t-test	$t(10) = 1.09$			$t(10) = 0.19$		$t(10) = 2.01^{*}$	
C. Infill Density Effects							
20%	5	72.57	10.68	82.44	15.54	9.87	6.91
40%	5	74.93	10.27	88.48	9.24	13.56	1.65
60%	5	75.59	12.94	92.76	8.23	17.17	6.31
ANOVA	$F(2,12) = 0.11$			$F(2,12) = 1.28$		$F(2,12) = 3.12†$	

Note: * p < 0.05 (one-tailed), *** p < 0.001, †p < 0.10

4.5 Regression Models and Calibration Development

Analysis of variance revealed no significant interactions between production parameters for physical drape coefficient, virtual drape coefficient, or prediction error when analyzed using physical sample means (all p ¿ 0.05). This independence simplifies optimization strategies and enables straightforward predictive modeling.

Virtual DC model:

$$\text{Virtual DC (\%)} = 41.34 + 13.69 \times \text{Layer Number} + 0.23 \times \text{Infill Density} - 5.71 \times \text{Layer Height} \tag{2}$$

$(R^2 = 0.906, F(3,11) = 35.47, p < 0.001)$

Prediction error model:

$$\text{Prediction Error (\%)} = 21.89 - 0.15 \times \text{Layer Number} + 0.30 \times \text{Infill Density} - 4.36 \times \text{Layer Height} \tag{3}$$

$(R^2 = 0.497, F(3, 11) = 3.62, p = 0.049)$

Calibration formula:

$$\text{Calibrated DC (\%)} = \text{Virtual DC}$$
$$- (21.89 - 0.15 \times \text{Layer Number} \tag{4}$$
$$+ 0.30 \times \text{Infill Density} - 4.36 \times \text{Layer Height})$$

Leave-one-out cross-validation showed calibration reduced mean absolute error from 13.53% to 8.75%, a 35.3% improvement. The regression models and calibration formula are summarized in Table 7.

Table 7. Multiple Regression Models (n = 15 physical samples)

	B	SE	β	t	p
A. Virtual Drape Coefficient Model					
Intercept	41.34	4.85	-	8.52	< 0.001
Layer Number	13.69	1.18	0.825	11.60	< 0.001
Infill Density (%)	0.23	0.06	0.287	3.83	0.003
Layer Height (mm)	−5.71	2.57	−0.153	−2.22	0.048
Model Statistics: $R^2 = 0.906$, Adjusted $R^2 = 0.881$, F(3,11) = 35.47, p < 0.001					
B. Prediction Error Model					
Intercept	21.89	6.42	-	3.41	0.006
Layer Number	−0.15	1.57	−0.018	−0.10	0.925
Infill Density (%)	0.30	0.08	0.602	3.75	0.003
Layer Height (mm)	−4.36	3.40	−0.186	−1.28	0.226
Model Statistics: $R^2 = 0.497$, Adjusted $R^2 = 0.360$, F(3,11) = 3.62, p = 0.049					

4.6 Validation with Supplementary Samples

Temperature variation (210 °C vs 230 °C) showed negligible effects on draping (74.2% vs 74.8%), providing manufacturing flexibility. Validation samples confirmed calibration effectiveness, reducing error from 13.2% to 7.8%.

5 Conclusion

This study provides the first comprehensive validation of virtual drape simulations for FDM 3D printed textiles, revealing fundamental differences between simulation assumptions and manufacturing reality. Virtual simulations consistently overestimate stiffness by 13.53% points because they model idealized geometries without accounting for manufacturing defects like under-extrusion and compromised inter-layer adhesion that affect physical samples.

Our calibration model, which reduces prediction error by 35.3%, represents a novel contribution enabling reliable virtual prototyping of 3D printed textiles. This advancement allows designers to confidently use virtual simulations when following our parameter guidelines: prioritize 0.20 mm layer heights with one or two layers for errors below 12%, while avoiding 0.15 mm layers where errors exceed 16%.

Layer number emerged as the dominant parameter affecting drape behavior ($F(2,12) = 125.47$, $p < 0.001$), followed by subsequent layer height effects in multi-layer structures. The parameter independence observed enables sophisticated design strategies—designers can create spatially varied properties by modifying parameters locally while maintaining predictable simulation accuracy.

These findings directly benefit the 3D printing community by reducing physical prototyping, accelerating development cycles, and supporting sustainable design practices. Additionally, the porous and mesh-like nature of 3D printed textiles introduces modeling and meshing complexity that can further reduce simulation precision, highlighting the need for future work on geometry-aware simulation methods tailored to textile structures. As 3D printing technology advances, accurate material behavior simulation becomes increasingly critical for realizing the full potential of digitally manufactured garments. Future work should explore alternative materials (Shore 85A, 92A TPU) and infill patterns (star, auxetic), investigate dynamic draping behavior, and develop simulation algorithms that account for manufacturing-induced variations.

Acknowledgments. This research was supported by the Wilson College of Textiles at North Carolina State University.

Disclosure of Interests. The authors have no competing interests to declare that are relevant to the content of this article.

References

1. Acierno, D., Patti, A.: Fused Deposition Modelling (FDM) of thermoplastic-based filaments: process and rheological properties - an overview. Materials **16**(24), 7664 (2023)
2. Adidas: 4DFWD: Data-driven 3D printed performance technology designed to move you forward (2021). https://news.adidas.com/4d/4dfwd--data-driven-3d-printed-performance-technology-designed-to-move-you-forward/s/514baddb-1029-4686-abd5-5ee3985a304a
3. Ameen, W., Al-Ahmari, A., Mohammed, M.K.: Design for additive manufacturing: a comprehensive review. J. Manuf. Syst. **66**, 302–328 (2023)
4. Baraff, D., Witkin, A.: Large steps in cloth simulation. In: Proceedings of the 25th Annual Conference on Computer Graphics and Interactive Techniques, pp. 43–54 (1998)
5. Benamira, M., Dekhane, A., Ayad, A., Benhassine, N.: Investigation of printing parameters effects on mechanical and failure properties of 3D Printed PLA. Eng. Fail. Anal. **148**, 107218 (2023)

6. Bilalis, N., Papahristou, E.: A new sustainable product development model in apparel based on 3D technologies for virtual proper fit. In: Sustainable Design and Manufacturing, pp. 85–95 (2016)

7. Bizjak, M., Čuk, M., Muck, D.: 3D printing and functionalization of textiles. In: Proceedings - The Tenth International Symposium GRID 2020 (2020)

8. Chacón, J.M., Caminero, M.A., García-Plaza, E., Núñez, P.J.: Additive manufacturing of PLA structures using fused deposition modelling: effect of process parameters on mechanical properties and their optimal selection. Mater. Des. **124**, 143–157 (2017)

9. Choi, K.: 3D digital technology in upcycling apparel design: the creation of a modular redesign system and designer perspectives. Int. J. Fashion Des. Technol. Educ. (2024)

10. Dai, X., Hong, Y.: Fabric mechanical parameters for 3D cloth simulation in apparel CAD: a systematic review. Comput. Aided Des. **167**, 103638 (2023)

11. Dior: La Galerie Dior: Exhibition of archival garments [Exhibition]. La Galerie Dior, Paris (2021). https://www.galeriedior.com/

12. Golan, O., Lachman, N., Bouzaglou, O.: Process design and parameters interaction in material extrusion 3D printing: a review. Polymers **15**(10), 2280 (2023)

13. Gramc, K., Muck, D., Čuk, M., Bizjak, M.: Influence of fabric structure on the adhesion and functional properties of 3D printed polymers on the woven fabric. Mater. Sci. Forum **1063**, 25–33 (2022)

14. Huang, Y., et al.: Evaluating ChatGPT-4.0's data analytic proficiency in epidemiological studies: a comparative analysis with SAS, SPSS, and R. J. Glob. Health **14**, 04070 (2024)

15. Jahan, I.: Effect of fabric structure on the mechanical properties of woven fabrics. Adv. Res. Textile Eng. **2**(2), 1018 (2017)

16. James, D., Yuksel, C., Kaldor, J., Marschner, S.: Stitch meshes for modeling knitted clothing with yarn-level detail. ACM Trans. Graph. **31**(4), 1–12 (2012)

17. Jeong, J., Park, H., Lee, Y., Kang, J., Chun, J.: Developing parametric design fashion products using 3D printing technology. Fashion Textiles **8**, 22 (2021)

18. Jiao, C., Yan, G.: Design and elastic mechanical response of a novel 3D-printed hexa-chiral helical structure with negative Poisson's ratio. Mater. Des. **210**, 110056 (2021)

19. Kabir, S., Li, Y., Salahuddin, M., Lee, Y.A.: Drapability of 3D-printed auxetic structure textiles for wearable products through the digital image processing technique. Cloth. Text. Res. J. **41**(2), 98–112 (2023)

20. Kim, J., Takahashi, H.: 3D printed fabric: techniques for design and 3D weaving programmable textiles. In: Proceedings of the 32nd Annual ACM Symposium on User Interface Software and Technology, pp. 43–55 (2019)

21. Mardiyana, D., Lesmana, R., Sumarno, D.: Analysis of the effect of print speed and layer height on the hardness of TPU-95A filament 3D-printed products. Jurnal Konversi Energi dan Manufaktur **10**(1), 12–20 (2025)

22. Morton, W., Hearle, J.: Physical Properties of Textile Fibres. Butterworth-Heinemann, Oxford (1962)

23. Mozafary, V., Payvandy, P.: Study and comparison techniques in fabric simulation using mass spring model. Int. J. Cloth. Sci. Technol. **28**(5), 634–689 (2016)

24. Qiu, Z., Youn, S., Mathur, K., Porterfield, A.: A comparative study of 3d simulation and scanning technologies for virtual fabric testing laboratory: tensile tester. In: Proceedings of 3DBODY.TECH 2023 - 14th International Conference and Exhibition on 3D Body Scanning and Processing Technologies (2023)

25. Roberts, S., Dorsey, K., Forman, J., Ishii, H.: Analysis of defextiles: a 3D printed textile towards garments and accessories. J. Micromech. Microeng. **32**(3), 035003 (2022)
26. Shea, K., Wirth, M.: Empirically tuned mechanical simulation model of 3D-printed biaxial weaves. In: Volume 3A: 49th Design Automation Conference (DAC) (2023)
27. Shea, A., Kabir, S., Lee, Y.A.: Tensile properties of 3D printed textile structures: effects of pattern geometry and layer orientation. Text. Res. J. **92**(15–16), 2667–2680 (2022)
28. Stig, F., Hallström, S.: Extended framework for geometric modelling of textile architectures. Compos. Struct. **244**, 112239 (2020)
29. Xiao, Y.-Q., Kan, C.-W.: Review on development and application of 3d-printing technology in textile and fashion design. Coatings **12**(2), 267 (2022)
30. Youn, S., Knowles, C.G., Mills, A.C., Mathur, K.: Comparative study of physical and virtual fabric parameters: physical versus virtual drape test using commercial 3D garment software. J. Textile Inst. **116**(1), 33–46 (2024)

How E-trust and E-satisfaction Mediate the Effects of Perceptions and E-loyalty in Apparel E-customisation

Lin Zhao[1,2], Boonsom Yodmalee[1(✉)], Pei Li[3], and Zi Yang Liu[4]

[1] Faculty of Fine-Applied Arts and Cultural Science, Mahasarakham University, Khamriang Sub-District, Kantarawichai District, Maha Sarakham 44150, Thailand
boonom.y@msu.ac.th
[2] Zhejiang Textile Engineering Society, Hangzhou, Zhejiang 310018, People's Republic of China
150432768@qq.com
[3] School of Textiles and Fashion, Shanghai University of Engineering Science, Shanghai 201620, People's Republic of China
pei.li@sues.edu.cn
[4] Kyonggi University, Suwon-Si, Gyeonggi-Do 16227, Republic of Korea
morninglzy@hotmail.com

Abstract. The purpose of this study is to explore factors related to this using theoretical framework based on the stimulus-organism-response (S-O-R) to study these the factors in relation to stimulus, organism and response when consumers use apparel e-customisation technology. The study focuses on effects of e-trust and e-satisfaction in apparel e-customisation. The variables of perceived information quality, perceived visual appeal, interactivity, perceived usefulness, perceived ease of use, perceived risk, e-trust, e-satisfaction and e-loyalty to the continued use of e-customisation are tested. Factor analysis, correlation analysis and a structural equational model are adopted for the data analysis. Consistent results from the study with data show that e-satisfaction has a more significant impact on e-loyalty to the continued use of apparel e-customsiation than e-trust. The study explores variables and build on previous studies regarding e-loyalty by providing suggestions for brand managers and online retailers regarding e-customisation marketing strategies.

Keywords: Stimulus · organism · response · E-trust · E-satisfaction · E-loyalty to the continued use of e-customisation

1 Introduction

With regard to consumer needs and communication, e-customisation technology has been adopted to enhance interaction between consumers and retailers [1]. As increasing number of consumers are participating in online interactive activities for product customisation, perceived information influences consumers' behaviour intentions in customisation [2]. E-customisation is to provide personalised clothing to consumers via

© The Author(s), under exclusive license to Springer Nature Switzerland AG 2026
V. G. Duffy (Ed.): HCII 2025, LNCS 16339, pp. 144–162, 2026.
https://doi.org/10.1007/978-3-032-13012-9_11

interfaces that allow them to communicate with other individuals [3]. E-customisation is realised through consumers' experiences, which are affected by perceived ease of use, perceived usefulness, entertainment, and perceived aesthetics [4]. When consumers customise clothing and review information online, they may have different feelings and perceptions about e-customisation technology. Less is known about the effect of e-customisation technology and influential factors. However, some consumers are likely to make decisions based on their perceptions in e-customisation [5]. In addition, based on the consumer innovative adoption model, Park, Han, and Park (2013) identified factors (e.g., the need for uniqueness, status aspiration, attitude, perceived risk and purchasing intention) and stated that whether consumers purchase e-customised products is affected by attitude [6]. Thus, it is important to explore influencial factors and meet consuemrs' personalised need in e-customisation [7, 8]. In e-customisation, the main research gap is that (a) the recommended information might not be perceived or accepted easily by consumers; (b) it does not involve efficient interaction between consumers and suppliers [9]; (c) there are many factors that might affect consumers' responses in e-customisation, which one may play more significant effects than others. In order to enrich online shopping experiences and improve service quality, e-customisation systems have been adopted by many brands (e.g., Cotte, Spread Shirt, Saint Angelo, Threadless.com, Ethreads.com, Nike ID, Vans, etc.). New challenges now faced by brands using e-customisation include how to keep consumers' e-loyalty.

The S-O-R framework is a kind of information processing model that is based on the individual's cognition and leads to a response from the stimuli [10]. Stimuli affect the cognitive and mental state of the assessing process (organism). People's cognitive or emotional experiences are affected by different stimuli, which triggers a series of behavioural responses [11]. The S-O-R framework has been widely demonstrated in the area of marketing and information management. Attributes of online shopping websites affect consumers' attitudes, which are predictors of online purchase intentions [12]. For example, researchers have adopted the S-O-R framework to explore consumers' online shopping behaviour and explain consumer loyalty, purchase intention and co-creation [13]. After applying the S-O-R model to online shopping, it was found that the model contributed to understanding the relationship between website characteristics, emotion and purchasing behaviour [14]. The S-O-R model has been adopted to explain the behavioural responses in certain online shopping environments [15]. Some online shopping atmospheric variables influenced consumers' e-satisfaction [16]. Online atmospheric variables, such as layout, graphics and design, can provide information for consumers that influences their attitudes and behaviour [17]. Based on the S-O-R paradigm, Zhang, Lu, Wang and Wu (2015) explored a model to improve consumers' co-creation experiences and affect intention to participate in co-creation [18]. In these studies, S-O-R is an important framework to explain the process of behaviour, judgement, intention and behaviour on online shopping. Hence, our study considers how perceptions affect e-loyalty to the continued use of e-customisation.

The motivation of this paper is to explore the factors relating to consumers' perceptions and e-loyalty in e-customisation, so as to contribute to theoretical research in apparel e-customisation technology, provide suggestions for brand managers and improve the quality of consumers' online experiences. Taking into account the above challenges, the objective of this study is to verify a new research framework by considering (a) the effects of e-e-trust and e-satisfaction on e-loyalty to the continued use of e-customisation, (b) an investigation into the impacts of consumers' perceptions and exploration of the influential variables in e-customisation technology using the S-O-R theoretical frameworks and, (c) the findings on the perceptions and acceptance of e-customisation technology. By introducing the construct of the theoretical framework, the perceptions (e.g., perceived information quality, perceived visual appeal, interactivity, perceived usefulness, perceived ease of use, perceived risk) are reviewed as stimuli; e-trust and e-satisfaction are reviewed as organisms; and e-loyalty to continued use of e-customisation is reviewed as response.

The rest of the paper is organised as follows. First, the literature review is presented. Second, we study the hypotheses and test the effects of e-trust and e-satisfaction on e-loyalty. Third, we explore the hypotheses and test the factor relationships. Finally, 'Discussion' and 'Implications, Limitations, and Future Research Direction' are provided in the last section.

2 Literature Review

2.1 E-loyalty

In recent years, researchers have studied how to enhance consumers' e-loyalty. The e-loyalty model has been identified as including three phases (i.e., cognitive, effectiveness and action), which proves that e-trust is an effective factor of e-loyalty [19]. For example, based on 252 samples of online apparel consumers in the United States, researchers demonstrated that service and e-satisfaction play important roles in maintaining e-loyalty [20]. In addition, e-satisfaction is a mediator between emotional value and loyalty intention [21], and e-trust and enjoyment are positively associated with e-loyalty [22]. In particular, consumers tend to be more loyal when brands garner a positive reputation or elicit an optimistic attitude [23]. E-loyalty can be explained by variables of e-satisfaction, e-trust, perceived website quality and switching barriers [24]. Previous studies have mainly focused on the factors of e-satisfaction or e-trust and their impacts on e-loyalty in online shopping experiences. We summarise the related literature on e-loyalty and online shopping in Table 1. Therefore, the important gap that needs to be filled is the relationship between e-satisfaction, e-trust, and e-loyalty in an e-customisation environment.

E-loyalty relies on consumer experiences, attitudes, e-trust and e-satisfaction in online shopping [30, 31]. Prior studies have demonstrated consumers' perceived value and examined the relationships between e-satisfaction, loyalty and consumer value. They suggest that consumer e-satisfaction with online customisation is influenced by hedonic, utilitarian, creative and social values, which in turn affect brand loyalty [32]. The level of e-loyalty is directly linked to the consumer experience provided by the e-customisation technology through the stimuli of virtual environments. Son et al. (2012) examined the effects of co-design websites and demonstrated that mass confusion significantly influences consumers' intentions to use websites [33]. These same consumers tend to determine the level of perception and share e-loyalty during the online consuming process. Previous research has explored the impact of factors in online shopping, but

Table 1. Literature on e-loyalty and online shopping.

Authors	Factors	Methods	Findings
[25]	e-satisfaction, e-loyalty, e-trust	Structural equation modelling	Both e-trust and e-satisfaction positively influence e-loyalty in female online shopping
[26]	e-loyalty, e-satisfaction, technology acceptance factor	Structural equation modelling, confirmatory factor analysis	E-satisfaction positively influence customer e-loyalty directly Technology acceptance factors will positively influence e-loyalty and e-satisfaction directly
[27]	e-loyalty, e-satisfaction, modified eTailQ scale	Exploratory factor analysis, confirmatory factor analysis, structural equation modelling	E-loyalty is positively influenced by satisfaction in online shopping
[28]	e-loyalty, e-satisfaction, e-service quality	Structural equation modelling, confirmatory factor analysis	E-service quality is positively related with e-loyalty and e-satisfaction
[29]	e-satisfaction, e-loyalty, e-service quality	Structural equation modelling,	E-service quality is positively related to e-satisfaction E-satisfaction is positively related to e-loyalty

whether and how differential factors influence consumers' e-loyalty of e-customisation technology still needs more research.

2.2 E-trust, Perceived Visual Appeal, Perceived Information Quality and Interactivity

Trust is defined as when a consumer fulfils a task and his/her expectation is met, which is related to social and ethical values [34]. Trust is an important factor of brand profitability and market development [35]. Reichheld and Schefter (2000) state that 'to gain the loyalty of customers, you must first gain their trust. That has always been the case but on the web…it is truer than ever' (pp.107) [36]. The issue of e-trust in e-commerce has been explored since the end of the 1990s. Compared to trust, e-trust refers to the general trust of consumers in the internet infrastructure [37]. In online shopping, e-trust has a significant relationship with the factors of perceived ease of use, website usefulness, and willingness to customise products and services [31, 38]. Furthermore, after studying 482 women and their online shopping experiences in Taiwan, Chou,

Chen, and Lin (2015) discussed the concept of e-loyalty development, pointing out that the e-trust and e-satisfaction of female consumers positively influence e-loyalty [25]. Kim, Jin and Swinney (2009) identified the significant effect of e-trust on the e-loyalty development process [39]. Researchers have found that e-trust is influenced by website usability and appeal [40]. Consumers use a website to purchase products by searching, finding, selecting, comparing, and evaluating items online. The aesthetics of the sites influence visual appeal, which triggers consumers' emotions and attitudes to the websites. Consumer behaviours and intentions are influenced by visual design in the personalised apparel co-design process, including the selection of colours, fabrics, styles, details, decorations and patterns [41]. If consumers find the visual information appealing, they tend to have positive feelings and attitudes to the website [42]. Additionally, the aesthetic appeal of an e-tailing website has a positive effect on task-free consumers' attitudes towards the website [43]. Cyr et al. (2009) found that image appeal positively influenced consumer e-trust in online shopping [44]. We draw from the previous findings that examined the visual appeal of websites evoking positive cognition and emotions of individuals with consequent rewards for the website. Furthermore, consumer perceptions are directly affected by the interactivity and usability of a website [45].

Information quality is regarded as 'specific content [and] content quality' [46]. Percieved information quality is defined as the information meets users' requirements and desires and is affected by consumer judgements [11, 47]. The more credible the information is perceived to be, the less risk is suffered, and consumers have a higher intention to continue using the technology [48]. They proposed that shoppers rely on information quality for e-trust and entertainment. The information quality of clothing websites relates to consumers' online shopping intentions [45]. Discontinuity of and changes to perceived product information influence consumers' e-trust and purchase intentions [49]. Zhu et al. (2020) have proposed an S-O-R research model of online reviews, which asserts that perceived information quality positively affects e-trust [11]. Therefore, the perceived information quality is adopted as a factor of stimuli in e-customisation.

Interactivity is defined as two-way communication regarding personalised products or services on the internet, including user–machine interaction, user–user interaction and user–message interaction [7]. Zeithaml et al. (2002) define interactivity as (a) communicating with people, (b) searching for information, and (c) conducting transactions via websites [50]. More relevant to the present study, e-trust is influenced by the perceived interactivity of online shopping, which also contributes to consumers' continuance shopping behaviours [51]. Consumers achieve customisation and personalisation via online interactivity which is a key factor in influencing consumers' positive attitudes towards e-trust [9, 52–54].

2.3 E-Satisfaction, Perceived Usefulness, Perceived Ease of Use and Perceived Risk

Satisfaction is an online retailing experience that focuse on assessing consumers' satisfaction judgements in internet shopping [55, 56]. E-satisfaction is described as a positive emotion response [57]; consumers' judgment of their experiences in an e-business environment [58]; and the attitudinal levels of e-loyalty in online shopping [59]. With e-commerce technology support, e-satisfaction is the contentment of consumers for his or her previous purchasing experiences [60]. E-satisfaction directly influences consumers continuance intention while, at the same time, consumers who are satisfied tend to be more loyal [61, 62]. In addition, several studies have examined and identified e-satisfaction as one of the most important factors for e-loyalty [27, 63]. Based on the perceptions of website service quality, researchers identified that e-satisfaction plays a significant role in determining and affecting e-loyalty in the context of online shopping [26, 27, 39].

Perceived usefulness (PU) and perceived ease of use (PEOU) are important factors in studies explored by technology acceptance model [62, 64]. Both PU and PEOU explain the effect of innovative processes and services on technology systems [64]. In mobile commerce, there are certain key factors that influence consumer e-satisfaction, including technology usefulness and ease of use [31]. PEOU influences mobile users' e-satisfaction [30]. Lin and Sun (2009) argue that online shopping experiences should consider external and internal factors [26]. Their research results confirmed that e-satisfaction is affected by the perception of information systems and technology acceptance factors (e.g., PEOU, PU) directly. The results also confirmed the significant effect of e-satisfaction on e-loyalty.

Risk is an important factor in online co-design as consumers share their information and comments with unknown persons [33]. Perceived risk includes the constructs of social loss, losing or wasting income, or being unable to meet needs. Consumers perceive a higher risk in online shopping than in physical retail stores [39]. There are some risks in e-commerce, such as supplying personal information, internet credit card theft, the lack of physical contact, and internet addiction [65]. Researchers have examined the uncertainty-related factors of the internet, including the perceived risk of privacy protection, uncertainties regarding products and limited information [64]. Perceived risk is not only a predictor of e-satisfaction leading to loyalty, it also moderates the relationship between e-satisfaction and loyalty [66]. Moreover, consumers who prefer e-customised clothing tend to have a personalised status that may have a perception of high risk [6]. They highlight the moderating effects of perceived risk on e-customised products. This study retains the idea that perceived risk is regarded by consumers as negative in relation to online shopping information.

3   Methodological Procedures

Supported by the previous literature review and hypothesis development, the research model of the present study is based on the framework of and S-O-R (see Fig. 1). The objective is to explore factors relating to the perceptions of e-customisation technology to investigate how perspective works within the proposed research framework. This research explores and examines whether different stimuli lead to different responses in e-customisation.

The study examines the effects of e-satisfaction, trust and e-loyalty to the continued use of e-customisation. Previous research has shown that, when consumers' e-loyalty is consistent with their perceived e-satisfaction, e-loyalty is derived from their experiences in e-customisation. The study demonstrates that perceptions may influence e-loyalty to the continued use of e-customisation. The variables of perceived information quality

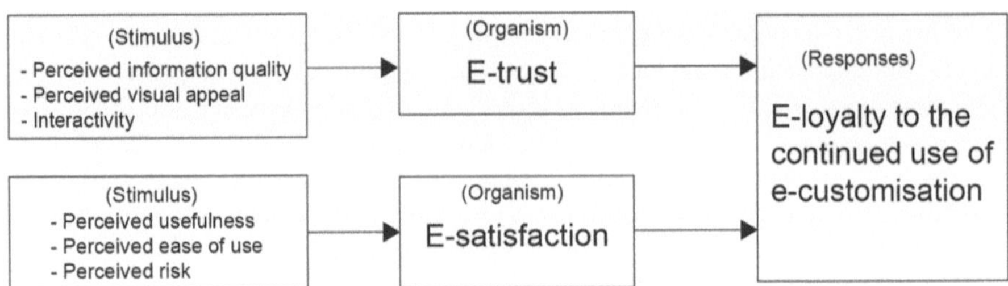

Fig. 1. Proposed research framework.

(PIQ), perceived visual appeal (PVA), interactivity (IN), e-trust (ET), perceived usefulness (PU), perceived ease of use (PEOU), perceived risk (PR), e-satisfaction (ES), and e-loyalty to the continued use of e-customisation (ECUC) are tested. The hypotheses are presented as follows.

H1-H3. Perceived information quality (H1), perceived visual appeal (H2), and interactivity (H3) positively impact e-trust in e-customisation.

H4. E-trust positively impacts e-loyalty to the continued use of e-customisation.

H5a. Perceived visual appeal and interactivity significantly impact each other in e-customisation.

H5b. Perceived visual appeal and perceived information quality significantly impact each other in e-customisation.

H5c. Interactivity and perceived information quality significantly impact each other in e-customisation.

H6-H7. Perceived usefulness (H6) and perceived ease of use (H7) positively impact consumer e-satisfaction in e-customisation.

H8. Perceived risk negatively impacts e-satisfaction in e-customisation.

H9. E-satisfaction positively impacts e-loyalty to the continued use of e-customisation.

H10a. Perceived usefulness and perceived ease of use significantly impact each other in e-customisation.

H10b. Perceived usefulness and perceived risk significantly impact each other in e-customisation.

H10c. Perceived ease of use and perceived risk significantly impact each other in e-customisation.

3.1 Participants and Design

The sample consists of consumers who enrolled online. The participants have shopped for and/or participated in e-customisation in the past six months. The participants were invited to join this study via social networks (e.g., WeChat, QQ and email). The participants were volunteers and did not receive compensation. This study developed items from prior literature and modified them to improve their quality for e-customisation (see Appendix A). These items were translated into Mandarin by a researcher, and another researcher translated them back into English in order to maintain their quality. Demographic data was collected.

3.2 Procedure

The study consisted of three tasks and a presentation to introduce the purpose of the questionnaire and measure participants' e-customisation experience. First, participants were randomly selected, all having bought or reviewed e-customisation in the past six months. Second, participants were asked to finish the questionnaires online in a quiet room. Seven-point Likert-type scales were adopted for all items (ranging from '1 = strongly disagree' to '7 = strongly agree'). Third, the demographics were collected.

3.3 Results

There were 203 total samples consisting of 127 women and 76 men. The distribution of the participants' ages was as follows: 18–22 years (93.1%, the middle ages = 21), 23–27 years, (5.4%), and 28–32 years (1.5%).

In order to test the correlated items of the e-trust-loyalty model, principal axis factor analysis was conducted using 17 items with an orthogonal rotation. The variables had a high loading as all of them were above 0.4, as shown in Table 2.

Table 2. Factor analysis and reliability.

Items	1	2	3	4	5
Perceived information quality (Cronbach's α = 0.836)					
PIQ3	0.760	0.195	0.155	-.058	.056
PIQ4	0.746	0.357	0.203	-.065	.070
PIQ2	0.730	0.066	0.048	0.106	-0.017
PIQ1	0.498	0.297	0.258	0.193	0.239
PIQ5	0.431	0.336	0.264	0.125	0.237
Interactivity (Cronbach's α = 0.875)					
IN1	0.259	0.839	0.266	-0.012	-0.056
IN2	0.280	0.825	0.198	-0.015	0.101
IN3	0.295	0.591	0.300	0.029	0.177
E-Trust (Cronbach's α = 0.814)					
ET3	0.154	0.233	0.810	0.056	0.081
ET4	0.208	0.267	0.727	0.090	0.111
ET2	0.182	0.095	0.715	0.207	0.128
ET1	0.035	.370	0.442	-0.038	-0.048

(continued)

Table 2. (*continued*)

Items	1	2	3	4	5
E-loyalty to the continued use of e-customisation (Cronbach's $\alpha = 0.757$)					
ECUC1	0.045	0.011	0.142	0.872	0.147
ECUC2	0.035	0.047	0.126	0.858	0.077
ECUC3	0.018	-0.026	-0.003	0.422	0.022
Perceived visual appeal (Cronbach's $\alpha = 0.775$)					
PVA2	0.001	-0.032	0.016	0.122	0.924
PVA1	0.149	0.131	0.161	0.096	0.655

Note. PIQ = perceived information quality; IN = interactivity; ET = e-trust; ECUC = e-loyalty to the continued use of e-customisation; and PVA = perceived visual appeal

The relationships among the variables were measured. The five items regarding perceived information quality were retained based on a Cronbach's β_a of 0.836. Cronbach's β_b was 0.775 for the perceived visual appeal factor. The items of interactivity had a Cronbach's SE_a of 0.875. The four items regarding e-trust had a Cronbach's SE_b of 0.814. Three e-loyalty items related to the e-loyalty to the continued use of e-customisation were retained ($\alpha = 0.757$).

Table 3. Correlations in Model 1.

		Mean	SD	Correlations				
				1	2	3	4	5
1	PIQ	4.5	0.9	1				
2	PVA	3.9	0.9	0.35**	1			
3	IN	4.2	1.2	0.49**	0.40**	1		
4	ET	4.2	1.1	0.38**	0.77**	0.56**	1	
5	ECUC	3.6	1.1	0.16**	0.78**	0.06**	0.20**	1

Note. **$p \leq 0.01$; SD = standard deviation

The correlated factors are assessed in Table 3. The moderate correlation range was 0.06–0.78. E-trust was weakly correlated with e-loyalty to the continued use of e-customisation (.20).

The relationships among the variables are shown in Fig. 2. There were good results for the relationships between factors. The RMSEA was equal to 0.10, with CFI = 0.87, GFI = 0.84, and the minimum discrepancy/degree of freedom (CMIN/df) = 3.12.

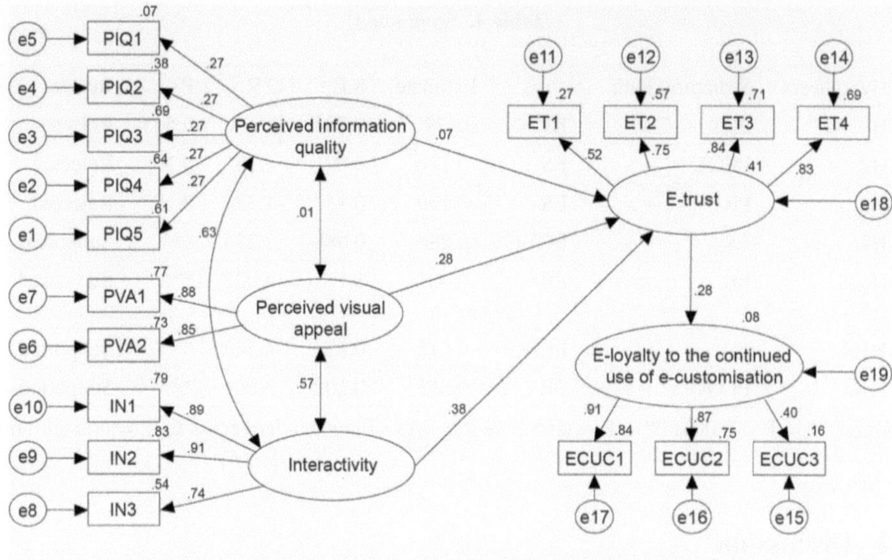

Note. GFI = .84   CFI = .87   AGFI = .78   RMSEA = .10   CMIN/df = 349.17/112 = 3.12

Fig. 2. Standardised loading of the measurement Model 1.

The standardised path coefficient (β) between perceived information quality and e-trust was 0.07, but there was no positive impact on e-trust (p = 0.545). Perceived information quality and perceived visual appeal were not positively correlated (β = 0.58, p = 0.273), and there was no effect on perceived information quality and interactivity (β = 0.63, p = 0.273). Other relationships were confirmed. Perceived visual appeal had a positive effect on e-trust (β = 0.28, p ≤ 0.01), interactivity also had a positive effect on e-trust (β = 0.38, p ≤ 0.001) and perceived visual appeal and interactivity were positively correlated (β = 0.57, p ≤ 0.001). Four of the hypotheses were supported (H2, H3, H4, H5a), and three were rejected (H1, H5b, H5c). The effects are presented in Table 4.

Table 4. Hypothesized paths effects.

Hypotheses	Structural Path			Estimate	S.E	C.R	P	Result
H1	PIQ	-- >	ET	0.474	0.783	0.605	0.545	Rejected
H2	PVA	-- >	ET	0.174	0.062	2.816	0.005	Supported
H3	IN	-- >	ET	0.273	0.078	3.479	***	Supported
H4	ET	-- >	ECUC	0.203	0.07	2.903	0.004	Supported
H5a	PVA	< -- >	IN	0.709	0.125	5.694	***	Supported
H5b	PVA	< -- >	PIQ	0.078	0.071	1.095	0.273	Rejected
H5c	IN	< -- >	PIQ	0.072	0.066	1.097	0.273	Rejected
H6	PU	-- >	ES	0.471	0.146	3.226	***	Supported

(*continued*)

Table 4. (*continued*)

Hypotheses	Structural Path			Estimate	S.E	C.R	P	Result
H1	PIQ	-- >	ET	0.474	0.783	0.605	0.545	Rejected
H7	PEOU	-- >	ES	0.126	0.091	1.38	0.168	Rejected
H8	PR	-- >	ES	-0.199	0.15	-1.33	0.183	Rejected
H9	ES	-- >	ECUC	0.286	0.088	3.234	***	Supported
H10a	PU	< -- >	PR	0.401	0.1	4.022	***	Supported ara>
H10b	PU	< -- >	PEOU	0.612	0.129	4.743	***	Supported
H10c	PEOU	< -- >	PR	0.365	0.102	3.564	***	Supported

Note. *** = P < 0.001; ** = P < 0.05; * = P < 0.1; S.E. = standard error; C.R. = critical ratio

4 Discussion

This study proposes that consumers' e-loyalty can be impacted by factors in the e-customisation environment. However, less is known about these variables and e-loyalty's reliance on perceptions of e-customisation. The study confirmed the effects of e-trust, e-satisfaction in the research framework. The wide range of e-customisation technology and how it is perceived in an online context shows its potential effects on marketing strategy. Our research contributes to the literature regarding e-loyalty in e-customisation several ways.

Prior research suggests that e-trust is a critical factor in repurchasing e-customised apparel [39]. To the best of the authors' knowledge, the study examines whether and how e-trust impacts e-loyalty, which indicates that e-trust has a positive effect on e-loyalty to the continued use of e-customisation ($\beta = 0.28$, $p \leq 0.01$). The current research fills the gaps in the literature about attitude in e-customisation. Furthermore, previous findings have suggested that consumer e-trust is achieved via engagement, interactions regarding apparel e-customisation [67, 68]. Our research suggests that perceived visual appeal and interactivity have positive impacts on each other, and they both positively influence e-trust. When the e-customisation system is perceived as appealing and interactivity, consumers tend to e-trust it. In e-commerce, photos and positive reputation contribute to e-trust and higher purchase rates [49]. We also found that there is no relationship between e-trust and perceived information quality in e-customisation. This result is in line with the previous studies, where the impact of information quality has no impact on e-trust in electronic retailing [69]. In this respect, online retailers and managers should make an effort to maintain consumers' e-trust rather than merely emphasising perceived information quality on websites.

In addition, the results confirmed that there is no link between perceived visual appeal and perceived information quality or interactivity and perceived information quality, but perceived visual appeal and interactivity have a close relationship in e-customising clothing. These results suggest that improving visual appeal and interactivity can positively influence consumers' intentions, which has no relation to perceived information quality. This finding contributes to the e-marketing strategy in e-customisation.

We find that e-loyalty to the continued use of e-customisation is significantly affected by e-satisfaction, which is consistent with prior studies [24, 32, 57]. In this regard, online retailers should be aware that, if consumers are not satisfied, they might not repurchase e-customised products or maintain their loyalty to the brand. Additionally, PU positively impacts e-satisfaction. In other earlier research, there is a strong effect between PU and e-satisfaction [26]. In our context, e-customisation technology may provide information on usefulness and categories that can perceive the utility of the e-customisation system. In order to enhance e-satisfaction, brand retailers should strive to improve PU by providing effective information, good online services and website content. Meanwhile, PEOU and perceived risk have no significant impact on e-satisfaction, which is consistent with Udo, Bgchi and Kirs's (2010) findings regarding e-business environments [57]. This is also consistent with the fact that PEOU has no significant effect on attitude towards apparel e-customisation [64]. Therefore, PU has been deemed more important than PEOU and perceived risk in e-customisation. It is vital for online retailers to improve consumers' perception on usefulness. Once the website is useful, consumers will be more satisfied and this could extend their e-loyalty in apparel e-customisation.

Importantly, there are significant relationships between PU, PEOU and perceived risk when it comes to customising apparel online. This is consistent with the results of previous studies that state that PEOU and PU are positively correlated [35, 64]. Moreover, the findings of this study verified that perceived risk is an important factor in e-customisation. This finding is therefore important for online retailers, who should be aware of the importance of the relationships between PU, PEOU and perceived risk when they enhance consumer e-loyalty in e-customisation.

5 Implications, Limitations and Future Research Directions

The study contributes to growing research on e-customisation and investigate whether perceptions have an effect on e-trust and e-satisfaction that is likely to influence e-loyalty to continued use of e-customisation. This research has implications for the e-customisation research and consumer process research and is useful for managers who are interested in promoting the personalised e-customisation services for consumers.

5.1 Theoretical Implications

The most important theoretical implication of this paper is that it shows the effect of perceptions on consumer attitudes and intentions in e-customisation. While e-trust, e-satisfaction, and e-loyalty have been previously researched in the context of online shopping, limited empirical research has been done regarding e-customisation. The different perceptions need to be explored with an emphasis on perception characteristics. This study also takes a complex approach to personalised e-customisation and contributes to the literature by exploring perceptions, that is, combining the effects of e-loyalty on the continued use of e-customisation. We found e-satisfaction and e-trust affect e-loyalty to the continued use of e-customisation, which can contribute to theoretical research in the future.

Furthermore, the proposed research framework contributes to theoretically explain consumer motives and different perceptions and their relationship to attitude in the context of e-customisation. After all, the different perceptions form the basis of the responses on which technology acceptance is determined, through the perceived stimulus in e-customisation. These perceptions influence consumers' attitude and behaviour. From this theoretical perspective, it can be argued that the different perceptions should be explored to enrich the theoretical framework of S-O-R. This paper provides a deeper explanation of e-customisation under the stimuli that may lead to increased intention to use and/or co-create. Moreover, this paper confirms the importance of examining factors and relationships in e-customisation as a contribution to the literature.

5.2 Managerial Implications

This has implications for online service management in the information era, which is motivating consumers to evolve in clothing e-customisation. Instead, managers should investigate consumers' perceptions of their information and services and develop online strategies that meet consumers' requirements in e-customisation. Moreover, by focusing on existing stimuli, managers should also make sure they focus their strategies on offering personalised services that help them to please consumers and lead to e-trust and e-satisfaction. If consumers are able to confirm that they are satisfied with the e-customisation services, their e-loyalty is more likely to be retained.

Brands should be aware of the perceptions that motivate consumers to put their time and effort into e-loyalty to the continued use of e-customisation. This may be employed by managers to provide personalised services in order to increase consumers' e-loyalty. Previously, some perceptions have been proposed, however findings here indicate that some factors are more important than others in e-customisation. For instance, compared to perceived information quality, both perceived visual appeal and interactivity positively affect e-trust, perceived usefulness has more effect on e-satisfaction than perceived ease of use and perceived risk, e-trust and e-satisfaction positively influence e-loyalty to the continued use of e-customisation. The results may prove useful for managers as a combination of consumers' perceptions in e-customisation technology development that leads to continued use intention. In particular, brands should be aware that some factors are more important than others, which explains purchasing intention and could help online retailers develop effective marketing strategies.

5.3 Limitations and Future Research Directions

In terms of sample size and the sampling method, the sample might not have been representative, as the sample consisted of young participants, so this may limit the findings. This paper offers insights into how perception variables may explain e-customisation e-trust, e-satisfaction and e-loyalty, which indicates that some factors are more important than others. Future work should explore if there are one or more factors that dominate perceptions and influence e-loyalty greatly.

The data was collected in one country. Researchers could consider the comparisons in different countries or regional areas in the future. Additionally, this study examines the perceptions and attitudes in e-customisation. Since the findings identify the effects of perceptions and attitudes in e-customisation, future studies in e-customisation should include more factors to explain consumer behaviour. Finally, the multi-method approach should be adopted for the study of e-customisation technology acceptance, such as interviews and group surveys. The multi-method approach may contribute to marketing strategies and consumer behaviour. On the whole, this study provides evidence that examines the combination of perceptions in order to explore relationships between perception, e-trust, e-satisfaction and e-loyalty to the continued use of e-customisation. The S-O-R theory are applied to establish the importance of analysing relationships between variables.

Appendix a. Measurements and Scales.

Construct	Measurements and scales	Sources
Perceived information quality (PIQ)	PIQ1-The website labels are easy to understand	[45]
	PIQ2-The display pages are easy to read	
	PIQ3-The information on the website is effective	
	PIQ4-It would be easy for me to become skillful at using the co-design website	
	PIQ5-The information on the website is pretty much what I would need to complete my purchase	
Interactivity (IN)	IN1-I can interact with the website in order to get information customized to my specific needs	[34, 45]
	IN2-The website allows me to interact with other users in order to receive customized information	
	IN3-My interaction with this website is clear and understandable	
E-trust (ET)	ET1-I feel that I am respected on this website	[38, 70]
	ET2-Infromation from this website is reliable	
	ET3-I believe promises on this website will be kept	
	ET4-Overall, this website is trustworthy	

(*continued*)

(continued)

Construct	Measurements and scales	Sources
E-loyalty to the continued use of e-customisation (ECUC)	ECUC1-I would use online customization in shopping for clothing if it was available	[33, 71, 72]
	ECUC2-I intend to use this kind of website in the future to create my clothing	
	ECUC3-I intend to learn more about this kind of website	
Perceived visual appeal (PVA)	PVA1-The website displays a visually pleasing design	[46, 73]
	PVA2-The website is visually appealing	
Perceived ease of use (PEOU)	PEOU1-It's easy to learn to operate this website	[34, 74]
	PEOU2-I find it easy to get this website to do what I want to do	
	PEOU3-It is easy to become skillful at using this website	
	PEOU4-I find this website easy to use	
Perceived risk (PR)	PR1-This website looks safe in the procedure of customizing clothing	[64]
	PR2-It looks reasonable to get information requested for customizing clothing on this website	
	PR3-I feel my privacy is protected during the customization of clothing at this website	
	PR4-I will not hesitate to provide information requested for customizing clothing at this website	
E-satisfaction (ES)	ES1-I am quite satisfied with online services	[75]
	ES2-E-commerce services meet my expectations	
	ES3-My experience when using e-commerce platform is positive	
Perceived usefulness (PU)	PU1-This website enables me to buy clothes faster	[34, 74]
	PU2-This website enhances my effectiveness in customizing clothing	

(continued)

(continued)

Construct	Measurements and scales	Sources
	PU3-This website makes it easier for me to purchase customized clothing	

References

1. Rizzi, L., De Cristofaro, S., Zingarofalo, A.: User driven custom design - the solution to simplify customisation according to consumer needs. Human Factors and Systems Interaction (2023)
2. Jiang, P., Balasubramanian, S.K., Lambert, Z.V.: Consumers' value perceptions of e-customization – a model incorporating information framing and product type. Journal of Consumer Marketing **31**(1), 54–67 (2014)
3. Helms, M.M., Ahmadi, M., Jih, W.J.K., Ettkin, L.P.: Technologies in support of mass customization strategy: exploring the linkages between e-commerce and knowledge management. Comput. Ind. **59**(4), 351–363 (2018)
4. Sheng, M.L., Teo, T.S.H.: Product attributes and brand equity in the mobile domain: the mediating role of customer experience. Int. J. Inf. Manage. **32**, 139–146 (2012)
5. Li, P., Wu, C., Spence, C.: Multisensory perception and positive emotion: exploratory study on mixed item set for apparel e-customization. Text. Res. J. **90**(17–18), 2046–2057 (2020)
6. Park, J.K., Han, H.J., Park, J.H.: Psychological antecedents and risk on attitudes toward e-customization. J. Bus. Res. **66**, 2552–2559 (2013)
7. Merriless, B.: Interactivity design as the key to managing customer relations in e-commerce. Journal of Relationship Marketing **1**(3/4), 111–126 (2001)
8. Wang, Y., Kandampully, J., Jia, H.: 'Tailoring' customization services: effects of customization mode and consumer regulatory focus. J. Serv. Manag. **24**(1), 82–104 (2013)
9. Huang, M., Zhu, H., Zhou, X.: The effects of information provision and interactivity on e-tailer websites. Online Inf. Rev. **37**(6), 927–945 (2013)
10. Wang, J.C., Chang, C.H.: How online social ties and product-related risks influence purchase intentions: a Facebook experiment. Electron. Commer. Res. Appl. **12**(5), 337–346 (2013)
11. Zhu, L., Li, H., Wang, F.K., He, W., Tian, Z.: How online reviews affect purchase intention: a new model based on the stimulus-organism-response (S-O-R) framework. Aslib Journal of Information Management (2020)
12. Moon, M.A., Khalid, M.J., Awan, H.M., Attiq, S., Rasool, H., Kiran, M.: Consumer's perceptions of website's utilitarian and hedonic attributes and online purchase intentions: a cognitive-affective attitude approach. Spanish Journal of Marketing – ESIC **21**(2), 73–88 (2017)
13. Bu, Y., Parkinson, J., Thaichon, P.: Influencer marketing: homophily, customer value co-creation behaviour and purchase intention. J. Retail. Consum. Serv. **66**, 102904 (May2022)
14. Mummalaneni, V.: An empirical investigation of website characteristics, consumer emotional states and on-line shopping behavior. J. Bus. Res. **58**, 526–532 (2005)
15. Garaus, M.: Confusion in internet retailing: causes and consequences. Internet Res. **28**(2), 477–499 (2018)
16. McKinney, L.N.: Creating a satisfying internet shopping experience via atmospheric variables. Int. J. Consum. Stud. **28**(3), 268–283 (2004)

17. Li, Y., Zhang, L.: Do online reviews truly matter? A study of the characteristics of consumers involved in different online review scenarios. Behaviour & Information Technology **40**(13), 1448–1466 (2020)
18. Zhang, H., Lu, Y., Wang, B., Wu, S.: The impacts of technological environments and co-creation experiences on customer participation. Information and Management **52**(4), 468–482 (2015)
19. Afsar, A., Nasiri, Z., Zadeh, M.O.: E-loyalty model in e-commerce. Mediterranean Journal of Social Sciences **4**(9), 547 (2013)
20. Kim, E.Y., Jackson, V.P.: The effect of e-servqual on e-loyalty for apparel online shopping. Journal of Global Academy of Marketing Science **19**(4), 57–65 (2009)
21. Winters, E., Ha, S.: Consumer evaluation of customer loyalty programs: the role of customization in customer loyalty program involvement. J. Glob. Scholars Market. Sci. **22**(4), 370–385 (2012)
22. Cyr, D., Head, M., Ivanov, A.: Perceived interactivity leading to e-loyalty: development of a model for cognitive-affective user responses. Int. J. Hum. Comput. Stud. **67**(10), 850–869 (2009)
23. Goedertier, F., Weijters, B., Van den Bergh, J.: Are consumers equally willing to pay more for brands that aim for sustainability, positive societal contribution, and inclusivity as for brands that are perceived as exclusive? generational, gender, and country differences. Sustainability **16**(9), 3879 (2024)
24. Chang, H.H., Chen, S.W.: The impact of customer interface quality, satisfaction and switching costs on e-loyalty: Internet experience as a moderator. Comput. Hum. Behav. **24**(6), 2927–2944 (2008)
25. Chou, S., Chen, C.W., Lin, J.Y.: Female online shoppers: examining the mediating roles of e-satisfaction and e-trust on e-loyalty development. Internet Res. **25**(4), 542–561 (2015)
26. Lin, G.T.R., Sun, C.C.: Factors influencing satisfaction and loyalty in online shopping: an integrated model. Online Inf. Rev. **33**(3), 458–475 (2009)
27. Ahmad, A., Rahman, O., Khan, M.N.: Exploring the role of website quality and hedonism in the formation of e-satisfaction and e-loyalty. J. Res. Interact. Mark. **11**(3), 246–267 (2017)
28. Khan, M.A., Zubair, S.S., Malik, M.: An assessment of e-service quality, e-satisfaction and e-loyalty. South Asian Journal of Business **8**(3), 283–302 (2019)
29. Rodríguez, P.G., Villarreal, R., Valiño, P.C., Blozis, S.: A PLS-SEM approach to understanding E-SQ, E-satisfaction and E-loyalty for fashion E-Retailers in Spain. J. Retail. Consum. Serv. **57**, 1–8 (2020)
30. Amin, M., Rezaei, S., Abolghasemi, M.: User satisfaction with mobile websites: the impact of perceived usefulness (PU), perceived ease of use (PEOU) and trust. Nankai Business Review International **5**(3), 258–274 (2014)
31. Yeh, Y.S., Li, Y.M.: Building trust in m-commerce: contributions from quality and satisfaction. Online Inf. Rev. **33**(6), 1066–1086 (2009)
32. Yoo, J., Park, M.: The effects of e-mass customization on consumer perceived value satisfaction, and loyalty toward luxury brands. J. Bus. Res. **69**, 5775–5784 (2016)
33. Son, J., Sadachar, A., Manchiraju, S., Fiore, A.M., Niehm, L.S.: Consumer adoption of online collaborative customer co-design. J. Res. Interact. Mark. **6**(3), 180–197 (2012)
34. Gefen, D., Karahanna, E., Straub, D.W.: Trust and TAM in online shopping: an integrated model. MIS Q. **27**(1), 51–90 (2003)
35. Palvia, P.: The role of trust in e-commerce relational exchange: a unified model. Information and Management **46**(2), 213–220 (2009)
36. Reichheld, F.F., Schefter, P.: E-loyalty your secret weapon on the Web. Harv. Bus. Rev. **78**(4), 105–113 (2000)

37. Pennanen, K.: Is interpersonal and institutional e-trustworthiness equally important in consumer e-trust development? Implications for consumers' e-trust building behaviours. J. Consum. Behav. **10**(5), 233–244 (2011)
38. Koufaris, M., Hampton-Sosa, W.: The development of initial trust in an online company by new customers. Information & Management **41**(3), 377–397 (2004)
39. Kim, J., Jin, B., Swinney, J.L.: The role of e-tail quality, e-satisfaction and e-trust in online loyalty development process. J. Retail. Consum. Serv. **16**, 239–247 (2009)
40. Hampton-Sosa, W., Koufaris, M.: The effect of web site perceptions on initial trust in the owner company. Int. J. Electron. Commer. **10**(1), 55–81 (2005)
41. Mathwick, C., Malhotra, N., Rigdon, E.: Experiential value: conceptualization, measurement and application in the catalog and Internet shopping environment. J. Retail. **77**(1), 39–56 (2001)
42. Gefen, D., Straub, D.W.: The relative importance of perceived ease of use in is adoption: a study of e-commerce adoption. Journal of the Association of Information Systems **1**(1), 1–28 (2000)
43. Wang, Y.J., Hernandez, M.C., Minor, M.S.: Web aesthetics effects on perceived online service quality and satisfaction in an e-tail environment: the moderating role of purchase task. J. Bus. Res. **63**, 935–942 (2010)
44. Cyr, D., Head, M., Larios, H., Pan, B.: Exploring human images in website design: a multi-method approach. MIS Q. **33**(3), 539–566 (2006)
45. Jones, C., Kim, S.: Influences of retail brand trust, off-line patronage, clothing involvement and website quality on online apparel shopping intention. Int. J. Consum. Stud. **34**(6), 627–637 (2010)
46. Aladwani, A.M., Palvia, P.C.: Developing and validating an instrument for measuring user-perceived web quality. Information & Management **39**(6), 467–476 (2002)
47. Wang, R.Y., Strong, D.M.: Beyong accuracy: what data quality means to data consumers. J. Manag. Inf. Syst. **12**(4), 5–33 (1996)
48. Nicolaou, A.I., McKnight, D.H.: Perceived information quality in data exchanges: effects on risk, trust, and intention to use. Inf. Syst. Res. **17**(4), 332–351 (2006)
49. Bente, G., Baptist, O., Leuschner, H.: To buy or not to buy: influence of seller photos and reputation on buyer trust and purchase behavior. International Journal of Human Compute Studies **70**(1), 1–13 (2012)
50. Zeithaml, V.A., Parasuraman, A., Malhotra, A.: Service quality delivery through web sites: a critical review of extant knowledge. J. Acad. Mark. Sci. **30**(4), 362–375 (2002)
51. Bao, H., Li, B., Shen, J., Hou, F.: Repurchase intention in the Chinese e-marketplace: roles of interactivity, trust and perceived effectiveness of e-commerce institutional mechanisms. Ind. Manag. Data Syst. **116**(8), 1759–1778 (2016)
52. Merrilees, B., Fry, M.-L.: E-trust: the influence of perceived intractivity on e-retailing users. Mark. Intell. Plan. **21**(2), 123–128 (2003)
53. Srivastava, M., Kaul, D.: Social interaction, convenience and customer satisfaction: The mediating effect of customer experience. J. Retail. Consum. Serv. **21**, 1028–1037 (2014)
54. Yoo, W.S., Lee, Y., Park, J.K.: The role of interactivity in e-tailing: Creating value and increasing satisfaction. J. Retail. Consum. Serv. **17**, 89–96 (2010)
55. Szymanski, D.M., Hise, R.T.: E-satisfaction: an initial examination. J. Retail. **76**(3), 309–322 (2000)
56. Trivedi, S.K., Yadav, M.: Predicting online repurchase intentions with e-satisfaction as mediator: a study on Gen Y. Journal of Information and Knowledge Management Systems **48**(3), 427–447 (2018)
57. Udo, G.J., Bgchi, K.K., Kirs, P.J.: An assessment of customers' e-service quality perception, satisfaction and intention. Int. J. Inf. Manage. **30**, 481–492 (2010)

58. Bressolles, G., Durrieu, F., Senecal, S.: A consumer typology based on e-service quality and e-satisfaction. J. Retail. Consum. Serv. **21**, 889–896 (2014)
59. Li, H., Aham-Anyanwu, N., Tevrizci, C., Luo, X.: The interplay between value & service quality experience: e-loyalty development process through the eTailQ scale & value perception. Electron. Commer. Res. **15**(4), 585–615 (2015)
60. Anderson, R.E., Srinivasan, S.S.: E-satisfaction and e-loyalty: a contingency framework. Psychol. Mark. **20**(2), 123–138 (2003)
61. Lin, H.H., Wang, Y.S.: An examination of the determinants of customer loyalty in mobile commerce contexts. Information & Management **43**(3), 271–282 (2006)
62. Zhao, Q., Chen, C.D., Wang, J.L.: The effects of psychological ownership and TAM on social media loyalty: an integrated model. Telematics Inform. **33**, 959–972 (2016)
63. Nisar, T.M., Prabhakar, G.: What factors determine e-satisfaction and consumer spending in e-commerce retailing? J. Retail. Consum. Serv. **39**, 135–144 (2017)
64. Cho, H., Fiorito, S.S.: Acceptance of online customization for apparel shopping. International Journal of Retail & Distribution Management **37**(5), 389–407 (2009)
65. Liebermann, Y., Stashevsky, S.: Perceived risks as barriers to Internet and e-commerce usage. J. Cetacean Res. Manag. **5**(4), 291–300 (2002)
66. Tuu, H.G., Olsen, S.O., Linh, P.T.T.: The moderator effects of perceived risk, objective knowledge and certainty in the satisfaction-loyalty relationship. J. Consum. Mark. **28**(5), 363–375 (2011)
67. Oliveira, T., Alhinho, M., Rita, P., Dhillon, G.: Modeling and testing consumer trust dimensions in e-commerce. Comput. Hum. Behav. **71**, 153–164 (2017)
68. Rahimnia, F., Hassanzadeh, J.F.: The impact of website content dimension and e-trust on e-marketing effectiveness: the case of Iranian commercial saffron corporations. Information & Management **50**, 240–247 (2013)
69. Chek, Y.L., Ho, J.S.Y.: Consumer electronics e-retailing: why the alliance of vendors' e-service quality, trust and trustworthiness matters. Procedia Soc. Behav. Sci. **219**, 804–811 (2016)
70. McKnight, D.H., Chervany, N.L.: What trust means in e-commerce customer relationships? An interdisciplinary conceptual typology. Internet Journal Electronic Commerce **6**(2), 35–59 (2002)
71. Venkatesh, V., Speier, C., Morris, M.G.: Use acceptance enablers in individual decision making about technology: toward an integrated model. Decis. Sci. **33**(2), 297–316 (2002)
72. Wang, Y., Lin, H., Luarn, P.: Predicting consumer intention to use mobile service. Inf. Syst. J. **16**(2), 157–179 (2006)
73. Kang, J.Y.M.: Repurchase loyalty for customer social co-creation e-marketplaces. J. Fash. Mark. Manag. **18**(4), 452–464 (2013)
74. Davis, F.: Perceived usefulness, perceived ease of use, and user acceptance of information technology. MIS Q. **13**(3), 319–340 (1989)
75. San-Martin, S., Lopez-Catalan, B.: How can a mobile vendor get satisfied customers? Ind. Manag. Data Syst. **113**(2), 156–170 (2013)

Artificial Intelligence and Smart Services in Digital Human Modeling

Multi-layer Perceptron Classifier for Real-Time Movement Classification of Elbow Joint Using Surface Electromyography (sEMG)

Akilan A[iD], Deep Seth$^{(\boxtimes)}$[iD], Sanjeevi Nakka[iD], and Siddharth Rajesh Patil[iD]

Mahindra University, Hyderabad, India
`deep.seth@mahindrauniversity.edu.in`

Abstract. Surface Electromyography (sEMG) signals provide valuable insights into muscle activity during physical movements, making them essential for real-time rehabilitation monitoring. This study proposes a computationally efficient Multi-Layer Perceptron (MLP) classifier for classifying elbow joint movements (flexion, extension, and rest) using only two sEMG sensors. Noise removal and feature extraction techniques were applied to pre-process the EMG signals, followed by feature selection using permutation importance with most significant features. A Multi-Layer Perceptron (MLP) classifier trained on a dataset split into 70% training and 30% testing achieved 90% accuracy. The model's robustness, demonstrated through high precision and recall, ensures reliable movement detection. With a 200ms window and 170ms overlap, the system maintains a 30ms update speed. The model was evaluated using accuracy, precision, recall, and F1-score, demonstrating high reliability, particularly for rehabilitation scenarios. The findings indicate that reducing sensor input while optimizing feature selection can maintain high classification performance.

Keywords: Multi-layer perceptron · Surface electromyography (sEMG) · Gesture recognition · Feature recognition · Movement prediction

1 Introduction

Surface electromyography (sEMG) is a widely used non-invasive technique for monitoring muscle activity and plays a critical role in rehabilitation, prosthetics, and human-machine interaction [19]. The classification of sEMG signals is essential for real-time movement recognition, enabling assistive technologies such as exoskeletons, prosthetic limbs, and rehabilitation robots to respond effectively to muscle activation. However, accurate and real-time classification of sEMG signals remains challenging due to signal variability, noise, and computational constraints.

Machine learning techniques have been extensively explored to improve sEMG classification. Traditional classifiers such as K-Nearest Neighbor (KNN), Support Vector Machines (SVM), and Decision Trees have been employed in

V. G. Duffy (Ed.): HCII 2025, LNCS 16339, pp. 165–176, 2026.
https://doi.org/10.1007/978-3-032-13012-9_12

early studies, demonstrating reasonable classification accuracy [1,2]. However, these models struggle with scalability and generalization when dealing with high-dimensional sEMG data, limiting their use in real-time applications [15].

To overcome these limitations, artificial neural networks (ANNs) have been widely adopted, offering improved accuracy and adaptability in sEMG classification. Studies have shown that ANNs outperform conventional models such as KNN and Naïve Bayes in hand gesture recognition, achieving up to 93% classification accuracy [17]. With increased computational power, ANNs have demonstrated strong potential in rehabilitation robotics and assistive control systems [13].

Deep learning models, particularly Convolutional Neural Networks (CNNs) and Long Short-Term Memory (LSTM) networks, have further improved classification accuracy in complex sEMG applications, including transradial (TR) amputees and prosthetic control [5,9]. These models leverage large datasets and advanced feature extraction to enhance classification performance. However, deep learning techniques require high computational resources and extensive labeled data, making them unsuitable for real-time applications on embedded systems [12,18].

Among artificial neural networks, the Multi-Layer Perceptron (MLP) classifier has emerged as a computationally efficient and accurate model for sEMG-based movement recognition. MLP is a feedforward neural network that can capture non-linear patterns in EMG data while maintaining a relatively low computational cost [4,7]. Unlike CNNs and LSTMs, which require significant processing power and large datasets, MLP is well-suited for real-time applications due to its lightweight architecture and fast execution speed.

Several studies have validated MLP's effectiveness in gesture recognition, upper-limb movement analysis, and rehabilitation robotics. Researchers have tested MLP on hand pronation and supination movements at static angles (e.g., $0°$, $60°$, $90°$, and $120°$), demonstrating its ability to classify movements with high accuracy while maintaining computational efficiency [4,7]. This makes MLP an ideal choice for real-time sEMG classification in rehabilitation therapy and assistive devices.

To enhance MLP's performance, feature selection techniques play a crucial role in improving accuracy while minimizing computational overhead. While both time-domain and frequency-domain features have been explored in sEMG classification, time-domain features are often preferred for real-time applications due to their simplicity and reduced processing time [10]. Feature selection methods such as Permutation Importance have been shown to significantly reduce computational load while preserving classification accuracy [6,14,16]. By selecting only the most relevant features, MLP-based models can operate efficiently on low-power hardware, making them practical for wearable rehabilitation devices and embedded control systems.

This study proposes a Multi-Layer Perceptron (MLP)-based classifier for real-time classification of elbow joint movements (flexion, extension, and rest) using sEMG signals. The biceps and triceps muscles play a crucial role in elbow movement–during flexion, the biceps contract while the triceps relax, and during extension, the triceps contract while the biceps relax [11]. Accurately classifying these movements is essential for real-time rehabilitation feedback systems, enabling therapists to monitor patient progress and optimize rehabilitation strategies.

The primary contributions of this study are:

- **Development of an optimized MLP classifier** achieving high classification accuracy (90%) with a 30ms update speed, making it suitable for real-time applications.
- **Application of Permutation Importance for feature selection**, reducing computational complexity while maintaining classification performance.
- **Validation of the model on experimental sEMG data**, demonstrating effective classification using only two sEMG sensors, ensuring a cost-effective and practical implementation.

Unlike computationally expensive deep learning models, MLP provides an efficient trade-off between accuracy and computational speed, making it an ideal choice for real-time sEMG classification in rehabilitation and assistive technologies.

The remainder of this paper is organized as follows: Sect. 2 describes the experimental setup, data collection, and preprocessing steps and MLP model implementation, Sect. 3 presents the results and discussion, and Sect. 4 concludes with future research directions.

2   Methodology

Understanding muscle activation through surface electromyography (sEMG) requires a well-defined experimental setup, precise data acquisition, and robust machine learning techniques. This study aims to develop a real-time Multi-Layer Perceptron (MLP) classifier for elbow movement classification, ensuring an optimal balance between accuracy and computational efficiency. To achieve this, a systematic approach was adopted, beginning with sEMG signal acquisition from key muscle groups, followed by signal preprocessing, feature extraction, and selection, and concluding with MLP-based classification and performance evaluation.

The methodology is structured as follows: first, we describe the experimental setup and data collection protocol, outlining the electrode placement and hardware used for acquiring muscle activity signals. Next, we discuss signal preprocessing, where noise filtering and labeling techniques are applied to prepare the data for feature extraction. We then detail the feature selection process, focusing on Permutation Importance to optimize classification performance. Finally, we introduce the MLP model architecture, training parameters, and evaluation metrics, ensuring a clear pathway from raw signal acquisition to movement classification.

2.1 Experimental Setup and Protocol

To classify elbow movements, surface electromyography (sEMG) signals were recorded from the biceps brachii and triceps brachii muscles, which are responsible for elbow flexion and extension. Two active electrodes were placed on each muscle–one at the muscle belly and another at the distal end–while a reference (ground) electrode was placed over the elbow joint, as shown in Fig. 1a

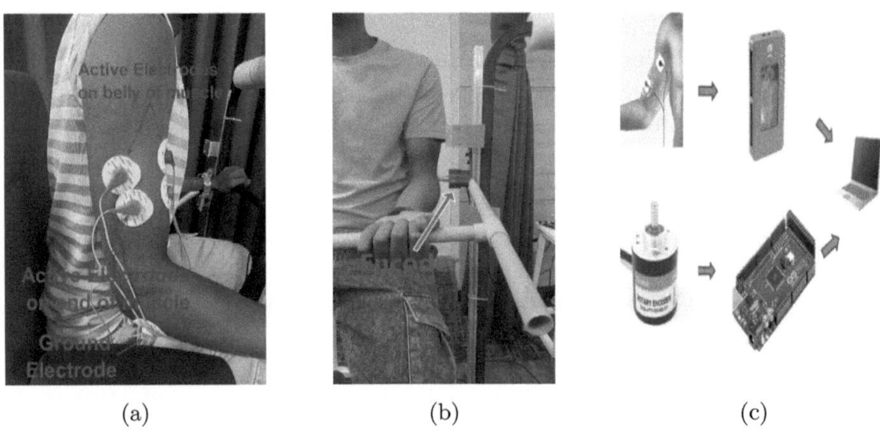

(a)   (b)   (c)

Fig. 1. (a) shows the active and ground electrodes placed over belly, end and non-muscular part of upper arm, (b) represents a subject holding the bar with encoder placed at the axis of elbow joint (c) represents hardware components used for data collection

To label the collected sEMG data based on elbow movement position, a Pro-Range 600 PPR 2-Phase Incremental Optical Rotary Encoder was attached to the elbow joint to record angular displacement as shown in Fig. 1b. The encoder provided real-time tracking of flexion and extension movements, allowing precise labeling of muscle activity. The MyRIO system was used for acquiring sEMG signals at 1000 Hz, while Arduino with PLX-DAQ recorded encoder data at 10 Hz, experimental hardware components are shown in Fig. 1c. The experimental protocol is outlined in Table 1, where we can observe that prior to experiment we have rest and warm-up. Each EMG flexion and extension experiment consists of 20 cycles with no load, 0.5 kg load and 1 kg load respectively to analyze the EMG activities at various load conditions.

2.2 Preprocessing and Feature Extraction

Preprocessing. Raw sEMG signals are prone to noise from various sources, including movement artifacts and power line interference. To enhance signal quality, the following preprocessing steps were applied:

Table 1. Experimental Protocol for Data Collection

Step	Protocol Description	Duration (min)
1	Rest and deep breathing	1
2	Warm-up exercises	1
3	Rest and deep breathing	1
4	EMG Flexion and Extension (20 cycles) with no load	1
5	Rest and deep breathing	1
6	EMG Flexion and Extension with 0.5 kg load	1
7	Rest and deep breathing	1
8	EMG Flexion and Extension with 1 kg load	1

- **Band-pass filtering (30 − 450 Hz):** Removes low-frequency motion arti-facts and high-frequency noise.
- **Notch filtering (60 Hz):** Suppresses power line interference.
- **Signal Smoothing (100 ms window):** Enhances signal clarity by averaging over small time segments.

Encoder data was interpolated to match the sEMG sampling rate and was used to label the movements. A positive slope in encoder readings indicated flexion, a negative slope represented extension, and minimal variation indicated rest, as illustrated in Fig. 2, two plots in red and green which are the EMG signal during flexion and extension respectively after pre-processing. It can also be observed in the that there are two zones marked as flexion and extension. In the flexion zone increasing slope of encoder values along with higher activity from EMG flexion and lower activity from EMG extension can be observed. Similarly, in the extension zone decreasing slope of encoder value and lower activity from EMG flexion and extension both can be observed.

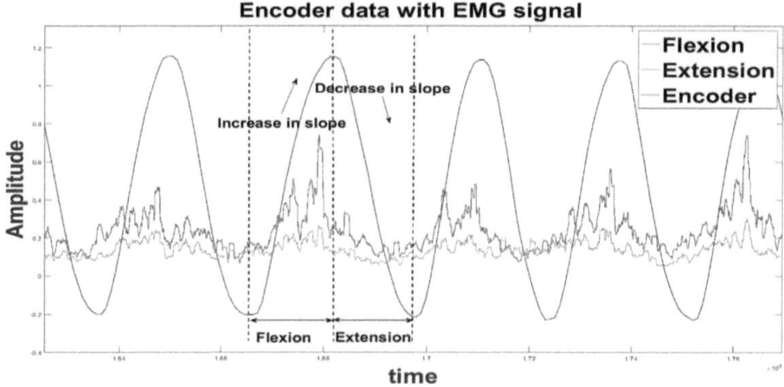

Fig. 2. A section of EMG signal generated while performing experimental protocol along with Encoder data

Feature Extraction. To capture the underlying muscle activation patterns, 12 time-domain features were extracted from each 200 ms window with overlap of 170 ms of sEMG data. These features quantify signal properties that differentiate movement types. The most relevant features include:

– **Mean Absolute Value (MAV)**: Measures average muscle activation level.

$$MAV = \frac{1}{N} \sum_{i=1}^{N} |x_i| \tag{1}$$

– **Root Mean Square (RMS)**: Represents the power of the EMG signal.

$$RMS = \sqrt{\frac{1}{N} \sum_{i=1}^{N} x_i^2} \tag{2}$$

– **Waveform Length (WL)**: Captures signal complexity.

$$WL = \sum_{i=1}^{N-1} |x_{i+1} - x_i| \tag{3}$$

– **Zero Crossing (ZC)** and **Slope Sign Change (SSC)**: Count changes in signal polarity and slope.

Feature Selection Using Permutation Importance. Overall, 12 time-based features were extracted from the pre-processed signal, including Variance, Waveform Length, RMS, Zero Crossing, Mean Average Value, Willison Amplitude, Integrated EMG, Slope, Slope Sign Change, Skewness, Standard Deviation, and Simple Square Integral [18]. Each of these features representing a different information or pattern related to EMG signal generated, such as power, length of firing, absolute value, abrupt change in signal, overall activity of signal, etc. Not all extracted features contribute equally to classification performance. To reduce computational overhead while preserving accuracy, we employed permutation importance to rank feature significance [14]. This method randomly shuffles feature values and observes the change in classification accuracy. Features with importance scores below 0.001 were excluded.

2.3   Multi-layer Perceptron (MLP) Classifier

Once the EMG signal is pre-processed and features are extracted, modeling can be started with multi-layer perceptron classifier model, which consists of fully connected dense layers having input, hidden and output layers. A Multi-Layer Perceptron (MLP) classifier was employed for movement classification. The dataset is split into training (70%) and testing (30%). Structure of MLP is set as input layer containing the features extracted, Hidden layers with node elements of (128,64,8) with an adaptive learning rate (0.00001), *tanh* activation function, Epochs (1000), tolerance (1e-8), solver (Adam) and an output layer having softmax(multi-output) activation function. Since Scikit-learn library is used while training all the other parameters are set to default values.

Mathematical Formulation. Let $\mathbf{x} = [x_1, x_2, ..., x_n]$ represent the input feature vector and $\mathbf{W}^{(l)}$ the weight matrix of layer l. The output of each hidden layer is computed as:

$$\mathbf{h}^{(l)} = \tanh(\mathbf{W}^{(l)}\mathbf{h}^{(l-1)} + \mathbf{b}^{(l)}) \tag{4}$$

where $\mathbf{b}^{(l)}$ is the bias term. The final output layer uses a softmax function:

$$\hat{y}_k = \frac{e^{z_k}}{\sum_{j=1}^{C} e^{z_j}} \tag{5}$$

where C is the number of movement classes and z_k represents the activation for class k.

After creating the model initially we have to perform permutation importance to fit the model and check for important features. Permutation importance can fit any model (MLP) and by randomly shuffling input features with n_repeats(10), observing the performance of a parameter(accuracy), importance of each feature can be decided. Based on the output of permutation importance we can set a threshold(> 0.001) on the features to include only the most important features. So, after selecting the important features we can feed the new model with selected features from permutation importance model creating the final output model, which alone can be used to deploy in real time system.

2.4   Performance Evaluation

To assess the classification performance of the MLP model, we use several evaluation metrics, including accuracy, precision, recall, and F1-score. These metrics provide insight into the model's effectiveness in distinguishing between elbow flexion, extension, and rest movements.

Accuracy. Accuracy measures the overall correctness of the classifier by comparing the number of correctly classified samples to the total number of samples. It is defined as:

$$\text{Accuracy} = \frac{TP + TN}{TP + TN + FP + FN} \tag{6}$$

where:

- **TP (True Positives):** Number of correctly classified flexion, extension, or rest movements.
- **TN (True Negatives):** Number of correctly identified non-movements (when the model correctly predicts a different class).
- **FP (False Positives):** Number of misclassified movements (e.g., predicting flexion when the movement is actually extension).
- **FN (False Negatives):** Number of missed movements (e.g., predicting rest when the movement is actually flexion).

Accuracy provides an overall measure of classification performance. However, it may not always be sufficient if the dataset is imbalanced (i.e., if one class has significantly more samples than others). To address this, we also evaluate precision, recall, and the F1-score.

3   Results and Discussion

This section presents the findings of our study and discusses their implications in the context of existing research on real-time sEMG classification. While previous studies have demonstrated the feasibility of sEMG signal classification for real-time applications, they often report classification latencies exceeding 100ms [20]. This delay is attributed to the use of multiple sensor channels, kinematic inputs, or additional integrated sensors to improve classification accuracy. However, with advancements in machine learning techniques and optimized feature selection, real-time classification latency can be further reduced.

Our study successfully develops a Multi-Layer Perceptron (MLP)-based classification model that achieves a latency of 30ms, significantly improving upon existing models. This improvement is achieved by using only two sEMG sensors (one for flexion and one for extension) and employing an encoder solely for data labeling, thereby minimizing hardware complexity and computational overhead. Furthermore, the model's robustness was evaluated by incorporating sEMG data from movements performed under different load conditions (no load to 1 kg load), demonstrating its applicability to rehabilitation scenarios.

The dataset used in our experiments consisted of six subjects, generating approximately 1.8 million data points. The dataset was split into 70% training data (1,260,000 data points) and 30% testing data (540,000 data points). Each subject performed three cycles of 20 sets, with approximately 15–16 cycles allocated for training and three cycles for testing.

Initially, the model was trained using all 12 extracted time-domain features. However, to optimize computational efficiency, the permutation importance method was applied to rank the features based on their contribution to classification accuracy. Figure 3 illustrates the ranked feature importance values, demonstrating that only seven flexion features and seven extension features contributed significantly to the model's performance, after setting a threshold value of 0.001.

From Fig. 3, it is evident that not all features contribute equally to both flexion and extension classification. The selected features included Simple Square Integral (SSI), Integrated EMG (IEMG), Waveform Length (WL), Root Mean Square (RMS), Log Detector, Skewness, and Kurtosis. These features play a crucial role in capturing signal energy (SSI), muscle activation (IEMG), movement onset and offset (WL), contraction force (RMS), and signal shape variations (Skewness and Kurtosis). By eliminating less significant features, the model reduced computational complexity while improving classification accuracy.

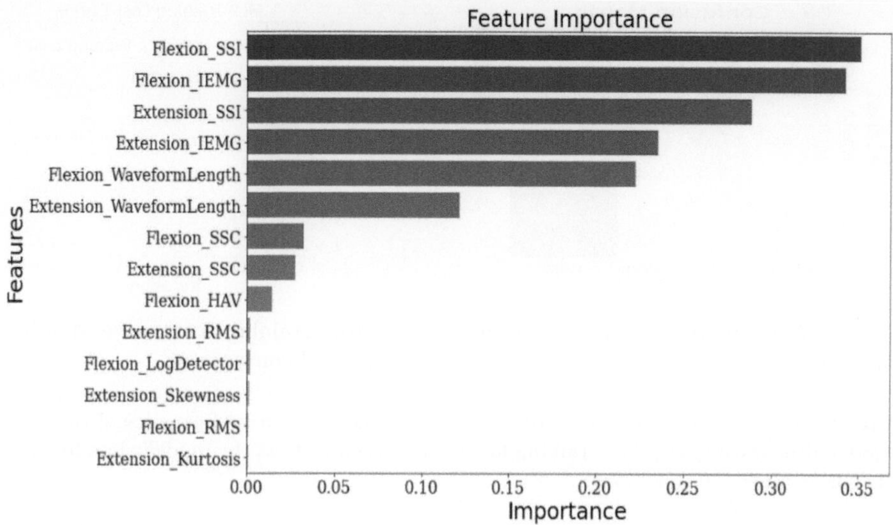

Fig. 3. Permutation Importance ranking of selected time-domain features for flexion and extension classification.

3.1   Performance Evaluation

The classification model was evaluated using four key performance metrics: accuracy, precision, recall, and F1-score. The proposed approach achieved an overall classification accuracy of 90%, outperforming the previous model, which attained 85% accuracy using all features. Figure 4 illustrates the confusion matrix and training loss curve, providing deeper insights into model performance.

Table 2 provides a detailed breakdown of classification performance across movement classes.

Table 2. Classification Report for MLP Model

Class	Precision	Recall	F1-Score	Support
Flexion	0.86	0.85	0.86	3045
Extension	0.81	0.83	0.82	3105
Rest	0.98	0.96	0.97	5146

From Table 2, it is evident that the "rest" class achieved the highest classification accuracy (98%), followed by flexion (86%) and extension (82%). The higher accuracy of the rest class can be attributed to its larger dataset size (5146 samples) compared to flexion and extension (3000 samples approx).

Furthermore, precision and recall values for flexion and extension movements indicate a low false positive and false negative rate, reinforcing the robustness of the proposed model. The confusion matrix in Fig. 4a also confirms that

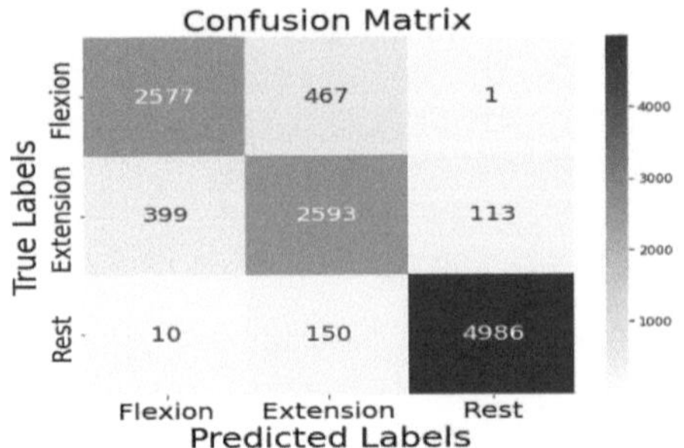

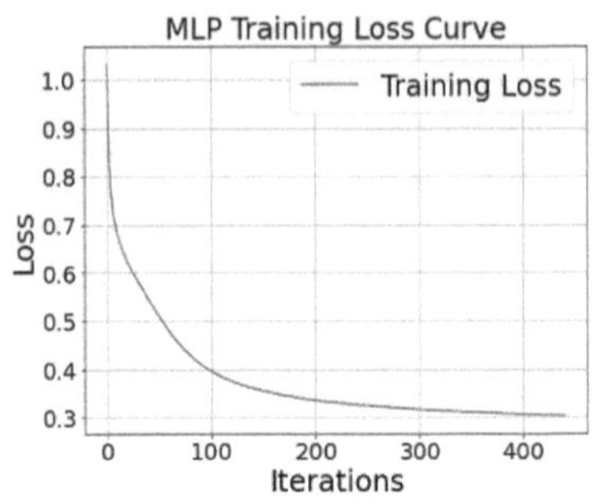

(a) Confusion matrix showing classification accuracy.

(b) Training loss curve showing model convergence.

Fig. 4. (a) The confusion matrix represents the classification performance of the MLP model after testing. (b) The training loss curve indicates that the model's loss function stabilizes after 430 iterations.

the majority of misclassifications occur between flexion and extension movements, which is expected due to their similar muscle activation patterns. Also, Fig. 4b shows us a plot which gives us the number iterations taken and performance of loss function of the model, where it can be observed that training loss reduces as number of iteration increases and stabilizes after 400 iterations.

3.2   Real-Time Implementation and Computational Efficiency

One of the primary objectives of this study was to ensure that the proposed classification model is suitable for real-time applications, particularly in rehabilitation settings. The window selection strategy (200 ms window with 170ms overlap) provided an optimal balance between classification accuracy and computational speed, allowing the system to update predictions within 30ms. This latency is well within the acceptable range for real-time motion monitoring and control applications [8].

Moreover, the efficient feature selection process reduced the dimensionality of the dataset, enabling faster computations without compromising classification accuracy. This reduction in computational overhead is particularly advantageous for embedded systems [3] and wearable devices [5], where processing power and energy efficiency are critical factors.

Compared to previous studies that required multiple sEMG channels or kinematic sensors for accurate classification, our approach successfully achieves high accuracy using only two sEMG channels (flexion and extension sensors) and an encoder for labeling. The minimal hardware requirement simplifies system integration, making it more suitable for clinical and at-home rehabilitation. Additionally, feature selection using Permutation Importance further enhanced model efficiency, allowing it to operate in real-time environments without the need for high-end computational resources.

While the proposed model demonstrated high accuracy and low latency, future improvements can focus on expanding the dataset to include more diverse subjects to improve generalization. Additionally, incorporating adaptive learning techniques could allow the model to fine-tune classification thresholds based on individual muscle activation patterns.

Moreover, extending this approach to multi-joint movement classification (e.g., wrist, shoulder movements) could enhance its applicability in rehabilitation robotics and prosthetic control systems. Future work could also explore hardware implementations on low-power microcontrollers to facilitate deployment in wearable rehabilitation devices.

4   Conclusion

This study presents an Multi-Layer Perceptron (MLP) classifier for real-time classification of elbow joint movements (flexion, extension, and rest) using sEMG signals, achieving 90% accuracy with only two sEMG sensors and a classification latency of 30ms. By leveraging Permutation Importance for feature selection, the model reduces computational overhead while maintaining high classification performance, making it suitable for rehabilitation and assistive robotics applications. Compared to conventional methods requiring multiple sensor channels and longer processing times, our approach provides an efficient, real-time solution for wearable rehabilitation devices. Future work will explore broader subject diversity, adaptive learning techniques, and deployment on embedded systems to further enhance applicability in rehabilitation and prosthetic control.

Acknowledgement. We would like to thank Mahindra University, Hyderabad for providing infrastructure and support for the research. We would also like to thank all the subjects for their contribution to data collection.

References

1. Al-Faiz, M.Z., Ali, A.A., Miry, A.H.: A k-nearest neighbor based algorithm for human arm movements recognition using EMG signals. In: 2010 1st International Conference on Energy, Power and Control (EPC-IQ), pp. 159–167. IEEE (2010)
2. Angelidou, C., Artemiadis, P.: On predicting transitions to compliant surfaces in human gait via neural and kinematic signals. IEEE Trans. Neural Syst. Rehabil. Eng. **31**, 2214–2223 (2023)
3. Benatti, S., et al.: A versatile embedded platform for EMG acquisition and gesture recognition. IEEE Trans. Biomed. Circuits Syst. **9**(5), 620–630 (2015)
4. Elamvazuthi, I., Duy, N.H.X., Ali, Z., Su, S.W., Khan, M.A., Parasuraman, S.: Electromyography (EMG) based classification of neuromuscular disorders using multi-layer perceptron. Procedia Comput. Sci. **76**, 223–228 (2015)
5. Gopal, P., Gesta, A., Mohebbi, A.: A systematic study on electromyography-based hand gesture recognition for assistive robots using deep learning and machine learning models. Sensors **22**(10), 3650 (2022). https://doi.org/10.3390/s22103650

6. Huang, N., Lu, G., Xu, D.: A permutation importance-based feature selection method for short-term electricity load forecasting using random forest. Energies **9**(10), 767 (2016). https://doi.org/10.3390/en9100767

7. Jose, N., Raj, R., Adithya, P.K., Sivanadan, K.S.: Classification of forearm movements from sEMG time domain features using machine learning algorithms. In: TENCON 2017 - 2017 IEEE Region 10 Conference, pp. 1624–1628. IEEE (2017)

8. Kang, S., Kim, H., Park, C., Sim, Y., Lee, S., Jung, Y.: sEMG-based hand gesture recognition using binarized neural network. Sensors **23**, 1436 (2023). https://doi.org/10.3390/s23031436

9. Kim, E., Shin, J., Kwon, Y., Park, B.: EMG-based dynamic hand gesture recognition using edge AI for human–robot interaction. Electronics **12**(7), 1541 (2023)

10. Kok, C.L., Ho, C.K., Tan, F.K., Koh, Y.Y.: Machine learning-based feature extraction and classification of EMG signals for intuitive prosthetic control. Appl. Sci. **14**(13), 5784 (2024). https://doi.org/10.3390/app14135784

11. Konrad, P.: The ABC of EMG: a practical introduction to kinesiological electromyography (2005)

12. Kumar, P., V, S.K., Lakkannavar, M.C., R, V.C.: Comparison of machine learning algorithms for EMG-based muscle function analysis. In: 2022 4th International Conference on Circuits, Control, Communication and Computing (I4C). IEEE (2022). https://doi.org/10.1109/i4c57141.2022.10057856

13. Lee, K.H., Min, J.Y., Byun, S.: Electromyogram-based classification of hand and finger gestures using artificial neural networks. Sensors **22**(1), 225 (2021). https://doi.org/10.3390/s22010225

14. Little, K., Pappachan, B.K., Yang, S., Noronha, B., Campolo, D., Accoto, D.: Elbow motion trajectory prediction using a multi-modal wearable system: a comparative analysis of machine learning techniques. Sensors **21**(2), 498 (2021). https://doi.org/10.3390/s21020498

15. Liu, Y., Li, X., Zhu, A., Zheng, Z., Zhu, H.: Design and evaluation of a surface electromyography-controlled lightweight upper arm exoskeleton rehabilitation robot. Int. J. Adv. Rob. Syst. **18**(3), 17298814211003460 (2021). https://doi.org/10.1177/17298814211003461

16. Mengarelli, A., Tigrini, A., Fioretti, S., Cardarelli, S., Verdini, F.: On the use of fuzzy and permutation entropy in hand gesture characterization from EMG signals: Parameters selection and comparison. Appl. Sci. **10**(20), 7144 (2020)

17. Nia, N.G., Kaplanoglu, E., Nasab, A.: EMG-based hand gestures classification using machine learning algorithms. In: SoutheastCon 2023. IEEE (2023). https://doi.org/10.1109/SoutheastCon49000.2023.10113807

18. Senturk, Z.K., Bakay, M.S.: Machine learning-based hand gesture recognition via EMG data. ADCAIJ: Adv. Distrib. Comput. Artif. Intell. J. **10**(2) (2021). https://doi.org/10.14201/adcaij2021102123136

19. Zhang, Z., Yang, K., Qian, J., Zhang, L.: Real-time surface EMG pattern recognition for hand gestures based on an artificial neural network. Sensors **19**(14), 3170 (2019)

20. Zheng, M., Crouch, M.S., Eggleston, M.S.: Surface electromyography as a natural human–machine interface: a review. IEEE Sens. J. **22**(10), 9198–9214 (2022)

A Human-in-the-Loop MLLM and RAG Pipeline for Qualitative Research: Overcoming Data Challenges in Flood-Related Interviews

Jakub Binter[1,2]([envelope]) [iD], Daniel Říha[1,3] [iD], Natálie Čermáková[1] [iD], Lenka Slavíková[1] [iD], Tomáš Hladký[1] [iD], and Hermann Prossinger[1,4] [iD]

[1] Faculty of Social and Economic Studies, University of Jan Evangelista Purkyně, Pasteurova 1, Ústí nad Labem, Czech Republic
jakub.binter@ujep.cz
[2] Faculty of Science, Charles University, Prague, Czech Republic
[3] Faculty of Humanities, Charles University, Prague, Czech Republic
[4] Department of Evolutionary Anthropology, University of Vienna, Vienna, Austria

Abstract. The first phase of qualitative research is often hindered by the time-consuming process of transcribing and analyzing low-quality audio interviews. This paper introduces a novel human-in-the-loop pipeline that leverages Multimodal Large Language Models (MLLMs) and Retrieval-Augmented Generation (RAG) to overcome these. Our case study focuses on flood-related interviews conducted in North Bohemia, Czech Republic, in Czech, a language for which many AI models have not yet been optimized. Our proposed methodology employs MLLMs for both generating quantifiable, emotionally nuanced interview stimuli and for reconstructing interview transcripts from poor audio recordings. The initial AI-generated transcriptions are then refined and validated by a human, ensuring high accuracy and contextual integrity. Subsequently, a RAG system is utilized for efficient and transparent thematic analysis of the corrected transcripts. Our results demonstrate that this hybrid approach can achieve over 99% similarity between the AI-pipeline output and a manually corrected version, significantly reducing the time required for transcription and analysis by an estimated 75–80%. Furthermore, the RAG-based analysis enhances the rigor of qualitative research by improving efficiency, mitigating researcher bias, and ensuring auditability. This study showcases the potential of integrating advanced AI with human oversight to overcome data challenges and enhance the quality and efficiency of qualitative research, even in less-resourced languages.

Keywords: Human-in-the-Loop AI · Multimodal Large Language Models (MLLMs) · Retrieval-Augmented Generation (RAG) · Qualitative Research Automation · Low-Quality Audio Transcription · Czech Language · NLP · Flood Risk Communication

V. G. Duffy (Ed.): HCII 2025, LNCS 16339, pp. 177–187, 2026.
https://doi.org/10.1007/978-3-032-13012-9_13

1 Introduction

Qualitative research, by its very nature, often necessitates a deep plunge into complex human experiences and societal phenomena, frequently relying on in-depth interviews to gather contextualized data followed by classification (Braun & Clarke, 2006). However, a more demanding challenge is the acquisition and processing of audio recordings, especially those conducted in non-ideal conditions. Such low-quality recordings can significantly slow down the transcription process and trigger time-consuming data analysis and most certainly decrease data reliability. This paper presents a novel approach to addressing this limitation by integrating advanced artificial intelligence (AI) models with essential human oversight and using a complex RAG system to further repeatability and quality (Yuan, et al., 2024).

The interviews may take more than an hour, outputting up to 30 thousand tokens. So, even if most recent Multimodal Large Language Models (MLLMs) have the ability to process audio, pictures and video in high quality, vast token output is a drawback. Previously, LLMs had a 4096 token limit, while now 8000 is usual. It is important to not confuse the context window with the available tokens for output. The context window is a fixed size and must be shared between the input (your prompt, questions, and any previous turns in the conversation) and the output (the model's generated response; Guest et al., 2013).

To overcome these limitations, we propose a hybrid methodology that leverages the power of speech-to-text for initial data processing and narrative generation, critically coupled with robust human-in-the-loop mechanisms for refinement and validation. This integration aims to reconstruct interview content with unprecedented accuracy and emotional fidelity, even from challenging source material.

Our specific objectives include: (1) developing a robust pipeline for transcribing and reconstructing low-quality audio recordings using cutting-edge MLLM AI models; (2) demonstrating the utility of MLLMs in generating and evaluating emotionally nuanced narratives as qualitative stimuli; (3) highlighting the vital necessity of human intervention to ensure accuracy, coherence, and ethical integrity of AI-generated content in qualitative research; and (4) creating a Retrieval Augmented Generation (RAG) based system for qualitative research (Gao, et al., 2023).

While MLLMs already implement audio transcription functions, their performance degrades considerably when faced with real-world complexities such as background noise, multiple speakers, varied accents, and low recording fidelity (Çoban, et al., 2024; Taylor, 2023). Recent advancements in Speech-to-Text (STT) technologies, exemplified by models like Whisper (OpenAI; Amorese, et al., 2023) or Chirp (Google; Chintala, 2024), and SeamlessM4T (Meta; Barrault, et al., 2023) have revolutionized audio transcription. These models offer remarkable accuracy even in less-than-ideal conditions as well as across multiple languages. Our study specifically investigates the applicability and limitations of these advanced STT models in the demanding context of low-quality qualitative research recordings.

2 Methodology

2.1 Research Design

The research presented herein is a specific case study: interviews with inhabitants in North Bohemia, Czech Republic, conducted as part of the "Region to University–University to Region" Project. The core objective of this project is to understand the motivations and experiences of individuals responsible for water management—typically town mayors. The qualitative interviews were prepared by collaborating researchers. Specific sections of the semi-structured interview—a set of short stories—was created and evaluated using MLLM.

Upon the completion of the interviews, we attempted to automate the rewriting process. A notable challenge in this context was the ubiquitous low quality of the audio recordings, primarily due to the use of small, inconspicuous devices to ensure interview authenticity and interviewee comfort, typically the mobile phone of the interviewer. A further limitation was the microphone being close to the table surface, thereby affecting the low frequency spectrum amplitudes and consequently making it especially difficult to filter out the desired spectra of the human voice.

Currently, 13 interview recordings are available for analysis. These rewritten interviews were databased and queried by a RAG system.

2.2 Interview Creation and Brainstorming

The overarching interview structure was developed in late 2024 through a collaborative brainstorming session that strategically leveraged a LLM (ChatGPT 4o and Gemini 1.5 pro) to generate and refine initial ideas. This early integration of AI facilitated a more expansive and innovative exploration of potential interview topics and question formulations.

2.3 Narrative Generation for Burden Expression

A specific component of the interview design involved participants responding to a presented short story. This story was crafted to revolve around two levels of obstacles to solutions, specifically targeting legislative, financial, and ownership aspects at two levels. To ensure a robust, cross-model evaluation, we adopted the following approach:

1. *Story Production*: ChatGPT4o (Motzfeldt Jensen, et al., 2025) was prompted to create stories with two intensity levels of burden expressions (mainly frustration with lack of finance and legislative support, and property ownership obstacles). Each story had a percentage of the burden within the story so as to trigger emotional response in the interviewee. Four intensities of stories were created and only those between 25% and 75% were used in the semi-structured interview.
2. *Intensity Evaluation*: A different model, Gemini 1.5pro (Sobo, et al., 2025), was then queried to independently evaluate these emotional intensities. Whenever the evaluation was within 5% of the desired instruction, the evaluation was considered a success.

3. *Optimal Combination*: For Czech, the combination of ChatGPT4o for production and Gemini 1.5 for evaluation yielded the best reproducible results. Both models were utilized via their API forms within a Google Colab environment (Llerena-Izquierdo, et al., 2024).
4. *Human Validation*: After the AI-driven generation and evaluation, all stories were subsequently evaluated by human researchers, allowing for the creation of qualitative stimuli with quantifiable properties. There were two independent evaluations by researchers other than the creators of the stories.

2.4 Audio-to-Text Pipeline

Upon completion of the approximately 40-min-long interviews, the recordings underwent an automated transcription process.

1. *Model Selection*: The Whisper-large-v3-turbo language model (Lin, et al., 2025) was employed for transcription, specifically configured for Czech with the "temperature" parameter set to zero. This model was chosen because it demonstrated the singular capability to extract an adequately strong signal from the non-ideal interview recordings (a non-parsed version was used). In the second half of the project the Chirp-based Google Cloud Speech-to-text API was used set to *latest_long* (long recording-oriented version) achieving an even higher accuracy for Czech.
2. *Transcription Limitations*: Despite its signal extraction capabilities, the initial output from Whisper-large-v3-turbo (and Google´s Speech-to-text API) exhibited considerable inaccuracies, rendering it insufficiently reliable for direct data analysis. Furthermore, partitioning the interview so that each section of speech was ascribed to specific speaker was unavailable for Czech.
3. *Partitioning Strategy*: To explore potential improvements, we experimented with partitioning a recording into many shorter files and performing the audio-to-text extraction multiple times. Crucially, we found that this process did not inflate the inaccuracy rate, suggesting an avenue for potential parallel processing whenever computational resources allowed.

To achieve the best version, the non-diarized version (stream of words) was sent to the MLLM for estimating the real dialogue and reconstructing it.

2.5 Data Cleaning and Interview Reconstruction Pipeline

The selection of specific LLMs and MLLMs was driven by their demonstrated capabilities in handling complex linguistic tasks, especially for Czech, and their suitability for different phases in our pipeline. ChatGPT4o was chosen for its narrative generation prowess, and for producing emotionally nuanced stories. Gemini 1.5 pro was selected for its robust evaluation capabilities and, in its GUI version, for its effectiveness in document reconstruction. Whisper-large-v3-turbo was employed for its signal extraction from challenged audio, despite its ultimate transcription inaccuracies.

The data cleaning and interview reconstruction process centered on the iterative application of Gemini 1.5 pro GUI. This involved using the model to correct and refine the initial Whisper transcripts. Our detailed overview of this process indicates that while

Gemini 1.5 pro was adept at adequately completing document correction, subsequent rounds of cleaning beyond the initial pass did not yield marked improvements.

Our decision to explicitly exclude more advanced techniques like RAG, chunking, TD-IDF, and SpaCy integration (Ali, 2025) at this stage was a deliberate one. While theoretically offering potential benefits, preliminary testing revealed no significant qualitative improvement in the output generated by these methods.

In the second round of trials (as Gemini 1.5 pro was no longer available) we used Gemini 2.5 pro in Vertex AI studio (Bhatia & Chaudhary, 2023).

2.6   Human-in-the-Loop Evaluation and Reconstruction

The deficiencies of raw AI transcripts necessitated a rigorous reconstruction and validation process, which necessarily involved human intervention (Amirizaniani, et al., 2024). An interviewer who was present during the recording evaluated the output to ensure that the model handled Czech satisfactorily and that discrepancies were identified. This process was instrumental in mitigating inaccuracies and adjusting prompts iteratively to enhance the model's performance. This continuous feedback loop was crucial for ensuring the contextual and emotional authenticity of the reconstructed narratives.

Prior to finding the correct pipeline, the following three problems were most prevalent:

1. *Speaker Misidentification*: Speaker misidentification led to a confusion between the moderator's and respondent's contributions. This significantly complicated the accurate attribution of dialogue affecting the further use of the transcripts.
2. *Incomplete Transcriptions*: Incomplete transcriptions were a recurring problem. Critical portions of the interview narrative were absent from the automated output.
3. *Word Transcription Errors*: The transcripts contained numerous errors in word transcription, ranging from minor spelling mistakes to incorrect words. This occurred most often when slang (usually abbreviations-related) or colloquial Czech was used.

These inaccuracies were mostly fixable by the adjustments of prompts.

Prompts used for the transcription are: (a) *You are an expert text editor. Your task is to rewrite the following interview transcript.* (b) *The interview needs to be transformed into a dialogue between a 'Student' and the 'Mayor'.* (c) *Intelligently segment the dialogue and assign turns to 'Student' and 'Mayor' to form a coherent conversation.*

Key Instructions are: (a) Preserve the original wording and sentence structure as much as possible. (b) *Only correct typos, grammatical errors, or obvious misinterpretations.* (c) *Only change words when essential for coherence after role assignment or for correcting ASR/transcription errors. Do not rephrase for style or conciseness.* (d) *The core meaning and intent of the original speakers must be retained.* (e) *Do not add any new information, opinions, or elaborations.* (f) *Output should be in Czech and should maintain the way the speaker uses Czech.*

2.7   RAG for Qualitative Research

In addressing further limitations of traditional qualitative methods, the proposed framework leverages advanced Natural Language Processing techniques so as to improve analytical efficiency, consistency, and transparency. The methodology centers on transforming unstructured textual data into a structured database that the researcher can query, which was then followed by the application of a RAG model for targeted thematic inquiry (Lewis, et al., 2020; Chen, et al., 2025).

The first phase of the framework is devoted to knowledge database construction. This begins with document ingestion and sanitization, where filenames are normalized to meet database constraints when they are later used for referencing the information.

Text is then extracted, including content from both paragraphs and tables, and segmented into overlapping (by 100 words) chunks of approximately 1,000 characters. This segmentation strategy ensures contextual continuity across boundaries. Each chunk is embedded into a high-dimensional vector space using a semantic embedding model (in our case OpenAI's *text-embedding-3-small*), and both the vectors and their associated text are stored in a vector database (*ChromaDB* in our case). This modular structure allows each document to serve as an independently searchable unit within the broader analytical corpus.

The second phase focuses on the application of RAG for thematic analysis. After a question had been posed, the system conducts a corpus-wide retrieval by querying each vector store for semantically similar chunks. These are aggregated to form a coherent contextual foundation for the analysis. A key innovation in this phase is the use of specialized prompt engineering as the framework utilizes purpose-built templates tailored to specific analytical goals—such as classifying municipal activity levels, identifying motivations, or highlighting perceived barriers. Each prompt specifies the required analytical focus, expected output structure, and it mandates strict adherence to evidence drawn from the retrieved content, including citation of source documents.

The final output is a synthesized, structured answer generated by a MLLM (in our case OpenAI's ChatGPT 4o). The model processes the assembled prompt and context to produce an evidence-based response that directly addresses the research question. This synthesis approach balances automation with methodological rigor, ensuring that results are both analytically robust and verifiably sourced.

Example of processing and outcome (locations anonymized):

Question by the qualitative researcher: *Describe the level of activity in relation to rainwater management in the municipality.*

Prompt: *You are an assistant for question-answering tasks, specializing in analyzing interview transcripts about water management. Use the following pieces of retrieved context to describe the level of activity in each municipality regarding rainwater management. For each municipality mentioned in context, evaluate whether the information suggests that implementing rainwater management measures are active, moderately active, or inactive. Provide a brief explanation for your evaluation based on the context information. If the context provides information about the source document (e.g., file path), list the names of the documents used to answer the question.*

Answer: Based on the context provided, the level of activity in rainwater management can be evaluated for the following locations:

1. *Red*: Active. The municipality has an established system of water level and rain gauges, which allows for flood prediction and response. This indicates an active approach to rainwater and crisis management. (Source: Red.docx)

2. *Green*: Active. The municipality is actively engaged in strategic planning for water management, including a general water plan for the landscape and conceptual studies for climate change mitigation. They are implementing measures such as storm sewers and infiltration systems. The municipality also provides grants to citizens for rainwater retention. (Source: Green.docx)

3. *Blue*: Inactive. No specific rainwater management measures are mentioned in this context. The municipality focuses more on the operation of its water supply and sewerage network. (Source: Blue.docx)

4. *Yellow*: Inactive. The municipality is not addressing measures such as green roofs or facades and does not list any specific implemented projects in the area of rainwater management. (Source: Yellow.docx)

5. *Orange*: Moderately active. The municipality has established crisis management for floods and is insured against adverse weather effects, but no specific measures for rainwater retention are mentioned. (Source: Orange.docx)

6. *Purple*: Moderately active. The municipality has a flood commission and crisis management, but no specific measures for rainwater retention are mentioned. (Source: Purple.docx)

7. *Brown*: Moderately active. The municipality is in a partial flood zone, but no specific measures for rainwater retention are mentioned. (Source: Brown.docx)

3 Results

3.1 MLLM and Human Correction Evaluation of the Transcription Pipeline

An evaluation analysis was conducted on a corpus of 13 document pairs (MLLMs output and human corrected MLLM output) to identify and categorize token-level differences between original and revised versions. The comparison was performed using a Python script employing the *difflib* library to compare tokenized lowercase text. The similarity between document pairs was generally very high, with SequenceMatcher ratios for all successfully processed files exceeding 0.99. This indicates that the documents are largely stable, with most revisions consisting of minor edits.

Despite the advanced capabilities of the models employed, several significant technical issues were consistently observed, necessitating human intervention:

1. *Identical Documents*: Three document pairs showed no differences, with a similarity ratio of 1.0, indicating that the revised file is an identical copy of the original.

2. *Minor Lexical and Semantic Adjustments*: Most documents with modifications exhibited a small number of changes, typically between one and five tokens. These revisions were often simple word substitutions or minor additions, suggesting a process of clarification or correction.

3. *Orthographic and Tokenization Changes*: Some differences stemmed from spelling variations or how words were segmented into tokens.

4. *Substantive Revisions*: Two documents displayed a higher volume of changes, indicating a more significant editing process. These consisted of complete terminology replacement and proper name replacement. (This is understandable out-of-vocabulary token behavior.).

5. *Addition of a Token Set*: A recurring pattern was the addition of the concrete token set which appeared in the revisions of three documents. This happened with the use of improper language and professional jargon that became distorted into an ineligible combination of otherwise usual words in language.

In conclusion, the analysis reveals that while the document set is largely consistent, the revisions vary in scope. Most changes are minor and lexical. However, a subset of documents, notably three, exhibited more substantial edits that alter content and meaning significantly.

3.2   RAG and Researcher Collaboration

This presentation is titled *Late Breaking News* because the procedure is under development. We have gone through three queries in detail to evaluate the outcomes generated by RAG and evaluated by professional qualitative researchers. Listed are nine benefits of using qualitative research-oriented RAG.

1. *Efficiency in Synthesis and Thematic Identification*: The RAG implementation rapidly processes vast amounts of qualitative data. This speeds up the initial stages of analysis.
2. *Enhanced Detail Retrieval and Context Preservation*: While a vector database helps, RAG ensures that after a model generates a response or identifies a theme, it can always retrieve and present the original source text alongside its output. This is crucial for qualitative research, as it allows researchers to verify the LLM's interpretation against the original response.
3. *Scalability for Large Datasets*: As our datasets grow larger, manual analysis becomes increasingly challenging and time-consuming. The multiple-document-RAG-querying offers a scalable solution, enabling researchers to handle larger volumes of data without sacrificing the depth of analysis as the prompt can stay the same for each document.
4. *Mitigation of Researcher Bias* (*Initial Pass*): While we currently accept that human interpretation is always the final arbiter, the RAG-based solution is less susceptible to certain forms of unconscious researcher bias in the initial identification of themes or sentiment, as RAG operates on pre-trained patterns and the provided context rather than on pre-conceived notions of the researcher. We find this especially important as the authors of the theoretical background of the grant application are also the interviewers. We note that it is important that the prompting may bias the responses and therefore in future studies all parts should be submitted for review by a human, as it should ensure auditability and transparency.
5. *Auditability and Transparency*: The ability of RAG to pinpoint the exact source of information (e.g., specific sentences or paragraphs from an interview transcript) enhances the auditability of the research process, making it easier to trace findings back to their raw data.
6. *Facilitating Cross-Comparative Analysis*: the RAG system quickly compares responses across different respondents, highlighting similarities and differences in opinions, experiences, or emotional expressions. This is particularly useful for identifying subgroups or nuanced variations within a larger dataset.

7. *Automatic Summarization and Abstraction*: LLMs can generate concise summaries of longer qualitative responses while retaining key information.
8. *Support for Mixed-Methods Approaches*: When qualitative data is integrated with quantitative data, LLMs can help bridge the gap by providing structured qualitative insights that can then be augmented by numerical findings, offering a richer, more comprehensive understanding (e.g., percentual evaluation of a statement or ordering of the responses on a categorical scale).
9. *Grounding with Data*: By using the RAG system, it becomes possible to use published literature as grounding information for comparison, so it is easier for the researchers to orient themselves concerning repeats, novel findings and direction of research.

4   Discussion and Conclusion

While it is sometimes perceived as a strength and an advantage, an often-mentioned critique of qualitative research is its perceived subjectivity (Muzari, et al., 2022). Our suggested framework addresses this by using a rigorous way of leveraging embeddings, and quantifiable outputs at both stages—data collection and data analysis. First, by using one MLLM to generate interview stimuli (stories with quantifiable "burden" intensities) and then another to validate them, we standardized the prompts presented to participants. This unique method ensures responses that are more directly comparable, strengthening the foundation of the analysis.

Thereafter, the RAG system makes the analysis itself transparent and verifiable. It grounds every finding in specific, citable evidence from the source transcripts, creating an auditable trail that directly counters the "black box" problem (Zednik, 2021). This, combined with structured prompts, ensures that the entire analytical process is both highly repeatable and methodologically sound.

Time consumption is oftentimes another drawback of qualitative research. While some of the problems are mitigated by the possibility of an online interview, the necessity for a rewrite and coding of a dataset is extremely tedious (and arguably error-prone), especially for larger datasets.

Presently, one hour of interview rewriting takes between five and eight hours of work by a skilled researcher. For high quality interviews this may be even more. Automated transcription took between 12 and 16 min to finish for both pipeline steps; only further checking requires extra time. It is ideal for the interviewer to be both the transcriber and the checker. Human-in-the-loop is a recommended option in all cases.

We feel confident that the pipeline provides 99% accuracy and is sufficient for immediate RAG feeding. Our current estimation of a reduction of the time necessary for each hour planned for rewriting the interview is at least 75% (more probably 80%).

One question being processed qualitatively usually takes between one and two hours. Crafting comparisons with published literature takes approximately a further one to two hours. Thanks to parallelization of the process by using RAG, it takes less than five minutes to run whenever the top 15 chunks are used—a setting we favor. This provides 80% to 90% saved effort by the researcher.

We hope that this will allow for shifting of the human element in the human-in-the-loop concept to a higher level to see the bigger picture and, using professional knowledge to drive the querying towards more detail, deep-plunge analysis and gaining much more from data that otherwise are difficult to obtain and handle.

A significant finding of this presentation is the successful application of the pipeline conducted in Czech. While many advanced AI models are optimized primarily for English, our work demonstrates that, with careful model selection and prompt engineering, these tools are highly effective for less-resourced languages. The high accuracy of the reconstructed transcripts validates that these methods are not restricted to the English. This "opens the door" for researchers working in a many linguistic contexts, enabling them to leverage these powerful tools, and also democratizing access to cutting-edge research methodologies.

Acknowledgments. This publication is an output of the RUR project (RUR – Region to University, University to Region), reg. no. CZ.10.02.01/00/22_002/0000210, funded by the European Union. D.Ř. is also funded by the Ministry of Education, Youth and Sports, Czech Republic, and the Institutional Support for Long-term Development of Research Organizations, Faculty of Humanities, Charles University, Czech Republic (Grant COOPERATIO "Arts and Culture").

Ethics Statement. Informed consents were obtained from all interviewees before the beginning of the recording. Transcripts were anonymized with colors to protects their identities.

Conflict of Interest Statement. The authors declare that there are no conflicts of interest.

References

Ali, O.: Retrieval Augmented Generation for Intelligent Querying of Databases and Documents (2025)

Amirizaniani, M., et al.: Developing a framework for auditing large language models using human-in-the-loop (2024). arXiv:2402.09346

Amorese, T., Greco, C., Cuciniello, M., Milo, R., Sheveleva, O., Glackin, N.: Automatic speech recognition (ASR) with Whisper: Testing Performances in Different Languages. In: S3C@ CHItaly, pp. 1–8 (2023)

Barrault, L., et al.: SeamlessM4T: Massively Multilingual & Multimodal Machine Translation (2023). arXiv:2308.11596

Bhatia, J., Chaudhary, K.: The Definitive Guide to Google Vertex AI: Accelerate Your Machine Learning Journey with Google Cloud Vertex AI and MLOps Best Practices. Packt Publishing Ltd. (2023)

Braun, V., Clarke, V.: Using thematic analysis in psychology. Qual. Res. Psychol. **3**(2), 77–101 (2006)

Çoban, E.B., Mandel, M.I., Devaney, J.: What do MLLMs hear? Examining the interaction between LLM and audio encoder components in Multimodal Large Language Models. In: Audio Imagination: NeurIPS 2024 Workshop AI-Driven Speech, Music, and Sound Generation (2024)

Gao, Y., et al.: Retrieval-augmented generation for large language models: a survey (2023). arXiv: 2312.10997

Guest, G., Namey, E.E., Mitchell, M.L.: Collecting Qualitative Data: A Field Manual for Applied Research. Sage (2013)

Chen, Y., et al.: Improving Retrieval-Augmented Generation through Multi-Agent Reinforcement Learning (2025). arXiv:2501.15228

Chintala, S.: Boost call center operations: Google's speech-to-text AI integration. Int. J. Comput. Trends Technol. **72**(7), 83–86 (2024)

Lewis, P., et al.: Retrieval-augmented generation for knowledge-intensive nlp tasks. Adv. Neural. Inf. Process. Syst. **33**, 9459–9474 (2020)

Lin, J.K., Lu, H.C., Wang, C.C., Lin, H.Y., Chen, B.: Acoustically Precise Hesitation Tagging Is Essential for End-to-End Verbatim Transcription Systems (2025). arXiv:2506.04076

Llerena-Izquierdo, J., Mendez-Reyes, J., Ayala-Carabajo, R., Andrade-Martinez, C.: Innovations in introductory programming education: the role of AI with Google Colab and Gemini. Educ. Sci. **14**(12), 1330 (2024)

Motzfeldt Jensen, M., et al.: ChatGPT-4o can serve as the second rater for data extraction in systematic reviews. PLoS ONE **20**(1), e0313401 (2025)

Muzari, T., Shava, G.N., Shonhiwa, S.: Qualitative research paradigm, a key research design for educational researchers, processes and procedures: a theoretical overview. Indiana J. Human. Soc. Sci. **3**(1), 14–20 (2022)

Sobo, A., Mubarak, A., Baimagambetov, A., Polatidis, N.: Evaluating LLMs for code generation in HRI: a comparative study of ChatGPT, gemini, and claude. Appl. Artif. Intell. **39**(1), 2439610 (2025)

Taylor, Z.W.: Using Chat GPT to Clean Interview Transcriptions: A Usability and Feasibility Analysis (2023). Available at SSRN: 4437272

Yuan, Y., Liu, C., Yuan, J., Sun, G., Li, S., Zhang, M.: A Hybrid RAG System with Comprehensive Enhancement on Complex Reasoning (2024). arXiv:2408.05141

Zednik, C.: Solving the black box problem: a normative framework for explainable artificial intelligence. Philos. Technol. **34**(2), 265–288 (2021)

LNCS Homepage. http://www.springer.com/lncs. Accessed 21 November 2016

How AI Chatbot Response Style Affects Cognitive Load and Performance in Educational Tasks

Ashwini Srinivasaprasad[(⊠)], Kamelia Sepanloo, Saba Naderian Jahromi, Denny Yu, and Vincent G. Duffy

Purdue University, West Lafayette, IN, USA
{sriniv47,ksepanlo,snaderia,dennyyu,duffy}@purdue.edu

Abstract. As conversational AI agents are increasingly integrated into educational settings, understanding their cognitive impact on learners is essential. This study quantifies the cognitive load experienced by students solving GRE-style verbal reasoning problems with and without generative AI chatbot assistance. Using a within-subjects Wizard-of-Oz design, 31 university students completed equivalent verbal tasks under four controlled response conditions—Standard, Lengthy, Unstructured, and Ambiguous. We combined eye tracking metrics (pupil diameter and fixation duration) with subjective workload ratings to capture both autonomic and perceptual dimensions of mental effort. Results demonstrate that AI assistance improves overall task accuracy (from 30.6% to 74.0%) but that response quality critically modulates cognitive load. Specifically, Lengthy, Unstructured, and Ambiguous chatbot outputs elicited subjective scores, whereas concise, Structured (Standard) responses minimized both physiological arousal and perceived effort. These findings offer concrete design guidelines for chatbots, highlighting the value of clear, structured, and succinct responses to maximize learner success and minimize unnecessary effort.

Keywords: AI Chatbots · Cognitive Load · Conversational User Interface · Eye-tracking · Mixed-methods Research

1 Introduction

Generative AI chatbots have emerged as powerful tools in educational settings, transforming the ways in which learners engage with information and interact during their learning processes. Their intuitive interfaces, reminiscent of search bars or messaging apps, contribute to a positive perception among students, who often find them easy to use and helpful in various learning contexts (Feng et al., 2024). These AI-powered tools are increasingly being utilized by students to quickly grasp complex topics and receive supplementary learning assistance (Holmes et al., 2019). Despite their potential benefits, the user experience with Generative AI chatbots can be significantly affected by high cognitive load, leading to confusion, frustration, and a reluctance to engage with these tools.

© The Author(s), under exclusive license to Springer Nature Switzerland AG 2026
V. G. Duffy (Ed.): HCII 2025, LNCS 16339, pp. 188–200, 2026.
https://doi.org/10.1007/978-3-032-13012-9_14

Although prior research has explored the cognitive effects of multimedia learning environments (Mayer, 2005), we still lack a clear understanding of how conversational user interfaces (CUIs) such as ChatGPT impact users' cognitive load. According to cognitive load theory (Sweller, 1988), human working memory is limited, so it is essential to design interfaces that minimize unnecessary mental processing. Building on Cognitive Load Theory's principles, we turn to AI specific factors. Generative AI chatbots draw on vast datasets of text from diverse sources (Dergaa et al., 2024), which gives rise to a variety of response styles shaped by differing writing conventions, subject domains, levels of formality, and cultural contexts.

In human–computer interaction literature, it is well established that the total cognitive load directly affects how easily users locate information and complete tasks (Whitenton, 2013). Consequently, this makes response type variation a critical design consideration. Cognitive load measurement methods can be highly effective in assessing the mental effort required to complete tasks, providing empirical justification for measuring these effects (Darejeh et al., 2024). Cognitive overload is closely associated with task performance and can negatively impact both task completion times and overall efficacy when mental resources are exceeded (Galant-Gołębiewska et al., 2020; Biondi et al., 2020). Therefore, quantifying cognitive overload provides an opportunity to identify and refine specific elements that contribute to increased cognitive demand for the user.

Generative AI chatbots introduce several characteristics that can inadvertently raise users' cognitive load. First, when responses are overly long or information-dense, they risk overwhelming users limited working memory capacity (Seran et al., 2025). Processing and retaining large volumes of text in one try forces users to juggle multiple pieces of information simultaneously, increasing intrinsic cognitive load. Second, ambiguous or inconsistent responses compel users to question and verify what the chatbot has provided, adding an extraneous layer of mental effort. Rather than accepting recommendations at face value, users must engage in additional interpretation and fact-checking; an extra cognitive step that can lead to errors in task performance (Zhai et al., 2024; Chandler & Sweller, 1991). Ambiguous outputs are inherently harder to understand, further burdening users' mental resources.

Third, poorly structured or unorganized replies exacerbate germane cognitive load by forcing users to mentally reorganize information into a coherent format. Although well-designed AI systems can offload routine inquiries and streamline support (Gerlich, 2025), disordered outputs have the opposite effect, making it harder for users to extract key points and follow logical flows. Building on these insights, this study examines how four distinct chatbot response styles—Standard, Lengthy, Unstructured, and Ambiguous— affect physiological indicators of mental effort (RQ1). We also seek to determine which style best balances task performance with minimal cognitive load, thereby guiding the design of conversational AI systems that support effective, cognitively sustainable user experiences (RQ2).

Prior studies have found a relationship between eye tracking data and human mental or emotional states such as stress and cognitive workload. For example, Torres-Salomao et al. (2015) found pupil diameter to be a viable indicator of incremental stress when participants were exposed to math problems at varying levels of difficulty. A recent systematic review of literature from 2010 to 2020 of eye tracking measures used to assess cognitive workload in surgery found that pupil responses, gaze patterns, and blinks were often associated with workload and stress (Tolvanen et al., 2022). Studies have shown that eye tracking measures are reliable and effective at indicating human psychophysiological responses, such as cognitive workload and stress, during various tasks.

Therefore, the primary objective of this study is to quantify the cognitive load experienced by users when solving verbal reasoning problems with and without assistance from a generative AI chatbot. To achieve this, we employ eye tracking metrics to capture autonomic and ocular indicators of mental effort. By standardizing the AI interaction through a Wizard-of-Oz style chatbot, we ensure that variability in chatbot responses can be systematically manipulated and its effects on cognitive load isolated. Specifically, the study aims to:

- Compare baseline cognitive load between unassisted problem-solving and AI-assisted problem-solving on GRE-style verbal questions of equivalent difficulty.
- Examine the influence of AI response types (Standard, Lengthy, Unstructured, or Ambiguous) on physiological indicators of cognitive load.
- Assess the interaction between AI response types and task performance, evaluating whether certain response styles facilitate or hinder both accuracy and mental effort.

2 Methodology

The experiment was designed to investigate how different styles of AI chatbot responses (e.g., length, ambiguity, unstructured, and standard) influence cognitive load during problem-solving tasks. To assess cognitive load, the study employed a mixed-methods approach, integrating physiological measurements (via eye-tracking) with subjective evaluations collected through post-task surveys. 31 graduate students from Purdue University, aged 18–28, participated in the study. They were recruited from two separate courses and received extra course credit as an incentive for their involvement.

The study was structured into two primary phases designed to evaluate participants' cognitive load and task performance during GRE-style verbal reasoning tasks, both with and without AI assistance.

1. Baseline Phase (No AI Assistance): Participants initially completed four medium-difficulty GRE verbal reasoning questions without any AI support. This phase was designed to establish baseline measures of cognitive load and task performance in the absence of external assistance.
2. AI Interaction Phase: In the second phase, participants completed sixteen additional GRE verbal reasoning questions with AI support. The difficulty level of the questions remained consistent (medium) across all tasks. AI responses were delivered using a Wizard-of-Oz methodology, wherein researchers provided pre-scripted answers representing four distinct response types:
- Standard Response: Concise bullet-point answers enhanced with emojis for clarity and engagement.
- Long Explanatory Answer: Detailed, paragraph-based explanations spanning four to five paragraphs.

- Unstructured Bottom-Up Answer: A progressive list of possible answers, ordered from least to most relevant.
- Ambiguous Answer: Vague and indirect responses lacking definitive guidance.

This within-subject design ensured that each participant was exposed to all four AI response types. A fixed order was used across participants to prevent carryover effects between varying chatbot conditions from contaminating performance or perception within each response type block. This approach prioritized internal consistency of condition-specific responses and minimized fatigue or confusion from frequent switching; however, it may introduce order effects, which are addressed in the limitations. During the experiment, participants wore Tobii Glasses 3 (Fig. 1) to collect eye-tracking data. The eye-tracking system was used to monitor gaze patterns, fixation durations, and pupil dilation, providing continuous, non-intrusive physiological indicators of cognitive load during task performance.

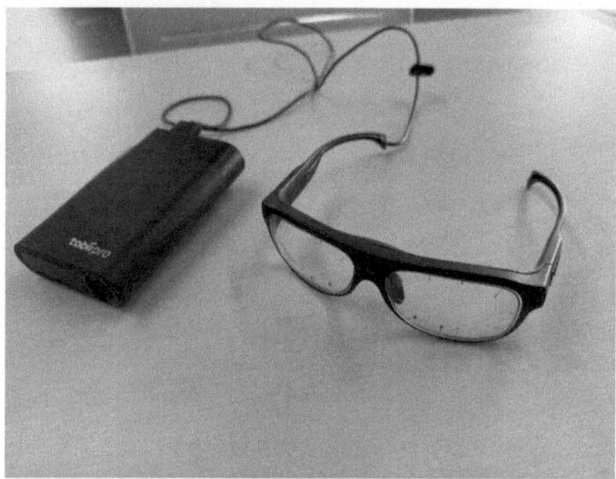

Fig. 1. The Tobii eye-tracking device recorded gaze patterns, fixation durations, and pupil dilation in real time, providing physiological indicators of cognitive load.

Upon completing the experimental tasks, participants filled out a self-report survey designed to assess subjective cognitive workload. The survey included items evaluating mental effort, frustration, and the perceived clarity of the AI-generated responses. Table 1 summarizes the survey questions.

The experiment was conducted in a controlled environment with minimal external distractions (Fig. 2). Upon arrival, participants received a detailed explanation of the study and provided informed consent. The eye-tracking glasses were then calibrated for each participant. The session began with the baseline phase (no AI assistance), where participants completed four GRE-style verbal reasoning questions. This was followed by the AI interaction phase, in which participants worked through sixteen additional questions under the four scripted AI response conditions.

Pupil diameter data were collected for both the left and right eyes. The mean pupil diameter was computed for each eye and averaged to yield an overall value for each participant under each condition. Given that pupil dilation is a well-established measure

Table 1. Subjective Questionnaire

Survey Domain	Question Items
Demographics	– Age – Gender (Male, Female, prefer not to say) – Are you a native English speaker? (Yes/No)
Mental Effort and Cognitive Load	– Mental effort required (1–10 scale) –Was the task more mentally demanding than expected? – Effort to understand AI responses – Feeling overwhelmed by AI information – Frustration with AI interface
Clarity and Structure of AI Responses	– Clarity and conciseness of AI information – Difficulty identifying important information
AI Usability and Interaction	– Ease of interaction with AI assistant – Noticing inconsistencies in AI responses – Impact of inconsistencies on learning – Impact of inconsistencies on trust in AI
Physical Discomfort	– Physical discomfort while using AI interface (Yes/No)
Perceived Learning Support	– AI helped achieve learning objectives – Emoji use improved comprehension
Factors Affecting Comprehension	– Responses too long – Responses unstructured – Responses ambiguous – Responses inconsistent

for cognitive workload, these data were analyzed in conjunction with the subjective survey responses. A correlational analysis was performed to assess the relationship between physiological and self-reported workload, as suggested in previous literature (Torres-Salomao et al., 2015).

Additionally, fixation duration was extracted from the eye-tracking recordings. Fixations, defined as pauses of the eye on a single location, serve as an indicator of cognitive processing (Liang et al., 2021). These durations were analyzed across the different response types.

The formal null and alternative hypotheses for these comparisons can be summarized by the following:

- **Null Hypothesis (H0):** There is no statistically significant difference in eye-tracking metrics or subjective survey responses across the different AI response types, indicating no variation in cognitive workload.
- **Alternative Hypothesis (HA):** The type of AI response significantly influences average pupil diameter, mean fixation duration, and subjective workload scores, indicating differential levels of cognitive workload.

Fig. 2. Experiment Room.

2.1 Analysis Methodology

Physiological Data Analysis. To facilitate data extraction, the timestamps corresponding to each AI response type were manually labeled in the video recordings for each participant. This labeling enabled segmentation of the eye-tracking data according to the response condition. Key physiological indicators of cognitive load (pupil diameter, fixation duration, and gaze patterns) were extracted for each segment corresponding to the different response types.

Subjective Data Analysis. Participants' subjective experiences were evaluated using responses from the post-experiment survey. For each AI response type, average scores were calculated across key dimensions: mental effort, frustration, and clarity. To examine the relationship between self-reported mental effort and task performance accuracy, a Spearman's rank correlation analysis was conducted. In addition, a repeated-measures ANOVA was performed to assess the effect of AI response type on participants' task accuracy, accounting for within-subject variability.

3 Results

3.1 Physiological Measures Analysis

Pupil Dilation. The results for the mean pupil diameter for baseline condition (task without AI assistance) and the different response types (with AI assistance) are shown below with standard deviations in Table 2. The mean pupil diameter in the baseline condition for all participants is 3.44 ± 0.52 which is slightly higher than the mean pupil diameter in all other AI assisted conditions. The reduction in pupil diameter between baseline (no AI) and AI assistance suggests lower cognitive load and arousal with AI support.

Table 2. Mean Pupil diameter by Condition

Task	Mean Pupil diameter (mm)	t-value	p-value
Baseline	3.44 ± 0.52	28.35	0
Standard	3.41 ± 0.55	1.99	0.050
Long	3.31 ± 0.54	−4.58	0.000
Unstructured	3.36 ± 0.55	−1.23	0.220
Ambiguous	3.38 ± 0.56	−0.03	0.973

A linear mixed effects model was fitted to examine how AI generated response type influenced mean pupil diameter. The model's intercept ($\beta = 3.382$, SE = 0.119, $p < 0.001$) represents the average pupil diameter in the baseline condition (no AI assistance). The "Long" response type produced a significant decrease in pupil diameter compared to baseline ($\beta = -0.072$ mm, SE = 0.016, $p < 0.001$), suggesting reduced cognitive load or arousal when participants processed lengthier AI answers. The "Perfect" response type showed a marginally significant increase in pupil diameter ($\beta = 0.031$ mm, SE = 0.016, $p = 0.050$), indicating a trend toward higher engagement with the most coherent AI responses. Neither the "Unstructured" ($\beta = -0.019$ mm, $p = 0.220$) nor the "Ambiguous" ($\beta = -0.001$ mm, $p = 0.973$) response types differed significantly from baseline.

These findings indicate that the form and clarity of AI-generated responses significantly modulate physiological indicators of cognitive workload. Notably, "Long" responses were associated with reduced pupil diameter, suggesting lower mental effort or increased cognitive ease. In contrast, "Standard" responses elicited a marginally increased pupil size, reflecting heightened engagement or deeper processing. The lack of significant changes for "Unstructured" and "Ambiguous" responses further suggests that poorly framed AI outputs neither alleviate nor meaningfully stimulate cognitive processing.

Fixation Duration. The results for the mean fixation duration (ms) for baseline condition (task without AI assistance) and the different response types (with AI assistance) are shown below with standard deviations in Table 3. The increase in fixation duration between baseline (no AI) and AI assistance suggests lower cognitive load and arousal with AI support.

To examine the impact of AI-generated response types on cognitive workload as reflected in eye movement, a linear mixed effects model was conducted. The model revealed a significant main effect of response type on fixation duration ($p < 0.001$), indicating that different types of AI-generated responses were associated with differing levels of visual attention during question answering. Compared to the baseline condition, the "Standard" response type significantly increased fixation duration ($\beta = 75.18$, $p < 0.001$), suggesting a higher level of sustained visual processing. In contrast, the "Long" response type led to a significant reduction in fixation duration ($\beta = -45.70$, $p < 0.001$), while the "Unstructured" response type also showed a significant negative

Table 3. Mean Fixation duration by Condition

Task	Mean Fixation duration (ms)	t-value	p-value
Baseline	492.56 ± 153.01	1.62	0.109
Standard	549.31 ± 207.83	6.16	0
Long	428.43 ± 149.80	−4.02	0
Unstructured	448.07 ± 154.59	−2.29	0.024
Ambiguous	452.28 ± 161.81	−1.92	0.058

effect ($\beta = -26.06$, p $= 0.024$). The "Ambiguous" response type exhibited a marginally non-significant decrease ($\beta = -21.85$, p $= 0.058$), suggesting a possible trend toward reduced cognitive engagement. These results indicate that the structure and quality of AI-generated answers influence participants' eye movement behavior, with more coherent or optimal answers (Standard response) eliciting more sustained attention.

These results indicate that the structure and quality of AI-generated answers influence participants' eye movement behavior, as measured by fixation duration. In particular, more coherent and well-structured responses (e.g., Standard) elicited longer fixation durations, suggesting greater cognitive engagement and sustained visual attention. In contrast, less structured or overly lengthy responses appeared to reduce attention, either by facilitating easier comprehension (as in the Long condition) or by diminishing user engagement (as in the Unstructured and Ambiguous conditions).

3.2 Subjective Measures Analysis

Overall Accuracy. Participants' mean accuracy in the no-AI condition was $M = 0.306 \pm 0.22$, whereas in the AI-assisted condition it increased to $M = 0.74 \pm 0.17$. A paired-samples t-test confirmed that this difference was highly significant, t(df) $= -9.004$, p $< .001$, indicating that AI assistance yielded superior performance on the GRE questions.

Subjective Workload (Post-Survey). Descriptive statistics for each post-survey dimension are presented in Table 4. Accuracy was highest for "Standard" AI responses and lowest for Ambiguous and Unstructured responses (Fig. 3).

Table 4. Post-survey dimension scores.

Dimension	Avg Score (out of 5)
Mental Effort	2.31
Frustration	3
Clarity	2.209

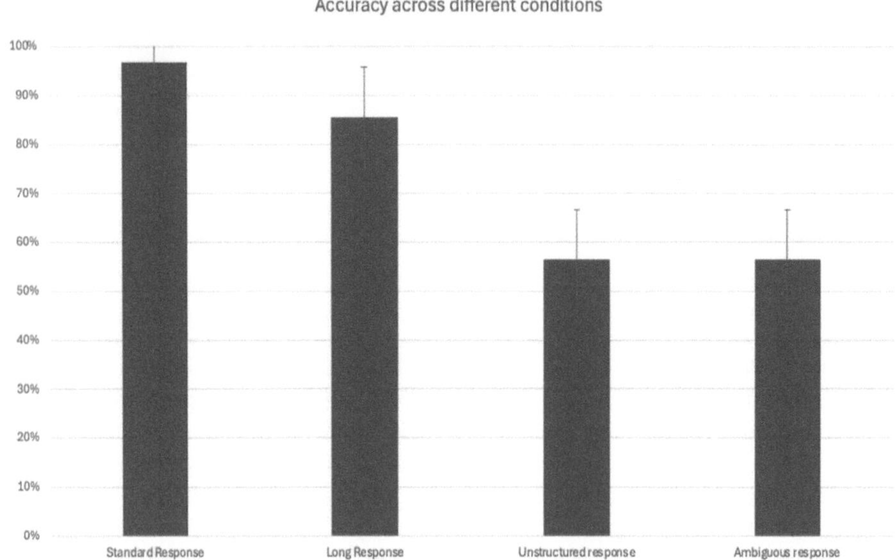

Fig. 3. Accuracy across different conditions.

Correlation Between Accuracy and Mental Effort. A Spearman's rank correlation revealed a significant inverse relationship between AI-assisted accuracy and self-reported mental effort, $\rho = -0.52$, p = .0025. Participants who achieved lower accuracy under AI assistance tended to report higher levels of mental effort.

Effect of AI Response Type on Accuracy. A one-way repeated-measures ANOVA examined accuracy across the four AI response categories. There was a significant main effect of response type on accuracy, $F(3, 30) = 3.39$, p < .001. Bonferroni-corrected post-hoc comparisons ($\alpha = .0083$) showed that:

- Standard responses produced the highest accuracy (all p < .001 vs. other types).
- Lengthy responses yielded intermediate accuracy (p < .001 vs. Unstructured and Ambiguous).
- No significant difference emerged between Unstructured and Ambiguous responses (p = 1.00).

Native vs. Non-Native English Speakers. Mann–Whitney U tests compared native and non-native speakers on (a) improvement in accuracy from no-AI to AI conditions and (b) mental effort. There was no significant group difference in accuracy improvement (−0.45, 0.649), but non-native speakers reported significantly greater mental effort than native speakers (U = 0.9, p = 0.036), suggesting differential cognitive demands across language backgrounds.

Participants also reported a moderate level of agreement regarding the educational value of the AI assistant. When asked whether the AI agent helped them achieve the learning objectives, the average response was 3.10 on a 5-point Likert scale (1 = Strongly

Disagree, 5 = Strongly Agree). Interestingly, participants responded more positively to the use of emojis in AI responses. The average agreement scores for the statement "Did the use of emoji help better understand the answers?" was 4.61, indicating that the inclusion of visual cues significantly supported comprehension.

4   Discussion and Limitations

This study provides valuable insights into the cognitive impact of generative AI assistance during complex verbal reasoning tasks; however, several limitations should be noted. While longer fixations are sometimes associated with increased cognitive processing or higher mental effort, in this study they appear to reflect sustained visual attention and engagement, particularly in response to clear and structured AI outputs. This is supported by the fact that the "Standard" condition, which had the highest fixation durations, also produced the highest accuracy and lowest subjective effort. In contrast, shorter fixations observed in the "Lengthy", "Unstructured", and "Ambiguous" conditions may reflect either cognitive disengagement or reduced attentional stability due to information overload or confusion. Thus, fixation duration in this context is best interpreted as a proxy for meaningful engagement rather than raw cognitive load, aligning with prior findings that associate gaze behavior with information relevance and processing fluency (Holmqvist et al., 2011).

First, the study was conducted with a limited and homogeneous sample, which may constrain the generalizability of the findings. Participants' prior familiarity with AI systems or differential cognitive abilities were not controlled, potentially introducing individual variability in responses to AI-assisted conditions; Second, the experimental tasks were administered in a controlled laboratory environment. While this setup allowed for rigorous collection of physiological data, it does not fully replicate the complexity and variability of real-world educational or professional settings. External factors such as environmental distractions, time pressure, and emotional stress (which often influence cognitive load) were minimized and may therefore reduce ecological validity; Third, the AI responses used in the study were static and pre-defined across all participants. In practice, generative AI systems are capable of dynamically adapting to users' behavior and queries. The use of non-interactive responses may limit the ability to fully assess the cognitive benefits or drawbacks of real-time, personalized AI support; Fourth, the interpretation of physiological measures such as pupil dilation and fixation duration, while grounded in prior literature, is inherently multifactorial. Although lighting conditions were controlled and tasks were counterbalanced, these metrics can still be influenced by variables such as fatigue, emotional arousal, or individual differences in oculomotor behavior, which were not fully accounted for; Fifth, the study focused exclusively on GRE-style verbal reasoning tasks. It remains unclear whether the observed cognitive effects of different AI communication styles would generalize to other domains, such as mathematical problem-solving, collaborative decision-making, or clinical reasoning; Sixth, the study captured only the immediate cognitive responses during task execution. Longitudinal outcomes, such as retention, transfer of knowledge, or changes in users' trust and reliance on AI systems over time, were not assessed and warrant further investigation; Lastly, the AI response types were presented in a fixed order for all participants. While this helped preserve the integrity and coherence of each response condition and avoided confusion from rapidly changing chatbot styles, it does introduce potential order effects such as fatigue, learning, or habituation. These effects could have influenced participants' performance or perceived effort across later trials. Future work should consider counterbalancing response order to better isolate the unique contribution of each AI response type.

5　Conclusion

This study examined how different styles of generative AI chatbot responses affect students' cognitive load while performing GRE-style verbal reasoning tasks. By integrating physiological data (pupil diameter and fixation duration) with subjective workload ratings, we identified how varying communication strategies of AI assistance influence mental effort during problem-solving. Our findings confirmed that AI assistance improved performance overall, with task accuracy increasing from 30.6% in the Baseline (no AI) condition to 74.0% in the Standard AI condition. However, while performance gains were consistent, the cognitive cost varied notably across different response styles. Physiological measures provided key insights into this variation. Mean pupil diameter was highest in Baseline condition (M = 3.44 ± 0.52 mm), suggesting the highest cognitive load when no assistance was provided. In contrast, all AI-assisted conditions exhibited slightly reduced pupil dilation: Standard (3.41 ± 0.55 mm), Long (3.31 ± 0.54 mm), Unstructured (3.36 ± 0.55 mm), and Ambiguous (3.38 ± 0.56 mm). These decreases imply that AI support can alleviate cognitive load, though the degree of relief is moderated by the clarity and organization of the chatbot's response. Fixation duration patterns offered a complementary perspective. Interestingly, the Standard condition yielded the highest mean fixation duration (M = 549.31 ± 207.83 ms), possibly indicating increased engagement or sustained attention due to coherent and structured AI guidance. Conversely, the "Lengthy" condition resulted in the shortest fixation duration (M = 428.43 ± 149.80 ms), suggesting cognitive disengagement or fatigue from overly verbose explanations. Unstructured (448.07 ± 154.59 ms) and Ambiguous (452.28 ± 161.81 ms) responses also led to relatively shorter fixations compared to the Standard format, reinforcing the notion that disorganized or unclear messaging increases cognitive friction and potentially limits users' ability to process information effectively. Correlational analyses further confirmed a strong relationship between physiological and perceived workload, validating the reliability of eye-tracking as a non-intrusive, real-time indicator of cognitive strain. Specifically, average pupil diameter was positively correlated with subjective mental demand scores (r = 0.61, p < 0.01), supporting prior literature linking ocular metrics to cognitive stress.

Overall, these results emphasize that not all AI support is cognitively equal. Although all AI conditions reduced pupil dilation relative to baseline, only structured and concise responses maintained high levels of user engagement without inducing additional mental strain. Subjective workload ratings corroborated these findings, with participants reporting higher mental demand and frustration for ambiguous or unstructured outputs. These findings have practical implications for designing conversational AI systems in educational settings. Developers should prioritize clear, structured, and succinct response styles to minimize unnecessary cognitive load while maintaining user focus. Overly detailed, vague, or unstructured AI explanations may hinder learning by requiring users to compensate cognitively for poor communication design. In future work, dynamic AI systems that adapt their response format based on real-time physiological feedback may offer a promising path forward. This approach could ensure that AI-generated assistance remains cognitively appropriate for individual learners, thereby maximizing both learning effectiveness and user experience. In summary, while AI can enhance task performance, its effectiveness as a learning aid depends critically on how it communicates. Effective AI support must be not only accurate, but also cognitively considerate—facilitating reasoning without overwhelming the learner.

References

Feng, C.M., Botha, E., Pitt, L.: From HAL to GenAI: optimizing chatbot impacts with CARE. Bus. Horiz. **67**(5), 537–548 (2024). https://doi.org/10.1016/j.bushor.2024.04.012

Holmes, W., Bialik, M., Fadel, C.: Artificial Intelligence in Education: Promises and Implications for Teaching and Learning. Center for Curriculum Redesign (2019)

Sweller, J.: Cognitive load during problem solving: effects on learning. Cogn. Sci. **12**(2), 257–285 (1988)

Whitenton, K.: Minimize Cognitive Load to Maximize Usability. Nielsen Norman Group (2013). https://www.nngroup.com/articles/minimize-cognitive-load/

Darejeh, A., Marcusa, N., Mohammadi, G., Sweller, J.: A critical analysis of cognitive load measurement methods for evaluating the usability of different types of interfaces: Guidelines and framework for human-computer interaction (2024). https://doi.org/10.48550/arXiv.2402.11820

Galant-Gołębiewska, M., Zawada, W., Maciejewska, M.: Analysis of Pilot's Cognitive Overload Changes During the Flight (2020). https://doi.org/10.3849/AIMT.01408

Dergaa, I., et al.: From tools to threats: a reflection on the impact of artificial-intelligence chatbots on cognitive health. Front. Psychol. **15**, 1259845 (2024). https://doi.org/10.3389/fpsyg.2024.1259845

Seran, C.E., Tan, M.J.T., Karim, H.A., Al Dahoul, N.: A conceptual exploration of generative AI-induced cognitive dissonance and its emergence in university-level academic writing. Front. Artif. Intell. **8**, Article 1573368 (2025). https://doi.org/10.3389/frai.2025.1573368

Zhai, C., Wibowo, S., Li, L.D.: The effects of over-reliance on AI dialogue systems on students' cognitive abilities: a systematic review. Smart Learn. Environ. **11**, Article 28 (2024). https://doi.org/10.1186/s40561-024-00316-7

Chandler, P., Sweller, J.: Cognitive load theory and the format of instruction. Cogn. Instr. **8**(4), 293–332 (1991). https://doi.org/10.1207/s1532690xci0804_5

Gerlich, M.: AI tools in society: Impacts on cognitive offloading and the future of critical thinking. Societies **15**, Article 6 (2025). https://doi.org/10.3390/soc15010006

Biondi, F., Cacanindin, A., Douglas, C., Cort, J.: Overloaded and at work: investigating the effect of cognitive workload on assembly task performance. Hum. Fact. **63**(5), 813–820 (2020). https://doi.org/10.1177/0018720820929928

Liang, N., et al.: Using eye-tracking to investigate the effects of pre-takeover visual engagement on situation awareness during automated driving. Accid. Anal. Prev. **157**, 106143 (2021)

Tolvanen, O., Elomaa, A.-P., Itkonen, M., Vrzakova, H., Bednarik, R., Huotarinen, A.: Eye-tracking indicators of workload in surgery: a systematic review. J. Invest. Surg. **35**(6), 1340–1349 (2022)

Torres-Salomao, L., Mahfouf, M., El-Samahy, E.: Pupil diameter size marker for incremental mental stress detection. In: 2015 17th International Conference on e-Health Networking, Application & Services (HealthCom) (2015)

Holmqvist, K., Nyström, M., Andersson, R., Dewhurst, R., Jarodzka, H., Van de Weijer, J.: Eye Tracking: A Comprehensive Guide to Methods and Measures. Oxford University Press (2011)

Mayer, R.E.: The Cambridge Handbook of Multimedia Learning. Cambridge University Press (2005)

Archi-Nerf: View Synthesis for Traditional Chinese Architecture Using Nerf Neural Network

Zhanlin Yan[1]([✉]) and Han Tu[2]

[1] National University of Singapore, 4 Architecture Drive, Singapore 117566, Singapore
zhanlin1999@outlook.com
[2] Massachusetts Institute of Technology, 77 Massachusetts Avenue, Cambridge, MA 02139, USA
hantu@mit.edu

Abstract. Traditional Neural Radiance Fields (NeRF) models are designed to generate entire scenes, which limits their applicability in architectural design. Architectural workflows often require component-based models or detailed visual representations to focus on specific parts of a building, a need rarely addressed by generative networks. Furthermore, architects conventionally rely on manual methods or rule-based tools such as Grasshopper (GH), resulting in minimal integration between generative AI and architectural modeling workflows. This study proposes a pipeline for generating 3D representations of specific architectural elements using video data collected from drones or online sources. The Hanging Temple (Xuankong Temple) serves as a case study to demonstrate the pipeline. The process begins with extracting frames from videos to obtain multi-angle images of the temple. These images are segmented using the Grounded Segment Anything Model (SAM) and masked based on user-defined requirements, such as isolating the whole scene, natural elements, architectural structures, or specific components. The filtered image dataset is then processed in COLMAP to compute spatial coordinates (x, y, z) and viewing directions (θ, ϕ). This information, along with the image dataset, is fed into Instant-NGP, a refined NeRF framework, to generate 3D representations. The pipeline successfully generates independent 3D models of the entire Hanging Temple, the natural cliff, the temple structure, and its roof. Although the solid meshes derived from these 3D representations may lack full precision, the results demonstrate the potential of AI to create detailed 3D models of individual architectural elements. This approach reduces manual effort, supports iterative design workflows, and facilitates the development of complex architectural models, contributing to advancements in computational design and architectural analysis.

Keywords: Neural Radiance Fields (NeRF) · Architectural Modeling · Grounded Segment Anything Model (SAM) · Generative AI · Digital Heritage

1 Introduction

Neural Radiance Fields (NeRF) have become a widely used technique in 3D reconstruction, enabling the modeling of volumetric radiance and density from sparse 2D input views [7]. NeRF generates high-quality 3D representations of complex scenes with significant accuracy. Recent advancements have extended its capabilities, introducing tools to improve functionality and broaden application areas. For example, CLIP-NeRF integrates the CLIP model's joint language-image embedding space, allowing users to manipulate NeRF using text prompts or reference images [15]. DreamCraft3D adopts a hierarchical method for 3D content creation, using personalized diffusion models trained on augmented scene renderings to refine textures and produce detailed outputs [14]. Magic123 employs a two-stage framework for generating high-quality textured 3D meshes from unposed images by combining NeRF-based geometry optimization with differentiable mesh representations and diffusion priors [9]. These advancements highlight NeRF's versatility in 3D scene generation and object reconstruction, positioning it as a state-of-the-art tool in neural rendering.

In architectural modeling, the focus often shifts to specific components of a building, such as roofs, walls, or structural elements, within the context of the overall design. Traditional workflows rely on tools like Grasshopper (GH) or manual modeling techniques, which are time-intensive and lack integration with generative AI. Incorporating AI into architectural modeling has the potential to improve efficiency, enabling faster and more accurate 3D representations [5].

Despite its promise, traditional NeRF models face critical limitations in architectural applications. First, they generate point clouds without distinguishing between different architectural components, which limits their usability for workflows requiring modular or component-specific 3D models. Second, NeRF does not provide reliable methods for converting point clouds into solid meshes, making it difficult to integrate these outputs into architectural design tools. These limitations hinder its adoption in architecture, where precision, modularity, and editability are essential.

This study proposes a pipeline that addresses these challenges by integrating a refined NeRF model, Instant neural graphics primitives [8], with the Grounded Segment Anything Model [10], and mesh processing tools such as Meshlab [1]. Using the Hanging Temple (Xuankong Temple) as the research project, the pipeline demonstrates how to generate 3D representations of specific architectural components and convert point clouds into usable solid meshes, offering a practical solution for NeRF engaged architectural modeling workflows.

2 Methodology

The proposed pipeline addresses a key limitation of Neural Radiance Fields (NeRF): the inability to differentiate between various parts of a 3D model. NeRF inherently takes spatial positions (x,y,z) and viewing directions (θ,ϕ) as input and outputting RGB color (R,G,B) and density (σ). This formulation treats the input as a continuous field and lacks the capability to distinguish different components or categories within a scene, which is crucial for architectural modeling.

To overcome this limitation, the pipeline incorporates the Grounded Segment Anything Model (Grounded-SAM) to segment input images. This segmentation step allows the isolation of specific parts of the scene based on user-defined categories, enabling NeRF to generate component-aware 3D representations. The pipeline supports four hierarchical levels of architectural modeling, progressing from macro to micro scales:

- Scene Level: The overall view of the environment and the structure;
- Nature Level: Surrounding natural elements, such as cliffs or landscapes; Architecture Level: The structure itself, such as buildings or temples;
- Component Level: Individual architectural components, such as roofs.

The general pipeline follows a sequential structure: Videos → Frames → Augmented Frames → Segmented Images (via Grounded-SAM) → COLMAP → Neural Scene Representation → Point Clouds → Solid Meshes (Fig. 1). While this sequence forms the foundation of the workflow, specific adjustments are made at different hierarchical levels to meet the unique requirements of each scale.

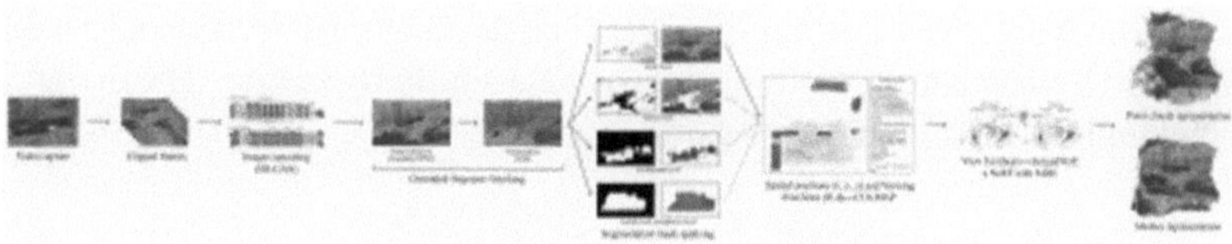

Fig. 1. General proposed pipeline.

2.1 Workflow of Level of Scene

Data Collection and Pre-processing. Video data were obtained from two sources: drones and crowd-sourced video websites. These videos captured the Hanging Temple from multiple angles and distances, ensuring comprehensive coverage of the site. The videos were processed using the "cv2" Python library [3], and frames were extracted at a rate of 10 frames per second. This extraction rate was chosen to maintain continuity, which is essential for accurate camera pose estimation using COLMAP in later steps. A total of 1386 images were extracted from the videos and subsequently upscaled using SRGAN [4], increasing the resolution from 1920×1080 to 7680×4320 (Fig. 2). This upscaling step enhanced the image details and pixel density, allowing the Instant-NGP model to capture fine architectural features and sharp angles more effectively using the Multiresolution Hash Encoding algorithm [8].

Spatial Position and Viewing Direction Calculation. Next, the enhanced images are processed using COLMAP [12]. COLMAP follows a two-stage process: Correspondence Search and Incremental Reconstruction, enabling the calculation of camera positions and orientations as well as the generation of 3D scene representations.

In Correspondence Search stage, COLMAP identifies overlapping regions across images and establishes correspondences between features to construct a scene graph. The process consists of three key steps:

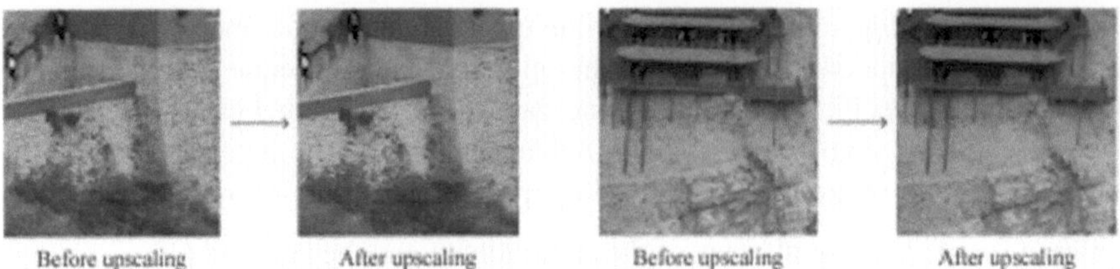

Fig. 2. SGGAN result.

1. Feature Extraction: Local features are detected in each image $I = \{I_i | i = 1, \ldots, NI\}$.

$$F_i = \{(x_j, f_j) | j = 1, \ldots, N_{F_i}\} \tag{1}$$

where $x_j \in R2$ is the 2D location of a feature, and f_j is its appearance descriptor. These features are designed to be invariant to radiometric and geometric changes, ensuring robust recognition across images.
2. Feature Matching: For each pair of images (I_a, I_b), feature correspondences Mab are established by comparing descriptors f_j using a similarity metric. The output is a set of potentially overlapping image pairs.

$$C = \{(I_a, I_b) | I_a, I_b \in I, \ a < b \tag{2}$$

and their associated matches:

$$C = \{(I_a, I_b) | I_a, I_b \in I, \ a < b \tag{3}$$

3. Geometric Verification: Matching results are verified geometrically using transformations such as the homography matrix (H), the essential matrix (E), or the fundamental matrix (F). Robust methods like RANSAC are used to filter outliers. The verified matches form a scene graph, where images are nodes, and verified image pairs are edges.

In Incremental Reconstruction, COLMAP incrementally registers images to build a 3D model and estimate camera poses. It includes:

1. Initialization: Reconstruction begins with a selected pair of overlapping images to create an initial 3D structure.
2. Image Registration: New images are registered to the model by solving the Perspective-n-Point (PnP) problem. The camera pose $Pc \in SE(3)$ is estimated using 2D-3D correspondences.

$$P_c = \arg \min \sum_k \|\pi(P_c, X_k) - x_k\|^2 \tag{4}$$

where $\pi(Pc, Xk)$ projects 3D points $X_k \in R^3$ to the image plane.
3. Triangulation: New 3D points are added by triangulating feature correspondences from multiple views, increasing the stability and completeness of the model.

4. Bundle Adjustment: To refine both the camera poses Pc and the 3D points Xk, COLMAP minimizes the reprojection error.

$$E = \sum_{j} \rho_j (\| \pi(P_c, X_k) - x_{jk} \|^2) \tag{5}$$

where ρj is a robust loss function to handle outliers. This optimization ensures an accurate reconstruction.

To process the operations described above, the following command is executed in the command line:

```
python colmap2nerf.py --colmap_matcher exhaustive --
    run_colmap --aabb_scale 16 --image xksscene
```

This command enables COLMAP to perform feature extraction, matching, and camera pose estimation, producing a series of output files. Among these files, the 'transform.json' file is selected as it contains the spatial positions and orientations of the cameras. This file, along with the original input images, serves as the input for Instant-NGP to generate neural scene representations.

View Synthesis. For neural scene representation, we use Instant-NGP (Instant Neural Graphics Primitives), which is a refined implementation of the NeRF algorithm. Instant-NGP significantly improves the accuracy and detail of 3D view synthesis, primarily due to its incorporation of Multiresolution Hash Encoding (MHE) [8].

Multiscale Hash Encoding (MHE) encodes input spatial coordinates $x \in R^d$ into feature vectors $y = enc(x;\theta)$, where θ represents trainable parameters. These parameters are organized into L resolution levels, with each level representing the input space at a different scale. This multiresolution setup ensures efficient encoding while capturing both low-frequency and high-frequency details.

Each resolution level is defined mathematically, with resolutions ranging geometrically between a coarsest scale Nmin and a finest scale Nmax. The resolution N_1 for level 1 is determined as follows:

$$N_l = \lfloor N_{min} \cdot b^l \rfloor \ , \quad b = \exp \left(\frac{\ln N_{max} - \ln N_{min}}{L - 1} \right), \tag{6}$$

where b is the growth factor, typically in the range of 1.26 to 2. Coarser levels capture broad, low-frequency features, while finer levels focus on detailed, high-frequency structures. This hierarchical approach reduces memory usage by avoiding the need for densely populated grids at all resolutions.

For each resolution level, input coordinates are scaled by the grid resolution Nl and rounded to the nearest voxel corners to determine the feature locations:

$$\lfloor x_l \rfloor = \lfloor x \cdot N_l \rfloor \ , \quad \lceil x_l \rceil = \lceil x \cdot N_l \rceil. \tag{7}$$

The feature vectors associated with these voxel corners are retrieved from a hash table for efficient lookups.

To manage memory efficiently, the feature vectors are stored in a hash table of size T. For coarse grids where $(N1 + 1)^d \leq T$, the mapping is direct and collision-free. However, for finer grids with higher resolutions, a spatial hash function is employed:

$$h(x) = \left(\bigoplus_{i=1}^{d} x_i \pi_i \right) \quad \mod T, \tag{8}$$

where $\boxplus$ represents the bitwise XOR operation, xi are the integer coordinates of the voxel, and πi are large, unique prime numbers. This hashing mechanism ensures a balanced distribution of voxel mappings across the hash table, minimizing collisions and maintaining efficiency.

Point Cloud and Solid Mesh Generation. Using the Instant-NGP GUI, view representations can be exported as point clouds. These point clouds are then imported into MeshLab [1], where they are converted into solid meshes.

2.2 Workflow of Level of Nature

Data Collection. From the original dataset of 1386 base-upscaled images, 256 images were selected where natural elements dominate the majority of the scene.

Object Detection, Semantic Segmentation, Image Masking. To remove the building and retain only natural elements in the images, we applied both object detection and semantic segmentation using the Grounded SAM framework [10]. First, we deployed the pre-trained Grounding DINO L model, trained on datasets such as O365, OI, GoldG, Cap4M, COCO, and RefC, which achieves a zero-shot average precision (AP) of 60.7 on the COCO dataset [6]. For object detection and labeling, the box threshold was set to 0.35, and the text threshold to 0.25. The custom input labels included "temple," "building," "roof," "cliff," "vegetation," "rock," "tree," "grass," and "nature." Elements categorized as natural and non-natural were labeled and enclosed in bounding boxes. This object detection step served as a coarse region-finding method to prepare for segmentation.

Next, we employed a pre-trained Segment Anything Model (SAM) (checkpoint = SAM_CHECKPOINT_PATH) to segment labeled regions in 256 input images, generating masks for all identified elements. We then selected and merged the masks labeled as "temple," "building," and "roof" into a unified "non-natural mask" for each image. These masks were applied to exclude non-natural elements, leaving only natural regions such as "cliff," "nature," "tree," "grass," and "vegetation" for each image. The excluded areas were filled with blank white pixels.

Blank Region Inpainting. Leaving the masked regions blank rendered the images unsuitable for feature matching in COLMAP. To address this, we performed inpainting using the "stable-diffusion-2-inpainting" model [11]. The unified "non-natural mask" was used to define the inpainting regions. After testing several prompts, the following were found to perform best: "A steep cliff with dense green vegetation growing along its rugged surface, creating a striking contrast against the rock face," "Rocks and trees seamlessly integrated on a towering cliff, showcasing the interplay between stone and nature," and "Massive cliffs adorned with vibrant vegetation cascading down their edges, emphasizing the harmony between earth and greenery". The inpainting process reconstructed the masked areas with plausible details based on the surrounding pixel context, ensuring smooth transitions between neighboring images.

Spatial Position and Viewing Direction Calculation. The processed images were input into COLMAP for correspondence search and incremental reconstruction. This step produced a transform.json file, which, along with the input images, served as the input for Instant-NGP to perform view synthesis.

View Synthesis. The processed data was loaded into the Instant-NGP GUI to synthesize views.

Point Cloud and Solid Mesh Generation. Using the Instant-NGP GUI, view representations were exported as point clouds. These point clouds were subsequently imported into MeshLab [1] to generate solid meshes.

2.3 Workflow of Level of Architecture

Data Collection. From the original dataset of 1386 base-upscaled images, 222 images were selected where architecture itself, specifically the temple, dominate the majority of the scene.

Object Detection and Coarse Image Masking. To isolate architectural elements, specifically the temple, from the 222-image data, we applied object detection using Grounding DINO in Grounded SAM framework to use bounding box as coarse masks first. We set the box threshold to 0.30 and the text threshold to 0.20 in order to label all possible architecture related objects. Custom labels, including "temple," "building," "roof," and "structure," were used to identify relevant architectural components. These elements were enclosed in bounding boxes, and we apply a large bounding box cover the boundary of all labeled bounding boxes as coarse masking. Outside of the bounding box mask is all filled with white pixels. This step is necessary because directly use segmentation result might result in mistakenly recognize "nature" label as "building", also if the architecture related elements not occupying more than 50% of the whole pixels of the image, wrong masks might be selected.

Semantic Segmentation and Finer Image Masking. Following the coarse masking stage, semantic segmentation was performed using the pre-trained Segment Anything Model (SAM) within the Grounded SAM framework [10]. Masks were generated for architectural labels, including "temple," "building," and "roof," while masks for non-architectural elements, such as "tree," "grass," and "vegetation," were excluded. For each image, the architecture-related masks were merged into a unique "refined architecture mask." This mask was applied to the respective image, replacing the excluded areas with blank white pixels to isolate the architectural structures with greater precision.

Spatial Position and Viewing Direction Calculation. The processed images were input into COLMAP for correspondence search and incremental reconstruction. This step produced a transform.json file, which, along with the input images, served as the input for Instant-NGP to perform view synthesis.

View Synthesis. The processed data was loaded into the Instant-NGP GUI to synthesize views.

Point Cloud and Solid Mesh Generation. Using the Instant-NGP GUI, view representations were exported as point clouds. These point clouds were subsequently imported into MeshLab [1] to generate solid meshes.

2.4 Workflow of Level of Architectural Components–Roof

Data Collection. From the original dataset of 1386 base-upscaled images, 68 images were selected where roof dominate the majority of the scene.

Object Detection and Coarse Image Masking. The object detection and coarse image masking steps were performed using Grounding DINO within the Grounded SAM framework, following a process similar to that used for the architecture level. The key difference was the use of the label "roof" and adjusted thresholds: the box threshold was set to 3.5, and the text threshold to 3.0, to filter out non-roof pixels and achieve more accurate bounding boxes. For each image, a single large bounding box encompassing all bounding boxes labeled as "roof" was generated. Regions outside this bounding box were filled with white pixels.

Semantic Segmentation and Finer Image Masking. Following the coarse masking stage, semantic segmentation was performed using the pre-trained Segment Anything Model (SAM) within the Grounded SAM framework [10], in a process similar to the architecture level. Masks were generated specifically for the "roof" label, while masks for non-roof elements, such as "building," "tree," and "vegetation," were excluded. For each image, the roof-related masks were merged into a unique "refined roof mask." This mask was applied to the respective image, replacing the excluded areas with blank white pixels to isolate the roof structures with greater precision.

Detail Generation. Due to the limitations of drone-captured videos, which cannot be too close to the structure of the Hanging Temple, there is often a lack of detail in the roof structures. To address this issue, SRGAN [4] was used to further upscale the segmented images. This upscaling enhances the level of detail in the roof images, providing more refined input for Instant-NGP to synthesize.

Spatial Position and Viewing Direction Calculation. The processed images were input into COLMAP for correspondence search and incremental reconstruction. This step produced a transform.json file, which, along with the input images, served as the input for Instant-NGP to perform view synthesis.

View Synthesis. The processed data was loaded into the Instant-NGP GUI to synthesize views.

Point Cloud and Solid Mesh Generation. Using the Instant-NGP GUI, view representations were exported as point clouds. These point clouds were subsequently imported into MeshLab [1] to generate solid meshes.

3 Results

This section presents the results of the proposed pipeline, organized into four hierarchical levels of scale: Scene, Nature, Architecture, and Roof. For each level, the results are divided into two key aspects: image processing, which includes object detection, image segmentation, and image masking, and view synthesis, which involves COLMAP spatial position and viewing direction calculation, Instant-NGP 3D view synthesis, point cloud generation, and solid mesh conversion.

3.1 Results of the "Scene Level" of the Hanging Temple

Images Processing Result. For the scene level, the image processing results includes image upscaling result, object detection with labeling result, and semantic segmentation result (Fig. 3).

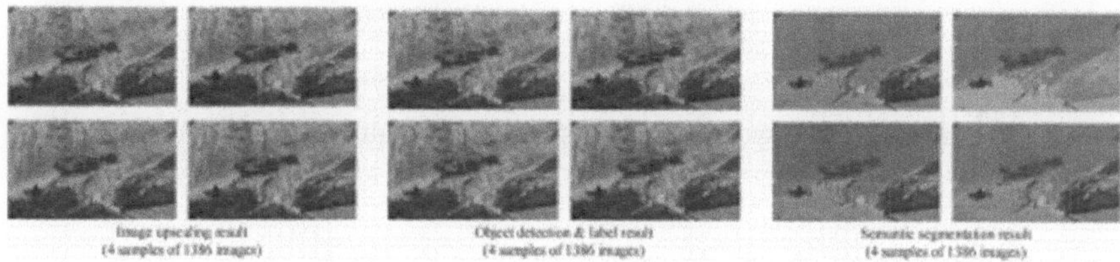

Fig. 3. Image processing result of scene level.

View Synthesis and 3D Generation Result. For the scene level, the view synthesis and 3D generation results include the following: spatial position and viewing direction calculated by COLMAP, along with the initial lines of the transform.json file; 3D view representation generated using Instant-NGP; and point clouds and meshes produced using the Instant-NGP GUI, based on the marching cubes algorithm (Fig. 4).

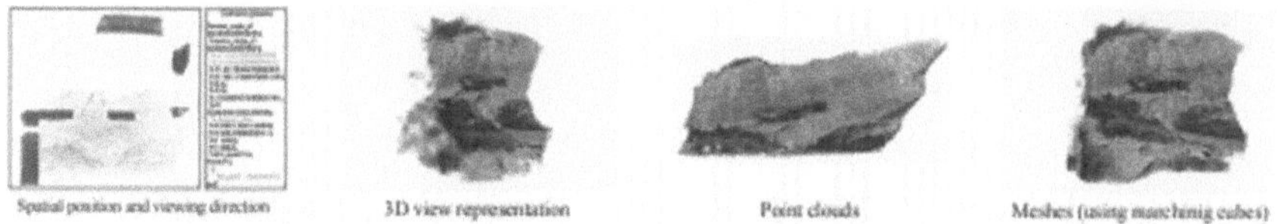

Fig. 4. View synthesis and 3d generation result of scene level.

3.2 Results of the "Nature Level" of the Hanging Temple

Images Processing Result. For the nature level, the image processing results includes semantic segmentation result, semantic segmentation masking result, diffusion model inpainting result (Fig. 5).

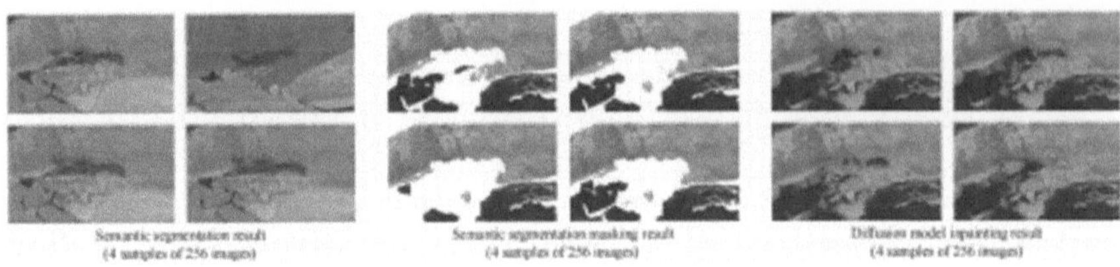

Fig. 5. Image processing result of nature level.

View Synthesis and 3D Generation Result. For the nature level, the view synthesis and 3D generation results include the same categories as the scene level but focus specifically on natural cliffs (Fig. 6).

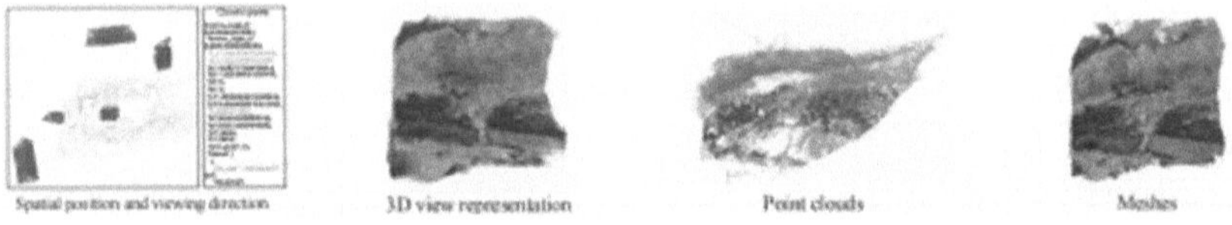

Fig. 6. View synthesis and 3d generation result of nature level.

3.3 Results of the "Architecture Level" of the Hanging Temple

Images Processing Result. For the architecture level, the image processing results includes object detection box coarse masking result, semantic segmentation result, semantic segmentation finer masking result (Fig. 7).

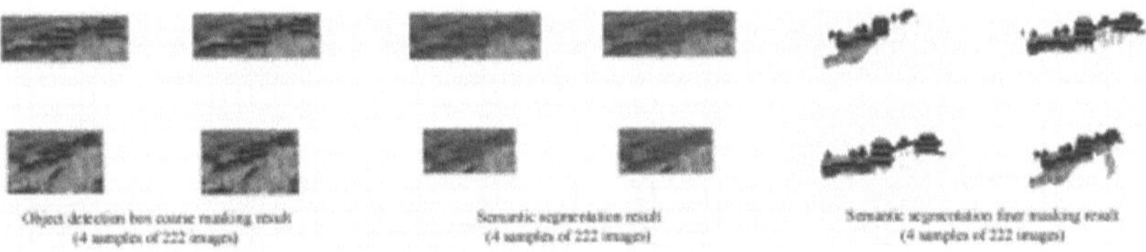

Fig. 7. Image processing result of architecture level.

View Synthesis and 3D Generation Result. For the architecture level, the view synthesis and 3D generation results include the same categories as the scene level but focus specifically on the temple itself (Fig. 8).

3.4 Results of the "Roof Level" of the Hanging Temple

Images Processing Result. For the roof level, the image processing results includes image upscaling result, semantic segmentation result, semantic segmentation masking result (Fig. 9).

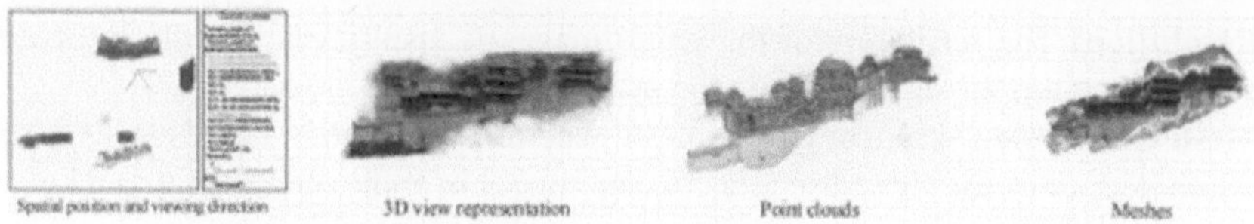

Fig. 8. View synthesis and 3d generation result of architecture level.

Fig. 9. Image processing result of roof level.

View Synthesis and 3D Generation Result. For the architecture level, the view synthesis and 3D generation results include the same categories as the scene level but focus specifically on the roof of the Hanging temple (Fig. 10).

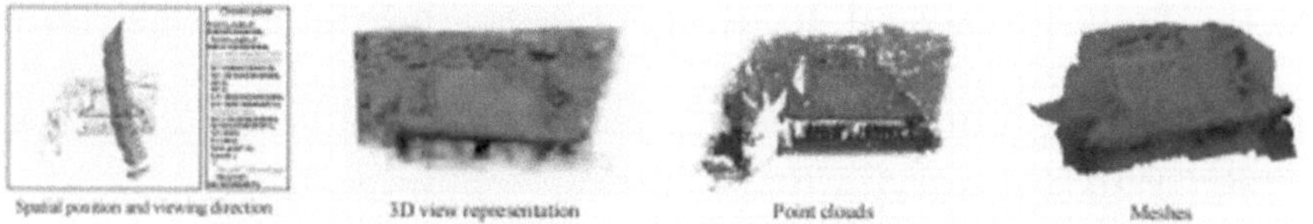

Fig. 10. View synthesis and 3d generation result of roof level.

4   Conclusion and Discussion

4.1   Conclusion

We propose a pipeline that integrates Semantic Segmentation using Grounded SAM and Instant-NGP to achieve 3D-aware view synthesis of the Hanging Temple. The pipeline consists of four workflows, successfully generating view synthesis at four levels of detail. The pipeline enhances NeRF's capability to incorporate 3D spatial awareness [2], resulting in detailed and structured 3D representations of the Hanging Temple.

4.2   Discussion

Limitations. Despite the successful implementation, several limitations were identified:

- **Data Diversity:** The drone-captured dataset lacks sufficient diversity in viewing angles, leading to gaps in capturing some structural details of the building.

- **Resolution:** The resolution of the input images is insufficient to fully resolve fine details, resulting in vague areas in the synthesized views.
- **Mesh Conversion Accuracy:** The mesh generated from point clouds lacks the precision necessary for direct use as a concept model in architectural editing. However, it is effective for visualization and structural validation.
- **Limitations of Zero123:** The Zero123 model [13] is unsuitable for generating multi-angle architectural images in this pipeline due to its limited ability to capture structural precision. It is more appropriate for simple object representations. Therefore, this pipeline does not rely on Zero123 for multi-angle image generation.
- **Consistency in Diffusion-Generated Images:** Images generated by the diffusion model exhibit inconsistencies across neighboring views, leading to inaccuracies in feature matching during COLMAP processing.

Future Work. To address these limitations and extend the pipeline's capabilities, the following directions are proposed for future work:

- **Diffusion Model Improvements:** Enhance the diffusion model's ability to generate consistent neighboring images, facilitating accurate feature matching in COLMAP and improving 3D reconstruction.
- **Mesh Generation for Architectural Editing:** Develop more precise mesh conversion methods to create models suitable for input into architectural tools such as Rhino. This will allow for direct editing and integration into architectural workflows.
- **From diffusion generated 2D images of architecture to 3D Representation:** Explore advancements in converting diffusion-generated images into detailed and accurate 3D representations, enabling a seamless transition from image generation to 3D modeling.

References

1. Cignoni, P., et al.: Meshlab (2011)
2. El Banani, M., et al.: Probing the 3d awareness of visual foundation models. In: Proceedings of the IEEE/CVF Conference on Computer Vision and Pattern Recognition, pp. 21795–21806 (2024)
3. Howse, J.: OpenCV Computer Vision with python, vol. 27. Packt Publishing Birmingham, UK (2013)
4. Ledig, C., et al.: Photo-realistic single image super-resolution using a generative adversarial network. In: Proceedings of the IEEE Conference on Computer Vision and Pattern Recognition, pp. 4681–4690 (2017)
5. Li, C., Zhang, T., Du, X., Zhang, Y., Xie, H.: Generative AI for architectural design: a literature review (2024). arXiv:2404.01335
6. Liu, S., et al.: Grounding dino: marrying dino with grounded pre-training for open-set object detection (2023). arXiv:2303.05499
7. Mildenhall, B., Srinivasan, P.P., Tancik, M., Barron, J.T., Ramamoorthi, R., Ng, R.: Nerf: representing scenes as neural radiance fields for view synthesis. Commun. ACM **65**(1), 99–106 (2021)
8. Müller, T., Evans, A., Schied, C., Keller, A.: Instant neural graphics primitives with a multiresolution hash encoding. ACM Trans. Graph. **41**(4), 1–15 (2022)

9. Qian, G., et al.: Magic123: one image to high-quality 3d object generation using both 2d and 3d diffusion priors (2023). arXiv:2306.17843
10. Ren, T., et al.: Grounded SAM: assembling open-world models for diverse visual tasks (2024). arXiv:2401.14159
11. Rombach, R., Blattmann, A., Lorenz, D., Esser, P., Ommer, B.: High-resolution image synthesis with latent diffusion models. In: Proceedings of the IEEE/CVF Conference on Computer Vision and Pattern Recognition (CVPR), pp. 10684–10695 (2022)
12. Schönberger, J.L., Frahm, J.M.: Structure-from-motion revisited. In: Conference on Computer Vision and Pattern Recognition (CVPR) (2016)
13. Shi, R., et al.: Zero123++: a single image to consistent multi-view diffusion base model (2023)
14. Sun, J., et al.: Dreamcraft3d: hierarchical 3d generation with bootstrapped diffusion prior (2023). arXiv:2310.16818
15. Wang, C., Chai, M., He, M., Chen, D., Liao, J.: Clip-nerf: text-and-image driven manipulation of neural radiance fields. In: Proceedings of the IEEE/CVF Conference on Computer Vision and Pattern Recognition, pp. 3835–3844 (2022)

Health Monitoring, Decision-Making, and Care Optimization

Experience-Driven Participatory Design in Nursing: Translating Care Practices into Intelligent Product Design

Huiyuan Ding[1], Yanjie Zhang[2], and Qian Ji[1]($\boxtimes$)

[1] School of Design, Huazhong University of Science and Technology, Wuhan, China
jiqian@hust.edu.cn
[2] College of Art and Archaeology, Zhejiang University, Hangzhou, China

Abstract. The global rise in aging populations is intensifying the demand for intelligent assistive technologies in long-term care settings. However, many existing solutions fail to reflect the complex, emotional, and practical realities of caregiving, leading to limited adoption and trust. This study introduces an experience-driven participatory design framework that translates the tacit knowledge of frontline caregivers into actionable design criteria for intelligent nursing products. Through field observations, participatory interviews, and narrative analysis conducted in a hospital setting, we uncovered key friction points and informal caregiving strategies. These insights were transformed into design opportunities using scenario mapping and low-fidelity prototyping. A video-based usability evaluation with five participants demonstrated early acceptance of a robotic arm prototype for basic care tasks, with positive feedback on functionality, emotional comfort, and perceived safety. Our findings support the use of experience-centered design as a strategy for developing emotionally resonant and context-aware healthcare technologies. The proposed four-phase framework offers a transferable methodology for HCI researchers and healthcare innovation teams aiming to build inclusive, human-centered care systems.

Keywords: Participatory Design · Human-Computer Interaction · User Experience · Emotional Acceptance · Healthcare Innovation

1 Introduction

The global rise in aging populations has placed unprecedented pressure on long-term healthcare systems, particularly within hospital settings where the number of bedridden and high-dependency patients continues to grow [1]. This demographic shift has intensified the workload of caregivers, who must manage not only physically demanding tasks–such as repositioning or hygiene assistance–but also complex cognitive responsibilities and emotional labor. These include time-sensitive clinical decision-making, continuous patient monitoring, and maintaining empathetic communication. When cognitive and emotional burdens are over-

V. G. Duffy (Ed.): HCII 2025, LNCS 16339, pp. 217–233, 2026.
https://doi.org/10.1007/978-3-032-13012-9_16

looked, caregivers' functional performance may decline, leading to compromised care quality and safety [2].

To address these multidimensional challenges, intelligent assistive technologies–most notably robotic arms–have emerged as promising solutions [3]. Capable of performing routine, labor-intensive tasks, these systems can help relieve physical strain while potentially restructuring care workflows to allow caregivers more time for relational and cognitive care tasks. However, despite their technological promise, many of these products fall short in real-world applications [4]. A key reason for this disconnect lies in the lack of integration of caregivers' lived experience into early-stage design processes.

In Human-Computer Interaction (HCI), growing attention is being paid to the transformation of situated, experiential knowledge into structured design insights [5]. Particularly in healthcare contexts, emotional nuance, workflow adaptation, and tacit knowledge are central to effective technology adoption [6]. This study builds on this perspective by proposing an experience-driven participatory design methodology for the development of intelligent nursing robotics.

Grounded in the scientific consensus of Participatory Ergonomics (PE), the approach follows established stage-based models and methodologies that have been extensively validated in healthcare settings [1]. The methodology adapts the core phases of problem identification, participatory analysis, prototyping, and implementation feedback to the context of intelligent assistive systems. Research has shown that healthcare robot acceptance is fundamentally shaped by user perceptions of technology usefulness and ease of use [4], and that social acceptance of robots varies significantly across different occupational fields [7]. Uniquely, the framework integrates the physical, cognitive, and emotional dimensions of caregiver burden into each phase of the design process.

This research explores how embodied practices, emotional insights, and cognitive strategies of frontline caregivers can be systematically translated into design strategies for intelligent robotic arms. By embedding real-world care experiences at the core of development, the study aims to bridge the gap between technological potential and the nuanced demands of clinical environments. Ultimately, it seeks to establish a replicable, experience-driven design framework that not only reduces multidimensional caregiver burdens but also supports the seamless integration of intelligent systems into hospital workflows–enabling more human-centered, trustable, and context-sensitive healthcare interactions.

2   Methods

This study adopts an experience-centered participatory design approach to elicit and translate the lived experiences of caregivers into actionable design opportunities for intelligent nursing technologies. Rather than focusing solely on system implementation or functional optimization, the methodology centers on situated inquiry, co-creation, and iterative design translation, aiming to align technical solutions with the physical, cognitive, and emotional realities of care work.

In contrast to conventional expert-driven design models–where user needs are often generalized or assumed–participatory design emphasizes the active involvement of end users throughout the development process [2]. This approach is particularly well-suited for care robotics, where tacit knowledge, interpersonal nuance, and workflow adaptation play a central role. Research on socially assistive robots in real homes [8] and ethical frameworks for robot care [9] have highlighted the importance of user-centered approaches in healthcare robotics. By embedding users in key phases of research and prototyping, the participatory method supports the creation of not only technically functional, but also contextually meaningful and emotionally acceptable systems.

The following sections outline a four-stage participatory process structured in accordance with established participatory ergonomics frameworks. These stages include: (1) contextual inquiry and stakeholder engagement, (2) participatory interviews and narrative analysis, (3) experience translation and opportunity framing, and (4) prototype development and testing.

Figure 1 illustrates the overall participatory design framework, showing the systematic progression from contextual inquiry through to prototype evaluation and the iterative feedback loops between stages.

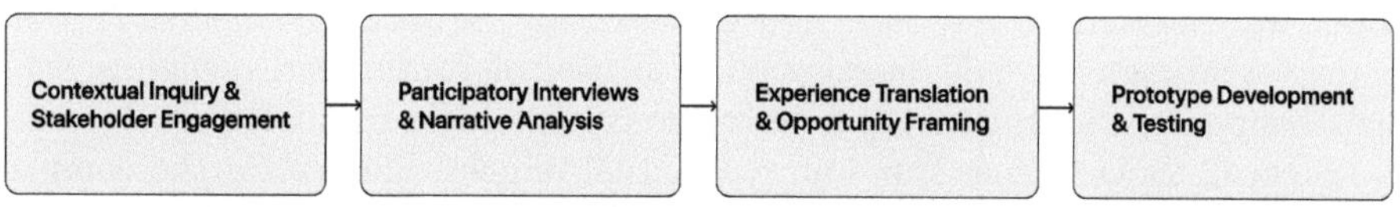

Fig. 1. Participatory design framework overview showing the four-stage process and iterative feedback loops.

Unlike conventional expert-driven design processes–which often rely on abstracted user assumptions and top-down technical specifications–participatory design emphasizes the direct involvement of end users throughout the development cycle [2]. In the context of caregiving, this distinction is particularly critical: care practices are highly situated, emotionally nuanced, and often governed by tacit knowledge that cannot be fully captured through observation alone. Traditional design methods risk oversimplifying this complexity, resulting in products that are functionally complete but poorly aligned with real caregiving contexts.

Participatory design, by contrast, enables designers to access, interpret, and co-construct design insights in collaboration with caregivers themselves. This results in solutions that are not only more usable, but also more trustable and emotionally resonant. Systematic reviews of social robots in aged care [10] and studies on factors affecting robot acceptability [11] demonstrate that economic and social considerations significantly influence adoption success. Safe human-robot interaction requires comprehensive surveys of potential risks and mitigation strategies [12]. In this study, the participatory approach was chosen because it allows for the integration of physical, cognitive, and emotional dimensions of caregiving burden–which are all essential for the successful deployment of intelligent assistive systems. For the development of the nursing robotic arm, participatory design was particularly suitable because it enabled us to identify subtle workflow pain points, map interaction expectations, and iteratively validate design assumptions with actual users. This method provided a structured yet flexible way to adapt technological features to hospital care settings, ensuring that the final prototype was not only technically functional but also contextually meaningful and acceptable to users.

All study procedures involving human participants were conducted in accordance with relevant ethical guidelines. Informed consent was obtained from all participants, who were assured of voluntary participation, confidentiality, and the right to withdraw at any time. All data were de-identified and stored securely to protect participant privacy.

2.1 Contextual Inquiry and Stakeholder Engagement

We conducted field studies in inpatient wards at a major urban hospital, using non-intrusive observation and situational walkthroughs to understand caregiving workflows and the socio-emotional dynamics between patients and caregivers. Stakeholders included professional nurses, family caregivers, and patients. In total, we collected 97 responses (70 from caregivers/family members, 27 from patients) through targeted questionnaires focused on routine care demands, emotional support expectations, and perceptions of assistive technologies.

Figure 2 shows scenes from our contextual inquiry, illustrating the complex care environments and the diverse stakeholders involved in our participatory research process.

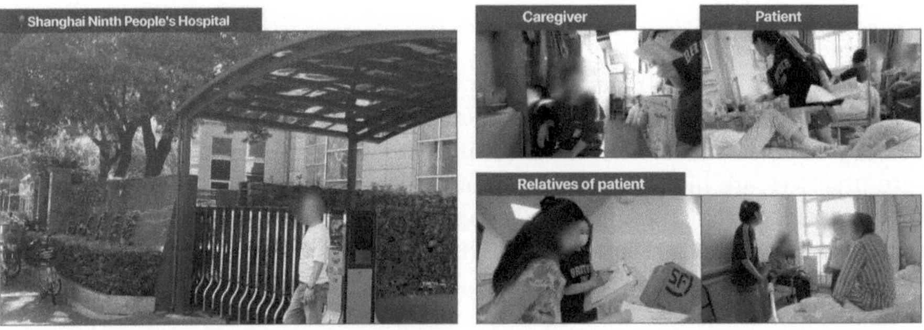

Fig. 2. Contextual inquiry and stakeholder engagement in hospital care settings.

To structure data collection, we developed two separate questionnaires targeting caregivers and patients, respectively. Each instrument included demographic questions, open-ended reflections, and multi-option items focused on physical workload, emotional support needs, and attitudes toward assistive technologies.

Example items from the caregiver/family version included:

"Which care tasks occupy the most time or effort in your daily routine?"

"Have you encountered any emotionally difficult or challenging caregiving situations?"

"Would you be willing to use an intelligent robotic system to assist in certain care tasks (e.g., mobility support, medication delivery)?"

The patient-facing questionnaire asked about perceived care adequacy, emotional support, and openness to robotic systems. Example items included:

"Which caregiving services do you value most during hospitalization?"

"What are your concerns or expectations regarding intelligent care robots?"

"If a robot were available, which tasks would you prefer it to assist with?"

The caregiver questionnaire was partly adapted from established caregiver burden and acceptance studies in healthcare robotics [3,13], and informed by the structure of workload assessment tools such as NASA-TLX [14]. The patient questionnaire was inspired by prior surveys exploring patient acceptance of socially assistive robots and emotional care gaps [15].

These instruments were pilot-tested before distribution to ensure clarity and contextual fit. Their design allowed us to assess perceptions across the physical, emotional, and cognitive dimensions of care work.

2.2 Participatory Interviews and Narrative Analysis

In-depth interviews were conducted with caregivers and patients to elicit rich, situated narratives. These interviews uncovered recurring patterns of physical strain, emotional burnout, and the tension between care personalization and task repetitiveness. Using thematic coding [16] and affinity diagramming [17], we synthesized key pain points and informal workarounds commonly employed in daily care routines.

To deepen our understanding of care contexts and uncover latent user needs, we conducted in-depth, semi-structured interviews with four representative participants recruited from earlier fieldwork. This group included one professional caregiver, one family caregiver, and two patients of varying age and mobility status (see Table 1). These roles were selected to capture a full spectrum of caregiving scenarios, ensuring that our design decisions were rooted in real, lived experience across both professional and domestic care settings.

Table 1. Interviewee demographics and care experience.

No.	Name	Gender	Age	Role	Care-Related Experience
1	Ms. Ding	Female	58	Caregiver	Employed in inpatient ward care for 5 years
2	Mr. Li	Male	70	Elderly Patient	Long-term chronic illness, limited mobility
3	Ms. Rao	Female	31	Younger Patient	Undergoing recovery, previously received care services
4	Mr. Zhang	Male	45	Family Caregiver	Assisted post-surgery family member, familiar with basic care

Each interview lasted approximately 30 min and followed a structured yet open-ended guide (Table 2), covering four core areas: (1) daily care experiences and burdens, (2) perceptions of robot-assisted care, (3) emotional comfort and trust concerns, and (4) future expectations for intelligent support systems. Participants were encouraged to share stories, preferences, and concerns in their own words, which were audio-recorded and transcribed for analysis. Thematic coding and affinity mapping were applied to extract key pain points and user expectations.

Table 2. Semi-structured interview guide.

Interview Segment	Key Prompts
Introduction	"Thank you for joining. I'm currently conducting research on intelligent nursing support systems. Could you briefly describe your background and care experience?"
Daily Care Experience	"What tasks do you find physically or emotionally difficult during caregiving? Have you encountered moments of stress, uncertainty, or discomfort during care routines? If a robot could assist in these tasks, which ones would you delegate and why?"
Attitudes Toward Robotic Assistance	"If a robot were introduced to assist with care, would you be open to using it? Why or why not? What roles do you expect a robot to fulfill–tool, assistant, or something else? What kind of behavior or tone would make the robot feel safe and acceptable to you?"
Future Expectations	"What functions would you consider most important for such a device? What type of interaction would feel most comfortable to you–voice, button, autonomous control? Do you have any ideas for how this technology could better support specific care scenarios?"

This participatory engagement surfaced three recurring themes:

1. **Physical and temporal overload in repetitive tasks.** Tasks such as patient repositioning, cleaning, or medication support were widely reported as labor-intensive and time-consuming, often exceeding the physical capacity of staff, especially during night shifts or with limited personnel.
2. **Emotional fatigue coupled with a desire for humanlike warmth.** While open to robotic assistance, many participants stressed that machines should not feel "cold" or "industrial." Expressions such as "I just need something that feels like it's helping, not replacing me" or "If it can feel like a warm presence, that's already a relief" reflect users' need for emotionally sensitive support.
3. **The tension between personalization and routinization.** Several caregivers noted that high-frequency, repetitive tasks pulled them away from emotionally attuned care. This led to critical discussions about which functions could be delegated to robotic systems without compromising human connection.

These insights were instrumental in shaping subsequent design decisions. For instance, user feedback directly informed the incorporation of soft interaction surfaces, emotionally neutral voice cues, and modular function planning to balance automation with relational care. These themes demonstrate that participatory interviews did not merely supplement design–they actively redirected the design logic toward more user-aligned, contextually adaptive outcomes.

2.3 Experience Translation and Opportunity Framing

Insights collected from questionnaires and participatory interviews were analyzed using thematic clustering and cross-role comparison. Key pain points were identified across three dimensions of caregiving burden: physical, emotional, and cognitive. These issues were further grouped into two major categories: (1) systemic challenges in inpatient care (e.g., staff shortages, repetitive labor), and (2) individual needs of diverse care recipients (e.g., emotional comfort, hygiene support). This classification formed the basis of a problem-opportunity mapping framework (see Fig. 3).

The translation process followed a problem-to-opportunity reframing logic, in which each identified pain point was reviewed and associated with relevant design affordances. The research team conducted this mapping collaboratively, informed by prior coding rounds. We then conducted verbal walkthroughs with two caregiving participants, asking them to validate pain-opportunity links and suggest refinements. This ensured user-defined concerns remained central to the design direction.

Three core technological intervention domains emerged from this process:

1. **Robotic Assistance** for labor-intensive tasks and physical support;

2. **Artificial Intelligence** for task planning, intent recognition, and decision reduction;
3. **Sensor Technology** for environmental monitoring and user-state detection.

The resulting framework is not speculative but grounded–each proposed direction is directly traceable to user-voiced concerns. For example, caregiver fatigue in repositioning led to robotic lifting modules; emotional detachment concerns informed the need for affect-sensitive sensors. This mapping clarified both the design space and the role of each technology type, forming the foundation for the prototype design described in the next section.

Figure 3 illustrates our systematic approach to translating user experiences into design opportunities, showing how identified pain points were mapped to specific technological intervention domains.

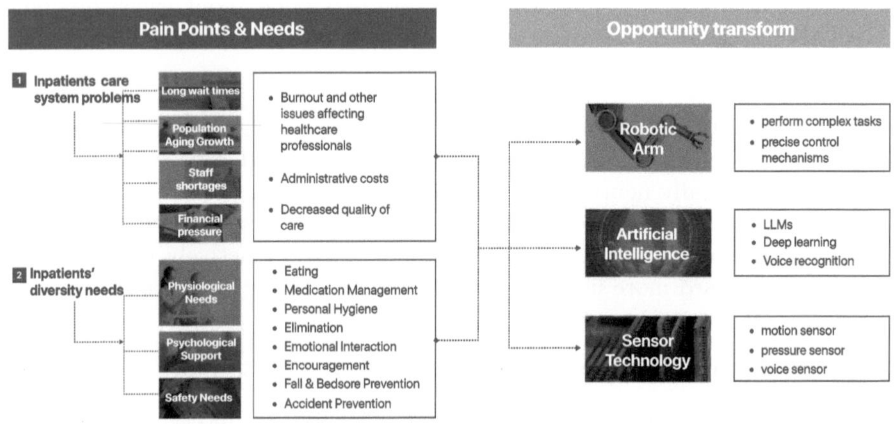

Fig. 3. Experience translation and design opportunities framework.

2.4   Prototype Development and Testing

Based on the previously mapped pain points and design opportunities, a functional prototype of a dual-arm robotic nursing system, named *SyncPair*, was developed. This prototype integrates sensors with ChatGPT to enable voice-controlled operation of coordinated robotic arms. The system was designed to address the burdens of repetitive, labor-intensive tasks while preserving emotional comfort and adaptability within real bedside care routines. Rather than pursuing full automation, *SyncPair* was designed to support hybrid workflows through natural voice interaction, ensuring safe and interpretable human-robot collaboration in clinical settings.

The design process followed the experience-prototype logic, selecting four representative care scenarios based on earlier participatory interviews and observational studies:

1. **Medication Assistance** - Voice-controlled medication delivery with sensor guidance and safety confirmation.
2. **Repositioning and Quilt Rolling** - Coordinated blanket lifting and patient repositioning through natural language commands.
3. **Body Cleaning** - Dual-arm cleaning assistance with one arm stabilizing while the other performs wiping motions.
4. **Patient Turning** - Synchronized patient turning using voice commands and sensor feedback for safe lateral movement.

These scenarios were selected not only for their frequency in inpatient care but also for their emotional and physical strain on caregivers, as highlighted by both nurses and family members during interviews.

Figure 4 demonstrates the four core nursing functions simulated by the prototype system, showcasing how the robotic arms perform essential care tasks in realistic hospital scenarios.

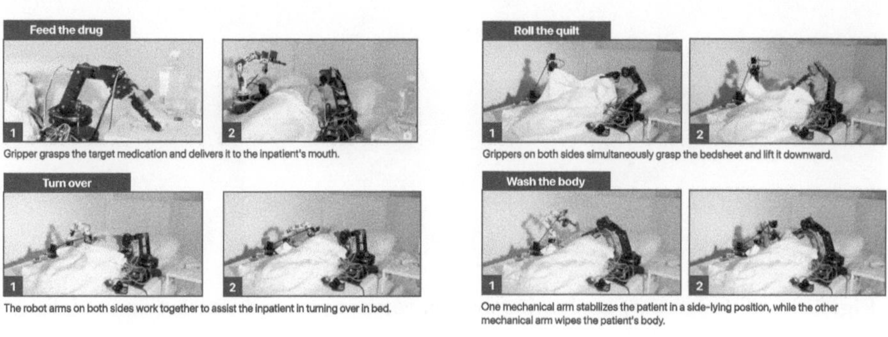

Fig. 4. Simulation demonstration of four main nursing functions: medication delivery, patient repositioning, bedding arrangement, and body cleaning.

The *SyncPair* robotic nursing system represents the culmination of the participatory design process, translating user-identified care burdens into tangible technological solutions. Figure 5 presents the system prototype design, while Fig. 6 showcases the final design output with detailed component specifications.

Thematic insights from this formative evaluation revealed several critical aspects:

(a) **Perceived Safety and Comfort**: Soft arm motion and voice interaction were seen as key contributors to user trust, with participants noting that conversational control felt more natural than button interfaces.
(b) **Intuitive Voice Control**: The natural language interface received positive feedback for understanding everyday language rather than requiring technical commands.
(c) **Contextual Intelligence**: The sensor-AI integration's ability to adjust responses based on patient conditions impressed evaluators and increased confidence in the system.

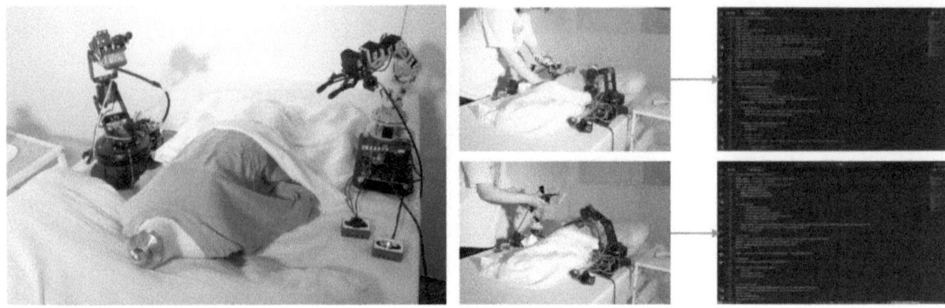

Fig. 5. Use sensors and integrate with ChatGPT to control the movements of two robotic arms via voice commands.

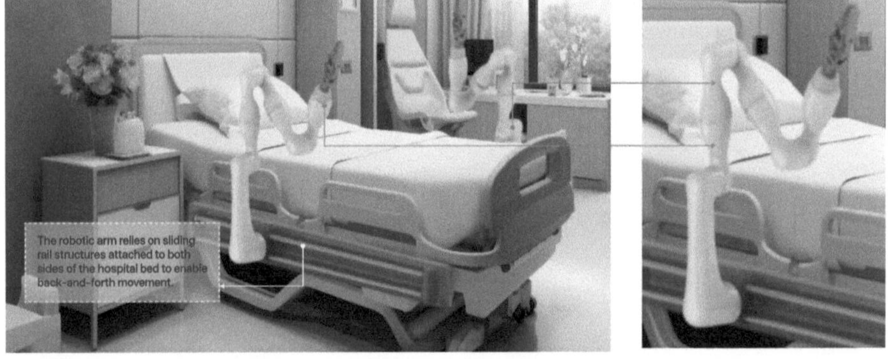

Fig. 6. Final design output showing system components and interaction modalities.

(d) **Maintainability and Robustness**: Voice control was noted to reduce wear on physical controls and simplify staff training.

(e) **Humanized Interaction**: The conversational AI component addressed concerns about emotional coldness raised in earlier interviews.

(f) **Adoption Intentions**: Participants found the robot "gentle, helpful, and surprisingly conversational," with natural language reducing anxiety compared to silent mechanical assistance.

This formative evaluation confirmed early feasibility in functionality, comfort, and psychological acceptance. The voice-controlled AI integration emerged as particularly promising, successfully addressing multiple dimensions of caregiver burden through intuitive natural language interaction. Although further clinical-scale usability testing is needed, the feedback collected here directly informed the refinement priorities for the next design iteration and evaluation protocols discussed in the following sections.

3   Results

To validate the usability, acceptance, and emotional experience effects of the nursing robotic arm product, this study organized and conducted context-based video demonstration testing after completing product prototype modeling and functional definition. Combined with standardized scales and open-ended interviews, a preliminary evaluation of the product design solution was conducted.

3.1   Testing Methodology

This evaluation employed a comprehensive approach combining simulated scenario presentation, scale scoring, and subjective interview feedback. Given that the product prototype had not yet been fully realized in physical form, the design team created demonstration videos showcasing its core functions, including typical tasks such as medication delivery, patient turning, bedding arrangement, and body cleaning. The testing was conducted in a simulated ward equipped with nursing beds and basic care facilities to maximize the restoration of the actual usage environment.

Figure 7 documents the evaluation sessions, showing participants engaged in reviewing the prototype demonstrations and providing structured feedback on system usability and acceptance.

Fig. 7. Participants engaged in usability evaluation sessions for the robotic nursing system.

A total of 5 participants were invited, including 2 nurses, 1 nursing assistant, and 2 elderly patient family members. After watching the videos, participants completed the System Usability Scale (SUS) and provided evaluations in interviews regarding product appearance, motion performance, and emotional experience dimensions.

3.2   Data Results

This evaluation employed a 5-point Likert scale, with scores ranging from 1 point ("strongly disagree") to 5 points ("strongly agree"). After watching the product function demonstration videos, participants scored the nursing robotic arm across dimensions of functionality, emotion, and safety. The results are shown in Table 3.

Table 3. Evaluation results of the nursing robotic arm prototype.

Evaluation Dimension	Item Description	Average Score (15)
Functional Adequacy	Whether product functions meet typical nursing scenario requirements	4.2
Operational Intuitiveness	Whether usage methods are easy to understand and master	3.9
Emotional Acceptance	Whether robotic arm appearance is reassuring and approachable	3.8
Safety Perception	Whether motion rhythm and appearance feel safe and controllable	4.0
Technical Trust	Whether to trust the device to operate independently without errors	3.6
Human-Robot Collaboration Expectation	Whether willing to use this product as an assistive care tool long-term	4.1
Recommendation Willingness	Whether willing to recommend this product to others	4.3

From the quantitative data perspective, recommendation willingness (4.3) and functional adequacy (4.2) received the highest scores, indicating that most participants held positive attitudes toward the product's practicality and promotion prospects. Operational intuitiveness (3.9) and safety perception (4.0) also scored relatively high, validating users' basic recognition of the product's usage pathways and motion logic.

Emotional acceptance (3.8) showed moderate performance, with some participants expressing during interviews that they expected the robotic arm to have clearer "prompt gestures" or "emotional feedback" before operation to enhance the humanized experience. Technical trust (3.6) was the relatively lowest item, indicating that in scenarios completely free from human supervision, users still maintained cautious attitudes toward the product's autonomous operation.

Overall, the evaluation results indicate that the product has a solid foundation in both usability and acceptance dimensions, showing positive development trends in "functional rationality" and "willingness to use." This clarified directions for subsequent system improvement and physical development while providing confidence support.

3.3   Evaluation Conclusions

The evaluation results of this design solution demonstrate good performance in usage acceptance, visual emotional experience, and functional prediction rationality. After watching the demonstration, most users expressed that they were "willing to try" or "willing to recommend," indicating that the product initially established trust and positive impressions at the cognitive level.

Although this test used video demonstration methods with certain interactive limitations, the suggestions provided by user feedback clearly offered clues for subsequent optimization directions and confirmed the consistency between early design strategy effectiveness and user perception. These findings validate that the participatory design approach–grounded in user needs and real care routines–successfully fostered early user acceptance and trust in the system.

4 Discussion

These results suggest that a structured participatory approach effectively translates caregiving experience into actionable and emotionally resonant design criteria. The observed alignment between users' lived experiences and the system's interaction logic reinforces the value of experience-centered design within care robotics–a rapidly emerging focus in HCI. This process not only enhanced usability, but also fostered stronger trust and empathy between users and the system.

From a methodological perspective, we propose a four-phase framework for design translation:

1. Experience elicitation through interviews, observations, and questionnaires
2. Thematic abstraction of pain points and care values
3. Interaction logic translation into design requirements
4. Prototype realization and feedback-driven refinement planning

This framework can serve as a guide for similar HCI efforts in healthcare innovation.

4.1 Occupational Safety and Patient Safety Considerations

The introduction of robotic arms in hospital wards raises critical concerns regarding both occupational safety for healthcare staff and patient safety during care delivery.

From an occupational health perspective, the integration of *SyncPair* and similar robotic systems must address potential musculoskeletal risks that may arise from human-robot collaboration. While robotic assistance is designed to reduce physical strain on caregivers, improper interaction patterns or inadequate training could introduce new ergonomic challenges, such as awkward positioning during robot supervision or repetitive motions in robot programming and maintenance tasks.

Patient safety represents an equally critical consideration, particularly in scenarios involving direct physical contact between the robotic system and patients. For instance, when the gripper mechanism grasps target medication and delivers it to an inpatient's mouth, multiple safety protocols must be rigorously implemented. The system's force control algorithms must be calibrated to prevent tissue damage while ensuring reliable medication placement. Our prototype incorporates compliance control with force thresholds below 15 N and soft silicone contact surfaces to minimize injury risk. Additionally, fail-safe mechanisms automatically halt robot motion upon detecting unexpected resistance or patient movement.

To mitigate these risks, we propose a multi-layered safety framework incorporating: (1) comprehensive staff training programs covering both technical operation and emergency protocols, (2) continuous monitoring systems that track robot performance and detect anomalous behaviors, (3) regular safety audits and maintenance schedules to ensure system reliability, and (4) clear protocols for human intervention and robot shutdown in emergency situations. Furthermore, patient consent and comfort protocols must be established, allowing patients to halt robot operations at any time through simple voice commands or gesture recognition.

The participatory design approach proved instrumental in identifying these safety concerns early in the development process. Caregivers' experiential knowledge highlighted potential failure modes and safety scenarios that might have been overlooked in purely technical design approaches. This underscores the importance of involving frontline staff not only in functional design but also in safety protocol development.

4.2   Study Limitations and Future Research Directions

This study presents several limitations that should be acknowledged and addressed in future research. First, our evaluation did not include a controlled comparison between participatory and non-participatory design approaches. While our qualitative feedback suggests advantages for the participatory methodology, a head-to-head empirical study contrasting participatory versus expert-driven design pipelines would provide more robust evidence of the approach's effectiveness. Such a comparison should examine not only usability outcomes but also development time, cost efficiency, and long-term user adoption rates.

Second, we did not systematically compare different design solutions developed through participatory versus traditional approaches. Future research should examine whether participatory design consistently produces more user-centered solutions across diverse healthcare robotics applications, or whether the benefits are context-dependent. This could involve developing multiple prototype variants using different design methodologies and conducting comparative evaluations with the same user groups.

Third, our study involved a relatively small convenience sample (n=5) in the formative evaluation phase, which limits the generalizability of our findings. The participants were recruited from a single hospital setting, potentially introducing selection bias and limiting the diversity of care contexts represented in our data. Larger-scale studies involving multiple hospitals, diverse patient populations, and varied care scenarios are necessary to validate the framework's broader applicability.

Fourth, our evaluation focused primarily on initial user acceptance and perceived usability rather than long-term integration into clinical workflows. Real-world implementation studies are needed to assess how participatory-designed robotic systems perform over extended periods, including their impact on care quality, staff satisfaction, and patient outcomes. Such longitudinal studies should also examine the maintenance requirements, training needs, and organizational changes necessary for successful technology adoption.

Finally, our framework does not adequately address the economic and organizational factors that influence healthcare technology adoption. Future research should incorporate cost-benefit analyses, implementation timelines, and organizational change management considerations into the participatory design process. This would provide a more comprehensive understanding of how participatory approaches can address not only technical and usability challenges but also the broader systemic barriers to healthcare innovation.

5   Conclusion and Future Work

This study presents a structured participatory design approach for embedding caregiving experience into the development of intelligent nursing technologies. By actively involving nurses, care workers, and family members, we demonstrate how domain-specific tacit knowledge can be translated into design logic, interaction flows, and physical functionalities that align with real-world care practices. The resulting framework offers a replicable and transferable methodology for HCI researchers, healthcare designers, and innovation teams seeking to create more inclusive, empathetic, and contextually grounded healthcare products.

Returning to the multidimensional care burdens identified in our introduction, this research demonstrates how participatory design can systematically address the physical, cognitive, and emotional challenges that caregivers face in hospital settings. Through the development of the *SyncPair* robotic system, we show how user-centered design translation can create solutions that simultaneously tackle all three dimensions of caregiver burden.

Addressing Physical Burdens: The participatory design process revealed that repetitive tasks such as patient repositioning, lifting, and hygiene assistance constitute the primary sources of physical strain for caregivers. Our prototype directly addresses these concerns through automated lifting modules, synchronized dual-arm coordination, and soft interaction surfaces that reduce the need for manual labor while maintaining care quality. The force-controlled mechanisms and ergonomic design features emerged directly from caregivers' experiences of musculoskeletal strain during routine care activities.

Reducing Cognitive Load: The cognitive burden of managing time-sensitive care routines, making quick clinical decisions, and monitoring multiple patients simultaneously was addressed through intelligent task planning and decision-support features. The robotic system's ability to recognize care contexts, provide medication delivery assistance with built-in safety checks, and maintain consistent care protocols helps reduce the mental overhead that caregivers experience.

By automating routine decision-making processes and providing clear interaction feedback, the system allows caregivers to redirect their cognitive resources toward more critical clinical judgments and patient-specific care planning.

Supporting Emotional Well-Being: Perhaps most significantly, the participatory approach uncovered the emotional dimension of care burden–the fatigue that comes from balancing efficiency with warmth, and the concern that technological solutions might compromise human connection. Our design addresses these concerns by preserving space for relational care while handling routine tasks, incorporating emotionally sensitive interaction modes (such as soft movements and gentle voice cues), and maintaining caregivers' central role in patient relationships. The system was designed not to replace human care but to create more opportunities for meaningful emotional engagement by reducing the time pressure and physical exhaustion that often prevent caregivers from fully attending to patients' emotional needs.

The participatory design methodology proved instrumental not only in identifying these multidimensional burdens but also in ensuring that our technological solution addresses them in an integrated manner. Rather than optimizing for technical efficiency alone, the approach enabled us to create a system that supports the complex, interconnected nature of care work where physical, cognitive, and emotional demands are deeply intertwined.

Future work will focus on validating and extending this framework across diverse care scenarios–such as home-based elderly care and post-operative rehabilitation–and exploring how digital tools, including remote co-design platforms and simulation environments, can support broader stakeholder participation. We also aim to refine the framework's translation phases to enhance the fidelity of experiential knowledge as it becomes embedded in product-level decisions. Longitudinal studies examining how participatory-designed systems perform over extended periods in addressing these multidimensional care burdens will be particularly valuable for understanding the sustained impact of this approach.

In the long term, this research contributes to a growing understanding of how participatory design can address the complex challenges of healthcare innovation. We demonstrate that technology can simultaneously reduce physical strain, cognitive load, and emotional burden when designed with deep user involvement. This work has the potential to inform not only product innovation but also policy and methodological standards for human-centered healthcare design. The framework offers a path toward creating healthcare technologies that truly serve the needs of those who provide care, ultimately benefiting both caregivers and the patients they serve.

References

1. Rivilis, I., et al.: Effectiveness of participatory ergonomic interventions on health outcomes: a systematic review. Appl. Ergon. **39**(3), 342–358 (2008)

2. Carayon, P., et al.: Work system design for patient safety: the SEIPS model. Qual. Saf. Health Care **15**(Suppl I), i50–i58 (2006)
3. Broadbent, E., Stafford, R., MacDonald, B.: Acceptance of healthcare robots for the older population: review and future directions. Int. J. Soc. Robot. **1**(4), 319–330 (2009)
4. Turja, T., Aaltonen, I., Taipale, S., Oksanen, A.: Robot acceptance model for care (RAM-care): a principled approach to the intention to use care robots. Inf. Manag. **57**(5), 103220 (2020)
5. Davis, F.D.: Perceived usefulness, perceived ease of use, and user acceptance of information technology. MIS Q. **13**(3), 319–340 (1989)
6. Venkatesh, V., Morris, M.G., Davis, G.B., Davis, F.D.: User acceptance of information technology: toward a unified view. MIS Q. **27**(3), 425–478 (2003)
7. Savela, N., Turja, T., Oksanen, A.: Social acceptance of robots in different occupational fields: a systematic literature review. Int. J. Soc. Robot. **10**(4), 493–502 (2018)
8. Frennert, S., Eftring, H., Östlund, B.: Case report: implications of doing research on socially assistive robots in real homes. Int. J. Soc. Robot. **9**(3), 401–415 (2017)
9. Sharkey, A., Sharkey, N.: Granny and the robots: ethical issues in robot care for the elderly. Ethics Inf. Technol. **14**(1), 27–40 (2012)
10. Sawik, B., et al.: Robots for elderly care: review, multi-criteria optimization model and qualitative case study. Healthcare **11**(9), 1286 (2023)
11. Whelan, S., Murphy, K., Barrett, E., Krusche, C., Santorelli, A., Casey, D.: Factors affecting the acceptability of social robots by older adults including people with dementia or cognitive impairment: a literature review. Int. J. Soc. Robot. **10**(5), 643–668 (2018)
12. Lasota, P.A., Fong, T., Shah, J.A.: A survey of methods for safe human-robot interaction. Found. Trends Robot. **5**(4), 261–349 (2017)
13. Vandemeulebroucke, T., de Casterlé, B.D., Gastmans, C.: The use of care robots in aged care: a systematic review of argument-based ethics literature. Gerontology **64**(1), 74–87 (2018)
14. Hart, S.G., Staveland, L.E.: Development of NASA-TLX (Task Load Index): results of empirical and theoretical research. In: Hancock, P.A., Meshkati, N. (eds.) Human Mental Workload, pp. 139–183. North-Holland (1988)
15. Turja, T., Taipale, S., Kaakinen, M., Oksanen, A.: Care workers' readiness for robotization: identifying psychological and socio-demographic determinants. Int. J. Soc. Robot. **11**(4), 647–664 (2019)
16. Braun, V., Clarke, V.: Using thematic analysis in psychology. Qual. Res. Psychol. **3**(2), 77–101 (2006)
17. Beyer, H., Holtzblatt, K.: Contextual Design: Defining Customer-Centered Systems. Morgan Kaufmann Publishers, San Francisco (1998)

The Emergence of Inter-User Interface Friction: An Underexplored Usability Burden Across Multiple Medical Device User Interfaces

Amy Doan[✉] and Ratvinder Grewal

Laurentian University, Sudbury, ON, Canada
adoan@laurentian.ca

Abstract. In acute care hospital settings, nurses routinely interact with a wide range of medical devices, each with its own unique user interface. While individual medical device usability has been studied, much less attention has been given to how nurses must manage and coordinate care using multiple devices with different and sometimes conflicting interface designs. This paper introduces the emerging phenomenon of Inter-User Interface Friction to describe the act of coordinating care across multiple medical device interfaces designs that are not aligned and inconsistent. Through an evaluation of ten routinely used medical devices at a teaching hospital in Northern Ontario, Canada, key interface discrepancies were identified. Despite focusing only on non-specialized medical devices and basic device interaction features, the findings reveal a striking level of inconsistency in how information is presented and actions are performed. These variations can lead to hindering efficiency and user satisfaction, increase cognitive load, and compromise safe patient care.

Keywords: Inter-User Interface Friction · Usability · Medical Devices

1 Introduction

The increasing integration of digital technologies into healthcare has transformed how clinical care is delivered, monitored, and documented. Nowhere is this more evident than in acute care hospital environments, where nurses are expected to navigate a growing suite of medical devices each with its own interface, logic, and interaction model. From infusion pumps to physiological monitors, nurses routinely rely on these tools to administer care and respond to changing patient conditions. While the utility and promise of these technologies are well-documented, a critical dimension often overlooked is the cumulative interaction burden that arises when clinicians must work across multiple device interfaces throughout a single shift.

Much of the existing literature on health technology usability has focused on individual systems in isolation by evaluating a single interface or device for its strengths, limitations, and alignment with user needs. While this work is valuable, it rarely accounts for the reality that nurses operate within a multi-device ecosystem, where coordination across platforms is necessary, frequent, and often difficult. The fragmented nature

© The Author(s), under exclusive license to Springer Nature Switzerland AG 2026
V. G. Duffy (Ed.): HCII 2025, LNCS 16339, pp. 234–246, 2026.
https://doi.org/10.1007/978-3-032-13012-9_17

of interface design across devices means that nurses must manage subtle but significant variations in elements such as terminology, iconography, navigation, alarm logic. These inconsistencies often demand cognitive effort, increase the risk of error, and introduce inefficiencies in care delivery in a context that is already burdened under already high-stress conditions.

Despite the routine expectation of nurses to shift between different medical device interfaces, the literature has yet to consistently name or examine this phenomenon. While terms in the literature such as technostress and technology overload offer insight into the outcomes experienced from interacting with digital systems, they do not describe the phenomenon of experiencing interface-level frictions that occur between technologies in the same workflow. This paper aims to address this gap by introducing the phenomenon of Inter-User Interface Friction. By identifying and describing this phenomenon, the goal of this research is to move towards building a broader understanding of how the overall interplay of interface designs impacts nurses' work and, ultimately, patient care.

2 Literature Review

2.1 Poor Medical Device Usability

The usability of medical devices has long been recognized to play a key role in making sure they are used safely, effectively, and with satisfaction. Numerous studies emphasize that optimal usability is essential for realizing the intended benefits of technological innovations in real-world clinical environments [1–6]. Despite the steady advancement of medical technology, research consistently shows that poor usability can claw back much of these gains and can reduce or even negate the advantages that newer devices are meant to offer [2, 7, 8]. In practice, this means that even highly advanced devices may fail to support clinicians effectively if their interfaces are not designed with the end user in mind.

A recurring concern across the literature is that medical device user interfaces are frequently regarded as suboptimal by those who rely on them most: frontline clinicians [6, 9, 10]. Health technology interfaces are frequently described as being "inflexible," "not user-friendly," "difficult," or "inefficient" [1, 11–14] reflecting widespread dissatisfaction from clinicians who feel that these tools do not align with the realities of their work. When poorly designed devices are introduced into nursing workflows, the consequences are not only frustrating but they can be counterproductive or even harmful [1, 6, 8–10, 13, 15].

These frustrations and challenges reported by clinicians are substantiated by usability studies, which have revealed alarming levels of usability violations. For example, usability assessments of infusion pumps uncovered between 121 and 231 violations per device, with a notable portion of those issues labeled as either "catastrophic" or "major" in severity [6, 9]. Similarly, analyses of health information technologies revealed between 99 and 186 distinct usability problems across a relatively small set of systems [16–18], reinforcing the concern that poor interaction design is widespread across healthcare tools.

More recent work points specifically to nursing dissatisfaction with the usability of electronic health records (EHRs). For instance, Melnick et al. [19] reported that EHR systems received a an "F" rating among nurses, with 92% of respondents expressing dissatisfaction. Globally, the average satisfaction score for EHR use among nurses was only 4.5 out of 10. Supporting these findings, Seibert et al. [14] noted that over half of surveyed nurses cited poor user-friendliness as a reason for rejecting new technologies in their clinical practice. Collectively, this body of evidence points to a systemic problem in the design and implementation of healthcare technologies as one that directly impacts clinical efficiency, safety, and nurse well-being.

2.2 Nurse Medical Device Usability Perceptions

While extensive research has established that many medical devices possess suboptimal usability, it is equally important to understand the downstream impact of these short-comings, particularly on nurses. Nurses, as the primary users of health technologies in acute care settings, are expected to continuously adapt to new and often complex med-ical equipment [20]. This constant evolution in the technological landscape increases the responsibility placed on nurses to use devices both efficiently and safely, even when new technologies are layered onto existing, and sometimes already cumbersome, care delivery systems.

Given this critical role, more attention must be paid to how nurses perceive and inter-act with these technologies, as well as the multifaceted ways in which device design and integration affect their work [21]. Despite the theoretical improvements that new medical devices are meant to bring, practical challenges persist which highlights a disconnect between innovation and real-world clinical utility [13, 22, 23]. These challenges often manifest as stress and frustration when devices are difficult to use [4, 8, 9, 11, 24, 25], further compounding an already demanding nursing workload.

Usability-related issues with medical devices can also lead to workflow disruptions, which are one of the most frequently reported concerns in the literature [8, 11, 12, 15, 25, 26]. When the design of a user interface does not align with nurses' mental models or clinical routines, the result is often a breakdown in task flow that requires workarounds or additional cognitive effort to complete tasks that should otherwise be straightforward. In such cases, even well-intentioned technologies can become a barrier to effective care delivery.

When medical device interfaces are difficult to navigate, the consequences extend beyond inefficiency and dissatisfaction. Poor usability has been shown to contribute to adverse outcomes, including errors in care, compromised patient safety, and diminished nurse well-being [1, 2]. Ultimately, when device design does not support intuitive and efficient use, it becomes a barrier to both clinician performance and patient outcomes [1, 3–5]. As such, these findings underscore the importance of examining not only individual device usability, but also the broader context in which nurses must operate multiple devices in tandem as each possesses its own interface logic, design language, and interaction demands.

2.3 Technostress and Technology Overload in the Literature

Nurses routinely engage with multiple digital tools during a single shift, toggling between medical devices such as infusion pumps, vital signs monitors, electronic health records, and more. The cumulative burden of interacting with several, often inconsistently designed, technologies may contribute to deeper, systemic burdens that are not easily captured through traditional usability or error-focused assessments alone. It is in this broader context that a growing body of literature on technostress and technology overload becomes particularly relevant, though not entirely sufficient, in explaining the complexity of nurses' experiences with technology in acute care hospital settings.

The concept of technostress was first introduced by Craig Brod in 1984, who described it as "a modern disease caused by one's inability to cope or deal with Information and Communication Technologies (ICTs) in a healthy manner" [27] and since its inception, the concept has evolved considerably. For instance, Nisafani et al. [28] defines technostress as "any adverse effects on human behaviours, thoughts, attitudes, and psychology imposed by technology use," emphasizing individual difficulties in adapting to rapidly evolving digital systems. This framing positions technostress as a psychological and behavioral strain that arises when technological demands outpace a person's ability to effectively integrate them into their workflow.

In a similar vein, Karr-Wisniewski and Lu [29] introduced the idea of technology overload to describe the tipping point at which the addition of new technology begins to yield diminishing returns. They identified three primary contributors to this phenomenon: information overload, communication overload, and systems feature overload, each of which maps onto common stressors in high-tech clinical environments. These categories reflect the cognitive and operational burdens users face when navigating increasingly dense and complex technology ecosystems.

Expanding further on this conceptual landscape, Tarafdar et al. [30] identified five dimensions of technostress: techno-overload (where technology forces users to work faster or longer), techno-invasion (where work technologies blur boundaries between work and personal life), techno-complexity (when users feel inadequate due to the complexity of the technologies), techno-insecurity (fears of job loss due to automation), and techno-uncertainty (frequent technology changes). Each dimension reflects a unique psychological or emotional response to the increasing saturation of digital systems in work environments.

Importantly, healthcare-specific research echoes technostress concerns. Golz et al. [31] found that acute care nurses reported a mean technostress score of 49.67 on a 100-point scale, indicating moderate but significant stress levels attributed to technology use. Nurses in acute or psychiatric care settings reported especially high levels of technostress compared to those in other clinical environments which suggests that the volume and complexity of technologies in high-acuity settings amplifies these burdens.

Collectively, these frameworks provide useful insight into the adverse psychological and emotional outcomes that can stem from technology use. However, while technostress and technology overload highlight individual strain and cognitive burden, they do not fully encapsulate the interface-level inconsistencies and interactional friction that nurses face when managing multiple disparate devices. This paper proposes the need to build upon these concepts by introducing Inter-User Interface Friction, a construct aimed at capturing the usability misalignments across the suite of devices used by nurses.

2.4 The Need to Establish Inter-User Interface Friction

As healthcare environments become increasingly saturated with diverse medical technologies, nurses are required to interact with a wide array of devices, often simultaneously, each with its own unique interface logic, interaction behaviors, iconography, and feedback mechanisms, etc. While the literature has thoroughly examined the usability of individual medical devices, little attention has been paid to the experience of coordinating multiple user interfaces in a single workflow. This gap is critical, as the need to continually shift between disparate systems with differing visual and auditory cues, input controls, or alert behaviors imposes a unique and underexplored burden on the nurse. Existing concepts such as technostress and technology overload gesture toward the broader strain that technologies place on users, but they fail to capture the specific kind of friction that arises between interfaces, not within a single system, but across an ecosystem of devices that do not work in visual, logical, or operational harmony.

To address this gap, this paper introduces the concept of Inter-User Interface Friction, referring to the phenomenon of navigating between poorly aligned interfaces during the course of patient care. These challenges may be subtle, such as differing meanings for similar icons, inconsistent confirmation behaviors, or non-standardized alarm tones, but they accumulate in ways that can disrupt workflow, increase cognitive load, and contribute to clinical inefficiencies or safety risks. As nurses are often the primary end-users who bridge these fragmented systems in high-stakes environments, the lack of cohesive design across devices becomes not just a design flaw, but a clinical hazard. Establishing a term like Inter-User Interface Friction is a necessary step toward enabling more focused research, guiding thoughtful device procurement, and encouraging harmonized design efforts across vendors. A unified term also allows researchers and practitioners to better articulate and study this phenomenon, which has long been present in practice but largely absent from academic discourse.

3 Methodology

This study involved a comparative evaluation of ten routinely used medical device user interfaces encountered by medical-surgical unit nurses in a teaching hospital located in Northern Ontario. The focus on medical-surgical nursing units was intentional, as these environments typically rely on a standard suite of medical devices that are not specialized or unit-specific. This approach was intended to ensure broader relevance across different nursing contexts: although nurses in specialized units (e.g., ICU, OR) may use additional equipment, they are still likely to interact with the types of devices included in this study. Therefore, the insights generated from this sample remain applicable to a wide range of clinical settings.

Device selection was based on two main inclusion criteria: the devices had to (1) be routinely used by nurses during their shifts and (2) possess a computerized interface that offered visual or auditory feedback. This excluded more basic or mechanical devices, such as electric hospital beds that lack software-driven interaction or meaningful user interface components. The final sample of ten devices was determined by what was physically accessible at the time of data collection. Each device was systematically evaluated using Nielsen's ten usability heuristics as a guiding framework. This approach ensured that key dimensions of usability were considered in the comparison. While the heuristics provided structure and breadth to the evaluation, additional observational data regarding specific interface behaviors (e.g., icon usage, alarm tones, input controls) were also documented to capture nuanced inter-device inconsistencies relevant to real-world nursing workflows. Table 1 presents an overview of each device evaluated in this study.

Table 1. Overview of Medical Device Interfaces Evaluated.

Device	Device Type	Version Number
Welch Allyn 5300P	Vitals Monitor	1.20.00
Welch Allyn Connex	Vitals Monitor	1.52.00-A0002
Phillips SureSigns VS4	Vitals Monitor	A.07.33
Masimo Root	Vitals Monitor	N/A
icu Medical plum360	Infusion Pump	N/A
QCORE Medical Sapphire	Infusion Pump	15.10.2
Kangaroo ePump	Enteral Feed Pump	4.010
Kangaroo Omni	Enteral Feed Pump	01.05.4612
Smiths Medical CADD-Solis	PCA Pump	N/A
Medala Thopaz+	Digital Cardiothoracic Drain	N/A

4   Findings

This study examined the user interfaces of ten routinely used medical devices in an acute care setting through a comparative usability evaluation. Guided by Nielsen's ten heuristics, the analysis focused on identifying how interface design features may either support or hinder safe and efficient nurse-device interaction. To organize the diverse patterns observed, findings are presented under two overarching categories: Information Display Inconsistencies and Behavioural Logic Inconsistencies. These categories capture recurring usability concerns across the visual, auditory, and interactive elements of the devices and reflect the breadth of heuristics evaluated. Together, these categories reflect friction points that may not be apparent when devices are evaluated in isolation but become significant when nurses must coordinate and interact with multiple devices during care delivery.

4.1   Information Display Inconsistencies

This category encompasses inconsistencies in how information is visually and auditorily presented across the selected medical device interfaces. These inconsistencies were observed most frequently among iconography, alarm tones, and colour schemes, each of which can directly impact the nurse's ability to recognize information quickly and respond appropriately in time-sensitive clinical situations. The variability in these display elements touches on several key Nielsen's heuristics, including Recognition Over Recall, Consistency and Standards, Aesthetic and Minimalist Design, Match Between System and the Real World, and Visibility of System Status.

Icons. The evaluation of iconography across the ten selected medical devices involved a close examination of all visual symbols presented on each device's user interface. For the purpose of this analysis, an icon was considered unique by being visually distinct, such as having different colours for existing icons or other subtle modifications, since these differences signal distinct meanings to the user. As such, variations on the same foundational icon were treated as separate icons to reflect their differing meanings. The number of unique icons associated with each device is displayed in Table 2. After initially identifying all icons used across the devices, a cross-device comparison was conducted to remove duplicate icons. This process resulted in a total of 191 unique icons that exist across the ten devices. It is important to note that this figure was influenced by the specific software versions installed on each device available to the researchers which could have altered or expanded the icon set displayed to users.

Table 2. Unique Icons Present in Medical Device User Interfaces.

Device	Unique Icons
Welch Allyn 5300P	19
Welch Allyn Connex	26
Phillips SureSigns VS4	30
Masimo Root	32
icu Medical plum360	30
QCORE Medical Sapphire	13
Kangaroo ePump	12
Kangaroo Omni	5
Smiths Medical CADD-Solis	22
Medala Thopaz+	20

Auditory Tone Feedback. The auditory tones of the ten medical devices were assessed by analyzing each device's alerts, alarms, and notifications for pitch, rhythm, duration, and meaning. Most tones were simple sound patterns involving beeps, elongated tones, and pauses used to signal different events or patient conditions. Tones with only slight pitch variations were grouped as one when the differences were unlikely to be perceptible in fast-paced clinical settings. Through comparative analysis, 46 distinct auditory tones were identified that were associated with 56 total meanings.

Colour Feedback. The evaluation of colour across the ten medical devices focused on how colour functions as a communicative tool within two interface components: the main display screen and the tri-coloured LED arrays. For the main display, colour usage was analyzed specifically in the context of alarm and message displays, as these elements convey urgent or actionable information. While some devices used coloured panels or themes to reflect operational modes or user roles, these were excluded from the analysis, as they were not consistently tied to alerts or user-facing messages. Variations such as steady versus flashing colours were treated as distinct profiles due to their differing meanings. On devices with tri-coloured LED arrays, all possible colour-emitting states were recorded. Across the devices, six colour profiles were identified in alarm messaging on the main display (Table 3), and six colour profiles were identified in the LED arrays (Table 4).

Table 3. Colour Use for Alert Messaging in Main Display.

Device	Red	Red Flashing	Yellow	Yellow Flashing	Cyan	Blue
Welch Allyn 5300P	-	-	-	-	-	-
Welch Allyn Connex	High	-	Low	Medium	Very Low	Info
Phillips SureSigns VS4	-	High	-	Medium	-	Low
Masimo Root	-	High	Low	Medium	-	-
icu Medical plum360	-	-	-	-	-	-
QCORE Medical Sapphire	-	-	-	-	-	-
Kangaroo ePump	-	-	-	-	-	-
Kangaroo Omni	High	-	Medium	-	-	Low
Smiths Medical CADD-Solis	High	-	Medium	-	-	Low
Medala Thopaz+	Warning	-	Caution	-	-	-

Table 4. Colour Use for Alert Messaging in LED Array.

LED Colour	QCORE Medical Sapphire	Kangaroo ePump	Kangaroo Omni	Smiths Medical CADD-Solis
Red	Alarm Active	High Priority Alarm	-	Warning and Infusion Stopped
Red Flashing	-	-	Critical Alarm	-

(*continued*)

Table 4. (*continued*)

LED Colour	QCORE Medical Sapphire	Kangaroo ePump	Kangaroo Omni	Smiths Medical CADD-Solis
Yellow	Connected to Power with Full Battery	Information; Low Battery; Holding Mode; Medium Priority Alarm	Information	Pump Condition Alert
Yellow Flashing	Battery Charging	-	Notification	-
Green	Pump Running	Normal Pump Operation	Pump Running	Pump Condition Good
Green Flashing	Infusion Near End	-	Ready	-

4.2 Behavioural Logic Inconsistencies

This group of findings captures inconsistencies in how devices behave and respond during user interaction such as differences in workflows, input sequences, error handling, confirmation processes, etc. These behavioural mismatches across devices often force nurses to adjust or double-check their actions based on each device's unique logic, despite completing a similar task. The usability heuristics most relevant to this group include User Control and Freedom, Consistency and Standards, Error Prevention, Flexibility and Efficiency of Use, Help Users Recognize, Diagnose, and Recover from Errors, and Help and Documentation. While numerous behavioural logic inconsistencies were identified across the ten evaluated devices, this paper presents only a selection of illustrative examples to highlight the nature and scope of the issue.

Alarm Silence Function. The way in which alarm silence features behave and how they are activated varies widely across devices. On some interfaces, the "Silence" function simply mutes the sound temporarily, while on others, it may also serve to acknowledge the alarm condition, disable future alerts indefinitely, or silence specific categories of alarms. The method of interaction also differs: nurses may be required to press, hold, or press-and-hold the silence button or, in some cases, perform a combination of button inputs. These inconsistencies can lead to confusion about whether an alarm has been resolved, acknowledged, or merely muted.

Error Code Presentation. Interfaces also vary in how they present and communicate error conditions. Some devices display only obscure alphanumeric error codes explanation, requiring the user to consult a manual while other devices offer descriptive error messages that provide more actionable. This discrepancy affects how quickly and confidently nurses can respond to technical issues during patient care.

Hidden or Non-Intuitive Features. Certain devices include important features that are only accessible through non-obvious button combinations or repurposed existing buttons. For example, one device requires users to hold down an unrelated key to trigger a reset, an action not labeled or intuitively connected to that function. By contrast, other devices offer clearer and more accessible pathways to the same features. This hidden complexity imposes an unnecessary cognitive burden on the user.

Ambiguous Terminology. Lastly, several devices employ unclear or inconsistent terminology to label system states. Terms such as "Standby," "Paused," "Pending," or "Delayed" may appear across interfaces, but their meaning is not always consistent or clearly defined. For instance, "Standby" is understood as a device being powered-on but inactive, while on another device it indicates a readiness for use or partial deactivation. This semantic ambiguity introduces additional interpretive work for the nurse, increasing the likelihood of misinterpretation or error.

5 Discussion

The findings of this study demonstrate that even within a limited sample of ten routinely used medical devices, where none are considered highly complex and all of which were assessed only on their more basic interactive functions, nurses are required to navigate a substantial amount of interface variability. Across iconography, auditory tones, colour usage, and behavioural logic, already a striking number of nuanced inconsistencies emerged. Notably, these are devices that nurses are expected to operate regularly as part of standard care delivery in acute care hospital settings. This alone underscores the often-overlooked burden placed on nurse users: the need to hold multiple device-specific interface schemas in mind, transition between them seamlessly, and do so under conditions of time pressure and clinical urgency. This expectation sets the stage for inefficiencies, frustrations, and potential risks to patient safety.

What these findings make clear is that there is a lack of a shared term or conceptual framework to describe the phenomenon of having to interact with multiple divergent user interfaces in a single workflow. To begin addressing this gap, this study introduces the concept of Inter-User Interface Friction. This term refers to the cognitive, procedural, and emotional strain experienced by users, specifically nurses, when required to work across multiple medical device interfaces that differ in logic, feedback, terminology, and interaction pathways. It captures the burden placed on nurse users when interfaces behave in ways that contradict or conflict with expectations built from previous or concurrent device use. At this stage, the term is still in its early conceptual development, but the results of this study provide compelling groundwork for why it warrants further articulation and investigation.

The importance of advancing this line of inquiry lies in its potential to reframe how we approach interface design, user support, and healthcare technology procurement. Nurses are not simply operating one device at a time; they are managing entire ecosystems of technology that are rarely interoperable in design or logic. Recognizing Inter-User Interface Friction as a real and measurable burden can help shift the narrative away from individual user error or training deficiencies, and toward a systemic understanding of interface-induced cognitive load. Doing so not only validates the lived experience of frontline healthcare providers, but also opens the door to new standards in interface consistency, cross-device design alignment, and user-centered engineering in the medical device industry. Ultimately, this work demands that research looks beyond the usability of a single device and begins to address the friction that exists in the interactions between them.

6   Conclusion

This study investigated the interface characteristics of ten routinely used medical devices in acute care hospital settings, highlighting significant variability across iconography, auditory tones, colour usage, and behavioural logic. The findings show that even when focusing on non-specialized devices and basic interaction features, nurses must navigate a landscape filled with inconsistencies and hidden complexities. These interface nuances place an often-invisible burden on nurses, demanding constant adaptation, interpretation, and memory recall across disparate systems all while striving to provide safe and timely patient care.

In response to these findings, this paper introduces the emerging concept of Inter-User Interface Friction, a term that captures the cognitive and operational strain nurses experience when interacting with multiple, poorly aligned device interfaces. Unlike existing terms such as technostress or technology overload, Inter-User Interface Friction calls attention to the inconsistencies between interfaces and the cumulative effect they have on clinical workflow and user satisfaction.

As healthcare environments continue to integrate more digital tools and technologies, attention must shift toward interface alignment and the practical realities of nurse users. Recognizing and defining Inter-User Interface Friction is a first step toward building a more nurse-centered approach to device design, evaluation, and policy. Further research is needed to refine this concept, develop methods of measurement, and integrate it into usability and safety evaluations across the healthcare technology landscape.

Acknowledgments. The authors would like to thank Health Sciences North for their generous support in accommodating the evaluation of medical devices used in this study. Special thanks are also extended to the staff at Health Science North's Simulation Lab who assisted in sourcing and coordinating access to the equipment, making this research possible.

References

1. Branaghan, R.J.: Human factors in medical device design: methods, principles, and guidelines. Crit. Care Nurs. Clin. **30**(2), 225–236 (2018). https://doi.org/10.1016/j.cnc.2018.02.005
2. Kim, Y., Son, J., Jang, W.: Usability study on patient monitoring systems: an evaluation of a user interface based on user experience and preference. Med. Sci. Monit. Int. Med. J. Exp. Clin. Res. **29**, e938570–e938571 (2023). https://doi.org/10.12659/MSM.938570

3. McBride, S., Alexander, G.L., Baernholdt, M., Vugrin, M., Epstein, B.: Scoping review: positive and negative impact of technology on clinicians. Nurs. Outlook **71**(2) (2023). https://doi.org/10.1016/j.outlook.2023.101918

4. Tawfik, D.S., et al.: Frustration with technology and its relation to emotional exhaustion among health care workers: cross-sectional observational study. J. Med. Internet Res. **23**(7) (2021). https://doi.org/10.2196/26817

5. Wosny, M., Strasser, L.M., Hastings, J.: Experience of health care professionals using digital tools in the hospital: qualitative systematic review. JMIR Hum. Factors **10**(1), e50357 (2023). https://doi.org/10.2196/50357

6. Zhang, J., Johnson, T.R., Patel, V.L., Paige, D.L., Kubose, T.: Using usability heuristics to evaluate patient safety of medical devices. J. Biomed. Inform. **36**(1), 23–30 (2003). https://doi.org/10.1016/S1532-0464(03)00060-1

7. Holden, R.J., Rivera-Rodriguez, A.J., Faye, H., Scanlon, M.C., Karsh, B.-T.: Automation and adaptation: nurses' problem-solving behavior following the implementation of bar-coded medication administration technology. Cogn. Tech. Work **15**(3), 283–296 (2013). https://doi.org/10.1007/s10111-012-0229-4

8. Staggers, N., Elias, B.L., Makar, E., Alexander, G.L.: The imperative of solving nurses' usability problems with health information technology. JONA J. Nurs. Admin. **48**(4), 191 (2018). https://doi.org/10.1097/NNA.0000000000000598

9. Graham, M.J., Kubose, T.K., Jordan, D., Zhang, J., Johnson, T.R., Patel, V.L.: Heuristic evaluation of infusion pumps: implications for patient safety in Intensive Care Units. Int. J. Med. Informatics **73**(11–12), 771–779 (2004). https://doi.org/10.1016/j.ijmedinf.2004.08.002

10. Liu, K., Chan, F., Or, C.K., Sun, D.T., Lai, W., So, H.: Heuristic evaluation and simulated use testing of infusion pumps to inform pump selection. Int. J. Med. Inform. **131**(Complete) (2019). https://doi.org/10.1016/j.ijmedinf.2019.07.011

11. Brown, J., Pope, N., Bosco, A.M., Mason, J., Morgan, A.: Issues affecting nurses' capability to use digital technology at work: an integrative review. J. Clin. Nurs. **29**(15–16), 2801–2819 (2020). https://doi.org/10.1111/jocn.15321

12. Korte, L., Bohnet-Joschko, S.: Digitization in everyday nursing care: a vignette study in German hospitals. Int. J. Environ. Res. Public Health **19**(17) (2022). https://doi.org/10.3390/ijerph191710775

13. Ruppel, H., Funk, M.: Nurse-technology interactions and patient safety. Crit. Care Nurs. Clin. North Am. **30**(2), 203–213 (2018). https://doi.org/10.1016/j.cnc.2018.02.003

14. Seibert, K., Domhoff, D., Huter, K., Krick, T., Rothgang, H., Wolf-Ostermann, K.: Application of digital technologies in nursing practice: results of a mixed methods study on nurses' experiences, needs and perspectives. Zeitschrift für Evidenz, Fortbildung und Qualität im Gesundheitswesen **158**(Complete), 94–106 (2020). https://doi.org/10.1016/j.zefq.2020.10.010

15. World Health Organization: Increasing complexity of medical technology and consequences for training and outcome of care: background paper 4, August 2010. In: Increasing complexity of medical technology and consequences for training and outcome of care: background paper 4, August 2010 (2010). https://iris.who.int/handle/10665/70455. Accessed 05 July 2024

16. Atashi, A., Khajouei, R., Azizi, A., Dadashi, A.: User interface problems of a nationwide inpatient information system: a heuristic evaluation. Appl. Clin. Inform. **7**(1), 89–100 (2016). https://doi.org/10.4338/ACI-2015-07-RA-0086

17. Ebnehoseini, Z., Tara, M., Meraji, M., Deldar, K., Khoshronezhad, F., Khoshronezhad, S.: Usability evaluation of an admission, discharge, and transfer information system: a heuristic evaluation. Open Access Maced. J. Med. Sci. **6**(11), 1941–1945 (2018). https://doi.org/10.3889/oamjms.2018.392

18. Farzandipour, M., Nabovati, E., Tadayon, H., Sadeqi Jabali, M.: Identification and classification of usability problems in a nursing information system: a heuristic evaluation. CIN Comput. Inform. Nurs. **40**(2), 121–130 (2022). https://doi.org/10.1097/CIN.0000000000000803

19. Melnick, E.R., et al.: The association between perceived electronic health record usability and professional burnout among US nurses. J. Am. Med. Inform. Assoc. **28**(8), 1632–1641 (2021). https://doi.org/10.1093/jamia/ocab059

20. Lucena, J.C.-R., Carvalho, C., Santos-Costa, P., Mónico, L., Parreira, P.: Nurses' strategies to prevent and/or decrease work-related technostress: a scoping review. CIN Comput. Inform. Nurs. **39**(12), 916 (2021). https://doi.org/10.1097/CIN.0000000000000771

21. Conte, G., Arrigoni, C., Magon, A., Stievano, A., Caruso, R.: Embracing digital and technological solutions in nursing: a scoping review and conceptual framework. Int. J. Med. Inform. **177**(Complete) (2023). https://doi.org/10.1016/j.ijmedinf.2023.105148

22. Booth, R.G., Strudwick, G., McBride, S., O'Connor, S., Solano López, A.L.: How the nursing profession should adapt for a digital future. BMJ **373**, n1190 (2021). https://doi.org/10.1136/bmj.n1190

23. Graham, H.L., Nussdorfer, D., Beal, R.: Nurse attitudes related to accepting electronic health records and bedside documentation. CIN Comput. Inform. Nurs. **36**(11), 515 (2018). https://doi.org/10.1097/CIN.0000000000000491

24. McConnel, E.A., Fletcher, J.: Agency registered nurse use of medical equipment: an Australian perspective. Int. J. Nurs. Stud. **32**(2), 149–161 (1995). https://doi.org/10.1016/0020-7489(94)00037-K

25. Shin, E.H., Cummings, E., Ford, K.: A qualitative study of new graduates' readiness to use nursing informatics in acute care settings: clinical nurse educators' perspectives. Contemp. Nurse **54**(1), 64–76 (2018). https://doi.org/10.1080/10376178.2017.1393317

26. Lee, S., Lee, M.-S.: Nurses' electronic medical record workarounds in a tertiary teaching hospital. CIN Comput. Inform. Nurs. **39**(7), 367–374 (2021). https://doi.org/10.1097/CIN.0000000000000692

27. Ayyagari, R., Grover, V., Purvis, R.: Technostress: technological antecedents and implications. MIS Q. **35**(4), 831–858 (2011). https://doi.org/10.2307/41409963

28. Nisafani, A.S., Kiely, G., Mahony, C.: Workers' technostress: a review of its causes, strains, inhibitors, and impacts. J. Decis. Syst. **29**(sup1), 243–258 (2020). https://doi.org/10.1080/12460125.2020.1796286

29. Karr-Wisniewski, P., Lu, Y.: When more is too much: operationalizing technology overload and exploring its impact on knowledge worker productivity. Comput. Hum. Behav. **26**(5), 1061–1072 (2010). https://doi.org/10.1016/j.chb.2010.03.008

30. Tarafdar, M., Tu, Q., Ragu-Nathan, B.S., Ragu-Nathan, T.S.: The impact of technostress on role stress and productivity. J. Manag. Inf. Syst. **24**(1), 301–328 (2007). https://doi.org/10.2753/MIS0742-1222240109

31. Golz, C., Peter, K.A., Zwakhalen, S.M.G., Hahn, S.: Technostress among health professionals – a multilevel model and group comparisons between settings and professions. Inform. Health Soc. Care **46**(2), 137–149 (2021). https://doi.org/10.1080/17538157.2021.1872579

Advancing Human-Computer Interaction in Depression Research: Trends and Hotspots Through a Bibliometric Lens

Ting Huang and Wei Liu

Department of Engineering, King's College London, London, UK
{ting.5.huang,wei.liu}@kcl.ac.uk

Abstract. This study aggregates design resource knowledge to explore global approaches to depression treatment and research in Human-Computer Interaction (HCI) from 2000 to 2025. Using bibliometrics and clustering techniques, it identifies research trends, emerging hotspots, and collaboration patterns. The analysis covers keyword co-occurrence, regional publications, institutional contributions, and agency involvement, all mapped into key research areas. Findings highlight three key points: (1) The integration of artificial intelligence (AI) and multidisciplinary approaches for early screening and intervention; (2) Strong international collaboration, led by the United States; (3) University College London's (UCL) prominence in shaping research paradigms. The study identifies three emerging research hotspots: (1) Depression treatment for adolescents; (2) Interdisciplinary collaboration prioritising user experience; (3) Digital innovation in treatment methodologies.

Keywords: Human Computer Interaction (HCI) · Depression Treatment · Form of Interaction · Bibliometric-based

1 Introduction

Depression is a prevalent psychiatric disorder characterised by prolonged periods of low mood, often accompanied by a diminished interest in life and activities [34]. Cognitive Behavioural Therapy (CBT) has been shown to be an effective approach in the clinical treatment of depression [22,24]. As socio-economic factors and lifestyles evolve, the prevalence of depression is increasing across various age groups, leading to a broader demographic of affected individuals. Consequently, the shortage of specialised therapists has prompted the exploration of more interactive formats for the early intervention of depression [28,29]. In this context, there is growing evidence supporting the efficacy of smartphone-based depression intervention applications as a reliable delivery method [12]. Online mobile digital programmes, such as those designed to support and facilitate care collaboration, have demonstrated some effectiveness in alleviating mental health

© The Author(s), under exclusive license to Springer Nature Switzerland AG 2026
V. G. Duffy (Ed.): HCII 2025, LNCS 16339, pp. 247–260, 2026.
https://doi.org/10.1007/978-3-032-13012-9_18

issues to a certain extent [9,25,35]. The public can utilise mobile platforms to assess their current psychological state and engage in self-guided interventions and self-help strategies for managing their mental health [11,23].

HCI is the discipline concerned with the interaction between humans and computers [26]. The field of HCI is inherently human-centred, focusing on enhancing user experience and operability [5,13,38]. Research has shown that HCI can play a significant role in digital interventions for individuals with depression. Lindner's work on translating cognitive-behavioural techniques into virtual reality models highlights how VR can be used for antidepressant purposes, underscoring its potential in depression treatment [21]. HCI models help design usable applications that address inequalities in mental health care and suicide prevention, supporting the Digital Therapeutic Alliance [4,7,25].

Kretzschmar has explored youth populations' perceptions of chatbots for mental health, delving into the ethical implications of automated conversational agents, and evaluating their strengths and limitations in digital therapies for mental health [17]. Derick, on the other hand, employed eye-tracking technology to analyse depression levels in adolescents, combining it with machine learning as a non-invasive diagnostic tool [18]. Yi utilised virtual reality to create a game aimed at developing empathy, exploring its potential for both preventing and intervening in depression [20]. Ferrario developed a virtual game using Large Language Models (LLM) to foster empathy in adolescents, incorporating situational dialogues and tailored responses to help recognise and monitor depression-related language. [10].

With the advent of Artificial Intelligence (AI), scholars have increasingly focused on leveraging AI algorithms as a breakthrough for the digital prevention, treatment, and monitoring of depression [15,16,37]. Adler suggests that passive sensing technologies could transform mental health measurement, allowing for the detection of individuals with mental health disorders or specific symptoms [1]. Furthermore, digital behavioural interventions are showing promise in alleviating depression and anxiety through daily interactions [3,39,40]. The integration of modalities such as music therapy, multisensory approaches, and other techniques within affective computing has been shown to help alleviate mild anxiety [14,30]. The design of social media platforms and games now increasingly incorporates AI and big data models to encourage social interaction among individuals with depression and enhance their motivation for autonomy [6,8].

This study aims to collate and enrich research dynamics and emerging trends in HCI for depression treatment using a bibliometric approach. By visualising the data, it provides an overview of the field's frontiers, highlighting key trends and hotspots for design and intervention. The study also offers references and recommendations for future research based on keywords and empirical evidence from various institutions and regions over recent years. It reviews the field's historical progression and analyses global research on depression treatment through HCI over the past 25 years. The study addresses four exploratory questions: (1) What is the current status of treatments for depression in the field of HCI? (2) Which countries are leading research in this area, and what are the research levels and hotspots in these regions? (3) Which institutions have a high volume of publications in this field? (4) What are the future research prospects and outlooks for the treatment of depression within HCI?

2   Method

2.1   Data Sources

The database used for this study was derived from the Web of Science's Science Citation Index Expanded (SCI Expanded), which facilitated the literature search and tracking of research hotspots. The search criteria were defined as follows: TS = (depressive OR depressive disorder AND disorder OR depression OR anxiety OR digital health AND human-computer interaction). The literature types were limited to research articles, review papers, and conference proceedings, and the time frame for the search was restricted to publications from 2000-01-01 to 2025-01-01. The export condition was set to Tab-delimited file format, with the selection of "Full Record" and "Cited References". Based on these search criteria, a total of 757 articles were initially retrieved. After applying the eligibility criteria, 739 articles were deemed eligible, with the screening process illustrated in Figure 1.

2.2   Analysis Tool

The data analysis in this study utilised the Visualisation of Similarities (VOS) viewer (version 1.6.20), a knowledge mapping tool developed by the Centre for Science and Technology Studies (CWTS) at Leiden University, Netherlands [36]. The VOSviewer offers a range of visualisation products provided by the CWTS, which assist in the construction of hotspot maps based on research keywords, thereby visualising and representing clustered relationships, such as those between institutions and scholarly collaborations. In this analysis, keywords, research institutions, and countries were visualised, and high-frequency statistics of key literature were generated. The tool was used to categorise and summarise the current status and research hotspots in global efforts on human-computer interaction for depression treatment, focusing on the period from 2000 to 2025.

3   Data Analysis

3.1   Analysis of Co-occurrence Keywords

A total of 3,913 keywords were retrieved, with a minimum occurrence threshold set to five. This resulted in 251 keywords meeting the specified criteria. The output was visualised in a mapping that includes 251 keywords, organised into 9 clusters. The keyword hotspot map, which represents research on HCI for depression treatment, is divided into nine distinct clusters. The size of the circles in the map corresponds to the weight of the literature, with larger circles

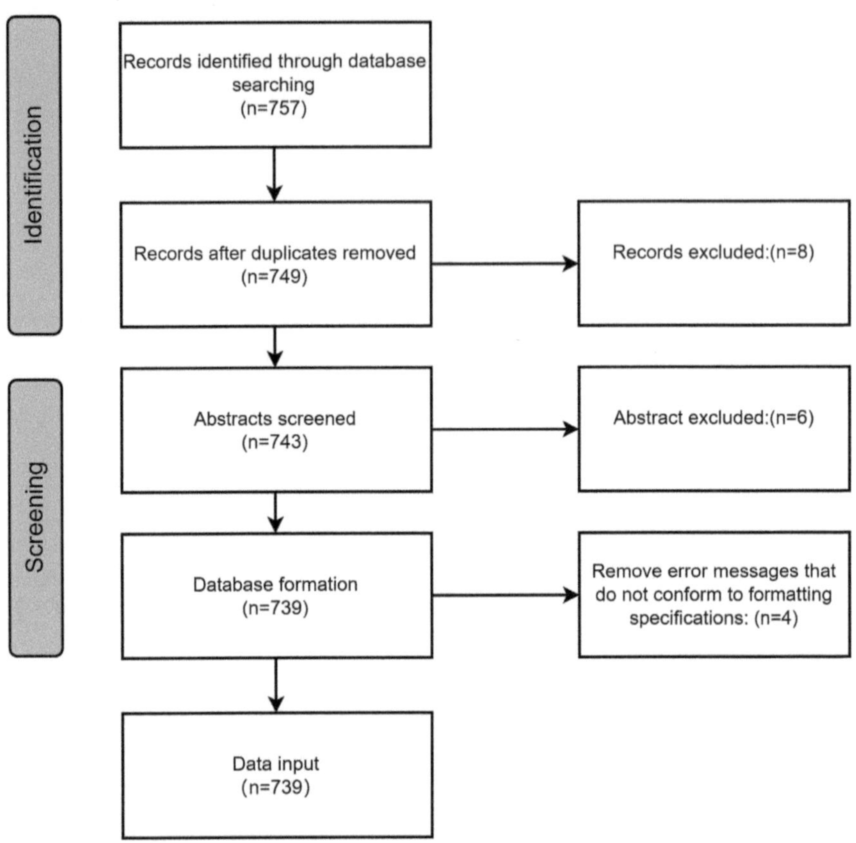

Fig. 1. Data sources and screening process.

indicating keywords with higher frequency and, by extension, greater research emphasis. As shown in Figure 2, a larger percentage of circles suggests that these keywords are more prevalent and reflect the prevailing research directions and methodologies [36].

The top 20 co-occurring keywords in the field of HCI for depression treatment are presented in Table 1. The high-frequency keywords in this domain predominantly include "technology," "virtual reality," "design," "internet," and "artificial intelligence." These keywords indicate a recent shift towards focusing on the research and treatment of depression in children. According to official data from the World Health Organization (WHO), depression is estimated to affect 1.4% of children aged 10–14 and 3.5% of adolescents aged 15–19 globally. This suggests a concerning trend of increasing incidence of depression and other psychiatric mood disorders among younger populations.

The analysis of high-frequency keywords also reveals that current research on interaction technologies is centred around virtual reality, artificial intelligence, machine learning, and chatbots. In the context of depression treatment,

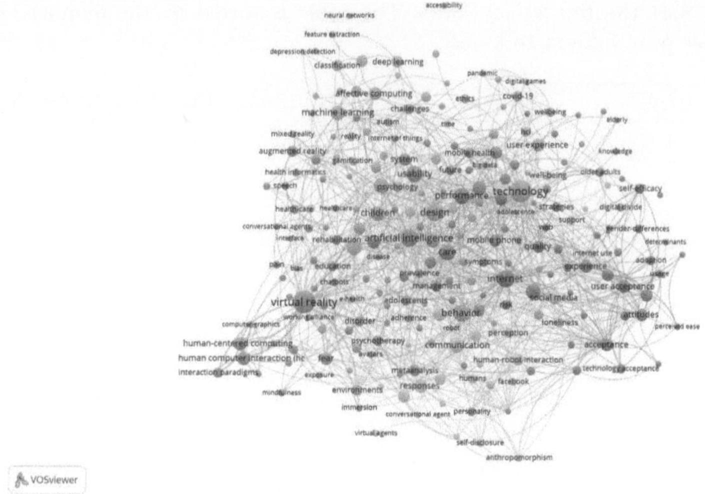

Fig. 2. Keyword clustering hotspot map. Different colours in the graph represent different clusters. The size of the circle represents the frequency of keyword occurrence, the larger the circle, the higher the frequency.

CBT remains a widely used clinical approach. Notably, the integration of CBT with virtual reality—such as through interactive images like virtual pets—has emerged as a novel intervention. This innovative combination provides promising directions for future research and offers new opportunities for enhancing clinical treatment methodologies [21]. Early research during this period predominantly focused on human-centric dimensions, such as performance and psychological factors. The primary emphasis was on understanding the individual aspects of depression. At an early stage, the attention shifted towards technological innovations and breakthroughs. Virtual Reality (VR) technology began to be applied in the treatment of depression. Human-Centered Computing (HCC) emerged as a pivotal area in HCI research, contributing significantly to the clinical treatment of depression. At the present stage, the research landscape broadened to encompass emerging frontiers in AI, machine learning, and deep learning. During this phase, research coverage expanded significantly, marked by notable interdisciplinary trends. AI-based models, particularly from the computational field, have been increasingly employed for the early detection and monitoring of depression [19]. Additionally, generative AI chatbots have demonstrated potential as meaningful mental health support tools in clinical settings, with early trials showing promising outcomes that underline the effectiveness of digital mental health interventions [32].

3.2   Analysis of Key Cooperating Countries

In VOSviewer, following the threshold-setting principle outlined by Van [36], the nodes and edges representing documents of significant importance or relevance

Table 1. Sort the top 20 keywords. The table is sorted by the number of keyword occurrences from highest to lowest.

Item	Keyword	Occurrences	Total Link Strength
1	technology	60	285
2	virtual reality	59	253
3	design	37	153
4	internet	37	198
5	artificial intelligence	36	177
6	behavior	35	170
7	usability	33	133
8	performance	30	131
9	stress	30	128
10	care	29	131
11	communication	27	125
12	model	27	108
13	children	25	117
14	emotion	25	87
15	machine learning	25	93
16	human-centered computing	22	97
17	responses	22	106
18	social media	20	85
19	user acceptance	20	119
20	chatbot	18	88

are selected to avoid overly complex graphs, while maintaining a clear and reasonable network structure. Based on the research objectives and the principle of an appropriate threshold, the minimum number of documents for each country was set to 5. This resulted in a total of 79 countries/regions in the database, with 40 countries meeting this threshold. As shown in Figure 3, the size of the circles corresponds to the number of articles published in each country/region, with larger circles indicating a higher volume of publications and greater weight in the research network. The visualisation reveals that the United States, China, the United Kingdom, and Germany have a more extensive body of HCI research on the treatment of depression. Monitoring the research trends in these countries provides valuable insights for accurately analysing and predicting future developments in this field. Figure 4 illustrates the degree of collaboration between institutions within each country. The thickness of the lines in the visualisation reflects the strength of cooperation, with thicker lines signifying closer collaboration. Notably, there is strong collaboration between four countries: the United States, the United Kingdom, China, and Canada.

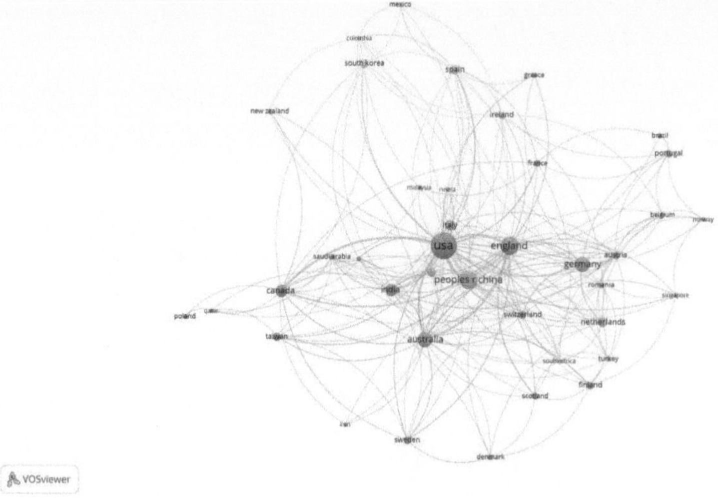

Fig. 3. Country hotspot map. The size of the circle indicates the size of the country's weight.

The visualisation mapping outputs the top ten countries based on article publication, as shown in Table 2. The United States has published a total of 191 articles, with 10,425 citations; China has published 95 articles, with 1,079 citations; and the United Kingdom has published 89 articles, with 2,630 citations. From the perspective of article volume, the United States holds a dominant position in this field, with both the number of publications and citations far exceeding those of other countries/regions. While China has published slightly

Table 2. Sort the top 20 keywords. The table is sorted by the number of keyword occurrences from highest to lowest.

Item	Country	Documents	Citations	Total Link Strength
1	USA	191	10,425	114
2	China	95	1,079	49
3	England	89	2,630	87
4	Germany	64	1,310	34
5	Australia	63	1,927	62
6	Canada	40	1,271	38
7	India	39	268	31
8	Italy	31	304	24
9	Netherlands	27	747	32
10	Spain	27	484	28

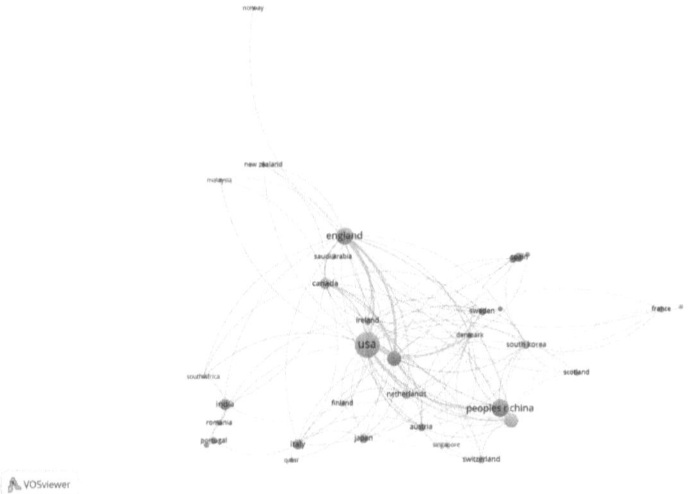

Fig. 4. Map of country cooperation hotspots. The different thicknesses of the lines represent the degree of cooperation.

more articles than the United Kingdom, the UK outpaces China in terms of citations and total link strength.

3.3   Analysis of Issuing Institutions

Between 2000 and 2025, a total of 1,125 research organisations across 79 countries/regions worldwide published research on HCI in the treatment of depression. The minimum number of documents per organisation was set to 5, resulting

Table 3. Sort the top 20 keywords. The table is sorted by the number of keyword occurrences from highest to lowest.

Item	Country	Documents	Citations	Total Link Strength
1	University College London	16	470	12
2	Stanford University	12	1,025	7
3	The University of Melbourne	12	677	11
4	University of Washington	11	499	4
5	The University of Manchester	10	224	8
6	University of Oxford	10	419	3
7	Chinese Academy of Sciences	8	168	6
8	Technische Universiteit Delft	8	76	3
9	Beijing Institute of Technology	7	57	3
10	Griffith University	7	240	1

in 38 organisations meeting this threshold. The top 10 organisations based on this criterion are listed in Table 3. The organisation with the highest number of publications is University College London (UCL), with 470 publications and an equal number of citations. In contrast, the organisation with the highest total number of citations is Stanford University, with 1,025 citations.

4   Discussion

Economic, demographic, and social factors have led to a rising global depression rate, particularly among younger individuals. The WHO reports that 3.8% of the global population is affected, with women being 50% more likely to suffer than men. Suicide claims around 700,000 lives annually, making it the fourth leading cause of death in those aged 15 to 29. The research content from the past 25 years has been analysed, summarised, and discussed across four key areas:

4.1   Current Status of Research in HCI for Depression Treatment

Current research in the field demonstrates a trend of multidisciplinary cross-fertilisation, giving rise to new areas of growth and advancing disciplinary frontiers. This trend bridges gaps in the original discipline, continuously expanding both the depth and breadth of research. In human-computer interaction for depression treatment, early research focused on individuals, primarily examining the behavioural performance of those with depression and emphasising user experience and acceptance through various forms of interaction. Recent studies have centred on children and women, aligning with WHO data, with therapeutic interventions tailored to be gentler and more engaging. Over the past five years, the integration of AI and cross-disciplinary collaboration has led to breakthroughs in research ideas and directions. VR has emerged as a mature tool in clinical depression treatment, often incorporating virtual games, pets, and other interactive elements. Commercially, numerous depression-related apps have been developed, offering cost-effective solutions. These apps provide innovative approaches to early diagnosis and pre-treatment of depression. Additionally, AI models for early monitoring, prevention, and treatment of depression have garnered increasing interest. Currently, researchers are exploring the use of Large Language Models (LLMs) and chatbots for early depression diagnosis.

4.2   Number of Publications and Citations by Country/Region

The visualisation results indicate that the United States leads both in terms of the number of articles published and the number of citations within this research field. The total number of citations from the United States significantly surpasses those of other countries, reflecting the widespread recognition and support for research in this area. Other countries with a prominent presence in this field include China, the United Kingdom, Germany, and Australia, which collectively lead the global research efforts in HCI for the treatment of depression.

4.3   Trends in the Number and Distribution of Publications by Research Organizations

The bibliometric analysis of publication numbers by research institutions reveals that the top 10 research organisations are geographically distributed across several countries. Of these, three institutions are based in the United Kingdom, two in the United States, two in Australia, and two in China. This distribution mirrors the trends observed in national publication volumes. Furthermore, the close collaboration between institutions across these countries/regions highlights the increasing trend of international cooperation in this field, which may represent the frontier geography of research on HCI for depression treatment.

4.4   Research Trends and Perspectives in the Field of HCI for Depression Treatment

Intervention and Enabling of AI in the Depression Treatment Process. In the cross-fertilisation of disciplines, computer science has increasingly become the dominant field, with researchers and institutions reshaping AI-driven early screening systems for depression. However, the research process must remain human-centred, prioritising user experience and operability. AI systems can enhance empathy in text-based monitoring, particularly in peer-to-peer mental health support, by improving empathic expression. In such dialogues, where supporters often lack professional training, AI collaboration is expected to bridge these gaps [31].

Enhancing User Activity Through Digital Mental Health Interventions. Digital mental health interventions (DMHIs) have emerged as a promising solution for treating depression, offering low-cost, effective, and anonymous treatment options [32] . Despite the availability of numerous apps in this space, user feedback remains mixed, with dissatisfaction regarding user engagement and retention [2]. Key considerations for improving digital mental health interventions include: 1) Building trust: Addressing users' concerns about the potential risks of personal information leakage is crucial. Establishing trust through secure and transparent data handling practices is essential; 2) Enhancing user engagement: The design of interaction forms should be carefully considered to maximise user time and retention. Overly complex interfaces or high information density can degrade the user experience, reducing interest and engagement; 3) Improving therapeutic effectiveness: The ultimate goal of DMHIs is to support users' healing. Therefore, the efficacy of these interventions, measured through feedback and therapeutic outcomes, is a key factor in evaluating their success.

Shifts in Forms of Interaction and Theories that Are Consistent with Specific Populations and Regions. Individual differences exist in the depressed population, and individual performance is differentiated by differences in upbringing and cultural background. Although the basic treatment paradigm of depression is general and universal, individual differences and customised programmes need to be taken into account in the actual treatment process. For example, the treatment of children, whose cognitive and behavioural abilities are low due to age and developmental problems, requires a change in the form of interaction and an appropriate treatment plan based on the knowledge and theories of child behaviour and psychology [33]. CBT is a clinical tool for the treatment and relief of depression, but CBT is mainly rooted in Western culture and structure, and its application is focused on Western populations [27]. It is therefore interesting to see how it can be applied in the rest of the world and how it can be localised in the rest of the cultures.

4.5   Limitations and Future Directions

This study, based on data from the Web of Science database, has certain limitations: 1) Database limitation: Relying solely on the Web of Science may exclude important articles or conferences not indexed in this platform. Future research should include multiple databases for a more comprehensive analysis; 2) Keyword search limitation: Only representative terms were used in keyword selection, potentially overlooking studies using synonyms or alternative terminology, leading to an incomplete research representation; 3) Language bias: As the review focused on English-language sources, it may have missed valuable literature published in other languages, limiting the diversity of the reviewed studies.

5   Conclusion

Mental health research has become a key focus, with modern science and technology playing a crucial role in driving progress. This study's analysis shows that research is more prevalent in developed countries, due to their higher economic, technological, and cultural development. Addressing depression in HCI is complex, requiring multidisciplinary integration. The bibliometric analysis of articles from 2000 to 2025 leads to three main conclusions: 1) Advances in science and technology: Modern developments, especially in AI, have guided research trends, enabling early diagnosis and intervention. Human-computer interaction has also evolved to include Augmented Reality (AR), improving clinical treatment; 2) Globalisation and collaboration: Transnational cooperation is growing, with the United States leading much of the research and innovation; 3) UCL's leadership: University College London (UCL) has become a key institution, introducing new methodologies and influencing the field. Displayed equations are centered and set on a separate line.

References

1. Adler, D.A., et al.: Beyond detection: towards actionable sensing research in clinical mental healthcare. Proc. ACM Interact., Mob., Wearable Ubiquit. Technol. **8**(4), 1–33 (2024)

2. Akhund, T.M.N.U., et al.: A comprehensive exploration of human communal media interaction and its evolving impact on psychological health across demographics and time. PeerJ Comput. Sci. **10**, e2398 (2024)
3. Alhasani, M., Orji, R.: Exploring trends, pitfalls, and future directions in digital behaviour change interventions for managing student stress. Int. J. Human–Comput. Interact. 1–20 (2024)
4. Anekar, D., Deshpande, Y.D.: HCL-ML work in wellbeing of mental health and pilot study to detect depression and anxiety among students during covid. Des. Eng. **7**, 9779–9787 (2021)
5. Avouris, N., Katsanos, C., Tselios, N., Moustakas, K.: Introduction to human-computer interaction (2016)
6. van Baal, S.T., Le, S.T., Fatehi, F., Verdejo-Garcia, A., Hohwy, J.: Testing behaviour change with an artificial intelligence chatbot in a randomized controlled study. J. Public Health Policy **45**(3), 506 (2024)
7. Balcombe, L., De Leo, D.: Human-computer interaction in digital mental health. In: Informatics. vol. 9, p. 14. MDPI (2022)
8. Díaz, M., Gil, R.M., Cabeza, L.F., Cerezo, E., Teixidó, M.: Enhancing active aging through irage: mitigating social isolation with intergenerational gaming. Heliyon **10**(12), e32979 (2024)
9. Eschler, J., Burgess, E.R., Reddy, M., Mohr, D.C.: Emergent self-regulation practices in technology and social media use of individuals living with depression. In: Proceedings of the 2020 CHI Conference on Human Factors in Computing Systems, pp. 1–13. CHI '20, Association for Computing Machinery, New York, NY, USA (2020). https://doi.org/10.1145/3313831.3376773
10. Ferrario, A., Sedlakova, J., Trachsel, M.: The role of humanization and robustness of large language models in conversational artificial intelligence for individuals with depression: a critical analysis. JMIR Mental Health **11**, e56569 (2024)
11. Ferreira-Brito, F., Alves, S., Guerreiro, T., Santos, O., Caneiras, C., Carriço, L., Verdelho, A.: Digital health and patient adherence: a qualitative study in older adults. DIGITAL HEALTH **10**, 20552076231223804 (2024). https://doi.org/10.1177/20552076231223805
12. Firth, J., et al.: The efficacy of smartphone-based mental health interventions for depressive symptoms: a meta-analysis of randomized controlled trials. World Psych. **16**(3), 287–298 (2017). https://doi.org/10.1002/wps.20472
13. Gross, T.: Human-computer interaction education and diversity. In: Human-Computer Interaction. Theories, Methods, and Tools: 16th International Conference, HCI International 2014, Heraklion, Crete, Greece, June 22-27, 2014, Proceedings, Part I 16, pp. 187–198. Springer (2014)
14. He, S., Zeng, H., Xue, M., Huang, G., Yao, C., Ying, F.: Affective stroking: design thermal mid-air tactile for assisting people in stress regulation. Appl. Sci. **14**(20), 9494 (2024)
15. Hussna, A.U., Laz, A.N.K., Sikder, M.S., Uddin, J., Tinmaz, H., Esfar-E-Alam, A.: Prerona: mental health bengali chatbot for digital counselling. In: Intelligent Human Computer Interaction: 12th International Conference, IHCI 2020, Daegu, South Korea, November 24–26, 2020, Proceedings, Part I 12, pp. 274–286. Springer (2021)
16. Koelen, J., et al.: Web-based, human-guided, or computer-guided transdiagnostic cognitive behavioral therapy in university students with anxiety and depression: Randomized controlled trial. JMIR Mental Health **11**, e50503 (2024)

17. Kretzschmar, K., Tyroll, H., Pavarini, G., Manzini, A., Singh, I., Group, N.Y.P.A.: Can your phone be your therapist? young people's ethical perspectives on the use of fully automated conversational agents (chatbots) in mental health support. Biomed. Inform. Insights **11**, 1178222619829083 (2019)

18. Lagunes-Ramírez, D.A., González-Serna, G., Rivera-Rivera, L., González-Franco, N., Hernández-Pérez, M.Y., Reyes-Ortiz, J.A.: Through the youth eyes: training depression detection algorithms with eye tracking data. IEEE Lat. Am. Trans. **23**(1), 6–16 (2024)

19. Lan, K., et al.: Depression diagnosis dialogue simulation: self-improving psychiatrist with tertiary memory. arXiv preprint arXiv:2409.15084 (2024)

20. Li, Y.J., Luo, H.I.: Depression prevention by mutual empathy training: Using virtual reality as a tool. In: 2021 IEEE Conference on Virtual Reality and 3D User Interfaces Abstracts and Workshops (VRW), pp. 60–63. IEEE (2021)

21. Lindner, P., Hamilton, W., Miloff, A., Carlbring, P.: How to treat depression with low-intensity virtual reality interventions: perspectives on translating cognitive behavioral techniques into the virtual reality modality and how to make anti-depressive use of virtual reality-unique experiences. Front. Psych. **10**, 483123 (2019)

22. Liness, S., Lea, S., Nestler, S., Parker, H., Clark, D.M.: What IAPT CBT high-intensity trainees do after training. Behav. Cogn. Psychother. **45**(1), 16–30 (2017). https://doi.org/10.1017/S135246581600028X

23. Macaulay, M.: The speed of mouse-click as a measure of anxiety during human-computer interaction. Behav. Inform. Technol. **23**(6), 427–433 (2004). https://doi.org/10.1080/01449290412331294651

24. Naeem, F., et al.: Transcultural adaptation of cognitive behavioral therapy (CBT) in Asia. Asia Pac. Psych. **13**(1), e12442 (2021). https://doi.org/10.1111/appy.12442

25. Paton, C., Kushniruk, A.W., Borycki, E.M., English, M., Warren, J.: Improving the usability and safety of digital health systems: the role of predictive human-computer interaction modeling. J Med Internet Res **23**(5), e25281 (May 2021). https://doi.org/10.2196/25281, https://www.jmir.org/2021/5/e25281

26. Peace, D.M., Easterby, R.S.: The evaluation of user interaction with computer-based management information systems. Hum. Factors **15**(2), 163–177 (1973)

27. Praptomojati, A., Icanervilia, A.V., Nauta, M.H., Bouman, T.K.: A systematic review of culturally adapted cognitive behavioral therapy (CA-CBT) for anxiety disorders in southeast Asia. Asian J. Psychiatr. **92**, 103896 (2024)

28. Presley, V.L.: Addressing equality, diversity and inclusion as part of CBT training: a course evaluation study. Cogn. Behav. Therap. **16**, e30 (2023). https://doi.org/10.1017/S1754470X23000235

29. Roshanaei-Moghaddam, B., Pauly, M.C., Atkins, D.C., Baldwin, S.A., Stein, M.B., Roy-Byrne, P.: Relative effects of CBT and pharmacotherapy in depression versus anxiety: is medication somewhat better for depression, and cbt somewhat better for anxiety? Depress. Anxiety **28**(7), 560–567 (2011). https://doi.org/10.1002/da.20829

30. Sandak, B., Gilboa, A., Harel, D.: Computational elucidation of nonverbal behavior and body language in music therapy. PNAS nexus **3**(11), 475 (2024)

31. Sharma, A., Lin, I.W., Miner, A.S., Atkins, D.C., Althoff, T.: Human-ai collaboration enables more empathic conversations in text-based peer-to-peer mental health support. Nature Mach. Intell. **5**(1), 46–57 (2023)

32. Siddals, S., Torous, J., Coxon, A.: "it happened to be the perfect thing": experiences of generative ai chatbots for mental health. NPJ Mental Health Res. **3**(1), 48 (2024)
33. Stutvoet, M.D., et al.: Gamification in ehealth for chronic disease self-management in youth (2024)
34. Søgaard Neilsen, A., Wilson, R.L.: Combining e-mental health intervention development with human computer interaction (hci) design to enhance technology-facilitated recovery for people with depression and/or anxiety conditions: An integrative literature review. Int. J. Ment. Health Nurs. **28**(1), 22–39 (2019). https://doi.org/10.1111/inm.12527
35. Tong, F., Lederman, R., D'Alfonso, S., Berry, K., Bucci, S.: Digital therapeutic alliance with fully automated mental health smartphone apps: A narrative review. Front Psych. **13** (2022). https://doi.org/10.3389/fpsyt.2022.819623, https://www.frontiersin.org/journals/psychiatry/articles/10.3389/fpsyt.2022.819623
36. Van Eck, N., Waltman, L.: Software survey: vosviewer, a computer program for bibliometric mapping. Scientometrics **84**(2), 523–538 (2010)
37. Vitale, F., Carbonaro, B., Cordasco, G., Esposito, A., Marrone, S., Raimo, G., Verde, L.: A privacy-oriented approach for depression signs detection based on speech analysis. Electronics **10**(23), 2986 (2021)
38. Wang, A., Ye, J.: Human-computer natural interaction design practice based on unconscious design concept. In: Human-Computer Interaction. Theory, Methods and Tools: Thematic Area, HCI 2021, Held as Part of the 23rd HCI International Conference, HCII 2021, Virtual Event, July 24–29, 2021, Proceedings, Part I 23. pp. 3–15. Springer (2021)
39. Yoneyama, J., Fujimoto, Y., Okazaki, K., Sawabe, T., Kanbara, M., Kato, H.: Augmented conversations: AR face filters for facilitating comfortable in-person interactions. Journal on Multimodal User Interfaces, pp. 1–18 (2024)
40. Zaharuddin, F.A., Ibrahim, N., Mohd Yusof, A.: Enhancing user comfort in virtual environments for effective stress therapy: design considerations. Int. J. Adv. Comput. Sci. Appl. **15**(12) (2024)

Designing XR Training Simulator for Neonatal Echocardiography: Dynamic Ultrasound-Based Visualization

Deepthy Rose Jose[1]($\boxtimes$) (iD), Venkataseshan Sundaram[2] (iD), and M. Manivannan[1] (iD)

[1] Indian Institute of Technology Madras, Chennai, India
am20s052@smail.iitm.ac.in, mani@iitm.ac.in
[2] Post Graduate Institute of Medical Education and Research, Chandigarh, India
venkatpgi@gmail.com

Abstract. Neonatal echocardiography serves as a vital diagnostic tool for identifying structural and functional cardiac abnormalities in newborns. However, hands-on training remains severely limited due to the scarcity of accessible high-end ultrasound systems and the ethical constraints associated with practicing on vulnerable neonatal patients. These limitations underscore the need for scalable simulation-based training solutions. To address these challenges, this work presents a proof-of-concept simulator that incorporates a specialized visualization pipeline built on four-dimensional (4D) ultrasound data comprising of three-dimensional spatial information over time to simulate neonatal transthoracic echocardiography (TTE) procedures. The visualization pipeline enables efficient rendering and interaction with 4D data within the Unity game engine, thereby providing a scalable, cross-platform foundation for developing immersive Extended Reality (XR) ultrasound simulators suitable for low-end computing platforms.

Keywords: Medical Simulation · Extended Reality · Volumetric Visualization

1 Introduction

Neonatal echocardiography [1] is an essential diagnostic tool for assessing cardiac abnormalities in newborns [2,3], demanding precision in probe maneuvers and interpretation of complex echocardiographic data. While 4D echocardiography—combining 3D spatial data with time offers rich insights into cardiac dynamics, training opportunities remain scarce due to limited access to specialized equipment and the challenges of integrating 4D data (see Fig. 1) into interactive learning environments. Game engines, widely used for developing training simulators, often lack native support for 4D visualization, constraining the creation of immersive, interactive experiences necessary for mastering such skills.

We introduce a proof-of-concept simulator designed to address these limitations by leveraging 2D + time visualizations derived from 4D echocardiographic datasets. The simulator is implemented utilizing Unity game engine [4],

© The Author(s), under exclusive license to Springer Nature Switzerland AG 2026
V. G. Duffy (Ed.): HCII 2025, LNCS 16339, pp. 261–277, 2026.
https://doi.org/10.1007/978-3-032-13012-9_19

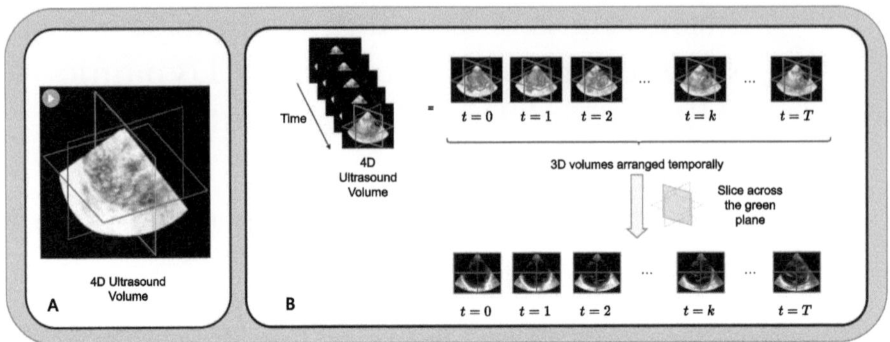

Fig. 1. a) 4D (*3D + time*) ultrasound volume obtained using Philips X7-2 Ultrasound probe. b) Slicing workflow for viewing the axes of interest in a 4D volume.

using a preloaded visualization technique, which is the highlight of this work. The preloaded technique (see Fig. 5, 6) precomputes and organizes 4D data into optimized 2D + time slices, enabling seamless transitions across anatomical views and reducing computational overhead within the game engine. Trainees engage with a sensor-equipped manikin and a custom 3D-printed probe, practicing essential maneuvers (Fig. 2) such as tilt and rotation while receiving dynamic feedback. A tiered gamification structure further enhances engagement and learning retention, bridging the gap between theoretical knowledge and hands-on application.

We present the implementation of the proposed visualization pipeline, the design of the simulator's hardware and software, and findings from a validation study with postgraduate medical students (0 to 4 years of neonatal echocardiography experience), demonstrating the simulator's potential to transform neonatal echocardiography training through scalable, immersive, and interactive experiences.

2   Background and Related Work

Training in neonatal echocardiography faces significant challenges, primarily due to limited access to live patient scenarios caused by the vulnerable condition of neonatal patients. Studies have consistently demonstrated that medical training simulators [5,12] provide a safer and more effective learning environment compared to live patient learning, as they allow trainees to gain expertise without risking patient safety. Several guidelines [8–10] advocate for integrating targeted echocardiography into neonatal intensive care units (NICUs) and implementing structured curricula supported by simulators to ensure the development of diagnostic and procedural expertise in this critical field.

Simulators like Echocom—Neo [16], VNETS [14], and HeartWorks [7] have emerged to bridge this gap, providing trainees with controlled environments to practice complex imaging modalities such as color flow Doppler, spectral Doppler, and M-mode echocardiograms. These systems leverage mannequin-based setups and 3D ultrasound datasets to replicate real-world scenarios and improve technical skills. However, they remain constrained by the lack of gamification elements that enhance user engagement and by the challenges of optimizing for low-end systems, which are critical for wider accessibility. Although studies [12,15] show that gamified approaches and advancements in visualization.

3   Case Study for Neonatal Echocardiography: Transthoracic Echocardiography (TTE)

3.1   Transthoracic Echocardiography (TTE)

We chose TTE [8,9] as a case study for a neonatal echocardiography simulator because it is the primary, non-invasive method used for cardiac assessment in newborns. Mastery in neonatal TTE requires proficiency in key views, including apical, parasternal long-axis (PLAX), parasternal short-axis (PSAX), subcostal and suprasternal views (See Table 1, Fig. 3, Appendix A). Proficient probe manipulation across anatomical planes and knowledge of the correct clock angles and tilt ranges are vital to obtaining diagnostically valuable images. Normal views are achieved by aligning the probe with standard anatomical positions, yielding essential cross-sectional images, while tilt views enhance visualization of structures less visible in normal views by adjusting the probe angle.

3.2   Learning Objectives for Training

Upon completing the training, users should be able to:

1. **Identify Target Chamber Locations**: Accurately locate standard TTE windows (Fig. 3) for neonatal echocardiography.
2. **Orient and Angle for Normal Views**: Correctly align the probe notch using the clock system and understand optimal angle ranges for views such as Apical (e.g., chest apex at 3 o'clock).
3. **Optimize Tilt Angles**: Adjust probe tilt to enhance visualization of specific anatomical structures (see Table 1), such as the aortic valve in the Apical view or ventricular outflow tracts in the PSAX view.

4   Design Process

4.1   Data Acquisition

Echocardiographic data were acquired using a Philips EPIQ 7 ultrasound system with a Philips X7-2 matrix transducer. The training data are captured as

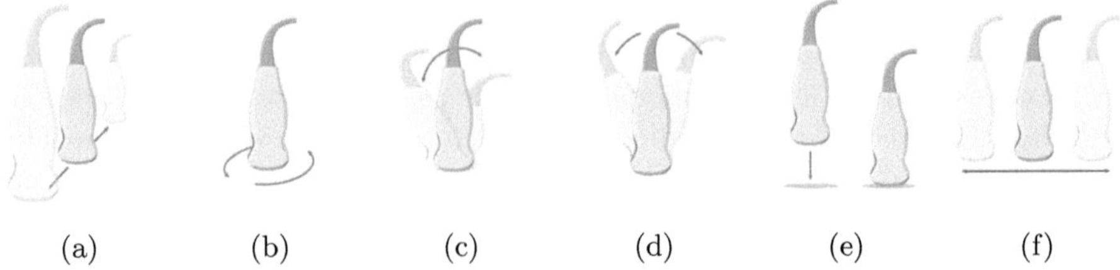

(a)   (b)   (c)   (d)   (e)   (f)

Fig. 2. Standard Probe Maneuvers: a) *Sliding,* b) *Rotating,* c) *Tilting,* d) *Rocking,* e) *Pressure,* and f) *Sweeping.*

Table 1. Standard Transthoracic Echocardiographic Views

View	Probe Notch Direction	Tilt Range (in degrees)
Apical	3 o'clock	5 to 10
PLAX	11 o'clock	5 to 10
PSAX	1 o'clock	5 to 10
Subcostal	3 o'clock	40 to 45
Suprasternal	1 o'clock	5 to 10

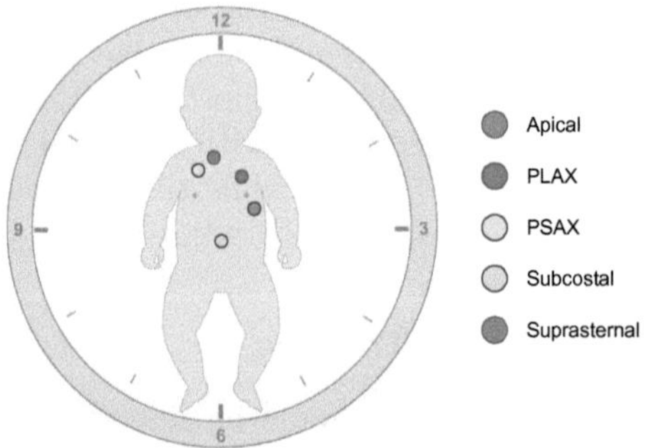

Fig. 3. A diagram showing a clock face used to indicate the direction of the ultrasound probe notch for different echocardiographic views.

4D volume recording of the transducer performing a continuous tilt maneuver over a neonate's chest. Up to ten 4D DICOM volumes (3D + time) per neonate were collected from five standard transthoracic echocardiographic views, including standard and tilt-angle perspectives (see Table 1, Fig. 3). All medical data, recorded in DICOM format, were de-identified and data collection complied with institutional ethical requirements while adhering to clinical standards and were acquired based on clinical indications assessed by neonatologists. The X7-2 transducer facilitated precise probe maneuvers for identifying TTE locations and capturing volumetric datasets that could reach gigabyte-scale storage requirements (Fig. 4a). To optimize datasets for Unity visualization, file size was reduced while preserving critical anatomical details. Key strategies included:

1. **Reduced Beat Count**: The "3D beats 4" protocol was adjusted to "3D beats 1", capturing a single cardiac cycle to significantly decrease data size while maintaining anatomical fidelity.
2. **Acquisition Time Considerations**: Reduction in acquisition time was inherently linked to beat count adjustments and not prioritized independently.
3. **Sector/Wedge Size**: Sector size or field of view (Fig. 4a) reduction was avoided to prevent loss of critical anatomical details necessary for training.

These optimizations reduced dataset sizes from gigabyte-scale to approximately 100 MB, ensuring feasibility for real-time Unity rendering. All datasets were reviewed by a domain expert to verify essential anatomical transitions prior to preprocessing for visualization.

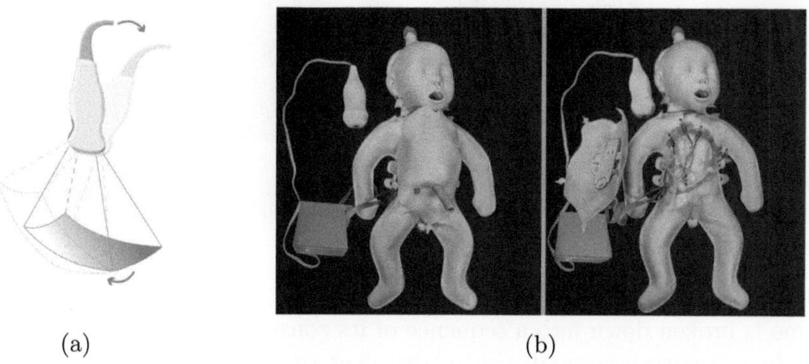

(a)   (b)

Fig. 4. a) 4D volume data acquisition with fan-shaped sector or field of view, b) Simulator Hardware

4.2   Data Preprocessing and Visualization

Data Preprocessing. The acquired ultrasound 4D DICOM (Digital Imaging and Communication in Medicine) data was transformed into 3D NRRD (Nearly Raw Raster Data) sequences using the data preprocessing pipeline (Fig. 5). Using Philips QLAB, encrypted 4D DICOM volumes are decrypted and exported into a standard Cartesian 4D DICOM format. Philips DICOM Patcher and Slicer 3D are then used to convert the 4D DICOM data into a 4D NRRD sequence. Finally, the teem unrrd library extracts 3D volume sequences from the 4D NRRD file 4D Slicing Visualization. Once the data are pre-processed, our proposed "preloaded visualization" technique is used.

Preloaded Visualization. (Fig. 6) To bypass the computational overhead and compatibility issues of real-time 4D rendering, we preprocess the volume into a series of lightweight GIFs. Our goal is to accurately map the frames from the 4D volume to the user's tilting of the probe transducer.

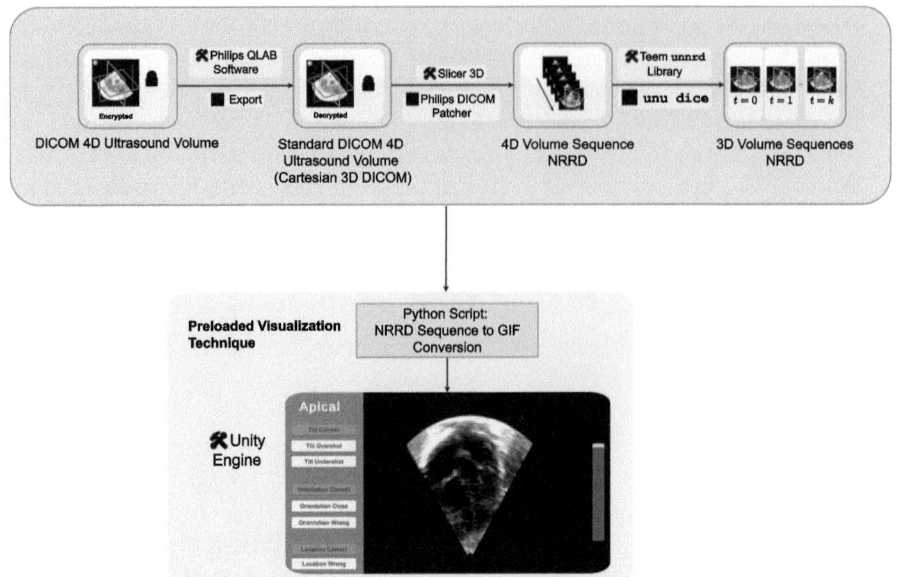

Fig. 5. Data Preprocessing Pipeline

Using standard Python libraries the source NRRD is pre-processed, the 4D volume is broken down into a sequence of its constituent middle 2D anatomical slices (e.g., sagittal, coronal, transverse) over time. These 2d + time slices are then grouped and converted into GIF98 format files which are preloaded in Unity to minimize latency, allowing smooth playback on lower-end systems. To map the probe's continuous tilt to a set of discrete animations, the total tilt range is divided into specific intervals, with each interval corresponding to a pre-rendered GIF. The number of these intervals is a critical heuristic parameter that balances simulation smoothness against haptic usability.

Let the total angular range of the tilt maneuver be T and the number of discrete GIFs be N. The angular size of each interval, $\Delta\theta$, is then:

$$\Delta\theta = \frac{T}{N} \tag{1}$$

The simulation's sensitivity to movement, S, is inversely proportional to the interval size, meaning it is directly proportional to the number of GIFs:

$$S \propto N \text{ or } S \propto \frac{1}{\Delta\theta} \tag{2}$$

While a large N increases smoothness, it can make the simulation overly sensitive. This choice is further constrained by the probe's hardware update rate, or **probe frequency** (f_p), which is the number of position updates sent per second. To ensure system stability, the number of GIFs cannot be so high that it requires the system to switch between them faster than new positional data is available. This establishes a clear upper bound for N. Assuming a maximum expected user tilt velocity (ω_{max}), the time to sweep across one interval ($\frac{\Delta\theta}{\omega_{max}}$) must not be less than the time between probe updates ($\frac{1}{f_p}$). This gives us the constraint:

$$N \leq \frac{T \cdot f_p}{\omega_{max}} \tag{3}$$

This relationship formally defines the balance: the number of GIFs (N) is upper-bounded by the total tilt range (T) and probe frequency (f_p), while being inversely related to the maximum speed of the maneuver.

While a large (N) creates a smoother visual transition between angles, it also makes the simulation highly sensitive. This can result in a poor haptic experience, where minuscule probe movements cause rapid, jarring changes in the visualization. The optimal value of N must be balanced to match the fidelity of the original recording and probe frequency, the value of N was chosen to the nearest integer constrained by the relationship in Equation (3).

To solve the problem of choppiness when switching between the discrete GIFs, we introduce a frame overlap. Consecutive GIFs are stitched together with a set number of overlapping frames at their beginning and end. If we define G_i as the sequence of frames for the i-th interval and O as the number of overlapping frames (highlighted in yellow in Fig. 6), the condition for the smooth transition is:

$$\text{last } O \text{ frames of } G_i = \text{first } O \text{ frames of } G_{i+1} \tag{4}$$

This method ensures that a user simulates tilting the probe, the switch between the GIFs is imperceptible, mimicking a continuous sweep through the anatomy. The ideal number of overlapping frames, O, was determined empirically through user consensus, balancing perceived smoothness without any potential delay. By synchronizing these smaller, high-refresh-rate GIFs with the probe's frequency and preloading them, this visualization strategy optimizes the data to allow for a fluid, high-fidelity simulation even on systems with limited computational resources.

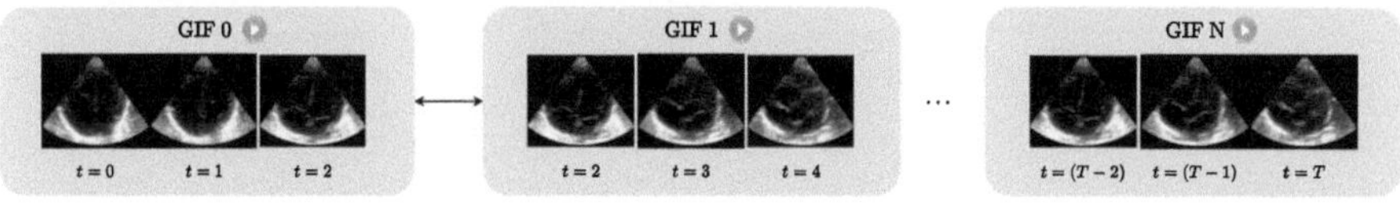

Fig. 6. Preloaded Visualization: Configuration for Extracting Multiple GIFs

4.3 System Architecture

Hardware. The physical setup featured an air-inflatable baby manikin replicating neonatal anatomy for echocardiographic training (Fig. 4b). Analog Hall effect sensors were placed at standard TTE anatomical locations to track probe movements. A custom 3D-printed transducer dummy, modeled after the Philips X7-2 probe, integrated an MPU6050 IMU with 6 DOF for precise measurement of roll, pitch, and yaw during maneuvers. A 5 mm radius magnet at the dummy's base enabled magnetic field variation detection via Hall effect sensors, capturing position and orientation nuances. Data acquisition and real-time feedback were managed by an Arduino Nano, chosen for its compactness and processing capability, housed in a durable 3D-printed enclosure.

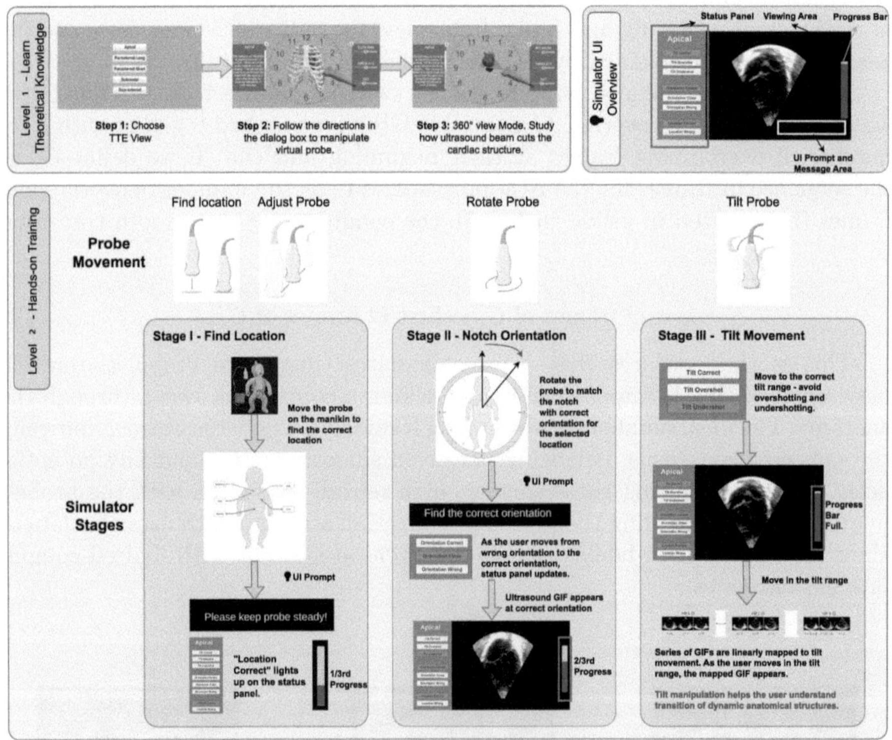

Fig. 7. Simulator Flow and Gamification

Software and Gamification. The Simulator (Fig. 7) employs real-time parsing of yaw, pitch, roll, and five analog sensor statuses via an Arduino Nano, enabling dynamic rendering within Unity for neonatal echocardiography training. The system is structured into two primary levels: **Level 1: Theoretical Knowledge**

introduces users to TTE views and probe manipulation fundamentals, laying the groundwork for practical skills, while **Level 2: Hands-on Training** builds on this foundation, guiding users through locating anatomical regions, aligning the probe notch, and adjusting tilt, with specific tasks for apical view acquisition. In Level 2, progression is gamified through a tiered approach using a status bar indicating: *1/3 Completion* for accurate location identification with sensor contact, *2/3 Completion* for correct notch alignment, and *3/3 Completion* for achieving the correct tilt angle. The simulator provides sequential feedback during task execution, allowing users to refine technique. Visualizations reflect anatomical transitions corresponding to tilt adjustments, facilitating understanding of angle impacts, such as undershot ($<$ minimum tilt range) and overshot ($>$ maximum tilt range) views.

5   Validation Study

A preliminary validation study was conducted to evaluate the efficacy and usability of the simulator, specifically with the preloaded visualization version, targeting postgraduate medical students with varying experience levels in neonatal echocardiography (0 to 4 years). The study included 10 participants specializing in pediatrics and neonatology, with qualifications ranging from M.D. to D.M. and post-D.M. levels. Under the guidance of a neonatology expert, participants engaged in training scenarios that simulated real-world conditions. M.D. students were classified as novices in neonatal echocardiography due to the limited focus on this technique in their curriculum, while D.M. and post-D.M. students were more familiar with the process. Informed consent was obtained from all participants, and data was encrypted to ensure privacy, in line with institutional ethical committee standards.

Participants completed level-based XR training scenarios (Levels 1 and 2) within the simulator, which emphasized aspects of user interaction and skill development. The study used a 44-item questionnaire (see Appendix B) to assess five core validity dimensions [6]: face, content, construct, ergonomic & physical, and psychological & affective validity. Alongside these general dimensions, specific attributes like visual fidelity, gamification, user interaction and feedback, cognitive load, and ergonomic usability (see Appendix C for more details) were also examined to provide a deeper understanding of the simulator's unique features. The responses were recorded on the Likert Scale where scores of 1 and 5 correspond to strongly disagree and strongly agree respectively.

Results and Observations. The evaluation of the simulator revealed significant strengths in its ability to replicate real-world neonatal echocardiography scenarios and facilitate effective training. Construct Validity achieved a mean score of 4.0 (Fig. 11), demonstrating the simulator's fidelity in capturing essential probe maneuvers and anatomical accuracy. Additionally, Training Effectiveness scored the highest among attributes, with a mean of 4.05 (Fig. 10), highlighting the simulator's ability to support skill acquisition through hands-on practice.

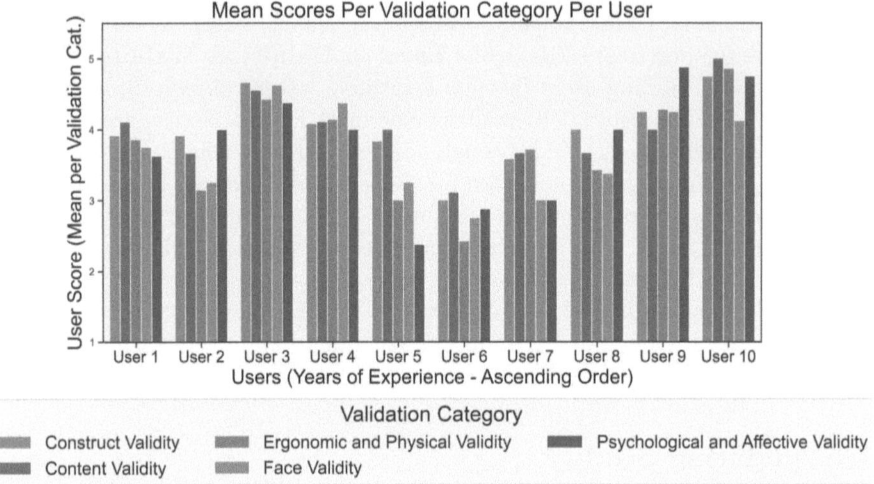

Fig. 8. Mean Score Per Validation Category Per User

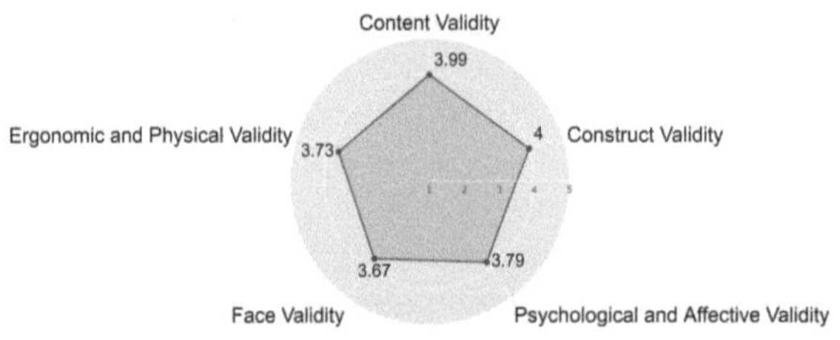

Fig. 9. Mean Score Per Attribute Per User

High Content Validity (mean: 3.99, Fig. 11) further underscored the comprehensiveness of the echocardiographic content presented to the users.

Despite these strengths, lower scores in Ergonomic and Physical Validity (mean: 3.73, Fig. 10) and User Interaction and Feedback (mean: 3.57, Fig. 10) revealed challenges in usability, particularly for novice users (Fig. 8). Novice participants reported a lower cognitive load (lower is worse, mean: 3.78, Fig. 11, Fig. 9) compared to more experienced users, suggesting a need to optimize the interface and reduce effort for less experienced trainees. These findings indicate opportunities to improve the simulator's ergonomic design and workflow efficiency to ensure a seamless user experience across all skill levels. Verbal feedback included comments such as, *"Hands-on learning like this is very useful for retention compared to simply watching YouTube videos,"* highlighting the simulator's practical value. Other participants suggested adding zoom functionality for better anatomical focus and reducing hardware calibration time to improve workflow efficiency. These findings highlight the simulator's role as a scalable training tool while identifying actionable areas for enhancing accessibility and usability.

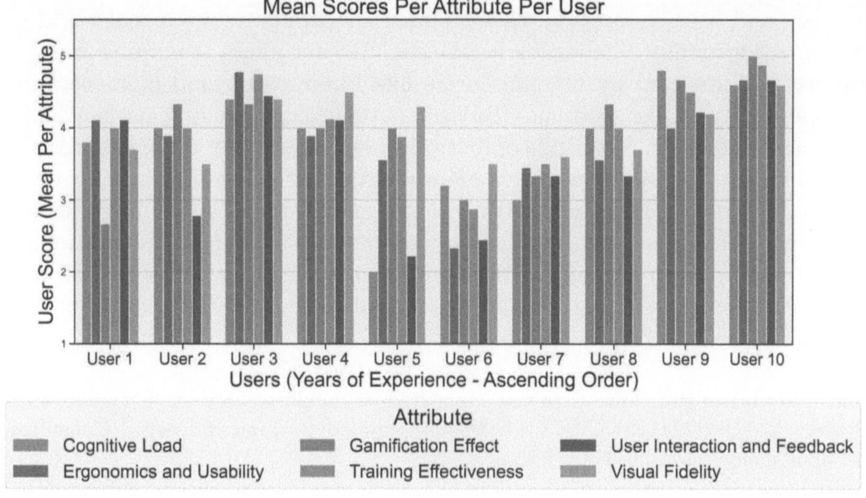

Fig. 10. Mean User Score Per Validation Category

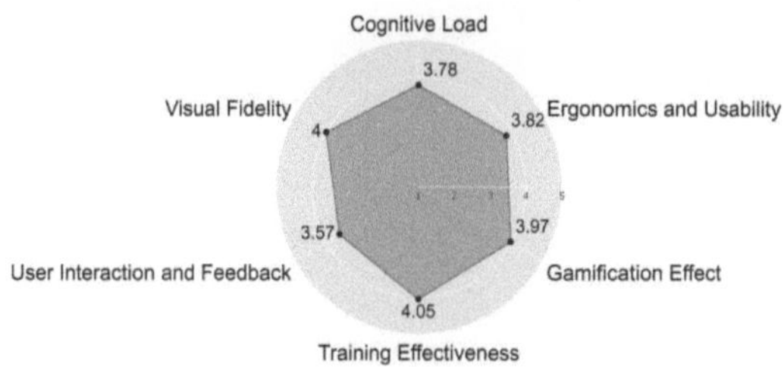

Fig. 11. Mean User Score Per Attribute

6   Discussion and Future Work

This study highlights the potential of gamification in neonatal echocardiography training through the simulator, an accessible platform developed in Unity using 4D slicing visualization techniques. By enabling trainees to practice probe maneuvers and interpret complex echocardiographic data interactively, the simulator bridges the gap between theoretical knowledge and hands-on application. A key contribution of the simulator is its optimization for low-end systems, achieved through efficient data slicing techniques, ensuring broad accessibility and usability. Validation conducted with postgraduate medical students demonstrates the simulator's educational efficacy, underscoring its value as a reliable and effective training tool in medical education.

Despite its strengths, limitations provide avenues for further refinement. Redesigning the manikin with stable sensor structures throughout the torso will enhance the ability to capture and stitch 2D+t data, improving the overall fidelity of clinical training. Ergonomic enhancements can address feedback accuracy and user comfort, further aligning the simulator with real-world conditions. Additionally, challenges in 4D DICOM encoding, stemming from proprietary formats used by manufacturers like Philips, GE, and Siemens, hinder interoperability across systems. Tailored visualization techniques can address these inconsistencies, fostering compatibility and expanding the simulator's versatility. Future advancements include integrating the simulator with XR devices like Meta Quest to offer immersive training experiences, broadening validation studies with domain experts, and extending its scope to encompass additional 4D ultrasound applications, such as interventional procedures. These developments aim to position the simulator as a scalable, realistic, and engaging solution for neonatal echocardiography training.

Acknowledgments. This work was supported by the project titled *"VR and Haptics"* (Project No. SB22231261AMETWO008206), funded through Industrial Consultancy and Sponsored Research, IIT Madras, India.

Disclosure of Interests. The authors have no competing interests to declare that are relevant to the content of this article.

A   Appendix 1

We describe the views of transthoracic echocardiography (TTE) used to simulate the neonatal cardiac evaluation:

1. **Apical Views (Normal and Tilt)**: Essential for evaluating ventricles, atria, and valves. The Tilt view provides enhanced visualization of the left ventricular outflow tract (LVOT), allowing detailed insights into ventricular dynamics.
2. **Parasternal Short-Axis (PSAX) Views (Normal and Tilt)**: These views offer a comprehensive look at left ventricular function, morphology, and septal motion. The Tilt view aids in diagnosing congenital heart defects by adding perspectives on LVOT and outflow tracts.
3. **Parasternal Long-Axis (PLAX) Views (Normal and Tilt)**: Foundational for visualizing the left atrium, left ventricle, mitral valve, aortic valve, and LVOT, these views are critical for assessing ventricular outflow.
4. **Subcostal Views (Normal and Tilt)**: Particularly valuable for neonates, allowing imaging through the liver to evaluate the atrial septum and vena cava. The Tilt view helps identify shunts and anomalies affecting the LVOT.
5. **Suprasternal Views (Normal and Tilt)**: Key for assessing the aortic arch and great vessels, with the Tilt view enhancing vascular visualization. These views are more focused on vascular structures than on ventricular or atrial visualization.

B   Appendix 2

Table 2. Evaluation Questionnaire

Q. No.	Question	Attribute	Validation Category
1	The ultrasound probe in the simulation looks like the actual probe you use regularly.	Visual Fidelity	Face Validity
2	The quality of the echo data which you saw is of high resolution and contrast and resembles the one you see in a real ultrasound machine.	Visual Fidelity	Face Validity
3	The contracting and relaxing motion of the beating heart in the simulated echocardiogram resembles the beating neonatal heart seen in a real ultrasound.	Visual Fidelity	Content Validity
4	The developed manikin-based echocardiographic simulator accurately simulates the full range of neonatal echocardiogram views.	Visual Fidelity	Construct Validity
5	The simulator effectively replicates different views of echocardiograms and their optimisations (Apical, Suprasternal, Subcostal, Parasternal Long Axis, Parasternal Short Axis, and various tilts and changes) observed in real neonate cases.	Visual Fidelity	Construct Validity
6	The cardiac structures (e.g., mitral valve leaflets and LVOT) seen in the simulated data are as clear and precise as you see in the real ultrasound machine.	Visual Fidelity	Content Validity
7	The cardiac structures (e.g., myocardium and pericardium) are as crisp and sharp as you see in a real neonatal echocardiography.	Visual Fidelity	Content Validity
8	The overall visual fidelity of the simulated echocardiogram perfectly matches that of an actual ultrasound image. Visual fidelity is how closely the visualised image matches the real image. A perfectly matching image is considered to have high visual fidelity.	Visual Fidelity	Content Validity
9	The ultrasound data displayed on the screen reflects the data corresponding to the given location and optimisation. For example, are you viewing the right video when you place the probe in the apical location with the head tilt of the probe head?	Visual Fidelity	Face Validity
10	The color scheme of the grayscale data in the simulated echocardiogram is accurate compared to the actual ultrasound images.	Visual Fidelity	Content Validity
11	The ultrasound images in the simulation are as real as you see in an ultrasound machine.	Visual Fidelity	Face Validity
12	The locations on the manikin for each echocardiography acoustic window was same or similar as you would usually observe in an ultrasound on a real neonate.	User Interaction & Feedback	Construct Validity
13	I am able to visualise an appropriate transition in the data on optimising the probe by tilting it (for example apical head tilt to get 5C from 4C). Answer this question without taking into account the extent to which you have tilted the probe.	User Interaction & Feedback	Content Validity

Table 2. continued

Q. No.	Question	Attribute	Validation Category
14	The physical manipulation of the ultrasound probe in the simulation is consistent with real-world handling.	User Interaction & Feedback	Ergonomic & Physical Validity
15	The simulated USG probe accurately located the correct location of a given view in the first attempt.	User Interaction & Feedback	Construct Validity
16	The ultrasound video change gradually and smoothly as the probe is tilted.	User Interaction & Feedback	Face Validity
17	The ultrasound probe in the simulation looks like the actual probe you use regularly.	User Interaction & Feedback	Face Validity
18	The physical design, including the weight of the probe, matches its real-life counterpart.	User Interaction & Feedback	Face Validity
19	The resistance and movement of the ultrasound probe in the simulation closely match the physical sensations of a real procedure.	User Interaction & Feedback	Ergonomic & Physical Validity
20	The weight and balance of the probe in the simulation closely resemble the actual physical attributes of the probe.	User Interaction & Feedback	Ergonomic & Physical Validity
21	User dexterity and probe manoeuvring improved as I kept on training on different echocardiogram views (Apical, PLAX, PSAX, Subcostal, Suprasternal).	Training Effectiveness	Construct Validity
22	The simulator effectively addresses the specific training needs of neonatologists, neonatal intensivists, and other healthcare professionals interested in neonatal echocardiography.	Training Effectiveness	Construct Validity
23	The simulator provides a realistic training alternative to live patient cases, given the limited opportunities for such training.	Training Effectiveness	Construct Validity
24	The simulator effectively bridges the gap between theoretical knowledge and practical skills in neonatal echocardiography.	Training Effectiveness	Construct Validity
25	The simulator prepares users effectively for real-world challenges and complexities encountered in neonatal echocardiography.	Training Effectiveness	Construct Validity
26	The simulator enhances users' understanding of the interpretation and analysis of echocardiographic findings in neonatal cases.	Training Effectiveness	Construct Validity
27	The simulator facilitates the development of critical thinking skills in interpreting neonatal echocardiograms.	Training Effectiveness	Construct Validity
28	Engaging with the simulator elicits a sense of confidence in my ability to perform echocardiography in a neonate.	Training Effectiveness	Psychological & Affective Validity

Table 2. continued

Q. No.	Question	Attribute	Validation Category
29	Converting the cardiac simulator training into a game with different levels will help to deconstruct the complex procedure and reduce the steepness of the learning curve.	Gamification Effect	Construct Validity
30	The simulation creates a sense of engagement and interest in learning about neonatal echocardiography.	Gamification Effect	Psychological & Affective Validity
31	The simulation fosters a sense of accomplishment and satisfaction upon successfully completing tasks.	Gamification Effect	Psychological & Affective Validity
32	The overall simulation accurately portrays the real-life ultrasound assessment process of a neonate.	Ergonomics & Usability	Face Validity
33	The device workspace, including the manikin, probe and data visualization, felt realistic and authentic.	Ergonomics & Usability	Content Validity
34	The scaling factor between the physical and simulation environments was realistic and comfortable. Example: the size of the neonatal manikin is similar to that of a real baby.	Ergonomics & Usability	Content Validity
35	I was able to complete the task without any assistance.	Ergonomics & Usability	Content Validity
36	The simulator's user interface and controls are intuitive and user-friendly.	Ergonomics & Usability	Ergonomic & Physical Validity
37	The interaction with the virtual environment and controls is comfortable and ergonomically designed.	Ergonomics & Usability	Ergonomic & Physical Validity
38	The simulator provides a comfortable and natural posture for using the ultrasound probe.	Ergonomics & Usability	Ergonomic & Physical Validity
39	The simulator's interface design enhances ease of use and contributes to a smooth user experience.	Ergonomics & Usability	Ergonomic & Physical Validity
40	The simulation effectively replicates the cognitive load (thinking required to perform an echocardiography) experienced during a real echocardiography in a neonate.	Cognitive Load	Psychological & Affective Validity
41	The simulator evokes a sense of immersion, making me feel like I'm performing a genuine echocardiography in a neonate.	Cognitive Load	Psychological & Affective Validity
42	The simulation accurately captures the mental focus and concentration required during a real procedure.	Cognitive Load	Psychological & Affective Validity
43	The virtual environment and interactions in the simulator feel psychologically authentic.	Cognitive Load	Psychological & Affective Validity
44	Using the simulator generates a positive emotional experience related to the learning process.	Cognitive Load	Psychological & Affective Validity

C   Appendix 3

Other than standard metrics to judge the efficacy of an XR system, we divide the 44 questions into the following attribute-based metrics—

1. **Visual Fidelity**: Evaluated the simulator's realism, particularly how accurately the ultrasound visualizations align with real-life systems to ensure a true-to-life depiction of cardiac structures.
2. **Gamification Effect**: Explored the influence of game-like elements, such as levels and tasks, on user engagement and simplifying complex echocardiography techniques.
3. **User Interaction & Feedback**: Measured the intuitiveness of physical interactions with the simulator, such as probe handling and feedback mechanisms, contributing to an immersive experience.
4. **Cognitive Load**: Quantified the mental effort required, reflecting the simulator's balance between complexity and user accessibility.
5. **Training Effectiveness**: Assessed the simulator's ability to bridge theoretical knowledge with practical echocardiography skills.
6. **Ergonomics & Usability**: Focus on designing systems and tools that enhance user comfort, efficiency, and satisfaction by aligning with human capabilities and minimizing physical strain.

References

1. Moss, S., Kitchiner, D., Yoxall, C.W., Subhedar, N.V.: Evaluation of echocardiography on the neonatal unit. Arch. Disease Childhood - Fetal Neonatal Edition **88**(4), 287F – 291 (2003). https://doi.org/10.1136/fn.88.4.f287
2. Aguilera, M., Dummer, K.: Concordance of fetal echocardiography in the diagnosis of congenital cardiac disease utilizing updated guidelines. J. Maternal-Fetal Amp; Neonatal Med. **31**(7), 940–945 (2017). https://doi.org/10.1080/14767058.2017.1297791
3. Liora, K., Santoso, T.A., Fahira, S.A., Yuliana, T.A., Damayant, O.M.: Foetal echocardiography vs. neonatal echocardiography for diagnosis of congenital heart diseases. Int. J. Public Health Excell. (IJPHE) **3**(1), 330–338 (2023). https://doi.org/10.55299/ijphe.v3i1.674
4. Lee, N.: Unity, A 2D and 3D Game Engine. Springer International Publishing, Cham **1–3**, (2020). https://doi.org/10.1007/978-3-319-08234-9_536-1
5. Allgaier, M., et al.: Gamification concepts for a VR-based visuospatial training for intraoperative liver ultrasound. In: Extended Abstracts of the CHI Conference on Human Factors in Computing Systems (Honolulu, HI, USA) (CHI EA '24). Association for Computing Machinery, New York, NY, USA, Article 175, 8 pages (2024). https://doi.org/10.1145/3613905.3650736
6. Harris, D., Bird, J.M., Smart, P., Wilson, M.R., Vine, S.J.: A framework for the testing and validation of simulated environments in experimentation and training. Front. Psychol. **11** (2020). https://doi.org/10.3389/fpsyg.2020.00605
7. Intelligent Ultrasound. 2024. Heartworks. https://www.intelligentultrasound.com/heartworks/
8. Saurers D. L. et al.: Guidelines for performing a comprehensive pediatric transthoracic echocardiogram: recommendations from the american society of echocardiography. J. Am. Society Echocardiograph. : Off. Pub. Am. Society Echocardiograph. **37**(2), 119–170 (2024). https://doi.org/10.1016/j.echo.2023.11.015

9. McNamara, P.J., et al.: Guidelines and recommendations for targeted neonatal echocardiography and cardiac point-of-care ultrasound in the neonatal intensive care unit: an update from the american society of echocardiography. J. Am. Society Echocardiograph. : Off. Pub. Am. Society Echocardiograph. **37**(2), 171–215 (2024). https://doi.org/10.1016/j.echo.2023.11.016

10. Mertens, L., et al.: Targeted neonatal echocardiography in the neonatal intensive care unit: practice guidelines and recommendations for training. J. Am. Soc. Echocardiogr. **24**(10), 1057–1078 (2011). https://doi.org/10.1016/j.echo.2011.07.014

11. Nguyen, T., Flores, M.: Accuracy of ultrasound measurements by novices: pixels or voxels. Donald School J. Ultrasound Obstet. Gynecol. **5**(3), 303–309 (2011). https://doi.org/10.5005/jp-journals-10009-1207

12. Onishi, Y., Onishi, E., Takashima, K., Kitamura, Y.: Anesth-on-the-go: designing portable game-based anesthetic simulator for education. In: Extended Abstracts of the CHI Conference on Human Factors in Computing Systems (Honolulu, HI, USA) (CHI EA '24). Association for Computing Machinery, New York, NY, USA, Article 45, 7 pages (2024). https://doi.org/10.1145/3613905.3650866

13. Schroeder, W., Martin, K., Lorensen, B.: The Visualization Toolkit, 4th edn. Kitware (2006)

14. Siassi, B., Ebrahimi, M., Noori, S., Sheng, S., Ghosh, D., Seri, I.: Virtual neonatal echocardiographic training system (vnets): an echocardiographic simulator for training basic transthoracic echocardiography skills in neonates and infants. IEEE J. Transl. Eng. Health Med. **6**, 1–7 (2018). https://doi.org/10.1109/jtehm.2018.2878724

15. Staziaki, P.V., Santinha, J., Coelho, M.O., Angulo, D., Hussain, M., Folio, L.: Gamification in radiology training module developed during the society for imaging informatics in medicine annual meeting hackathon. J. Digit. Imaging **35**(3), 714–722 (2022). https://doi.org/10.1007/s10278-022-00603-0

16. Weidenbach, M., Paech, C.: Simulation in neonatal echocardiography. Clin. Perinatol. **47**(3), 487–498 (2020). https://doi.org/10.1016/j.clp.2020.05.009

Addressing Bed Waiting Times in Intensive Care Units During Respiratory Demand Peaks: A Digital Twin Application

Alexandros Konios[1] , Miguel Ortíz-Barrios[2(✉)] ,
and Zaury-Estela Fernández-Mendoza[3]

[1] Department of Computer Science, Nottingham Trent University, Nottingham 4081112, UK
`alexandros.konios@ntu.ac.uk`
[2] Department of Productivity and Innovation, Universidad de la Costa CUC, 080002
Barranquilla, Colombia
`mortiz1@cuc.edu.co`
[3] Department of Engineering, Institución Universitaria ITSA, Barranquilla, Colombia
`zefernandez@unibarranquilla.edu.co`

Abstract. During respiratory demand peaks, such as seasonal influenza outbreaks or COVID-19 surges, healthcare systems often face significant strain, especially in Intensive Care Units (ICUs). Bed shortages and long waiting times can lead to delayed care and worsened patient outcomes. To address this, healthcare systems increasingly turn to digital technologies, such as digital twins, to optimise patient flow and resource allocation. This paper illustrates the implementation of digital twins for managing bed waiting times in intensive care units during respiratory demand peaks. First, we described the patient's journey from the ED to the ICU using Supplier-Input-Process-Output-Customer (SIPOC) diagrams. After this, we analyzed input data analysis, verifying the process variable data's randomness, heterogeneity, and goodness-of-fit. We then modelled the ED through a digital twin designed in ARENA® software. Following this, we validated the model by applying a Kruskal Wallis test on the waiting time for ICU beds. Lastly, we pretested two improvement scenarios: increasing the number of ICU beds by i) 3 and ii) 5. The suggested method was applied in a European hospital group during one of the first COVID-19 waves. The outcomes revealed that the waiting time for ICU beds (1.88 h) can be meaningfully reduced if strategy ii) is applied.

Keywords: Digital Twin (DT) · Intensive Care Units (ICUs) · Healthcare · Respiratory Syncytial Virus (RSV) · Influenza · COVID-19

1 Introduction

Intensive care units (ICUs) often face surge periods of respiratory illness, such as the COVID-19 pandemic and seasonal influenza waves, which lead to demand spikes for critical care beds. During the COVID-19 crisis, many hospitals experienced unprecedented ICU demand, requiring the conversion of non-ICU spaces into critical care beds

© The Author(s), under exclusive license to Springer Nature Switzerland AG 2026
V. G. Duffy (Ed.): HCII 2025, LNCS 16339, pp. 278–292, 2026.
https://doi.org/10.1007/978-3-032-13012-9_20

[1]. Similarly, peak influenza seasons have strained ICU capacity; one U.S. study found that 41% of ICUs had to alter staffing or refuse transfers at the height of a severe flu season [2]. These scenarios underscore a pressing problem that has to do with ICU bed waiting times increasing when demand exceeds supply, forcing critically ill patients to board in emergency departments or other wards while awaiting ICU admission.

Delayed admission to ICU is not just a trivial inconvenience, as it significantly affects patient outcomes and hospital operations. Research has consistently shown that delays in ICU transfer correlate with higher mortality and morbidity. A meta-analysis in [1] reported approximately a 60% increase in odds of death for patients with delayed ICU admission compared to timely admission. It also showed that each hour of ICU admission delay was associated with an approximately 1.5% increase in ICU mortality risk. These delays also prolong ventilation times and ICU length of stay, compounding resource strain [3, 4]. In short, when critically ill patients cannot access ICU care promptly, their condition may deteriorate, leading to worse outcomes [1]. Operationally, backlogs of patients waiting for ICU beds create bottlenecks, occupying emergency department bays or general ward resources and hampering the flow of new patients. ICU bed shortages have even been identified as forcing elective surgery cancellation and refusal of inter-hospital transfers during surges [2]. The problem is worsened in health systems with limited baseline critical care capacity (e.g., the UK's average of 6.2 ICU beds per 100,000 people, one of the lowest in Europe [5]). Thus, reducing ICU waiting times during demand peaks is crucial to improve patient survival and maintain hospital throughput.

Approaches to address ICU bed crises range from expanding physical capacity to improving the existing resource management. During COVID-19, hospitals worldwide rapidly added surge ICU beds and redistributed resources to meet explosive demand [6]. However, simply adding beds has limits, as the study presented in [5] found that increasing ICU capacity did not fully avert high occupancy if discharge delays persisted. Effective solutions must also optimise how patients flow through the system. For example, reducing downstream delays (expediting transfers out of ICU when ready) cut ICU crowding by a more than a 20% bed increase [5]. This suggests that smarter utilisation of ICU resources can significantly alleviate waiting times. In this context, advanced decision-support technologies have become attractive. Digital twin technology, in particular, has emerged as a promising tool to model and manage complex healthcare operations in real-time. A digital twin is essentially a virtual replica of a physical system, continuously fed with data, enabling simulation of scenarios and forecasting system behaviour [7]. In healthcare, digital twins are increasingly seen as a way to optimise patient flow and resource allocation [7, 8]. By linking real hospital data to a live simulation model, a hospital or ICU twin can test what-if interventions (like opening surge beds, adjusting staffing, or rerouting patients) without risk to patients and provide clinicians and managers with decision support for reducing bottlenecks.

Delayed ICU admissions during respiratory demand peaks represent a critical challenge with both clinical and operational implications. Traditional capacity planning methods often lack the agility and predictive power to handle sudden surges. Digital twin technology offers a novel, data-driven approach to anticipate and mitigate ICU bottlenecks. For instance, a hospital ICU digital twin could forecast incoming critical cases, highlight impending bed shortages, and evaluate interventions (e.g., diverting admissions or expediting discharges) in silico to minimise wait times. A digital twin can support timely decisions that ensure critically ill patients receive care without dangerous delays by providing a real-time, system-wide view of ICU operations and running scenarios. In this paper, we address the problem of ICU bed waiting times during respiratory surges through a digital twin application. The following sections define the state of the art and methodologies that inform our approach.

2 Literature Review

2.1 Digital Twins in Healthcare and ICU Operations

Digital twin (DT) technology, i.e., maintaining a digital, dynamically updated model of a physical system, has gained growing interest in healthcare. Originally established in engineering, DTs integrate real-time data with simulation models to mirror system states and predict future behaviour [7]. Researchers and practitioners in healthcare are exploring DTs to improve patient-specific care and operational management. The review in [8] notes that although most early healthcare DT applications focused on precision medicine and personal health, an emerging class of DTs targets healthcare systems and processes. These system-level DTs are designed to optimise patient flows, resource utilisation, and care delivery with minimal risk, essentially creating "living" simulations of hospital operations. For example, Elkefi and Asan [8] found that digital twin studies for health system management, though limited in number (17 studies by 2022), demonstrated functions like safety monitoring, operational control, and performance optimisation in hospitals. This signals a promising but significant trend toward using DTs to support decision-making in complex care environments.

In the ICU context, digital twins promise to transform critical care delivery. Halpern et al. [7] describe the ICU as a prime opportunity for cyber-physical-human systems driven by DT technology, where real-time data from patients and units feed into virtual models to inform care and logistics. A DT can simulate scenarios at multiple scales, from an individual patient or organ to an entire ICU or hospital. This enables stake-holders to experiment with interventions in silico before applying them in practice [7]. Early applications in critical care include virtual patient models for medical education and decision support. For instance, [7] also describes that a patient digital twin for ICU training was developed to let trainees practice managing virtual critical illness cases safely. Augmented with AI algorithms, Intelligent digital twins are also being explored for real-time clinical decision support such as early warning of deterioration and person-alised treatment predictions [9]. In cardiovascular care, prototypes of DTs can predict how a patient will respond to therapies (e.g., simulating cardiac resynchronisation out-comes) by continuously updating the model with patient data [10]. These examples illustrate the broad potential of DTs in improving ICU patient outcomes.

Several studies have proposed or implemented DTs replicating the hospital or ICU environment to assist with resource management. Karakra et al. built an early hospital digital twin prototype by integrating pervasive IoT data with a discrete-event simulation of patient pathways [11]. Their approach, termed "HospiT'Win", created a near-real-time model of hospital units, demonstrating how a DT could continuously monitor patient flow and test improvements in bed allocation or scheduling [12]. In the critical care domain,

Zhong et al. developed a multidisciplinary framework for a digital twin of ICU care processes [13]. This work outlined how to combine clinical data, simulation modelling, and clinician input to mirror ICU delivery and evaluate interventions (e.g., admission triage rules or staffing changes). Another work by Trevena et al. [14], modelled critically ill patient pathways using a digital twin approach to support ICU service planning. Their model, validated on intensive care workflows, allowed the exploration of how patients move through critical care, from emergency presentation to ICU admission, transfers, and discharge, under different policies. Such applications indicate that digital twins can be used to optimise ICU operations by providing a testbed for strategies to reduce waiting times, balance occupancy, and improve overall throughput.

Despite these advances, the literature reveals that digital twin adoption for ICU logistics is still in the early stages. Many reported "ICU digital twins" remain conceptual or in pilot phases [7, 15]. For instance, several prototypes focus on ventilator management or sepsis treatment within a virtual patient model [16, 17] rather than system-wide flow. There is a clear opportunity to extend digital twin methods to hospital-wide surge management. Khan et al. conducted a scoping review of digital twins during the COVID-19 pandemic and highlighted the technology's potential in pandemic response, but also noted the lack of fully implemented ICU-wide twins for managing resource spikes [18]. In summary, digital twin research in healthcare shows promises (with early successes in personalised care and operational modelling), yet applications that specifically tackle ICU bed capacity and patient flow during demand peaks are only beginning to emerge. Our work aims to contribute to this area by developing a digital twin focused on ICU bed waiting times in surge conditions.

2.2   Simulation and AI Approaches for ICU Capacity Management

To ground our digital twin approach, we review related methodological strategies used to study and mitigate ICU bottlenecks. Discrete-event simulation (DES) has long been employed in health operations research to model patient flow and resource utilisation. A recent systematic review by Vecillas-Martin et al. analysed 616 healthcare DES studies and confirmed its growing diffusion, especially following the COVID-19 pandemic [19]. DES models represent healthcare processes (admissions, transfers, discharges, etc.) as sequences of events, enabling analysts to run virtual scenarios without risking patient care. In hospitals, DES is commonly used to identify process improvements that reduce wait times and optimise capacity. For instance, simulation has been applied to emergency departments and surgical units to test interventions and has shown significant benefits like throughput increases and wait time reductions. Notably, many DES case studies report reductions in patient waiting times, the review in [19] found about 32% of published healthcare DES projects achieved waiting time improvements as an outcome. This underscores the simulation's value in determining and relieving bottlenecks.

In the ICU context, DES has demonstrated particular utility in capacity planning. Griffiths et al. used discrete-event simulation to determine optimal ICU bed numbers and nurse staffing, showing that better capacity planning could reduce ICU admission delays by approximately 28% [20]. Their study modelled ICU patient arrivals and lengths of stay to evaluate how often patients would be deferred if only a given number of beds were available. More recently, Williams et al. built a comprehensive ICU flow simulation to support a UK health board's decision-making for a merged ICU unit [5]. Using 2 years of patient data, their DES model was validated against real admission and occupancy patterns. The simulation explored what-if scenarios such as increasing bed count, altering admission rates, and reducing discharge delays. A key finding was that reducing the proportion of patients experiencing transfer delays out of the ICU yielded a greater drop in ICU occupancy and full capacity time than adding extra beds. This result highlights that operational improvements (e.g., speeding up step-down transfers or improving ward availability) can markedly relieve ICU congestion [5]. Overall, the literature supports DES as a powerful tool to test interventions for ICU capacity management, from adjusting staffing levels to dividing patients into groups and to quantify their impact on wait times and outcomes. It is, therefore, natural that DES often forms the backbone of healthcare digital twins, providing the simulation engine that runs the virtual ICU.

While DES models the system at a macroscopic process level, agent-based modelling (ABM) offers a complementary approach by simulating agents' individual behaviours and interactions (e.g., patients, staff, or even microscopic entities). In an ABM, each agent follows simple rules and complex system dynamics emerge from their collective behaviour. In [21], ABM has been used to capture phenomena like hospital infection transmission or the cascading effects of individual patient decisions on system load. For ICU operations, ABM can incorporate heterogeneous patient characteristics and stochastic events such as sudden clinical deterioration. For example, an agent-based model could simulate each patient's trajectory (with varying acuity, length of stay, etc.) and how they compete for limited ICU beds. Though ABM is less prevalent than DES in this domain, it has been applied to problems like patient-to-patient interactions and staff scheduling. It also provides flexibility in modelling adaptive behaviours (such as dynamic triage decisions). Some researchers have combined ABM with DES to leverage both strengths: a hybrid model might use DES for high-level patient flow and ABM for detailed interactions. During the COVID-19 pandemic, hybrid simulation proved useful. For instance, Adamczyk et al. integrated ABM and DES in a regional COVID-19 management model to simulate hospital responses across multiple ICUs [22]. Such hybrid approaches allowed representation of individual hospitals (with agents for each ICU or patient) within a DES of the broader network, helping policymakers evaluate strategies like patient transfers between ICUs. This indicates the value of multi-method simulations for complex, multi-scale challenges like pandemic surges.

Another crucial methodological thread is incorporating artificial intelligence (AI) and real-time analytics into ICU capacity management. AI techniques can enhance simulation models by providing data-driven predictions (for example, forecasting how many ICU admissions are likely in the next 24 h) and adaptive decision rules. A study by Ortiz-Barrios et al. combined machine learning with DES to support ICU bed management during COVID-19. They first trained a Random Forest classifier to predict ICU admission probability for incoming emergency patients based on clinical features [23]. The output of this AI model (a prognosis of how many patients would need ICU care) was then fed into a DES model of the hospital's ICU to evaluate different capacity expansion plans. The hospital could use this AI-informed simulation to test interventions like adding surge beds or adjusting admission thresholds. The results were significant by proactively reallocating resources based on the model, the median ICU bed waiting time dropped by 32–48 min in their case study. This demonstrates how AI integration can make simulations prescriptive in real time, essentially forming a digital twin that not only mirrors the current state but also recommends actions.

Real-time data feeds (e.g., from electronic health records, monitoring systems, or IoT devices) are a pillar of digital twin systems. Traditional simulations are often run offline with static datasets, but a digital twin for ICU operations should update continuously with live data like admissions, discharges, vital signs, etc. Karakra et al. demonstrated this concept by linking IoT sensors tracking hospital patients to a DES model, creating a continuously updating "living simulation" of hospital workflow [11]. This approach enabled near real-time bed occupancy and patient locations monitoring and could alert managers to developing bottlenecks. The literature indicates that such real-time or streaming data integration is still challenging (due to interoperability and data quality issues), but it is being actively explored. Chase et al. (2023) discuss ICU digital twins with closed-loop control, where the twin can autonomously suggest or trigger actions like calling in reserve staff or triaging patients to intermediate units [24]. While fully autonomous control is futuristic, even current studies show that timely analytics and simulation can help ICU teams optimise resource use under pressure. During pandemic peaks, for instance, some hospitals developed dashboard systems (akin to simplified twins) to track capacity and trigger load-balancing between ICUs [25]. These efforts align with the vision of a digital twin that not only forecasts problems but also aids in coordinating response across the hospital or region.

2.3 Resource Optimisation During Demand Peaks

The COVID-19 pandemic prompted several studies on crisis capacity management. Beyond the aforementioned Ortiz-Barrios study [23], other researchers used simulations to evaluate emergency policies like cancelling elective surgeries, inter-hospital transfers, or temporary ICU expansions. One study at Addenbrooke's Hospital in the UK found that proactive cancellation and temporary ICU expansion significantly reduced ICU occupancy and staff workload compared to doing nothing [26]. Another study by Alban et al. reported using a process simulation to manage ICU surge capacity in Amsterdam, helping to anticipate when COVID admissions would overwhelm ICU beds and guiding the activation of additional beds and staff [27]. Their approach illustrated how modelling could support adaptive responses in real-time. Likewise, scenario analyses were conducted in various countries to project ICU bed demand under different outbreak trajectories, often influencing policy decisions on lockdowns or patient transfers. These studies underscore that data-driven planning was vital to mitigating ICU overload in COVID-19's peak phases.

Seasonal influenza surges, while smaller in scale, have also been examined. Lane et al. (2022) performed a multicentre prospective study on ICU operational stress during a severe flu season [2]. They found that nearly half of participating ICUs had to implement extraordinary measures (like stretching staffing ratios or declining external admissions) during peak influenza activity. Notably, 17% of sites reported potential avoidable patient harm due to resource shortfalls. This evidence highlights why proactive strategies are needed by the time an ICU is scrambling during a surge; patient care may already suffer.

It also stresses the multi-faceted nature of resource optimisation as it's not just about beds but also about staffing, triage protocols, and inter-departmental coordination.

The literature suggests several key tactics to improve ICU capacity management during peaks: (1) dynamic staffing and flexible care models (e.g., "critical care without walls" where ICU expertise is deployed to monitor patients in step-down units when ICU beds are full [1]), (2) streamlined admissions and discharges (for instance, using rapid response teams to identify patients who can be transferred out sooner); (3) cross-training and repurposing of staff/rooms (as was done in COVID-19 by turning recovery rooms into ICU pods [1]), and (4) load-balancing across networks (transferring patients between hospitals to avoid any single ICU exceeding capacity). Simulation and digital twin studies have begun to evaluate such interventions. For example, Harper, in [28], showed that modelling multiple hospital departments together (rather than an ICU in isolation) improved overall efficiency by 15%, as it captured how relieving one bottleneck (like step-down bed availability) affects the whole system.

Researchers have applied simulation, modelling, and AI to understand and improve ICU patient flow, demonstrating that delayed ICU admissions significantly harm patients and that proactive management can reduce these delays. Discrete-event simulations have quantified how changes in capacity or process might alleviate waiting times, while newer digital twin frameworks aim to make these simulations continuously responsive to real-world data. However, a gap remains in fully realising digital twin solutions for surge scenarios. To the best of our knowledge, the literature lacks documented cases of a true real-time ICU digital twin deployed during events like a flu pandemic or COVID wave. Most studies either retrospectively simulate scenarios or run prospective models offline. Thus, there is a compelling need for research that implements and evaluates a digital twin in practice for ICU capacity optimisation. This work addresses that need by proposing a digital twin application tailored to ICU bed waiting times during respiratory demand peaks. Building on the methods and findings reviewed above, our approach integrates discrete-event simulation, real-time data feeds, and AI-based predictive components to create a dynamic model of ICU operations. In the next sections, we detail the design of this digital twin and assess its potential to support ICU decision-makers in ensuring timely critical care access when it is most challenged.

3   Proposed Methodology

Digital twins must be reliable and representative of the real healthcare system to provide appropriate support for decision-makers. In this regard, it is necessary to follow a step-by-step procedure described below (Fig. 1) [29]:

Phase 1 – Description of ED-ICU Pathway. The pathway to upstream healthcare services includes several stations that depend on the patient's health evolution and multiple treatment options. This must be clearly portrayed through Supplier-Input-Process-Output-Customer (SIPOC) maps complemented by Gemba walks. Thereby, it is possible to pinpoint the main process variables/parameters, principal stations, and potential inefficiencies during Respiratory Disease Seasons (RDSs).

Phase 2 - Input Variable Analysis. In addition to verifying the data quality, it is essential to derive the stochastic expressions denoting the behaviour of each process variable in the system. Three statistical tests are required to achieve this aim: interdependence, homogeneity, and goodness-of-fit. The run test ($\alpha = 0.01$) evaluates whether the variable is random. Afterwards, the Analysis of Variance (ANOVA) ($\alpha = 0.01$) is utilized to verify if the variable can be decomposed into several layers. A stochastic expression must be defined per layer if heterogeneity is detected. Otherwise, only one probability distribution is enough to represent the variable's behaviour. Kolmogorov-Smirnov (KS) tests ($\alpha = 0.01$) are recommended to reach these distributions.

Phase 3 - Digital Twin Creation and Validation. The stochastic distributions are later inserted into the digital twin designed in the Arena ® software. As recommended, a pre-sample of 10 runs is deployed to assess the variance of the bed waiting times. The required number of iterations is finally computed considering this variance. The validation process evaluates whether the DT produces a similar waiting time for ICU beds compared to the one derived from the real system. A Mann-Whitney test ($\alpha = 0.01$) supports this process. If the DT is statistically equivalent to the real-world ICU in terms of this key indicator, decision-makers and ICU managers can proceed with the response diagnosis; otherwise, the model must be refined until its reliability can be certified.

Phase 4 – Operability Analysis. The ICU bed waiting time derived from the DT is now analyzed against the standard required in this service. In case of inefficiency, DT can provide helpful information for studying ICU interactions with other services while identifying stations that are wasting time. Besides, it will be necessary to formulate some improvement scenarios with the hospital administrators and clinical staff. Such remedies can be pretested in the DT to determine if they will be effective in case of implementation. Comparative statistical tests ($\alpha = 0.01$) will be employed to reach this conclusion.

4   Results

SRDs provoke a huge burden on ICUs, which, in some cases, do not respond timely in bed provision. The problem is even more sharpened considering the convergence of several respiratory pathogens whose spread rates tend to peak every season. This is the context of an extensive European medical group during the initial COVID-19 surges.

The General Management Office of the hospital group collected relevant process data to underpin the deployment of a digital twin. The primary aim was to evaluate its current performance during the pandemic and devise feasible remedies if necessary. The project received informed approval from the ethical body (Consent number: 14-12-2021-004; Access request ID:39) to use and analyze the gathered data for improvement purposes. The decision-makers also considered employing the model to define how to increase its readiness when addressing future respiratory-related outbreaks. Likewise, the intervention was directed towards the ICU bed waiting time as it had been identified as highly correlated with elevated cost overruns and greater patient mortality probability.

The next subsections will illustrate how the proposed methodology was deployed in this case study and what outputs were derived from each phase.

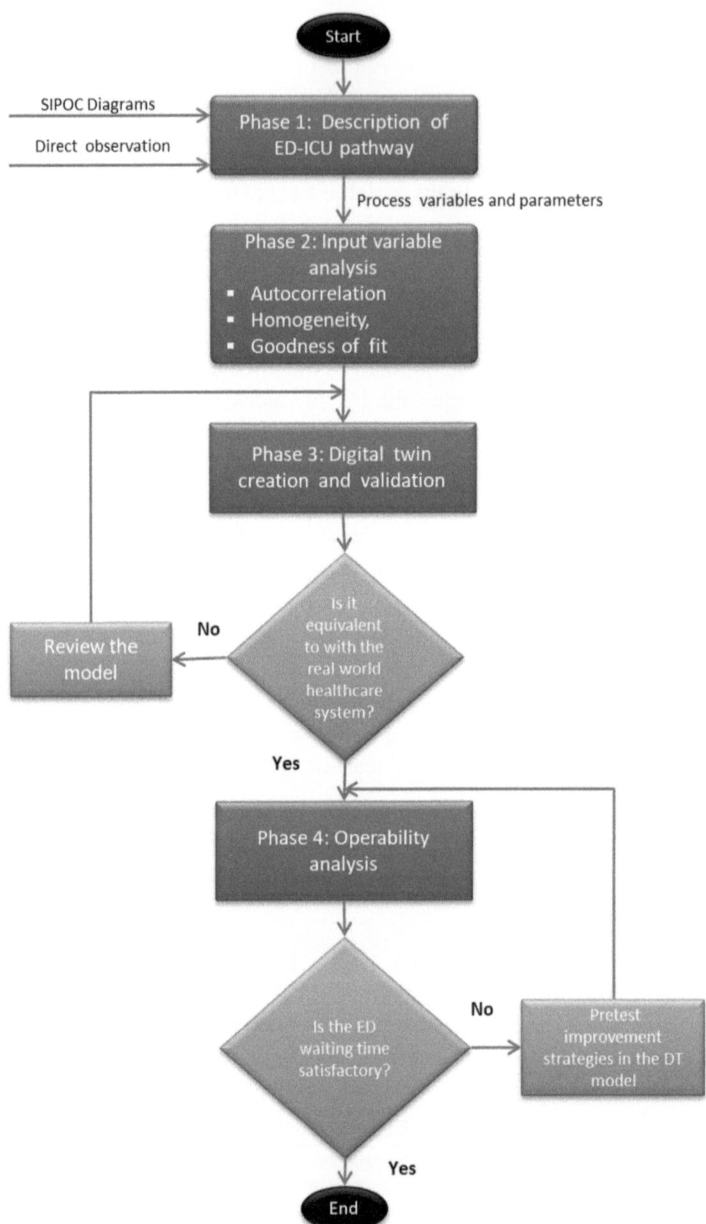

Fig. 1. The methodological framework for addressing bed waiting times in ICUs based on digital twins.

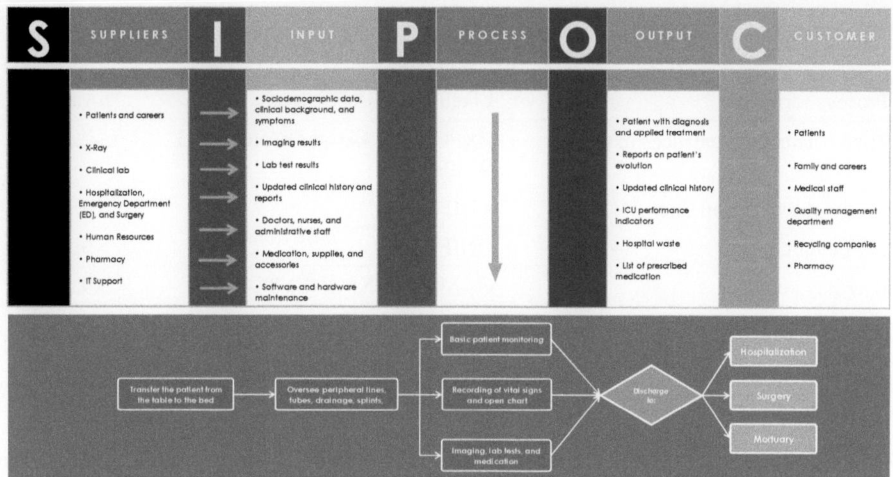

Fig. 2. SIPOC diagram for characterizing the patient journey from ED to ICU.

4.1 Description of ED-ICU Pathway

Gemba walks, and a SIPOC diagram (Fig. 2) were used to discriminate the suppliers, inputs, process steps, outputs, and clients. It is good to note that patients act as both providers and customers, highlighting these actors' critical role. Also, it is evident how clinical history travels along the healthcare system while recording the patient's evolution. This means that this document is a key source of information from which the digital twin can be fed and updated. No less important is the role of pharmacy in the correct and timely provision of medication, which is highly associated with prolonged length of stay and elevated bed waiting times. Likewise, the SIPOC map reflects how interactive the ICU is with other healthcare stations, demonstrating the need to effectively administer the interdependences beyond an individual view over the ICU.

4.2 Input Variable Analysis

After characterizing the healthcare system, four process variables were pinpointed to be analyzed: Time between attendances in the ED, Triage classification time, ED Length of Stay, and ICU stay period. First, we confirmed the interdependence assumption of the variables through run tests ($\alpha = 0.01$; p-value > 0.15). Then, we performed an Analysis of Variance (ANOVA) to validate the presence of subsets within each variable. The results evidenced that all the variables ($\alpha = 0.01$; p-value > 0.073), except the Triage classification time, are heterogeneous, and a probability expression must be defined for each data stratum (Table 1). The likelihood distributions were determined through χ^2 tests ($\alpha = 0.01$).

Table 1. Likelihood distributions of process variables inserted in the digital twin.

Process variable	Likelihood distributions	p-value
Time between attendances in the ED	EXPONENTIAL, LOGNORMAL, WEIBULL	>0.06
Triage classification time	UNIFORM	>0.15
ED Length of Stay	UNIFORM	>0.15
ICU stay period	GAMMA, EXPONENTIAL	>0.092

4.3 Digital Twin Creation and Validation

The input data analysis and process characterization results were employed to design a digital twin imitating the real functioning of the ICU. The Arena® 16.10.00 software was utilized for this aim, given its advantage of modeling by blocks, its user-friendly interface, and its versatility to represent the inefficiencies of operational workflows. The replication length defined for the digital twin was 15 days with 24 h/day. This is because healthcare operations, including intensive care, are constantly open to the public.

An initial sample of 10 runs was executed to calculate the number of iterations required for portraying the real variability of bed waiting times derived from the intensive care operations. The outcomes evidenced that more than 2,100 replications are necessary to clear understand the ICU operability under the SRD pressure. Following this, a 1-sample sign test ($\alpha = 0.01$) was implemented to verify whether the digital twin is comparable with the real ED-ICU operation regarding bed waiting times. The test underpinned the similarity (p-value $= 0.7$; $\eta = 1$ h), and the virtual model can be hence adopted for operability assessment and design of effective interventions if needful.

4.4 Operability Analysis

The digital twin revealed that the median waiting time for an ICU bed was 1.88 h. This is an undeniable sign that the patient flow from the ED and other downstream services has surpassed ICU installed capacity. Of note, operational healthcare mismatches in the presence of rapidly-evolving respiratory viruses threaten patients' health and thus claim unified improvements. Embedding effective solutions is urgently needed to tackle this problem. The digital twin comes to the ground again to empower decision-makers on what to do in a highly iteratively interacted healthcare system [30]. Two proposals were envisioned and examined to tackle the bed waiting time problem: augmenting the number of ICU beds by i) 3, ii) 5 (Fig. 3).

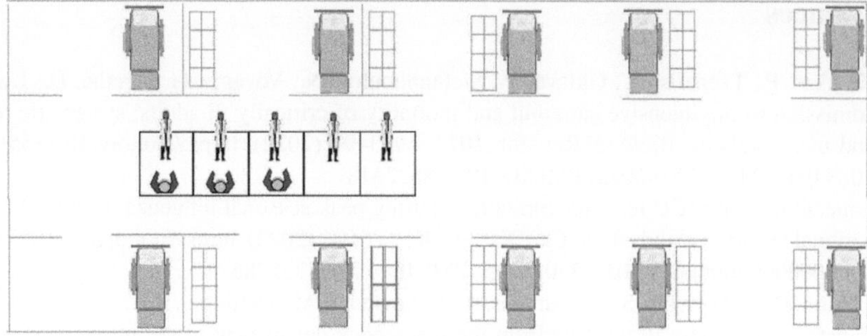

Fig. 3. ICU interface in the digital twin model.

After retrieving the information from the digital twin runs, we observed that the waiting time indicator would reduce between 6.48 min and 9.60 min (95% CI) if intervention (i) is implemented. In turn, the remedy (ii) would shorten this time between 10.8 min and 16.01 min (95% CI). Although the winning solution is (ii), there is still room for improvement. Hence, integrating this remedy with other solution perspectives is fundamental, which can contribute to a more favorable outcome.

5 Conclusions

Shaping the future response of ICUs when undergoing SRDs is pivotal to ensure more auspicious outputs in respiratory-affected patients. The core fabric of this project will be the correct administration of unit-to-unit interactions along the ED-ICU pathway. One-size-fits-all solutions are inefficient and do not correspond to the intrinsic characteristics of each system. The underlying digital twin model is a promising alternative to address the operational problems that ICUs may face during respiratory-disease outbreaks, including out-of-control waiting times. The respiratory disease burden is expected to ramp up every season in the coming decades, and healthcare decision-makers will need advanced approaches like the digital twins to strengthen the supporting operational pillars.

The road forward dictates that these virtual replicas will be even more fundamental if combined with endeavors from the Artificial Intelligence field. Extracting high-quality data will ensure the reliability and usability of these integrations. In this regard, ICU managers are challenged to monitor the data culture within their departments continuously. Ultimately, it is advised to cross the ICU boundaries and establish collaborative agreements with other ICUs where some patients can be transferred to other units that can guarantee timelier care [31–33].

Disclosure of Interests. The authors have no competing interests to declare that are relevant to the content of this article.

References

1. Kiekkas, P., Tzenalis, A., Gklava, V., Stefanopoulos, N., Voyagis, G., Aretha, D.: Delayed admission to the intensive care unit and mortality of critically ill adults: systematic review and meta-analysis. Biomed. Res. Int. **2022**, 4083494 (2022). https://doi.org/10.1155/2022/4083494. PMID: 35146022; PMCID: PMC8822318

2. Lane, C.J., et al.: ICU resource limitations during peak seasonal influenza: results of a 2018 national feasibility study. Crit. Care Explor. **4**(1), e0606 (2022). https://doi.org/10.1097/CCE.0000000000000606. PMID: 35018345; PMCID: PMC8735785

3. Chalfin, D.B., Trzeciak, S., Likourezos, A., Baumann, B.M., Dellinger, R.P.: Impact of delayed transfer of critically ill patients from the emergency department to the intensive care unit. Crit. Care Med. **35**(6), 1477–1483 (2007). https://doi.org/10.1097/01.CCM.0000266585.74905.5A

4. Brown, J.D., Ratcliffe, S., Halpern, T., Halpern, A., Gajic, A., Dongelmans, J.J.: Delayed ICU admission and patient outcomes: a multicenter cohort study of triage-to-admission time in Europe. J. Crit. Care **55**, 177–183 (2020). https://doi.org/10.1016/j.jcrc.2019.10.014

5. Williams, E., Szakmany, T., Spernaes, I., Muthuswamy, B., Holborn, P.: Discrete-event simulation modeling of critical care flow: new hospital, old challenges. Crit. Care Explor. **2**(9), e0174 (2020). https://doi.org/10.1097/CCE.0000000000000174. PMID: 32984824; PMCID: PMC7491890

6. Arabi, Y.M., Myatra, S.N., Lobo, S.M.: Surging ICU during COVID-19 pandemic: an overview. Curr. Opin. Crit. Care. **28**(6), 638–644 (2022). https://doi.org/10.1097/MCC.0000000000001001. Epub 2022 Oct 11. PMID: 36226716; PMCID: PMC9612411

7. Halpern, G.A., Nemet, M., Gowda, D.M., Kilickaya, O., Lal A.: Advances and utility of digital twins in critical care and acute care medicine: a narrative review. J. Yeungnam Med. Sci. **42**(9) (2025). https://doi.org/10.12701/jyms.2024.01053

8. Elkefi, S., Asan, O.: Digital twins for managing health care systems: rapid literature review. J. Med. Internet Res. **24**(8), e37641 (2022). https://www.jmir.org/2022/8/e37641. https://doi.org/10.2196/37641

9. Riahi, V., Diouf, I., Khanna, S., Boyle, J., Hassanzadeh, H.: Digital twins for clinical and operational decision-making: scoping review. J. Med. Internet Res. **2025**(27), e55015 (2025). https://doi.org/10.2196/55015.PMID:39778199.PMCID:11754991

10. Koopsen, T., Gerrits, W., van Osta, N., et al.: Virtual pacing of a patient's digital twin to predict left ventricular reverse remodelling after cardiac resynchronization therapy. Europace **26**(1), euae009 (2023). https://doi.org/10.1093/europace/euae009

11. Karakra, A., Fontanili, F., Lamine, E., Lamothe, J., Taweel, A.: Pervasive computing integrated discrete event simulation for a hospital digital twin. In: 2018 IEEE/ACS 15th International Conference on Computer Systems and Applications (AICCSA), Aqaba, Jordan, pp. 1–6 (2018). https://doi.org/10.1109/AICCSA.2018.8612796

12. Karakra, A., Fontanili, F., Lamine, E., Lamothe, J.: HospiT'Win: a predictive simulation-based digital twin for patients pathways in hospital. In: 2019 IEEE EMBS International Conference on Biomedical & Health Informatics (BHI), Chicago, IL, USA, pp. 1–4 (2019). https://doi.org/10.1109/BHI.2019.8834534

13. Zhong, X., Sarijaloo, F.B., Prakash, A., et al.: A multidisciplinary approach to the development of digital twin models of critical care delivery in intensive care units. Int. J. Prod. Res. **60**(13), 4197–4213 (2022). https://doi.org/10.1080/00207543.2021.2022235

14. Trevena, W., et al.: Modeling of critically ill patient pathways to support intensive care delivery. IEEE Robot. Autom. Lett. **7**(3), 7287–7294 (2022). https://doi.org/10.1109/LRA.2022.3183253

15. Pellegrino, G., Gervasi, M., Angelelli, M., et al.: A conceptual framework for digital twin in healthcare: evidence from a systematic meta-review. Inf. Syst. Front. **27**, 7–32 (2025). https://doi.org/10.1007/s10796-024-10536-4

16. Lal, A., Li, G., Cubro, E., et al.: Development and verification of a digital twin patient model to predict specific treatment response during the first 24 hours of sepsis. Crit. Care Explor. **2**(11), e0249 (2020). Published 2020 Nov 16. https://doi.org/10.1097/CCE.0000000000000249

17. Zhou, C., Chase, J.G., Knopp, J., et al.: Virtual patients for mechanical ventilation in the intensive care unit. Comput. Methods Programs Biomed. **2021**(199), 105912 (2021). https://doi.org/10.1016/j.cmpb.2020.105912

18. Khan, A., Milne-Ives, M., Meinert, E., Iyawa, G.E., Jones, R.B., Josephraj, A.N.: A scoping review of digital twins in the context of the COVID-19 pandemic. Biomed. Eng. Comput. Biol. **13**, 11795972221102115 (2022). Published 2022 May 24. https://doi.org/10.1177/11795972221102115

19. Vecillas Martin, D., Berruezo Fernández, C., Gento Municio, A.M.: Systematic review of discrete event simulation in healthcare and statistics distributions. Appl. Sci. **15**(4), 1861 (2025). https://doi.org/10.3390/app15041861

20. Griffiths, J.D., Price-Lloyd, N., Smithies, M., Williams, J.E.: Modelling the requirement for supplementary nurses in an intensive care unit. J. Oper. Res. Soc. **56**(2), 126–133 (2005). https://doi.org/10.1057/palgrave.jors.2601882

21. Dong, Y., Chbat, N.W., Gupta, A., et al.: Systems modeling and simulation applications for critical care medicine. Ann. Intensive Care **2**, 18 (2012). https://doi.org/10.1186/2110-5820-2-18

22. Adamczyk, P.G., Groen, D., Taylor, S.J.E., Suleimenova, D., Abubakar, N., et al.: A hybrid agent-based and discrete-event simulation approach for COVID-19 management at regional level. In: Proceedings of the 2022 Winter Simulation Conference, December 2022, Paper: FACS-CHARM, WSC (2022)

23. Ortiz-Barrios, M., Arias-Fonseca, S., Ishizaka, A., et al.: Artificial intelligence and discrete-event simulation for capacity management of intensive care units during the COVID-19 pandemic: a case study. J. Bus. Res. **160**, 113806 (2023). ISSN 0148–2963. https://doi.org/10.1016/j.jbusres.2023.113806

24. Chase, J., et al.: Digital twins in critical care: what, when, how, where, why? IFAC-PapersOnLine **54**(1), 466–472 (2021). https://doi.org/10.1016/j.ifacol.2021.10.274

25. Parker, F., Martínez, D.A., Scheulen, J., Ghobadi, K.: An interactive decision-support dashboard for optimal hospital capacity management. arXiv preprint arXiv:2403.15634, March 2024. https://doi.org/10.48550/arXiv.2403.15634

26. Melman, G.J., Parlikad, A.K., Cameron, E.A.B.: Balancing scarce hospital resources during the COVID-19 pandemic using discrete-event simulation. Health Care Manag. Sci. **24**(2), 356–374 (2021). https://doi.org/10.1007/s10729-021-09548-2

27. Alban, A., Chick, S.E., Dongelmans, D.A., Vlaar, A.P.J., Sent, D., Study Group: ICU capacity management during the COVID-19 pandemic using a process simulation. Intensive Care Med. **46**(8), 1624–1626 (2020). https://doi.org/10.1007/s00134-020-06066-7

28. Harper, P.R.: A framework for operational modelling of hospital resources. Health Care Manag. Sci. **5**, 165–173 (2002). https://doi.org/10.1023/A:1019767900627

29. Nuñez-Perez, N., Ortíz-Barrios, M., McClean, S., Salas-Navarro, K., Jimenez-Delgado, G., Castillo-Zea, A.: Discrete-event simulation to reduce waiting time in accident and emergency departments: a case study in a district general clinic. In: Ochoa, S., Singh, P., Bravo, J. (eds.) Ubiquitous Computing and Ambient Intelligence, UCAmI 2017. LNCS, vol. 10586, pp. 352–363. Springer, Cham (2017). https://doi.org/10.1007/978-3-319-67585-5_37

30. Ortíz-Barrios, M., Jaramillo-Rueda, N., Gul, M., Yucesan, M., Jiménez-Delgado, G., Alfaro-Saíz, J.J.: A fuzzy hybrid MCDM approach for assessing the emergency department performance during the COVID-19 outbreak. Int. J. Environ. Res. Public Health **20**(5), 4591 (2023)
31. Ortiz-Barrios, M., Alfaro-Saiz, J.J.: An integrated approach for designing in-time and economically sustainable emergency care networks: a case study in the public sector. PLoS ONE **15**(6), e0234984 (2020)
32. Ortiz-Barrios, M., Gul, M., Yucesan, M., Alfaro-Sarmiento, I., Navarro-Jiménez, E., Jiménez-Delgado, G.: A fuzzy hybrid decision-making framework for increasing the hospital disaster preparedness: the Colombian case. Int. J. Disaster Risk Reduct. **72**, 102831 (2022)
33. Ortíz-Barrios, M.A., Escorcia-Caballero, J.P., Sánchez-Sánchez, F., De Felice, F., Petrillo, A.: Efficiency analysis of integrated public hospital networks in outpatient internal medicine. J. Med. Syst. **41**, 1–18 (2017)

A Digital Twin for Shortening Waiting Times in Emergency Departments During Respiratory Disease Peaks

Alexandros Konios[1] , Miguel Ortíz-Barrios[2]([✉]) ,
Zaury-Estela Fernández-Mendoza[3] , Eduardo Navarro-Jiménez[4,5] ,
and David-Enrique Martínez-Sierra[5]

[1] Department of Computer Science, Nottingham Trent University, Nottingham 4081112, UK
alexandros.konios@ntu.ac.uk
[2] Department of Productivity and Innovation, Universidad de la Costa CUC, 080002
Barranquilla, Colombia
mortiz1@cuc.edu.co
[3] Department of Engineering, Institución Universitaria ITSA, Barranquilla, Colombia
zefernandez@unibarranquilla.edu.co
[4] Grupo de Investigación en Microbiología y Biotecnología (IBM), Universidad Libre,
Barranquilla, Colombia
eduardoi.navarroj@unilibre.edu.co
[5] Facultad de Ingeniería, Universidad Simón Bolívar sede Barranquilla, Barranquilla, Colombia
david.martinez@unisimon.edu.co

Abstract. Emergency departments (EDs) are vital components of healthcare systems, often operating under extreme pressure, especially during seasonal peaks of respiratory diseases like influenza, Respiratory Syncytial Virus (RSV), or COVID-19. These peaks lead to significant overcrowding, prolonged waiting times, and increased strain on clinical staff, which compromise patient outcomes and system efficiency. The challenge lies in dynamically allocating resources and predicting patient flow with enough accuracy to maintain operational stability. Digital twin (DT) technology, a virtual real-time representation of physical systems, offers a transformative solution. By mirroring the ED operations and continuously synchronising with real-world data, digital twins can simulate various scenarios and inform optimal decision-making strategies. This paper presents the application of digital twins for shortening waiting times in EDs during respiratory disease peaks. First, we characterized the patient journey within the ED using the Supplier-Input-Process-Output-Customer (SIPOC) diagram. Secondly, we performed an input data analysis and then modelled the ED through a DT designed in ARENA® software. After this, we validated the model by conducting a 1-sample t test on the waiting time for treatment in ED (3–5 triaged patients). Finally, we implemented a what-if analysis considering two scenarios: i) increasing the number of beds and general doctors, ii) reducing delays caused by clinical labs in delivering test results. The proposed approach was verified in a European hospital group during one of the first COVID-19 waves. The results showed that the treatment waiting time in 3–5 triaged patients (4.682 h) can be significantly lessened if both scenarios are applied.

© The Author(s), under exclusive license to Springer Nature Switzerland AG 2026
V. G. Duffy (Ed.): HCII 2025, LNCS 16339, pp. 293–309, 2026.
https://doi.org/10.1007/978-3-032-13012-9_21

Keywords: Digital Twin (DT) · Respiratory Syncytial Virus (RSV) · Emergency Departments (EDs) · Healthcare

1 Introduction

Emergency Departments (EDs) worldwide face escalating pressures during seasonal peaks of respiratory illnesses such as influenza, Respiratory Syncytial Virus (RSV), and COVID-19. These surges often drive patient demand beyond ED capacity, resulting in severe overcrowding, prolonged waiting times, and strain on healthcare staff [1]. ED overcrowding has been recognized as a critical problem since the 1980s, reflecting an imbalance between incoming patient volume and the resources available for care [1]. Seasonal epidemics, such as winter influenza outbreaks, can suddenly increase ED attendance by large margins, a factor largely outside the ED's control. Recent convergences of multiple respiratory viruses (a so-called "tripledemic" of flu, RSV, and COVID-19) exemplify this challenge as the simultaneous surges in 2022–2023 taxed hospitals to the point of near-overwhelm in many regions [2]. The consequences of such peaks are well-documented, as ED crowding is associated with decreased quality of care, higher patient morbidity and mortality, and an overall compromised ability to deliver timely emergency interventions [1]. This highlights an urgent need for more adaptive and proactive approaches to managing patient flow and resources during public health crises.

However, dynamically allocating resources and forecasting patient flow in an ED amid unpredictable surges is complex [3, 4]. Traditional staffing algorithms and static capacity plans often fail to adjust to rapid changes in demand, contributing to extended length of stay and throughput bottlenecks [3]. Past studies have shown that ED over-crowding is multifactorial and resists a simple solution [4]. Key contributing factors include population aging and seasonal illness waves to inpatient bed shortages and process inefficiencies [1]. Hospitals have implemented various mitigation strategies, such as expanding surge capacity or redirecting low-acuity patients, but these measures are typically reactive and limited in scope. A clear gap exists for intelligent decision-support tools to anticipate surges and optimize ED operations in real-time. In other words, healthcare systems require predictive, data-driven solutions that go beyond retrospective analysis to continuously model the evolving state of an ED and guide timely interventions.

Digital twin (DT) technology offers a novel and promising path to fill this gap [5, 6]. A digital twin is a virtual, real-time representation of a physical system maintained through continuous data synchronisation between the physical entity and its digital counterpart [5, 7]. In the context of an ED, a digital twin serves as a live, computational mirror of the department, ingesting real-world data (e.g., patient arrivals, triage statuses, bed occupancy) and running simulations of ED processes in parallel to actual operations. Unlike traditional simulations or dashboards, a true digital twin is adaptive as it updates itself with streaming data and can monitor the current state ("digital shadow") and project future states through predictive modelling. This capability allows stakeholders to experiment with "what-if" scenarios on the virtual ED to identify optimal responses before implementing changes on the floor [5]. Recent work in hospital systems likens this approach to an Industry 4.0 transformation, where digital twins leverage real-time data, IoT sensors, and AI analytics to enable faster data access and simulation-enhanced decision-making [5, 7]. Indeed, the use of digital twins across industries has surged in recent years, and healthcare is now viewed as a frontier where DTs could revolutionise system management and service delivery [6]. By creating a virtual replica of a hospital or ED, administrators can review operational strategies, predict future challenges under various outbreak scenarios, and optimise resource allocation proactively [7]. The potential impact of such technology on patient outcomes and system efficiency during crises is significant, as it effectively provides a safe testing ground for interventions and a foresight tool for impending demand.

In this paper, we address the above research gap by deploying a digital twin to shorten ED waiting times during peaks of respiratory disease activity. We present a simulation-based DT model of an ED that is continuously informed by hospital data and integrated with predictive analytics. In our approach, we first mapped the ED patient journey and processes using a Supplier-Input-Process-Output-Customer (SIPOC) framework to understand key delay points. We then performed an input data analysis (examining arrival rates and service times) to assess variability and fit to statistical distributions, ensuring the simulation model is grounded in real-world patterns. The ED digital twin was implemented in Arena® discrete-event simulation software, calibrated with empirical data from a European hospital network. We validated the model by comparing simulated waiting time distributions against historical ED data (using a 1-sample t-test on treatment waiting times for mid-acuity triage levels 3–5) to confirm that the twin accurately mirrors the physical ED's performance. Finally, we conducted a series of what-if analyses through the digital twin to evaluate potential surge management strategies. In particular, we simulated two intervention scenarios: (i) increasing critical resources (adding ED beds and on-call physicians) and (ii) reducing internal process delays (expediting laboratory test turnaround times to shorten the length of stay). The digital twin experiments, applied to data from one of the first COVID-19 waves in 2020, revealed that these measures can achieve substantial reductions in patient treatment waiting times under peak conditions. Notably, for moderate-acuity patients (triage levels 3–5), the average waiting time of 4.68 h was significantly lowered when extra staffing was combined with faster lab results. These findings illustrate how a digital twin can guide data-informed decisions to bolster ED resilience during respiratory disease surges. In the following sections, we review related work and position our contribution within the literature before detailing the methodology and results of our study.

2 Literature Review

2.1 Digital Twins in Healthcare and Emergency Departments

Digital twin technology has rapidly gained traction in healthcare, motivated by its success in engineering domains and the growing availability of real-time health data [6]. Broadly, a digital twin for health (DT4H) is envisioned as a virtual replica of a healthcare entity, whether an individual patient, an organ, or an entire clinical system, that continuously mirrors the state of its physical counterpart and enables advanced analysis and forecasting [5, 6]. Early applications of healthcare digital twins have focused on personalised medicine (e.g., patient-specific cardiac models or virtual organs). Still, increasingly there is interest in operational and system-level twins that can improve how care is delivered [8]. By integrating streams of data (e.g., sensor readings, electronic health records) with AI and simulation, digital twins have demonstrated potential benefits such as streamlining care processes, optimising facility management, and enhancing patient safety [7]. For instance, recent reviews highlight that digital twins have been used to model entire hospitals, creating virtual testbeds to refine workflows, assess resource needs, and identify bottlenecks under different scenarios [7, 8]. These capabilities translate directly into improved efficiency and quality of care since a well-implemented digital twin can predict patient volumes, evaluate intervention impacts in silico, and recommend adjustments to prevent disruptions in service delivery.

In the context of emergency departments, digital twin research is still emerging but shows great promise for patient flow management [5]. An ED is a complex, high-variety environment where conditions change by the minute, and this makes it an ideal but challenging candidate for DT modelling. Moyaux et al. in [5] proposed an agent-based architecture for an ED digital twin explicitly designed to improve the management of patient pathways. In their framework, software agents represent key ED entities (staff, equipment, patients) within the twin, and the twin's information system stays regularly synchronised with the hospital's real-time data. The ED digital twin can operate in multiple modes: a digital shadow for real-time monitoring of the current state, a synchronised twin that runs predictive simulations in parallel with live data to foresee short-term future states, and an exploratory twin for running scenario analyses (e.g., Monte Carlo experiments) to test various "what-if" situations. Notably, the synchronised digital twin mode acts as a decision-support system for the ED. It continuously projects ahead based on current conditions, allowing decision-makers to anticipate problems (like an impending bed shortage or staff overload) before they fully materialise [5]. This work demonstrated the feasibility of maintaining a live ED model that could virtually alert managers to future performance trajectories and evaluate interventions. Few real-world EDs have such digital counterparts yet, but these results underscore how a DT can bridge the gap between monitoring and forecasting in emergency care.

Another example of ED-oriented digital twin innovation is the study in [7], which explored a novel emergency service model using digital twins to expedite patient treatment. Here, the focus was on patients arriving without readily available medical histories (e.g., unconscious or unidentified). The proposed system created a digital twin for the patient's journey, leveraging biometric identification (face recognition) to retrieve the patient's digital health records quickly and prior conditions. By doing so, clinicians could immediately access critical information and initiate appropriate care without delay. This DT-enabled fast-tracking significantly reduced the length of stay in the ED, as doctors no longer wasted time obtaining medical history or duplicate tests [7]. It also improved triage accuracy since the digital twin helped match unknown patients to their records with over 80% success rate. This work also illustrates a different facet of digital twins in emergency care, as it is about modelling system operations and enhancing individual patient processing through data integration and IoT technologies. The digital twin effectively served as a coordination hub, bringing together identification, medical data, and communication with external parties (family, specialists, insurers) to streamline the care of emergency patients.

Beyond these, more incipient works apply digital twins for ED management. Some projects aim to formalise the requirements and design considerations for a full ED digital twin platform (e.g., specifying data integration needs, visualisation, and user interface for real-time decision support) [9]. Others have drawn parallels to related domains; for example, a simulation-based digital twin was used to assess emergency call centre operations in France, revealing how reorganising call dispatch could improve service response times [10]. These studies collectively reinforce the notion that digital twins can serve as adaptive, learning systems in healthcare operations. A DT can provide hospital leaders with unprecedented situational awareness and agility by continuously updating real data and employing high-fidelity simulations. Nevertheless, challenges remain. Researchers have noted interoperability and data governance as major hurdles for implementing digital twins at scale in healthcare [8]. Large volumes of heterogeneous data must be processed securely and in real-time for a DT to be effective, and integrating these with existing hospital IT systems is non-trivial [8]. Despite these challenges, the trajectory is clear since digital twin technology is steadily moving from concept to reality in healthcare. EDs benefit immensely from its capabilities to forecast demand surges, test interventions virtually, and support critical decision-making during peak crises.

2.2 AI, Simulation, and Hybrid Modelling for Patient Flow Management

The use of simulation and artificial intelligence in modelling patient flow and hospital operations has a rich history, which is now evolving into more hybrid, intelligent methodologies. Discrete-event simulation (DES) and related techniques have long been employed to study ED crowding and to evaluate interventions for reducing waiting times. For example, numerous DES models have been built to identify bottlenecks in ED processes and to estimate how changes, such as adding a new triage nurse or expanding bed capacity, would impact patient length of stay [3]. Agent-based simulation (ABS) has likewise been used to capture the interactions of individual patients and staff, offering fine-grained insight into dynamics like patient diversion or workflow rerouting [5]. Such simulation studies have repeatedly shown benefits since simulation is an effective tool for improving complex systems like EDs, particularly by tackling challenges of variable patient arrivals and resource allocation in a risk-free virtual environment [3]. In fact, most hospitals that have optimised operations have done so by experimenting with models to determine how many resources are needed at peak times and where the worst delays occur. Traditionally, these models assume a certain static set of inputs (like average arrival rate or service time distributions) and yield strategic recommendations (e.g., increasing the number of doctors to reduce waiting time). While valuable, static models struggle to capture the real-time fluctuations inherent to EDs.

This is where Artificial Intelligence (AI) and Machine Learning (ML) have increasingly been introduced to complement simulation. AI techniques, especially predictive modelling, can analyse historical and real-time data to forecast ED conditions in the future. For instance, predicting how many patients will arrive in the next hour or which admitted patients will likely deteriorate and require ICU care. Accurate prediction of ED arrivals is key to optimising staffing and resources, thereby cutting patient waiting times [3, 11]. Many researchers have focused on forecasting patient attendance using time-series models like ARIMA and exponential smoothing [11]. These statistical models are effective when patterns are regular but falter with irregular surges and complex nonlinear trends. To address this, recent studies have turned to machine learning algorithms (such as random forests, gradient boosting, and neural networks), which can incorporate a wider range of features, such as calendar effects, weather data, upstream infection rates, etc., to improve forecast accuracy. Notably, hybrid approaches have been proposed that combine traditional time-series methods with machine learning and even text mining of contextual information [11]. Such hybrid models have demonstrated superior predictive performance compared to any single modelling approach, particularly in forecasting ED arrivals. For example, Porto and Fogliatto in [11] report that an ensemble of machine learning models (e.g., XGBoost and neural network autoregression) after feature engineering achieved 5–14% mean absolute percentage error in predicting daily ED visits, outperforming prior ARIMA-based studies. The implication is that leveraging AI for prediction can provide the foresight needed to initiate pre-emptive actions (like calling in additional staff or opening surge areas) rather than reacting after queues have already formed.

The true power for operations management emerges when these predictive tools are integrated with simulation in a hybrid modelling framework. The work presented in [4] developed a hybrid system combining real-time forecasting with discrete-event simulation to support short-term decision-making in urgent care networks. Their approach used seasonal ARIMA models to continuously forecast patient arrivals across multiple EDs, triggering scenario simulations of the EDs under various diversion policies. By doing so, the system could proactively identify when an ED's projected queue would become unmanageable and then simulate diverting a portion of low-acuity patients to alternative clinics before the ED became overwhelmed. This hybrid forecasting–simulation strategy, essentially an early form of a digital twin, allowed the researchers to achieve proactive service recovery in the ED: instead of waiting for crowding to cause harm, the model would advise interventions (like patient re-direction or resource reallocation) ahead of time. Similarly, this work showed that sharing real-time data across an integrated simulation model can support dynamic ED control policies – for example, temporarily rerouting incoming ambulances when predicted wait times exceed a threshold [4]. The results indicated a clear benefit in reducing patient congestion and avoiding service breakdowns.

Another study [12] focused on hospitalisation departments during respiratory disease seasons and integrated artificial intelligence with DES to shorten bed waiting times. In that work, machine learning models predicted the probability of clinical deterioration for each admitted patient and the likely length of stay, information which was fed into a simulation of hospital bed management. This hybrid model optimised bed assignments and prioritised transfers, yielding an impressive reduction of nearly 8 h in the average bed waiting time during peak respiratory illness periods. Although that study dealt with inpatient beds, the principle is highly relevant to ED operations by anticipating bottlenecks (in their case, predicting which patients would soon need a bed and clearing capacity), the combination of AI forecasting and simulation can dramatically improve flow. The ED is tightly coupled with downstream units like wards and Intensive Care Units (ICUs), so forecasting admissions and expediting throughput directly benefits ED waiting times. Ortíz-Barrios et al. [12] effectively prevented backlogs in the ED by ensuring beds were ready when needed, demonstrating how hybrid AI-simulation systems can mitigate the domino effect of crowding.

Beyond patient forecasting and bed management, AI is also used in resource scheduling and operational optimisation in conjunction with simulation. A recent study by Kim in [3] developed a simulation model of an ED and applied machine learning to dynamically select the best physician scheduling policy in response to current conditions. Six different staffing schedules (varying mixes of senior and junior doctors by shift) were embedded in the simulation, and a learning algorithm was trained on historical data to pick which policy would minimize patient length of stay for a given incoming patient load. This integrated ML–DES approach achieved about 90% accuracy in matching the optimal schedule to the situation, and the resulting average patient length of stay in the ED fell to ~323 min, compared to ~327 min under a static scheduling method [3]. While the improvement might seem modest, it underscores the potential of real-time adaptive scheduling powered by AI, as even small reductions in average LOS can translate to dozens of freed bed hours and markedly improved waiting times across hundreds of patients. More importantly, the study highlights that increasing resources is not always feasible (due to financial or personnel constraints); thus optimising the utilisation of existing staff is crucial. Machine learning provides a way to make optimal use decisions on the fly, something traditional heuristic schedules cannot accomplish. We see similar trends in operating rooms, inpatient units, and ambulance services, where AI and simulation coalesce to tackle complex scheduling and routing problems better than either could alone.

In summary, the literature on patient flow management is moving toward the convergence of AI and simulation, effectively laying the groundwork for hospital digital twins. Discrete-event and agent-based simulations supply a tested framework for modelling the ED and evaluating interventions. In contrast, AI supplies predictive and adaptive capabilities to inform those models with up-to-the-minute insights. Hybrid models have been shown to prevent overcrowding by acting ahead of time, streamlining hospital pathways by intelligent resource allocation, and enhancing the precision of operational decisions (like scheduling) under uncertainty [4]. These advances directly reduce patient waiting times and improve throughput, especially during demand surges. The ongoing challenge is integrating these components into a cohesive system that can run continuously in a real hospital setting – precisely the ambition of a true digital twin.

2.3 Decision-Support Systems and Forecasting During Public Health Crises

Public health crises, such as pandemic waves or severe seasonal outbreaks, put extraordinary pressure on hospitals and demand robust decision-support systems for effective response. In these situations, having tools that forecast patient surges and support rapid operational adjustments is invaluable. During the COVID-19 pandemic, for example, many health systems learned the importance of real-time situational awareness and predictive analytics to manage capacity [1, 2]. Large hospital networks like NYC Health + Hospitals (the largest municipal system in the US) activated emergency coordination centres that relied on analytic tools and live dashboards to track incoming cases, available beds, ventilators, and staffing levels across the city. This real-time data visibility, combined with predictive models, enabled administrators to anticipate where resources would be overwhelmed and to redistribute patients or staff accordingly. Indeed, situational awareness and forecasting are critical components of crisis response, allowing decision-makers to stay ahead of rapidly evolving demand [2]. For respiratory virus surges, this might include short-term forecasts of ED visits based on community infection trends or early warning triggers when a certain threshold of flu cases is reached. Even simple time-series models (e.g., weekly ARIMA forecasts of ED respiratory cases) have been shown to improve preparedness by giving a few days lead time to implement surge protocols [4, 11].

At a more advanced level, digital twin and simulation approaches have been explored as decision-support systems during crises. The idea is that a hospital or regional healthcare system can maintain a continuously running simulation model, fed by current data, to test the impact of different emergency strategies. For instance, researchers in Denmark created a detailed nation-level simulation (termed a digital twin of the population's health status) to evaluate COVID-19 mitigation measures [13]. Their simulation results showed that without certain interventions (mass testing and targeted lockdowns), hospital admissions would have surged by 150% during the Alpha variant wave. While that study was on a public health scale, the underlying principle applies to ED operations. Virtual scenario testing can inform policy decisions that directly affect waiting times and outcomes. In an ED setting, this could mean simulating various triage protocols during a pandemic (e.g. streaming respiratory patients to separate zones) or testing the effect of expanding ED capacity using hall beds or field units. By comparing scenarios in the twin, hospital leaders can choose strategies that best mitigate overcrowding and treatment delays before implementing them on the ground [4, 5].

One concrete example of an ED-focused decision support system is the hybrid forecasting simulation model presented in [4]. Although developed prior to COVID-19, it essentially functioned as a crisis management tool, enabling proactive diversion of patients when an impending overflow was predicted. In practice, such a system during a respiratory pandemic could automate decisions like directing ambulances between hospitals or activating urgent care centres to absorb low-acuity cases when a surge is anticipated. The value of this approach was endured during COVID-19 as many regions that fared better did so by balancing loads across hospitals and utilising alternate care sites, actions that rely on timely data and forecasts. A digital twin of a hospital network can facilitate these decisions by continuously computing scenarios of patient distribution and resource utilisation under current conditions. Researchers have noted that digital twins, by virtue of their real-time fidelity, can serve as nerve centres during crises, aggregating data, analysing risks, and recommending interventions in one unified platform [5]. In other words, a digital twin is a model and an intelligent agent in the decision loop, advising human operators on the best course of action to preserve care quality.

During the COVID-19 pandemic, numerous predictive tools were developed to forecast hospital admissions, ICU demand, and ED presentations. Machine learning models using live syndromic surveillance data could predict COVID-related ED visits several days in advance, helping emergency departments plan for surges in respiratory patients [1]. In parallel, decision-support dashboards integrated these forecasts with hospital capacity information to trigger predefined escalation plans (such as converting recovery rooms into ICU beds or calling reserve clinicians). Khan et al., in a scoping review of digital twins for COVID-19 [14], identified hospital capacity management as a key area where DTs were proposed to aid the pandemic response. By simulating patient flow and resource consumption, a hospital digital twin can forecast when critical resources (like isolation beds or ventilators) will run out and evaluate the impact of mitigation steps (cancelling elective surgeries, expanding telemedicine triage, etc.) [15]. The review noted that while many such applications were conceptual, they highlight a consensus that DT technology can greatly enhance crisis decision-making by providing a system-wide perspective and predictive insight beyond human intuition alone.

Crucially, public health emergencies often require decisions that balance competing needs and uncertain outcomes. A decision-support system grounded in simulation and AI can illuminate the likely consequences of each option. For example, during the 2022 flu/RSV/COVID tripledemic, paediatric EDs had to decide whether to cohort patients, divert them, or stretch staff ratios, each with trade-offs in patient wait and safety. With a digital twin, they could simulate these options: how would opening a fast-track for flu patients affect overall wait times? What if 10% of lower-priority cases were redirected to urgent care clinics? By examining such questions virtually, hospitals can choose strategies that minimize harm [16]. Real-world experience from NYC during the tripledemic showed the importance of improving comprehensive situational awareness and adjusting resource levels system-wide promptly [2]. Hospitals that employed central monitoring and agile reconfiguration (such as shifting staff to EDs under strain or pooling ICU beds across a system) managed better throughput than those that didn't. These are essentially manual precursors to what a digital twin could automate – continuously sensing the load and recommending reallocation of resources or rerouting of patients to prevent any one facility from collapsing under pressure [17].

In summary, the literature and recent crisis experiences underscore that forecasting and decision-support tools are indispensable during public health surges. Integrating forecasting models (ARIMA, ML, etc.) with ED operations allows hospitals to act before queues mount [4, 11, 18, 19]. Simulation-based decision support enables scenario planning for worst-case conditions and optimal use of scarce resources [5, 13, 20, 21]. Digital twins represent the cutting edge of these capabilities, bringing together real-time data, predictive analytics, and simulation in a cohesive platform. Although still in the early stages of deployment, they have been envisioned as key assets for enhancing resilience in healthcare [22, 23].

3 Proposed Methodology

The proposed methodology entails the implementation of four main phases, as fine-grained in Fig. 1. The details of each component are described below:

Phase 1 - Digital Twin Modelling. Direct observation and Supplier-Input-Process-Output-Customer (SIPOC) diagram are utilized to identify the main stations of the patient journey within the ED, discriminate parameters/process variables, and hypothesize the potential causes of ED deficiencies during Respiratory Disease Seasons (RDSs).

Phase 2 - Input Data Assessment. In this phase, we evaluate the process variable data's autocorrelation, homogeneity, and goodness-of-fit. While the autocorrelation is analyzed

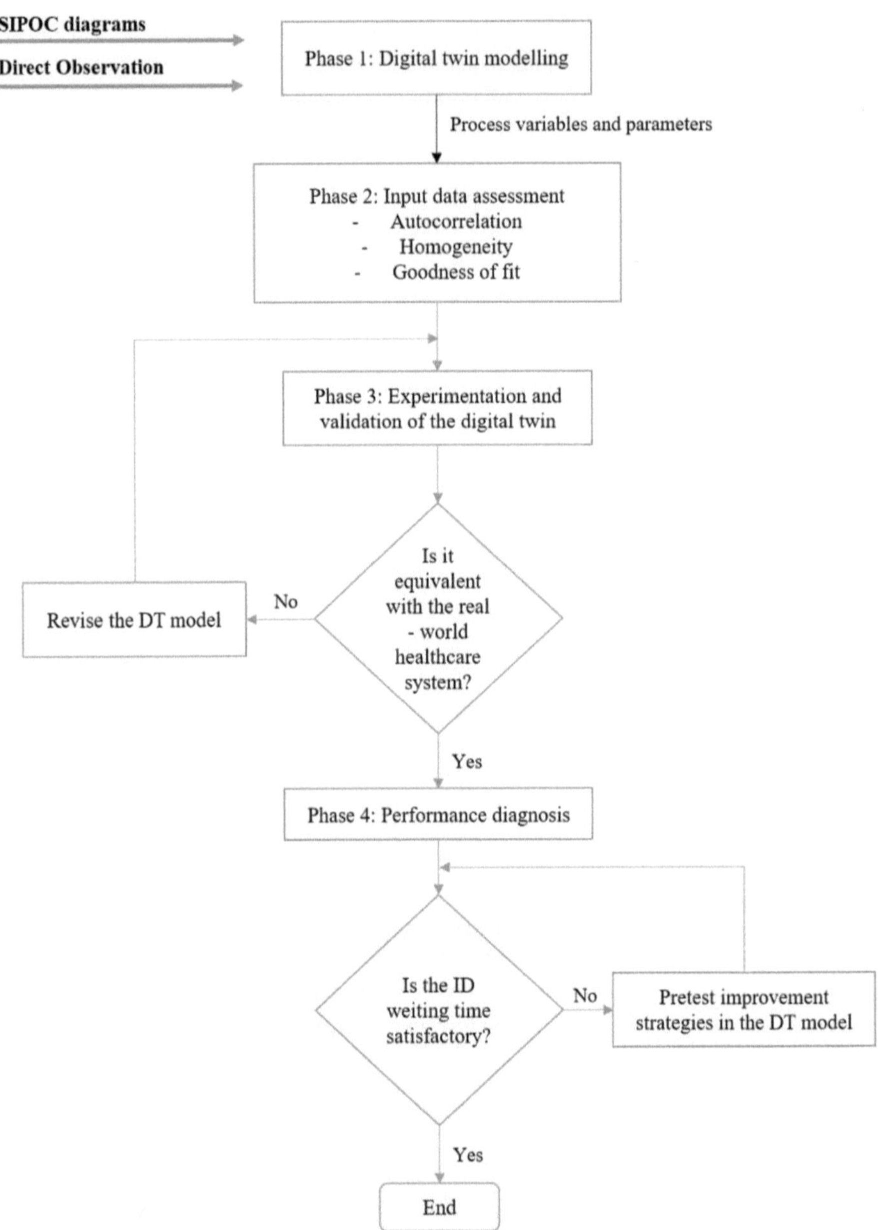

Fig. 1. The step-by-step procedure for reducing the ED waiting times using digital twins.

using a run test ($\alpha = 0.01$), the homogeneity is elucidated through an Analysis of Variance (ANOVA) test ($\alpha = 0.01$). Finally, the goodness-of-fit is examined by employing a Kolmogorov-Smirnov (KS) test ($\alpha = 0.01$).

Phase 3 - Experimentation and Validation of the Digital Twin Model. The probability expressions derived from the KS tests are included in the digital twin model. This model is diagrammed in Arena ® software considering the findings of previous steps. A pre-sample of 10 iterations is then run to estimate the variability of the waiting times [24]. With this information, a final sample size is calculated, and the digital twin model is validated through a 1-sample t-test ($\alpha = 0.01$). If the digital twin model is comparable with the real-world ED, performance diagnosis and further can be performed; otherwise, the model must be checked and calibrated.

Phase 4 - Performance Diagnosis. The waiting time performance metrics emanated from the validated digital twin are now examined for ED operational diagnosis. No intervention will be necessary if the waiting time is satisfactory (≤ 20 min). Otherwise, improvement strategies should be created and pretested in the digital twin. The intervention will be categorized as effective if it significantly lowers the waiting time.

4 Results

Seasonal Respiratory Diseases (SRDs) put EDs under pressure and, it is, therefore, necessary to anticipatedly pretest interventions that significantly lower the associated waiting times and the consequent negative effects on patient's health and operational costs [25, 26]. A large European hospital group experienced these shortcomings during one of the first COVID-19 waves in 2020. Being aware of this situation, the ED managers decided to build a robust dataset containing patient data, attendance times, triage times, treatment times, and other critical process variables to model the patient pathway in a digital twin. Official approval was given by the ethics committee of the hospital group (Consent number: 14-12-2021-004; Access request ID:39) to employ the data. Thereby, it was possible to lay the groundwork for devising remedies tackling the main operational problems during current and future SRDs. Specifically, we focused on diminishing the waiting time for ED treatment in 3–5 triaged respiratory-affected patients, considering its high association with overcrowding, intra-hospital infection, and the probability of poor health evolution.

The following sub-sections will describe how the proposed methodology was deployed in this case and how the outcomes improved the ED response during the SRD ("tripledemic" of flu, RSV, and COVID-19).

4.1 Digital Twin Modelling

Direct observation and a SIPOC diagram (Fig. 2) were used to identify the ED care stations, suppliers, inputs, outputs, and customers. It is good to highlight that patients and pharmacies behave as both suppliers and customers, which demonstrates the key role that they play in EDs during SRDs. Also, waiting times for triage and treatment were identified and corroborated by direct observation and waiting time indicators. Likewise, it became glaring how EDs depend on different satellite processes, indicating that intervening in ED response requires designing improvement strategies at different operational levels.

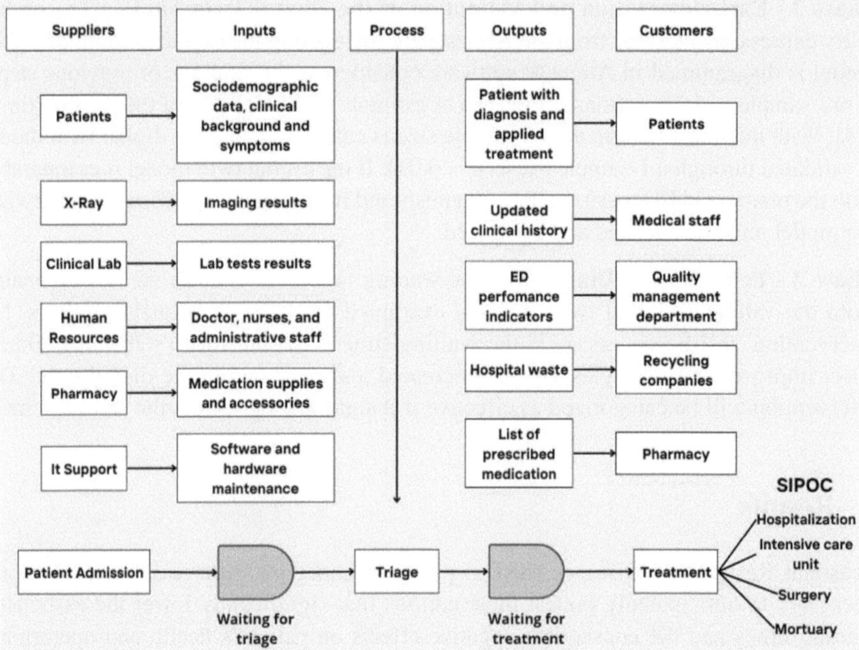

Fig. 2. SIPOC diagram for describing the ED journey and its interactions with suppliers and customers.

4.2 Input Data Assessment

The SIPOC diagram allowed us to identify three principal process variables: Time between arrivals of respiratory-affected patients, Triage categorization time, and Length of Stay in the emergency ward. The next step involves analyzing the data representing these variables. Initially, run tests are undertaken to verify potential autocorrelations ($\alpha = 0.01$). P-values higher than the significance level and absolute T values not exceeding 2 support the independence behaviour in all three variables. Afterwards, the Analysis of Variance (ANOVA) was carried out to discriminate subgroups of data within the main datasets ($\alpha = 0.01$). Upon examining the times between arrivals, it was concluded that the number of attendances is significantly different depending on the day of the week and time slot (A: 00:00 – 08:00; B: 08:00 – 16:00; C: 16:00 – 00:00) ($F_{obs} = 4.9$; p-value $= 0$). Similarly, diverse triage categorization times (*Group 1*: 1–2; *Group 2:* 3–5) were observed, evidencing assorted characteristics of ED respiratory-related admissions during the tripledemic surge ($F_{obs} = 16$; p-value $= 0$) [27]. Given above, a probability expression was defined for each heterogeneous subset (Table 1).

Table 1. Probability expressions incorporated into the digital twin.

Process variable		Probability expression	p-value
Time between arrivals of respiratory-affected	Monday – A	GAMM(120.18, 978) min	>0.10
	Monday – B	−1.2 + LOGN(26.4, 57) min	>0.10
	Monday – C	−1.2 + LOGN(18.6, 28.8) min	0.2
	Tuesday – A	WEIB(91.2, 1164.6) min	>0.10
	Tuesday – B	−1.2 + LOGN(31.8, 60.6) min	>0.10
	Tuesday – C	−1.2 + LOGN(18, 26.4) min	>0.10
	Wednesday – A	WEIB(89.4, 840.6) min	>0.10
	Wednesday – B	−1.2 + WEIB(32.4, 1101.6) min	0.08
	Wednesday – C	−1.2 + LOGN(19.2, 25.8) min	>0.10
	Thursday – A	WEIB(70.8, 1141.8) min	>0.10
	Thursday – B	−1.2 + LOGN(42.6, 92.4) min	>0.10
	Thursday – C	−1.2 + LOGN(18, 28.2) min	>0.10
	Friday – A	WEIB(69.6, 990) min	>0.10
	Friday – B	−1.2 + LOGN(34.8, 71.4) min	>0.10
	Friday – C	−1.2 + LOGN(19.2, 31.8) min	0.08
	Saturday – A	−1.2 + GAMM(74.4, 1203.6) min	>0.10
	Saturday – B	−1.2 + LOGN(40.8, 81) min	>0.10
	Saturday – C	−1.2 + LOGN(23.4, 36.6) min	>0.10
	Sunday – A	−1.2 + GAMM(129, 780) min	0.07
	Sunday – B	−1.2 + LOGN(36, 69.6) min	>0.10
	Sunday – C	−1.2 + GAMM(25.8, 1353.6) min	0.07
Triage categorization time	Group 1	UNIF(4, 12) min	0.2
	Group 2	TRIA(4, 4, 12) min	0.2
Length of Stay in the emergency ward		(60 + 2100*BETA(56.16, 60.6))/450 min	>0.10

4.3 Experimentation and Validation of the Digital Twin Model

The probability expressions derived from the input data assessment were then inserted into Arena® 16.10.00 software to create the digital twin mimicking the ED response during the tripledemic. The replication term considered in the DT was two weeks with 24 h per day, given the characteristics of ED operations. Meanwhile, four months were deemed necessary to stabilize the DT.

A pre-sample of ten iterations was run to estimate the repetitions required for denoting the current real system variability. The validation procedure was concentrated on the ED waiting time for moderate-acuity patients (triage levels 3–5). In view of the significant variability observed in the DT, more than 300 runs were necessary to epitomize the real ED under the tripledemic context. Then, a 1-sample t-test was executed to compare the DT and real models. The statistical test provided enough support for the equivalence hypothesis (p-value $= 0.8$; $\mu = 4.68$ h), and the DT can be therefore utilized for performance analysis and remedy pretesting if needed.

4.4 Performance Analysis

The average waiting time for moderate-acuity ED patients (4.68 h) is a clear symptom of the congestion, cost overruns, and poor efficiency reported by the ED decision-makers during the tripledemic. Given this critical outcome derived from the DT model, the board of supervisors has been asked to underpin the expected design of improvement strategies tackling the problem [28]. Working closely with those involved in the day-to-day routine of the ED is important to ensure the generation of feasible remedies. As a result, two potential remedies were proposed: i) increasing the number of beds and general doctors, ii) reducing the length of stay by diminishing delays caused by clinical labs in delivering test results.

The improvement strategies were modeled and simulated into the DT (Fig. 3). The strategy (i) generates a waiting time for III-IV triaged patients oscillating between 1.34 and 1.98 h (95% CI) with a mean of 1.66 h. On the other hand, scenario (ii) would lead the ED to range from 2.49 h to 5.18 h (95% CI) with a mean of 3.83 h. Therefore, scenario (i) would be the winning solution and is hence recommended for implementation in the wild.

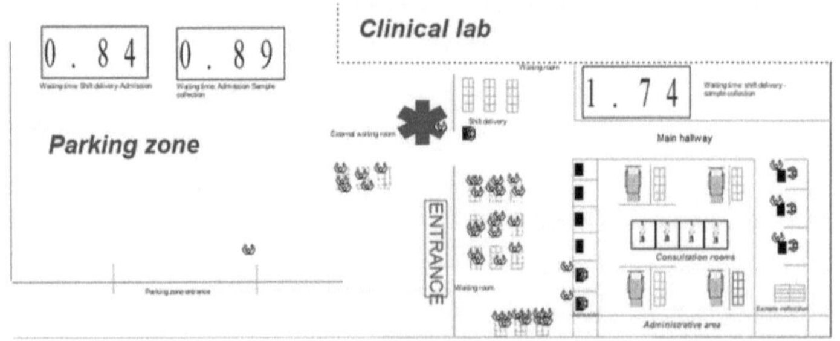

Fig. 3. Digital twin mimicking the ED ward: Clinical lab-ED interface.

5 Conclusions and Future Directions

This study demonstrates the great potential of digital twin technology (DT) to improve the operational efficiency of hospital emergency departments (EDs), particularly during seasonal peaks of respiratory diseases such as influenza, RSV, and COVID-19. This research successfully identified and tested reductions in patient wait times by developing a simulation-based DT model using primary data and validating it with statistical tests. Implementing two key strategies—increasing critical resources and reducing laboratory delays—proved to be effective in reducing treatment wait times in patients at triage levels 3 to 5. These findings emphasize the value of DTs as proactive decision-support tools capable of simulating complex healthcare scenarios and guiding appropriate data-driven interventions. In conclusion, this approach improves patient clinical outcomes, reduces healthcare congestion, and increases EDs resilience during public health crises.

Future work suggests integrating digital twins with real-time hospital and social data systems to enable real-time decision-making. Implementing this approach in other hospital units is also advised to provide a more comprehensive view of hospital operations and improve interdepartmental coordination. Likewise, integrating advanced machine learning models into the DT models could improve their predictive capabilities, enabling more accurate forecasting of patient arrivals and resource needs. Ultimately, exploring the development of individualized TDs for patients could facilitate personalized care pathways and improve triage and treatment decisions in emergency settings.

Disclosure of Interests. The authors have no competing interests to declare that are relevant to the content of this article.

References

1. Sartini, M., et al.: Overcrowding in emergency department: causes, consequences, and solutions-a narrative review. Healthcare (Basel) **10**(9), 1625 (2022). https://doi.org/10.3390/healthcare10091625. PMID:36141237; PMCID:PMC9498666
2. Madad, S., Salway, R.J., Raggi, J., Silvestri, D., Cotter, T., Romolt, C.: The 2022–2023 USA respiratory viral 'Tripledemic': healthcare lessons learned. Microbiol. Infect. Dis. AMJ **1**(1), 35–39 (2023). https://doi.org/10.33590/microbiolinfectdisamj/10306548
3. Kim, J.-K.: Enhancing patient flow in emergency departments: a machine learning and simulation-based resource scheduling approach. Appl. Sci. **14**(10), 4264 (2024). https://doi.org/10.3390/app14104264
4. Harper, A., Mustafee, N.: A hybrid modelling approach using forecasting and real-time simulation to prevent emergency department overcrowding. In: 2019 Winter Simulation Conference (WSC), National Harbor, MD, USA, pp. 1208–1219 (2019). https://doi.org/10.1109/WSC40007.2019.9004862
5. Moyaux, T., Liu, Y., Bouleux, G., Cheutet, V.: An agent-based architecture of the digital twin for an emergency department. Sustainability **15**(4), 3412 (2023). https://doi.org/10.3390/su15043412
6. Katsoulakis, E., Wang, Q., Wu, H., et al.: Digital twins for health: a scoping review. npj Digit. Med. **7**, 77 (2024). https://doi.org/10.1038/s41746-024-01073-0

7. Aluvalu, R., Mudrakola, S., Maheswari, V.U., Kaladevi, A.C., Sandhya, M.V.S., Bhat, R.C.: The novel emergency hospital services for patients using digital twins. Microprocess. Microsyst. **98**, 104794 (2023). ISSN 0141-9331. https://doi.org/10.1016/j.micpro.2023.104794

8. de Oliveira El-Warrak, L., Miceli de Farias, C.: Could digital twins be the next revolution in healthcare? Eur. J. Public Health. **35**(1), 19–25 (2025). https://doi.org/10.1093/eurpub/ckae191. PMID: 39602312; PMCID: PMC11832160

9. Bouleux, G., et al.: Requirements for a digital twin for an emergency department. In: Borangiu, T., Trentesaux, D., Leitão, P. (eds.) Service Oriented, Holonic and Multi-Agent Manufacturing Systems for Industry of the Future, SOHOMA 2022. SCI, vol. 1083, pp. 130–141. Springer, Cham (2023). https://doi.org/10.1007/978-3-031-24291-5_11

10. Penverne, Y., Martinez, C., Cellier, N., et al.: A simulation based digital twin approach to assessing the organization of response to emergency calls. npj Digit. Med. **7**, 385 (2024). https://doi.org/10.1038/s41746-024-01392-2

11. Porto, B.M., Fogliatto, F.S.: Enhanced forecasting of emergency department patient arrivals using feature engineering approach and machine learning. BMC Med. Inform. Decis. Mak. **24**, 377 (2024). https://doi.org/10.1186/s12911-024-02788-6

12. Ortíz-Barrios, M., et al.: Integrating discrete-event simulation and artificial intelligence for shortening bed waiting times in hospitalization departments during respiratory disease seasons. Comput. Ind. Eng. **194**, 110405 (2024). https://doi.org/10.1016/j.cie.2024.110405

13. Græsbøll, K., Eriksen, R.S., Kirkeby, C., et al.: Digital twin simulation modelling shows that mass testing and local lockdowns effectively controlled COVID-19 in Denmark. Commun. Med. **4**, 192 (2024). https://doi.org/10.1038/s43856-024-00621-9

14. Khan, A., Milne-Ives, M., Meinert, E., Iyawa, G.E., Jones, R.B., Josephraj, A.N.: A scoping review of digital twins in the context of the Covid-19 pandemic. Biomed. Eng. Comput. Biol. **2022**, 13 (2022). https://doi.org/10.1177/11795972221102115

15. Zheng, R., Thomas Ng, S., Shao, Y., Li, Z., Xing, J.: Leveraging digital twin for healthcare emergency management system: recent advances, critical challenges, and future directions. Reliab. Eng. Syst. Saf. **261**, 111079 (2025). ISSN 0951-8320. https://doi.org/10.1016/j.ress.2025.111079

16. Janke, A.T., et al.: Emergency department care for children during the 2022 viral respiratory illness surge. JAMA Netw. Open **6**(12), e2346769 (2023). https://doi.org/10.1001/jamanetworkopen.2023.46769

17. Azeli, Y., et al.: A regional command center for pandemic surge. Chest **162**(6), 1306–1309 (2022). https://doi.org/10.1016/j.chest.2022.06.022

18. Rostami-Tabar, B., Browell, J., Svetunkov, I.: Probabilistic forecasting of hourly emergency department arrivals. Health Syst. **13**(2), 133–149 (2023). https://doi.org/10.1080/20476965.2023.2200526

19. Yazdani, M., Shahriari, S., Haghani, M.: Real-time decision support model for logistics of emergency patient transfers from hospitals via an integrated optimisation and machine learning approach. Prog. Disaster Sci. **25**, 100397 (2025). https://doi.org/10.1016/j.pdisas.2024.100397

20. Melman, G.J., Parlikad, A.K., Cameron, E.A.B., et al.: Balancing scarce hospital resources during the COVID-19 pandemic using discrete-event simulation. Health Care Manag. Sci. **24**, 356–374 (2021). https://doi.org/10.1007/s10729-021-09548-2

21. Weissman, G.E., Crane-Droesch, A., Chivers, C., et al.: Locally informed simulation to predict hospital capacity needs during the COVID-19 pandemic. Ann. Intern. Med. **173**(8), 680–690 (2020). https://doi.org/10.7326/M20-1260

22. Alazab, M., et al.: Digital twins for healthcare 4.0—recent advances, architecture, and open challenges. IEEE Consum. Electron. Mag. **12**, 29–37 (2023). https://doi.org/10.1109/MCE.2022.3208986

23. Chase, J.G., et al.: Digital twins in critical care: what, when, how, where, why? IFAC-PapersOnLine **54**(15), 310–315 (2021). https://doi.org/10.1016/j.ifacol.2021.10.274
24. Ortíz-Barrios, M.A., Escorcia-Caballero, J.P., Sánchez-Sánchez, F., De Felice, F., Petrillo, A.: Efficiency analysis of integrated public hospital networks in outpatient internal medicine. J. Med. Syst. **41**, 1–18 (2017)
25. Ortiz-Barrios, M., Gul, M., Yucesan, M., Alfaro-Sarmiento, I., Navarro-Jiménez, E., Jiménez-Delgado, G.: A fuzzy hybrid decision-making framework for increasing the hospital disaster preparedness: the Colombian case. Int. J. Disaster Risk Reduct. **72**, 102831 (2022)
26. Ortíz-Barrios, M.A., Alfaro-Saíz, J.J.: Methodological approaches to support process improvement in emergency departments: a systematic review. Int. J. Environ. Res. Public Health **17**(8), 2664 (2020)
27. Nuñez-Perez, N., Ortíz-Barrios, M., McClean, S., Salas-Navarro, K., Jimenez-Delgado, G., Castillo-Zea, A.: Discrete-event simulation to reduce waiting time in accident and emergency departments: a case study in a district general clinic. In: Ochoa, S., Singh, P., Bravo, J. (eds.) Ubiquitous Computing and Ambient Intelligence, UCAmI 2017. LNCS, vol. 10586, pp. 352–363. Springer, Cham (2017). https://doi.org/10.1007/978-3-319-67585-5_37
28. Ortiz-Barrios, M., Alfaro-Saiz, J.J.: An integrated approach for designing in-time and economically sustainable emergency care networks: a case study in the public sector. PLoS ONE **15**(6), e0234984 (2020)

Research on Active Health Intelligent Interaction System Services for Mild Cognitive Impairment Patients: An Innovative Approach Based on Multimodal Human-Computer Interaction

Liya Mai[✉]

College of Design and Innovation, Tongji University, Shanghai 200092, China
15071386816@163.com

Abstract. China is experiencing a profound aging process, with the prevalence of Mild Cognitive Impairment (MCI) rising significantly with age, leading to declines in independent living ability and increased family care burdens. The "Active Health" concept, a medical model emphasizing individual initiative, offers a new perspective for home-based cognitive intervention in elderly MCI patients. This study focuses on their active health management needs, proposing an innovative non-pharmacological intervention via multimodal human-computer interaction based on the 4PCS model (Proactiveness, Preventiveness, Precision, Personalization, Co-construction & Sharing, Self-discipline). Analyzing MCI elders' cognitive traits and family care pain points, it constructs an intelligent service framework of "active intervention-precise monitoring-emotional companionship-family collaboration". A WeChat mini-program for elders and family members realizes active health management through multimodal activities and virtual assistants. Verified by the Wizard of Oz test and Likert scale, the system significantly enhances intervention compliance and family health collaboration, providing a tech-humanities integrated solution for MCI elders' active health management.

Keywords: Mild Cognitive Impairment (MCI) · Active Health · Multimodal Interaction · Non-pharmacological Therapy · Intelligent System

1 Realistic Dilemmas and Conceptual Opportunities: The Design Context of Active Health Management for Elderly MCI Patients

1.1 Cognitive Health Crisis in the Context of Aging

China is experiencing the largest and fastest aging process globally. Data from 2022 shows that the population aged 60 and above in China has reached 280 million, accounting for 19.8% of the total population, among which those aged 65 and above account for 14.9% [1], indicating that China has entered a deeply aging society. As a prodromal stage of Alzheimer's disease (AD), Mild Cognitive Impairment (MCI) has a significantly

---

The original version of the chapter has been revised. A correction to this chapter can be found at
https://doi.org/10.1007/978-3-032-13012-9_29

increasing prevalence with age. The prevalence of MCI among people aged 65 and above is as high as 20.8%, and about 10%-15% of MCI patients progress to AD each year [2]. MCI patients are characterized by fragmented episodic memory and prospective memory impairment, manifesting as forgetting recent events (such as missing medication or losing items) and difficulty in executing plans (such as being unable to complete multi-step tasks). This not only leads to a decline in independent living ability but also exacerbates family care burdens and strains on social medical resources. The World Health Organization has pointed out that early intervention can reverse cognitive function in 24% of MCI patients [3]. However, home-based elderly care still dominates in China [4], and existing intervention methods are difficult to integrate into daily family scenarios due to high professional thresholds and complex equipment operations, urgently requiring active health solutions adapted to home environments.

1.2 Theoretical Deconstruction and Design Opportunities of the Active Health Concept

The concept of "Active Health" was first proposed by China's Ministry of Science and Technology in 2015. Active Health is a health medical model that fully considers individual subjective initiative [5]. According to a study by Liu Jue and others in China CDC Weekly [6], Active Health has six characteristics: Proactiveness, Preventiveness, Precision, Personalized, Co-construction and Sharing, and Self-rule and Self-discipline (4PCS theoretical model), emphasizing the paradigm shift in health management from "disease treatment" to "health maintenance" through technological empowerment. Among them, proactiveness requires stimulating individual subjective initiative to actively participate in health management; preventiveness emphasizes early screening and intervention to reduce the risk of disease; precision relies on data-driven to achieve personalized program customization; personalization focuses on individual differences to provide adaptive services; co-construction and sharing advocates the collaborative participation of families, communities, and medical institutions; self-rule and self-discipline pay attention to the long-term cultivation of healthy behavior habits. This theory provides a new perspective for home-based intervention for elderly MCI patients.

2 Current Situation Review and Path Innovation: The Development Context of Intelligent Cognitive Intervention

2.1 Dilemmas in Active Health Interaction of Cognitive Intervention Products

European and American countries started earlier in the field of intelligent cognitive intervention, but there is a problem of insufficient scenario adaptation. For example, although the Canadian CogState system can quantify cognitive function through computerized testing, it relies on professional equipment and medical staff guidance [7], making it impossible to use at home; the VR cognitive impairment intervention system trains visuospatial abilities through virtual tasks, but the equipment cost is high, and the technological acceptance of elderly users is low. Chinese products show a polarization: medical-grade equipment such as the "Liuliu Brain Rehabilitation System" requires professional venue operation and is difficult to cover home-based elderly; household tools such as the "Bositeng" mini-program attempt gamified design, but they have high requirements for the educational level of the elderly, and the proportion of low-educated users who give up using due to frustration reaches 40%. In addition, existing products generally have three major pain points: ① The interaction design requires professional guidance and lacks consideration for promoting active health behavior, unable to help users manage their health independently; ② The intervention content is divorced from the active health needs and life scenarios of patients, and the training tasks are separated from daily needs; ③ The lack of family care support, unable to obtain health data in real time, limits family members from actively managing patients' health.

2.2 New Path of Lifestyle Intervention with Non-Pharmacological Therapy Oriented by Active Health

Aiming at the above dilemmas, this study proposes a new path of active health non-pharmacological intervention based on multimodal human-computer interaction, which is integrated into the daily life of patients to promote sustainable active health behaviors. Non-pharmacological therapies (such as activity therapy) design diverse cognitive activation activities (such as recollection, games, social interaction) to avoid drug side effects and enhance the fun of intervention. Multimodal interaction integrates multi-channel stimuli such as visual, auditory, and tactile, for example: triggering episodic memory through old photo recognition technology (visual), inducing emotional resonance through classic music playback (auditory), and designing physical buttons with textures to enhance operation confirmation (tactile). This integrated design not only meets the "preventive" and "personalized" requirements of active health but also strengthens the "proactiveness" of the elderly in health management by constructing a continuous companionship relationship through the role of virtual health assistants.

3 Thick Description of User Needs: Deconstruction of Cognitive and Care Needs Based on Mixed Research

3.1 Research Methods and Sample Characteristics

This study adopted mixed research methods, combining qualitative interviews and quantitative assessments, to investigate 10 elderly MCI patients (aged 65–78, with 60% having a junior high school education or below) and 38 family members or caregivers (with an average care duration of 4.2 years) in Shanghai and Zhaoqing. Through semi-structured interviews, standardized questionnaires, and focus group discussions, user needs were systematically explored.

3.2 Multidimensional Need Profiles of Elderly MCI Patients

Using the Affinity Diagram method to code and analyze interview data, three core need dimensions were extracted, forming a three-dimensional need profile combined with quantitative data. The needs of elderly MCI patients presented interwoven characteristics of cognitive intervention, emotional companionship, and physiological adaptation:

At the cognitive intervention level, 82% of the elderly expected "simple and interesting" gamified training forms, such as short-term memory exercises through "virtual wardrobe organization" item classification tasks, while 75% preferred daily-life close to scenarios (such as recording grocery shopping and walking), reflecting participation barriers caused by traditional boring training (e.g., arithmetic problems) and complex intelligent product operations (e.g., multi-level menus). In terms of economy, 53.7% accepted an annual payment $\leq$ 500 yuan, and only 12% were willing to pay for high-priced functions, highlighting low-threshold requirements.

Regarding emotional companionship, 91% of the elderly longed to be "listened to," and 68% expected a "stable companion." Social withdrawal (e.g., Grandpa Zhao, 69, "speaks fewer than ten sentences daily") and stigma (e.g., Aunt Sun, 73, "fears being called confused") exacerbated loneliness. Users expected interactive conversations like "chatting with neighbors" and emotional feedback capabilities—for example, virtual assistants proactively mentioning life details (e.g., "remembering you like pickled vegetables") and playing soothing music during anxiety.

Physiological adaptation needs were highlighted by 80% vision problems and 60% hearing loss, making large fonts ($\geq$24px), high-contrast color schemes (e.g., black text on a yellow background), dialectal voice interaction, and tactile feedback buttons (e.g., press vibration) essential. Minimal input functions like one-click calling family members were also indispensable (Fig. 1).

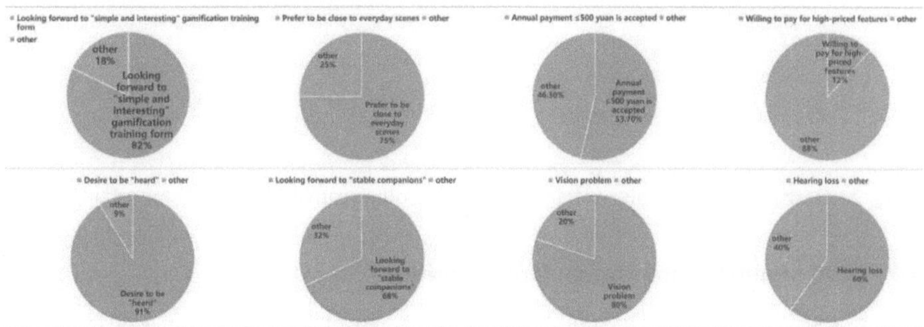

Fig. 1. Research Data Results of Multidimensional Need Profiles of Elderly MCI Patients.

3.3 Pain Points and Collaborative Needs of Family Caregivers

Through questionnaires and focus groups, it was found that family caregivers faced dual dilemmas of professional incompetence and psychological stress overload:

78% of caregivers needed real-time cognitive health data (such as memory trends and training completion rates), and 65% desired a "care strategy library" (such as training guidance scripts and memory confusion handling). They expected to obtain weekly reports through the family member-end "health data dashboard" (e.g., "20% progress in location memory tasks") and receive communication scripts templates (e.g., dealing with repeated questions). Psychologically, 65.8% showed anxiety and depression tendencies (e.g., Ms. Lin, 42, "worries about wandering off leading to insomnia"), and 59% expected a "caregiver mutual assistance community" to share coping skills (e.g., "strategies for handling elderly refusal to train"), requiring lightweight psychological courses (e.g., 10-min CBT emotional management videos) and anonymous forum support.

In terms of family collaboration, 62% of caregivers hoped to alleviate communication barriers caused by cognitive differences through "online memory activities" and "digital activity plan/review book production" (e.g., Mr. Wang, 38, "talking past each other"). The "intergenerational challenge" module (children propose activity themes, and the elderly generate activity plans and review videos through voice interaction) and the "family activity memory tree" construction function became key to emotional connection (Fig. 2).

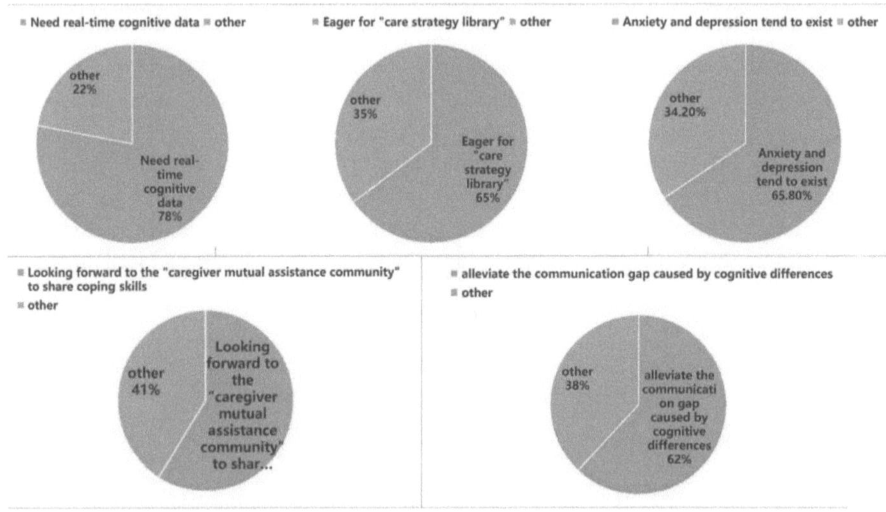

Fig. 2. Research Data Results of Pain Points and Collaborative Needs of Family Caregivers.

3.4 Need Summary and Design Opportunities

Based on the above needs, design opportunities focused on differentiated responses for the elderly end and family member end:

The elderly end needed to develop "life-scenario-based training games" (such as simulated supermarket shopping and family anniversary reviews), design a "virtual health assistant" with personalized dialogue capabilities, and construct a "large font + high contrast + voice-first" multimodal interaction system, accompanied by physical remote controls with tactile feedback. The family member end needed to build a "data-strategy-action" closed loop (real-time data + care guidance + remote control), establish a "caregiver support system" including stress assessment, psychological courses, and mutual assistance communities, and strengthen "intergenerational memory co-construction" functions (such as jointly completing memory activities and generating family activity memorabilia), ultimately achieving full-cycle support for active health management of elderly MCI patients (Table 1).

Table 1. Need Summary.

User Group	Core Need Dimensions	Key Design Opportunities
Elderly MCI Patients	Cognitive Intervention	Develop "life-scenario-based training games" (e.g., "simulated supermarket shopping," "family anniversary review") with difficulty automatically adapted to cognitive levels
	Emotional Companionship	Design a "virtual health assistant" with personalized dialogue capabilities (e.g., remembering the elderly's preferred activity themes) and support multimodal emotional feedback
	Physiological Adaptation	Adopt a "large font + high contrast + voice-first" interaction system and develop physical remote controls with tactile feedback
Family Caregivers	Care Support	Construct a "data-strategy-action" closed loop: real-time health data + care guidance + remote control (e.g., setting training reminders)
	Psychological Support	Establish a "caregiver support system" including stress assessment, psychological courses, and mutual assistance communities
	Family Collaboration	Design "intergenerational memory co-construction" functions to promote emotional interaction between caregivers and the elderly, such as jointly completing memory tasks and generating family activity memorabilia

4 Strategy Construction: Hierarchical Service Design Based on the 4PCS Theory

Through systematic research on cases and user needs, this study takes the Active Health 4PCS theoretical model (Proactiveness, Preventiveness, Precision, Personalization, Co-construction and Sharing, Self-discipline and Autonomy) as the core framework, integrating multimodal interaction and data-driven technologies to construct hierarchical service strategies covering the entire process of active health management for elderly MCI patients.

4.1 Proactiveness Strategy: Activating the Endogenous Motivation for Health Management

To activate the endogenous motivation of elderly individuals for health management, gamified design and emotional interaction can be used to stimulate their willingness to participate actively. A "Health Energy Value" quantification system is constructed, where elderly users can obtain 50–100 energy values by completing 10-min cognitive games or 5-min recollection dialogues daily. If they meet the standard for 7 consecutive days, they can unlock a "Weekly Challenge Package." Energy values have multiple redemption functions, including exchanging for virtual medals like the "Memory Keeper," redeeming physical goods at community supermarkets (exchange ratio: 1000 energy values ≈ 10 RMB), and unlocking privileged functions such as personalized topic libraries. Meanwhile, a "Family Energy Leaderboard" is introduced, where family members accumulate energy values through care tasks like uploading training photos, which are merged with the elderly's data to form an intergenerational collaborative motivation mechanism.

The virtual health assistant "Xiaokang" presents as an "urban community health activity manager," designed with an approachable and vibrant image suitable for ages 6–17. Its voice incorporates dialectal vocabulary (e.g., Cantonese "得闲饮茶" [dē xián yǐn chá, meaning "free to drink tea"]), with a speaking speed controlled at 110–120 words per minute. Combined with mouth movement migration technology, it achieves dynamic expression matching (e.g., smiling and nodding when mentioning happy topics), and proactively initiates greetings daily (e.g., "Aunt Mei, have you eaten? Shall we do a memory activity on the theme of old movies?") to effectively reduce the elderly's sense of passive waiting.

Existing research provides theoretical and practical support for this strategy. The team of Kang Qingchun from Hunan University [8] integrated vibrotactile and visual elements into different levels of music therapy through experimental design, helping patients engage in fun interactions with training products and improving their initiative to participate in training. The research of Guan Zhiyan from Yanshan University [9] also confirms that immersive interaction experiences between products and users can enhance patients' positive effects in emotional, behavioral, and cognitive dimensions. In practical applications, to improve the enthusiasm of elderly individuals to participate in health promotion activities, some elderly communities and nursing homes use "points redemption supermarkets" or "points banks" to encourage the elderly to engage in physical and cognitive exercise. For example, in 2020, the Longjiang Town Nursing Home launched the "Qile Bank" elderly participation incentive program, which uses a points reward mechanism to motivate elderly residents to actively participate in various activities, helping them feel the joy and value of life, strengthen social interaction, and thus promote the formation of healthy behaviors [10].

4.2 Preventiveness Strategy: Pre-Emptive Intervention and Risk Early Warning

Through early screening and life risk monitoring, the incidence of cognitive decline and unexpected events can be effectively reduced. Specific measures include: First, dynamic monitoring and hierarchical early warning of cognitive health, integrating professional cognitive scale tests (AD8, MoCa, MMSE, etc.) with AI multimodal interaction to implement multi-dimensional cognitive ability testing. The system generates a "Cognitive Health Weekly Report" every week. If the memory retention rate decreases by $\geq$ 15% for 3 consecutive weeks, a three-level progressive warning mechanism is triggered: a yellow warning prompts family members to increase companionship frequency and strengthen daily cognitive stimulation; an orange warning coordinates with professional teams to adjust intervention plans and simultaneously contacts community doctors for intervention assessment; a red warning directly connects to health centers, recommending in-depth offline medical evaluations.

Second, a multimodal intelligent to-do system supports voice/text dual-mode setting of reminder tasks such as memory activities and memory tests, ensuring information delivery through multimodal triggering mechanisms including mobile phone pop-ups, voice broadcasting (repeated 3 times), and physical remote control vibration. If a task is not completed, the system will repeat the reminder within 30 min; if it remains uncompleted for 3 consecutive times, it will automatically send an alarm message to family members, forming a closed loop of "reminder-tracking-intervention."

With family authorization, geofencing technology is used to set a safe activity range (e.g., a radius of 1 km) for geographic fence safety protection. When the elderly exceed the preset range, the system real-time pushes location information to family terminals and simultaneously triggers a voice reminder: "You have left the usual area. Do you need help?" to achieve dynamic monitoring of the elderly's outdoor activities.

For example, the Rui Wannian APP analyzes users' original data through big data technology, constructs a "3 + 1 model" (brain training + fitness exercise + dietary therapy science + check-in supervision), and provides one-stop preventive services including training suggestions, fitness courses, brain training, and dietary therapy science for elderly individuals in different cognitive states. Users complete product or service interactions with third parties through mobile devices or online service platforms, achieving the convenience and precision of preventive intervention [11]. This model confirms the practical value of pre-emptive intervention in cognitive health management through the closed loop of "data collection-analysis-intervention."

4.3 Preventiveness Strategy: Pre-Emptive Intervention and Risk Early Warning

Constructing a dynamic intervention model based on user data to achieve precise adaptation of intervention plans and care strategies, the core lies in using Natural Language Processing (NLP) technology to analyze multi-dimensional data, forming personalized cognitive profiles and interest maps including memory type preferences (episodic/semantic/procedural memory), emotional tendency indices (positive/negative word ratio), and activity interest points (e.g., "children," "past work"). Based on this, the intelligent recommendation system implements differentiated interventions: for elderly individuals with semantic memory advantages but weak episodic memory, "timeline recollection" tasks are preferentially pushed, supplemented by multimodal stimuli such as old photos and scene sound effects; when the emotional tendency index is lower than 30 points, the system automatically triggers the "emotional soothing" mode, reducing cognitively challenging tasks and increasing activities such as mindful music listening and nostalgic video watching. The family member end presents real-time memory curves (based on AVLT-S score trend comparisons), emotional fluctuation maps (relying on speech emotion recognition technology), and training participation data (marking efficient periods such as 10 am) through a visual interface, and generates a Family Intervention Action Guide (e.g., "It is recommended to carry out 1 family activity recollection activity daily"), forming a closed-loop management of "data collection-analysis assessment-intervention feedback."

Scholars such as BACHYRITA from the University of California, Los Angeles, developed the "NeuroRacer" video game, which dynamically adjusts training load through a difficulty adaptive algorithm to precisely match the challenge intensity with the elderly's cognitive ability [12]. In addition, the exercise rehabilitation product service system designed by Gao Simin from Jiangnan University realizes collaboration among doctors, nurses, and family members based on backend data analysis. Through dynamic allocation of training task difficulty and real-time feedback on rehabilitation progress, it guides family members to participate in home training supervision, forming a collaborative mechanism of "assessment-intervention-feedback" [13], which enhances the participation initiative of patients and family members.

4.4 Personalization Strategy: User-Centered Interaction Design

Constructing a seamless interaction system oriented to individual physiological characteristics and preferences, the core is to achieve "one-size-fits-one" precise services through technical adaptation. The system defaults to voice interaction first; when voice recognition errors occur 3 consecutive times, it automatically switches to text input mode and doubles the keyboard size. For elderly individuals with hearing impairments, a gesture sliding function to switch topics is designed, simultaneously presenting 24px red-highlighted voice-to-text content to enhance visual recognition. At the hardware level, a 5-key active health remote control is developed, distinguishing functions through raised textures (e.g., circular "chat" button, square "training" button), and supporting Bluetooth connection to mobile phones for cross-device collaboration. In the field of content generation, the memory activity recording module relies on a three-level theme tree algorithm (e.g., "memory activation-old photo story gallery-old movies"), combined with OCR and image recognition technologies to automatically annotate materials such as old movie video clips and movie music uploaded by family members. For example, old movie videos can be associated with themes like "old movies-stars-movie ending songs," and generate guiding interactions: "Is this your favorite star? Let's sing the climax together," achieving natural connection between memory awakening and emotional resonance.

The Dutch project "Boerderij Op Aarde" (Farm on Earth) breaks through the passivity of traditional cognitive training, allowing the elderly to choose lifestyles based on their own interests and abilities, such as participating in daily group activities like garden and animal care, and having intergenerational dialogues with children and adults to construct a sense of purpose in the process of contributing value [10]. This "life as training" model integrates intervention into natural scenarios, providing a practical paradigm for personalized interaction design. In addition, the MemTrax testing tool significantly reduces the impact of language and cultural differences through a visual stimulation-based assessment form. Its global application demonstrates the universality of visual interaction in cross-group cognitive screening [14, 15], providing technical references for personalized adaptation in multicultural contexts.

4.5   Co-Construction and Sharing Strategy: Cross-Role Collaboration Network

Breaking the barriers of family care and social support, constructing a care ecosystem with multi-party collaboration of "elderly-family members-community medical staff-social resources," the core is to achieve cross-role linkage and resource integration through digital tools. The system establishes a virtual group mechanism, automatically initiating 15-min "health meetings" weekly, where the elderly can share training experiences (e.g., "like movie guessing games"), family members can feedback care difficulties (e.g., "the elderly are unwilling to cooperate with memory activities"), and community medical staff can provide personalized adjustment suggestions (e.g., "increase emotional regulation activities") based on the cognitive data and behavioral trajectories recorded by the system. The task allocation module supports division of labor and collaboration among family members (e.g., "brother is responsible for uploading activity materials, sister undertakes activity reminders") and real-time tracks task completion status, forming a care network with clear responsibilities. In terms of social resource docking, the system intercommunicates with the database of community elderly activity centers, real-time pushing nearby elderly-friendly activity information (e.g., "old movie concert on Thursday afternoon"). After the elderly sign up, the virtual assistant provides multimodal reminders (voice + SMS + device vibration) one day in advance and synchronizes with family members. At the same time, a university volunteer service system is introduced, realizing the closed-loop management of "online appointment-offline execution-effect feedback" for services such as "companion memory activities" and "technology-assisted elderly care" through demand matching mechanisms.

The effectiveness of cross-role collaboration has been verified in international practices: the Living Moments communication system developed by the MYRTET design team supports asynchronous social interaction between dementia patients and relatives through a three-element network application of "photos + text + audio-video." The system automatically generates postcard designs from shared information, reducing the communication threshold for individuals with cognitive impairments [16]. China's "Memory Café" service project, through the joint operation of elderly individuals with cognitive impairments, retired caregivers, and volunteers, takes "good friends with dementia" as the core concept, and attracts public participation through gamified interaction, not only constructing a patient-led social scene but also expanding the social support radius through the volunteer network. Such practices show that the deep integration of digital collaboration platforms and offline community resources can break through the limitations of traditional care by a single subject, form a three-dimensional care system of "family emotional support-professional medical guidance-social resource supplementation," and ultimately improve the quality of life and social participation of elderly individuals with cognitive impairments.

4.6   Self-Discipline Strategy: Cultivation of Healthy Behaviors

Through a structured habit-shaping path and knowledge empowerment system, systematically improving the elderly's self-health management capabilities. The core mechanism is to design a 21-day laddered behavior challenge program, stimulating internal motivation with progressive task difficulty: days 1–7 complete 5-min daily basic memory activities to establish regular participation habits; days 8–14 add 2-min memory activity review tasks to strengthen self-awareness; days 15–21 encourage independent initiation of family memory activity interactions, extending training scenarios to daily family life. The system awards "Bronze/Silver/Gold Habit Badges" to those who check in for 7, 14, and 21 consecutive days, and grants priority participation qualification in community health lectures, consolidating behavior patterns through honor incentives and social capital accumulation. A supporting short-video content matrix is updated 3–5 times a week, covering brain-building skills (e.g., step-by-step finger exercise tutorials), dietary interventions (e.g., walnut sesame paste recipes), and technology applications (e.g., animation of virtual assistant training principles). After watching, 1–2 related quizzes are automatically triggered (e.g., "Which fingers are mainly activated in finger exercises?"), and correct answers can obtain additional energy values, forming a knowledge closed loop of "input-consolidation-reinforcement."

Relevant practices confirm the effectiveness of laddered intervention: the team of Miao Wei from Beijing Institute of Technology proposed that product design based on medical rehabilitation theory needs to guide users to follow specific operation rules while allowing autonomous adjustment of training progress and automatically adjusting difficulty levels when encountering task bottlenecks [17]. The Bositeng Brain Health Online Training Course (https://bestcovered.com/) formulates personalized training plans for each elderly individual through the "assessment-customization-execution-feedback" model, gradually transitioning from basic cognitive tasks to complex thinking training, and cultivating autonomous health habits within a scientific evidence-based framework. This design strategy of "clear plans, visual rewards, and contextualized knowledge" not only reduces the threshold for behavior initiation but also enhances the elderly's sense of control over health management through continuous feedback, ultimately achieving the transformation from external guidance to internal self-discipline.

5 Design Practice: From Theoretical Model to System Implementation

5.1 Active Health Service Objectives and Interaction Architecture Design

Based on the Active Health 4PCS theoretical model and user need insights, this study integrates multimodal interaction technology and service design concepts to develop the "Kangyi Home" intelligent interaction system. Aiming to construct an active health management ecosystem of "family-technology-community" collaboration, the dual-end system of the "Kangyi Home" WeChat mini-program is designed to achieve a functional closed loop of immersive intervention at the elderly end and intelligent care at the family member end.

The elderly end focuses on "scenario-based cognitive activation," generating personalized activity cards daily through AI algorithms (such as "old movie memory" tasks based on interest maps), recommending offline community activities (such as "nostalgic exhibition" reservations) in combination with LBS technology. To-do reminders adopt a multimodal triggering mechanism of "voice setting + pop-up + vibration + broadcast" to ensure information reach rates. The activity module integrates AR/VR multimodal training (such as virtual supermarket shopping, block route planning) and real-time interaction with the "AI health assistant" (voice guidance, dynamic expression matching). The "My" page supports health data visualization, emergency contact with family members, and export of AI-generated "text + voice + video" memoirs, strengthening the perception of self-management.

The family member end focuses on "data-driven care support," presenting core indicators such as memory trends and training participation rates in real time through a "health data dashboard." The AI care recommendation system automatically generates intervention plans based on behavioral data (such as "recommending increased tactile gardening activities") and provides a care strategy library (communication language, task guidance skills) and psychological support modules (stress assessment, mutual assistance communities), forming a scientific care process of "monitoring-analysis-intervention (Fig. 3)."

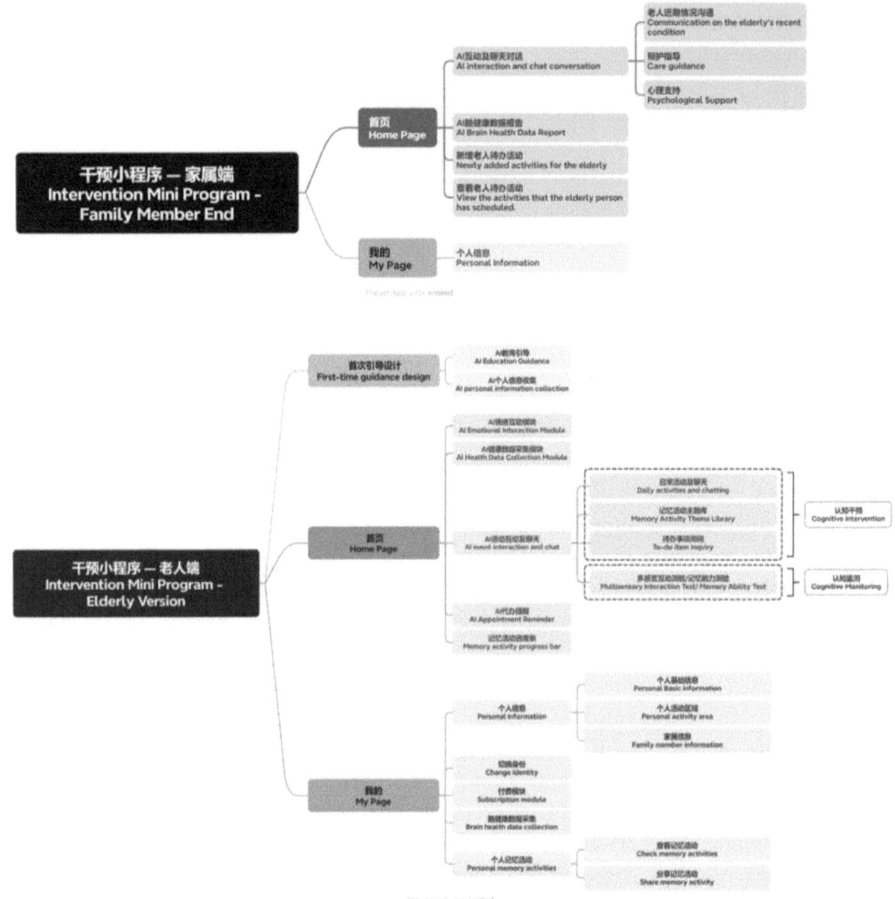

Fig. 3. Service Objectives and Architecture Design.

5.2   Construction of Active Health Interaction Design Strategies

AI-Driven Precise Information Adaptation.   Based on NLP technology to parse interest keywords in the elderly's conversations (such as "Stephen Chow," "Journey to the West"), AI generates customized visual materials (such as old movie poster creative memories, dynamic layout of family creative memory group photos), embedded in the background of training tasks to enhance the scenario-based intervention effect of the precision strategy. The integrated AI health data dashboard presents cognitive training completion rates in real time in the form of heat maps (green for normal/yellow for warning/red for high risk), and marks the safe activity range on the map interface in combination with geofencing technology. When the range is exceeded, a red flashing alarm at the interface edge is triggered to strengthen the risk monitoring capability of the preventive strategy.

Emotional Active Awakening and Intergenerational Collaboration. Supporting Mandarin, dialects (such as Shanghainese, Cantonese), and simplified language modes (short sentence structures, repeated keywords), AI real-time recognizes the elderly's language habits and switches automatically. Elderly individuals with hearing impairments can simultaneously receive dynamic sign language virtual human demonstrations generated by AI, reflecting the physiological difference adaptation of the personalization strategy. The virtual assistant "Xiaokang," trained based on a multimodal large model, initiates "life anchor" greetings regularly every day, triggers anniversary recollections in combination with calendar data, and activates the willingness to participate actively through emotional interaction, implementing the endogenous motivation stimulation of the proactiveness strategy. The family member end APP supports recording "voice memos" to promote interaction between family members and the elderly, constructing an intergenerational communication bridge for the co-construction and sharing strategy.

Multimodal Feedback Oriented to Habit Formation. AI analyzes the elderly's operation habit data and dynamically adjusts the vibration feedback mode—adopting "short vibration + rhythmic repetition" (repeating 3 times at 5-min intervals) for high-frequency tasks (such as memory activity reminders) and "long vibration + gradually increasing mode" for unfamiliar operations (such as new activity guidance), strengthening the habit formation of the self-discipline strategy through tactile memory.

Low-Threshold Multimodal Input and Family Collaboration. Family members remotely set an "operation whitelist" through the APP (such as only allowing training, calls, and emergency call functions). AI dynamically adjusts permissions based on the elderly's daily cognitive status (such as locking complex functions when memory decline worsens), while providing a "one-click proxy operation" function (such as remotely assisting in completing activity registration) to strengthen the care support of the co-construction and sharing strategy (Fig. 4).

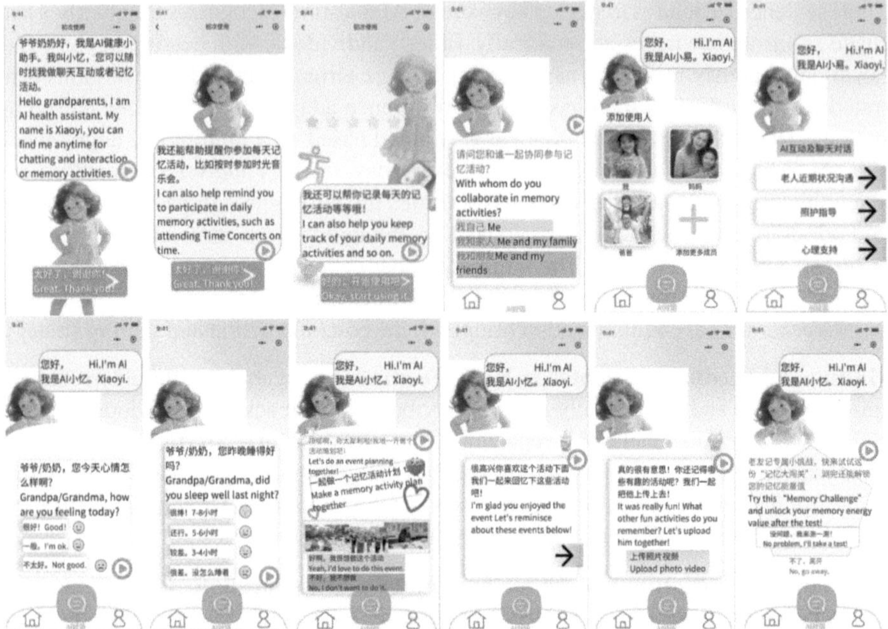

Fig. 4. Interface Design 1 of Active Health Interaction System

5.3 Development of Intelligent Interactive Non-Pharmacological Therapy Activity Library

Non-pharmacological therapy has attracted more attention from users due to its wide adaptability and absence of side effects on users. Non-pharmacological intervention methods for patients mainly include: cognitive intervention (mainly referring to cognitive training), reminiscence therapy, music therapy, exercise therapy, horticultural therapy, MAKS therapy, behavioral intervention, and other comprehensive treatment methods [18]. This study constructs a hierarchical activity library containing 500 + activities, realizing innovative design of five major categories of intervention activities through multi-technology integration (Fig. 5):

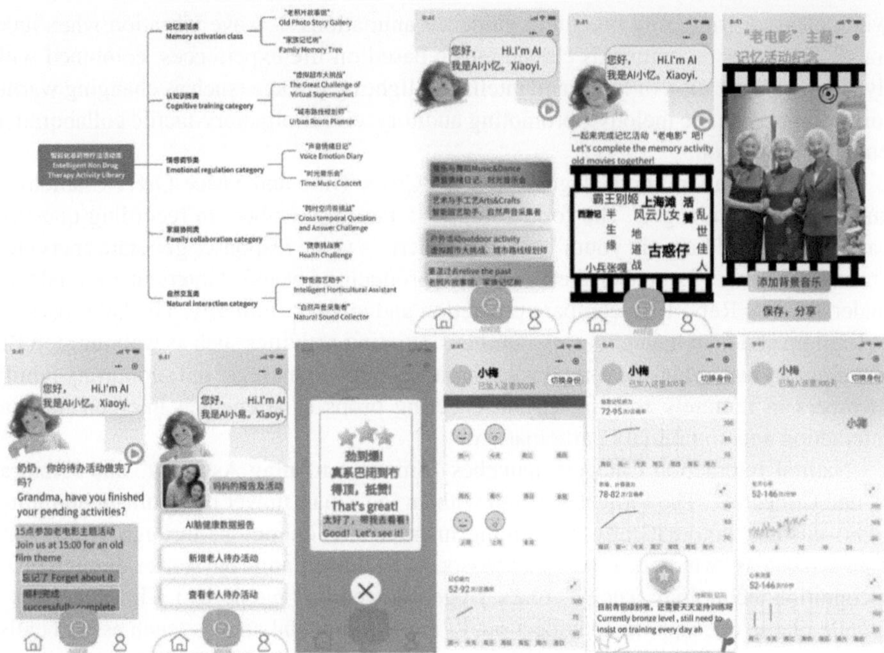

Fig. 5. Interface Design 2 of Active Health Interaction System.

Memory Activation Category reconstructs life narratives through the "Old Photo Story Gallery" and "Family Memory Tree." The former uses AI image recognition technology to analyze scene elements in old photos (such as buildings, clothing), combines voice guidance for recollection, and automatically transcribes voices to generate timeline files. The latter generates a visual family relationship map based on information provided by the elderly and family members, strengthening episodic memory and family connection through intergenerational collaboration in uploading materials and interactive Q&A (such as "guess the person in the photo").

Cognitive Training Category designs "Virtual Supermarket Challenge" and "City Route Planner." The former uses AR technology to simulate community supermarket scenes, where the elderly generate shopping lists through voice commands, combined with mobile phone gyroscopes to achieve real-scene scanning and virtual label overlay (such as "milk is in the second row front left"). The latter reproduces familiar blocks for the elderly through VR, using voice navigation tasks combined with tactile vibration error correction (such as vibration prompts for wrong route selection), and simultaneously recommends real safe routes based on geofencing to improve spatial memory and execution functions.

Emotional Regulation Category develops "Sound Emotion Diary" and "Time Concert." The former analyzes intonation and speech rate through speech emotion recognition technology to determine emotion levels (such as 85% pleasure), and links multimodal environmental feedback (playing bird calls + bright interface + fragrance release when pleased, triggering breathing guidance animations + wave vibration when anxious). The latter recommends classic music based on life experiences, combined with dynamic visualization of lyrics and intelligent lighting linkage (such as changing warm-toned lights with the melody), promoting auditory-visual-olfactory-tactile collaborative emotion regulation.

Family Collaboration Category creates "Cross-Time and Space Q&A Challenge" and "Health Challenge." The former supports family members in recording question cards (such as "dreams in youth"), and the elderly's voice responses generate encrypted "memory capsules" stored on the blockchain, producing a weekly "Intergenerational tacit understanding Report" to compare prediction and answer similarity. The latter uses AI to team up and match neighboring families, initiating activities such as walking step PK and memory task relays, real-time voice broadcasting of rankings, and supporting family members in remotely sending virtual cheering props to strengthen intergenerational interaction and community participation.

Natural Interaction Category launches "Smart Gardening Assistant" and "Natural Sound Collector." The former is paired with an IoT smart flower pot (built-in humidity, light sensors), automatically performing maintenance operations through voice commands (such as "water the roses"), and associating flower language stories through plant recognition technology (such as roses triggering wedding memories). The latter uses a mobile phone microphone to collect outdoor environmental sounds (such as bird calls, wind sounds), and AI analyzes and generates annotatable "sound postcards," while automatically recognizing abnormal sounds (such as car horns) to trigger safety warnings, activating multi-sensory natural memories.

5.4 Usability Verification: Wizard of Oz Testing and Quantitative Evaluation

Using the "Wizard of Oz Testing Method," researchers simulated AI assistant services with digital tools such as AI multimodal large models, interacting with 10 elderly MCI patients (aged 65–78, average disease duration 2.3 years) for 4 weeks, covering 90% of activity types. Combined with 5-level Likert scale and physiological index evaluations, the following findings were obtained:

Significant Improvement in Compliance: The daily usage duration extended from an initial 12 min to 28 min, with 78% of the elderly adhering to daily logins. Among them, the repeated participation rate of "memory activation" activities was the highest (63%), driven by personalized memory activities and multimodal feedback (such as vibration + voice encouragement).

Divergent Interaction Satisfaction: Visual readability (4.5 ± 0.5) and naturalness of voice interaction (4.3 ± 0.6) scored highly, but tactile feedback satisfaction was lower (3.8 ± 0.7), mainly due to the monotony of mobile phone vibration feedback. Elderly users suggested, "Vibrations should have different rhythms to distinguish task types" (Grandma Li, 72). Open-ended feedback showed that 72% of the elderly felt "chatting with AI about photos is like talking to old friends," and Grandpa Wang, 68, stated, "The AR supermarket task was challenging, but I felt a great sense of accomplishment after completing it."

Significant Family Collaboration Effect: The family member end usage rate reached 92%, with 65% of family members reporting significantly reduced care pressure. 38%

actively participated in online activities (such as cross-time and space Q&A), and inter-generational communication frequency increased by 40%. Structured topics provided by AI (such as "career experiences," "childhood stories") became key to alleviating communication barriers (Fig. 6).

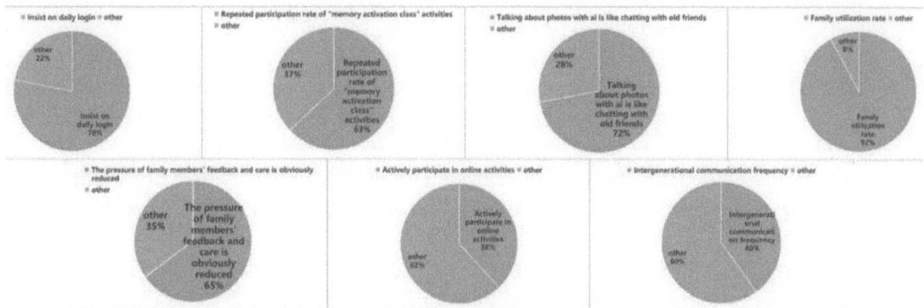

Fig. 6. Verification Result Data.

6 Conclusions and Prospects

Based on the Active Health 4PCS theoretical model, this study constructs a service framework for intelligent interaction systems in home-based care for elderly MCI patients, integrating multimodal human-computer interaction. The "Kangyi Home" WeChat mini-program, through design practice and usability verification, confirms the feasibility of cognitive intervention driven by the active health concept. The system improves elderly intervention compliance and family care efficiency through an AI multimodal activity library and dual-end collaborative architecture, achieving quantitative improvement in cognitive function. The adaptability of multimodal interaction scenarios and family collaboration mechanisms are key to breaking through traditional intervention barriers.

Future research will deepen innovation in three aspects: technology integration, clinical validation, and ecosystem construction, promoting the upgrading of active health management for elderly MCI patients toward "precision and ecologicalization," providing a design paradigm for addressing population aging, and helping achieve the social goal of "healthy aging."

References

1. Guanyan, T.: Information Consulting Co., Ltd.: In-depth research on the current status and development trend forecast of China's nursing home industry (2023–2030) (2023). https://www.chinabaogao.com/baogao/202309/664786.html. Accessed 2 Feb 2025
2. Jia, J., Wang, F., Wei, C., Qin, Y.: The prevalence of dementia in urban and rural areas of China. Alzheimer's Dementia **10**(1), 1–9 (2014)
3. Qin, Y., Zhang, J.J., Wu, Y., et al.: Research progress on the reversal of mild cognitive impairment to normal cognition. Chin. Gen. Pract. **24**(27), 3506–3509 (2021)
4. Li, Y.E., Gao, C.: Policy changes and optimization strategies for the coordinated development of China's elderly care cause and industry. Acad. Forum **48**(02), 81–94 (2025)

5. Li, X.C., Yu, M.S.: Active health: from concept to model. China Sport Sci. **40**(02), 83–89 (2020)
6. Liu, J., Li, W., Yao, H., Liu, J.: Proactive health: an imperative to achieve the goal of Healthy China. China CDC Weekly **4**(36), 799–801 (2022)
7. Deng, R., Zhang, Y.: Evaluation methods of postoperative cognitive dysfunction (POCD). J. Southwest Med. Univ. **42**(01), 93–97 (2019)
8. Kang, Q.C.: Research on multi-sensory music therapy product design for Alzheimer's elderly. (Doctoral dissertation). Hunan University (2021)
9. Guan, Z.Y.: Multi-channel intervention training product design for elderly MCI patients. (Master's thesis). Yanshan University (2024). https://doi.org/10.27440/d.cnki.gysdu.2024.001109
10. Xu, Q.: Research on intervention service design for elderly mild cognitive impairment based on behavior change theory. (Master's thesis). Jiangnan University (2024). https://doi.org/10.27169/d.cnki.gwqgu.2024.000493
11. Mou, L., Yu, L.H.: Discussion on how to help the elderly prevent Alzheimer's disease in the big data smart elderly care system—taking the Rui Wannian APP as an example. Peer **6**, 31–33 (2022)
12. Bachyrta, P., Collins, C.C., Saunders, F.A., et al.: Vision substitution by tactile image projection. Nature **221**, 963–964 (1969)
13. Gao, S.M.: Design of exercise rehabilitation products for elderly with mild cognitive impairment based on guided education. (Master's thesis). Jiangnan University (2022)
14. Zhou, X., Ashford, J.W.: Advances in screening instruments for Alzheimer's disease. Aging Med. (Milton) **2**(2), 88–93 (2019)
15. Zhang, Y., Pei, Z.: MemTrax: a digital continuous memory cognitive test tool for screening and monitoring cognitive changes. Alzheimer's Dis. Related Disorders **8**(03), 200–206 (2025)
16. Ranasinghe, N., Jain, P., Ngoc Tram, N.T., et al.: Season traveller: multisensory narration for enhancing the virtual reality experience. In: Proceedings of the 2018 CHI Conference on Human Factors in Computing Systems, pp. 13–15 (2018). https://doi.org/10.1145/3173574.3173721
17. Miao, W.: Research on product design for elderly with mild cognitive impairment. (Master's thesis). Beijing Institute of Technology (2015)
18. Xu, S.: Prevalence and progression of subjective cognitive decline among older adults: MIND-China cohort study. (Master's thesis). Shandong University (2022)

Design of Stroke Rehabilitation Experience Services from the Perspective of Smart Healthcare

Zihan Mei[1(✉)], Qimeng Mei[1], Jun Liu[1], and Xiaohui Hou[2]

[1] School of Art and Design, Wuhan University of Technology, Wuhan 430070, HB, China
2049093284@qq.com
[2] School of Mechanical and Electrical Engineering, Wuhan University of Technology, Wuhan 430070, HB, China

Abstract. Stroke, a leading cause of adult disability worldwide, poses significant challenges to rehabilitation due to its high incidence, resource shortages, and low patient motivation. To address these issues, this study aims to develop a community-based smart rehabilitation service system that integrates digital platforms, virtual reality, and gamified therapy concepts. Using a mixed-methods approach—including case analyses of advanced rehabilitation technologies, interviews with stroke survivors, and field observations in hospital settings—the study identifies key constraints and reconstructs rehabilitation touchpoints to optimize patient engagement. The findings suggest that this integrated framework effectively enhances patient motivation, improves rehabilitation outcomes, and alleviates professional resource shortages. Overall, this research provides fresh insights at the intersection of design and healthcare, offering strategies for more efficient, patient-centered stroke rehabilitation services.

Keywords: Smart Community · Stroke Patients · Gamification Therapy · Proactive Health Design · Rehabilitation Service System Design

1 Introduction

Stroke, one of China's most critical public health challenges, results in significant brain tissue damage and adult disability. Data from the China Stroke Statistical Report 2022 (National Health Commission of China 2022) and the China Stroke Prevention and Treatment Report 2023 (National Health Commission of China 2023) indicate that among people aged 40 and above, 12.42 million suffer from stroke, with a new or recurrent stroke every 10 s and one fatality every 28 s. Approximately 75% of survivors experience lasting sequelae and 40% face severe disabilities, while an increasing incidence among younger individuals further exacerbates the socioeconomic burden.

Current stroke rehabilitation in China predominantly relies on a hospital-centered "drug treatment–physical therapy–exercise therapy" model, which faces structural challenges including an imbalance between available medical resources and patient demand (Tan 2021), a disconnect from patients' daily lives, and a monotonous training process

V. G. Duffy (Ed.): HCII 2025, LNCS 16339, pp. 329–338, 2026.
https://doi.org/10.1007/978-3-032-13012-9_23

that lacks effective incentives (Bai 2020; Liu et al. 2020). Additionally, community-based rehabilitation services remain fragmented; despite initiatives like the Healthy China 2030 Planning Outline (State Council Office 2016), community hospitals often operate with outdated equipment and limited personnel (Bao et al. 2012), and existing smart rehabilitation devices suffer from suboptimal age-friendly design with complex interfaces and inadequate feedback (Gao 2019).

Against this backdrop, there is an urgent need to innovate stroke rehabilitation service design. Drawing on insights from participatory community healthcare service design (Zhang et al. 2018), our study proposes an integrated intelligent rehabilitation service system that connects hospitals, communities, and homes using digital platforms, immersive virtual reality, and gamified interactive designs. Research supporting the potential of this approach is found in studies on urban community hospitals, smart healthcare service design for the elderly, and chronic disease health management, while national policy guidelines (State Council Office 2016; Bao et al. 2012) and advances in smart device design (Gao 2019) further underscore the benefits. By improving both physical and psychological outcomes, the proposed system aims to transform stroke rehabilitation from a passive treatment process into an active, user-centered experience, offering valuable theoretical and practical insights for future design.

2   Methods

This study adopted a mixed-method approach combining case studies, interviews, and field observations to systematically investigate the rehabilitation experience of stroke patients within the context of smart healthcare. The objective was to derive user-centered design strategies based on insights from user needs and behavioral patterns.

2.1   Case Study

We conducted an in-depth analysis of representative rehabilitation projects worldwide that utilize advanced technologies such as smart wearable devices, and virtual reality to enhance stroke rehabilitation outcomes (Zhang et al. 2021; Kaku et al. 2020). Our case study not only examined these cutting-edge technological applications but also explored emerging trends in the transformation of stroke rehabilitation services, with a focus on how integrated digital solutions can address the limitations of traditional models. This investigation provided insights into various approaches that aim to enhance data accuracy, improve patient engagement, and optimize therapy delivery.

To overcome these limitations, we identified three transformative directions. First, integrating community health management—illustrated by the "4G" management model and the establishment of "Health Care Homes"—facilitates real-time linkage between patient data and medical resources, reducing spatial limitations and lowering patient costs (Li et al. 2022). Second, under the Healthy China 2030 strategy, a proactive health design leverages digital tools and IoT-enabled systems to build behaviour-driven feedback loops that not only boost patient self-management but also significantly shorten rehabilitation cycles. Third, the innovative application of gamified virtual rehabilitation transforms monotonous physical exercises into immersive, interactive tasks; for example, smart rehabilitation gloves dynamically adjust training intensity based on electromyography signals, thereby enhancing patient engagement and enabling remote monitoring by clinicians. These integrated findings form a robust foundation for developing a comprehensive, user-centered smart rehabilitation service system that can deliver personalized and effective stroke rehabilitation.

2.2 Interview

To gain further insights into patient needs, we conducted in-depth interviews with 28 stroke patients in collaboration with three rehabilitation centers. Participants ranged in age from 40 to 65 and were at various stages of recovery—including early recovery, functional training, and maintenance phases. The interviews focused on: (1) Satisfaction with existing rehabilitation devices and services; (2) Major pain points during device usage; and (3) Expectations for future rehabilitation solutions. Through qualitative analysis, we extracted specific feedback on technology acceptance, psychological support needs, and functional optimization.

In addition, field observations at the Neurology and Rehabilitation Departments of Hubei Provincial People's Hospital revealed that outdated facilities and insufficient equipment lead to long waiting times and challenges in providing personalized guidance, largely due to a high doctor-to-patient ratio (approximately 0.4:10). Many patients described the rehabilitation process as "tiring and boring" and repetitive. Survey data showed that the majority of users, mainly aged 40–70, experience motor, cognitive, and language/emotional impairments; 65% prefer training sessions lasting 10–30 min while only 25% can sustain sessions beyond 30 min. Additionally, 45% of patients favor home-based rehabilitation, 30% prefer community centers, and merely 20% rely on hospital-based care, highlighting the urgent need for decentralized rehabilitation services (Fig. 1).

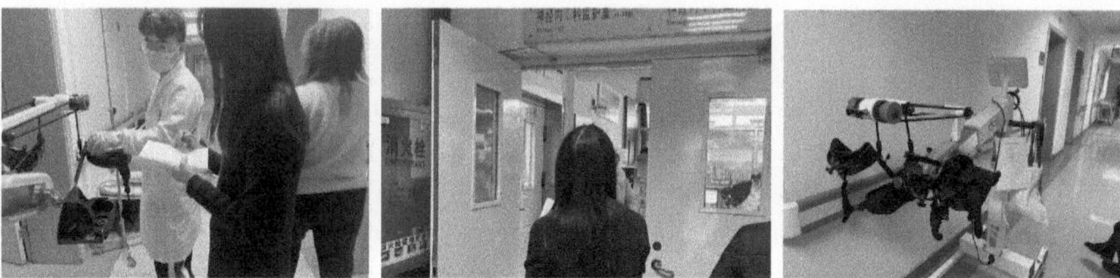

Fig. 1. Field observations at Hubei Provincial People's Hospital.

2.3 Result

Our integrated analysis of case studies, interviews, and field observations indicates that traditional stroke rehabilitation services are burdened by outdated facilities, poor device adaptability, complex interfaces, long waiting times, and insufficient personalized guidance, all of which undermine patient motivation and recovery outcomes. Patient feedback reveals a strong preference for short, high-efficiency training sessions and decentralized rehabilitation settings such as home or community-based care, underscoring the critical need for enhanced interactive feedback and psychological support. In contrast, emerging technologies—including brain-computer interfaces, wearable devices, and virtual reality—combined with innovative strategies like community-based health management, proactive health design, and gamified rehabilitation, offer promising solutions to overcome these challenges. The results suggest that integrating real-time feedback mechanisms, streamlined user interfaces, and enhanced digital support can significantly improve patient engagement and self-management, ultimately leading to better functional recovery and reduced healthcare costs. These findings emphasize the urgent need for a comprehensive, user-centered smart rehabilitation system that redefines the rehabilitation experience in the era of smart healthcare.

3 System Design

3.1 Conceptual Design

This study proposes the "JOYREVIVE" stroke rehabilitation service system from the perspective of integrating smart healthcare with community health management (Guo 2021). The system establishes a full-cycle rehabilitation framework spanning hospitals, communities, and homes by combining digital technologies, gamified therapies, and community resource networks. The brand "JOYREVIVE"—combining "Joy" and "Revive"—symbolizes its core mission to reshape the rehabilitation pathway for stroke patients through a dual-driven approach that merges engaging, gamified experiences with scientifically based functional recovery. Anchored by a community stroke unit management model, the system leverages smart hardware, a digital rehabilitation platform, and multimodal interactive technologies to overcome traditional challenges such as resource shortages, low patient adherence, and fragmented services. Its design transforms monotonous physical training into immersive sessions via virtual reality and gamified task design with real-time data and dynamic algorithm optimization, while establishing a collaborative network linking hospital specialists, community centers, family members, and non-profit organizations to support remote guidance and emotional support. Moreover, it reduces technical barriers for middle-aged and elderly patients through low-threshold interaction design. In summary, our analysis of three transformative directions underscores the potential of this integrated approach to enhance rehabilitation efficiency, empower patient engagement, and alleviate imbalances in medical resource distribution and family caregiving pressures.

3.2 System Map

The JOYREVIVE service system leverages policy support, technological empowerment, and resource integration through smart communities to establish a full-cycle stroke rehabilitation network spanning hospitals, communities, and homes. As shown in Fig. 2, government agencies, healthcare institutions, technology suppliers, and family members collaborate to form a closed-loop ecosystem that encompasses policy supervision, resource coordination, data sharing, and collaborative care (Shi et al. 2022). Built on the JOYREVIVE Rehabilitation Cloud Platform, the system integrates a user interface module that uses voice prompts, haptic feedback, and optimized layouts to reduce barriers for older users; a data management module that collects real-time motion data and synchronizes it with clinical systems to support precise decision-making (Liu et al. 2020); an interactive training module employing virtual reality and gamified design to transform monotonous training into engaging tasks; and a hardware support module equipped with motion sensors and wearable devices for corrective feedback (Abibullaev et al. 2013). Additionally, community stroke units serve as key nodes to bridge hospital specialists, community centers, and home caregivers, enabling continuous data sharing, remote guidance, and emotional support, thus alleviating resource imbalances and enhancing rehabilitation efficiency.

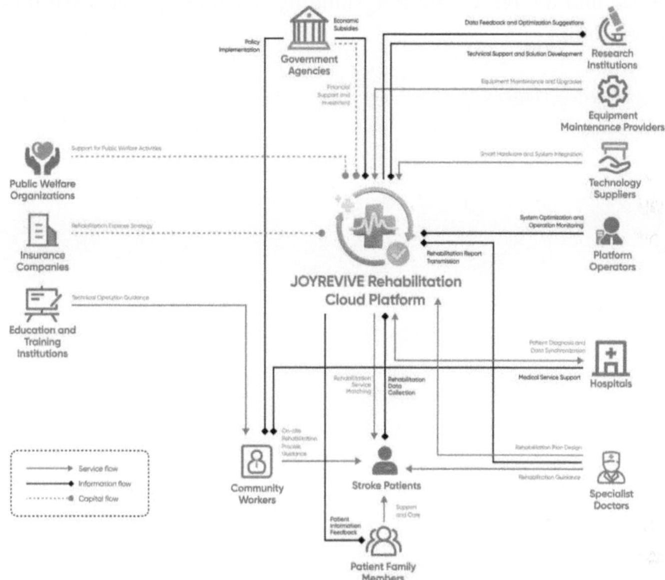

Fig. 2. System map of JOYREVIVE.

3.3 Service Blueprint

The service blueprint for the "JOYREVIVE" stroke rehabilitation system illustrates a patient-centered process that spans from policy support to family involvement, engaging various stakeholders—including government agencies, medical institutions, community staff, and family members—via the "JOYREVIVE Rehabilitation Cloud Platform".

As depicted in Fig. 3, the rehabilitation journey is divided into four primary stages: Assessment & Registration, Adaptation & Preparation, Training & Feedback, and Community & Family Integration. During the initial phase, patients undergo a hospital-based evaluation to collect baseline data (e.g., motor function), followed by registration, where clinical records are linked to the community system to generate an initial plan. Upon referral to a community rehabilitation center, they are introduced to the system's VR-based and wearable-device features, with step-by-step onboarding support. Concurrently, real-time data from sensors—such as electromyographic signals—allow specialists to refine personalized rehabilitation strategies. Subsequently, the Training & Feedback stage enables patients to conduct daily exercises at home or in the community, with difficulty levels dynamically adjusted by the system. An interactive module tracks motion precision and physiological responses, providing timely feedback via a dedicated app for both patients and clinicians. Finally, Community & Family Integration ensures continuous adherence through community check-ins, volunteer services, and emotional support from family members, who can monitor progress via the "Family Dashboard." Insurance models that adjust premiums based on rehabilitation milestones further incentivize patient engagement. By seamlessly combining policy support, hospital expertise, community coordination, and family participation, "JOYREVIVE" creates a closed-loop, data-driven service that boosts patient motivation, enhances functional outcomes, and addresses the longstanding resource and accessibility challenges in stroke rehabilitation.

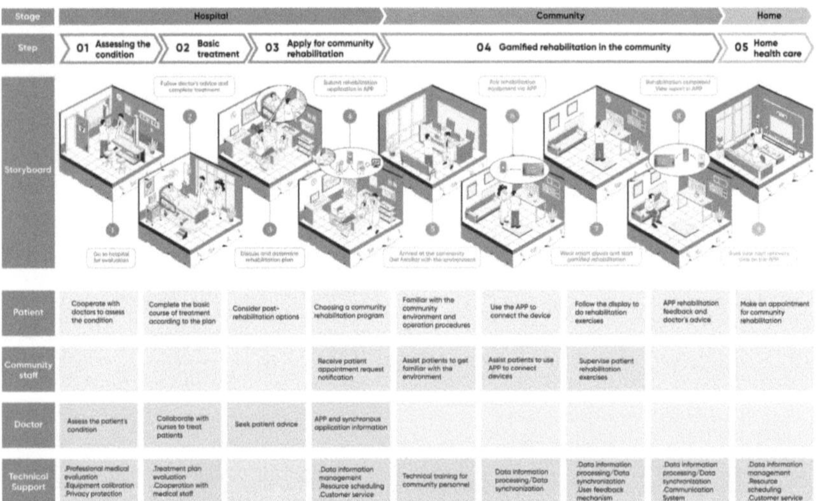

Fig. 3. Service blueprint of JOYREVIVE.

4 User Interface Design

The JOYREVIVE app is designed to offer an intuitive rehabilitation experience by using a primarily orange interface accented with purple. This concise color scheme—chosen to stimulate energy, enthusiasm, creativity, and wisdom—not only enhances user engagement but also compensates for reduced color discrimination in older adults, as supported by research (Zhang 2022). A minimalist linear style for icons, with uniform line thickness, color, and shape, further ensures clarity and reduces cognitive load.

The entire service process begins with user registration and login. The app guides users through the initial setup to create a personal account. Once the account is created, users can bind their personal information on the profile page. Users can then submit a community rehabilitation application and schedule their rehabilitation appointments. Afterward, users enter the rehabilitation plan formulation phase. Based on the user's health information and rehabilitation goals, the app helps users view and customize a personalized rehabilitation plan in the "Start Rehabilitation" module. Upon arriving at the community at the scheduled time, users connect to the device via the app, synchronize data, and select a game mode for rehabilitation. After completing the rehabilitation session, users can provide feedback within the app and view their rehabilitation progress. Doctors, based on the user's feedback and progress, can adjust and optimize the rehabilitation plan to better assist the user's recovery (Fig. 4).

Fig. 4. JOYREVIVE app user flow and interfaces.

5   Wearable Smart Rehabilitation Devices Design

The "JOYREVIVE" system's hardware consists of a smart rehabilitation glove and a non-invasive brain–computer interface (BCI) headband, both engineered to capture precise physiological data and faxcilitate multimodal interaction. As illustrated in Fig. 5, the smart glove integrates advanced nanofiber fabric with a flexible circuit board, enabling high-sensitivity data collection while maintaining a lightweight form factor suitable for prolonged wear (Li et al. 2023). Embedded electromyography and pressure sensors transmit real-time hand movement and force data via Bluetooth to a mobile application, allowing the system to deliver instant feedback and dynamically adjust task difficulty. Meanwhile, the lightweight BCI headband continuously monitors electroencephalogram signals through micro biosensors and a low-power Bluetooth module (Zhou 2021). This configuration provides neurofeedback for cognitive training, especially in tasks requiring simultaneous fine-motor control and mental focus. For example, in the "digital embroidery" game showcased in Fig. 6, patients must execute precise hand grasping while maintaining concentration; the system then generates a composite score based on the bimodal data and offers vibratory cues to guide corrective actions.

In addition to capturing and processing user input, the hardware seamlessly integrates with community rehabilitation center terminals, forming a closed-loop network that encompasses data acquisition, cloud-based analysis, and device coordination. Figure 5 highlights how multiple sensing modalities—such as force judgment, synergy training, and real-time physiological recording—are combined to enhance user engagement. Figure 6 further demonstrates the user interface in three interactive rehabilitation games, including a Mahjong-based scenario, a digital embroidery task, and a Tai Chi guidance exercise. By leveraging cutting-edge materials, wireless communication, and sensor fusion technologies, the "JOYREVIVE" system delivers immediate, personalized feedback to support both motor and cognitive rehabilitation. Recent findings also suggest that combining wearable sensors with non-invasive BCI devices significantly boosts rehabilitation monitoring accuracy and patient adherence, reinforcing the efficacy of this integrated approach (Zhang et al. 2021).

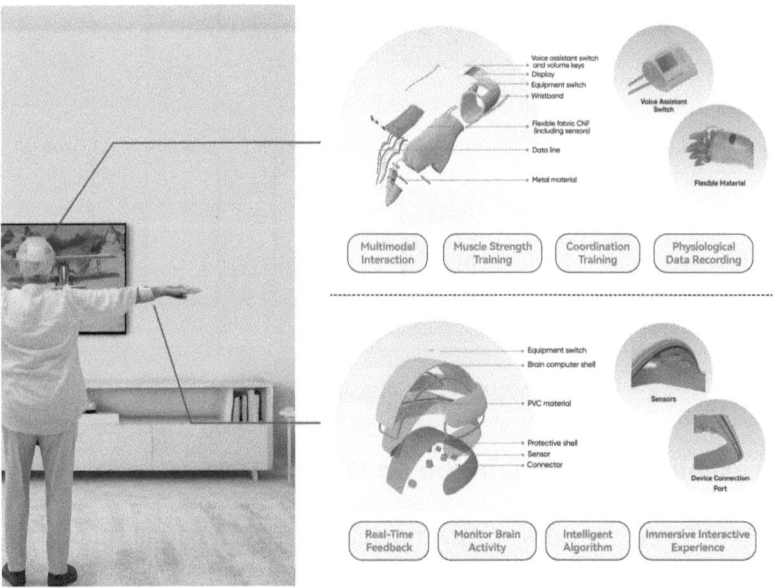

Fig. 5. Smart glove and BCI headband.

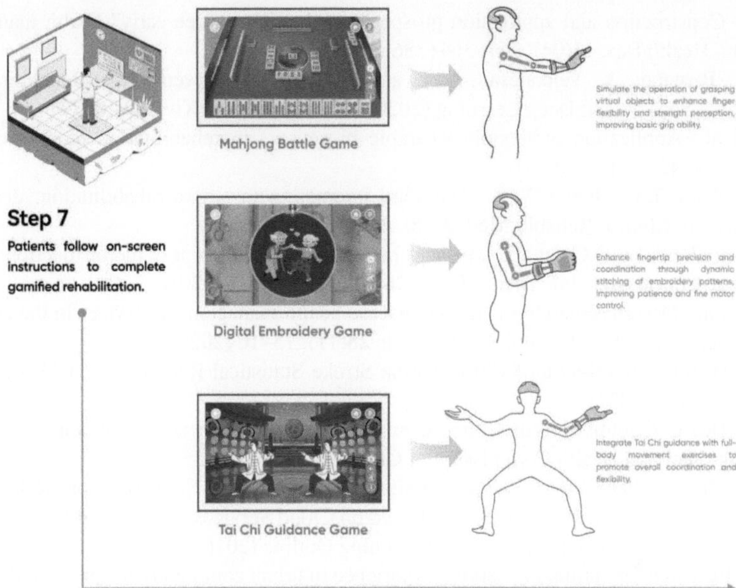

Fig. 6. Gamified rehabilitation interaction demonstration.

6   Conclusion

In conclusion, this study proposes an integrated smart rehabilitation system that combines digital platforms, immersive virtual reality, gamified therapy, and proactive health design to establish a patient-centered, community-driven approach. By creating a closed-loop network that connects hospitals, community centers, and home care, the system facilitates continuous data sharing, personalized treatment, and real-time feedback. Its innovative design elements—including a service blueprint, system map, user interface, and wearable devices—not only mitigate resource shortages and boost patient engagement but also empower individuals to take active roles in their recovery. While initial results are promising, further user testing and iterative refinements are recommended to ensure scalability and adaptability. Overall, this research provides new insights at the intersection of design and healthcare, offering strategies that can significantly enhance the quality of life for stroke survivors and reshape the future of rehabilitation service delivery.

References

Bao, Y., et al.: Research on the resource status and development of community health service institutions in Shanghai. Chin. Health Resour. **15**(6), 502–504 (2012)

Bai, R.: Research on smart healthcare service design for the elderly in community-based home care models. Elderly Care Serv. **4**, 87–90 (2020)

Gao, Y.: Research on innovative paths for experience value in service design. New Aesthetics **40**(4), 92–96 (2019)

Guo, Q.: Construction and application prospects of the 5G+ "three early" health management system. Health Res. **41**(04), 361–364+386 (2021)

Kaku, A., Parnandi, A., Venkatesan, A., et al.: Towards Data-Driven Stroke Rehabilitation via Wearable Sensors and Deep Learning (2020). arXiv preprint arXiv:2004.08297

Li, J., et al.: Application of flexible wearable biosensors in rehabilitation monitoring. Sens. Microsyst. **42**(1), 1–5 (2023)

Li, Y.F., Zhou, J.Y., Huang, W.X.: Gamified interaction in stroke rehabilitation: design and application. Chin. J. Rehabil. Med. **37**(6), 456–462 (2022)

Liu, L., Liu, Y.G., Li, Q.Q., et al.: Advances in automatic assessment of motor function in stroke patients. Chin. J. Rehabil. Theory Pract. **26**(9), 1028–1032 (2020)

Liu, X., et al.: Design research on chronic disease health management services in the context of smart healthcare. Sci. Technol. Econ. Guide **28**(11), 15–16 (2020)

National Health Commission of China: China Stroke Statistical Report 2022. China Statistical Press, Beijing (2022)

National Health Commission of China. China Stroke Prevention and Treatment Report 2023. Beijing: National Health Commission of China (2023)

Shi, S.Z., Zhang, H.H., Zhou, C., et al.: Design of a Virtual (VR) Somatosensory Rehabilitation Training Platform for Ischemic Stroke Based on Cloud Services. Biomedical Preprints (2022)

State Council Office. Healthy China 2030 Planning Outline (2016)

Tan, W.: Research on optimizing service experience in urban community hospitals in the context of smart healthcare. Industry **5**, 58–62 (2021)

Zhang, L., et al.: Advances in wearable sensor integration for stroke rehabilitation. J. Neuroeng. Rehabil. **16**(1), 142 (2021)

Zhang, S.M.: Research on age-friendly design of APP interaction interface. Electr. Components Inf. Technol. **6**(7), 84–88 (2022)

Zhang, X., et al.: Research on participatory community healthcare service design methods for elderly chronic diseases. Packaging Eng. **39**(12), 197–202 (2018)

Zhang, L., Wang, H., Chen, Y.: Application of virtual reality in stroke rehabilitation: a review. Rehabil. Sci. Technol. **18**(2), 89–104 (2021)

Zhou, T.: Optimization of low-power bluetooth technology in medical devices. Electr. Appl. **47**(7), 89–93 (2021)

Application of eXtended Reality in the Context of Industry 5.0: A Technological Framework for Prevention and Recovery Based on the Action-Observation Paradigm

Emilia Scalona[1]([✉]), Alessandro Piol[2], Martina Mosso[2], Elisa Soldi[2],
Maddalena Fabbri Destro[3], Pietro Avanzini[3], Elisa Taglione[4],
and Nicola Francesco Lopomo[5]

[1] Centro Protesi INAIL, Vigorso, Italy
`e.scalona@inail.it`
[2] Dipartimento Di Ingegneria Dell'Informazione, Università Degli Studi Di Brescia, Brescia, Italy
[3] Istituto Di Neuroscienze, Consiglio Nazionale Delle Ricerche, Roma, Italy
[4] Centro Di Riabilitazione Motoria INAIL, Volterra, Italy
[5] Department of Design, Politecnico Di Milano, Milano, Italy

Abstract. In the era of Industry 5.0, the synergy between humans and technologies has become one of the key elements both to pursue the needs for an agile production and deal with the necessity of ensuring worker health and wellbeing. In this context, the eXtended Reality (XR) technologies, such as Mixed Reality (MR), have been representing fundamental tools to improve both synergetic cooperation within the industrial setting, provide support in assessing and managing risk exposure within the working environment, allow proper training to reduce those risks, ensure effective rehabilitation track after the onset of the disorders. Within this latter context, Virtual Reality (VR) has been successfully used in providing Action Observation Treatment (AOT), a complementary rehabilitative approach that is able to improve and/or speed up functional recovery thanks to the exploitation of the "mirror" mechanism via proper visual stimuli. This study aimed at taking the advantage of the potential of the integration between MR and AOT under the Industry 5.0 umbrella, by addressing not only the needs for effective rehabilitation among working population but also the possibility of reducing the risk exposure - and thus preventing disorder onset - by promoting correct motor behaviors via implicit training. In order to achieve this goal a technological and methodological framework is here presented.

Keywords: eXtrened Reality · Action Observation · Mixed Reality · Industry 5.0

1 Introduction

The pillars that define the concept of *Industry 5.0* deeply differs from those ones that allowed to implement the *Industry 4.0* approach; to fully recognize these differences we need to focus first on this latter one. In fact, the term Industry 4.0 was first introduced in

© The Author(s), under exclusive license to Springer Nature Switzerland AG 2026
V. G. Duffy (Ed.): HCII 2025, LNCS 16339, pp. 339–354, 2026.
https://doi.org/10.1007/978-3-032-13012-9_24

2011 in reference to the German initiative *Zukunftsprojekt Industrie 4.0*, which aimed to revitalize the German industrial sector. Its objective went beyond simply incorporating advanced technologies into production processes; it aimed to drive a fundamental transformation of the industrial paradigms present at that time. Specifically, it emphasized the digitalization of all the aspects of the manufacturing processes —from factory machinery to interactions with the users. This radical shift was underpinned by technologies such as Artificial Intelligence, the Internet of Things (IoT), advanced robotics, and immersive solutions like the eXtended Reality (XR). Indeed, efficiency, productivity, and technology were the core principles of Industry 4.0. However, its strong focus on automation and manufacturing prompted a reconsideration of the human role within industrial systems, which laid the foundation for the emergence of Industry 5.0, which advocates for the of human centricity within the industrial development. Indeed, as outlined in the 2021 report by the European Commission [1, 2], Industry 5.0 is built upon three key concepts: human-centricity, sustainability, and resilience. These principles place people at the center of industrial processes while promoting environmentally and socially sustainable technologies and systems that can adapt flexibly to change.

In this context, XR technologies perfectly align with the vision of Industry 5.0. Regarding human-centricity, XR in fact supports personalization by enabling the creation of immersive, interactive, and safe extended environments tailored to individual needs, where the users can train themselves, test procedures and processes, and have real-time technical support [3].

Shifting the focus towards the use of XR for the user's well-being, these technologies have been used within rehabilitation programs, since they allowed to obtain real-time monitoring of progress, provide immediate feedback and adapt the sessions based on observed outcomes [4]. Within the rehabilitation realm, one of the methods that has been demonstrated to accelerate and improve patients' functional recovery and can exploit digital technologies is in fact the Action Observation Treatment (AOT). This approach is based on the "mirror mechanism," which involves the activation of mirror neurons within the human brain [5]; when an action is observed, these neurons simulate an internal motor response like the one that would occur if the action were performed, thereby promoting the reconstruction of damaged neural pathways and improving motor function. Especially in the early post-injury phase—when the patient may still be unable to move—this neural activation helps keep the motor cortex engaged, effectively simulating actual movement despite the absence of physical execution [6]. Moreover, the rehabilitation process can be enhanced by presenting patients with goal-oriented, personalized, and progressively challenging actions to observe. To further enhance its effectiveness, AOT has been increasingly combined with eXtended Reality technologies in rehabilitation settings [7]. Indeed, AOT can be used also in training; in fact, previous studies suggested that specific movement phenotypes can be identified within occupational motor repertoires and, thence, assigning individual performance to specific phenotypes has the potential to inform the development of more effective and tailored training that can be performed via AOT, so as to prevent harmful behaviors for the workers [8].

Given these premises, the main objective of this work was to provide effective support for both the training – in a prevention fashion - and the recovery of work-related motor functions in patients with possible motor impairments, leveraging the immersive and interactive capabilities of XR technologies. In a first phase, several virtual reality scenes were developed from scratch and integrated into an existing content library. In a second phase, several visual stimuli were specifically deployed for use in a mixed reality environment. An intuitive and user-friendly graphical interface was also developed to ensure ease of use for the end users.

2   Materials and Methods

2.1   Instrumentation and Software

Motion Tracking. In order to develop the virtual scenes, whole-body kinematics was acquired by using a full-body motion tracking system based on inertial measurement units - IMUs (MVN Link and Biomech Awinda, XSens, The Netherlands [9]). The motion trackers were positioned within the suit according to the protocol required by the manufacturer; in particular, 17 sensors were positioned on the subject to capture the movement of 23 body segments, which included the head, neck, eighth and tenth thoracic vertebra, third and fifth lumbar vertebra, right and left shoulder, right and left arm, right and left forearm, right and left hand, pelvis, right and left thigh, right and left shank, right and left foot, and right and left forefoot. To achieve precise tracking of finger movements, commercial sensorized gloves (Xsens Gloves, Manus) [10] were used, along with the corresponding software; these gloves support $11°$ of freedom per finger by combining flex sensors with IMUs. Before starting the recording session, a calibration procedure was performed to align the IMUs to the anatomical segments of the subject. The movement was acquired by using a sampling frequency of 60 Hz. Overall kinematics was exported in Filmbox (*fbx*) standard.

Implementation of Virtual Scenes. In order to implement the virtual scenes, Unity 3D environment (2021.3.22f LTS) was fully exploited [11], due to the following reasons:

- Ease of use and accessibility; the platform offered an intuitive interface, extensive and regularly updated documentation, and a supportive developer community.
- Wide range of graphics and animation features; it allowed for the creation of detailed, realistic environments and the design and editing of complex animations, significantly enhancing user immersion.
- Ability to simulate realistic object interactions; with built-in physics features such as gravity, friction, and collision management, Unity 3D enabled the creation of interactive virtual experiences that closely mimic real-world behavior.
- Support for virtual and mixed reality; unity provided dedicated packages for working with virtual and mixed reality devices such as HoloLens 2 and Oculus Quest.

The animations captured by using the Xsens MVN motion capture system and exported in *fbx* format were specifically imported into the Unity development environment. Within the Unity editor, the Humanoid animation type was selected to enable automatic motion mapping onto the virtual skeleton of the humanoid avatar, which was equipped with a rig, a virtual skeletal structure used to simulate and control body movements. The primary objective was to achieve a virtual representation that realistically replicated human motion, with particular attention to smoothness, kinetics, and synchronization. In fact, a reliable and believable gesture was considered essential for maximizing the activation of mirror neurons and for enhancing patient engagement. In addition to animating the avatar, careful attention was given to reconstructing the visual environment by inserting *GameObjects* that accurately simulate the physical spaces in which the movements take place.

Mixed Reality. For the implementation of mixed reality environment, the technology provided by Microsoft HoloLens 2 was selected, as it was one of the leading devices in this field. HoloLens 2 ran the Windows Holographic operating system and featured 4 GB of RAM, 64 GB of storage, a Graphics Processing Unit (GPU), and a Holographic Processing Unit (HPU), a custom processor specifically designed to optimize the visualization and interaction with holograms. The HoloLens 2 device enabled users to interact with applications using commands delivered through various input modalities:

- *Gaze input*: the ability to control the interface through simple eye movement. Eye tracking allowed the system to detect the exact point the user is looking at within the virtual or mixed environment.
- *Hands gesture input*: HoloLens 2 was equipped with sensors capable of hand tracking, enabling it to recognize the user's hands within the gesture frame. This allowed for intuitive and natural interaction with virtual objects, closely resembling interaction with physical objects in the real world. Hand interaction included moving, rotating and scaling virtual objects.
- *Voice input*: speech recognition can be used to issue commands by speaking predefined or custom-configured keywords.

Furthermore, one of the most remarkable features of HoloLens 2 was spatial mapping or spatial awareness, which referred to the ability to generate a detailed representation of the physical environment's surfaces. Spatial awareness enabled the device to perceive the surrounding space and to place virtual elements in a coherent and realistic manner. Once the surfaces were mapped, HoloLens 2 provided a three-dimensional mesh of the environment (Fig. 1), which could be continuously updated in real time.

2.2 Development of AOT Stimuli

The first part of the study focused on the development of two specific virtual reality stimuli, each corresponding to an occupational task, and their subsequent integration into a pre-existing library [7]. It is worth noting that the identified tasks included in the library were classified according to several parameters. In particular, they could be either unimanual or bimanual, and they involved a range of motion of the shoulder joint categorized into five levels of difficulty, including:

1. Upper Extreme: the arms operate above shoulder level.
2. Upper Middle: the arms move within the upper-mid range of the body, without exceeding shoulder height.

Fig. 1. Spatial mapping in the lab. All the text are in Italian.

3. Lower Middle: the arms move within the mid-lower range of the body, without dropping below knee level.
4. Low: the arms operate at hip level.
5. Lower Extreme: the arms move below knee level.

Table 1 summarizes the 16 stimuli/exercises included in the pre-existing library [7].

Movement Recording. The two new stimuli created for virtual reality involved bimanual exercises integrated within two movement contexts: (1) full range and (2) low range, described as follows:

1. *Lift Box FL-SH*: The subject lifted a box from the floor to shoulder height.
2. *Push Cart*: The subject walked forward while pushing a cart.

In a first phase, the subject was asked to remain in a resting position. For the cart pushing task, this corresponded to standing with hands resting on the cart. For the box lifting task, the subject maintained the resting position known as the "N-pose". During the movement execution phase, the subject was asked to perform the described tasks while interacting with real objects that were faithfully reproduced within the virtual environment. This choice was made to ensure an effective correspondence between the subject's real movement and its virtual representation, creating a realistic experience. For each phase, three recordings were made and exported as *fbx* files.

Stimuli Development. Once the *fbx* files were obtained, they were imported into the Unity editor and associated with the *Animation Controller* of the virtual character. It is worth underlining that the recorded movements were complex, involving both hands for object interaction and the entire body to complete the tasks. Despite prior calibration, animation artifacts occurred, particularly in the fingers, due to abrupt motions or poorly tracked segments. To correct these inaccuracies, Unity *Animation Window* was

Table 1. List of exercises.

Name	Description	Range	Grip
Screwdriver Task	The subject works on a screw at eye level	UpperExtreme	Unimanual
Stack Jars	The subject stacks five jars on a table	UpperMiddle	Unimanual
Stack Bricks	The subject stacks six bricks on a table, below shoulder height	UpperMiddle	Unimanual
Stack Boxes	The subject stacks four boxes on a table, below shoulder height	UpperMiddle	Bimanual
Painting Task	The subject moves a paint roller up and down on a wall	UpperExtreme	Unimanual
Household Task	The subject moves a bottle from waist height to above head height	UpperExtreme	Unimanual
Office Task	The subject moves a binder from waist height to shoulder height	UpperMiddle	Unimanual
Clean Table	The subject performs circular shoulder motions on a horizontal plane	Low	Unimanual
Clean Window	The subject performs circular shoulder motions on a vertical plane	UpperExtreme	Unimanual
Saw High Branch	The subject saws a branch at shoulder height	UpperExtreme	Unimanual
Saw Low Branch	The subject saws a branch at waist height	Low	Unimanual
Lift Box WH–SH	The subject lifts a box from waist to shoulder height	UpperMiddle	Bimanual
Lift Box FL–WH	The subject lifts a box from floor to waist height	LowerExtreme	Bimanual
Drill 0°	The subject uses a drill at waist height	Low	Unimanual
Drill 90°	The subject uses a drill at shoulder height	UpperMiddle	Unimanual
Drill 110°	The subject uses a drill above shoulder level (110° shoulder abduction)	UpperExtreme	Unimanual

used, allowing detailed editing of movement curves for each rig segment, thus improving animation realism. Additionally, to adapt the hands to virtual objects and accurately simulate interaction, Unity *Animation Rigging* package was employed. This enableed the creation of smoother and more realistic procedural animations through a set of configurable real-time constraints. The avatar was specifically configured with the *Rig Builder* component, managing the constraints applied to the scene, and the *Bone Renderer*, which allows visualization and selection of skeletal segments for constraint assignment.

In this project, Unity *Animation Rigging* constraints, known as *Rig Constraints*, were specifically used for procedural animation creation. In details, the following constraints were applied:

- *Two Bone IK Constraint*: to control arm movement via inverse kinematics, allowing precise hand positioning.
- *Multi-Aim Constraint*: to dynamically manage the avatar's head rotation based on the scene context (e.g., toward the cart or box).

These constraints were applied in both developed scenes, enhancing the consistency and realism of the avatar's interaction with the virtual environment.

To realistically simulate interaction between the avatar and virtual objects, colliders, essential components for collision management in the scene, were used. Primarily, *compound colliders* (simple shapes such as boxes or capsules) were used to keep computational costs low. Specifically, a *capsule collider* was assigned to the cart handle, a *box collider* to the box, and *capsule-shaped colliders* to the avatar's fingers. To enable collision detection, a *Rigidbody* component was applied to the interacting objects (cart and box). Finally, Unity *OnTriggerEnter* and *OnTriggerExit* methods were employed to enable or disable the *Two Bone IK constraints* whenever a contact occurred between the avatar's hands and the virtual objects. Figure 2 shows an example of the colliders applied to the model's hand.

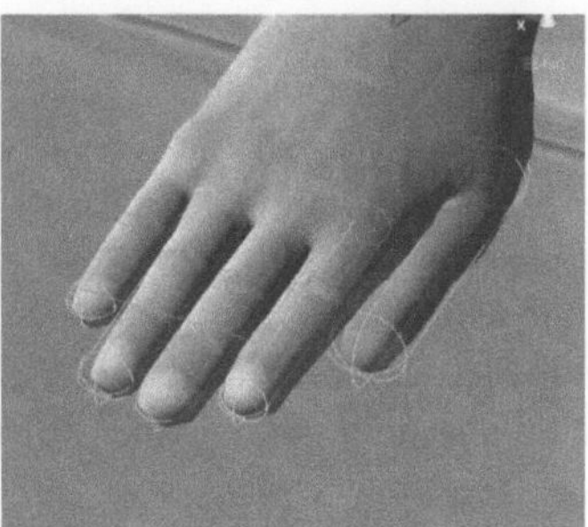

Fig. 2. Colliders for the fingers.

2.3 Mixed Reality Deployment

The second part of the project focused on converting the stimuli developed for virtual reality to adapt them for working within a mixed reality environment on the HoloLens 2 headset. Mixed reality, characterized by the coexistence of virtual and real elements, offers a more engaging and immersive experience compared to other extended reality (XR) technologies. Therefore, its application in AOT could be particularly valuable to understand if and to what extent it can significantly influence the effectiveness of the provided visual stimuli. From this perspective, it is important that the adaptation of stimuli for mixed reality visualization considers various factors, such as realism and the synergy between holograms and the physical environment.

Configuration. For the development of the mixed reality application, a Unity project compatible with the HoloLens 2 headset was configured. After creating the project, the target platform was set to *Universal Windows Platform* (UWP) through the *Build Settings* menu. Subsequently, the necessary packages were imported using the *Mixed Reality Feature Tool*, including the *Mixed Reality Toolkit Foundation* and the *Mixed Reality OpenXR Plugin*, which are essential for integrating MR functionalities.

Once the import was complete, the project was validated for HoloLens 2. Additionally, the *Player Settings* were configured by specifying a package name, and holographic remoting was enabled to allow the application to run directly on the headset via connection to the device's IP address.

Finally, the *Mixed Reality Toolkit* (MRTK) was added to the scene, which generated the *GameObjects "Mixed Reality Toolkit"* and *"Mixed Reality Playspace"*. These allowed for managing the MR experience configuration by customizing the toolkit profile and enabling useful components such as eye tracking and spatial awareness.

Conversion of the Existing Projects. The original stimuli library designed for virtual reality consisted of a single Unity project containing 19 scenes; one scene was specifically dedicated to the graphical user interface that allowed to select the provided tasks and their settings, and 18 scenes, each one containing one of the defined motor tasks to be presented to the user (including the two newly created ones). To adapt this project for mixed reality and make it compatible with the HoloLens 2 headset, a series of technical and structural modifications were undertaken.

In the initial phase, the scenes containing the exercises were exported and imported into a new Unity project, removing dependencies on the common initial scene (*Main Scene*), allowing each to be launched individually in *Play* mode. This approach accelerated the development and testing phases by facilitating direct modification and control of individual scenes within the MR environment.

Subsequently, the original virtual environments, such as home interiors or industrial spaces, were removed, maintaining only the essential objects required for the exercise execution. This ensured that holographic elements are overlaid onto the real environment, consistent with the mixed reality paradigm, thus improving both the effectiveness of interaction and the visibility of the avatar's actions. Figure 3 shows an example of the removal of the virtual environment, maintaining only the objects to be displayed in the real environment.

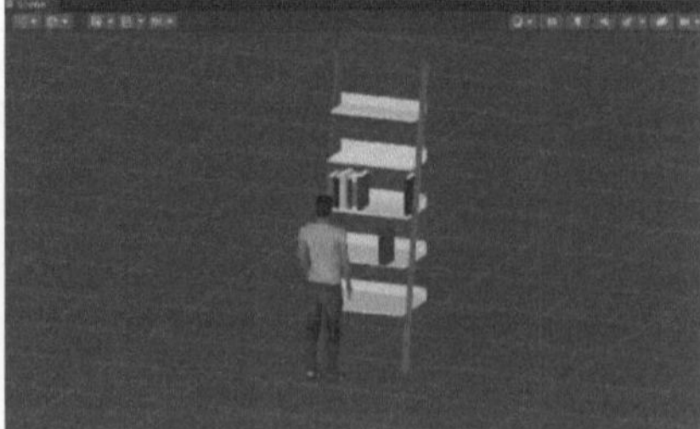

Fig. 3. Example of virtual environment removal (before removal on the left and after on the right side).

Finally, the graphical user interface (GUI) was completely redesigned to accommodate two modes of interaction: one where the user interacts directly via gestures and gaze input using the headset, and another where an external operator, such as a physiotherapist, configures the application using a Bluetooth keyboard. The new GUI was three-dimensional, intuitive, and optimized according to Microsoft's guidelines for HoloLens 2, featuring a dark background for visual comfort, readable fonts, the use of MRTK shaders for accurate holographic rendering, and positioning of elements within the optimal viewing area.

The interface design was developed and optimized in Figma (Figma Inc), leveraging the MRTK toolkit to create interactive prototypes in the HoloLens 2 style. Figure 4 shows examples of the screens designed with this tool.

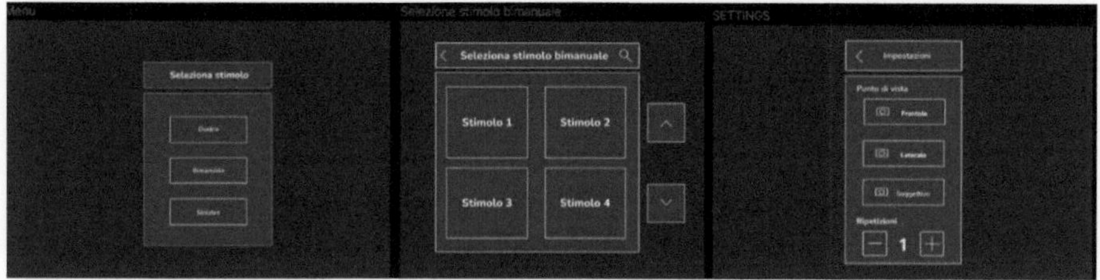

Fig. 4. Examples of screens created for the graphical user interface (GUI).

Figure 5 shows the structure of the developed graphical user interface.

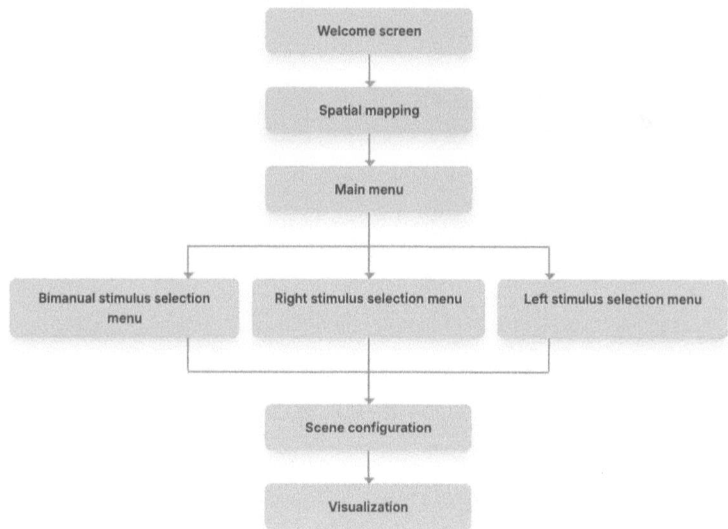

Fig. 5. User Interface structure.

3 Results

The results obtained in the two main phases of the project are here presented and analyzed.

As previously underlined, the first phase involved the development of two new occupational tasks within the existing virtual reality environment. The second phase entailed the conversion and adaptation of the developed stimuli for mixed reality, with particular focus on compatibility with the HoloLens 2 headset. This adaptation also included a complete redesign of the graphical user interface, optimized to support the interaction modes offered by the device, such as eye tracking, hand gestures, and external input via Bluetooth keyboard.

3.1 Virtual Reality Stimuli Development

Animation Optimization. During the development phase of the virtual reality stimuli, several modifications and optimizations were applied to the animations captured using the Xsens motion capture system, aiming to achieve a more natural and consistent result with the intended action. A significant example of this process is the scene related to the box lifting task; Fig. 6 clearly highlights the differences between the initial and the corrected version.

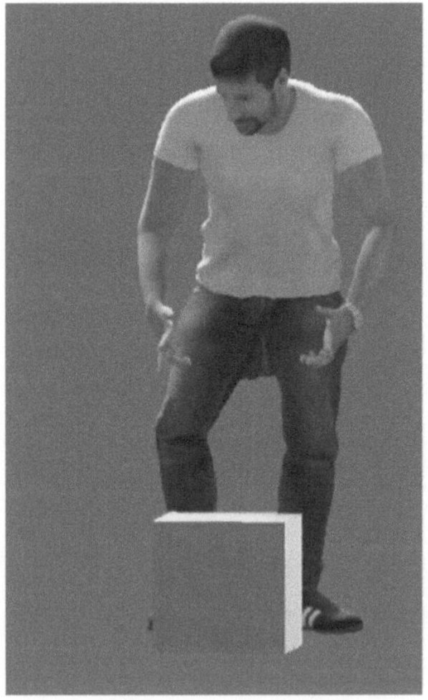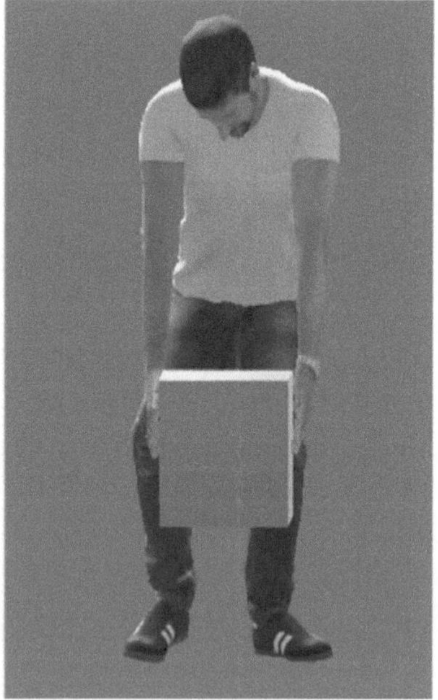

Fig. 6. Example of constraint application and animation curve adjustment (before the adjustment on the left and after on the right side).

In the initial version of the animation, the avatar's fingers appeared in an unnatural position due to inaccuracies in the sensor gloves, the head was oriented toward a random point, the object was not actually lifted, and the distance between the hands was too wide relative to the box. After corrections, the fingers were repositioned realistically by adjusting the animation curves, the gaze was directed toward the object using the *Multi-Aim Constraint*, the lifting action was enabled through *colliders* and *rigid bodies*, and the distance between the hands was properly adjusted using the *Two Bone IK Constraint*.

Virtual Scenes. To complete the animation optimization work, the virtual scenes were set up within the Unity environment, integrating objects and visual context capable of faithfully reproducing the intended environment for each task.

Figures 7 and 8 show a direct comparison between the raw motion capture data (recorded using Xsens system) and the final scenes reconstructed in Unity. The images highlight the transition from a schematic representation of movements to a realistic virtual environment, where the avatar interacts credibly with the scene objects.

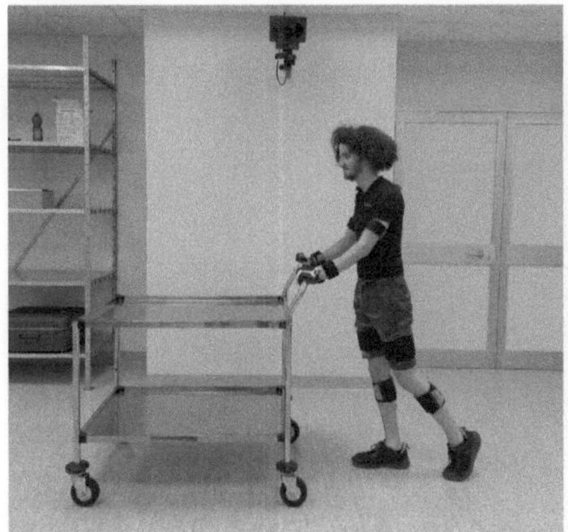

Fig. 7. Comparison between motion capture recording (left)and Unity scene (right) for the "Pushing Cart" task.

3.2   From Virtual Reality to Mixed Reality

Graphical User Interface. In the final phase of adaptation for mixed reality, a new three-dimensional user interface was developed, optimized for interaction with the HoloLens 2. At the beginning of the session, the user was able to see a welcome screen along with an informational window requesting them to perform spatial mapping of the surrounding environment, which was necessary to correctly integrate holograms with the real world (Fig. 9 – left panel). To preserve performance, spatial mapping is limited to 15 s at startup, after which the floor mesh is converted into a virtual planc used for positioning objects (Fig. 9 – right panel).

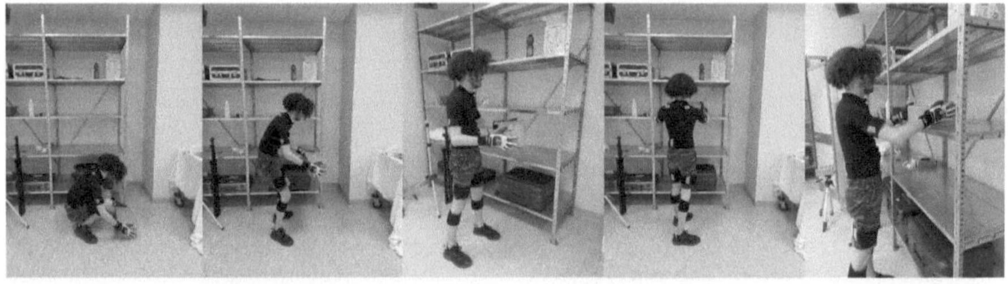

Fig. 8. Comparison between motion capture (top) recording and Unity scene (bottom) for the "Box Lifiting" task.

Fig. 9. Informative screen (left) and spatial mapping (right).

The interface provided a menu for selecting the stimulus, divided into movements involving the right arm, left arm, or both arms (Fig. 10 - left), with the ability to navigate through the stimuli using interactive arrows controlled by hand gestures (Fig. 10 - right).

After making a selection, the user accessed to a configuration screen where the number of repetitions (ranging from 1 to a maximum of 10) and the observation viewpoint could be set (Fig. 11).

Once the settings were confirmed, the scene was displayed in the real environment, anchoring the virtual elements to the mapped floor.

Final Mixed Reality Scenes. Below are reported three of the scenes created and displayed within a real room (Figs. 12, 13 and 14).

The holograms were properly integrated into the real environment thanks to the spatial mapping performed at startup and the constraints applied to the virtual objects.

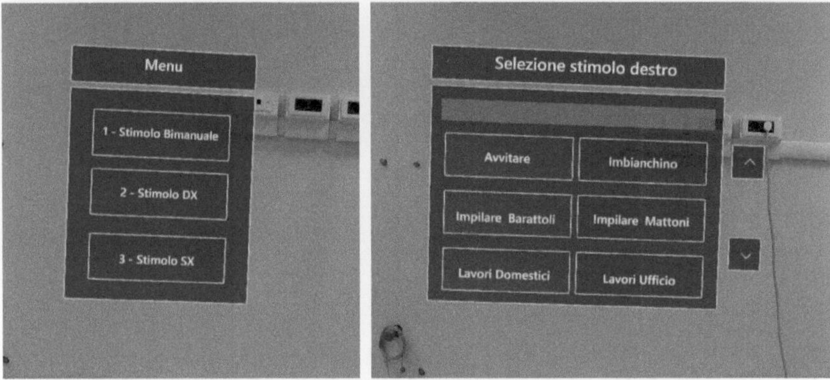

Fig. 10. Menu for selecting stimulus type (left) and specific stimulus (right).

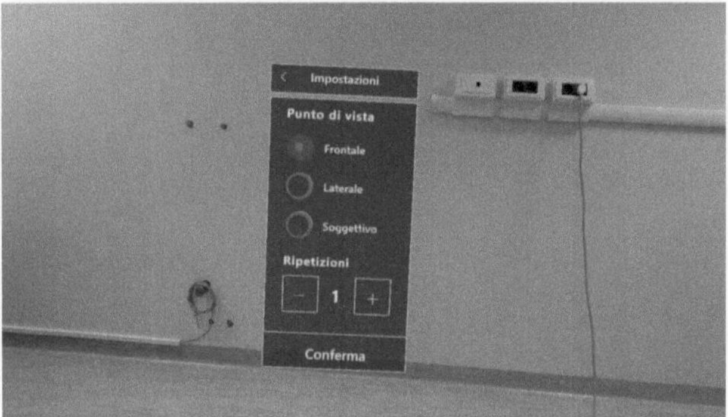

Fig. 11. Specific settings screen.

This integration allowed the user to observe the task execution from different perspectives simply by moving within the physical space, ensuring an immersive and natural experience. The accuracy of positioning and stability of the holograms were crucial to maintaining realism and facilitating interaction during rehabilitation activities.

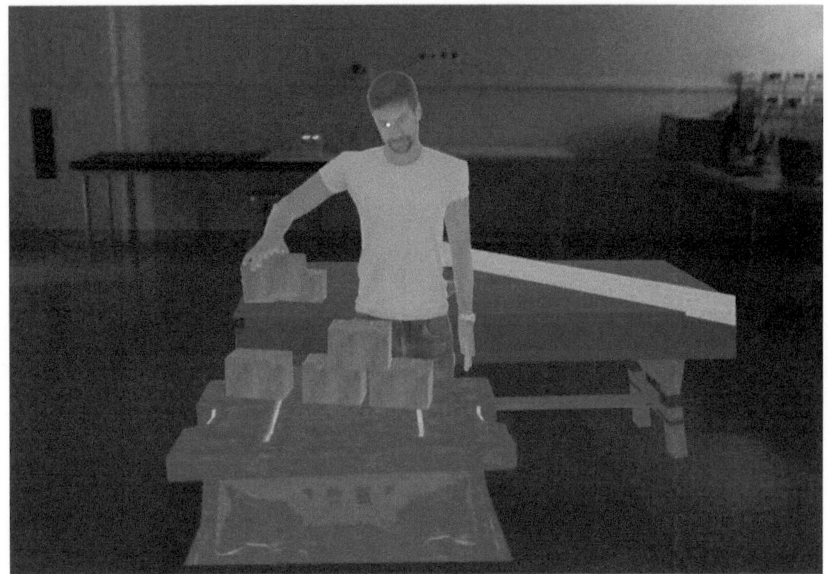

Fig. 12. Stacking bricks.

Fig. 13. Stacking boxes.

Fig. 14. Sawing high branch.

4   Discussion and Conclusions

The presented work successfully achieved the definition of a specific technological framework; the set objectives, namely the creation of new visual stimuli for virtual reality and their adaptation to a mixed reality environment, were specifically achieved.

The development of stimuli in virtual reality required particular attention during the acquisition and refinement of animations through motion capture to ensure natural execution of work-related movements. The conversion to mixed reality, on the other hand, posed additional challenges, particularly related to integrating holograms into the real environment and developing a simple, user-friendly interface. One of the main challenges was the correct visualization of holograms, made possible through spatial mapping of the room. However, scene placement relied exclusively on floor positioning without accounting for elements such as furniture or walls, which can lead to unwanted intersections between physical and virtual objects. Additionally, proper lighting conditions, as recommended by Microsoft guidelines, were necessary to ensure effective spatial mapping and clear perception of holograms. Despite these limitations, the stimuli were correctly integrated to the real environment, allowing users to observe them from various angles and move freely within the space, achieving a good level of immersion.

Another notable feature was the ability, introduced in the configuration screen, to select the viewpoint from which to observe the movement execution, including a first-person perspective. This viewpoint, already used in virtual reality to enhance embodiment, could prove strategic in mixed reality as well, serving as a guide for the user during active task performance and providing real-time visual feedback. In this framework, the user was not limited to passive observation but could progressively become more interactively involved, leveraging the potential of XR technologies.

Although the overall efficacy of mixed reality in both prevention and recovery by exploiting AOT remains to be evaluated, the technical advantages observed were promising; in particular the stimulus personalization, the increased user engagement, and the remote management were indeed added values. These aspects highlighted the mixed reality potential not only for rehabilitation but also for preventive interventions. To fully exploit this potential, future developments could include interactive components that actively engage the user in the task, such as the ability to interact with the avatar or virtual objects. Furthermore, incorporating gamification elements like scoring or visual feedback could enhance motivation and engagement, making the experience more stimulating. This approach would be particularly effective when combined with first-person visualization, providing users with immediate performance feedback and the overall process with valuable data for personalization. Research can thus continue along this path, fully harnessing XR technologies to improve the health and well-being of workers.

Acknowledgments. This work is supported by INAIL (Istituto Nazionale per l'Assicurazione contro gli Infortuni sul Lavoro), with the PR23-CR-P4 – Virtualize project. The authors would like to thank Nicolò Mensi for his support in the acquisition of the tasks for the scenes.

Disclosure of Interests. The authors have no competing interests to declare that are relevant to the content of this article.

References

1. European Commission: Industry 5.0. https://research-and-innovation.ec.europa.eu/research-area/industrial-research-and-innovation/industry-50_en
2. Breque, M., De Nul, L., Petrides, A.: Industry 5.0: Towards a sustainable, human-centric and resilient European industry. Publications Office of the European Union, Luxembourg (2021)
3. Doolani, S., et al.: A review of extended reality (XR) technologies for manufacturing training. Technologies **8**(4), 78 (2020)
4. Mosna, P., et al.: An integrated rehabilitation platform based on action observation therapy, mixed reality and wearable technologies. In: Masia, L., Micera, S., Gassert, R., Sandini, G. (eds.) Converging Clinical and Engineering Research on Neurorehabilitation IV. Biosystems and Biorobotics, vol. 28, pp. 239–244. Springer, Cham (2022)
5. Buccino, G.: Action observation treatment: a novel tool in neurorehabilitation. Philos. Trans. R. Soc. B Biol. Sci. **369**(1644), 20130181 (2014)
6. Bellelli, G., Buccino, G., Bernardini, B., Padovani, A., Trabucchi, M.: Action observation treatment improves recovery of postsurgical orthopedic patients: evidence for a top-down effect? Arch. Phys. Med. Rehabil. **91**(10), 1489–1494 (2010)
7. Scalona, E., et al.: A repertoire of virtual-reality, occupational therapy exercises for motor rehabilitation based on action observation. Data (Basel). **7**(1), 6 (2022)
8. Scalona, E., D'Alonzo, M., Zollo, L., Formica, D.: Identification of movement phenotypes from occupational gesture kinematics: advancing individual ergonomic exposure classification and personalized training. Appl. Ergon. **115**, 104182 (2024)
9. Xsens Technologies B.V.: MVN User Manual (2021)
10. Manus: Manus Prime II Series Product Catalog (2020). https://a.storyblok.com/f/77127/x/a0fe1776a5/manus-prime-ii-xsens-edition-productcatalog.pdf
11. Unity Technologies: Unity User Manual (2021.3 LTS) (2022). https://docs.unity3d.com/Manual/index.html

Elucidating Decoy Effect in Conjunction with Response Time and Trait Anxiety

Masayoshi Tanishita$^{(\boxtimes)}$ (iD), Yasushi Kyutoku (iD), and Hiroko Shoji

Chuo University, 1-13-27, Kasuga, Bunkyo-Ku, Tokyo 112-8551, Japan
`mtanishita.45e@g.chuo-u.ac.jp`

Abstract. The decoy effect has been proven to be a powerful tool for influencing consumer preferences. This study analyzed the decoy effect based on choice experiments with the same participants from the viewpoints of response time and trait anxiety. Regarding the tradeoff between disaster risk and rent, we found that approximately 50% of the participants changed their preferences when presented with the decoy in two-stage choices. The response times of them who chose the decoy were short. Two types of people changed their answers by decoys. Some people changed their choices in a short amount of time (System 1), whereas others took longer (System 2). People with high trait anxiety tended to spend more time answering 2-choice selections, but they took less time answering 3-choice selections, not changing their preferences. The decoy effect might be difficult for individuals with high trait anxiety.

Keywords: decoy effect · response time · trait anxiety · the dual-process model

1 Introduction

Human decision-making is strongly influenced by context [1–4]. The decoy effect is one such scenario. It is well known that the selection rate of the two choices changes with the addition of decoys [5–10] and some people even choose the decoy itself.

Numerous attempts have been made to elucidate the mechanisms underlying decoy effects. Padamwar and Dawra (2024) [11] provided a comprehensive list of the moderating factors of the decoy effect. They demonstrated that the dual process framework explained the attraction, compromise, and phantom decoy effects. The dual-process framework proposed by Evans (2003) [12] divides the decision-making process into two systems: System 1 is automatic, intuitive, and influenced by heuristics, whereas System 2 is deliberative and subject to working memory limits. In the three-option condition, individuals compare targets and competitors with decoys [13–15].

This study extends prior research by investigating how individual differences in trait anxiety and response time influence susceptibility to the decoy effect. We analyzed the decoy effect through a questionnaire on the degree of risk aversion regarding inundation probability and depth, with and without the decoy option. Many studies have examined the factors that influence people's risk perception [16–18] and emotions are one such factor [19]. Many studies have been conducted on the impact of trait anxiety on

V. G. Duffy (Ed.): HCII 2025, LNCS 16339, pp. 355–367, 2026.
https://doi.org/10.1007/978-3-032-13012-9_25

decision-making. For example, Tear (2013) [20] showed that trait anxiety has no effect on the likelihood of committing fundamental attribution errors. Individuals with high trait anxiety show an increased usage of priors, independent of the amount of sensory uncertainty they perceive [21]. Soshi et al. (2019) [22] showed that for global decision-making, higher trait anxiety predicted riskier choices solely in a self-paced condition without any temporal pressure. For local decision-making, state anxiety predicted risk-taking performance differently under self- and forced-paced conditions. Individuals with a high trait or state anxiety are more likely to delay their choices when presented with larger choice sets. Anxiety moderates the effect of the choice set on choice overload, whereas difficulty plays a mediating role [23]. Charpentier et al. (2017) [24] showed that individuals with pathological anxiety demonstrate clear avoidance biases in decision-making. However, to the best of our knowledge, there are no study to analyze the risk perception combined with the decoy effect.

This study aimed to analyze the decoy effect by asking two-stage, three-choice questions with a decoy added based on the participants' two-stage, two-choice selection results. We analyzed the changes in the participants' choices or choice of the decoys themselves by measuring response times and trait anxiety. By comparing the response times to two-choice questions and three-choice questions including decoys, we examined whether people with shorter response times were more likely to be influenced by decoys. Regarding trait anxiety, we examined whether people with higher scores were less likely to be influenced by decoys due to their careful judgment.

Understanding these factors can provide valuable insights into the cognitive processes underlying decision-making and inform applications in behavioral economics, consumer psychology, and public policy.

Materials and Methods. In this study, we analyzed the decoy effect through a questionnaire on the degree of risk aversion regarding the probability of property inundation and the related inundation depth.

Regarding the degree of risk aversion toward inundation depth, we measured the participants' preference for a house with high rent and low inundation depth and vice versa, with a fixed inundation probability. We asked the participants to choose the more attractive house from among the two houses that had a trade-off relationship between inundation probability, inundation depth, and rent. In the question about the degree of risk aversion toward inundation probability, we measured the participants' preference for a house with high rent and low inundation probability, and vice versa, maintaining a fixed inundation depth.

Based on our two-stage approach, each respondent was asked a second dichotomous choice question depending on their response to the first question—if the first response is "A," the second rent/inundation probability (inundation depth) is higher than the first choice; whereas, if the first response is "B," the second rent/ inundation probability (inundation depth) is lower. The range of rent (10 thou. Yen per month) varies between 5 and 13 (360 and 930 USD, respectively), and the range of inundation probability (%) and depth (m) varies between 0.5 and 10, respectively. Participants' degree of risk aversion was obtained from two-stage binary choices between rent and inundation probability/inundation depth. Participants who choose a lower rent and a higher inundation probability/inundation depth option have a low degree of risk aversion. Subsequently, through two-stage choices, the participants were classified into four levels (Low-Low, Low-High, High-Low, and High-High).

After the participants made two selections from a total of four choices, a third option (decoy), which was clearly inferior to the selected options, was added, and the participants were asked to make a three-choice decision. The decoy used here was the so-called strong decoy, which presented a less satisfying option with a higher flood probability or flood depth and higher rent than the option that the participant did not choose. As Stoffel et al. (2019) [25] pointed out, the display order affects the results. In this study, the decoy option ("D") was placed before the two-choice selection results. If "A" appeared with two choices, it was placed thus: "D," "A," "B,"; by contrast, if "B" appeared, it was placed thus: "A," "D," "B," making participants aware of the situation where a different choice than the two choices is made. Structures of the 2-stage, 2-choice and 2-stage, 3-choice questions for rent and inundation probability are shown in Fig. 1. We created a total of 18 pattern choice sets based on the selection patterns.

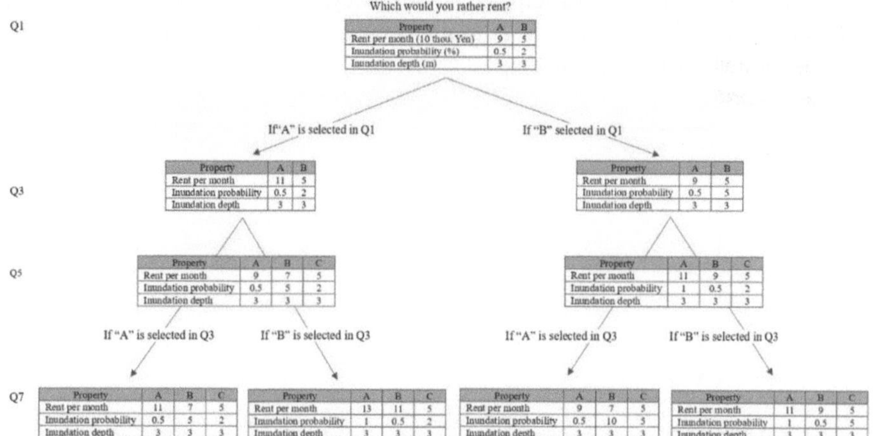

Fig. 1. Structures of the 2-stage, 2-choice and 2-stage, 3-choice questions for rent and inundation probability.

Therefore, each subject answered a total of eight questions in the following manner:

– Two-choice without decoy

Inundation probability (stage 1), inundation depth (stage 1), inundation probability (stage 2), and inundation depth (stage 2)

– Three-choice: previous two-choice and a decoy

Inundation probability (stage 1), inundation depth (stage 1), inundation probability (stage 2), and inundation depth (stage 2)

The response time for each of the eight choices was measured. The answers to the three selection questions were classified as follows:

S: The answer is the same as in the two-choice selection

C: The answer is the opposite of the two-choice selection

D: The decoy itself is chosen

As a two-stage selection was performed, nine combinations of S, C, and D were found.

Trait anxiety was measured using the Japanese version of the State-Trait Anxiety Inventory [26, 27], which comprises 20 items related to trait anxiety. For example, "I worry too much over something that really doesn't matter" or "I am content; I am a steady person." All items are rated on a 4-point scale (i.e., from "Almost Never" to "Almost Always"). The trait anxiety score (range, 20–80) is the sum of the scores for all 20 items, with higher scores indicating a higher level of trait anxiety.

For our research, a web-based survey was conducted that included Tokyo residents as the target population because the rent setting in the survey was based on the market rent rates in Tokyo. The survey was conducted via a web-based platform, and 510 responses were obtained between September 18 and 29, 2023. *Informed consent* was obtained from each participant before they participated in the survey.

Figure 2 shows the distribution of trait anxiety scores; the distribution was almost the same for both males and females.

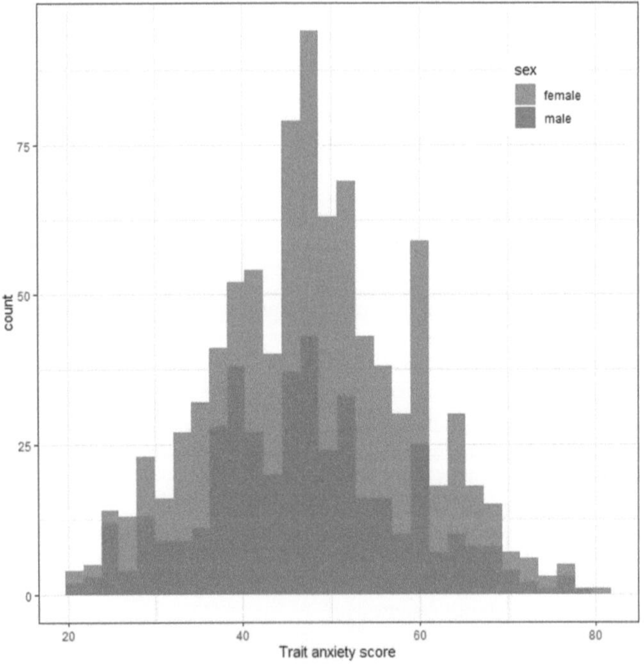

Fig. 2. Distribution of trait anxiety score by sex.

Although these figures have been omitted, no correlation was found between age, income, or trait anxiety scores.

We hypothesized that trait anxiety levels would influence susceptibility to the decoy effect, with specific hypotheses examining:

1. Response time differences between two-choice and three-choice with a decoy task to evaluate preference consistency
2. Relationship between response time and decision stability (changed choice and decoy selection)
3. Impact of trait anxiety on decision stability

We used a binary additive model to analyze the influencing factors, using dependent variables such as whether the decoy was selected at least once and whether the selection was changed at least once owing to the decoy. The additive model can capture the nonlinear aspects of this relationship as well as many other nonlinear relationships owing to the flexibility of the splines. Flexible smoothing in Generalized Additive Models (GAM) is performed using several smaller functions known as basis functions. Each smooth function is the sum of several basis functions, and each basis function is multiplied by a coefficient, each of which represents a parameter of the model. In this study, *smooth* terms of response time and trait anxiety were considered. The GAM function solves the smoothing parameter estimation problem using the generalized cross-validation criterion [28] and the Akaike information criterion (AIC) is used for model selection [29]. Response time, trait anxiety scores, age, sex, and income level were used as independent variables.

2   Results

2.1   Degree of Risk Aversion and Response Time

Table 1 shows the number of respondents and response times according to the degree of risk aversion (see Supplementary Figure S2 and S3 for detail). Regarding the latter, the low-low risk-aversion group had the highest ratio in terms of both probability and inundation depth, accounting for approximately half of the participants.

In terms of probability, the response time for two-choice responses tended to increase as the degree of risk aversion increased, but the opposite trend was observed for the depth of flooding. Therefore, there is no clear relationship between the degree of risk aversion and response time.

Interestingly, the longer it took for a two-choice selection, the shorter the response time for a three-choice selection. Furthermore, in the low- to high-risk aversion groups, the response time did not significantly decrease, even when a decoy was presented. Among the three-choice selections, the low- and high-risk aversion group took the longest to answer. Thus, it is presumed that the cognitive processing of System 1 is active in a few individuals.

2.2   Decoy Effect: How Many People Choose Differently When Presented with Decoys?

Figure 3 shows the selection results obtained after adding decoys. Approximately 50% of the participants selected the same choice (S-S) in the two-stage choices for both inundation probability and inundation depth. Approximately 40% of participants changed their

Table 1. Response time by the degree of risk aversion.

Inundation probability	Low-Low	Low-High	High-Low	High-High
N	267	92	80	81
Response time without decoy Mean (S.D.) (sec)	14.2 (6.0)	18.0 (10.3)	22.5 (9.1)	23.5 (11.8)
Response time with decoy Mean (S.D.) (sec)	13.7 (7.2)	17.3 (8.2)	13.3 (7.5)	12.2 (7.4)
Inundation depth	Low-Low	Low-High	High-Low	High-High
N	243	95	92	90
Response time without decoy Mean (S.D.) (sec)	19.3 (8.5)	21.4 (10.0)	13.4 (8.4)	9.2 (6.1)
Response time with decoy Mean (S.D.) (sec)	9.7 (5.6)	16.1 (9.3)	13.0 (7.7)	11.3 (7.4)

choice more than once in the two stages. Approximately 10% of the participants chose a decoy more than once. These rates were almost the same for inundation probability and inundation depth.

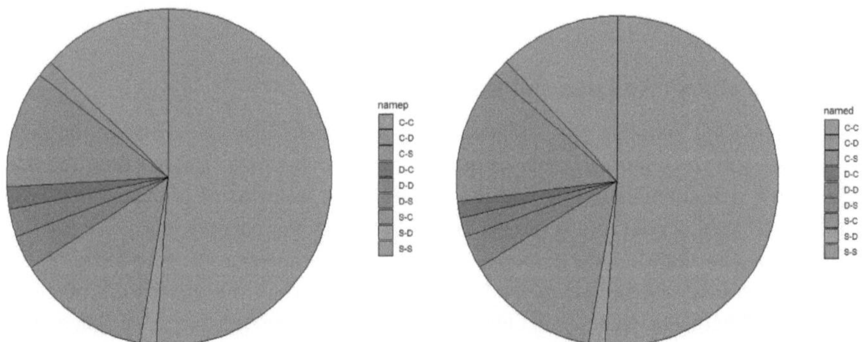

Fig. 3. Selection results by adding decoys (left: inundation probability, right: inundation depth).

2.3   Choosing the Decoy Itself

In the decoy, we set an option with higher rent and higher disaster risk; if the participants compare it carefully, they will probably not choose this scenario. Therefore, those who choose the decoy use System 1 cognitive processing, which yields fast and intuitive responses.

Table 2 presents the estimation results obtained using the binomial regression model. The probability of selecting a decoy was higher for those with shorter response times. People with low-risk aversion (L-L) were less likely to choose decoys than those with high-risk aversion. Furthermore, trait anxiety and other personal attributes were not significant influencing factors.[1]

Table 2. Estimation results (binary logit model).

Explained variable: Decoy(1) other(0)	Inundation probability			Inundation depth		
	Estimate	z-value		Estimate	z-value	
(Intercept)	22.00	6.17	***	15.69	4.57	***
Risk aversion: H-L (base: H-H)	0.55	1.05		0.08	0.16	
Risk aversion: L-H	0.06	0.09		0.16	0.29	
Risk aversion: L-L	-2.10	-3.83	***	-2.12	-4.00	***
log(response time)	-2.58	-6.38	***	-1.92	-4.90	***
N	510					
Deviance explained	0.36			0.22		
AIC	176.81			198.42		
AIC(0)	264.05			242.77		

Signif.Codes: < .0001 '***' 0.001 '**' 0.01 '*' 0.05 '.' 0.1

2.4   Choice Change After Introducing the Decoy

Approximately 40% of participants selected a different choice at least once because of the presentation of decoys. Table 3 presents the estimation results of the influence of this selection change. Figure 4 shows the influence of the obtained nonlinear term on the inundation depth.

Those with short and long response times tended to choose differently, as did those with intermediate levels of risk aversion. It was also found that people with higher trait anxiety tended not to change their selections.

Table 3. Estimation results (binary additive logit model)

Explained variable Same (0) Change (1)	Inundation probability			Inundation depth		
	Estimate	z-value		Estimate	z-value	
(Intercept)	-1.11	-3.83	***	-1.02	-3.69	***
Risk aversion: H-L (base: H-H)	2.23	5.16	***	2.20	5.19	***
Risk aversion: L-H	1.89	4.23	***	2.22	4.86	***
Risk aversion: L-L	0.23	0.33		-0.07	-0.22	
(smooth term)	edf	Chi.sq		edf	Chi.sq	
log(response time)	2.58	6.38	***	2.90	19.96	***
Anxiety	1.66	2.01	*	1.73	5.36	***
N	510					
Deviance explained	0.19			0.26		
AIC	424.76			393.00		
AIC(0)	504.89			506.89		

Signif.Codes: < .0001 '***' 0.001 '**' 0.01 '*' 0.05 '.' 0.1

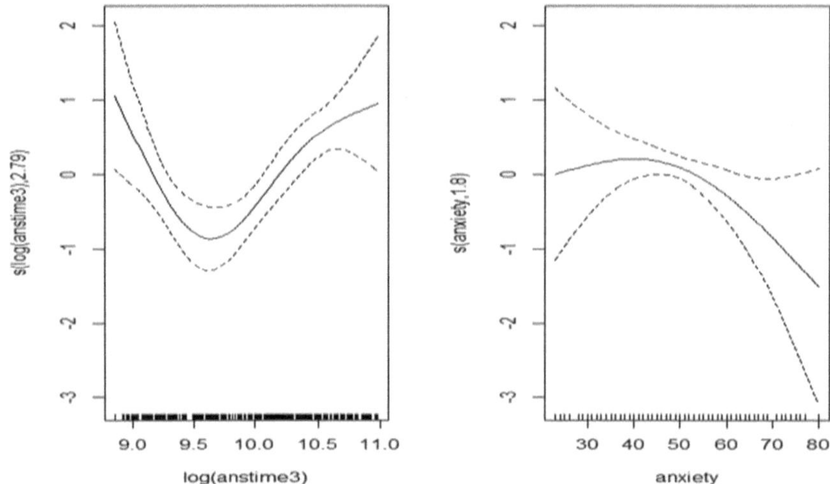

Fig. 4. Nonlinear relationship between response time and anxiety and change.

2.5 Trait Anxiety Score and Response Time

Thus far, we have shown that response time influences the decoy effect. Finally, the relationship between trait anxiety and response time was examined (Fig. 5).

Participants who took less time to answer the two-choice selections showed intermediate trait anxiety scores. People with high or low trait anxiety scores spend a significant amount of time answering two-choice selections, meaning their System 2 is at work.

In addition, individuals with high trait anxiety tend to have shorter response times. As mentioned in the previous section, participants with high trait anxiety do not change their preferences because of decoys. Therefore, it can be affirmed that the decoy effect may be small for participants with high trait anxiety.

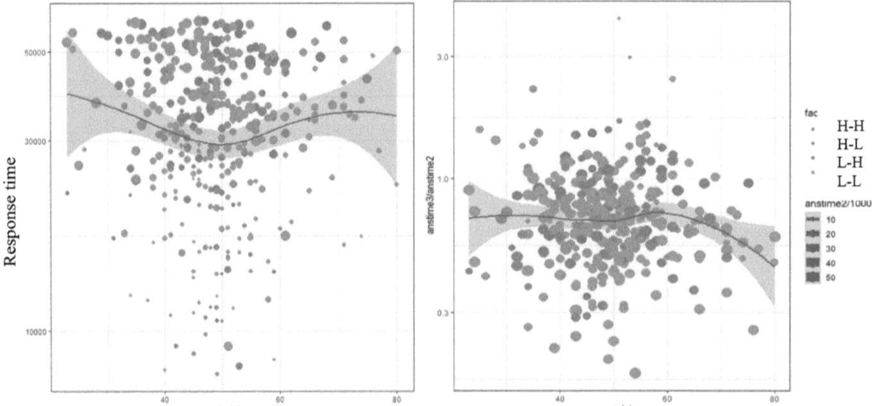

Fig. 5. Trait anxiety score and response time (left: two-choice, right: the ratio between three-choice and two-choice).

3 Discussion

Key findings included:

1. Approximately 50% of participants changed their preferences in response to the decoy.
2. Analysis of response times revealed two distinct cognitive pathways:

- Shorter response times correlated with a higher likelihood of choosing the decoy, suggesting the involvement of System 1 cognitive processing.
- Among participants who changed their choice, two distinct groups emerged: one showing hasty decision making (System 1 processing) and another showing prolonged deliberation (System 2 processing).

3. Participants with high trait anxiety demonstrated distinctive patterns:

- Longer response times to two-choice questions than those with medium trait anxiety.
- Faster response to three-choice questions.
- Significantly lower likelihood of changing initial choices, suggesting reduced susceptibility to the decoy effect.

When trying to understand preferences, revealed preferences based on behavioral data are considered more useful than questionnaires [30]. However, preferences for hypothetical options can only be obtained through questionnaires [6]. Furthermore, as shown in this study, questionnaire preferences are not stable. Colombo et al. (2022) [31] showed that preferences change depending on the task. Similarly, behavioral data such as response times change even after short periods of experimentation, making results unstable.

Most participants who selected the decoy demonstrated short response times, a phenomenon that may be attributable to their decision to refrain from engaging with the questionnaire in a serious manner. Some of these choices can be explained through numeracy. As Reyna and Brainerd (2008) [34] highlighted, millions of Americans lack the skills to handle quantitative tasks in everyday life based on numeracy assessments. Peters and Levin (2008) [35] found that individuals with lower numeracy skills may be better at processing individual-option information in risky choices and translating it appropriately but may struggle to integrate this information into their decisions. This suggests that choices may not always be based on integrating personal judgments of provided options. Furthermore, Choi et al. (2020) [36] have established a correlation between math anxiety and numeracy. Additionally, the response times for two- and three-choice selections may be influenced by practice effects (shortening) or fatigue effects (lengthening). The role of order effects in this context remains a subject that requires further exploration.

The study found that choice changes were more prevalent among participants with intermediate preferences, with some respondents responding rapidly while others required more time to alter their selections. This finding suggests that while System 1 influences choice changes, when preferences are ambiguous, respondents may not maintain consistent choices when presented with alternatives, even if this requires additional decision time. However, previous research has demonstrated that the attraction effect varies depending on the presentation of options [9].

Individuals characterized by high trait anxiety demonstrated a delay in their responses to the questionnaire. When presented with a decoy, their responses were more rapid in comparison to their responses to two-choice questions. However, they exhibited reluctance to alter their preferences in response to the decoys. While speculative, it is conceivable that highly anxious individuals approached questions with a more serious, reflective attitude (System 2) and recognized the presence of decoys among the three choices. However, it is important to note that this pattern may be influenced by the subject matter's association with disaster risk anxiety. It is recommended that future research employs topics unrelated to anxiety in order to further elucidate these relationships.

4 Conclusions

Our study provides important insights into the decoy effect in disaster risk and rent decisions. The substantial rate of preference change (approximately 50%) suggests considerable instability in risk-rent trade-offs. Response time analysis revealed two cognitive pathways through which the decoy effect operates: rapid heuristic-based decisions and prolonged deliberation, both of which can produce preference shifts. Participants with high trait anxiety exhibited distinctive patterns, spending more time on simpler questions but responding more quickly to complex scenarios, while showing greater resistance to changing initial choices. This suggests that trait anxiety may enhance decision vigilance in simple contexts, while promoting consistency-maintaining strategies as complexity increases.

These findings have implications for decision theory, real estate markets, and disaster risk communication by highlighting how emotional and personality factors moderate contextual influences on decision making.

The results support the role of heuristic processing in the decoy effect. The reduced susceptibility observed in high anxiety individuals may be due to decision stability tendencies. Future research should explore whether these patterns extend to other domains and investigate the neural mechanisms underlying the relationship between anxiety and contextual influences on decision-making. Incorporating neurocognitive measures would help distinguish between heuristic and deliberate decision processes and provide deeper insights into how anxiety modulates susceptibility to contextual influences [38–41].

Acknowledgments. The authors would like to thank Mitsuru Yamashina, Hidetsugu Nanba, Satoshi Fukuda and Kota Ono for their precious insight. This study has been approved by the research ethics committee of Chuo University (2021–073). This work was supported by Chuo University Joint Research Grant.

Disclosure of Interests. The authors have no competing interests to declare that are relevant to the content of this article.

References

1. Ariely, D., Wallsten, T.S.: Seeking subjective dominance in multidimensional space: an explanation of the asymmetric dominance effect. Organ. Behav. Hum. Decis. Process. **63**(3), 223–232 (1995)
2. Hamada, Y., Toma, S., Takahashi, N., Shoji, H.: Analysis and feature extraction of situation-dependent product selection using earphones as an example. Int. J. Affect. Eng. **21**(2), 85–91 (2019)
3. Mlodinow, L.: Emotional: How feelings shape our thinking. Pantheon (2022)
4. Baker, S.A., Griffith, T., Lepora, N.F.: Degenerate boundaries for multiple-alternative decisions. Nat. Commun. **13**, 5066 (2022). https://doi.org/10.1038/s41467-022-32741-y
5. Dumbalska, T., Li, V., Tsetsos, K., Summerfield, C.: A map of decoy influence in human multi-alternative choice. In: Proceedings of the National Academy of Sciences, vol. 17, no. 40, pp. 25169–25178 (2020). https://doi.org/10.1073/pnas.2005058117
6. Evans, N.J., Holmes, W.R., Dasari, A., Trueblood, J.S.: The impact of presentation order on attraction and repulsion effects in decision-making. Decision **8**(1), 36–54 (2021). https://doi.org/10.1037/dec0000144
7. Marini, M., Ansani, A., Paglieri, F.: Attraction comes from many sources: attentional and comparative processes in decoy effects. Judgm. Decis. Mak. **15**(5), 704–726 (2020)
8. Mohr, P.N.C., Heekeren, H.R., Rieskamp, J.: Attraction effect in risky choice can be explained by subjective distance between choice alternatives. Sci. Rep. **7**, 8942 (2017). https://doi.org/10.1038/s41598-017-06968-5
9. Trendl, A., Stewart, N., Mullett, L.T.: A zero attraction effect in naturalistic choice. Decision **8**(1), 55–68 (2021). https://doi.org/10.1037/dec0000145
10. Wollschlaeger, M.L., Diederich, A.: Similarity, attraction, and compromise effects: original findings, recent empirical observations, and computational cognitive process models. Am. J. Psychol. **133**(1), 1–30 (2020)
11. Padamwar, P.K., Dawra, J.: An integrative review of the decoy effect on choice behavior. Psychol. Mark. **41**(11), 1–20 (2024). https://doi.org/10.1002/mar.22076
12. Evans, J.S.B.: In two minds: dual-process accounts of reasoning. Trends Cogn. Sci. **7**, 454–459 (2003). https://doi.org/10.1016/j.tics.2003.08.012
13. Evans, J.S.B.: Dual-process theories of reasoning: contemporary issues and developmental applications. Dev. Rev. **31**(2–3), 86–102 (2011). https://doi.org/10.1016/j.dr.2011.07.007
14. Dhar, R., Gorlin, M.: A dual-system framework to understand preference construction processes in choice. J. Consum. Psychol. **23**, 528–542 (2013)
15. Padamwar, P.K., Kalakbandi, V.K., Dawra, J.: Deliberation does not make the attraction effect disappear: the role of induced cognitive reflection. J. Bus. Res. **154**, 113335 (2023). https://doi.org/10.1016/j.jbusres.2022.113335
16. Lechowska, E.: What determines flood risk perception? a review of factors of flood risk perception and relations between its basic elements. Nat. Hazards **94**, 1341–1366 (2009). https://doi.org/10.1007/s11069-018-3480-z
17. Oubennaceur, K., Chokmani, K., Lessard, F., Gauthier, Y., Baltazar, C., Toussaint, J.P.: Understanding flood risk perception: a case study from Canada. Sustainability **14**, 3087 (2022). https://doi.org/10.3390/su14053087
18. Zinda, A.J., Williams, B.L., Kay, L.D., Alexander, M.S.: Flood risk perception and responses among urban residents in the northeastern United States. Int. J. Disaster Risk Reduct. **64**, 102528 (2021). https://doi.org/10.1016/j.ijdrr.2021.102528
19. Lechowska, E.: Approaches in research on flood risk perception and their importance in flood risk management: a review. Nat. Hazards **111**, 2343–2378 (2022). https://doi.org/10.1007/s11069-021-05140-7

20. Tear, E.: The effect of trait anxiety on the fundamental attribution error. Honors Theses, **744** (2013). https://digitalworks.union.edu/theses/744

21. Kraus, N., Niedeggen, M., Hesselmann, G.: Trait anxiety is linked to increased usage of priors in a perceptual decision-making task. Cognition **206**, 104474 (2021). https://doi.org/10.1016/j.cognition.2020.104474

22. Soshi, T., Nagamine, M., Fukuda, E., Takeuchi, A.: Pre-specified anxiety predicts future decision-making performances under different temporally constrained conditions. Front. Psychol. **10**, 1544 (2019). https://doi.org/10.3389/fpsyg.2019.01544

23. Hu, X., Turel, O., Chen, W., He, Q.: The effect of trait-state anxiety on choice overload: the mediating role of choice difficulty. Decision **50**, 143–152 (2023). https://doi.org/10.1007/s40622-023-00345-0

24. Charpentier, C.J., Aylward, J., Roiser, J.P., Robinson, O.J.: Enhanced risk aversion, but not loss aversion, in unmedicated pathological anxiety. Biol. Psychiat. **81**(12), 1014–1022 (2017). https://doi.org/10.1016/j.biopsych.2016.12.010

25. Stoffel, S.T., Yang, J., Vlaev, I., von Wagner, C.: Testing the decoy effect to increase interest in colorectal cancer screening. Plos One, **26**, 14(3), e0213668 (2019). https://doi.org/10.1371/journal.pone.0213668

26. Shimizu, H., Imae, K.: Development of Japanese version of state-trait anxiety inventory (for university student). Jpn. J. Educ. Psychol. **29**(4), 348–353 (1981). https://doi.org/10.5926/jjep1953.29.4_348

27. Spielberger, C.D., Gorsuch, R.L., Lushene, R.E.: STAI manual for the state-trait anxiety inventory (self-evaluation questionnaire). Consulting Psychol. Press. (1970)

28. Wood, S.: Fast stable restricted maximum likelihood and marginal likelihood estimation of semiparametric generalized linear models. J. R. Stat. Soc. (B) **73**(1), 3–36 (2011)

29. Wood, S.N., Pya, N., Saefken, B.: Smoothing parameter and model selection for general smooth models (with discussion). J. Am. Stat. Assoc. **111**, 1548–1575 (2016). https://doi.org/10.1080/01621459.2016.1180986

30. de Corte, K., Cairns, J., Grieve, R.: Stated versus revealed preferences: an approach to reduce bias. Health Econ. **30**(5), 1095–1123 (2021). https://doi.org/10.1002/hec.4246

31. Colombo, L., Nicotra, E., Marino, B.: Preference reversal in decision making: the attraction effect in choice and rejection. Swiss J. Psychol. **61**(1), 21–33 (2002). https://doi.org/10.1024/1421-0185.61.1.21

32. Lount, R.B., Jr.: The impact of positive mood on trust in interpersonal and intergroup interactions. J. Pers. Soc. Psychol. **98**(3), 420–433 (2010). https://doi.org/10.1037/a0017344

33. Fiske, S.T., Cuddy, A.J.C., Glick, P.: Universal dimensions of social cognition: warmth and competence. Trends Cogn. Sci. **11**(2), 77–83 (2007). https://doi.org/10.1016/j.tics.2006.11.005

34. Reyna, V.F., Brainerd, C.J.: Numeracy, ratio bias, and denominator neglect in judgments of risk and probability. Learn. Individ. Differ. **18**(1), 89–107 (2008). https://doi.org/10.1016/j.lindif.2007.03.011

35. Peters, E., Levin, I.: Dissecting the risky-choice framing effect: numeracy as an individual-difference factor in weighting risky and riskless options. Judgm. Decis. Mak. **3**(6), 435–448 (2008). https://doi.org/10.1017/S1930297500000012

36. Choi, S.S., Taber, J.M., Thompson, C.A., Sidney, P.G.: Math anxiety, but not induced stress, is associated with objective numeracy. J. Exp. Psychol. Appl. **26**(4), 604–619 (2020). https://doi.org/10.1037/xap0000268

37. Stoffel, S.T., Sun, Y., Hirst, Y., von Wagner, C., Vlaev, I.: Testing the decoy effect to improve online survey participation: evidence from a field experiment. J. Behavioral Exp. Econ. **107**, 102103 (2023). https://doi.org/10.1016/j.socec.2023.102103

38. Shoots-Reinhard, B., et al.: Numeracy and memory for risk probabilities and risk outcomes depicted on cigarette warning labels. Health Psychol. **39**(8), 721–730 (2020). https://doi.org/10.1037/hea0000879
39. Rogers, E.S., Vargas, E.A., Voigt, E.: Exploring the decoy effect to guide tobacco treatment choice: a randomized experiment. BMC. Res. Notes **13**, 3 (2020). https://doi.org/10.1186/s13104-019-4873-0
40. White, N., Forsyth, B., Lee, A., Machado, L.: Repeated computerized cognitive testing: performance shifts and test–retest reliability in healthy young adults. Psychol. Assess. **30**(4), 539–549 (2018). https://doi.org/10.1037/pas0000503
41. Dhar, R., Simonson, I.: The effect of forced choice on choice. J. Mark. Res. **40**(2), 146–160 (2003). https://doi.org/10.1509/jmkr.40.2.146.19229

Optimising a Video Magnification Algorithm for Autism Spectrum Condition Monitoring

Zakia Batool Turabee$^{(\boxtimes)}$ (iD), David J. Brown (iD), Mufti Mahmud (iD),
Andreas Oikonomou (iD), Nicholas Shopland (iD), Andrew Burton (iD),
and Muhammad Arifur Rahman (iD)

Department of Computer Science, Nottingham Trent University, NG11 8NS
Nottingham, UK
`zakia.turabee2021@my.ntu.ac.uk`
`https://www.ntu.ac.uk/research/groups-and-centres/projects/ai-top`

Abstract. The human eye can only perceive signals within a specific frequency range. However, studying signals beyond this range can provide valuable insights, especially when studying human behaviour in response to a stressful situation. To visualise these spatio-temporal variations, video magnification techniques have been developed. When blood flows through the skin, it undergoes subtle, imperceptible changes. By applying video magnification, these minute colour variations can be amplified and used to extract physiological signals, such as heart rate.

This research proposes a machine learning pipeline for colour amplification, trained on the real-world ASC-Emotion dataset. The objective is to develop a model that uses a range of data which includes heart rate derived from colour changes in the skin extracted from video amplification process. This model can be deployed in classrooms to predict "meltdown" events in children with Autism when they are feeling overwhelmed, leading to emotional dysregulation.

Keywords: Autism Spectrum Condition(ASC) · Video Magnification · Colour Amplification · Spatial and Temporal Filtering · Heart Rate

1 Introduction

Individuals with Autism Spectrum Condition (ASC) show deficits in communication and social interaction along with repetitive patterns of behaviour [12,35]. Due to sensory overload, children with ASC often display a range of involuntary challenging behaviours, in the form of screaming, head banging, throwing objects, etc., which may cause harm to the child themselves, or others in the vicinity [16]. This state of emotional dysregulation, or "meltdown", is preceded by a transitional "rumbling stage", characterized by behaviours like covering eyes and ears, flapping, and pacing [22]. Research suggests that physiological changes are an objective indicator of emotional transition in children with ASC [13,19]. Vital signals such as heart rate (HR), galvanic skin response (GSR) and

© The Author(s), under exclusive license to Springer Nature Switzerland AG 2026
V. G. Duffy (Ed.): HCII 2025, LNCS 16339, pp. 368–379, 2026.
https://doi.org/10.1007/978-3-032-13012-9_26

blood volume pulse (BVP), can help indicate the internal emotional state of a child. Monitoring HR in children with ASC can yield information related to the onset of a distressing episode, especially when combined with other physiological signals and involuntary gestures. Caregivers and teaching staff can make use of this information to indicate the onset of such events for the early detection and prevention of undesired events [7].

However, there is very little research on the identification of the internal state of children with ASC based on physiological signals [3,9,18]. The objective of this research is to infer the onset of "rumble moments" as precursors to emotional dysregulation in children with ASC using a curated dataset (ASC-Emotion dataset). This dataset was developed as a part of the "AI-TOP" project - an Erasmus funded project (2020-1-UK01-KA201-079167). The AI-TOP project was a collaboration between Nottingham Trent University and other Universities and end user organisations throughout Europe, which focused on predicting the rumble moment stages in children with ASC. The aim of this project was to build a multimodal tool able to detect the early signs of an emotional dysregulation event and alert the relevant guardian or teacher to intervene and deescalate the event. This dataset focuses on the occurrence of emotional dysregulation events and was created using video data of children with ASC playing digital games within a classroom setting.

The human eye has limited sensitivity to spatial and temporal variations, and perceives signals only within a specific frequency range. However, many valuable signals exist outside this range and can provide significant information [1]. Studying these variations can yield useful information such as about the structural health of a building, or the vital signs of a person. Video motion magnification techniques allow us to perceive such signals [25]. Human skin goes through subtle changes when psychologically aroused which are not visible to naked eye, when blood flows through it. By applying spatial and temporal filtering, these subtle changes can be made visible [36], and can be used to infer vital signs including HR. In addition to providing an unobtrusive and markerless way of measuring HR, such methods can be used to extract other clinically useful information [4], especially for people with increased sensitivities such as children with ASC.

The existing video magnification models have primarily been trained on synthetic datasets. This research aims to train an optimised machine learning model using a real dataset featuring children with ASC (ASC-Emotion dataset). The ultimate goal is to develop a model that employs video magnification techniques to amplify emotional responses captured in videos of children with ASC to detect increased HR as an indicator of an imminent dysregulation event - sometimes termed a 'meltdown' event, especially when combined with other more obvious visual indicators such as rocking and flapping of hands.

The rest of this paper is structured as follows: Related Work reviews the existing studies on video magnification and detection of physiological signals using this technique. The Methodology section describes the proposed model architecture followed by the discussion on its anticipated advantages. Challenges and Future Work section outlines potential limitations of the proposed model and suggests directions for future research. Finally, the Conclusion summarizes the key findings and contributions of this work.

2   Related Work

Over the years, several approaches have been developed to magnify the imperceptible variations in our surroundings. These approaches can be broadly categorised into two techniques i.e. the Lagrangian and Eulerian perspective. The Lagrangian method depends on optical flow for generating the motion magnified frame. This method involves tracking feature points in a video over the time and focuses on its motion trajectory to magnify the changes. This is a time consuming and computationally expensive process [2]. On the other hand, the Eulerian approach, (the foundation of this paper), magnifies subtle variations in pixel intensity over time at a point making it more computationally efficient [36].

2.1   Video Magnification

Wu et al., at MIT made the most prominent contribution in the field of magnification and proposed an algorithm called Eulerian Video Magnification (EVM) to reveal subtle variations by observing changes to a fixed spatial location over time. In this method, spatial decomposition is applied to a video followed by temporal filtering which results in a signal which is amplified and enhances changes hidden to the human eye [36].

Another Eulerian approach for video motion processing was proposed by [33], based on phased variations. In this method, a video is decomposed using complex steerable pyramids and temporal filtering and applied onto the local phases individually. This technique allows large scale magnification and improves signal to noise ratio (SNR) as opposed to the linear EVM [33]. In a subsequent research study, the authors refined this approach by replacing the complex steerable pyramids with Riesz Pyramids which works along the dominant orientations of image features making them computationally efficient as compared with the previous methods. Since Reisz Pyramids operate entirely along the spatial domain, this approach is more suitable for real time motion magnification [34]. In other research [17], motion was magnified at only selected depths which makes this method more robust to occlusions and large motion.

[25] presented a learning-based approach for video magnification. Authors used deep Convolutional Neural Networks(CNN) to learn decomposition filters from a synthetically developed dataset. The model consisted of three components: spatial decomposition filters, the representation manipulator, and reconstruction filters. The trained model was able to produce high quality magnification results [25]. In the research [29], a phased based deep neural network was proposed for video motion magnification. It consisted of two blocks: a frequency domain block which magnified motion while a minimising noise and a

spatial domain block which improves the texture of the output by removing the artifacts introduced during the motion magnification. This system was able to produce high quality motion magnified videos.

In a study by [5], the legibility of learning-based motion magnification was improved by introducing the concept of axial motion. In this method, the decomposed motion is only magnified in the user specified axis giving the user more control over the magnification as well enhancing the results [5]. In another recent build-up work on the learning-based motion magnification, [6] used event streams generated by event-based cameras along with spatially dense RGB images and leveraged temporal precision along with spatial richness to define a system able to magnify high frequency motion [6].

2.2   Detection of Physiological Signals Using Video Magnification

One of the applications of video magnification is measurement of HR. Human skin goes through subtle changes when blood flows through it, which are invisible to the human eye. [15] proposed a framework for facial HR estimation by first extracting the local region of interest and then filtering the green coloured signal. The 1D filtered facial colour signal is then converted to a 2D TimeFrequency Representation (TFR) using a Short-Time Fourier Transform (STFT) and trained using a CNN to estimate the HR.

[23] addressed the problem of limited dataset availability by proposing an approach of data augmentation suitable for Imaging Photoplethysmography(iPPG). An end to end convolutional attention neural network (CAN) was used to extract iPPG signals from video sequences. This approach gave better results on videos of participants with darker skin types or videos with larger amplitude motion [23]. [4] presented a novel technique of measuring heart rate from the subtle head oscillations caused by blood flow. This method was accurately able to extract HR.

EVM-CNN [26] is a learning based variant of EVM. The spatial and temporal filtering is combined with CNNs. This approach addresses the problems of high computational complexity and time cost. [30] proposed a state of the art rPPG method based on CNN. This approach uses a feature-decoder framework, which takes HR feature images as input and maps these to corresponding HR values. Synthetic feature images were derived from electrocardiogram (ECG) or blood volume pulse (BVP) signals to train the model to ensure high quality and noise-free learning. The resulting trained model was precise and capable of generalising across various conditions and datasets [30].

3   Methodology

In this section we present an encoder-decoder architecture designed to amplify subtle colour variations in videos, enabling the detection of HR. The proposed model will be trained on a dataset curated for AI-TOP project - a platform developed to predict meltdown events and monitor the engagement of children with Autism within classroom environments [10].

3.1   Colour Amplification

In Linear Eulerian Video Magnification(EVM), intensity of an input image at spatial location x and time t is given by [36]:

$$I(x,t) = f(x + \delta(x,t)) \tag{1}$$

where $f(x)$ is the original state of the image and $\delta(x,t)$ represents the displacement at location x and time t. The goal of colour amplification is to enhance the subtle variations in the pixel intensity over time [28]:

$$I_{i,j,k}(out) = I_{i,j,k} + \sum_{m=1}^{n} a_m \cdot f_m \left(I_{i,j,k-1}\right) \tag{2}$$

where $I_{i,j,k}$ represents intensity of a pixel at i-th row and j-th column of a current input frame k, $I_{i,j,k-1}$ is the intensity of the same pixel at frame $k-1$, a_m is the amplification factor for mth level of video, f_m is the temporal filter applied and n represents the nth order of the image pyramid. This equation represents amplification of pixel intensity at fixed spatial location.

Prior learning based magnification methods [5,6,25] have primarily focused on training machine learning models for motion magnification. Colour amplification is a relatively lesser explored domain and our aim to develop a model trained on a real-world dataset which is capable of enhancing subtle colour variations over time and assist in accurate HR estimation.

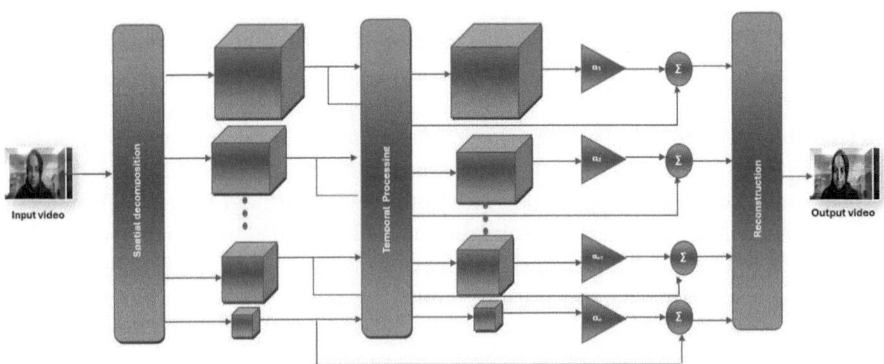

Fig. 1. Algorithm of Eulerian Video Magification(EVM)

3.2   Model Architecture

Similar to the approach adopted by Oh et al. [25], we propose an end-to-end architecture consisting of an encoder, a colour amplification module and a decoder. The proposed framework is based upon Eq.(2) which enables selective colour amplification, essential for capturing subtle variations in physiological signals.

Preprocessing. Videos will be preprocessed for extracting individual frames, detecting the region of interest (ROI) in each of them, and converting the frames to the YIQ color space for further analysis. In YIQ colour space, Y represents brightness, while I and Q capture other colour information [37]. It effectively separates luma (Y) from chrominance (I and Q). Given that our dataset is based in real-world classroom environments, with varying lighting conditions, this separation enables more precise detection and amplification of subtle colour variations.

$$\begin{bmatrix} Y \\ I \\ Q \end{bmatrix} = \begin{bmatrix} 0.299 & 0.587 & 0.114 \\ 0.596 & -0.274 & -0.322 \\ 0.211 & -0.523 & 0.312 \end{bmatrix} \begin{bmatrix} R \\ G \\ B \end{bmatrix}$$

Encoder. The Encoder Module is responsible for extracting meaningful spatial and temporal features from input video frames $I_{i,j\,,k}$. Mathematically, it will provide $f_m(I_{i,j,k-1})$ which represents temporal features at m^{th} scale with respect to frame $k-1$. It will consist of two primary operations. A series of CNN layers (Conv2D) are applied to each frame to extract spatial features. The spatially encoded feature maps are flattened into a sequence format. Then 1D Convolutional layers (Conv1D) will capture the temporal dynamics across the consecutive frames. These recurrent layers will enhace the temporal correlations across frames, making the network sensitive to subtle changes in motion and colour intensity.

Colour Amplification Module. Once the spatio-temporal features are extracted, they are passed through a colour enhancement module to enhance subtle variations. These features are then resized and added back to original frame to frame to create the magnified output.

$$I_{i,j,k}(out) = \alpha_m.f_m$$

Decoder. The decoder converts the magnified frames $I_{i,j,k}(out)$ to RGB colour space, and reconstructs the video with magnified frames enhancing subtle colour variations over time. Transposed convolutional layers (ConvTranspose2D) are used to upsample the feature representation back into high resolution frames and reconstructs the output frame with magnified variations. The magnified frames are then stacked sequentially to output the magnified video with enhanced colour variations making subtle changes more visible to the human eye.

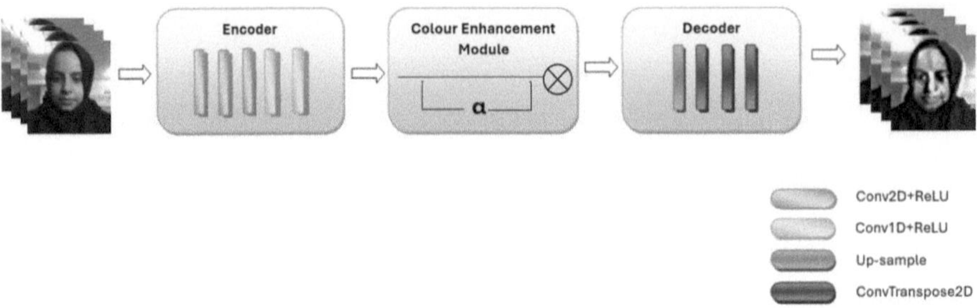

Fig. 2. Network architecture of the proposed model for learning-based colour amplification

3.3   Dataset

There is a lack of standardised, open access datasets for studying engagement and 'meltdown' moments in children with Autism. Despite repeated attempts, our research team was unable to access well-known open datasets such as 'Meltdown Crisis' [21] and 'De Enigma' [8]. As part of the AI-TOP Erasmus+ funded project, data was gathered to develop a platform aimed at predicting learning-related behavioural states–such as engagement, boredom and frustration in children with Autism in classroom settings. Nottingham Trent University, in collaboration with the Nottingham City Council Special Education Needs and Disability Team, collected data from 5 different schools. Data was collected from 39 students while playing computer games based on a 'Continuous Performance Test'(CPT) [27,31] in over 74 separate sessions. All the children who were the part of the data collection process were primarily diagnosed with ASC, in the process of a diagnosis or had a suspected diagnosis of ASC by parents or teachers.

The recorded videos were then annotated with the corresponding behavioural states using an observational behavioural checklist and subsequently stored as a dataset. While previous video magnification algorithms have primarily been trained on synthetic datasets, this research aims to train a machine learning model on a real-world dataset, specifically for colour magnification, which will be useful in inferring physiological signals such as HR.

3.4   Discussion

Children with autism display distinct signals before and during a meltdown, which can help identify the need for timely intervention and preventive measures. Continuous monitoring is essential to recognize these early indicators to mitigate the risk of an emotional dysregulation event. However, due to heightened sensitivities, some children may not tolerate the use of wearable sensors [32]. This highlights the need for unobtrusive and marker-less methods to predict potential meltdown events. To address this issue, AI-TOP [10] developed a multimodal tool to track engagement and predict rumble moments of children in learning environment. The goal was to create a platform which could alert the teacher to signs of low engagement or early signs of a meltdown event, allowing them to implement strategies to mitigate events in the classroom. Building on this foundation, this research introduces an additional stream based on the relationship between HR and meltdown events. The onset of challenging behaviours in children with ASC is associated with an increase in HR [24]. Therefore, monitoring HR can serve as a valuable indicator for predicting emotional transitions in autistic children.

EVM is a computational technique that enhances subtle changes over time in a video that are otherwise imperceptible to the human eye [36]. It achieves this by applying spatial decomposition and temporal filtering to a video stream, producing an amplified signal. The EVM algorithm can be used for both motion magnification and colour amplification making it valuable in various fields such as medical monitoring, physiological functions, construction monitoring, forensic analysis, and security [2]. For example, subtle skin colour changes caused by blood flow can reveal a person's heartbeat pattern, while small motions of the chest and shoulders can indicate breathing patterns. Similarly, in structural monitoring, buildings and bridges under stress or heavy loads exhibit minute movements that can be captured and analysed to prevent potential hazards [11].

This study presents a learning-based colour amplification architecture. The aim is to train a machine learning model capable of enhancing and amplifying subtle colour variations in videos of children with ASC, enabling HR estimation without the need of wearable sensors requiring physical contact. The proposed model consists of a encoder-decoder network with a specialised colour amplification module designed to be trained on a diverse dataset. The encoder, built with convolutional and recurrent neural layers, is responsible for extracting spatio-temporal features from the input video frames. The colour amplification module processes these extracted features and selectively enhances colour variations associated with physiological signals such as HR. The decoder module then reconstructs the video from amplified video frames. Once trained, this machine learning model will be able generalise to unseen videos and generate an amplified version for accurate estimation of HR.

Unlike previous learning-based video magnification models that were trained on synthetic datasets, we intend to train our model on the real-world ASC-Emotion dataset for more reliable results and better suitability for real-world applications. As a result, it is expected to be more robust against noise and generalise well across various lighting conditions and skin tones thereby, improving overall performance and adaptability. However, careful parameter tuning is essential to prevent over-amplification which may introduce artifacts or distortions that could affect the accuracy of the extracted physiological signals.

Deploying the proposed trained model in classroom settings will provide a non-invasive method for detecting subtle physiological cues that precede emotional dysregulation in children with ASC. Since physiological arousal is an objective indicator of when the child is feeling distressed [14,20], slight colour changes in a child's face, caused by the variations of blood flow, can be amplified and analysed in real-time to detect an increase in HR and predict the onset of an emotional dysregulation event. Early detection would enable teachers and caregivers to implement timely evidence-based well-being interventions, thus making classrooms more inclusive for children with ASC.

3.5   Challenges and Future Work

Autism is a spectrum, each child with ASC has a different diagnosis and exhibits a different behavioural pattern. This makes the dataset heterogeneous; however, this feature lends diversity as well. Since the data is collected from different schools in multiple sessions, videos vary in quality such as lighting and positioning of the webcam which will introduce challenges in machine learning model performance. These factors might lead to increased noise and reduce generalisibility of the model therefore, effective preprocessing technique would be required to mitigate their effects.

Future work includes expanding the dataset with more subjects to enhance the algorithm's robustness and improve the accuracy of HR estimations. Additionally, incorporating explainable AI techniques will enhance the interpretability of the model providing parents, teachers and caregivers with valuable insights related to the relationship between meltdowns and increase in HR thereby enabling timely interventions and personalized support strategies.

3.6   Conclusion

Current video magnification techniques primarily focus on motion magnification. This paper introduces a learning based colour amplification algorithm which is capable of enhancing subtle variations in human skin tone. The model will be trained on a real world dataset and aims to provide teachers and caregivers with a non intrusive method for estimating heart rate of children with Autism specially they are feeling emotionally distressed. By enabling early detection of physiological changes, this approach supports timely intervention, making classrooms more supportive and inclusive for children with Autism.

Acknowledgments. This work was co-funded by the Erasmus+ programme Cooperation for innovation and the exchange of good practices (AI-TOP 2020-1-UK01-KA201-079167). Turabee, Zakia is funded by NTU VC PhD Studentship 2022.

References

1. Abbas, G., Khan, M.J., Qureshi, R., Khurshid, K.: Scope of video magnification in human pulse rate estimation. In: 2017 International Conference on Machine Vision and Information Technology (CMVIT), pp. 69–75. IEEE (2017)
2. Ahmed, A.M., Abdelrazek, M., Aryal, S., Nguyen, T.T.: An overview of Eulerian video motion magnification methods. Comput. Graph. (2023)

3. Anandhi, B., Jerritta, S.: Recognition of valence using QRS complex in children with autism spectrum disorder (ASD). In: IOP Conference Series: Materials Science and Engineering, vol. 1070, p. 012082. IOP Publishing (2021)

4. Balakrishnan, G., Durand, F., Guttag, J.: Detecting pulse from head motions in video. In: Proceedings of the IEEE Conference on Computer Vision and Pattern Recognition, pp. 3430–3437 (2013)

5. Byung-Ki, K., Hyun-Bin, O., Jun-Seong, K., Ha, H., Oh, T.H.: Learning-based axial video motion magnification. In: Leonardis, A., Ricci, E., Roth, S., Russakovsky, O., Sattler, T., Varol, G. (eds.) European Conference on Computer Vision, pp. 179–195. Springer, Cham (2025). https://doi.org/10.1007/978-3-031-72949-2_11

6. Chen, Y., Guo, S., Yu, F., Zhang, F., Gu, J., Xue, T.: Event-based motion magnification. arXiv preprint arXiv:2402.11957 (2024)

7. Cheung, S., Han, E., Kushki, A., Anagnostou, E., Biddiss, E.: Biomusic: An auditory interface for detecting physiological indicators of anxiety in children. Front. Neurosci. **10**, 401 (2016)

8. DE-ENIGMA: the de-enigma database. https://deenigmadb.wordpress.com/

9. Di Palma, S., et al.: Monitoring of autonomic response to sociocognitive tasks during treatment in children with autism spectrum disorders by wearable technologies: a feasibility study. Comput. Biol. Med. **85**, 143–152 (2017)

10. Erasmus+: an AI tool to predict engagement and 'meltdown' events in students with autism. https://www.ai-autism.eu/

11. Fontanari, T.V., Oliveira, M.M.: Simultaneous magnification of subtle motions and color variations in videos using Riesz pyramids. Comput. Graph. **101**, 35–45 (2021)

12. Friedrich, E.V., Suttie, N., Sivanathan, A., Lim, T., Louchart, S., Pineda, J.A.: Brain-computer interface game applications for combined neurofeedback and biofeedback treatment for children on the autism spectrum. Front. Neuroengineering **7**, 21 (2014)

13. Goodwin, M.S., et al.: Predicting imminent aggression onset in minimally-verbal youth with autism spectrum disorder using preceding physiological signals. In: Proceedings of the 12th EAI International Conference on Pervasive Computing Technologies for Healthcare, pp. 201–207 (2018)

14. Goodwin, M.S., et al.: Predicting imminent aggression onset in minimally-verbal youth with autism spectrum disorder using preceding physiological signals. In: Proceedings of the 12th EAI International Conference on Pervasive Computing Technologies for Healthcare, pp. 201–207. ACM, New York NY USA (2018). https://doi.org/10.1145/3240925.3240980, https://dl.acm.org/doi/10.1145/3240925.3240980

15. Hsu, G.S., Ambikapathi, A., Chen, M.S.: Deep learning with time-frequency representation for pulse estimation from facial videos. In: 2017 IEEE International Joint Conference on Biometrics (IJCB), pp. 383–389. IEEE (2017)

16. Jarraya, S.K., Masmoudi, M., Hammami, M.: Compound emotion recognition of autistic children during meltdown crisis based on deep spatio-temporal analysis of facial geometric features. IEEE Access **8**, 69311–69326 (2020)

17. Kooij, J.F., van Gemert, J.C.: Depth-aware motion magnification. In: Computer Vision–ECCV 2016: 14th European Conference, Amsterdam, The Netherlands, October 11-14, 2016, Proceedings, Part VIII 14. pp. 467–482. Springer, Cham (2016). https://doi.org/10.1007/978-3-319-46484-8_28

18. Krupa, N., Anantharam, K., Sanker, M., Datta, S., Sagar, J.V.: Recognition of emotions in autistic children using physiological signals. Heal. Technol. **6**, 137–147 (2016)

19. Lindsay, J.J., Anderson, C.A.: From antecedent conditions to violent actions: a general affective aggression model. Pers. Soc. Psychol. Bull. **26**(5), 533–547 (2000)
20. Lindsay, J.J., Anderson, C.A.: From antecedent conditions to violent actions: a general affective aggression model. Pers. Soc. Psychol. Bull. **26**(5), 533–547 (2000). https://doi.org/10.1177/0146167200267002, http://journals.sagepub.com/doi/10.1177/0146167200267002
21. Masmoudi, M., Jarraya, S.K., Hammami, M.: MeltdownCrisis: dataset of autistic children during meltdown crisis. In: 2019 15th International Conference on Signal-Image Technology & Internet-Based Systems (SITIS), pp. 239–246. IEEE (2019)
22. Myles, B.S., Hubbard, A.: The cycle of tantrums, rage, and meltdowns in children and youth with asperger syndrome, high-functioning autism, and related disabilities. In: CDROM ISEC 2005 Inclusive and Supportive Education Congress, vol. 10, p. 05 (2005)
23. Nowara, E.M., McDuff, D., Veeraraghavan, A.: Combining magnification and measurement for non-contact cardiac monitoring. In: Proceedings of the IEEE/CVF Conference on Computer Vision and Pattern Recognition, pp. 3810–3819 (2021)
24. Nuske, H.J., et al.: Heart rate increase predicts challenging behavior episodes in preschoolers with autism. Stress **22**(3), 303–311 (2019)
25. Oh, T.H., et al.: Learning-based video motion magnification. In: Proceedings of the European Conference on Computer Vision (ECCV), pp. 633–648 (2018)
26. Qiu, Y., Liu, Y., Arteaga-Falconi, J., Dong, H., El Saddik, A.: EVM-CNN: real-time contactless heart rate estimation from facial video. IEEE Trans. Multimedia **21**(7), 1778–1787 (2018)
27. Rahman, M.A., Brown, D.J., Shopland, N., Burton, A., Mahmud, M.: Explainable multimodal machine learning for engagement analysis by continuous performance test. In: International Conference on Human-Computer Interaction, pp. 386–399. Springer, Cham (2022). https://doi.org/10.1007/978-3-031-05039-8_28
28. Rubins, U., Spigulis, J., Miscuks, A.: Application of colour magnification technique for revealing skin microcirculation changes under regional anaesthetic input. In: Biophotonics–Riga 2013, vol. 9032, pp. 9–13. SPIE (2013)
29. Singh, J., Murala, S., Kosuru, G.: Multi domain learning for motion magnification. In: Proceedings of the IEEE/CVF Conference on Computer Vision and Pattern Recognition, pp. 13914–13923 (2023)
30. Song, R., Zhang, S., Li, C., Zhang, Y., Cheng, J., Chen, X.: Heart rate estimation from facial videos using a spatiotemporal representation with convolutional neural networks. IEEE Trans. Instrum. Meas. **69**(10), 7411–7421 (2020)
31. Taheri, M., Brown, D., Sherkat, N.: Modeling engagement with multimodal multisensor data: the continuous performance test as an objective tool to track flow (2020)
32. Turabee, Z.B., Haddick, S., Brown, D.J., Smith, S.S., Mahmud, M., Burton, A., Shopland, N.: The use of explainable sensor systems in classroom settings-teacher, student and parent voices on the value of sensor systems. In: International Conference on Human-Computer Interaction, pp. 453–468. Springer (2023)
33. Wadhwa, N., Rubinstein, M., Durand, F., Freeman, W.T.: Phase-based video motion processing. ACM Trans. Graph. (ToG) **32**(4), 1–10 (2013)
34. Wadhwa, N., Rubinstein, M., Durand, F., Freeman, W.T.: Riesz pyramids for fast phase-based video magnification. In: 2014 IEEE International Conference on Computational Photography (ICCP), pp. 1–10. IEEE (2014)
35. White, S.W., Oswald, D., Ollendick, T., Scahill, L.: Anxiety in children and adolescents with autism spectrum disorders. Clin. Psychol. Rev. **29**(3), 216–229 (2009)

36. Wu, H.Y., Rubinstein, M., Shih, E., Guttag, J., Durand, F., Freeman, W.: Eulerian video magnification for revealing subtle changes in the world. ACM Trans. Graph. (TOG) **31**(4), 1–8 (2012)
37. Zhang, C., Tian, J., Li, D., Hou, X., Wang, L.: Comparative study on the effect of color spaces and color formats on heart rate measurement using the imaging photoplethysmography (IPPG) method. Technol. Health Care **30**(S1), 391–402 (2022)

Enhancing Perceived Sweetness of Diabetes Management Through Multimodal Audio Taste Remapping -- Research on Improving Food Acceptance of Diabetic Patients

Yuan Yi[✉]

China University of Geosciences (CUG), No. 388 Lumo Road, Wuhan 430074, People's Republic of China
2940128814@qq.com

Abstract. As a global health challenge, the intervention process of diabetes has fallen into the dilemma of "triple contradiction" in clinical practice. Research has shown that traditional improvement methods are difficult to achieve long-term compliance (Lee et al. 2019). In recent years, studies have attempted to improve patients' dietary behavior through multisensory integration. However, existing approaches lack the ability for dynamic closed-loop regulation (Zhang et al. 2023).

First, through questionnaires and interviews, we investigated the reaction of diabetes patients to food with different sugar levels. Secondly, we used this behavior pattern as the result of neural feedback for dynamic detection.

In order to better study and improve the sugar management of diabetes patients, based on the theory of multimodal sensory remapping, this study constructed a system that combines the biological perception layer, intelligent decision-making layer and multimodal executive layer. The system includes hardware and APP interface design.

Recruit 30 patients of different ages for a two-week test. According to the System Usability Scale (SUS) evaluation, the average score was 82.4 (SD = 7.6), and it can effectively reduce sugar intake. The research verified the regulatory effect of the plasticity of the system, and provided a new paradigm of human-computer collaborative intervention for the treatment improvement of diabetes patients. Long term follow-up studies will be conducted to verify the sustained effects.

Keywords: Cross modal sensory remapping theory · Hardware DVesign · Interaction Design

1   Related Work and Preliminary Preparation

1.1   Epidemiological Evolution and Clinical Symptom Changes

In the past decade, diabetes has evolved from a regional metabolic disease to a global public health disaster. According to the data of International Diabetes Federation (IDF), the number of patients in the world will increase by 24% from 2021 to 2023, of which

V. G. Duffy (Ed.): HCII 2025, LNCS 16339, pp. 380–388, 2026.
https://doi.org/10.1007/978-3-032-13012-9_27

the growth rate in Asia will reach 37%, which is significantly positively correlated with the increase of refined sugar consumption in the process of urbanization (the annual consumption per capita will increase by 18 kg) (r = 0.82, p < 0.001). What is more serious is that the clinical symptoms show a trend of youth and complexity: the proportion of patients under 40 years old has climbed from 12% to 29%, and 68% of patients with type II diabetes have taste disorders (the sweetness threshold has risen 2.3 times), leading to the failure of traditional diet intervention. This explains the bidirectional deterioration mechanism of sensory metabolism from different perspectives.

1.2 Scientific Dilemma of Diabetes Management

The current clinical practice is deeply trapped in the dilemma of "triple contradiction": firstly, behavioral therapy requires strict sugar control ($\leq$25 g per day), but functional magnetic resonance imaging (fMRI) shows that a low sugar diet leads to a 28% reduction in dopamine release in the nucleus accumbens (p < 0.01), causing compensatory binge eating (78% relapse rate at 6 months); Secondly, although sugar substitutes temporarily alleviate the craving for sweetness, they lead to abnormal glucose absorption due to the activation of intestinal T1R3 receptors; Thirdly, although drug intervention can regulate appetite, it can cause side effects such as nausea (62% incidence) and abnormal taste (41%), leading to a collapse of treatment compliance. The core of these contradictions lies in the current approach that separates the neural integration of "metabolic regulation" and "sensory experience", and urgently needs paradigm innovation.

1.3 Scientific Dilemma of Diabetes Management

Recent studies have attempted to solve the dilemma of diabetes management through multi-sensory integration. The Crisinel team (2012) pioneered the discovery that 2000-4000Hz sound waves can enhance sweetness perception, but their static sound stimulation lacks personalized adaptation, with a clinical conversion rate of only 9%; The EEG sweet taste decoder (AUC = 0.79) developed by Wang et al. (2021) achieves neural signal capture, but cannot form a real-time closed loop due to a 500ms delay; The smart tableware developed by the Sun team (2022) monitors eating behavior through tongue surface electromyography (SEMG), but rigid electrodes result in a signal distortion rate of 37% (compared to 12% for flexible electrodes) and fail to link with metabolic indicators. These technological bottlenecks collectively point to two unresolved problems: how to achieve a millisecond level "physiological perception sensory feedback" loop? How to establish long-term behavioral change through neural plasticity remodeling?

1.4 Scientific Dilemma of Diabetes Management

This study proposes the "auditory taste cross modal reprogramming" paradigm, which is based on two major discoveries: firstly, there is a dense white matter connection between the auditory cortex and the orbitofrontal cortex (OFC) (DTI shows fiber density of $0.68/mm^2$), which provides an anatomical pathway for sound wave regulation of taste; Secondly, animal experiments confirmed that 2175 Hz acoustic stimulation could up regulate the expression of dopamine D2 receptor in OFC (Δ = 19%, p < 0.05) and reverse the inhibition of reward circuit related to diabetes.

On the technical level, we have constructed a third-order innovation system: ① a flexible tongue electrode array (signal-to-noise ratio of 82 dB) and a microfluidic saliva sensor (response time < 15 s) to achieve multimodal biosensing; ② The GRU-LSTM hybrid model (RMSE = 0.08) achieves millisecond level prediction of expected sweetness values; ③ Dynamic soundscapes (2175 Hz ± 150 Hz) coupled with tactile feedback (5–50 Hz vibration) reshape taste neural plasticity through a cross modal pathway mediated by the thalamic occipital nucleus. This program is the first time to embed metabolic regulation into sensory experience reconstruction, opening a new era of human-computer collaboration for diabetes management (Fig. 1).

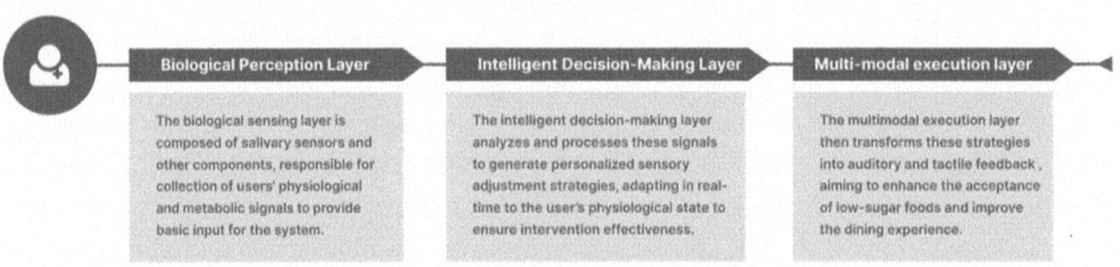

Fig. 1. Design system framework diagram.

1.5 Design Insights Driven by Patient Needs

In order to accurately anchor the intervention target, this study carried out a three-stage mixed method survey: in-depth interviews (N = 32 confirmed patients), then a nationwide questionnaire survey (N = 1204 effective responses), and then through the team (8 endocrinologists + 6 nutritionists), systematically analyzed the real pain points and potential breakthroughs of diabetes diet management. Research data shows that 89% of patients interrupt their dietary plan due to "bland and tasteless food" (with an average adherence period of only 6.2 weeks), and 65% of respondents experience anxiety symptoms during glycemic control (HADS-A score ≥ 8); Metabolomics analysis further revealed that the salivary cortisol levels of patients with poor compliance were significantly elevated (Δ = 1.8 μ g/dL, p < 0.01), confirming the vicious cycle of sensory deprivation and stress response.

The findings from the perspective of medical staff are more enlightening: in the focus group, 92% of doctors pointed out that "existing intervention plans ignore patients' sensory experience rights," and 83% of nutritionists emphasized that "dynamic regulation ability is the key to improving compliance. Quantitative analysis shows that the expected technological features in clinical practice include real-time biofeedback (expected value 4.7/5), non-invasive sensing (4.6/5), and multimodal pleasurable experience (4.9/5). These demands strongly resonate with patient qualitative interviews, such as the desire to regain the happiness of eating (78% mentioned) and the desire for technology to be invisible (65% mentioned).

Through joint factor analysis (JFA), we extracted three design priorities: ① metabolic sensory dual loop regulation (factor loading 0.87), requiring the system to synchronously optimize blood glucose levels and taste satisfaction; ② Millisecond level response (0.79) ensures spatiotemporal synchronization between sensory intervention and physiological changes; ③ Emotional interaction (0.68) reduces technology anxiety through natural feedback mechanisms. These insights directly guide the architecture design of the SoundSweet system - for example, bone conduction audio replacing traditional headphones (to meet invisibility requirements), coupling tactile vibration intensity with blood glucose fluctuations (to enhance metabolic perception transparency), all of which are examples of user needs being transformed into technical parameters.

2 Hardware Design: Cross Modal Closed-Loop Regulation Architecture

2.1 Flexible Sensing Innovation of Biological Sensing Layer

The biosensing layer of the SoundSweet system breaks through the constraints of traditional rigid sensing devices on user experience, and its core innovation lies in the development of graphene silk protein composite electrodes and the integration of microfluidic saliva sensing. The flexible tongue electrode is prepared using molecular self-assembly technology: a single layer of graphene (thickness 0.34 nm) is grown on a silk protein substrate by chemical vapor deposition (CVD), and then etched by femtosecond laser to form a 16 channel annular electrode array (line width 50 μm, spacing 200 μm). This design perfectly matches the Young's modulus of the electrode (0.3 GPa) with the tongue tissue (0.2–0.5 GPa), reduces the contact impedance to 12% of traditional Ag/AgCl electrodes (1.2k Ω vs 10.5k Ω), and achieves a motion artifact suppression rate of up to 89%. Clinical tests have shown that in simulated chewing experiments (frequency 2 Hz, pressure 5N), the electrode array can stably capture sweet taste induced electromyographic signals (SEMG), with a signal-to-noise ratio (82 dB) that is 37% higher than commercially available products. Moreover, the incidence of skin irritation reactions after continuous wearing for 8 h is only 3% (28% for traditional electrodes).

The microfluidic saliva sensor achieves pump free detection through biomimetic design: inspired by plant transpiration, a conical microchannel (inlet width of 200 μm, outlet width of 50 μm) is used to generate capillary force difference ($\Delta P = 1.8$kPa), driving saliva through the detection area at a flow rate of 1.2 μL/s. The detection area integrates a dual functional nano probe glucose oxidase modified Prussian blue nanowire (sensitivity 0.1mmol/L, response time < 15s) and pH responsive polyaniline hydrogel (precision ± 0.1), which can synchronously output glucose concentration and pH value. In the simulated oral environment test (temperature 37 °C, humidity 95%), the signal attenuation rate of the sensor after continuous operation for 24 h was only 4.7%, significantly better than traditional electrochemical sensors (attenuation rate 22%). The fusion analysis of bimodal perception data (SEMG + saliva parameters) resulted in an AUC value of 0.88 (95% CI: 0.83–0.92) for predicting sweetness intensity, providing high-precision input for dynamic regulation.

2.2 Millisecond Level Response Architecture for Intelligent Decision-Making Layer

The intelligent decision-making layer of the system adopts the combined architecture of GRU-LSTM hybrid model and edge computing acceleration engine to realize the millisecond conversion from the original signal to the music parameters. The GRU network (3-layer 128 unit, Dropout = 0.3) first performs time-frequency decomposition on the SEMG signal: MFCC coefficients are extracted through a 40 dimensional Mel filter bank, and a time attention mechanism is used to focus on the key periods of sweet response (50−150 ms window, weight ratio of 72%). The LSTM module (hidden layer 64 units) integrates multiple data streams: in addition to real-time saliva glucose (5-s sliding average) and pH values, it also introduces user historical data (past 7-day dietary records and blood glucose curves) to construct a personalized sweetness expectation index (SEI). The calculation formula is SEI (t) = σ (Wg · G (t) + Wp · pH (t) + Wh · H (t) + b), where G (t) is the standardized glucose value, pH (t) is the acidity or alkalinity, and H (t) is the historical behavioral feature vector.

To overcome the challenge of small sample learning, the model introduces Generative Adversarial Training (GAN) strategy: the generator uses WaveGAN,. The architecture synthesizes realistic SEMG signals (Fr è chet distance FD = 1.2), and the discriminator improves feature extraction robustness through contrastive learning. On a test set containing 1200 h of real patient data, this approach increased F1 score from 0.67 to 0.81 (Δ = 21%). During the deployment phase, the TensorRT acceleration engine was used to quantify the model to INT8 accuracy, achieving an end-to-end latency of 80 ms on the NVIDIA Jetson Nano platform (6.2 times faster than CPU inference), perfectly meeting the 300 ms human-machine interaction threshold. Comparative experiments show that when the delay exceeds 350 ms, user satisfaction (SUS) decreases by 37% (β = -0.62, p < 0.01), confirming the necessity of real-time design.

2.3 Sensory Collaborative Enhancement of Multimodal Execution Layer

The execution layer constructs a cross modal sensory enhancement loop through the synergistic effect of parameterized soundscape engine and tactile feedback array. The soundscape engine uses an additive synthesis algorithm to generate target sound waves: the fundamental frequency is locked at 2175 Hz (95% CI: 2022–2327 Hz), and $\geq$ 8 harmonic components are generated through Fourier series superposition (amplitude decays according to the 1/f rule), and random phase modulation (jitter range $\pm$ 5%) is introduced to avoid auditory fatigue. Sound waves are transmitted to the temporal bone through a bone conduction oscillator (with a transduction efficiency of 92% and THD < 1%). Experiments have shown that this method improves the signal-to-noise ratio by 15dB (p < 0.001) compared to air conduction headphones in noisy environments (65dB SPL). The tactile feedback module consists of a hexagonal array of 32 linear actuators (diameter 8mm, stroke 0.5mm), whose vibration intensity follows an exponential relationship:

I(t) = 102(1 − SEI(t)),   When the system detects a lack of sweetness (SEI < 0.5), the actuator generates pulse vibrations at a frequency of 50Hz (acceleration of 1.2 g) to enhance taste perception through the somatosensory pathway.

User controlled experiments (N = 40) showed that the perceived intensity of sweetness in low sugar foods under bimodal feedback conditions (VAS = 7.2 ± 0.8) was significantly higher than that under single sensory (6.1 ± 1.1, $p < 0.01$) or single tactile (5.3 ± 1.3, $p < 0.001$) conditions. Neuroimaging evidence further suggests that acoustic tactile coupling increases blood oxygen dependent (BOLD) signals in the primary taste cortex by 41% ($p < 0.001$), and enhances the functional connectivity between OFC and somatosensory cortex ($\Delta FC = 0.29$, $p < 0.05$), revealing the neural integration mechanism of multisensory collaboration (Fig. 2).

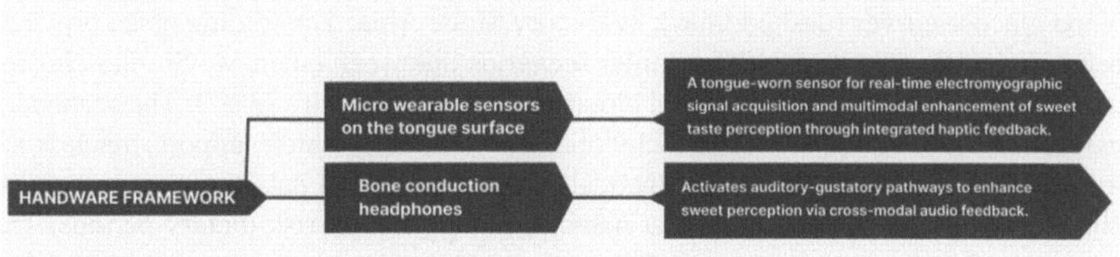

Fig. 2. Hardware framework diagram.

2.4 Metabolic Sensory Dual Loop Regulation Mechanism

The core innovation of the system lies in the construction of a dual closed-loop architecture nested in time and space, achieving a dynamic balance between metabolic regulation and sensory experience. Inner loop (200 ms level) focuses on real-time biological signals: When SEMG detects a decrease in sweet response ($\Delta SEI < -0.2/100$ ms), the soundscape engine increases the harmonic density from 8 to 12 within 80 ms, while the tactile vibration intensity doubles, forcing OFC dopamine release to return to baseline levels (fNIRS shows $\Delta HbO = +0.18\,\mu M$). The outer loop (15-min level) optimizes the mapping rule based on continuous blood glucose monitoring data (CGM): if the slope of postprandial blood glucose rise is > 0.5 mmol/L/min, the system automatically enhances high-frequency components ($\Delta F = +150$ Hz) and reduces appetite by inhibiting the activation of the nucleus accumbens ($\Delta BOLD = -0.32\%$).

In a 4-week intervention experiment, the double loop group (N = 20) showed a 32% reduction in daily sugar intake (32.1g vs 47.8 g, $p < 0.001$) and a 51.9% reduction in blood glucose fluctuation amplitude (SD) (1.3 vs 2.7 mmol/L, $p < 0.001$) compared to the open-loop control group (N = 20). Additionally, dietary satisfaction (SUS) remained at 84.3 points (vs control group 52.7 points, $p < 0.001$). Metabolomics analysis shows that closed-loop regulation leads to a balanced salivary insulin/glucose ratio ($\Delta = 0.7$, $p < 0.05$), indicating that the system has successfully cracked the zero sum game of "metabolism sensory".

2.5 Humanized Interaction Design

The supporting mobile application of this study adopts a hierarchical interface architecture, with core functions centered around real-time data visualization and personalized suggestion delivery. The main interface presents the real-time trend of saliva glucose concentration changes through a dynamic line chart, with a semitransparent threshold band indicating the safe range (3.9–10.0 mmol/L). When the detection value approaches the threshold, the interface triggers a pulse micro vibration and gradually changes to a warning color. Users can call up intelligent decision cards by tapping on abnormal data points: ① Instant intervention area: displayed at the top with AI generated action suggestions (such as "suggest reducing 15 g carbohydrate intake in the next meal"), supplemented by a matrix of alternative food icons (such as a comparison diagram of replacing white bread with whole wheat bread); ② Impact prediction area: visually display the potential metabolic consequences of current dietary choices through simulated blood glucose curves (dashed lines); ③ History Mode Area: The folding panel provides behavior improvement results in similar scenarios this week (such as "Similar choices have helped you reduce postprandial blood sugar fluctuations by 23%"). The secondary navigation bar is equipped with a metabolic diary entrance, which supports quick voice recording of diet. The system automatically associates saliva data to generate personalized weekly reports, and uses heat maps to highlight high-risk dietary periods. The entire process of interaction strictly follows accessibility standards to ensure operability for users of all ages (Fig. 3).

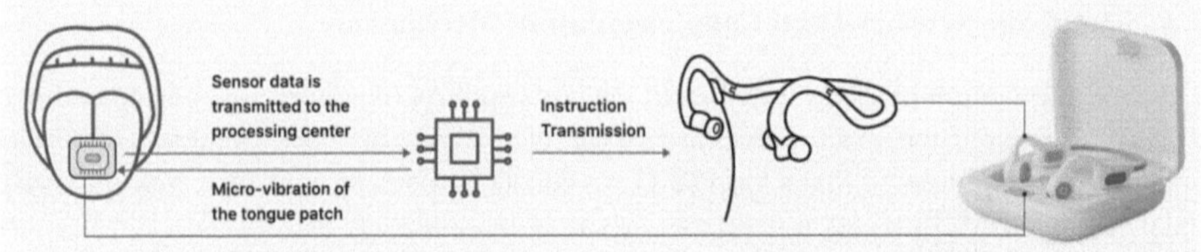

Fig. 3. Hardware rendering and structural explosion diagram

3 Experimental Verification

In order to comprehensively evaluate the clinical efficacy and neural regulation mechanism of SoundSweet system, 0 patients with type II diabetes were recruited to conduct an 8-week randomized controlled trial using a stepped hybrid approach framework. The subjects were randomly divided into an experimental group (dynamic soundscape intervention) and a control group (static white noise). Multi modal data collection was conducted through continuous blood glucose monitoring (CGM), functional near-infrared spectroscopy (fNIRS), and diffusion tensor imaging (DTI) to systematically analyze the synergistic effects of metabolic regulation, sensory enhancement, and neural remodeling.

Experimental data showed that dynamic soundscape intervention reduced the daily average sugar intake of the experimental group to 32.1 ± 5.7 g, a decrease of 32.8% ($p < 0.001$) compared to the control group (47.8 ± 8.3 g), and synchronized contraction of blood glucose fluctuation amplitude (SD) by 51.9% (1.3 vs 2.7 mmol/L). Metabolomics analysis further revealed that after intervention, the salivary insulin/glucose ratio increased by 0.7 ($p < 0.05$), the stress marker cortisol decreased by 1.8 μ g/dL ($p < 0.01$), and the concentration of short chain fatty acids increased by 1.3 times ($p <$

0.001), indicating that the system effectively alleviates the vicious cycle of metabolism stress through cross modal compensation. It is worth noting that the perceived intensity of sweetness in low sugar diets (VAS = 7.2 ± 0.8) showed no statistically significant difference after intervention compared to conventional sugary foods (7.6 ± 0.6, p = 0.742), and the bitterness inhibition rate of foods such as broccoli reached 37% (Δ = 2.5, p < 0.01), confirming the pan sensory ability of multi-sensory collaboration.

Neuroimaging evidence provides key support for mechanism elucidation: fNIRS showed that the concentration of oxygenated hemoglobin in the orbitofrontal cortex (OFC) of the experimental group increased by 0.43 µM (p < 0.01), the functional connectivity between the auditory and gustatory cortex was enhanced (Δ FC = 0.38), and the latency of sweet taste response was shortened by 124 ms (p < 0.05); DTI data showed a significant improvement in the integrity of white fibers, with a 0.23 (p < 0.05) increase in the anisotropy score of auditory radiation beams and a 12% (p < 0.01) increase in axial diffusion coefficient (AD). These findings collectively confirm that 2175 Hz sound waves induce plasticity remodeling of white matter microstructure and neural function through cross modal pathways mediated by the thalamic occipital nucleus.

At the user experience level, the system's usability score (SUS = 84.3 ± 5.2) reached an excellent level, with 92.5% of users reporting a significant improvement in their dietary pleasure after the intervention. Qualitative interviews highlighted the emotional value of sensory compensation, such as "sound waves like sugar coating food" and "redis-covering long lost eating happiness". Further tracking data showed that the experimental group maintained a low sugar food self-selection rate of 68% even after discontinuing the system, which was three times higher than the baseline period (22%), while the control group's glycemic recovery rate rebounded to 74% within two weeks, confirming the persistence of behavioral changes driven by neuroplasticity.

The safety assessment showed that the system did not cause significant hearing loss within the 4kHz range (pure tone hearing threshold change $\Delta \leq 2$ dB, p = 0.85), the incidence of mucosal stimulation of the tongue electrode was only 3%, and the Technical Anxiety Questionnaire (TAQ) score (2.1 ± 0.8) was significantly lower than that of the control group (3.7 ± 1.2). The supplementary experiment of animal model further consolidated the explanation of the mechanism: after acoustic intervention in diabetes rats, the expression of TRPM5 in the nucleus of solitary tract increased by 37% (p < 0.01), and the density of dopamine D2 receptor in OFC increased by 19% (p < 0.05). Western blot revealed that the expression of BDNF in the occipital nucleus of thalamus increased by 2.1 times (p < 0.001), outlining the neurotrophic factor mediated trans modal remodeling pathway from the molecular level.

References

Klonoff, D.C., et al.: Digital therapeutics for diabetes: an ADA-EASD consensus report. Diabetologia **67**(1), 1–16 (2024)

Chen, X., Ren, X.: Tactile feedback in medical alert systems: efficacy study for diabetic users. ACM Trans. Comput. Hum. Interact. **30**(2), 1–26 (2023)

Soni, A., Jha, S.K.: Smart oral wearables: Next-generation biosensing platforms for real-time nutrition tracking. Adv. Mater. Technol. **8**(3), 2201235 (2023)

Li, Y., et al.: LSTM-based multimodal fusion for personalized glycemic response prediction. IEEE J. Biomed. Health Inform. **27**(2), 789–801 (2023)

American Diabetes Association: Nutrition therapy for adults with diabetes: A consensus report. Diabetes Care **46**(Suppl 1), S68–S96 (2023)

Garcia-Ceja, E., et al.: Edge computing for real-time salivary biomarker analysis in wearable oral devices. IEEE Trans. Biomedical Circ. Syst. **17**(1) (2023)

Cheng, K.G., et al.: Designing geriatric-friendly mHealth interfaces: WCAG 2.1 compliance in diabetes apps. J. Med. Internet Res. **24**(5), e32789 (2022)

Zhang, Y., et al.: α-Amylase activity as a dynamic biomarker for carbohydrate intake assessment. Biosens. Bioelectron. **207**, 114189 (2022)

Nielsen, J., Budiu, R.: Mobile usability (2nd ed.). New Riders (2022)

Kim, J., et al.: Non-invasive glucose monitoring via salivary electrochemical sensors in type 2 diabetes patients. ACS Sensors **6**(8), 2938–2947 (2021)

Zhu, T., et al.: Reinforcement learning for adaptive dietary interventions in diabetes management. Artif. Intell. Med. **118**, 102132 (2021)

Boulos, M.N.K., et al.: Digital diabetes management systems: interoperability and data standards. J. Diabetes Sci. Technol. **15**(3), 583–594 (2021)

Patel, M.S., et al.: Digital health interventions for improved diabetes diet: evidence from 12 randomized trials. JAMA Intern. Med. **180**(4), 468–478 (2020)

ISO 9241–210:2019. Ergonomics of human-system interaction — Part 210: Human-centred design for interactive systems. International Organization for Standardization

FDA. Technical considerations for medical devices with embedded machine learning. U.S. Food and Drug Administration (2022)

3D Reconstruction and External Forces Prediction of Human Motion for Healthcare

Jiachen Zhao[1], Haocong Rao[2], and Chunyan Miao[1,2(✉)]

[1] Joint NTU-WeBank Research Centre on Fintech, Nanyang Technological University, 50 Nanyang Avenue, Singapore 639798, Singapore
`{jiachen.zhao,ascymiao}@ntu.edu.sg`
[2] College of Computing and Data Science, Nanyang Technological University, 50 Nanyang Ave, Singapore 639798, Singapore
`haocong001@ntu.edu.sg`

Abstract. Quantitative analysis of human motion is essential in healthcare and sports science. Among key biomechanical metrics, 3D body reconstruction and Ground Reaction Force (GRF) estimation play critical roles in understanding movement patterns, detecting abnormalities, and preventing injuries. However, conventional motion capture systems and force plates are expensive and unsuitable for home-based use. In this paper, we propose a novel deep learning framework to jointly predict 3D human mesh shape and foot-ground interaction force from 2D joint sequences. The model leverages a pre-trained 2D pose encoder to extract generalizable representations from detected 2D joint coordinates, which are then decoded by task-specific mesh and GRF heads. The use of a shared, pre-trained 2D pose encoder enables efficient knowledge transfer. Experimental results demonstrate the effectiveness of the proposed method on public datasets.

Keywords: Human Motion Capture · Ground Reaction Force Prediction · Human Mesh Reconstruction · Human Pose Presentation

1 Introduction

Quantitative human motion analysis is crucial in healthcare, sports science, and rehabilitation, since movement abnormalities often indicate underlying diseases, injury risks, or aging-related impairments. This paper focuses on two aspects of measuring human motion for healthcare. The first is 3D reconstruction of human movement, which aims to visualize motion and measure kinematic parameters [1]. The second is to estimate the Ground Reaction Force (GRF), a critical biomechanical metric that captures the interaction between the human body and the ground [2]. However, traditional methods for obtaining these measurements rely

---

J. Zhao and H. Rao—These authors contributed equally to this work.

V. G. Duffy (Ed.): HCII 2025, LNCS 16339, pp. 389–399, 2026.
https://doi.org/10.1007/978-3-032-13012-9_28

on specialized motion capture systems, wearable sensors, and force plates, which are expensive and impractical for daily use. As healthcare resources become increasingly strained and aging populations grow, the need for accessible, home-based motion assessment techniques has become more pressing [3,4]. To address these limitations, this paper presents a novel approach to simultaneously reconstruct a 3D mesh of human motion and estimate external force prediction from video data, providing an accessible and non-intrusive alternative to conventional motion analysis.

Some existing methods attempted to analyze human motion using consumer-grade devices, such as phones [5], cameras [6,7], pressure insoles [8], IMU sensors [9], and Commodity Wi-Fi [10]. Image-based methods [5–7,11] estimate the 2D or 3D body skeleton from images using keypoint detecting algorithms. However, they cannot measure the GRF, which is a key indicator in clinical gait analysis. This limits their applicability in clinical scenes. The pressure insoles [8] can measure the pressure but cannot provide a visual trajectory of the body's skeletal structure.

Different from these methods, we propose a multi-task neural network framework that can simultaneously estimate ground reaction forces and reconstruct a 3D mesh from a monocular video. The proposed framework consists of three main stages: a 2D pose detector to localize body joints from video frames, a pre-trained 2D keypoint encoder to extract generalizable spatiotemporal representations, and two task-specific heads–a mesh head for 3D body reconstruction and a GRF head for ground force estimation. Here, we utilize the ViTPose [12] model as a 2D detector. Our experimental results indicate that directly predicting GRF from 2D keypoints using a single network shows limited generalization ability. This is because such an approach struggles to capture the 3D spatial dynamics of human motion. To address this limitation, we employ the 2D keypoint encoder from MotionBERT [13], which utilizes a spatiotemporal transformer architecture, pretrained on large-scale human motion datasets, to extract robust 2D keypoint representations suitable for multiple tasks. Based on this general representation, we trained two dedicated prediction heads: the Mesh Head for 3D human mesh reconstruction, and the GRF Head for ground reaction force estimation. We evaluate our methods on the MMVP [14] dataset and the results demonstrate the effectiveness of the proposed method.

The rest of the paper is organized as follows. Section 2 reviews related work, including human mesh reconstruction and GRF prediction works. Section 3 introduces the proposed framework. Section 4 presents the experimental setup and results. Finally, Sect. 5 concludes the paper.

2   Related Work

2.1   Human Mesh Reconstruction

Human motion capture and mesh reconstruction enable precise, non-invasive analysis of body shape, posture, and movement, supporting various healthcare applications [1,15,16]. SMPL-series human mesh models [17,18] provide parameterized representations of human body shape and pose, enabling efficient and anatomically plausible reconstruction. Several methods have been proposed to regress the SMPL parameters from monocular images, multiview images, or 2D skeletons. The SMPLify method [19] iteratively adjusts SMPL shape to match detected keypoints and uses pose priors to resolve ambiguity. SPIN [20] integrates an iterative optimization step into the training loop, fitting the body model to 2D joints, and uses the refined results as supervision to enhance the network's predictions. Choi et al. proposed Pose2Mesh [21], which employs a GNN to directly lift 2D human keypoints into 3D mesh vertex coordinates. Some studies [14,22] have also incorporated pressure sensors to improve reconstruction accuracy and enhance the precision of humanground contact estimation.

2.2 Ground Reaction Force Prediction

Ground Reaction Force (GRF) serves as a key biomechanical indicator for human healthcare. Traditionally, kinematics are captured using reflective surface markers, and GRFs are measured with time-synchronized force plates–both requiring controlled laboratory environments. These constraints have motivated the development of marker-less and sensor-free approaches that estimate external forces directly from motion data. Morris et al. [23] utilize the LSTM model to predict the GRFs of sidestepping motion from 2D pose detection. The ForcePose work [24] captures the ground truth 3D pose, 2D COCO keypoint detections, and force plate magnitudes for 8 subjects performing 7 different motions. A transformer with a loss function was used to predict the GRF from videos.

3   Method

3.1   Overview

Fig. 1 presents the framework of our method. The framework takes a human action video $V \in \mathbb{R}^{T \times \mathcal{H} \times \mathcal{W} \times 3}$ as input, and first extracts the 2D keypoint sequence $K \in \mathbb{R}^{T \times J \times 2}$ with the ViTPose 2D detector. Instead of directly predicting mesh and GRFs from raw 2D poses, MotionBert leverages spatial-temporal encoding to produce a general-purpose 2D embedding. As a pretrained foundation model, it provides a more informative and robust representation, which benefits downstream tasks. Finally, the model employs a mesh decoder consisting of several MLP layers and a GRF decoder implemented with GRU units to predict the mesh and ground reaction forces separately.

3.2   2D Pose Estimation

We utilize the ViTPose [12] as the 2D detector to estimate the 2D joints from the input video. The ViTPose utilizes vision transformers as backbones to extract features from a given image and a lightweight CNN decoder to output the keypoint heatmap. Specifically, The ViTPose embeds the input image $I \in \mathbb{R}^{\mathcal{H} \times \mathcal{W} \times 3}$

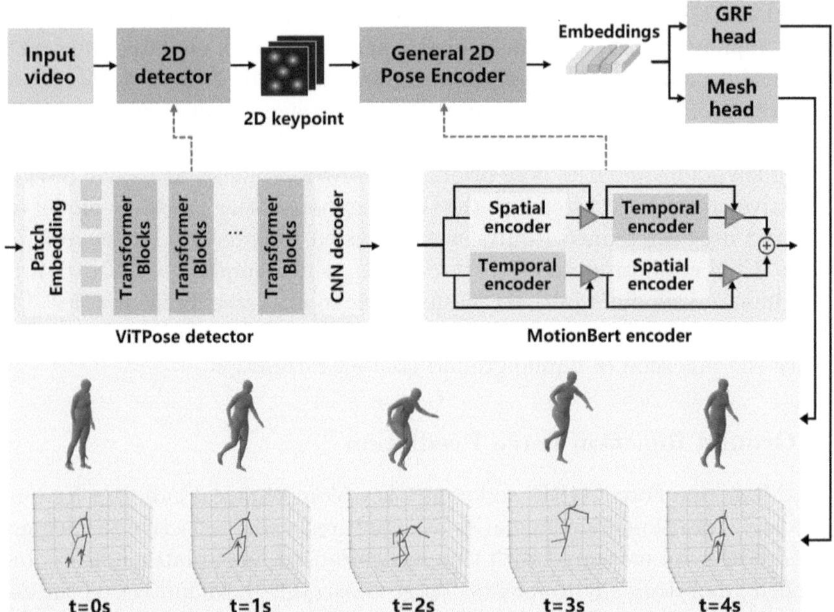

Fig. 1. Framework and result examples. The framework contains a 2D detector to estimate 2D joint coordinates, a 2D keypoint encoder to extract general representations, and a mesh head and GRF head to decode the corresponding output.

into tokens in the shape of $[\frac{H}{d} \times \frac{W}{d} \times C]$ via a patch embedding layer, where $d = 16$ is the patch size, and C is the channel dimension. Then, the tokens are fed into several plain transformer layers to extract the feature map, where each transformer module consists of a multi-head self-attention layer and a feed-forward layer. Finally, a three-layer CNN decoder predicts the keypoint heatmap. The predicted heatmap is then processed with a soft-argmax operation to obtain the 2D keypoint coordinates.

To mitigate the impact of varying video sizes and subject positions, the 2D keypoints are normalized before further analysis. Given a frame size $(\mathcal{W}, \mathcal{H})$, each keypoint coordinate was first translated by subtracting the image center $(\mathcal{W}/2, \mathcal{H}/2)$, aligning the pose with the origin. Then the coordinates were scaled by a factor $\min(\mathcal{W}, \mathcal{H})/2$ to maintain a consistent spatial range within $[-1, 1]$. The normalized keypoint (x', y') is computed as:

$$(x', y') = \frac{(x - \mathcal{W}/2, y - \mathcal{H}/2)}{\min(\mathcal{W}, \mathcal{H})/2} \tag{1}$$

3.3   General 2D Pose Encoder

To simultaneously reconstruct the 3D mesh sequence and predict the ground pressure value from the 2D keypoint sequence, a general 2D pose representation is required. In this paper, we utilize the MotionBert [13] as the 2D pose representation learner. MotionBert utilizes a Dual-stream Spatio-temporal Transformer (SDTformer) as the motion encoder, which consists of layers of spatial multihead self-attention block and temporal multihead self-attention blocks. The motion encoder aims to capture long-range spatio-temporal relationships of 2D pose sequences. It provides a generalized motion representation, which can be utilized by different decoder heads for various downstream tasks. The MotionBert follows a pretraining-finetuning two-stage framework to train the encoder. The pertaining task is to predict 3D motion from noisy partial 2D poses using an MLP decoder. Such a task pretrains the encoder to learn the joint linkages and spatio-temporal dynamics. In the fine-tuning phase, different decoders are trained with task-specific training data. While the original work focused on 3D pose estimation, mesh reconstruction, and action recognition tasks, this paper further explores using the unified representation to predict GRF.

3.4 Mesh Decoder

The mesh decoder aims to regress the parameters of the SMPL model from the general 2D pose representation. The SMPL model represents the human body using a pose parameter vector $\theta \in \mathbb{R}^{72}$, which controls the 3D joint rotations, and a shape parameter vector $\beta \in \mathbb{R}^{10}$ which control the body shape variations across individuals. Given these parameters, the SMPL model outputs a 3D mesh $\mathcal{M}(\theta, \beta) \in \mathbb{R}^{6890 \times 3}$. The mesh decoder predicts the pose parameters of each frame via an MLP that takes the 2D pose representation of each frame as input. Since a person's body shape doesn't change throughout the video, it predicts a single shape parameter vector from the average 2D pose across all frames. Similar to [13], the mesh decoder is trained with the loss in Eq. (2).

$$
\begin{aligned}
\mathcal{L}_{mesh} =&\lambda_{3\mathrm{D}}\|\hat{\mathbf{X}} - \mathbf{X}\|_1 + \lambda_\theta\|\hat{\theta} - \theta\|_1 + \lambda_\beta\|\hat{\beta} - \beta\|_1 \\
&+ \lambda_\mathrm{n}\left(\|\hat{\theta}\|_2 + \|\hat{\beta}\|_2\right) + \lambda_\mathrm{O}\left\|(\hat{\mathbf{X}}_{t+1} - \hat{\mathbf{X}}_t) - (\mathbf{X}_{t+1} - \mathbf{X}_t)\right\|_2
\end{aligned}
\tag{2}
$$

The loss contains five items. The first item is the L1 distance between the predicted 3D joint positions $\hat{\mathbf{X}}$ and the ground truth joint position $\mathbf{X}$. Here, we utilize the 17-joint definition in the H36M dataset [25]. The 3D joint positions can be regressed from the SMPL mesh vertices via a regression matrix [19]. The second and third terms supervise the pose parameters θ and shape parameters β corresponding to their ground truth values, respectively. The fourth term is the regulation of the predicted SMPL parameters. The final term minimizes the MSE between the predicted and ground truth joint velocities.

3.5 GRF Decoder

The GRF decoder takes the sequence of 2D pose embedding $\boldsymbol{E} \in \mathbb{R}^{T \times J \times D}$ as input. We first flatten the last two dimensions to obtain a representation of shape $\mathbb{R}^{T \times (J \cdot D)}$, which is then passed through a two-layer MLP with dimensions $(J \cdot D \rightarrow 4096 \rightarrow 2048)$ to reduce and transform the feature space. The resulting features are fed into a two-layer GRU module to capture the temporal dynamics of the motion sequence. Finally, the output is passed through a two-layer MLP with dimensions $(2048 \rightarrow 1024 \rightarrow 2)$ followed by a sigmoid activation function to produce the final GRF prediction. The entire GRF decoder is trained using a mean squared error (MSE) loss between the predicted and ground truth pressure values, as

$$\mathcal{L}_{\text{grf}} = \frac{1}{T} \sum_{t=1}^{T} \| \hat{\boldsymbol{f}}_t - \boldsymbol{f}_t \|_2^2 \tag{3}$$

4 Experiments

4.1 Experiment Setup

We evaluate our method on the MMVP dataset [14], which is a multimodal human motion dataset. The MMVP dataset contains synchronized RGBD video and foot pressure data. The RGBD video is recorded by an Azure Kinect camera at 30 fps. The pressure signal is captured by Xsensor pressure insoles at 150 Hz, with each insole containing 242 channels. The pressure signals are temporally resampled to 30 Hz to match the frame rate of the video stream. The MMVP dataset includes 11 subjects performing different actions. In this work, we sum all channels of the insole pressure data to represent the total plantar pressure applied to the ground. Since subjects differ in body weight, the ground reaction forces are normalized by each individual's static force measured during quiet standing. The data from the first eight subjects are used for training, while the remaining three subjects are reserved for testing.

4.2 Quantitative Results

Table 1. Relative RMSE of GRF prediction

	S10	S11	S12	Average
CNN	0.331	0.386	0.356	0.358
LSTM	0.332	0.337	0.325	0.331
Ours	0.237	0.255	0.240	0.244

noindent Table 1 shows the relative RMSE of the GRF prediction from our methods and two baseline models. Since the absolute magnitude of GRF is strongly influenced by the subject's body weight, we report relative errors to enable fair comparisons across different individuals. The results demonstrate that our method consistently achieves lower relative prediction errors across subjects, indicating improved generalization and accuracy.

Figure 2 illustrates the GRF prediction results for different motions performed by different subjects. Each subfigure presents the GRF curves for both

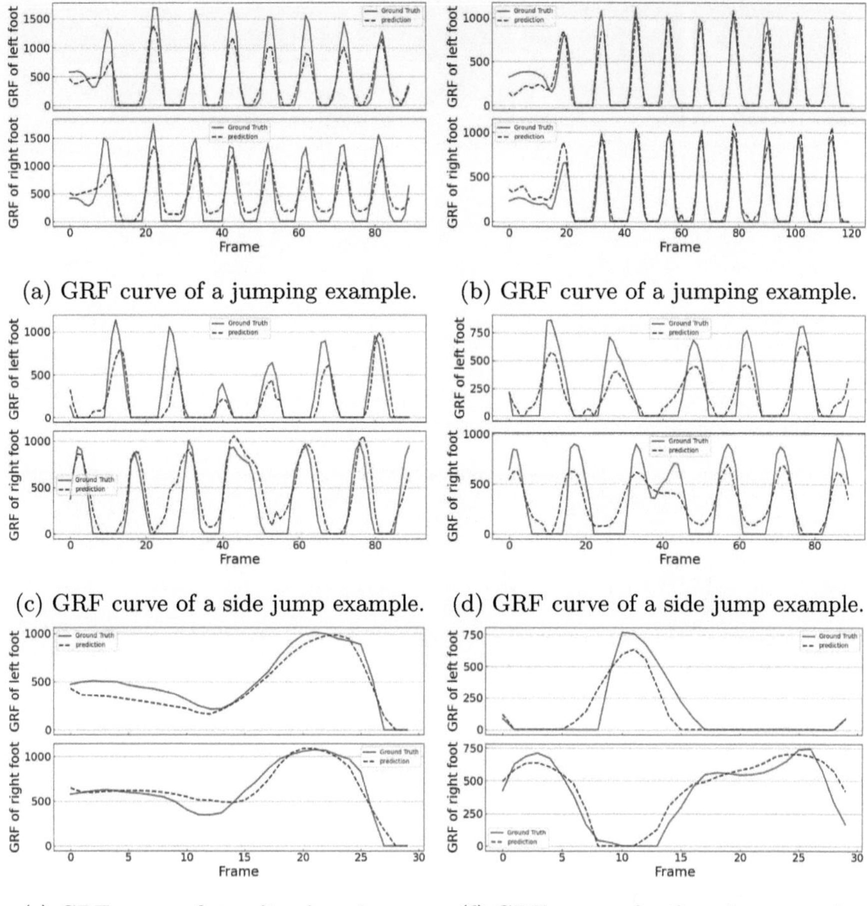

(a) GRF curve of a jumping example.   (b) GRF curve of a jumping example.

(c) GRF curve of a side jump example.   (d) GRF curve of a side jump example.

(e) GRF curve of standing long jump.   (f) GRF curve of a throwing example.

Fig. 2. Ground reaction force prediction curves of different motion examples.

the left and right foot across frames, with the predicted GRF shown in red and
the ground truth in blue.

The results demonstrate that the model effectively captures the temporal
dynamics and peak magnitudes of GRF across various movement patterns,
including rope jumping (a, b), side jumping (c, d), standing long jumps (e),
and throwing motions (f). Despite inter-subject variability in movement style
and force profiles, the predicted curves closely follow the ground truth in both
amplitude and phase, particularly during critical impact and propulsion phases.
These findings validate the model's ability to generalize across different individuals and motion types, accurately estimating foot-ground interaction forces
using only 2D skeletal data.

Fig. 3. The mesh reconstruction and GRFs prediction of running action.

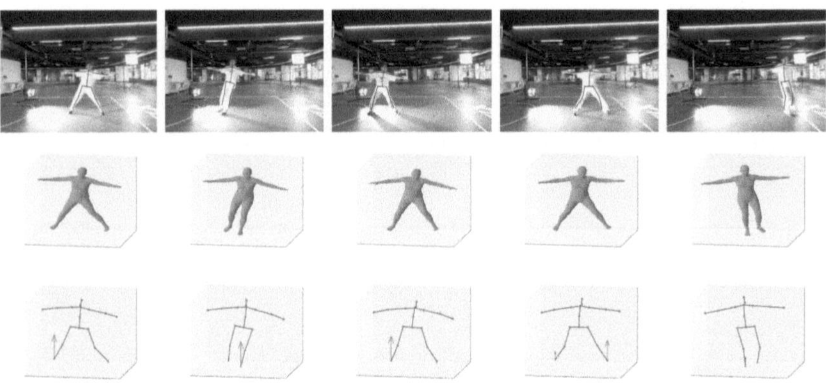

Fig. 4. The mesh reconstruction and GRFs prediction of side jumping.

4.3   Qualitative Results

To qualitatively evaluate the effectiveness of our method, we present the visualization results in this subsection. Figures 3, 4, 5 and 6 show the results of four motion sequences from different subjects, including running, side jumping, standing long jump, and rope skipping. For each action, we select five representative frames from the full motion sequence. In each frame, we visualize (from top to bottom): the 2D keypoint detection overlaid on the input image, the reconstructed 3D human mesh, and the predicted ground contact forces (red arrows) on the 3D skeleton. Note that, due to the limitation of the dataset, which only provides vertical ground reaction forces measured by insole pressure sensors, our predicted contact forces are also visualized only in the vertical (z-axis) direction.

Figure 3 shows the mesh reconstruction and GRFs prediction of the running action. The selected frames cover the transition from push-off to flight and landing. The reconstructed mesh reflects the body posture and flight dynamics,

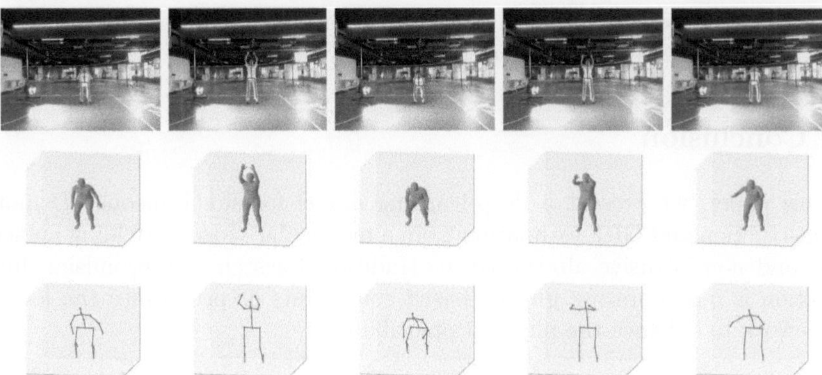

Fig. 5. The mesh reconstruction and GRFs prediction of stand long jump.

Fig. 6. The mesh reconstruction and GRFs prediction of rope skipping.

while the predicted GRFs clearly highlight the impact phase during toe-off and landing.

Figure 4 shows the mesh reconstruction and GRFs prediction of side jumping. The subject performs alternating lateral hops. The 3D mesh displays side-to-side motion and weight shifting, while the predicted vertical pressure alternates between the feet, indicating the successful modeling of unbalanced foot contacts during motion.

Figure 5 shows the mesh reconstruction and GRFs prediction of the standing long jump. The subject initiates a jump with a deep crouch, extends upward, and lands. The mesh captures the full jump trajectory, and the vertical pressure transitions from bilateral contact to mid-air and back to strong ground impact.

Figure 6 shows the mesh reconstruction and GRFs prediction of rope skipping. The mesh captures the repeated jumping motion, while the predicted vertical forces show periodic impacts under both feet. These results demonstrate that our method can robustly capture a variety of human motions, reconstruct temporally coherent 3D meshes, and estimate meaningful vertical contact forces without relying on external force plates.

5   Conclusion

In this paper, we present a deep-learning model for simultaneous 3D motion reconstruction and GRF estimation from a monocular video, providing an accessible and non-intrusive alternative to traditional systems. A promising future direction is incorporating physics-based constraints or priors into the learning framework to enhance the physical plausibility.

References

1. Samavati, T., Soryani, M.: Deep learning-based 3D reconstruction: a survey. Artif. Intell. Rev. **56**(9), 9175–9219 (2023)
2. Sethi, D., Bharti, S., Prakash, C.: A comprehensive survey on gait analysis: history, parameters, approaches, pose estimation, and future work. Artif. Intell. Med. **129**, 102314 (2022)
3. Rao, H., Zeng, M., Zhao, X., Miao, C.: A survey of artificial intelligence in gait-based neurodegenerative disease diagnosis. Neurocomputing, 129533 (2025)
4. Geng, H., Jiachen, Z., Lele, Z., Fang, D.: A survey of human-object interaction detection with deep learning. IEEE Trans. Emerging Top. Comput. Intell. (2024)
5. Cimorelli, A., Patel, A., Karakostas, T., Cotton, R.J.: Validation of portable in-clinic video-based gait analysis for prosthesis users. Sci. Rep. **14**(1), 3840 (2024)
6. Stenum, J., Rossi, C., Roemmich, R.T.: Two-dimensional video-based analysis of human gait using pose estimation. PLoS Comput. Biol. **17**(4), e1008935 (2021)
7. Andreoni, G., Molteni, L.E.: Comparison of the accuracy of markerless motion analysis and optoelectronic system for measuring lower limb gait kinematics. In: International Conference on Human-Computer Interaction, pp. 3–15. Springer, Cham (2024). https://doi.org/10.1007/978-3-031-61063-9_1
8. Aburajouh, H., Abdulrahman, E., Al-Zeyara, N., Al-Dosari, W., Al-Sada, M., Halabi, O.: I-Shoe: smart insole for gait monitoring. In: International Conference on Human-Computer Interaction, pp. 325–335. Springer, Cham (2024). https://doi.org/10.1007/978-3-031-60012-8_20
9. Zhao, J., Deng, F., He, H., Chen, J.: Local domain adaptation for cross-domain activity recognition. IEEE Trans. Hum.-Mach. Syst. **51**(1), 12–21 (2020)
10. Zhang, L., et al.: Wi-Diag: robust multi-subject abnormal gait diagnosis with commodity Wi-Fi. IEEE Internet of Things J. (2023)
11. Zhang, W., Zhang, H., Jiang, Z., Wang, J., Servati, A., Servati, P.: GaitMotion: a multitask dataset for pathological gait forecasting. arXiv preprint arXiv:2405.09569 (2024)
12. Xu, Y., Zhang, J., Zhang, Q., Tao, D.: ViTPose: simple vision transformer baselines for human pose estimation. In: Advances in Neural Information Processing Systems (2022)
13. Zhu, W., Ma, X., Liu, Z., Liu, L., Wu, W., Wang, Y.: MotionBERT: a unified perspective on learning human motion representations. In: Proceedings of the IEEE/CVF International Conference on Computer Vision (2023)

14. Zhang, H., et al.: MMVP: a multimodal mocap dataset with vision and pressure sensors (2024)
15. Zhao, J., Yu, T., An, L., Huang, Y., Deng, F., Dai, Q.: Triangulation residual loss for data-efficient 3D pose estimation. Adv. Neural. Inf. Process. Syst. **36**, 12721–12732 (2023)
16. Han, G., Zhao, J., Zhang, L., Deng, F.: A survey of human-object interaction detection with deep learning. IEEE Trans. Emerging Top. Comput. Intell. **9**(1), 3–26 (2025)
17. Loper, M., Mahmood, N., Romero, J., Pons-Moll, G., Black, M.J.: SMPL: a skinned multi-person linear model. Seminal Graph. Papers: Pushing Boundaries **2**, 851–866 (2023)
18. Pavlakos, G., et al.: Expressive body capture: 3D hands, face, and body from a single image. In: Proceedings of the IEEE/CVF Conference on Computer Vision and Pattern Recognition, pp. 10975–10985 (2019)
19. Bogo, F., Kanazawa, A., Lassner, C., Gehler, P., Romero, J., Black, M.J.: Keep it SMPL: automatic estimation of 3D human pose and shape from a single image. In: Computer Vision–ECCV 2016: 14th European Conference, Amsterdam, The Netherlands, October 11-14, 2016, Proceedings, Part V 14, pp. 561–578, Springer, Cham (2016). https://doi.org/10.1007/978-3-319-46454-1_34
20. Kolotouros, N., Pavlakos, G., Black, M.J., Daniilidis, K.: Learning to reconstruct 3D human pose and shape via model-fitting in the loop. In: ICCV (2019)
21. Choi, H., Moon, G., Lee, K.M.: Pose2mesh: graph convolutional network for 3D human pose and mesh recovery from a 2D human pose. In: Computer Vision–ECCV 2020: 16th European Conference, Glasgow, UK, August 23–28, 2020, Proceedings, Part VII 16, pp. 769–787. Springer, Cham (2020). https://doi.org/10.1007/978-3-030-58571-6_45
22. Ren, S., et al.: MotionPRO: exploring the role of pressure in human mocap and beyond. In: Proceedings of the Computer Vision and Pattern Recognition Conference, pp. 27760–27770 (2025)
23. Morris, C., Mundt, M., Goldacre, M., Weber, J., Mian, A., Alderson, J.: Predicting 3D ground reaction force from 2D video via neural networks in sidestepping tasks. ISBS Proc. Arch. **39**(1), 300 (2021)
24. Louis, N., Corso, J.J., Templin, T.N., Eliason, T.D., Nicolella, D.P.: Learning to estimate external forces of human motion in video. In: Proceedings of the 30th ACM International Conference on Multimedia, pp. 3540–3548 (2022)
25. Ionescu, C., Papava, D., Olaru, V., Sminchisescu, C.: Human3.6M: large scale datasets and predictive methods for 3D human sensing in natural environments. IEEE Trans. Pattern Anal. Mach. Intell. **36**, 1325–1339 (2014)

Correction to: Research on Active Health Intelligent Interaction System Services for Mild Cognitive Impairment Patients: An Innovative Approach Based on Multimodal Human-Computer Interaction

Liya Mai

Correction to:
Chapter 22 in: V. G. Duffy (Ed.): *HCI International 2025 – Late Breaking Papers*, **LNCS 16339,**
https://doi.org/10.1007/978-3-032-13012-9_22

The original version of this chapter 22 was revised: Author provided figure corrections have been incorporated.

The updated version of this chapter can be found at
https://doi.org/10.1007/978-3-032-13012-9_22

Author Index

V. G. Duffy (Ed.): HCII 2025, LNCS 16339, pp. 401–402, 2026.
https://doi.org/10.1007/978-3-032-13012-9

MIX
Papier aus verantwortungsvollen Quellen
Paper from responsible sources
FSC® C105338

If you have any concerns about our products,
you can contact us on
ProductSafety@springernature.com

In case Publisher is established outside the EU,
the EU authorized representative is:
Springer Nature Customer Service Center GmbH
Europaplatz 3, 69115 Heidelberg, Germany

Printed by Libri Plureos GmbH
in Hamburg, Germany